THE LIFE MODEL
OF SOCIAL WORK
PRACTICE

CAREL B. GERMAIN
ALEX GITTERMAN

THE LIFE MODEL
OF SOCIAL WORK
PRACTICE

ADVANCES IN THEORY & PRACTICE

·

SECOND EDITION

 COLUMBIA UNIVERSITY PRESS · NEW YORK

In Memoriam
Carel B. Germain
October 23, 1916–August 3, 1995
A note from the publisher:
Shortly after completing her work on this book, Carel Germain died. As her many friends and colleagues would expect, she revised her sections of *The Life Model of Social Work Practice* with her customary concern that it serve its readers and sustain a standard for social work that her own efforts in the field brilliantly defined.

Columbia University Press

New York   Chichester, West Sussex

Library of Congress Cataloging-in-Publication Data

Germain, Carel B.
  The life model of social work practice : advances in theory and
practice / Carel B.Germain, Alex Gitterman.—2nd ed.
    p. cm.
  Includes bibliographical references and index.
  ISBN 0-231-06416-0 (alk. paper)
  1. Social case work. 2. Man—Influence of environment.
  I. Gitterman, Alex. II. Title.
HV43.G47 1996
361.3'2—dc20   95–41023

                                          CIP

Casebound editions of Columbia University Press books are printed on permanent and durable acid-free paper.

Printed in the United States of America

c 10 9 8 7 6 5 4 3 2 1

CONTENTS

PREFACE

In the fifteen years since *The Life Model of Social Work Practice* was first published, there have been dramatic changes in the profession and in the societal context of new social problems, new populations, and new public attitudes. Social workers today deal with profoundly vulnerable populations, overwhelmed by oppressive daily struggles with poverty, discrimination, and various life circumstances that they are powerless to control. Social workers in the 1990s and in the new century will confront daily the devastating impact of AIDS and other grave illnesses, homelessness, substance abuse, chronic mental disorders, child abuse, unemployment, family and community violence. While social problems are growing more intractable, resources to mitigate them continue to decrease. In this new book we respond to these pervasive changes and present a more fully-developed life-modeled practice, i.e., a practice modeled on natural life processes. While retaining and refining the core of our previous work, we make use of new concepts and new content. We believe this book provides social work practitioners and students with the necessary knowledge base and practice guidelines to deal with the many professional, societal, theoretical, and ethical issues they face.

We remain committed to our original conceptions, and have broadened and deepened them. The ecological metaphor continues to provide concepts that illuminate the continuous exchanges between people and their environments. We now adopt a *life course* concept of human development and functioning. In contrast to traditional stage models of development, this concept takes into account diversity in race, ethnicity, sex, age, socioeconomic status, sexual orientation, and physical/mental challenges, and environmental diversity within historical, societal, and cultural contexts. "Life course" is a multidisciplinary concept (in anthropology, social psychology, social history, biology, psychiatry, and sociology), adapted here for social work. We use "life course" to replace the traditional, linear "life cycle" models and their assumption that emotional and social development proceed in fixed, sequential, universal stages without reference to the diversity of life experience, culture, and environments in North American society.

In this book we develop an integrated practice we believe more effectively incorporates the ecological perspective for practice. The belief rests on our conviction that professional specialization should not determine whether a client receives individual, family, group, or community services, but rather the service should be based on client needs and preferences. Two formulations are particularly helpful in developing an integrated life-modeled practice.[1] The first, *degree of client choice*, differentiates common professional methods and skills in the initial phase by the auspice of the service (i.e., whether the client sought the service or an agency offered or mandated a service) rather than by a particular modality. The second, *life stressors—stress-coping*, supports an integrated practice related to the assessment of and intervention in varied life stressors rather than to an agency's service mode.

As a result of their commitment to the life model, many practitioners originally educated in social casework, social group work, or community organization took on a "new" identity as social workers and a deepened understanding of professional assessment and intervention processes. We offer new content throughout this book and new chapters dealing with these processes. They pay greater attention to specifying the common base of social work assessment and interventions as well as the methods and skills specific to each practice modality.

Readers of the previous edition of this book might recall our promise to include material on community and neighborhood practice in any future work. In this book, we develop our ideas about community/neighborhood practice in a new chapter. Social workers whose practice is life-modeled are increasingly engaged in community or neighborhood practice. Some clinical social workers are introduced to community practice when they volunteer or are called upon to help residents and communities after natural or person-made disasters. When working with individuals, families, and groups, many life-modeled practitioners expand their practice to community or neighborhood populations of similarly affected persons, helping them to undertake social action and develop preventive and growth-promoting programs.

If social work clinicians in face-to-face services are to practice effectively, in addition to knowledge of individuals, families, and groups, they require (a) an understanding of the structures and functioning of commu-

nities and their influence on residents; (b) knowledge of the programs, services, policies that affect the life of the community and shape their own
practice, including issues of power/oppression and empowerment/libera-
tion at individual, family, group, and community levels; and (c) the ability
to analyze the intended and unintended consequences of programs, services, and policies for the people served.[2]

We believe that social work services in today's complex world are
enhanced by an integrated social work practice that serves people—individuals, families, groups, or communities—and engages them in their desired
efforts at change. All social workers should be prepared to practice at whatever level a particular situation begins and wherever it may lead. Life-modeled practice, however, is not simply a conglomerate of little bits from each
of the earlier specializations, but a reconceptualized practice that reflects
the continuous transactions among individual, collective, environmental,
and cultural processes in human development and functioning, and integrates the modalities required to improve or sustain those transactions. Our
perspective on practice is difference-sensitive, empowering, and ethical.

We continue our commitment to practice that mirrors natural life
processes and builds upon people's strengths. In our earlier book we developed the concept of *problems in living* to organize our ideas about professional
assessment and intervention. We now discard that concept because we think
it may unwittingly imply a deficit in the individual or the collectivity. We substitute the more neutral *life stressor—stress-coping* paradigm (Lazarus and
Folkman 1984). Life stressors and associated stress include (a) difficult life
transitions and traumatic life events; (b) harsh social and physical environments; and (c) dysfunctional interpersonal processes in families and groups,
and between workers and clients. Recent research and practice reveal that
managing a life stressor of any kind can involve simultaneous changes in (a)
social, psychological, and biological functioning; (b) interpersonal processes;
and (c) altered environmental processes requiring new responses.

While we realize that any separation of phenomena distorts the reality of
simultaneous processes, we think analyzing them separately has distinct
advantages. Social work practitioners are overwhelmed by the nature, range,
and intractability of life stressors faced by the people they serve. The life
stressor—stress-coping paradigm covers an almost limitless variety of human
plights, and provides a useful schema for specifying, grouping, and organizing data throughout the helping process. The paradigm also provides heuris-
tic guidelines that focus and direct interventions at any point during the helping encounter. It also links clinical practice with practice in growth-promo-
tion and prevention programs. We caution readers that life stressors often
must be managed simultaneously or, at least, any one of them may need to be
managed in such a way as to have a positive impact on the others.

The oppression experienced by many of those we serve leaves their families, networks, and communities vulnerable to deprivation and deteriora-

tion. These realities have required us to work more intensely on building bridges between the clinical and social reform traditions of the profession. We make a determined effort in this book to explore the connections between people's life stressors and community, organizational, and legislative influence and change.

The book is divided into three parts. Part I offers a theoretical and methodological overview. Chapter 1 reviews the ecological perspective, including new concepts of habitat and niche, life course, vulnerability, misuse of power, and social and technological pollution. Chapter 2 presents an overview of the defining characteristics and anatomy of life-modeled practice at this point in its development. It briefly delineates modalities, methods, and skills used to help people to cope with or meliorate life stressors.

Part II presents the knowledge, values, methods, and skills of life-modeled practice with individuals, families, formed groups, organizations, and social networks. Chapter 3 examines the initial phase of working together, that is, of getting started with individuals and collectivities. Chapters 4 through 8 cover the ongoing phase. Specifically, chapter 4 discusses helping individuals and collectivities deal with difficult life transitions and traumatic life events. Chapter 5 considers the interrelated dimensions of helping individuals and collectivities negotiate their organizational, social network, and spatial and temporal environments. Chapters 6 and 7 explore the questions of helping the family and groups reduce dysfunctional interpersonal processes that prevent the fulfillment of members' individual and shared needs. Chapter 8 explores interpersonal stress in the worker-client relationship, particularly the processes that interfere with helpfulness. Chapter 9 considers the ending phase, or termination of the work together, and evaluation of practice.

Part III examines life-modeled practice at community, organizational, and political levels. Chapter 10 focuses on helping communities and neighborhoods to achieve desired improvement in their quality of life. Chapter 11 discusses professional issues and methods of influencing organizational operations that do not serve their intended beneficiaries. Chapter 12 presents the knowledge and skills of legislative, regulatory, and electoral politics. Social work's purpose and its value system require us to help change oppressive life conditions of many clients. We therefore regard community, organizational, and political advocacy for social justice as the responsibility of all social workers.

The epilogue examines the societal and cultural contexts of contemporary practice.

Carel B. Germain
Alex Gitterman

ACKNOWLEDGMENTS

We are deeply grateful to our baccalaureate, masters, and doctoral students—and to administrators and practitioners whom we met in the course of our consultation work—for their generosity in permitting us to use their practice excerpts. We especially appreciate the remarkable richness and relevance of their materials to grave social issues facing North American society and to the struggles of our profession to meet increasingly complex human needs. We are indebted to faculty colleagues throughout Canada and the United States who have influenced our work in many ways. We especially thank Professors Emeriti George Brager and Irving Miller of the Columbia University School of Social Work, Professor Joan Laird and Emerita Dean Ann Hartman of the Smith College School of Social Work, Professors Toby Berman-Rossi and Jacqueline Mondros of the Barry University School of Social Work, Professor Judith A. B. Lee of the University of Connecticut School of Social Work, and Professor Lawrence Shulman of the Boston University School of Social Work for sharing their creativity and practice acumen with us over the years.

We are also indebted to our late, beloved, Columbia colleagues, Professors Lucille N. Austin, Mary Funnyé Goldson, William Schwartz, and Hyman J. Weiner for their remarkable contributions to social work theory and practice. Their ideas continue to influence the profession and our own work.

We are grateful to our families for their continuous love and support during the writing of this book. Alex is grateful for the professional contributions of his wife, Naomi, as well as her abiding support and that of their children, Daniel and Sharon. His mother, late father, late stepfather, aunt, cousin, and mother-in-law, taught him the meaning of courage and the value of life.

TRIBUTE

Professor Carel Bailey Germain died on August 3, 1995, just as we were editing the final manuscript of this book.

Our collaboration began in 1972 as faculty colleagues developing the first integrated practice course at the Columbia University School of Social Work. This led to a twenty-three year writing collaboration and close friendship. The effort to develop and express our ideas about practice forged an enduring bond between us.

Professor Germain was internationally recognized for her brilliant scholarship. She drew on numerous academic disciplines to develop ideas about human ecology. Her body of work reflects an uncommon intellect and erudition. She bequeaths a lasting gift to the profession.

Professor Germain held fast to her ideas, never cutting her cloth to suit the fashion of the day. She was graceful, gentle, and gallant. Her understated wit was illuminating and often trenchant.

This book's epilogue ends with "And so our journey continues!" Without Carel the journey will be lonelier, but her originality, powerful ideas, and loyalty will be a source of continuing strength.

Alex Gitterman

THE LIFE MODEL
OF SOCIAL WORK
PRACTICE

OVERVIEW

Part 1 introduces the current conceptual framework of the ecological perspective for social work practice. It also offers a brief overview of life-modeled practice, its defining features, modalities, methods, and skills.

Chapter 1 reviews and expands the original four sets of ecological concepts that underlie life-modeled practice:

1. Person:environment exchanges and relationships (the colon is used to repair the conceptually fractured relationship suggested by the hyphen in person-environment)

2. Varied levels of fit between people's needs, goals, and rights, and their environment's qualities and processes, within a historical and cultural context; adaptedness and adaptation, achieved by making changes in the self, the environment, or both, in order to improve or sustain the level of fit; maladaptivness leading to dysfunctional perceptions, emotions, thinking, and action; and positive and negative feedback processes

3. Life stressors that threaten the level of fit and lead to associated emotional or physiological stress, and the coping tasks that require personal skills and environmental resources for managing the life stressor and reducing the associated stress

4. Human relatedness (connection to others), competence, self-concept and self-esteem, and self-direction are positive attributes generated by past and current person-environment relationships

Three new sets of concepts are now added to the ecological perspective:

5. Vulnerability, oppression, abuse or misuse of power, and social and technological pollution
6. Salutary and nonsalutary human habitats and niches
7. The "life course" conception of nonuniform pathways to human development and functioning, replacing traditional formulations that consider development a journey through fixed, sequential, universal stages. The "life course" conception incorporates human, environmental, and cultural diversity, and it is applicable to individuals and groups. It also makes use of temporal concepts—historic, social, and individual time—in considering psychosocial functioning.

Chapter 1 demonstrates how these seven sets of ecological concepts, used throughout the book, reflect particular person:environment relationships. These varied sets do not refer to persons alone or environment alone. Hence, each can only be considered in relation to the other, not just in theory but in life-modeled social work practice.

Chapter 2 provides a brief overview of the origins and characteristics of life-modeled practice. Ten features, in unique combination, define life-modeled practice: (1) professional purpose and function which includes community, organizational, and political advocacy; (2) professional aims of diversity-sensitive, empowering, and ethical practice; (3) worker:service recipient relationship regarded as a partnership; (4) agreements, assessments, and life stories; (5) integrated modalities, professional methods, and skills; (6) focus on personal and collective strengths; (7) pervasive significance of social and physical environments and culture; (8) emphasis on client action and decision-making; (9) consistent attention to the unique dimensions of the life course of individuals, families, and groups; (10) evaluation of practice and contribution to knowledge-building.

Life-modeled practice is structured by the initial, ongoing, and ending phases of work, even in one-session and episodic services, where the phases are temporally collapsed. Life-modeled practice focuses on (a) painful life transitions and traumatic life events; (b) poverty, oppression, and unresponsiveness or harshness of social and physical environments; and (c) dysfunctional interpersonal processes in families or groups and sometimes between the practitioner and the people served. The life stressor—stress-coping paradigm in particular clearly expresses the relations and exchanges between the psychological and social factors that practitioner and client seek to improve through the use of enhanced personal and environmental coping resources. These and many other aspects are considered in greater detail and depth in Parts 2 and 3.

We hope that the brief examination of ecological concepts and overview of the totality of life-modeled practice in Part 1 will help the reader move confidently and eagerly into Parts 2 and 3 and their detailed study of a complex professional practice. It is complex because it is designed to prepare students and seasoned practitioners to move knowledgeably and skillfully among varied modalities (individual, family, group, neighborhood and community, organizational, and political) as needed.

ONE

THE ECOLOGICAL PERSPECTIVE

Our earlier work drew on several major sets of ecological concepts, including: (1) exchange or transaction; (2) person:environment fit, adaptedness, and adaptation; (3) life stressors, stress, and coping; (4) relatedness (attachments and social affiliations or connectedness), competence, self-concept, self-esteem, and self-direction (formerly termed autonomy). The first section of this chapter reviews and expands on those concepts. The second section presents refined and newly added concepts: (5) vulnerability, oppression, abuse or misuse of power, and social and technological pollution; (6) habitat and niche; and (7) life course.[1] Together, these seven sets of ecological concepts form the current theoretical foundation of life-modeled practice.

Review of Ecological Concepts

Ecology is the biological study of relationships among components of a biotic community. This community includes flora and fauna, as well as features of the physical environment such as terrain, climate, and natural disturbances. Because it emphasizes the interdependence of organism and environment, ecology is especially suitable as a *metaphor* for social work, given our historic commitment to the person-in-environment concept. The ecological metaphor helps the profession enact its social purpose of helping people and promoting responsive environments that support human growth, health, and satisfaction in social functioning. Human beings act within a physical environment, a society, and a culture. Physical settings include the natural world, structures built by people, the space which supports, contains, or arranges these structures, and the rhythms of environmental and human biology. Social settings include friendships, other dyads, and larger groups such as the family; social networks of two or more significant people; organizations, institutions, and the community (which are also physical settings), and society itself, including its political, economic, social structures, and the law. Culture is part of the environment, part of the person, and is expressed through each person's values, norms, beliefs, and language. "Culture is variously defined. It often refers to the fact that human groups differ in how they structure their behavior, their worldview, their perspective on the rhythms of life and their concept of the essential nature of the human condition." (Devore and Schlesinger 1995:903)

From a holistic view, people (and their biological, emotional, and social processes) and physical and social environments (and the characteristics of those environments) can be fully understood only in the context of the relationship between and among them, in which individuals, families, and groups and physical/social environments continually influence the operations of the other. It must be remembered that this dynamic array of linked influences always occurs in a cultural context.

Ecology also rests on an evolutionary, adaptive view of the development of human beings and the characteristics of the species. Human cultures enabled people to transcend limitations imposed by environmental conditions or the genetic structure of the species developed in the evolutionary past. There were, however, some negative consequences to human development through cultural instead of genetic change. We became disassociated from the rhythms of nature that had shaped our physiology and psychology, and we were exposed to conditions of our own creation that were very different from those in which our earlier organic evolution had proceeded over the millennia. Our psyches and bodies still conform to a model that was adapted to suit a Pleistocene environment. Because of our ability to adapt, we tolerate our technological environment and our depersonalizing mass societies. In doing so, we pay a high price in chronic illnesses, emotional disturbances, impaired social functioning, and planetary degradation. The evolutionary, adaptive point of view is important for social workers to understand because it accounts for the complexity in understanding human behavior in terms of heredity versus environment. The relative contribution to biological, social and emotional functioning made by heredity (genetic endowment) and by past and present environmental experiences of individuals and the species is still largely unknown. The matter is further complicated by degrees of human freedom from both.

Ecological Thinking

Ecological thinking focuses on the reciprocity of person-environment exchanges, in which each shapes and influences the other over time. This mode of thought differs markedly from the linear thinking that now pervades our language, culture, education, and systems of ideas. According to linear thinking, we assume that an antecedent variable, A, leads to an effect on B at a certain point in time, while A remains unchanged. There is a certain inescapable determinism in this: given A, effects on B necessarily follow. Unquestionably, linear thinking explains some simple human phenomena, but ecological thinking explains more complex phenomena, such as those encountered in social work practice.

For example, a teenage son is striving for an age-appropriate degree of autonomy from parental control. The parents, not aware of or not accepting of the teen's normal desire for greater independence, try to keep their son close and compliant with their wishes. Rather than seeing either the parents or the son as the cause of escalating battles (linear thinking), the life-model social worker, using ecological thinking, is likely to hold the view that the age-appropriate behavior of the son evokes stringent countermeasures from the parents, particularly from the father. These lead to the son's increased rebellion, which eventually may take the form of total rejection of parental values and expectations—a situation that neither son nor parents want. Each stride toward such an undesirable end leads to further restrictions on the son, which then tends to encourage his rebellious behavior. This pattern becomes a closed circle of negative exchanges.

Instead of attributing the escalation of anger and resentment to either party, the social worker focuses with the family on the exchanges and how they lead to the maladaptive behaviors of parents and son. At the same time the social worker is sensitive to environmental factors, such as possible help or interference from kin and friends, the nature of school and peer forces, and workplace and health issues.

Ecological thinking also recognizes that given A, predicted effects on B may not necessarily follow, reflecting the indeterminacy or unpredictability of complex human phenomena. More important, A and B are in a reciprocal relation rather than a linear or unidirectional one. A may act in a way that leads to change in B, whereupon that change in B leads to change in A, which in turn affects B—it is a continuous loop of reciprocal influences over time. Each element in the loop directly or indirectly influences every other element. As a consequence, simple linear notions of cause and effect lose their meaning.

Ecological thinking suggests that we should be less concerned with causes than with consequences, and that we should concentrate on helping change maladaptive relationships between people and their environments (Duhl 1983). We should ask the questions "What is going on?" rather than

"Why is it going on?" and "How can the 'what' be changed?" rather than "the 'who'?." In the previous example, the worker may learn that the father has recently lost his managerial job due to cutbacks in his company. Attempts to find other work have been fruitless. He is ashamed and depressed. The new behaviors of his son now seem a personal affront. We now can see that the *what* includes job loss, and the worker's tasks will need to include encouraging the father to join community support groups, helping him with resumés, networking, examining his potential for retraining, and so on.

Person:environment exchanges (transactions) can be positive, negative, or neutral. Furthermore, all of the fundamental ecological concepts described in this chapter are based in such transactions in nature. That is, they express reciprocal relationships among people and their environment. They do not refer simply to a lone characteristic of an individual or the environment, but to particular relationships between them. The complexity of these relationships is captured in the following quote:

> Psychological phenomena are best understood as holistic events composed of inseparable and mutually defining psychological processes, physical environments and social environments, and temporal qualities. There are no separate actors in an event; the actions of one person are understood in relation to the actions of other people, and in relation to spatial, situational and temporal circumstances in which the actors are embedded. These different aspects of an event are so intermeshed that understanding one aspect requires simultaneous inclusion of other aspects in the analysis.
>
> (Werner, Altman, Oxley, and Haggard 1987:244)

Person:Environment Fit

When there is a poor fit between a person's environment and his or her needs, capacities, rights, and aspirations, personal development and functioning are apt to be impaired and the environment may be damaged. When there is a good fit, both person and environment flourish. A condition of *adaptedness* exists when the environment provides resources and experiences at the appropriate time and in the appropriate form to assure people's optimum biological, cognitive, sensory, perceptual, emotional, and social development and functioning (Dubos 1968).

When the fit between person and environment is unfavorable, or merely adequate, the person—alone or with help—may, by changing the self or the environment, improve the level of fit. Put another way, *adaptive* person:environment exchanges support and release human potential and growth, health, and satisfaction. *Dysfunctional* exchanges fail to support adaptedness or interfere with the potential for adaptedness. Ultimately, maladaptive exchanges may lead to an unfavorable fit, impairing development and functioning, perhaps even damaging the environment. However,

Table 1.1	Original Life Model Concepts and Their Definitions
• *Exchanges:*	Continuous transactions between people and their environments, in which each shapes the other over time
• *Person-environment fit:*	Favorable or unfavorable fit between the needs, capacities, behavioral styles, and goals of people, and the characteristics of the environment
• *Adaptedness:*	A favorable person:environment fit that supports human growth and well-being, and preserves and enriches the environment
• *Adaptation:*	Actions designed to achieve personal change, environmental change, or both, in order to improve the level of person:environment fit
• *Adaptive:*	Person:environment exchanges that release and support human potential for adaptedness

the degree of adaptedness between person and environment is not fixed: the relationship between them is constantly changing in large and small ways.

Adaptation refers to behaviors that move an individual toward adaptedness. These behaviors may have biological, cognitive, emotional, social, or cultural bases. Adaptations are active efforts to (a) change oneself in order to meet the environment's expectations or its demands that are perceived as unalterable, or to take advantage of environmental opportunities; or (b) change the environment so that the social and physical environments are more responsive to one's needs and goals; or (c) change the person:environment relationship in order to achieve an improved fit.

Adaptations may be needed when the environment is changing. Sometimes they reflect an active search for a more responsive environment, as when people emigrate. Whatever the adaptation, people must continue to adapt to the changes they or the environment have made. Hence, adaptation is a never ending process. Social work values support the profession's preference for person:environment exchanges that release people's potential for further growth and promote diverse, supportive environments that release human potential.

"Adaptedness" and "adaptation" are sometimes confused with passive or conservative adjustments to the status quo. But in the ecological social work perspective and in life-modeled practice, adaptedness and adaptation are firmly action-oriented and change-oriented. Neither adaptedness nor adaptation avoids the issues of conflict and power that are as prominent in nature as they are in society. Table 1.1 summarizes the concepts discussed so far.

Life Stressor, Stress, Coping, and Challenge

Practice suggests that people who seek social work services are trying to manage a stressful issue, even though they do not necessarily present their request for service in those terms. The same may be said for those who are referred for services by a third party and those for whom services are mandated by an outside agency or institution. Lazarus, the foremost theorist and researcher in stress and coping, believes that the concepts of stressor, stress, and coping have now achieved the status of a paradigm, "a set of interrelated assumptions . . . about certain classes of phenomena and . . . also a closely linked set of methods or procedures" (1980:28).

Because the stressor—stress-coping paradigm takes account of the characteristics of the person and the operations of the environment, as well as the exchanges between them, it fits well with social work's mission, the ecological perspective, and the life-modeled practice that is derived from it. Like all ecological concepts, the paradigm also helps the social worker to maintain a focus on both person and environment. Hence, we present the stressor—stress-coping paradigm in detail; its assumptions, methods, and procedures are applied throughout this book.

Life stressor and life stress are two concepts that differ from *stress management*, a popularized term that denotes day-to-day control of tensions, annoyances, and frustrations at work, home, or elsewhere through self-administered, learned techniques such as relaxation exercises and biofeedback. This focus on symptoms usually ignores the uniqueness of people, their environments, and the ongoing person:environment relationship. Stress management tends to overlook emotional and cultural features of stress.

> Self-control of physiological responses painstakingly acquired during biofeedback training is readily disrupted by stresses encountered outside the laboratory. . . . People simply are unable to exert control over specific physiological responses while they are engaged in transactions with the environment that generate the very same responses.   (Holroyd and Lazarus 1982:24)

The one exception noted by Holroyd and Lazarus is that the symptoms of migraine headaches can be lessened. These two researchers believe that the improvement in migraine is due to biofeedback indirectly inducing patients to change the way they cope with headache-related stressors, and not that training enables them to control symptom-related physiological responses more directly.

External life stressors and internal stress are expressions of negative relationships between person and environment. The *life stressor*, which is externally generated, takes the form of a harm or loss, or threat of a future harm or loss (e.g., illness, bereavement, job loss, difficult transition, interpersonal conflict, or countless other painful life issues and events). The resulting *stress*, which is internally generated, may have physiological or emotional consequences. Frequently, it has both. Stress should not be equated with internal anxiety because anxiety is only one possible internal response to an external life stressor.

We agree with Lazarus's view that physiological and emotional stress are the consequence of people's appraisal that a difficult life transition, traumatic life event, or other critical life issue exceeds their personal *and* environmental resources. Stressful feelings aroused by the stressor are negative and usually immobilizing. They may include anxiety, guilt, anger, despair, helplessness, or depression.

The stress caused by difficult life transitions and traumatic life events is related to dimensions of the stressor and its meaning to the person. These dimensions include the following:

Whether a stressor is chronic or acute affects its impact. Negative feelings associated with divorce, for example, are largely a function of chronic conflict and disruption in family relationships before and after the divorce (Rutter 1986).

At times, a person may be ambivalent about the stressor and its resolution. For example, a woman may be stressed by the suffering of her partner from severe injuries in an automobile accident. She may feel ambivalent about the possibility of her partner's death. Her understandable ambivalence may further complicate the difficulty of coping.

Whether a critical event is anticipated or unexpected can affect the amount of time available for a person to prepare for the life change. Unpredictable life events are more difficult to cope with than predictable ones. For example, nursing home patients moved to another nursing home with little or no preparation suffer higher death rates than those who receive individual and group preparation and visit the new facility beforehand (Kasl 1972).

Lack of control over a stressor has a profound effect. For example, the diagnosis of terminal cancer in a child evokes severe anxiety in the parents, who may feel helpless or hopeless about helping their child die.

Timing, the point on the life course at which the stressor strikes, is a significant factor in the degree of stress experienced. Most of us anticipate that certain events will take place in accord with certain social or biological expectations (Neugarten 1979). Stressful timing can include the arrival of puberty either very late or very early so that one is painfully different from peers, or inability to find work after graduation.

Expected desired events may not take place, as when an engagement is broken, a miscarriage occurs, or a promised job does not materialize.[2]

When we encounter any difficult life issue we engage in *primary appraisal*, which may be conscious or unconscious. If we ask ourselves, "What is the meaning of this issue?" or "Am I in trouble or is this a challenge?," the appraisal results in a judgment that the issue is irrelevant, benign, or a stressor (Lazarus 1980). If we decide that the issue is a stressor, further appraisal determines whether it represents a harm or loss, a threat of harm or loss (life stressors), or a challenge. Harm or loss refers to current damage and suffering, while threat refers to an anticipated future loss or harm, such as an announced factory closing. In the case of a harm or a loss, efforts to cope are directed to overcoming, reducing, or tolerating the stressor. In the case of threat, efforts to cope are directed to maintaining the current state of affairs, preventing an anticipated harm or loss, or easing the effects. Careful planning of the use of time and financial resources following an announced factory closing or an upcoming but unwanted retirement is an effective coping measure.

We appraise a life issue as a *challenge* when we believe we have the personal and environmental resources to master it. Although challenge can be stressful, it is nevertheless accompanied by feelings of zest, relatedness, competence, and self-direction. In contrast, a stressor is accompanied by a sense of being in jeopardy. A stressor may interfere with problem-solving, and levels of self-esteem, sense of competence, relatedness, and self-direction are apt to drop.

One person may experience a traumatic life issue as a stressor while another may experience the same issue as a challenge. Challenge is experienced by some people even under the most adverse conditions. These differences appear to arise from the interplay of personality, physical condition, environment, past experiences, personal and culturally-based meaning of a serious life issue, availability of resources for coping, and absence of too many concurrent stressors. People who experience a difficult life issue as a challenge are probably less likely to seek social work services than are people who experience the same life issue as a severe stressor.

Sometimes our initial appraisal contains an error in perception or thinking. For example, we may believe that a life issue is a stressor when it is not, or we may think the environment is hostile when it is supportive. We may overestimate our resources for dealing with the stressor and thereby fail to cope with it successfully, or underestimate our resources and believe that the situation is hopeless. Such a belief is often seen in instances of *internalized oppression*, with consequent self-hatred or lowered self-esteem (Lee 1992). Erroneous beliefs, perceptions, and thoughts may intensify the stress. Both in assessment and intervention, the client and the social worker need to determine whether appraisals of stressor and resources are accurate and, if they are not, work on developing greater accuracy. However, the determination must also take account of the influence of the appraisal on morale, social functioning, health, and preservation of options for future coping. It is important to avoid merely considering the truth or falsity of the cognitions (Coyne and Lazarus 1980). For example, defenses falsify situations, yet they can be adaptive over the short term.

Once a life issue is appraised as a stressor that exceeds a person's resources, the *secondary appraisal* asks, "What can I do about this state of affairs?" We respond to secondary appraisal by initiating *coping measures*. Coping occurs over time. Some stressors may pass quickly, as when a firing is followed by another job. Or stressors may be present for a long time, as in mourning, raising an autistic child, or in the case of a solo mother living in poverty. Coping efforts may demand frustrating delays (Lee 1992), or the toleration of a lengthy interval between meeting the demands posed by the stressor and the onset of relief. Now and again, demands may momentarily exceed personal resources because of temporary depletion of an individual's usual capability. Progress is often characterized by ups and downs, especially in some chronic illnesses. Coping expresses a person's person:environment relationship since both personal and environmental resources are required.

Personal resources for coping include motivation; problem-solving and relationship skills; a hopeful outlook; optimal levels of self-esteem and self-direction; the ability to identify and use information from the environment about the stressor and how to deal with it; self-restraint; and an ability to seek environmental resources and to use them effectively. Wheaton (1983) suggests that flexibility is also a personal coping resource. Like hope, it reflects a recognition of positives despite the stressor, a trust in the certainty of future satisfaction, and seeking and accepting help when needed. Also important are optimism (Lazarus and Folkman 1984) and self-attention (Suls and Fletcher 1985).

Environmental resources include formal service networks such as public and private agencies and institutions. Their availability depends on society's and the community's social provisions, eligibility requirements, hours of service, and transportation facilities. Supports also include informal networks of relatives, friends, neighbors, workmates, and coreligionists. Such informal support networks serve as buffers against stress. Even the perception of their availability can make it easier to cope with a life stressor by altering appraisals (Whethington and Kessler 1986:78). However, some formal and informal support systems may be unresponsive or cease to be supportive. Hence, their responsiveness must be evaluated by client and social worker, just as personal resources are evaluated. The social and physical environments involved in coping must be assessed as well: they may not contribute to physical and emotional well-being, support coping efforts, provide therapeutic influences, needed information, or opportunities for personal decision-making and action.

When efforts at coping are ineffective, physiological and emotional stress are likely to be intensified and may lead to physical, social, or emotional dysfunction. The stress generated in one area may cause other stresses, so that multiple stressors become involved. For example, stressful family relationships may affect a child's school performance and thereby make school an additional stressor. It should be noted that stress alone does not cause dysfunction. Rather, a maladaptive outcome depends

Table 1.2	Original Life Model Concepts and Their Definitions
• *Life stressor:*	Life transitions, events, and issues which disturb the level of person:environment fit or a prior state of relative adaptedness
• *Stress:*	Internal (physical or emotional) responses to a life stressor that exceeds one's perceived personal and environmental resources to cope with it
• *Primary appraisal:*	Conscious or unconscious processes through which a person judges whether an issue is irrelevant, benign, or a stressor. If the latter, whether it poses a harm or loss (damage already suffered), a future threat of harm or loss associated with an anticipated life issue, or a challenge (anticipated mastery). A stressor is associated with negative feelings, while a challenge is associated with positive feelings.
• *Secondary appraisal:*	Consideration of measures and resources to deal with a life stressor
• *Coping:*	Behavioral and cognitive measures to change some aspect of oneself, the environment, the exchanges between them, or all three, in order to manage the negative feelings aroused
• *Feedback:*	Error-correcting internal and external signals and cues from a person's cognitions and sensory perceptions and from the environment about the effectiveness of the coping efforts

on either personal vulnerability or ineffective coping. Some coping attempts are doomed to fail, and their outcomes become added stressors. For example, alcohol or drug use may represent an effort to cope with a life stressor and may result in temporary relief. However, chemical substances do not eliminate the stressor or change the person-environment relationship; excessive use can intensify the stress and generate additional stressors.

Most people can cope relatively well with serious life stressors. In some instances, the stressor is ameliorated or its consequences mastered. Many people grow as a result of coping with stressors; their self-esteem and sense of competence, relatedness, and self-direction are strengthened by their triumph over adversity. This growth is much the same as that achieved in mastery of challenge, although challenge is accompanied by less pain and personal and familial upset in the process.

Relatedness, Competence, Self-esteem, and Self-direction

These attributes refer to positive outcomes of adaptive person:environment relationships in past and current environments. Hence they help social workers to maintain simultaneous attention to person and environment in accord with the profession's mission. They are desired outcomes of all practice, in addition to goals specific to a particular person, family, group, or situation. Life-modeled practice assumes that social workers think, feel, and act in ways that support, restore, or increase their clients' experience of these four vital attributes.

We believe that these attributes are interdependent—each is critical to the development of the others. However, relatedness could be considered the central attribute. All cultures seek to support relatedness. But kinship structures and the norms governing rights and obligations of social relations in family and community life, and behavioral responses to friends and strangers may be defined differently in different cultures and subcultures. Similarly, all societies seek to prepare their young for competent performance in the valued roles of its culture, although definitions of competence may vary across age, gender, culture, society, historical era, and within complex multicultural societies such as those of Canada and the United States. Self-esteem and self-direction may be lodged less in the individual and more in the family or tribe in some cultures but they too appear to be universal human characteristics that arise from adaptive person:environment relationships.

The concept of *relatedness* is based on Bowlby's (1973) attachment theory, which proposes that relatedness is an innate capacity of human beings, built into the genetic structure of the species over evolutionary time because of its survival value. Attachment behaviors in the infant (crying, rooting, sucking) elicited reciprocal, caregiving responses in the mother (feeding, care, soothing). These reciprocal behaviors maintained proximity between the pair and, together with the social affiliations of a small band of kin and others, protected the infant from predators. Hence, babies equipped with attachment behaviors and whose mothers reciprocated the behaviors were more apt to survive and reproduce their kind than those not so equipped. Attachment behaviors also include vocalization, smiling, and gazing by baby and caregiver (Stern 1977).

Attachment remains vitally important throughout adulthood as well. As adults our attachments are restricted to a few people (Weiss 1982). The need for proximity to those people is strong, and temporary separations may be painful. Permanent loss can be profoundly debilitating.

Relatedness also incorporates ideas about loneliness, isolation, and supportive social networks. Beginning in toddlerhood and continuing through adulthood, human beings form friendships that reflect a growing capacity for relatedness. Friendship, however, does not necessarily imply attachment. As the child grows, the circle of friends grows and becomes in youth and adulthood a network of affiliations that may consist of friends and relatives as well as neighbors, work mates, religious affiliates, and so on. Such social networks can become very important support systems that buffer the impact of life stressors or serve as coping resources for both problem-solving and managing negative emotions in the face of life stressors.

The power of these informal systems derives from their communicating to their members that each is valued, esteemed, and even loved. On the other hand, a network can be a negative influence, as in violent teenage gangs or adult groups of drinking companions. Other networks may be emotionally destructive because of hostile attitudes toward a person, family, or group. Therefore client and worker need to assess the network and its support capacity.

Weiss (1973) makes an important distinction between emotional ties (attachments) and social ties (friendships and other relationships). Emotional isolation and loneliness at separation or loss can only be relieved by developing a new attachment after mourning has been completed. This is particularly clear in the loss of a child, parent, spouse, or partner. The social network may be helpful at the time of loss, but the members cannot help ease the profound pain of bereavement. That requires the bereaved person's own mourning.

Social isolation and loneliness caused by separation or loss can only be relieved by developing a new social network. Children, teens, and adults can suffer the stress of social loneliness, even though their personal attachment—to parent, spouse, or lover—remains available. The distinction between emotional and social isolation must be kept in mind in assessing loneliness so that social work help is appropriate and effective. Ecomaps (Hartman and Laird 1983) and network maps (Swenson 1979) are useful assessment and intervention tools when looking at relatedness, loneliness, and isolation.

We also experience relatedness with the natural world. Searles (1960) believes that human beings not only must respect the natural world, our life-sustaining environment, but must remain in touch with its restorative, healing and spiritual forces. According to Searles, relatedness with the natural world:

1. ameliorates various painful and anxious feelings
2. fosters self-realization
3. deepens one's feeling of reality
4. fosters the appreciation and acceptance of other people.

These ideas help explain the feelings of serenity and wonder felt by people visiting mountains, seashore, and countryside. It also explains the powerful influence of wilderness programs, organized camping, and nature excursions on people suffering from physical or emotional disorders. We are also coming to recognize the value of companion animals for the chronically ill, those confronting physical or mental challenges, and the isolated aged. Horticultural programs also bring pleasure and a sense of competence to people of all ages.

The sense of *competence* as a bio-psychological concept was developed by White (1959) out of his discontent with the psychoanalytic idea that effective action derives from libidinal and aggressive drives. White proposed that all living organisms are innately motivated to have an effect on their environment in order to survive. The motivation is most highly developed in human beings. For example, even very young babies experience having an effect on the environment when their caregivers respond promptly and ungrudgingly to their signals of distress.

The desire to have an effect on the environment also appears to require novelty, complexity of stimuli, and satisfying responses from the environment. Babies enjoy the environmental consequences of their actions as they bat a mobile, bang pots and pans, drop cups of milk, splash bath water, and otherwise explore and manipulate the environment.

Accumulated experience of competent action, perhaps together with an ability to seek and accept help on one's own terms when needed, eventually leads to a sense of competence over the life course. Innate competence motivation is an important hypothesis for social workers: it suggests that the client's motivation to be effective in the environment can be mobilized even after life experiences have dampened it. The sense of competence and experiences of success or failure as narrated by the client are part of assessment, while the ongoing phase of the work together must include opportunities for the further development of competence.

Unfortunately, social work and other human service professions do not have all the needed knowledge and skills to help some people mobilize their competence motivation. Moreover, values affect how competence is defined. Nevertheless, in many situations it is possible for social worker and client to devise opportunities for effective action that will mobilize, enhance, or restore the sense of competence and heighten relatedness, self-esteem, and self-direction.

Self-esteem represents the extent to which one feels capable, significant, effective, and worthy. It is the most important dimension of self-concept (Coopersmith 1967; Rosenberg 1979) and is a major influence in human thinking and behavior. High self-esteem is intrinsically satisfying and pleasurable because it reflects self-respect and feelings of self-worth. Low self-esteem reflects lack of self-respect, and feelings of worthlessness, inadequacy, and inferiority. Clinically, low self-esteem and depression are often associated. The initial level of self-esteem must be assessed by client and worker, and then continually noted throughout the contact. Social workers quickly come to recognize the significance of their own empathic attentiveness, encouragement, and appropriate reassurance in restoring or supporting a client's self-esteem.

Self-esteem has its start in infancy, as the behavior toward the baby by the parents or caregiver conveys their feeling that the baby is lovable and is loved by them. self-esteem is especially important in childhood and adolescence, and it continues to develop and change in adulthood. The level of self-esteem shifts from time to time, given the ups and downs of life. self-confidence in one's abilities may contribute to self-esteem but should not be equated with it. For example, many people who live in poverty have positive self-esteem, although some may have less self-con-

Table 1.3	Original Life Model Concepts and Their Definitions
• *Relatedness:*	Innate capacity of human infants to form attachments and, later, to form friendships and other social affiliations. In adulthood an attachment may or may not include a sexual relationship.
• *Efficacy:*	Feeling state resulting from a positive experience of having an effect on the environment
• *Competence:*	Inner sense derived from accumulated experiences of efficacy and, at times, associated with the ability to seek and accept help when needed
• *Self-concept:*	Totality of a person's thoughts and feelings about oneself
• *Self-esteem:*	Extent to which a person feels capable, significant, and worthy of respect and love
• *Self-direction:*	Sense of having some control over one's life and ability to take responsibility for one's decisions and actions, while respecting the rights and needs of others

fidence in their ability to affect their environment in the face of formidable barriers.

Self-direction refers to the sense of having some measure of control over one's life, and feeling able to take responsibility for one's decisions and actions while respecting the rights and needs of others. Self-direction must be supported throughout childhood, youth, and adulthood by the family and community. Age-appropriate opportunities for making decisions and taking action foster self-direction and help sustain self-esteem and the sense of competence. Toddlers and preschoolers develop the ability to do things for themselves if opportunities are provided by the caregivers and the child's successes are recognized and valued. Social workers need to help clients develop opportunities to make decisions and act effectively on their decisions (however modest) in light of age, physical and psychological condition, environmental features, and culture. Issues of personal power and powerlessness are critical to the exercise of self-direction. When people's life circumstances narrow their options so that personal choices are meaningless, and they have no control over life events or financial security, then self-direction, self-esteem, and the sense of competence may be threatened. Some may succumb to the passivity of impotent, chronic rage, or to feelings of despair, helplessness, hopelessness, self-hate, or acts of violence. Powerlessness is particularly cruel since poor and oppressed people are apt to suffer many more disruptive life stressors than the rest of the population. At the same time, far fewer environmental resources are available to them for modifying disruptive, stressful life issues or coping with their consequences.

We must not overlook the substantial evidence of effective coping, energetic activity, and aesthetic variety in the functioning of poor communities. These strengths include the use of music and humor in the face of grinding life issues, renewed efforts in response to defeat, recourse to sacred and secular ideologies for psychological strength, resourceful devices to manipulate social structures for maximum benefit, and mobilization for large-scale change, and kin and non-kin networks for emotional and material support (Comer and Hamilton-Lee 1982; Stack 1974; Valentine and Valentine 1970).

Table 1.3 summarizes the additional original ecological and life model concepts:

Additions to the Ecological Perspective

Three sets of new concepts are explained in this section. One set describes the maladaptive societal and community processes that have serious consequences for individuals, families, groups, and communities. The second set examines the importance of habitat and niche. The third set provides a definition of the life course.

Power, Powerlessness, and Pollution

While power and its abuse may have always been a part of collective life, the decade of the 1980s saw corporate abuses of financial power to an extent not seen since the 1880s and 1890s. Even in public bureaucracies, abusive power excludes and oppresses large segments of our population. Such power is the antithesis of growth-promoting, self-healing life forces.

Dominant groups withhold power from vulnerable groups on the basis of their personal or cultural characteristics (such as color, ethnicity, gender, age, sexual orientation, religion, socioeconomic status, or physical or mental conditions). The result is oppression (prejudicial discrimination) of vulnerable people and groups. This abuse of power creates and maintains such social pollution as poverty, institutional racism and sexism, repressive gender roles in family, work, and community life, homophobia, and physical and social barriers to community participation by those with disabilities. The abuse of economic and political power also leads to poor schools, chronic unemployment or underemployment of those whom the schools failed to educate, lack of affordable and safe housing, homelessness, inadequate health care, and differential rates of chronic illness and longevity among people of color as compared to whites. These conditions form the context of life for large segments of our population, and the social worker who serves these populations must possess appropriate advocacy skills.

Private corporations and governmental agencies pollute our air, food, water, and soil. Toxic materials continue to be present in our dwellings, schools, and workplaces, especially in blue-collar and poor communities. Social workers are coming to understand that some of these perils must be foci of change efforts by the profession and individual social workers in cooperation with other groups.

Disempowerment and technological pollution are major stressors that afflict the entire population, but their burden falls heaviest on the vulnerable, disenfranchised, and excluded. Disempowerment and pollution threaten health, social wellbeing, and life itself. They impose enormous adaptive tasks on the oppressed. They are expressions of destructive relationships between person and environment, in which the social order permits some to inflict grave injustice and suffering on others. The concepts and principles of an empowering practice with the oppressed are incorporated into life-modeled practice.

Habitat and Niche

These two concepts are particularly useful in work with communities (Germain 1985), although they also help us understand an environment's impact on the individuals, families, and groups we serve. In ecology, habitat and niche are neutral concepts, but as applied in this book they may be neutral, supportive, or can carry great negative force.

In the science of ecology, *habitat* refers to the places where the organism can be found, such as nesting places, home ranges, and territory. Metaphorically, human beings' particular physical and social settings within a cultural context represent their habitat. For humans, physical habitat may be rural or urban, and include dwellings, transportation systems, workplaces, schools, religious structures, social agencies, and hospitals, and amenities such as parks, recreation facilities, entertainment centers, libraries, and museums, and aspects of the natural world. Habitats that do not support the growth, health, and social functioning of individuals and families, and do not provide community amenities to an optimum degree, are likely to produce isolation, disorientation, and helplessness. Thus habitats may interfere with basic functions of family and community life and require joint work of client and practitioner.

Niche refers to the position occupied by a species of organisms within a biotic community, that is, their place in a community's web of life. Odum (1964), an ecologist, wrote that the habitat is the organism's "address" and the niche is its "profession." In this book, niche refers to the status occupied in a community's social structure by its groups and individuals. What constitutes a growth-supporting, health-promoting human niche is defined differently in various societies and in different historical eras. In the United States, a niche is generally thought to be shaped by a set of rights, including the right to equal opportunity (DeLone 1979). Yet millions of children and adults occupy niches that do not support human needs, rights, and aspirations—often because of some personal or cultural characteristic devalued by society.

These niches are shaped and sustained by society's tolerance of the misuse of power in political, social, and economic structures. Community niches that interfere with health, morale, and social functioning are critical environmental elements in community social work. In order to help reconstruct damaging niches, social workers and social agencies must participate in efforts to influence local, state, and federal policies through professional associations, political coalitions, the press, and activity as individual concerned professionals (Germain and Gitterman 1987, 1995).

Life Course

The concept of life course is probably the most far-reaching advance in life-modeled practice. The term refers to the unique pathways of development that each human being takes—from conception and birth through old age—in varied environments and to our infinitely varied life experiences. "Life course" replaces the traditional "life cycle" models of human development in which so-called "life stages" are assumed to be fixed, sequential, predictable, and universal.[3] The term "life cycle" is a misnomer, because human development is not cyclical, yet the term persists. Stage models conceal the fact that stages and developmental tasks originate in the social norms of a particular society in a particular historic context. They view psychological transformations as due exclusively to natural processes of psychological growth and ignore the formative influence of society's practices, interpersonal exchanges, and socialization processes (Broughton 1986) and, we add, diverse cultures and subcultures.[4]

By contrast, the life course conception rests on an ecological view of nonuniform, indeterminable pathways of biopsychosocial development within diverse environments and cultures.[5] Hence, as adopted for life-modeled practice, the life course conception readily incorporates and emphasizes the following elements:

1. Human diversity (race, ethnicity, gender, culture, socioeconomic status, religion, sexual orientation, and physical/mental states). The life course conception permits us to individualize personal and collective life experience, instead of forcing all people into predetermined, universal developmental stages. Human behavior is indeterminate.
2. The self-regulating, self-directing, indeterminable nature of human beings and their innate push toward growth and health.
3. Environmental diversity (economic, political, social, and historical), taking account of the effects of poverty or prejudicial discrimination on human development and functioning.
4. Newly emerging family forms and their special tasks and developmental issues in addition to those faced by traditional family forms.
5. Rapid shifts in societal and community values and norms in today's world.
6. The critical significance of global and local environments.

Because it is a system of ideas drawn from many disciplines, the life course conception readily assimilates new data (and new meanings attributed to older data) about the observed and almost infinite diversity in human development and functioning. The life course conception has biological, social, cultural, and environmental emphases that fit neatly with social work's historic commitments and with the ecological perspective. It also emphasizes such strengths as cognition and perception, emotions and motivations, spirituality, the capacity to attribute meaning to life experiences, self-help, and mutual aid (Gitterman and Shulman, 1994; Lee and Swenson 1994).

Perhaps most significant of all, the life course conception can be organized around matters of life stressors, stress, and coping that are generated by difficult life transitions, traumatic life events, poverty, and prejudicial discrimination. Life transitions, for example, are then viewed not as isolated, separable, fixed developmental stages but as ongoing biopsychosocial processes, occurring or recurring at any point in the life course. They may be expected or unexpected, and they may be stressful or challenging, depending on the unique interplay of personal, historic, cultural, and environmental factors. The resolution of these processes leads to growth, while the lack of resolution can lead to the physical, emotional, or social dysfunction and possible disorganization of family, group, or community (Germain 1990).

Life course theorists place human development and social functioning in a matrix of historical, individual, and social time (Hareven 1982). *Historical time* refers to the formative effects of social change on birth cohorts (segments of the population born at the same historical point) that help account for generational and age differences in biopsychosocial development, opportunities, and social expectations. For example, cohorts of North American women born between 1970 and 1980 differ—in psychosocial development, opportunities, expectations of marriage, parenting, and work—from earlier cohorts. Social workers need to understand the differences across cohorts, in addition to the more telling differences in personality, culture, and life experiences, which are understood in terms of individual and social time.

Individual time refers to the experiences, meanings, and outcomes of personal and environmental factors over the life course, within a given historical and cultural context. Individual time in this sense is reflected in the self-constructed life stories or narratives, about which more will be said in a later chapter. For now, we merely note Neugarten's observation (1969: 123) that predates by a quarter of a century practitioners' current interest in narrative theory:

> The adult, surely by middle age, with his highly refined powers of introspection and reflection, is continually busying himself in making a coherent story out of his life history. He reinterprets the past, selects and shapes his memories, and reassesses the significance of past events in his search for coherence. An event which, at the time of its occurrence, was 'unexpected' or arbitrary or traumatic becomes rationalized and interwoven into a context of explanation in its retelling 20 years later.

Table 1.4	New Ecological Concepts and Their Definitions
• *Coercive power:*	Withholding of power by dominant groups from other groups on the basis of personal or cultural features
• *Exploitative power:*	Abuse of power by dominant groups that creates technological pollution around the world, endangering the health and well-being of all people and communities and, most especially, poor people and their communities
• *Habitat:*	Place where an organism is found. Used metaphorically, all the physical and social settings of human individuals or groups
• *Niche:*	Position occupied by a species in a biotic community. Used metaphorically, the social status occupied in a human community by an individual or a group
• *Life course:*	Unique, unpredictable pathways of development that humans take within diverse environments and cultures, and their diverse life experiences from conception and birth to old age
• *Historical time:*	The historical contexts of social change and its differential formative effects on different birth cohorts (segments of the population born in the same decade or period of time)
• *Individual time:*	The life experiences of the individual, the meanings attributed to them and their outcomes, within a given historical context and a particular culture (exemplified by people's life stories)
• *Social time:*	The expected and unexpected transitions, traumatic events, and other life issues in a family, group, or community, and the consequent positive transformations of the collectivity or grave disorganization that may occur

Social time refers to the timing of collective life issues in a family, group, or community, and the transformations or disorganizations that occur as consequences of individual and collective processes, shifts in issues facing the group, and the myths and rituals families, groups, communities, and organizations develop to explain their experiences. Many groups such as school-age and adult peer groups develop cherished rituals, and some create myths about their origin and experiences. A community may also develop rituals such as parades or ethnic celebrations, and myths about early events such as its founding or its catastrophes.

Until the 1960s, social time consisted of "timetables" that prescribed the timing of certain life transitions: the proper time to enter school, leave home, marry, have a child, retire. Such timetables are no longer viable, a manifestation of the accelerated rate of social change (historical time). The early childhood education movement is creating a new age group—preschoolers—who attend nursery school, Head Start, and so on. Elders go back to school for high school certificates or college degrees, grown children remain at home after finishing college, some children bear and rear children, while some adults postpone childbearing until the last possible moment. Many elders do not regard themselves as old until their late seventies or eighties. These and other life transitions are becoming age-independent.

In parallel fashion, and related to historical, individual and social time, the phenomenon of gender crossover is slowly expanding. Gendered family roles are changing in some families in regard to childrearing, household management, and so on. Gender crossovers also appear in the workplace as women enter previously male-dominated occupations and professions such as truck driving and medicine, and men take on previously female-dominated work such as nursing, office support, and so on.

In adapting to life experiences accumulated over historical, individual, and social time, human beings change themselves and their environments for good or ill. To understand the positive and negative changes, we must understand the interplay of personal, environmental, cultural, and historical factors that produces change. The implication of these and other elements of the life course conception are expanded in subsequent chapters through their application to practice methods and skills.

Table 1.4 summarizes new ecological concepts and their definitions.

THE LIFE MODEL OF
SOCIAL WORK PRACTICE:
A Brief Overview

Origins of Life-Modeled Practice

The term *Life Model* of social work practice was initially inspired by the work of the late Bernard Bandler, a Boston psychiatrist who worked closely with social workers. In advancing ego-supportive practice in social work, Bandler introduced the idea of modeling practice on "life itself, its processes of growth, development, and decline, its methods of problem-solving and need-satisfaction as understood in the trajectory of the life span" (1963: 42–43). Such a life-modeled practice fits the social work profession's purpose of releasing the potential for growth and satisfying social functioning of individuals, families, and groups, while increasing the responsiveness of their environments to people's needs, rights, and aspirations.

> Two major tendencies in all people from birth to death . . . are ceaselessly in opposition. These [are] the progressive and regressive trends in human nature. . . . Other things being equal, progressive forces are the stronger. . . . We must identify the progressive forces with which we can ally ourselves and which, at the appropriate time, we can help mobilize.

Bandler challenged social workers to learn from people who cope effectively with the inevitable stressors in life and from those who nurture their children well. Instead of relying on artificial clinical processes, social workers can utilize these real-life processes in interventions that will mobilize forces of health and continued growth and also relieve environmental pressures. Indeed, recent studies (Germain 1991a, 1990) disclose many natural life processes now used in life-modeled practice with such critical stressors as family discord, divorce and custody matters, severe, acute, and chronic physical illness, and some emotional disorders. However, many other critical life issues also enter the social work domain, but without research and practice experience that might suggest potential helping methods derived from natural life processes. These particular stressors are mainly large-scale issues such as poverty, unplanned teenage pregnancy, drug addiction, youth gangs, family violence, structural unemployment, and many child welfare dilemmas. Nevertheless, some social workers and social agencies are developing experimental programs and services and studying their outcomes; their pioneering may disclose real-life processes of repair and restoration (Lightburn and Kemp 1994).

Defining Characteristics of Life-Modeled Practice

Ten features, in their unique combination, characterize life-modeled practice.

1. Professional function which includes practice with individuals, families, groups, communities, and organizational and political advocacy.
2. Diversity-sensitive, empowering, and ethical practice.
3. Client:worker relationship regarded as a partnership.
4. Agreements on all aspects of the work, life stories, and assessments.
5. Integrated modalities, methods, and skills.
6. Focus on personal and collective strengths.
7. Emphasis on client action and decision-making.
8. Pervasive significance of social and physical environments and culture.
9. Consistent attention to the unique dimensions of the life course of individuals, families, and groups served.
10. Evaluation of practice and contributions to knowledge.

1. Professional function

The purpose of life-modeled practice is to *elevate the level of fit* between people and their environments, especially between human needs and environmental resources. In providing direct services to individuals, families, and groups, the social work purpose is to (a) eliminate, or alleviate life stressors and the associated stress by helping people to mobilize and draw on personal and environmental resources for effective coping; and (b) influence social and physical environmental forces to be responsive to people's needs.

Over the life course, most people confront life stressors in one or more aspects of living: difficult life transitions and traumatic life events, environmental pressures (including poverty and oppression), and dysfunctional processes in family, group, or community. Life transitions include developmental (biological) and social changes in status and role. Traumatic life events, often unexpected, include grave losses such as bereavement, job loss, loss of a home, rape, AIDS and other illnesses.

Environmental pressures can arise from the lack of resources and social provisions on the part of some social and physical environments. This might include destructive or nonsupportive social networks, organizations that arbitrarily withhold resources, and societal toleration of poverty, violence, and other major social problems. Physical settings can be serious life stressors because of deteriorated dwellings and neighborhoods that may lack amenities of any kind. Dysfunctional arrangements in families, communities, human services, and organizations might also be serious life stressors.

When a life stressor strikes and is not successfully managed, additional stressors can erupt in other areas of life.

The Williams family, African-Americans, consists of the parents and two daughters, one in high school and the other in kindergarten. Mr. Williams was a valued employee of a moving company until he began to suffer migraine and fainting spells, accompanied by progressive alcoholism. Eventually, he was suspended from his job. Nevertheless, his employer is eager for his return—but only with medical assurance that the fainting spells and alcoholism are under control. However, Mr. Williams's health care is not coordinated. He receives large doses of different medications, prescribed by several doctors, on which he is becoming increasingly dependent. He is immobilized by debilitating migraines and fainting spells. When Mr. Williams lost his job, he also lost the status and self-esteem he had gained as a successful professional mover. This undermined his sense of competence, intensified his depression, and worsened his drinking problem. He also needs help in considering hospital detoxification programs. Mrs. Williams works part-time in a fast-food restaurant and has become the dominant force in the family as her husband's condition deteriorated. Life stressors appear in the following areas:

The family faces eviction because Mr. Williams's troubles resulted in nonpayment of rent and complaints about his noisy behavior.

Mr. Williams now occupies a community niche of "helpless alcoholic." He enacts the role of victim, sleeping late and withdrawing from family life. Reciprocally, Mrs. Williams encourages him to stay away from home, treats him as if he were a naughty child, scolding him, and withholding money. Their conflict becomes increasingly severe and is marked by physical violence, emotional explosions, and absence of sexual intimacy.

Mr. Williams is withdrawing from his children, and the children are beginning to withdraw from both parents. The older daughter is beginning to have difficulties in school.

These stressors are interrelated, but each takes on a life of its own. Together, they can overwhelm the individual, group, family, or community. This family is in need of immediate help to prevent its disorganization. Life-modeled practice would intervene at individual, family, and environ-

Figure 2.1   Professional Function and Life Stressors

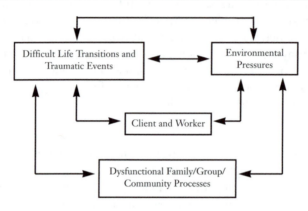

mental levels. Family members would be asked to set priorities among the stressors to be worked on immediately, and the social worker would seek out personal, family, and environmental strengths. The professional function is represented in figure 2.1.

In mediating the exchanges between people and their environments, social workers daily encounter the lack of fit between people's needs and the environment. Thus the purpose of life-modeled practice also includes

Figure 2.2   The Life Model Social Change
                    Conception of Professional Function

professional responsibility for bearing witness against social inequities and injustice. This is done by *mobilizing community resources* to influence quality of life in the community, by *influencing unresponsive organizations* to develop responsive policies and services, and by *politically influencing local, state, and federal legislation and regulations* to support social justice (figure 2.2).

2. Diversity-sensitive, empowering, and ethical practice

Social work values are a set of beliefs that define what the profession considers to be desirable and good. Most social workers, for example, hold the basic value of "maximum realization of each individual's potential for development throughout . . .[the client's] lifetime" (Gordon 1965:38). This and other values, such as respect for individual worth and dignity, self-determination, justice and equality, constitute the value base of all social work practice.

Sensitivity to difference. Social workers must consistently accept and respect each client's (a) race, ethnicity, socioeconomic status, and religion; (b) sexual orientation; (c) gender; (d) age; and (e) mental and physical states. Such sensitivity requires a high level of self-awareness and specialized knowledge about a particular population or person being served by the practitioner.[1]

The combination of self-awareness and specialized knowledge helps to assure a practice that is sensitive to difference and is responsive to the needs and aspirations of vulnerable and oppressed populations and to the consequences of discrimination. Sensitivity to difference also requires respect and understanding of people whose characteristics and values may differ from those of the group around them or of the worker.

Sensitivity to race and ethnicity. Social workers must familiarize themselves with the characteristics of the cultural groups whom they serve (*Bridging Cultures: Southeast Asian Refugees in America 1981*; Devore *1983*; Drachman and Shen-Ryan *1991*; Germain *1991*; Gitterman and Schaeffer *1972*; Hardy-Fanta and MacMahon-Herrera *1981*; McGoldrick, Pearce, and Giordano *1981*; Pinderhughes *1989*; *Social Casework 1974, 1976*, and *1980* issues; *Social Work 1982* issue). Formal social work education now provides general information about people of color, and perhaps more specific information regarding minorities within the region served by an educational program. Nevertheless, all social workers must continually update their knowledge about the history and culture of the racial and ethnic groups whom they serve. In the case of recent immigrants, for example, the practitioner needs to be aware of

- civil war, revolution, traumatic expulsions, mass murders, atrocities
- regional and class differences within the group
- characteristics of family structure, gendered role expectations, the status of women, and generational relationships
- values, attitudes, and beliefs, and the significance of religion
- health and illness patterns, the meaning attributed to physical and mental symptoms, and natural helping traditions
- worldview and the social construction of reality

- the group's acculturation experience in North America
- the ways in which a particular individual or family differs from cultural patterns usually found in the group.

Sensitivity to gender.   The feminist movement has explored the pervasiveness of institutional sexism in education, work, health care, and family and community life (Tice 1990; Cole 1986; Van Den Bergh and Cooper 1986; Weick and Vandiver 1982). Gender-sensitive practice requires enlightened avoidance of compliance with male and female clients' expectations of male dominance. Not all women are dissatisfied with their gender roles and subjugation or wish to change such limitations. Nevertheless, techniques of consciousness-raising and renaming do help many to recognize the social source of their troubles and how their personal and social lives can become more fulfilling or satisfying.

Sensitivity to differing developmental issues.   The practitioner must possess extensive knowledge of normative biological development over the life course, as well as of psychological and social development. Fortunately, most social work educational programs are beginning to furnish information in this area, and a rich and growing literature is readily available.

Sensitivity to chronic conditions.   All social workers—and not only those in the fields of health and mental health care—must be knowledgeable about major physical and mental conditions and the impact of discrimination. Social workers, regardless of their field of practice, are likely at times to be professionally engaged with individuals, families, groups, and communities struggling with severe, chronic mental and physical disorders. Practitioners must familiarize themselves with the nature, course, and prognosis of the condition, and the stressors faced by those who directly or indirectly suffer from it. (Anderson, Reiss, and Hogarty 1980; DeJong 1979; Germain 1991b, 1984; Gitterman 1991a; Gliedman and Roth 1980; Kerson and Kerson 1985; Mahaffey 1987).

Sensitivity to sexual orientation.   Current practice requires knowledge of the effects of oppression on gay and lesbian people, the strengths and resources within gay and lesbian communities, the process of coming out and its personal costs and joys, gay and lesbian family life, alternative lifestyles, and gay and lesbian rights (Moses and Hawkins 1982). Homophobia (fear and hatred of homosexual people) is widespread in North America, even among social workers, despite some enlightened progress made in some communities. The professional literature on gays and lesbians is rapidly increasing (Lee 1994). So too are novels, short stories, dramas, and poetry by openly gay and lesbian people, and published personal journals of AIDS patients. All are important sources for the development of empathy with gay people. Sadly, not all agencies and services are ready to serve this population. Their gay and lesbian staff members may even be afraid to come out and risk losing their jobs. The following is an entry in an employed social work student's journal:

> I am extremely lucky that I have been able to be open about my sexual prefer-
> ence in my agency with no apparent negative backlash. It's not only a matter of
> luck but also my willingness to take some risks. I think that one of the strongest
> factors in reaching that decision was the knowledge that if another social
> worker were to verbalize or react negatively to some aspect of homosexuality, I
> would be ready to point out that the profession is ethically mandated to be
> open-minded, tolerant of all differences, and prepared to help all who are in
> need regardless of personal values, beliefs, and cultural traditions. To process
> the values of difference without practicing them and making them part of our
> core beliefs, is not a position of strength. I am never really sure if my openness
> is accepted or simply tolerated. But I have made a beginning by giving my fel-
> low workers the opportunity to re-evaluate the concept of homosexuality and
> the stereotypes and attitudes which they grew up with. In the near future, I
> hope to organize a workshop on homosexuality within my agency. It is long
> overdue.

Social workers must confront their own prejudices and stereotypes about gay and lesbian clients. Recently, a colleague was invited to consult at an agency providing services to gay and lesbian clients. In the elevator, he felt the stares and smirks of a few workmen. He was in touch with his discomfort and wanted to inform the workmen that he was not gay. He was unsettled by these thoughts and feelings, and, confronting his own homo-phobia, he began the consultation with agency staff by sharing his experi-ence with them. They, in turn, appreciated his candor and their work together began in a real and moving way.

Finally, we should note that knowledge and self-understanding must be supplemented by reflection on racism, sexism, ageism, able-ism, etc., that is, by reflection on the abuse and misuse of power, the effects of powerless-ness, and the need for an empowerment practice (Lee 1994; Pinderhughes 1989; Simon 1994).

Empowerment practice. Various social work traditions deal with the issues of power and powerlessness. On a micro level, the concept of empower-ment is limited to the development of *personal power* (Pernel 1985, Sherman and Winokur 1993). On a macro level, empowerment is limited to the development of collective action and *political power* (O'Connel 1979). Life-modeled practice is committed to helping people gain both types of power. Empowerment practice in the life model is conceived as the help given by social work practitioners and administrators to clients and colleagues to increase their personal, interpersonal, or political power for greater control over their lives.

We have been greatly influenced by Bertha Reynolds's (1934) belief that the client has the right to decide when help is needed, what help will be useful, and when it is no longer needed. She suggests that social workers find their professional goals on the client's own road. She does not deny that the worker has the power of knowledge, skill, and resources, but she reminds us that those served also have knowledge and skills. Their knowledge of their environment and culture, for example, exceeds that of the worker. Together the person served and the worker are better able to achieve agreed upon goals and tasks than either would be alone. Reynolds also believed that the practitioner must be willing and ready to discuss a client's victimization by injustice.

Solomon's work on disempowerment, powerlessness, and empowerment in social work practice in oppressed African-American communities advanced the conception of an empowering practice (Solomon 1982, 1976). Later, other social work theorists (Breton 1984; Germain 1991b; Gitterman 1991; Kelley, McKay and Nelson 1985; Lee 1994; Mondros and Wilson 1994; Pinderhughes 1983; Simon 1994; Shapiro 1983; Weick 1982) made important contributions to empowerment practice. Gutierrez (1990), for example, described an empowering relationship between client and worker as one of shared power; workers need to perceive themselves as enablers, organizers, consultants, or compatriots. Empowering skills include accepting people's definitions of their life issues; identifying and building on existing strengths; engaging in a power analysis of their situation; mobilizing resources and advocating with and on their behalf; teaching specific skills such as problem-solving, community and organizational change, parenting, job-seeking, assertiveness, competence, and self-advocacy. When helping clients develop these skills the worker consults, facilitates, or guides; the worker should not instruct. This avoids replicating the power relationships that worker and service user are attempting to overcome.

Sensitivity to difference and empowerment practice are inseparably and intimately connected to ethical practice. Each supports the other two.

Ethical practice.   Ethical practice, always a professional concern, is gaining increased attention among social workers because of new and rapidly emerging ethical and moral dilemmas. Ethical practice is firmly rooted in professional values, the NASW CODE OF ETHICS, and laws and legal rulings. The NASW CODE OF ETHICS (1993) provides a codified statement of every day obligations and guidelines for professional behavior. The Code consists of prescriptive ethical principles (i.e., what a social worker must do) and proscriptive ethical principles (i.e., what a social worker mut not do). The Code also serves as a guide for adjudication when the conduct of social workers is alleged to deviate from the profession's standards. See Appendix

A for the NASW CODE OF ETHICS (1993) and the Canadian Association of Social Workers *Code of Ethics* (1994).

While the Code is a helpful guide, the contemporary social worker often confronts contradictory and competing professional obligations that create ethical conflicts and dilemmas such as: truthfulness in client—worker relationships (should the worker respond truthfully to a dying patient who seeks a frank answer to the question, "Am I going to die?" when the family refuses to have such information shared with the patient); the worker's obligations to the employing institution versus obligations to the client (obeying a formal rule or informal policy that seems unjust versus acting in the client's best interests); ethical issues arising from confidentiality and privileged communication, not only in court situations but in family practice and team practice; informed consent (when ending services against a client's wishes because the client is not cooperating or is not benefiting from the service); self-determination (imposing services that were mandated by court, or imposed on a person who refuses help while living on the streets without shelter, food, and needed medical care) (Dean and Rhodes 1992; Reamer 1994, 1990, 1987).

Ethical issues proliferate with the application of computer technology that restricts individuals' ability to make decisions as in computer-generated Diagnostic Related Group (DRG) regulations that determine what is best for a patient (Cwikel and Cnaan 1991). Organizations, professionals, and technology increasingly determine what is best for clients (Walden, Wolock, and Demone 1990). Organizational operations can undermine selfdetermination and competence motivation, and ethical principles of autonomy and self-determination (Abramson 1989; 1985).[2] While at times such paternalistic interventions might be necessary for the person's well-being, too often they are used to exercise social control on behalf of social order or to support an organization and its practices.

Ethical conflicts permeate prevention programs in health, mental health, and other social services. For example, much is known about the effects on fetal well-being of such maternal behaviors as smoking, alcoholism, drug abuse, and inattention to treatment of diabetes. Many social workers are engaged with pregnant women. When fetal and maternal health conflict, the health of the mother is usually the first priority. But what should be done where maternal behavior is endangering fetal health? Does the fetus, when the mother intends to carry it to term, have the right to be born healthy? In situations where the mother fails to discontinue dangerous behavior, what is to be done? Two courses of action are available: pursuing civil commitment to restrain the mother, or seeking custody of the fetus (and hence of the mother) under child protection laws (Mackenzie, Collins, and Popkin 1980). What should the social worker's ethical stance be toward conflicting and competing claims, rights, and responsibilities in this situation?

Ethical issues also arise in social welfare policy. For example, should an agency open a group home for offenders or mentally disturbed people in the face of neighborhood protests? Conflicts between the service ethic and the profit motive will confront social workers as growing number of proprietary organizations enter the human services. Ethical issues in research can arise in truth-telling, methods, analysis, and inferences. Ethical issues in social action and advocacy are connected to truth-telling and informed consent, and client vulnerability and risk (Torczyner 1991).

Ethical concerns in collegial relations include the extent of a practitioner's responsibility for reporting colleague incompetence or wrongdoing to supervisors or other authorities (whistle-blowing) (Reamer 1995). Reamer (1983:33) cites Bok: "To weigh all the dilemmas of whistle blowing—where the cause is a just one, where responsibility is openly accepted, and the whistle blower is above reproach—is rare."

Practice concepts, principles, and methods are not sufficient to resolve ethical issues and value conflicts when they do appear (Reamer 1995, 1990). In recent years, social work scholars have created guidelines for ethical decision-making (Lewis 1984; Joseph 1985; Reamer 1995, 1990; Siporin 1983). Such guidelines can help social workers identify the ethical dimensions of a practice situation and understand particular ethical positions. Four social work approaches to ethical decision-making provide practical guidelines (Loewen-berg and Dolgoff 1992; Reamer 1990, 1994; Joseph 1985; Levy 1976).

When confronting an ethical dilemma, Loewenberg and Dolgoff (1992) suggest that the first step is to examine the NASW Code of Ethics to determine if any of its rules apply. However, since most ethical dilemmas confronted by workers are not directly dealt with by the *Code*, Loewenberg and Dolgoff developed an "Ethical Principles Screen" to help social workers deal with ethical conflicts.

Their ethical principles are presented in the order of priority. In making ethical decisions, "the satisfaction of higher-order principle takes precedence over the satisfaction of a lower-order principle" (60).

1. *Protection of life*. Protecting a client's life and the lives of others takes precedence over any other professional obligation. A severely diabetic adolescent, for example, refuses life-saving insulin injections and diet restrictions because they interfere with her quality of life. Using the ethical principle screen, the worker is justified in compromising the girl's privacy because protecting her life is of primary importance. In such situations, the client must be told what is being done and why.

2. *Equality and inequality*. "Equal people have the right to be treated equally and non-equal persons have the right to be treated differently if the inequality is relevant to the issue in question" (61). In the case of an abused child, the child is not in an equal position relative to the abuser. The worker's obliga-

Table 2.1	Loewenberg and Dolgoff Ethical Principles Screen

- the protection of life
- equality and inequality
- autonomy and freedom
- least harm
- quality of life
- privacy and confidentiality
- truthfulness and full disclosure

tion to protect the child is of a higher order than the rights to privacy and confidentiality of the child and the abusing adult.

3. *Autonomy and freedom.* The profession has an unyielding commitment to support and foster a client's autonomy and freedom. In order to be autonomous, people must be able to act in accordance with their own decisions. Others (especially the social worker) have to respect and support the person's right to do so. However, this principle is superseded when people plan to harm themselves or others.

4. *Least harm.* The worker is required to choose the option that "will result in the least harm, the least permanent harm, or the most easily reversible harm" (57). For example, before a social worker suggests that a client withhold rent payment to protest dilapidated housing conditions, less risky alternatives should be attempted.

5. *Quality of life.* The social worker should not ignore a client's poor quality of life, but client and practitioner should work together to improve it to a reasonable degree.

6. Privacy and confidentiality. Social workers must make ethical decisions that "strengthen every person's right to privacy. Keeping confidential information inviolate is a direct derivative of this obligation." (62)

7. *Truthfulness and full disclosure.* This demands that social workers speak the truth and fully disclose all significant information to those served.

The authors present a vignette of a twelve-year-old sixth grader who is ten weeks pregnant. The school nurse referred her to the social worker. The youngster said she does not want an abortion and does not want her parents to know that she is pregnant. The worker confronts an ethical dilemma: to respect the child's wishes for confidentiality or to respect the parents' right to protect their daughter from potential health risks. In reviewing the Code of Ethics (the authors' suggested first step), no discussion is directly applicable to this situation. In the ethical principle screen, principle 6 states that a social worker should not violate a person's right to privacy and confidentiality without permission. Ethical principle 3 emphasizes respect for an individual's right to be self-ruling. These principles support honoring the youngster's decision about pregnancy and her right to confidentiality. However, since pregnancy poses an immediate danger to a 12-year-old, the worker is justified in violating the principle of confidentiality and notifying her parents. Ethical principle 1 "requires decisions that protect a person's life and survival" (62). The social worker should tell the youngster first that her parents have to be notified, affording her time to tell them herself, or in the company of the social worker.

Maintaining or violating confidentiality is a common ethical dilemma (Berman-Rossi and Rossi 1991, Kopels and Kagle 1994). Abramson (1990) found that it is a major issue for social workers serving people with AIDS or who are HIV-positive. When their clients refuse to inform sexual partners of their infection, workers confront a difficult ethical issue. In these situations, workers have to examine legal statutes as well as ethical guidelines. For example, does the ethical principle screen justify a violation of confidentiality? Or does the ruling in *Tarasoff v. The Regents of the University of California* (1976) (cited further in this chapter) require the worker to warn the third party? Or does a state law prohibit the social worker from notifying the third party, and solely entrust that responsibility to the physician?

Joseph (1985) notes that we must consider our own values and ethics in relation to those whom we serve: our clients, the profession, the agency, and society. Joseph provides this example: A social worker is counseling a 16-year-old girl on a regular basis about her interpersonal relationships. The young woman discloses that she has been shoplifting, and she insists that the information be kept in strict confidence. The initial contract included confidentiality of all content except suicidal or homicidal threats. The parents were being seen by another worker in the agency. Must the worker maintain confidentiality or is she obliged to reveal the information to the parents and to her colleagues? And what of her obligation to society? The NASW Code of Ethics states that sharing information without the client's consent cannot be done except for "compelling professional reasons." Are the reasons in this case compelling? The Code also obliges the worker to fully inform those served about the limits of confidentiality. Is the promise implicit in the contract? This dilemma poses one good, the teenager's right to confidentiality, versus another good, the right of the family and society to this information. After reviewing the data, reflecting on the values, and analyzing the dilemma and alternative actions one might argue that "the parents, on the basis of their authority, have a right to the information . . . based on the claim that the well-being of the adolescent takes precedence over her right to confidentiality. . . . On the other hand, one might argue in favor of the client's right to confidentiality on the basis of the fiduciary relationship and the contract, a further moral force. (214)

As the author points out, this example demonstrates the interaction of practice knowledge and skill with ethical concerns. For instance, failure to be precise in the original contract regarding confidentiality may lead to the dilemma. Also, practice skill might encourage the young woman to discuss the shoplifting with her parents. Joseph contrasts this to the action of a less skilled worker who might, on the basis of the parents' authority or because of personal discomfort, have given the information to the parents without prior discussion with the client.

The following conversation took place between a social work student in an elementary school placement and an eleven-year-old pupil, Robert. She had been seeing the boy weekly for two months, following his mother's vague complaints about his lack of friends. Robert volunteered nothing and nothing had been achieved. The worker continually pushed for problems, and Robert consistently denied having any. Yet the field instructor urged her to continue with Robert; and the pushing went on, capped by the following violation of ethical practice:

> WORKER: Did you wonder why I was at your apartment yesterday?
> ROBERT: Yeah.
> WORKER: Did you talk to your mom at all about that?
> ROBERT: No.
> WORKER: Well, the reason why I went was to find out if you had mentioned anything or if your mom had any ideas about what we should be talking about. I notice that when we get together you don't seem to have things that you want to talk about. What do you think about that?
> ROBERT: Well, I really don't have anything to talk about.
> WORKER: Yeah. (Silence)
> WORKER: Well, when I asked your mom about it, she said that you told her you were having problems with friends, that sometimes you don't have friends to play with.
> ROBERT: Yeah.
> WORKER: What's up with all that stuff?
> ROBERT: I don't know. (Silence)

The worker continues to badger the boy to no avail. Ethical issues are twofold: gaining Robert's informed consent to the worker's visit to his mother was not considered or even mentioned. Nor did the worker tell Robert she was going to visit his mother.

Violations of *ethical boundaries* are extremely serious forms of professional misconduct. Social work practitioners' sexual misconduct with clients are blatant examples of what are called boundary violations. The NASW Code of Ethics states, "The social worker should under no circumstances engage in sexual activities with clients," and several states have passed laws imposing penalties for such transgressions. "But beyond sex violations, the boundaries become less clear, and many violations do not fall neatly under the guidelines of any code of ethics . . . NASW's National Committee on Inquiry reviews about 90 cases of alleged ethics violations each year. . . . The number seems to be growing" (NASW News 1992:3).

Two books on boundary violations—Peterson (1992) and Milgrom, Milgrom, et al. (1989)—urge social workers to avoid risky behaviors and to "be especially aware of inappropriate touching of clients or of disclosing information about themselves" (NASW News, 1992:3). Milgrom suggests that if social work practitioners feel uneasy, it may indicate that they should not keep doing whatever they are doing that makes them uncomfortable. Peterson notes that social workers who change their own rules for a particular client by taking calls late at night or giving a client a ride or money may be engaging in potential violations of ethics.

Laws sanction organizations and professionals to serve the public. Laws also provide users of services certain protections such as privileged communication. Laws assure minimum professional standards through licensing, and they mandate certain professional behaviors such as reporting suspected child abuse (Sales and Shuman 1994). Kutchins (1991) suggests that the relationship between client and worker, as a fiduciary relationship (a relationship of trust), offers the client legal protection including *confidentiality and privileged communication* (with important limitations); and *informed consent.* While a client's right to confidentiality is an ethical principle rather than a legal one, its violation by a social worker can result in a lawsuit. In *MacDonald v. Clinger*, for example, a psychotherapist divulged personal information to a patient's wife. A court ruled this a breach of confidentiality and allowed the patient to sue for damages (Kutchins 1991).

Privileged communication is a legal exemption that limits the government's right to force a social worker to break confidentiality. Whether a practitioner is protected from disclosing confidential material is primarily determined by state law (Smith-Bell and Winslade 1994). If a client is abusing a child, for example, a worker's actions are legally mandated: all fifty states have mandatory reporting statutes, and many specify the reporting as an exception to client privilege. A social worker might be expected also to breach confidentiality if the client represents a danger to others (Kopels and Kagle 1993). In one case, a client told his psychologist, who was employed by a university hospital, that he planned to kill his former girlfriend when she returned from her summer vacation (Weil and Sanchez 1983). The psychologist informed the campus police, seeking their help in having the client committed to a psychiatric hospital for observation. The police judged the client to be rational and released him after he assured them that he would not harm his former girlfriend. Subsequently, he murdered her. In *Tarasoff v. The Regents of the University of California* (1976), the girl's parents sued the psychologist, campus police, and the university for their failure to warn their daughter and them (Givelber, Bowers, and Blitch 1984). On appeal, the California State Supreme Court ruled that the psychologist had a legal obligation to warn the victim and failed to exercise reasonable care. Since state statutes differ, employing organizations and social workers must be familiar with their respective state laws.

Informed consent protects clients' rights to self-determination and privacy. Reamer (1995:164) identifies six standards that must be met to meet the requirements of valid informed consent:

1. absence of worker coercion
2. capability of client to provide informed consent
3. consent is specific
4. consent forms are clear and understandable
5. clients must feel they have the right to refuse or withdraw consent
6. client decisions must be based on sufficient information

While these standards reflect a consensus on what constitutes informed consent, exceptions exist. State statutes, for example, differ on the legal rights of parents to make decisions for their children, and how much autonomy their children are granted to make decisions for themselves. In some states, an adolescent is allowed to provide her own consent for contraception, an abortion, or to enter substance abuse treatment. In other states, however, parents have to be notified, and only they may give consent. The employing organization and the worker, therefore, must know how to acquire informed consent and the limitations of and exceptions to consent. The process includes furnishing information to clients over time and engaging them in a dialogue about assessment and interventions. Informed consent is much more than simply securing a signature.

3. Relationship between client and worker

In life-modeled practice the professional relationship is conceived as a humanistic partnership, with power differences between the partners reduced to the greatest degree possible. Thus, the relationship between client and worker shifts from subordinate recipient and superior expert to a relationship characterized by mutuality and reciprocity. Social workers bring professional knowledge and skill to the therapeutic encounter. Those served bring experiential knowledge of their life issues and their life stories. They are responsible for work on their goals and tasks; social workers are responsible for creating conditions that will facilitate clients' work.

To be effective, the relationship also must be strongly rooted in empathy. Absence of empathy inevitably leads to therapeutic errors and failures, and to client drop-out.

In order to empathize, one must have a well-differentiated sense of self in addition to an appreciation of and sensitivity to the differences as well as sameness of the other. Empathy always involves surrender to feelings and active cognitive structuring; in order for empathy to occur, self-boundaries must be flexible [to allow] perception of the other's affective cues (both verbal and non-verbal) followed by surrender to affective arousal in oneself. . . . For empathy to be effective, there must be a balance of affective and cognitive, subjective and objective, active and passive.   (Jordon 1991:69)

The author also suggests that empathy may be relative rather than absolute. For example, some people may be empathically attuned to certain feelings but not to others, to sadness but not to anger, to pride but not to shame. With practice experience, however, social workers' ability to empathize with most clients is expected to increase. But if one cannot empathize with certain people or their feelings, this limitation must be recognized and a transfer must be arranged so that a person with whom one cannot empathize will not be deprived of needed service.

Mr. Chapman is a 38 year old, white, divorced, unemployed artist receiving welfare. For four months, he was seen by a young, female social worker, having been referred following his complaints that the psychotherapy group he attended was not helpful. Mr. Chapman had experienced two short-term psychiatric hospitalizations and five emergency room contacts. He complained of anxiety, racing thoughts, sleep disturbances, and suicidal ideation. The student social worker records:

During our work over two months, Mr. Chapman was typically late for appointments, guarded, hostile, anxious, and unwilling or unable to respond to the gentlest of questions about his past or current difficulties. He once came between sessions, complaining of racing thoughts and paranoid ideas, and he was given a thorazine elixir. Following this event he became more anxious about our sessions and his content was highly eroticized. He spoke of past relationships with women in a flamboyant, emotional style. His stories depicted himself as either passionately in love or obsessively angry at their imagined mistreatment of him. He left me written material between meetings—love letters from former girlfriends, lists of sexual techniques, and letters complaining about my comments to him. I occasionally saw him in the building and felt he was there for safety and to see me by chance. After my three-week vacation, Mr. Chapman anxiously complained that he could not get me out of his mind and that I had become associated with unpleasantness. He requested transfer to another practitioner. When I suggested we talk about this, he left my office and terminated contact.

This usually sensitive, empathic social work student committed a practice error that led to client drop-out. In her later reflections, the student decided that the failure was due to her erroneous focus on the anxiety and early history, instead of recognizing with Mr. Chapman his artistic talent, high intelligence and intellectual curiosity, and what she described as an engaging relational style. She felt that given these strengths, he would have been better served by a supportive approach, including encouragement in selling his excellent paintings through his many contacts in the arts community. This would have given him financial security and increased self-esteem, as it clearly had all through his twenties. Help in gaining control over his environment and its available resources, and learning new methods of coping were more likely to have been effective than was the internal focus she adopted because of her interest in psychoanalysis.

Inexperience, together with lack of empathy, may occasionally lead to underestimating people's strengths and their potentials for growth. This is especially true in settings that serve profoundly disturbed people. A beginning social work student reports on how her low expectations were turned around:

My client in a day treatment program for those suffering from chronic schizophrenia was riding with me in the program's van. The driver stopped the van and asked my client to go across the street to buy a pack of cigarettes. I began to argue that Matthew does not speak, cannot make change, and doesn't know how to cross the street. The driver said, "Gee, I didn't know that. If I had, I wouldn't have asked him, but he's been getting my cigarettes for me for weeks now."

I think I had been seeing my clients as bundles of symptoms rather than as living, growing human beings. Our driver didn't know about the "hopelessness" of the symptoms and therefore he set his expectations higher and more accurately than mine. This was an important lesson for me.

4. Agreements, life stories, and assessments

Mutual agreements and assessments are characteristic of many practice approaches. In life-modeled practice, social worker and client are partners as they work together throughout the contact. When the worker-client partner relationship is defined and manifested as it is in life-modeled practice, resistance, testing, withdrawal or unplanned termination in the initial phase are minimized.

Agreements. All helping in life-modeled practice rests on shared definitions of life stressors and explicit agreements on foci, priorities, selection of modality, goals, plans, next steps, and other arrangements of the work. In themselves, an applicant's statement of need, or an agency's offer of service, or a mandated service do not represent agreement until the applicant and worker reach a shared, specific, and clear understanding about their foci and methods. Reaching agreement is a critical aspect of the initial phase of social work practice and continues in the ongoing and ending phases.

Agreement between worker and client protects the client's individuality, enhances self-direction, and strengthens coping skills. Most important, arriving at an agreement structures and focuses the work, decreases anxiety associated with the fear of the unknown and the ambiguity inherent in beginnings, and mobilizes energy for work. It also reduces some of the power discrepancy between client and worker at a time when the client is vulnerable to manipulation or misuse at the hands of the agency or professional authority.

Life stories.   The life stories that we tell to ourselves and others over our life course are natural, real-life processes—our human way of finding meaning and continuity in life events. "One's identity, then, is built on the sense one can make of one's own life story" (Laird 1989:430–431). The truth of life stories lies in the connections these stories create among life events, lending coherence to individual and family life (Cohler 1982; Spence 1982). With the empathic, active listening of the social worker, a life story gains increased intelligibility, consistency, and continuity. The teller of the story reinterprets and reconstructs a narrative which ultimately will contain new conceptions of oneself and of relationships with others (Stern 1985). Because they are offered voluntarily after trust is established, life stories become part of the work. The extensive "life histories" taken by the practitioner in intake interviews are obtained from probing questions before a trusting relationship is in place; as a result, they yield less significant content.

Assessment.   Assessment is an essential attribute of all practice approaches. Social workers must make informed choices as the helping process begins, including where and how to enter an individual's, family's, or group's situation, what modality and temporal arrangements to suggest, which client messages to explore, and when to work on factual content or feelings, or on verbal or nonverbal material, or on goal-setting and next steps. Assessment relies on reasoned thought when making judgments at any moment during the session, and when constructing a formal assessment of person:environment exchanges following several sessions. To be valid and useful, clinical decisions and the assessment itself must be rooted in logical reasoning, and inferences based on available evidence (Gambrill 1992; Meyer 1993).

To develop reliable and clinical judgments, social workers must construct assessments in partnership with those served. Their shared tasks include:

1. Collecting salient data on the nature of the life stressors and their degree of severity, the person's perception of and responses to the stressor, and personal and environmental resources available for coping. Data are also collected that clarify the operation of cultural and historical contexts, and biological, emotional, perceptual, cognitive, and environmental factors in the current situation. Strengths and limitations must be identified.
2. Organizing data in ways that reveal significant patterns. Social workers can be overwhelmed by their clients' overwhelming life stressors. Therefore, a system is needed that can organize data in a way that clarifies their meaning and reveals significant patterns.
3. Analyzing and synthesizing the data in order to draw inferences about client strengths and limitations, environmental resources and deficits, and level of fit between person and environment.

These assessment tasks are common to all practice approaches. However, a few underlying beliefs are distinct to life-modeled practice. First, life-modeled practice strongly values and encourages *client participation* in the assessment tasks. Involvement ensures shared focus and direction, and supports a difference-sensitive, empowering, and ethical practice.

Second, life-modeled practice emphasizes assessment of the *level of fit* between human needs and environmental resources. For example, Mrs. Stein, a sixty-year-old widow, has suffered a stroke. How much stress and difficulty she will experience when discharged from the hospital and confined to a wheel chair will depend on her: physical condition (extent of physical loss, stamina); inner resources (motivation, outlook on life, coping skills, meaning of the illness); access to organizational resources (competent medical staff, homemaker, nursing care, physical rehabilitation, speech therapy); availability of social support networks (family, relatives, friends, neighbors); supportive physical environment (wheel chair accessibility of building and apartment); and financial resources. Figure 2.3 suggests the

Figure 2.3   Person: Environment Fit

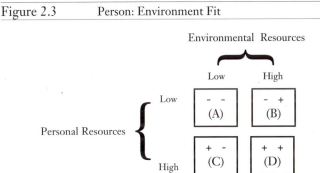

combined impact of a client's internal resources and limitations and environmental resources and limitations (Gitterman 1991).

If Mrs. Stein has strong internal and external coping resources (D), the social worker's activity might be limited to uncomplicated referrals, suggestions, and emotional support. In contrast, if Mrs. Stein has limited personal resources (cognitive impairment, chronic depression, lack of physical strength), and limited environmental and financial resources (no children, few friends) (A), she is at serious risk for disorientation, deterioration, and disorganization. In this case, the immediate attention of an active and directive social worker with sufficient time to become a critical resource for an extended period would be called for. If Mrs. Stein has limited personal resources and strong external resources (B), it is essential to find organizational and network resources to compensate for her biopsychosocial deficits. Finally, if Mrs. Stein has strong personal but limited environmental resources (C), the social worker might help her to seek alternative resources or construct new ones. By jointly assessing the person:environment level of fit, social workers and clients can make informed decisions about focus and direction.

Finally, life-modeled practice emphasizes assessment as a moment to moment process. In the helping encounter, the worker faces an array of simultaneous issues and varied cues. At any moment, the practitioner must determine which ones to respond to, which to ignore, and which to put aside. There is little time to think about a "correct" intervention. Conceptualizing life issues and stressors as difficult life transitions and traumatic life events, environmental pressures, and dysfunctional family and group processes provides a schema for *moment to moment* assessment. To illustrate, at an early moment in the fourth session with Mrs. Stein, she complains about her loneliness and isolation. The social worker has to obtain additional data (e.g., "Can you tell me a little more?") in order to determine with Mrs. Stein whether at this particular moment she is asking for help in:

> exploring her grief and requesting help with mourning her loss of physical mobility and independence (seeking help with a life transition)
>
> exploring her feeling of social isolation from her friends and family and asking for help with reaching out to natural support systems, or help in constructing new support systems (seeking help with the environment)
>
> complaining obliquely about the worker's inattentiveness and subtly pressing for attention to their own transactions and obstacles to communication between them (seeking help with the interpersonal)

From one moment to another, the focus may change, demanding the worker's ability sensitively and skillfully to assess and follow Mrs. Stein's cues.

5. Integrated modalities, methods and skills

Life-modeled social work practice consists of eight modalities: work with individuals, families, groups, social networks, communities, physical environments, organizations, and politics. Contemporary practitioners must be equipped to work effectively within all eight modalities, moving readily and skillfully from one to another as situations require and with client (individual, family, group, or community) agreement. In life-modeled practice, client needs, goals, interests, and life stressors govern the selection of modality at any particular point, and that then guides the selection of methods and skills.

Some methods and skills are common to all modalities, others are specific to one. Commonly-held methods and skills are used for developing explicit agreements and exploring client concerns. Specific methods and skills are those used to form groups, develop mutual aid, and deal with internal group obstacles; help families change dysfunctional relationships processes; help communities or neighborhoods acquire needed resources, networks, and self-help groups; create needed programs and services; and influence organizational and legislative activity.

Practitioner style and creativity are indispensable in life-modeled practice. Clients respond best to social workers who are willing to reveal their humanness, vulnerability, and spontaneity (Shulman 1991). Clients do not expect social workers to be models of perfection and virtue. A practitioner's empathy, commitment, and desire to be helpful speak louder than any possible awkwardness or mistake. Successful practitioners are "dependably real" rather than "rigidly consistent" (Rogers 1961:50).

Professional education and socialization sometimes stiffen practice and discourage purposeful and spontaneous humor. Yet, used appropriately, humor might relieve a client's (and the worker's) tensions, anxiety, and embarrassment. For instance, after heart surgery, a blue collar worker was very anxious about possibly being impotent. He had been unable to discuss the concern with his physicians. The social worker dealt with the awkward silences between them by asking with a smile, "Are you worried about whether the lead has run out of your pencil?" He responded with laughter, and a frank discussion followed (Gitterman 1987).

6. Practice focus on personal and collective strengths

In life-modeled practice, the focus is on individual and collective strengths rather than on deficits. All people have strengths and resilience, although for some, those strengths have been dampened by circumstances. Practitioners must identify, mobilize, and build on people's strengths and resilience. When social workers are preoccupied with deficits, psychopathology, and diagnostic labels, individuals, families, and groups are merely broken objects to be "fixed" (treated) by powerful experts. This obscures the humanity of both clients and practitioners. Life-modeled practice, as closely as possible, mirrors natural life processes, builds on people's strengths, and seeks to remove or reduce environmental obstacles.

7. Emphasis on client action and decision-making

All people need opportunities to make decisions about their own situations and take action on their own behalf. When people have an effect on their environment, take responsibility for an aspect of their situation, or make decisions in significant areas of life, their self-esteem and sense of competence are strengthened, and skills for continued mastery are developed. In life-modeled practice, the worker helps individuals, families, and groups to mobilize their motivation and follow through with action. Tasks, activities, and actions are carefully considered to ensure that they are achievable and appropriate to the client's lifestyle, interests, and capacities. Risks of failure must be minimized.

8. The pervasive significance of the environment

Society's varied social and physical structures are often closed to some populations by virtue of race, ethnicity, social class, gender, sexual orientation, physical and mental challenges, or age, generating many painful life stressors. Organizations designed to meet fundamental needs (welfare, schools, health care systems) are frequently life stressors because of their harsh or unresponsive policies and procedures. A social network of relatives, friends, or neighbors might be emotionally and materially supportive, or might be unresponsive, or the network is characterized by interpersonal conflict. A network might not even exist, and the person or family is socially isolated.

Physical habitats must support human needs for stimulation, comfort, challenge, family and community life, and provide access to the natural world. They become life stressors when they create overcrowding; fail to provide sufficient protection from the hazards of crime and pollution; or lack of affordable housing that supports family life.

9. Consistent attention to unique dimensions of the life course of individuals, families, and groups as they move through difficult life transitions and traumatic life events

The life course conception is applicable to individuals, families, and to some degree to groups and communities. It proposes that individual processes coalesce into collective processes . We recognize that such merged processes do not rule out other processes that may be distinctive to families, groups, and communities.

10. Evaluation of practice and contribution to knowledge

In the ending phase of life-modeled practice, social workers engage clients in a joint evaluation of the service, including satisfactory and unsatisfactory elements. This is usually termed outcome research. The evaluations may help workers further develop positive aspects and correct negative ones.

Over time, accumulated evaluations may suggest interesting questions to the worker: what seems to work best with certain life issues but not with others? with certain individuals, groups, or cultures but not with others? Questions that arise from practice experience can lead the practitioner to undertake a quantitative study that may yield contributions to social work theory.

Qualitative research also contributes to social work theory and practice through studies of exchanges between people and their environment (Coulton 1979, Lee 1990, Patterson et al. 1988, 1992, 1995). See Appendix B for a discussion of social work practice research traditions.

Three Phases of Life-Modeled Practice

Initial Phase: Getting Started

Empathy. Even before the first session, social workers need to prepare themselves to enter applicants' or clients' lives by reflecting on available information concerning the probable objective situation, its possible cultural meaning, and its potential impact on the first session. Practitioners need also to reflect on an applicant's or client's subjective reality by empathizing with their likely perceptions and feelings. Drawing on such anticipatory processes readies the social worker to "hear" both manifest and latent content. A high level of professional empathy is correlated with a high level of client sharing (Truax and Carkhoff 1967). Social workers must demonstrate empathy by showing interest and concern through nonverbal and verbal means and paying close attention to the client. The more anxious and vulnerable a client feels, the greater the need for demonstrating empathy.

Stressor definition. The client and worker must first identify and define the life stressor(s): how the life stressor is defined largely governs what will be done about the issue. In some cases multiple stressors lead to disorganization, as with the Williams family described earlier in this chapter. Sometimes, effective work on one life stressor supports coping with others. At other times worker and client may agree to rank order the stressors and work on them one by one. Occasionally, however, the shared work is simultaneously directed to two or more stressors, as in the following example, in which the client himself defines the stressors.

I was assigned to work with Mr. Hall, age 87, a childless widower. He came to America from Russia with his mother when he was seven. He is a high school graduate who, at age 65, retired as a bridge toll collector.

He entered the institution after two strokes left him paralyzed on one side. He has chronic heart failure, limited vision due to glaucoma, and a hearing impairment. Before her sudden death three years ago, his wife visited daily. They had divorced four years ago so that Mr. Hall could receive Medicaid without her becoming penniless. He rarely socializes with other residents and infrequently leaves his room. When I read his chart, the nurse told me "he turns off anyone who tries to help." My field instructor also warned me that Mr. Hall is angry, manipulative, self-destructive, and rude. As I prepared to meet him, I reminded myself that people are often unfairly labeled.

When I introduced myself to Mr. Hall, I met a friendly, receptive, elderly man. I explained who I was, my role, and how long I would be at the institution. He said he was desperate to have someone to speak with. In our early sessions, Mr. Hall expressed some feelings and concerns and gave me small, select glimpses into his past. During those times he frequently tested my loyalty and the boundaries of our relationship. I understood his occasional gruffness and was undaunted by it.

Mr. Hall wished to work on three painful life issues:

1. his wife's death [a traumatic life event and difficult life transition]. She died in the winter—Mr. Hall is confined to a wheelchair, and he has never visited her grave. Hence he has not been able to work through his grief and to experience a sense of closure with her death.

2. a change of room [environment]. Mr. Hall feels he is "shriveling up" on the third floor where the most limited reside. He wants to move to a more independent floor.

3. institutionalization and loss of personal control [a painful life transition and environmental stressor]. Mr. Hall's ultimate life stressor is his sense of lost control over his mind and body due to his disabilities and being institutionalized.

Degree of choice. The initial phase is strongly influenced by the degree of choice about the service. People usually seek professional help, taking on the applicant or client role, when stressors become unmanageable (Alcabes and Jones 1985). They are propelled into social work services either out of their own quest for help or out of the concern of other people or organizations who then initiate referral. When services are *sought*, finding common ground among client's and practitioner's definitions of the life stressor(s) and goals, and the agency services, is usually easier to achieve than when client choice is more constricted.

When services are *offered* to pre-selected groups or populations as in outreach programs, the social worker must maintain an ethical balance between active presentation of anticipated benefits and people's right to refuse service. By identifying and relating to people's perceptions and def-

Table 2.2	Social Worker Skills in the Initial Phase
• *In general:*	Prepare to enter the applicant's or client's life by reflecting on available information concerning probable objective and subjective realities, their possible cultural meanings, and potential impact on the first session
	Create an accepting and supportive environment by demonstrating empathy by showing interest, curiosity, and concern through nonverbal and verbal means and paying close attention to what client is saying and doing
	Define people's life issues and stressors as expressions of relationships between people and environment and emphasize increased adaptive capacity and increased environmental responsiveness
• *In sought services:*	Create welcoming atmosphere when client *seeks* services; encourage applicants or clients to share their concerns; reach for details and explore possible doubts and hesitations about the agency and the worker
• *In services offered:*	Identify the applicant's or client's potential perceptions and definitions of life issues and stressors when offering services; maintain an ethical balance between active presentation of anticipated benefits and people's right to refuse *offered* service
• *In mandated services:*	Acknowledge the *mandate* when offering services; deal directly with the implications of both the nature of the mandate and the extent of possible sanctions for violations, and locate and respond to client discomfort
• *In all:*	Describe and explain agency services and social work procedures, and invite client questions and discussion
	Develop a tentative shared assessment of person:environment exchange
	Develop explicit initial agreement on next steps, tentative goals, priorities, reciprocal tasks and responsibilities, and other arrangements affecting the proposed work together

initions of their needs, practitioners are more likely to engage them in the offer of service.

When services are *mandated* by a court order or other authoritarian institutions and their representatives, the practitioner must acknowledge the mandate and directly deal with its implications. Both the nature of the mandate and the extent of possible sanctions on violations must be specified. Efforts to locate and respond to people's discomfort with mandated services are also important.

In a first session, practitioners need to describe and explain agency services and social work procedures, and invite client questions and discussion about them. Exploring and defining the life stressor(s) then begins. A tentative shared assessment of person:environment exchanges, including coping skills and environmental resources, may be reached in the first and other early sessions of the initial phase (or in the only session in one-session and episodic services). Explicit initial agreement on next steps, tentative goals, priorities, reciprocal tasks and responsibilities, and other arrangements affecting the proposed work together, must also be covered in the initial phase. Clients' active participation in these processes is empowering because it enhances the sense of competence, relatedness, self-esteem, and self-direction. Table 2.2 summarizes worker skills used in the initial phase.

These professional skills are differentially applied according to applicants' and clients' life experiences and level of functioning, the particular practice modality in use at a given point, and temporal arrangements.

Ongoing Phase: Working Toward Goals

Methods.   Strengthening and supporting person:environment relationships (such as level of fit and personal coping skills and environmental resources required for managing life stressors) are central in the ongoing phase. Modalities were briefly described earlier in this chapter and are more fully examined in the next chapter. Methods and skills associated with the various modalities are more fully examined and illustrated throughout Part 2 of this book.

Supporting and strengthening people's adaptive capacities and problem-solving abilities can be achieved through the methods of enabling, exploring, mobilizing, guiding, and facilitating. *Enabling* mobilizes or strengthens clients' motivation to deal with the difficult life stressors and the associated stress it arouses. Enabling clients to elaborate their concerns requires skills that include using minimal responses to encourage; waiting out silence; reaching for facts; verbalizing feelings; legitimizing and universalizing thoughts, reactions, and feelings; emphasizing and highlighting specific cues; rephrasing concerns; using metaphors; using appropriate humor; and sharing one's thoughts and feelings as appropriate. Other skills such as identifying strengths, conveying hope, and offering realistic reassurance help clients to mobilize and sustain their motivation and personal strengths.

Exploring and *clarifying* provide focus and direction to the work. Conveying "Can you help me understand your situation?" the social worker draws on skills such as developing focus; specifying concerns; reaching for underlying meaning; clarifying ambivalence; identifying discrepant messages; patterning concerns; offering interpretations; providing and inviting feedback; and inviting self-reflection. Exploring and clarifying deepen the "therapeutic conversation" between the partners.

Mobilizing is used to strengthen people's motivation to deal with difficult life stressors and manage the associated disabling feelings. In dealing with painful life issues and events, people need help with mobilizing their personal strengths and motivation based on skills such as identifying strengths, offering realistic reassurance, and conveying hope.

Guiding helps clients learn the steps in the problem-solving aspects of coping. Social workers must attend to the different ways in which people learn. Some learn primarily by doing, others learn primarily by summarizing—visualizing and organizing perceptions into patterns and images. Still others learn primarily by abstracting and conceptualizing (Bruner 1966). Effective guidance depends on providing opportunities for activity, modeling, and role play, and discussion and exchange of ideas. The following skills guide problem-solving: providing needed information regarding the stressor and coping tasks; clarifying misinformation; offering advice when requested; supporting clients' accurate interpretations; discussing, visualizing, acting; specifying action tasks; and planning for task completion (Gitterman 1988).

Facilitating encourages clients to remain committed to the work. Some will be reluctant to examine and work on difficult issues. Avoidance is indicated by passive behaviors such as withdrawal, over-compliance, and extreme diffidence, or by such nonpassive behaviors as provocation, intellectualization, interruption, verbosity, and seductiveness, or flight behaviors such as changing the subject, withholding information, and minimizing concerns. If avoidance persists, the worker needs to challenge and demand purposive work, by commenting on the avoidance pattern; challenging illusions of mutual agreement; and remarking on discrepant messages. These interventions can stimulate and mobilize energy for the work. However, if used indiscriminately, they may increase defensiveness or lead to drop-out.

All life stressors require work with the environment. Social work methods for this work include: coordinating, mediating, advocating, innovating and organizing, and influencing organizational and legislative policies and regulations.

In *coordinating*, the social worker links clients to available resources. After bringing about agreement on shared tasks, the worker draws on skills including: preparing the way for informed consent and involvement; defining a division of labor; evoking and drawing on clients' energy and personal resources; and lending the worker's professional status to the client.

When the environmental pressure arises from distorted exchanges, the worker *mediates* between the client and the organization or social network so they effectively connect to each other. Skills of the external mediating method include developing and using informal and formal contacts; demonstrating understanding of the perspectives held by other organizational staff; knowing and using formal policies, procedures, and precedents; and persevering.

If mediation fails, worker and client consider potentially adversarial actions through the use of *advocacy*. Because both client and worker are often vulnerable to retaliation, probity and caution are necessary. Before

Table 2.3   Professional Methods and Skills Associated with the
                   Ongoing Phase

LIFE STRESSORS	PROFESSIONAL METHODS	SKILLS
Difficult Transitions and Traumatic Events	Enabling	use minimal responses to encourage; wait out silence; reach for facts; verbalize feelings
	Exploring	develop focus; specify concerns; reach for underlying meaning; clarify ambivalence
	Mobilizing	offer realistic reassurance and hope
	Guiding	provide information regarding stressor and coping tasks; clarify misinformation
	Facilitating	comment on avoidance patterns; challenge illusion of mutual agreement; generate anxiety to promote movement
Environmental Issues	Coordinating	prepare the way for informed consent and involvement; define a division of labor; educe and draw on client energy
(organizations, social networks, natural world, built world)	External Mediating	develop and use system contacts; demonstrate understanding of others' perspectives
	External Advocacy	imply further action; organize protests; refuse compliance; report to other organizations and the media
	Innovating	assess need; develop program in response; acquire organizational and community support
	Influencing	build coalitions, position, lobby, testify
Maladaptive Interpersonal Processes	Internal Mediating	identify and comment on dysfunctional patterns; challenge collective resistance
(family, group, worker:client)	Internal Advocating	invite and sustain conflict; establish protective ground rules; lend support

taking an adversarial position the social worker needs to evaluate available organizational, professional, and personal resources for dealing with potential consequences. In using external advocacy, the social worker assumes a polite, respectful stance, rather than one of outraged righteousness. Ethical practice requires an adversarial position and external advocacy when essential entitlements are denied or client rights are violated regardless of risks. The method includes such skills as hinting plans of further action; organizing protests; refusing compliance; and reporting to the media, civil rights groups, and NASW.

Through *innovation*, the social worker seeks to fill gaps in services and resources and to help establish preventive and growth-promoting programs. When clients lack a social network or communities lack informal networks, the practitioner can organize social support and self-help groups centered on members' common life stressors, interests, or tasks. Social support groups help members assume an active role in reducing the stress generated by social and emotional isolation and loneliness. Self-help groups focus on a shared painful stressor such as job loss, bereavement, a physical or mental disorder, or family violence. Innovation skills include assessing need; developing programmatic response; acquiring organizational consent and support; identifying community leaders; and recruiting the population in need.

Social workers and clients seek to influence organizational practices and legislation on social policies and regulations at local, state, and national levels in the cause of social justice. The *influencing* method includes such skills as coalition-building; positioning; lobbying: and testifying.

In responding to difficult life transitions and harsh environments, families, groups, and communities can encounter interpersonal obstacles such as maladaptive behaviors, conflicted relationships, and blocked communication. Withdrawal, factions, alliances, and scapegoating are examples of dysfunctional patterns in groups. Dysfunctional patterns in families include misuse of power and authority, violence, neglect, and sexual abuse. Dysfunctional patterns in communities include unfair allotment of scarce resources, inter-group hostilities, and power structures that exclude vulnerable residents. Helping groups, families, and communities to change these and other dysfunctional patterns is a critical arena for preventive and restorative interventions. The social worker helps members to recognize obstacles, learn to communicate more openly and directly, and attain greater mutuality, trust, and concern for collective well-being. *Internal mediating* and *advocating* skills include identifying and commenting on dysfunctional patterns; challenging collective resistance; inviting and exploring conflicting ideas; establishing protective ground rules; lending support and crediting work. Social work methods and skills associated with the ongoing phase are summarized in Table 2.3.

Natural Life Processes.   Clients are not responsible for "confirming and conforming to our interests; our professional responsibility is to join their natural life processes, to follow their leads and to be responsive to their cues" (Shulman and Gitterman 1994:25). The following provides an example of joining natural life processes in life-modeled practice with a family (a solo mother and her 12-year-old daughter). It also illustrates how by-passing serious pathology facilitates this joining and releases the potential for growth and social functioning.

When I arrived at Mrs. Richards's home for the first visit, she seemed to be under considerable stress, complaining of sleepless nights and an increasing inability to concentrate on anything besides her "noise problem," caused by "vicious upstairs, downstairs, and next-door neighbors." The neighbors all persist in "ganging up" on her by "purposely annoying" her, beginning at 5:00 A.M. and continuing until 1:00 A.M. the following day. They speak loudly, play TV and radios on high volume, repeatedly drop shoes, and "go out of their way" to walk very heavily. Mrs. Richards also refuses to pick up mail, fearing a bomb may have been mailed to her. Further proof of the "conspiracy" against her is the notice she just received from the landlord that her lease is being terminated because neighbors have complained of noise coming from her apartment. Mrs. Richards has also received a summons from a neighbor charging her with harassment. Mrs. Richards admits she rings her neighbors' bells frequently to ask them to be quiet. She views the termination of the lease as an act by "malicious people who are jealous" of her because she is so quiet.

After my visit, Mrs. Richards had another agency call the department to verify I had no secret intent to harm her. In the second visit, Mrs. Richards told me she always did well in school, but all her life she has felt out of place and inferior to those around her. She states her social life consists of Debbie and one friend, whom she rarely sees. Debbie also has only one friend and prides herself on being a "bookworm." Mrs. Richards also said that for ten years she has lived in various buildings with "noisy, inconsiderate neighbors," whom she has often unsuccessfully taken to court, but the present noise level is the most bothersome of all because she can't rest or even think of anything else.

In Mrs. Richards's transactions with her environment, disturbances and disruptions occur frequently. She perceives a powerful imbalance between external demands placed on her by the environment and her self-defined ability to meet these demands with her own external and internal resources. This imbalance creates intense stress and anxiety. These transactional imbalances create daily transitional, environmental, and interpersonal stressors (Gitterman and Germain 1976; Germain and Gitterman 1979, 1986). The worker viewed Mrs. Richards's paranoia as poor perceptions of the inside and outside worlds preventing adaptive interchanges between Mrs. Richards and her environment and impairing her ability to cope with the tasks of adulthood. Mrs. Richards saw the problem as "vicious people out to get me." The consulting psychiatrist, noting that Mrs. Richards had been a patient in a state hospital twenty years before, defined the problem as a long-standing psychosis exacerbated by threat of eviction. Life-modeled practice puts an emphasis on the troubles Mrs. Richards is experiencing. Whatever her diagnosis, she nonetheless has to manage serious life issues. The life-modeled emphasis helps the worker to find common ground so Mrs. Richards could have what she calls "a friend" to talk with her about her "noise problem," since she is alone all the time and has no one with whom to discuss the problem. They agree on the goal of a solution to Mrs. Richards's discomfort with her environment. Accepting Mrs. Richards's environmental concerns is the "ticket" into the work. It provides the worker with time to assess Mrs. Richards's level of functioning and her capacity to explore such life issues and transitions as thwarted tasks of adulthood, or to accept the status of a person with an illness who might need medication to improve her daily functioning, or interpersonal issues of establishing appropriate boundaries between her daughter and herself.

10/24—I asked Mrs. Richards if she has thoughts about the possibility that she has to move. She says she has, and she has begun to look in the papers to see if anything is available in the neighborhood. She stated she had seen what sounded like a beautiful apartment advertised in the paper, and when she called up it was already taken. Mrs. Richards feels sure the vacancy never existed at all, and that they played a trick on her so that she'd call and inquire about a more expensive apartment. I agreed that might be possible, but wondered if the apartment had sounded so attractive to her that someone else might have thought so, too, and telephoned before her. Mrs. Richards said that she doubted that—she's pretty sure it was all a "gimmick" to trick her. On further discussion, she remembered she had, in fact, bought the newspaper late in the day, and said, yes, maybe I was right.

During the next month at Mrs. Richards's request the worker accompanied her to court several times. Each time they went to a coffee shop afterward. Whenever Mrs. Richards's anxiety mounted, the worker offered support.

11/11—Mrs. Richards stated that she was not at all sure why she had asked me to come, since there was nothing that I could do to help her with her case. I said I knew sitting alone in a courtroom is not the most pleasing thing, and I would not like to wait alone. Mrs. Richards then turned and thanked me for coming with her today.

When the case was postponed a week, Mrs. Richards expressed fear that her attorney might not come back.

She seemed very anxious about this, saying she wouldn't know who else to call. I then told Mrs. Richards that if he couldn't make it for the 19th, the date of her next appearance in court, I would try to help her find another lawyer. She said that she would appreciate that. She stated again that her noisy neighbors are "picking on" her. I told Mrs. Richards that while she may be bothered by the noise, it is something that we must all put up with while living in the city. Mrs. Richards did not deny this, but expressed fear that she would have to go through moving again. She anxiously stated that she's afraid that she "won't live through" the court case. I reassured her that she will, and that if she has to move I will be there to help her clear things through the Department of Welfare. Mrs. Richards then seemed much calmer and said it was nice to talk to me, adding that Mrs. Peterson at the other agency really hadn't understood her, and she would like to have coffee with me again.

At the next court hearing, after a long wait:

11/19—Mrs. Richards seemed to be getting more and more nervous and suddenly, sounding as if she were going to cry, stood up and said "What will happen to me if I get thrown out? I have no family, no one to go to, I'm all alone." I immediately reassured her that whatever happens, she won't be out on the street. If she is evicted, I will make sure that everything is cleared at the welfare center. Mrs. Richards then worried that she won't get permission to move because she has not been living in her present apartment for the required two years. I assured her that under the circumstances, the time element will not count, and that I will try to have everything arranged for her quickly. Mrs. Richards looked at me, smiled, and thanked me for being there with her today.

The case was postponed indefinitely, and afterward, at the coffee shop, Mrs. Richards asked if the worker would go looking for an apartment with her.

I pointed out that she may not even have to look for another place to live—she may not be evicted at all. Mrs. Richards then asked if she would be able to move even if she weren't evicted. I said that I had been under the impression that she wanted to stay in her apartment. She said she does, but she can't stand her "vicious neighbors." I reminded her that wherever she would move in the city she'd be faced with neighbors and noise. Mrs. Richards said I was right, even the lawyer had said the same thing, and she'd been bothered by neighbors for ten years. I reinforced this, and wondered if she would feel less aggravated by trying to get out of the house a little more. Mrs. Richards nodded and said that maybe that's what she should be doing, and she'll try it. Mrs. Richards then said she did not want to discuss it today, but asked if on Thursday we might discuss the possibility of her getting a part-time job because she wants to be more independent. As we walked together to the corner, Mrs. Richards thanked me again many times, and before my leaving, she turned to me and said, "I like you." I said I liked her too.

A month later, Mrs. Richards reported some changes in her situation.

She said she sometimes still hears her neighbors, but they "seemed to be bothering her" less. She is trying not to pay so much attention to them, she "has her own life." Mrs. Richards said that all day yesterday she hadn't been home, having gone to the Y for swimming, and then to the library. I said that was good, and she might find the more she continues to pay attention to other things, the less bothered she may be by her neighbors. Mrs. Richards nodded in agreement. She said she know she is "smart" because she has an IQ of 132, but she always felt inferior to others. She could never mingle or feel at home with others. She remembers reading that people who are smart are good in everything, and should be able to get along well with others. She said that she has been thinking about it lately, and there's no reason for her to think she's not as good as everyone else. I nodded in support, and she said she's thinking of being more independent and getting some part-time work. She asked if I could find out if this would be possible under the WIN [Womens and Infants Nutrition] program.

Not only did the worker focus on Mrs. Richards's strengths, but she successfully bypassed the pathology. While it may not always be possible to bypass pathology, we believe that the social work focus should always be on the daily hassles and serious life stressors rather than on "treating" the pathology. Instead of treating a paranoid schizophrenic person, the worker, a life modeled practitioner, viewed Mrs. Richards's difficulties as arising from exchanges between her and the environment. The worker sought to interrupt transactional processes that had created and sustained the present life stressors, and did this successfully by a focus on strengths. She purposefully increased Mrs. Richards's badly damaged self-esteem while engaging her perceptual-sensory capacity by distinguishing between inner and outer experiences at every opportunity. Together these two areas of work created a beginning trust in interpersonal relationships.

As Mrs. Richards's anxiety diminished, progressive forces in her personality were released. She began to feel better about herself; her thinking, perceptions, and behavior began to change. The behavioral changes elicited different responses from her environment (neighbors, landlord), thus supporting the restitution process. Within two months, Mrs. Richards began to transact differently with her environment. Instead of spending her days frantically listening for traces of noise, she readied herself for taking action that could lead to learning and competence. Several months later, with the social worker's help, she successfully planned for Debbie to attend summer camp, made arrangements for her own vocational counseling at the division of vocational rehabilitation, and was expressing an interest in meeting men.

Mrs. Richards was able to relinquish her preoccupation with inner phenomena and to reestablish connections with the outer world through the worker's support and clarifications provided. Her sense of herself as a worthwhile person was nurtured by the social worker's caring, respect, and positive expectations. Successful experiences led to growth, and growth increased the likelihood of further successes. The previous cycle of frustration and failure in transactions with the environment was interrupted. Mrs. Richards was beginning to build a sense of trust and was more ready to take action for developing competence in the tasks of adulthood.

To identify and pursue an appropriate focus, the worker first identifies the client's perceptions of her *most pressing and stressful life issues*. By paying close attention to the client's own sense of her greatest vulnerabilities, the worker is provided with critical points of entry into her life situation. Mrs. Richards's possible eviction and the risk of becoming homeless represented the most serious threat to her and her daughter's survival. Therefore, joining and supporting her in coping with the eviction hearing was the crucial point of entry into her life situation.

Second, the social worker *avoids mobilizing defenses*. With reluctant or ambivalent clients, for example, the practitioner focuses on safer and more comfortable definitions of life issues, thereby fostering credibility and trust. Accepting Mrs. Richards's initial definition of "noisy neighbors" avoided mobilizing her defenses and her paranoia. In contrast, if parents initially define their child as the "problem," unconsciously avoiding an underlying conflict between themselves, the worker's redefinition of stressors in the marriage is likely to mobilize defensiveness and withdrawal.

Third, the worker and client *select tasks that provide opportunities for success*. Success is a powerful motivator for involvement in the partnership, the development of hope, and commitment to the work. When Mrs. Richards confronted an overwhelming environmental stressor, the worker divided it into manageable tasks. The partners could begin with the simpler ones and experience some success before tackling the more complex tasks.

The Ending Phase: Bringing the Shared Work and the Relationship to a Close

The ending phase includes the carefully planned termination of the work together and the worker:client relationship. As part of ending, practitioner and client consider organizational, temporal, modality, and relationship factors that affect phases of termination such as avoidance; negative feelings; sadness; and release. Each phase requires distinctive skills used in a timely fashion.

Avoidance is a conscious effort to ward off pain or loss; denial is an unconscious defense against pain or loss. With the worker's help, clients can begin to relax the avoidance effort and allow feelings of anger and sadness to surface. Social workers must remain empathic and sufficiently detached for this to happen. They need to maintain sufficient empathy to understand the aroused feelings. At the same time, they must move far enough away from the experience to invite the expression of negative thoughts and emotions. As the reality of ending is directly confronted, both client and social worker are freed to experience their positive feelings and their shared sadness at ending. Not all clients will feel sad; some will feel relieved, neutral, or cheated. Workers must be careful to avoid forcing an expression of feelings that may not exist.

Having faced and shared the termination, the social worker next helps the client evaluate gains and consider whether some work is still to be done; develop plans for the future such as transfer or referral; and say goodbyes and disengage.

In the following vignette, the social worker is ending with Grace after eight months of weekly sessions. Grace divorced her first husband of 13 years and recently separated from her second husband of ten years. He had adopted her children, who are now adults, but had sexually molested the daughter as a child. He was also verbally abusive toward Grace during most of the marriage, undermining her confidence in herself.

Grace and the worker had identified two major goals: reaching a decision about divorcing her second husband and feeling better about herself. Her low self-esteem was partly due to socialization, her past promiscuity and drugs, and her experiences in two disastrous, abusive marriages.

I began termination five weeks before our final session. We discussed whether she wanted to continue with someone else. She preferred to stop, feeling she has learned enough for now about how to handle herself. She knows she can return to the agency if she begins to feel unsure of herself again. In a couple of sessions she expressed anger and sadness about my leaving. We also began to review the gains she has made. She highlighted her ability to trust her own judgment as a major new skill. She also feels much better about her past and commented that while she knew she was trying to get affection, it was really good to have someone else tell her too. She feels she now knows what gets her into trouble with herself—letting herself be discounted. While she knows that she may not always prevent it, she continues to work on it.

Areas not fully resolved include complete disengagement from her husband and her feelings about her children. Her husband continues to call her and she allows this more than she thinks she should. In part, she is still mourning the loss and, in part, she is testing how strong she is. She knows that he has little effect on her feelings and decisions any more, and that feels good. Serious issues about the children will probably continue for a while. We talked of this, and I suggested writing down her feelings and even letting herself cry as a sign of caring about herself and the hurts. I also recommended some readings and emphasized her intelligence and capabilities.

I told her how much I valued knowing her and knowing also that she feels stronger and more competent. She said that she now feels safe and able to trust, and is grateful for having successfully resolved very painful issues. We have one more session, and my plan is to refer to the sadness in separating and whatever that may evoke.

PART TWO

THE HELPING PROCESS
IN LIFE-MODELED
PRACTICE

Like life itself, life-modeled practice is phasic. Three phases, initial, ongoing, and ending, constitute the processes and operations of the practice. These processes ebb and flow in response to the interplay of personal and environmental forces. While the phases are separated in order to organize our presentation, they are not always distinct in actual practice.

Chapter 3 examines the professional processes of skillfully entering people's lives. Beginning a professional relationship requires careful preparation in order to accomplish two simultaneous professional tasks essential to entering another's life. One is to create a supportive environment. People must feel safe and accepted before they can trust and confide in a professional. The other is to develop a commonality of purpose. All helping efforts rest upon shared definitions about concerns, needs, and explicit agreement about goals, tasks, and reciprocal roles.

The ongoing phase is ushered in by the joint recognition that client and worker have reached a shared, possibly tentative, understanding of the nature of the stressor and its amelioration.

In the ongoing phase, the professional purpose is to help people effectively cope with the biological, social, emotional, cognitive, and behavioral demands posed by life transitions and events and to influence the social and physical environments. Effective help requires attention to (1) painful life transitions and traumatic life events; (2) associated environmental stressors; and (3) dysfunctional interpersonal processes. An interpersonal focus applies when the social worker is involved with a family or group system or sub-system. If a social worker, for example, is working with an abused woman, but not with the partner, the focus is on life transitional concerns (e.g., separation, grief) or environmental concerns (e.g., linkage with community resources, negotiating with her partner, securing a court Order of Protection). By contrast, a focus on dysfunctional interpersonal communication and relationship patterns requires conjoint work with both partners or the children.

The reader will see in the bereavement group presented in chapter 4 that the worker and members had to work simultaneously on the traumatic life event and the interpersonal tensions that erupted in the group, while at the same time constructing a safe social environment that could support the painful grief work. For purposes of discussion, however, we believe that considering the three arenas of practice in separate chapters yields greater clarity. We ask the reader to remember that actual practice is not as separated as our presentation might seem to imply.

Ending a professional relationship also requires careful preparation to deal with the feelings aroused by the ending; a review of what has been accomplished and what has yet to be achieved; planning for the future including, where indicated, transfer to another worker or referral to another agency; and evaluation of the service that was provided. Like the initial and ongoing phases of helping, the ending phase requires sensitivity, knowledge, careful planning, and a range of skills on the part of the social worker.

THREE

BEGINNINGS:

Auspice, Modalities,
Methods, and Skills

Initiating a professional relationship with another person requires careful preparation, ready compassion, and professional skills burnished by creativity. All helping rests on shared definitions about life stressors and explicit agreement on goals, plans, and methods.

Creating an Accepting and Supportive Service Environment

Anticipatory Empathy

The worker creates an accepting and supportive service environment by demonstrating empathy—the capacity to get "inside" another person's life and to experience how the person is feeling and thinking. To convey empathy, the practitioner begins by examining available data.

For example, a hospital social worker receives a referral from a nurse of a 60-year-old, unmarried, African-American patient who had spent her working life as a domestic. She had been admitted to the hospital a month earlier for a severe circulatory disorder related to chronic diabetes. Her gangrenous foot was amputated; shortly thereafter a further amputation of the leg to the knee was performed. The patient refuses to talk or to follow medical orders, and is regarded as a management problem. The worker reflects on this information. He considers the assault of losing a limb, piece by piece. He thinks about the impact of age and age-specific tasks related to loss of work and financial independence looming ahead. He wonders how the surgery was explained to her, what social supports she can call on, and what discharge options are available to her. He reflects on the fact that the patient is African-American while the physicians, nurses, and social workers are white. And he considers the culture of the particular ward, including staff's tolerance of difficult behavior.

Essential to this preparation was his viewing the world from the patient's probable perception of reality and the meaning she might attribute to her current situation. A social worker's struggle to achieve empathic feeling and thinking within another's frame of reference is an ongoing one (Goldstein 1983). Achieving this level of empathic understanding is aided by the process of *anticipatory empathy*. The four steps in anticipatory empathy are: (1) identification, through which the social worker experiences what the client is feeling and thinking; (2) incorporation, through which the worker feels the experiences as if they were personal; (3) reverberation, through which the worker tries to call up personal life experiences that may facilitate understanding those of the client; and (4) detachment, through which the worker engages in logical, objective analysis (Lide 1966).

Practitioners might find it difficult to identify with life circumstances such as poverty, grave injury, racism, homophobia, or job loss if they have not themselves experienced such conditions. They can evoke parallel memories of their own—for example, the worker's childhood memory of a parental divorce can parallel to some degree the client's mourning the death of a loved one. However, this can also lead social workers to project their own emotions and thoughts onto the client. Social workers must move "inside" another's experience *as if* it were their own, but "without losing the 'as if' quality" (Rogers 1961:284). They must also anticipate their own characteristic patterns of handling certain situations and life issues. Detachment permits a pulling back and reestablishment of a more objective view of the client's situation. Detachment takes into account the tentative assessment of available information, knowledge, and empathy.

A student assigned to a former client returning to the agency for help with several life issues began by reviewing the case folder:

After reading the folder, I had misgivings about working with Mrs. Stein. Early entries portrayed her as a physical and emotional invalid: cerebral palsy, chronic paranoid schizophrenia, legal blindness, mental retardation, and placement as a foster child. As I read, I became emotionally removed, hiding my fears in diagnostic speculations. Then I allowed myself to become curious about the person rather than the labels. This time her life story as a human being unfolded. I found myself feeling her feelings of being overwhelmed, alone, and scared. I sensed her inner strength and her capacity to endure despite numerous traumas. I pictured her sitting next to me, and I wondered what she would be like and how she would react to me. If I were she, I would be curious about why I was getting a new worker. She might feel that the change of workers was her fault, a reflection of her unworthiness. She might be angry and upset about beginning anew with another social worker. At the same time she might be curious about me and hopeful that I could help. As I anticipated her possible reactions, several opening statements occurred to me: explaining why I was assigned to her, eliciting her understanding of why the other worker left, listening for her feelings about starting with someone new, sharing what I know about her situation, and inviting her to bring me on board her current situation.

The student's sensitive preparation virtually assured engagement and prevented the possibility of provocative, prolonged testing of the worker, nonverbal expressions of anxiety, unresponsiveness, or the client's failure to return.

Another student described how she prepared to meet with Mr. Sachs, whose wife was terminally ill with cancer.

In preparing for the first session, I considered how to introduce likely issues that might be of concern to Mr. Sachs. I also tried to anticipate his reactions. The interview itself confirmed my anticipation. However, I stopped short of dealing with his wife's approaching death, and failed to invite discussion in this area. At the time, I was aware of what I was doing, yet I continued to avoid the painful topic, thus undermining my intention to help. In preparing for my interview and Mr. Sachs' possible reactions to his wife's death, I had not included my own reactions. I "forgot" to consider how the loss of a loved one would make me feel.

Practitioners' preparation for understanding clients' life issues and feelings needs to be flexible, individualized, and multi-dimensional. At the same time, workers must be careful that the anticipatory preparation does not become a rigid script. Effective empathy always remains open to additional data and impressions, and avoids stereotypes and preconceptions.

Cohort history can also play a part in anticipatory empathy. For example, a school social worker plans to reach out to seriously troubled, 13-year-old Laura, who is repeating the sixth grade because of extensive truancy. Laura, her 11-year-old brother and their alcoholic, diabetic mother are on welfare. They share a bedroom in a small, dilapidated, dirty, 3-bedroom house in a dangerous and impoverished neighborhood. Also living in the household are a cousin, her boyfriend and her two children, ages 12 and 13.

Interfamily conflict is continuous. Laura and her 16-year-old boyfriend spend much time together, but she denies sexual involvement. Laura's parents were divorced when she was 5 years old. Her father remarried and now has two young children. Laura occasionally visits her father and his family.

As the social worker prepares to meet with Laura, she considers cohort history. Laura and her cohort grew up in the 1980s, a decade in which the poor became poorer. These children arrived at puberty and adolescence in the 1990s, when drugs and guns were devastating the United States. Divorced parents, blended families, and solo-parent families are also a reality for these young people. We need to be sensitive to: (1) what it meant to Laura to grow up poor in a decade when greed and wealth were glorified; (2) the reality of illicit drugs and alcohol as part of Laura's life, peer pressures involved in their use and in early promiscuity, and pervasive fears in living in a dangerous neighborhood; (3) the possible influences of the several differing family forms in her home.

By locating Laura in the context of a historical cohort, the worker gains greater empathy for her life issues.

Demonstrating Empathy

Cognitive understanding and anticipatory empathy are important in the creation of a supportive, accepting service environment. However, the most significant task remains to demonstrate understanding and empathy in the sessions with the applicant or client. The social worker must communicate attitudes of caring and being emotionally "with" the person. Social workers convey interest, curiosity, concern, and caring through numerous nonverbal and verbal behaviors. Nonverbal skills are presented in this section; verbal skills are presented in later sections and chapters.

Nondefensiveness and self-exploration manifested by clients have been found to be directly related to high levels of practitioner empathy (Truax and Carkhoff 1967; Duehn and Proctor 1977). The more vulnerable and anxious applicants or clients feel in the early sessions the more necessary is the worker's immediate demonstration of interest, concern, and caring.

Practitioners must always take account of physical, developmental, and cultural influences—and their own biases—in order to avoid misinterpreting nonverbal behaviors (Coleman 1991). Most people are initially reluctant to express thoughts and feelings directly to a stranger, even a professional. Empathic practitioners note significant shifts and changes in nonverbal behaviors that might reflect intense discomfort (eye contact, posture, gestures, facial expressions, physical reactions, changes in vocal qualities). For example, when a social work student probed the recent murder of a client's husband, she observed the client's sudden rigid body posture, uncontrolled perspiration, frequent body shifts, and increase in voice volume and pitch. All these behaviors indicated intense discomfort. The worker uses posture, gestures, and facial expressions to show attentiveness, and maintains eye contact during discussion of tabooed or painful material. In such moments, the social worker can comment on the painfulness of the material and ask clients if they prefer exploring the difficult area later. This is done without directing attention to a particular behavior which might intensify the client's self-consciousness.

The worker observes and listens for discrepancies between nonverbal and verbal behavior, and between the manner of speaking and the verbal content. Observing an applicant or client smiling while her body is rigid, or asserting she is not upset or angry in an agitated tone of voice suggests that she has not grasped or fully processed her emotional reactions. In a first session, the worker might demonstrate empathy by supportive verbal and nonverbal means rather than by directly confronting the discrepancies. However, commenting on discrepancies is usually necessary and helpful in later sessions.

An important professional nonverbal behavior is touching. Shaking hands, guiding the client to the office by the elbow, patting a child, touching a hand during a crisis or an emotional upset, are nonverbal demonstrations of empathy (Greene and Orman 1981). The worker must be cautious that an applicant or client does not confuse warmth with sexual interest, or perceive it as a threat. It is wise, in the current social climate, to limit touching to the very young or the very old.

Empathy is also demonstrated by the social worker's manner of speaking. A soft and gentle tone can show caring and sadness for client pain; a louder and animated tone can suggest pleasure in client accomplishment. A bland tone conveys indifference. Language that is forced or unnatural is pitched above or below the client's level increases distance between client and worker. The social worker must speak directly, clearly, and without jargon.

And finally, empathic practitioners create a welcoming atmosphere in their offices by adding plants and pictures and providing alternative seating arrangements. They are also careful to assure uninterrupted time for sessions by minimizing telephone calls and other interruptions.

Table 3.1 summarizes anticipatory empathy skills and nonverbal skills used to demonstrate empathy.

Developing Mutual Focus

Degree of Choice

People seeking services are applicants until they accept the agency's service and the agency agrees to provide it (Alcabes and Jones 1985). People who are offered the service by an agency become clients only when they agree to a need for the service and to the specified conditions. Even when service is mandated, the person's participation and acceptance of the service are equally necessary. Even continuing clients, when transferred to new workers, must agree to re-involve themselves. Engaging clients in a social work service and in contracting with them depend on the choice people have in

Table 3.1	Skills of Anticipatory Empathy and Demonstrating Empathy Nonverbally

- examine available data
- understand the person's perception of reality through identification, incorporation, reverberation, and detachment
- respond to nonverbal cues and manner of speech
- observe discrepancies between nonverbal and verbal behavior, and between manner of speech and content
- demonstrate interest and concern through responsive body postures, facial expressions, and hand gestures
- welcome the applicant or client by attractively and comfortably setting up one's office
- provide uninterrupted meeting time
- use responsive tone of voice
- speak directly, clearly, and without jargon

accepting or rejecting the service (Maluccio and Marlow 1974; Seabury 1979, 1976).

Services Sought. Applicants usually seek social work services at the point when life stressors have become unmanageable. The act of seeking help can itself be another stressor. In a society that values self-reliance, a need for help might be interpreted as personal inadequacy and loss of control over one's affairs. A sense of shame or fear of how one will be received by the social worker mingles with hope that needs will be met, the stressor resolved, and stress eased. Hence, many applicants face the first session with ambivalence.

After introductions, the applicant is invited to tell his or her story and specific concerns and needs. The approach is nonthreatening and encourages specific responses. The worker may ask, "Tell me what brings you here?" The question focuses attention, yet gives the applicant latitude in replying. When the person readily shares concerns, the worker uses minimal encouragers to invite elaboration with sounds such as "Uh huh," "Ah," and "Mmm" and words such as "I see," "Go on," and "I understand." Such minimal encouragers are "like the pats you give to a swing in motion to keep it in motion" (Kadushin 1983:160). Where needed to help applicants continue, the worker makes supportive statements: "You were badly hurt," "That was rough," "Most parents would worry about that." Inability to follow clients' presentations in these ways is significantly related to drop-out (Duehn and Proctor 1977).

When an applicant falls silent, the worker waits out the silence. Silence is uncomfortable for most people, but effective social workers are cautious about rushing to fill it. Judiciously waiting it out might release the applicant's expression of underlying painful life issues. The wait, however, has to be brief (although it may not feel short) because prolonged silence intensifies the person's anxiety. Social workers should not engage in power struggles over who will talk first. Timing is critical: not to respond too quickly and thus cut off thinking, nor too slowly and thus increase anxiety.

When uncertain about the meaning of a silence, reach directly for its meaning. For example, "I wonder what you are thinking at this moment?" invites further exploration. Unfortunately, our own discomfort leads us away from silence and from the applicant's concern that it expresses. Shulman (1991; 1978) found that the skill of reaching for silence is one of the least used of all the skills that he studied.

Mrs. Carlini, age 32, Italian-American, sought help from a community mental health center. She left her husband a year ago when he told her he was seeing another woman. She described herself as feeling depressed, and began to tell her story:

As good as the weekend had been, she still had to go home alone and face the reality of her husband's leaving her for another woman. What made it worse was her feeling that she had failed miserably as a wife, as a lover, companion, source of support, and failed as a mother since her children would no longer have their father at home. She felt alone and pessimistic. She would have a hard time "getting it together with another man" and added that she can't get it out of her mind that she was to blame. "I'm even a failure at getting better." (During this time I responded nonverbally, occasionally nodding or making short comments to show that I understood what she was saying. She related her story without emotion in her voice, but I did not comment on this.) After a brief silence, I asked Mrs. Carlini what she was thinking at this moment. She said she was thinking about her expectations of what a woman was supposed to do—get married, run a household, raise kids, give support to her husband. She must have failed him in some way for him to leave her for another woman. I said that the last few months must have been very painful for her, especially with thoughts of failure on her mind.

She said she worked hard in her marriage to make things work, but they didn't, and all of a sudden he told her he was seeing someone else. She was surprised and is still shocked because she thought he was a "man of integrity." I responded, "He hurt you very badly." She had hoped that he would be willing to discuss and work on whatever problems existed in their marriage. She realized that he might think about leaving but never expected him to go so far. For that to have happened, she really must have botched things up. I said "Mrs. Carlini, you are taking a tremendous amount of responsibility onto yourself." She nodded and said others tell her the same thing, but she can't seem to get rid of that idea.

As Mrs. Carlini speaks, the worker picks up nonverbal messages that might indicate anxiety, depression, guilt, or relief. He notes what is emphasized, what is left out, any discrepancies between verbal and nonverbal communication, and also considers the client's affect. When people actively seek service, minimal, supportive interventions usually suffice. In these situations, "less is more."

When people begin to describe their troubles, workers must sort the ensuing data into three areas: (a) the life stressor, its nature and duration; (b) what was done or not done to manage or resolve the stressor; and (c) how the client is reacting to the situation. By requesting facts, objective and subjective (feelings are also facts), the worker invites further details for greater range and depth of the applicant's presentation of concerns. Open-ended questions—what, how, when, and where—encourage further exploration. For example, "What happened then?"; "How did you respond?"; "When did she say that?"; "Where was she when she saw him?"

Questions that ask "why" should be avoided; they are usually experienced as challenges or accusations, and they encourage self-justification and rationalization. Asking why someone is depressed may imply there is something inappropriate in that feeling, or that the person is expected to produce an insightful answer. The question *Why* is usually unanswerable, and blocks applicants' spontaneity in discussing their situation.

Closed-ended questions such as "Did you tell your husband how you felt?" result in a restrictive "Yes" or "No" response. Gitterman's content analysis of case recordings by student and experienced workers suggests that interviews characterized by closed-ended questions take on an investigative flavor. The worker maintains substantial control of the interview and the applicant follows the worker's direction and structure rather than the reverse. Occasionally, however, closed-ended questions do help applicants get started and can also slow down premature "spilling" and overconfiding.

In the early presentation of their stories, people might include subtle, indirect, or qualified messages, such as "I thought he was a man of integrity," "He beats me but I am generally satisfied with him," or "I'm kind of pleased with what she has done." By repeating a key phrase, "A man of integrity?" "Generally satisfied?" "Kind of pleased?" the worker highlights the hidden message. Rephrasing and paraphrasing in the form of a question, "Are you saying that for once she . . . ?" "Does what I am hearing mean that he is doing . . . ?" communicate the worker's interest in understanding the hidden message. They also encourage further elaboration.

As people explain the factual aspects of their concerns, the associated feelings are usually also expressed. Thus, for example, when a worker asks a youngster about being thrown out of his class, his anger mounts as he tells his story and he may shout or raise his voice while reliving the experience. An empathic response, "He embarrassed you in front of your classmates" or "You have felt all along that he picks on you," may help the youngster to continue his story. Our profession has a tendency to verbally overspecify people's feelings. The youngster's anger does not have to be labeled. Telling the youngster, "You must have been angry" when he is shouting is superfluous. Minimal encouragement, supportive statements, waiting out silence, reaching for the meaning of silence, and securing more data are often more likely to elicit the associated feelings.

When people have difficulty expressing feelings, putting the feeling into words is helpful ("You felt very hurt"). Verbalizing and acknowledging the person's feeling encourages continued development of the narrative. For example, reaching for a specific feeling, "How did your husband's behavior with the children make you feel?," highlights a feeling and invites further discussion as the focus shifts from the situation to reactions.

In telling their life stories, some people feel shame about events and situations in their lives such as incest, violence, or drug use. Legitimizing and universalizing the client's thoughts, emotions, and reactions facilitates continued elaboration. Comments such as "Most people in such an experience would feel abandoned," or "Many people wrongfully blame themselves when such things happen," convey acceptance and invite further discussion.

Metaphors and figures of speech demonstrate understanding and invite further discussion. When clients are stuck in their perceptions, thinking, and verbalizations, the social worker can use a parallel situation, an analogy, to achieve release. For example, a father unable to understand a child's embarrassment at being yelled at in class by her teacher, might learn from the worker's analogy of being yelled at by his boss in front of others at the workplace. Parents who are defensive and vulnerable in an intake interview for the hospitalization of their adolescent schizophrenic son might respond to a worker's analogy to diabetes (i.e., both having a biochemical and genetic nature, and both conditions being activated by stress).

Telling one's troubles to a stranger is uncomfortable and painful for many people. If the worker is detached and impersonal, pain and anxiety mount. The ability of workers to share their thoughts and feelings was ranked by clients as the most important skill in Shulman's 1978 study. Social workers' self-disclosures often invite further and deeper disclosures by clients (Doster and Nesbit 1979). Appropriate sharing of the worker's personal feelings that are neither too powerful nor too superficial bridges the distance between worker and client. Statements such as "I also get upset when . . ." or "I understand your pain, for I also lost my father . . ." must always be responsive to the person's need and not to the worker's efforts to be liked.

At the right moment, gentle humor can relieve anxiety or embarrassment and ease suffering (Siporin 1984). Humor helps to equalize power and to normalize the helping process. Feeling more at ease and not judged, clients are more likely to share their thoughts, feelings, and experiences. However, humor is risky unless it comes naturally to the worker, and it should never be couched in sarcastic or hostile terms.

After the applicant or client has shared considerable material, the worker briefly summarizes concerns and life issues, bringing salient themes to the foreground, consolidating lengthy messages, and providing continuity within the first session and from session to session (Hepworth and Larsen 1986). A statement such as "Let me pull together what we have talked about to make sure I understand . . ." provides an opportunity for clients to amplify messages not heard by the worker, take stock, and continue the exploration.

As the social worker helps applicants and clients describe the stressful life issues they are facing, they are actually working together on the beginnings of a mutual assessment of the life issues (stressors), how they are manifested, and the personal and environmental resources available for coping with them. Together, applicant and worker consider a stressor's onset, duration, and intensity, what has been done about it so far, and the results. By maintaining balance between a focus on the life stressor(s) and responsiveness to verbal and nonverbal cues, the worker encourages applicants and clients to tell their story in their own way. This gives a beginning sense of the interplay of forces in the life situation. The practitioner might then be able to tentatively confirm the applicant's definition of the life stressor(s), suggest an alternative definition to consider, or agree to postpone further exploration to a later time. Then they together examine what each believes might be helpful, including objectives, priorities, respective tasks, and next steps.

Only when applicant, practitioner, and agency agree to work together does an applicant become a client. At this point, given the tentative assessment, practitioners may again describe the agency's function, the social work purpose, and how the work together will proceed. The description must be concise, explicit, and clear (Gitterman and Shulman 1994; Gitterman 1989a). Table 3.2 summarizes the skills applicable to services sought:

Services Offered. In offering a service, social workers begin with a clear, concrete, description of the agency and of social work services and professional purpose, without falling into jargon and with due attention to the potential clients' values and life styles. The worker suggests how the offered service connects to the person's life situation. Next, the worker invites the potential client(s) to respond in terms of that connection. People who are well informed about what is offered are less apt to fear a hidden agenda, such as a practitioner describing one service while intending another.

For example, in a psychiatric hospital serving adolescents and their families, social workers were expected to interview parents for the stated purpose of securing a developmental history of their teenager. The latent purpose, however, was to engage parents in treatment:

In our first session I explained to Mr. and Mrs. Dalton that the hospital provides regular interviews with a social worker in order to secure developmental and family history and information about recent events in the patient's life. Families are informed about patient progress and their questions answered, and their help with discharge plans is sought. Mr. and Mrs. Dalton accepted my invitation and agreed to provide the necessary information. In subsequent interviews, however, they resisted my

Table 3.2   Skills Related to Degree of Client Choice: Service Sought

- invite person to identify concerns
- use minimal encouragers to invite elaboration
- provide supportive statements
- wait out silence
- reach directly for the meaning of silence
- invite facts
- ask open-ended questions
- repeat key phrases
- rephrase and paraphrase questions
- acknowledge and verbalize feelings
- reach for specific feelings
- legitimize and universalize feelings
- use figures of speech and analogies
- share own thoughts
- use selfdisclosure when appropriate
- use timely humor when appropriate
- summarize discussion
- explain agency function and services
- describe and explain social work service and professional purpose

efforts to "treat" them. I had never acknowledged the covert aim of our meetings. I was too uncomfortable to state directly that they may be partially responsible for their son's disturbance.

Most parents worry about their possible roles in their child's illness. A practitioner's covert agenda mobilizes their anxiety and defenses and closes off any possibility of engagement. Contrast the Daltons' experience with that of Mr. and Mrs. Parker, an African-American couple whose daughter, age 16, was hospitalized for schizophrenia after attempting to strangle her 4-year-old foster sister:

I discussed the purpose of our getting together and mentioned that parents often have worries about how their children became ill and also what happens to them in the hospital. They also wonder what to expect when their child goes home for the weekend. I said I would like to help them with any worries and questions they may have, and at the same time, I need their help with our efforts to understand Linda's illness.

Mrs. Parker responded that Linda as a baby had no troubles, tantrums, or feeding problems. "We always thought she was a happy child and it's hard for us to understand what went wrong. I want to know what went wrong. What caused this to happen? Can you tell us or don't you know? Or do you know and won't tell us?"

I replied, "We don't really understand how this came about, but I will always share with you anything I know. Right now, we want you to know that in this disorder there is usually no single factor, no single experience that one can point to as the cause. There are biochemical and genetic factors which are still not fully understood. There may be emotional experiences that only Linda perceived to be significant, yet they could have triggered this reaction. She might have felt pressure that built up anxiety, and you and I need to understand that too." Mr. Parker noticeably relaxed and shared some recollections of when he began to suspect that Linda was having trouble.

The direct statement that all parents have natural worries was both reassuring and welcoming. It relieved the parents' fears of negative judgments and blame.

Social workers' discomfort with intruding in people's privacy is readily conveyed to clients. A worker might focus on forming a positive relationship with the intent of easing gradually into the "serious" business later. This erroneously assumes that a relationship is the goal of the work. Overlooked is the fact that the relationship can only arise out of the quality of the work together. Preoccupation with forming a "good relationship" deflects the client's concerns and hinders the worker's ability to help.

Inviting potential clients to accept an agency service requires anticipatory empathy to understand potential clients' perception of their life situations. Introducing the service by correspondence, telephone calls, or personal contact requires conveying genuine concern and responsiveness to those perceptions. When an agency decides to offer a service, someone has already decided that a need exists, or a source of funding has become available. However, perception of needs will vary. For example, a child is referred by a teacher for being a "troublemaker." While the teacher calls the child troublesome, the worker calls him troubled, and the child says he is being picked on. Similarly, while developmentally challenged young adults are likely to be upset by a social worker identifying them as "mentally retarded," they will be much more likely to engage in a discussion of how the status effects their lives—being teased for being slow, being treated like a child, labeled as "retarded." By verbalizing the potential clients' perceptions of their life issues, the worker demonstrates empathic understanding and, thereby increases the likelihood that the potential client will accept the agency's services.

People offered a service may already be experiencing stress and are vulnerable in the face of any manipulation or misuse of authority by agency or practitioner. Hence, in offered (outreach) social work services, establishing mutuality is essential to the acceptance and engagement of potential clients, many of whom already feel powerless and perhaps resentful of the offer. A worker's offer of service is not formalized until potential clients and the worker reach explicit agreements about goals, means, and mutual responsibilities. Setting priorities among life stressors and translating them into coping tasks offer worker and potential clients a focus for their work. The first priority is given to the most critical life issue. If potential clients face eviction, a medical emergency, or lack of food, such issues must be immediately addressed. Beginning with the person's definition of the life issue minimizes resistance. If parents declare their child to be the stressor but the worker immediately redefines it as a marital issue, the couple's defenses will be mobilized. Trust and credibility must be in place before a fixed system can become more flexible. Then the worker considers which tasks might successfully resolve or reduce the stressor; success is a powerful motivator.

Six women, ages 24 to 35, were present for the meeting. Five were African-American, one was Hispanic. We put chairs in a circle and began. I asked their names and ages. I told them I was a teacher at a school of social work, working here voluntarily on a part-time basis because I wanted to help—there were so many people here, and not enough help to go around. "You can say that again" and "There's *no* help" were the replies. I told them I felt concerned that they were in such trouble and living under these conditions. Maybe I could help them to help each other. This group, if they wanted to become a group, would talk about making this place better and about getting out and back on their feet again. As I spoke they were saying "yeah" and "right on."

Then Iris angrily and very loudly said she didn't want to meet with me as a go-between—I should send them the director or the big boss of all the shelters. I said I couldn't do that today, and I couldn't promise fast results, but I would act as mediator or go-between if they wanted. Iris reluctantly agreed. They all expressed fear of reprisals for coming to this meeting—staff would get them for it. I said I didn't know if that were so or not, but they should tell me if anything did happen. I asked for their concerns and they began.

In a steady stream, Iris, Jean, and Carla shared the problems. Ana and Dora agreed by nodding. There was a list of fifteen distinct grievances. The women spoke of filth, hunger, sexual harassment and rape by the guards, violence by staff toward the mentally ill residents, and fear of being killed. Sheryl seemed uncomfortable with the tone and the barrage. At various points I turned to her to get her in. I related to the feelings behind all the statements with empathy, naming the feelings of anger, helplessness, and outrage.

CARLA: We're all treated like we're crazy or in prison. It's hard enough to be down and out, but to be treated like dirt gets you desperate.

JEAN: This place is tense, it's going to explode. [Everyone else agreed.]

IRIS: I feel really close to hurting somebody and going to jail.

WORKER: I understand how angry you all are. Iris, do you really want to go to jail?

IRIS: No.

WORKER
[TO ENTIRE GROUP]: What do you think Iris could do then?

JEAN: Just what we're doing, talk about it here. I'm so glad you came. I don't explode, but I'm so depressed.

WORKER: I hear your pain and I wonder how the rest of you feel. [Everyone agreed to being very depressed.]

CARLA: You need hope, you need to know your options, how you can get out of here. If you don't, who knows what you'll do?

SHERYL: People who feel they're so angry they can hurt somebody should get some help. A lot of them wouldn't hurt anybody, and don't want to be hurt themselves.

WORKER: I hear you and understand. You don't feel like that and it's scary when other people do. But everyone here is hurting in her own way.
[. . .]

JEAN: There's a lack of compassion here. Everything is hard and tough and soon you become hard and tough. You get treated like dirt, so you feel like dirt. Being treated like a criminal is the worst part. You already hate yourself for messing up and landing here. Where's the compassion?

WORKER: I agree. [Everyone nodded.] I see that you care about each other and that's why I brought you together as a group.

JEAN: God bless you for coming here. This is the first time I talked my heart out and felt caring from anyone since I got here. [Everyone agreed.]

WORKER: Thank you for giving me a chance to hear you and be with you and share your pain and frustration. Maybe we can become a group here and take care of each other. I honestly don't know how much I can do about the shelter system, but I'll be pleased to try. But I do know you could care for each other and I could help with that.

JEAN: It's happening right here, right now. I'm so glad I spoke up this morning.
[Iris starting joking and singing about everyone needing a little love.]

My interventions were aimed at helping the group members tell the story of life there and to reach for and show understanding of the pain they were feeling. I tried to welcome the expression of anger not only to bring relief but because I wanted to model an authority that did not punish them for their anger and who could "take it." I also let them know that the demand to change the system overnight would be hard, but that I would try. We also defined some of the next steps for social action on their grievances. (Lee 1987:11)

Table 3.3 summarizes social work skills in offered services.

Services Imposed or Mandated. Increasingly, social workers serve involuntary clients (Rooney 1992). Imposed service presents ethical dilemmas that arise from the dual social work functions of care and social control. Hutchison (1987) suggests that care for individuals and control of the general social welfare are complementary rather than antithetical and ethical practice requires that "social workers, especially in mandated settings, remain sensitive to the inherent dangers of becoming repressive forces in support of the dominant special interests" (590).

Mandated social work services range from completely involuntary to somewhat involuntary. Court-mandated services carry prescribed consequences for clients if they fail to comply with court orders (coercion). To some extent, the court's legal authority is transferred to the agency and the social worker. Compliance becomes the minimal condition for escaping a status of parolee, probationer, or juvenile offender or for achieving a desired goal such as return of one's child from foster care or discharge of a child from institutional care. While legally mandated services are the most coercive, institutions or agencies can also impose a social work service as a condition for methadone maintenance, homemaker service, or adopting or fostering a child.

While institutional sanctions may be less restrictive than legal mandates, they can nonetheless be formidable threats to prospective clients. The authoritarian nature of a particular agency can create ambiguity about the extent of client choice. For example, a welfare recipient might feel compelled to accept a group service for fear of jeopardizing the assistance grant. Public housing tenants may accept service lest they be evicted. Hospitalized

---

Table 3.3	Skills Related to Degree of Choice: Service Offered

- define and describe agency function and services
- describe professional function
- describe the service being offered
- identify person's potential perceptions of his or her life issues or needs
- reach for doubts, hesitations, ambivalences
- the elaboration skills listed in table 3.2
- establish priorities
- specify respective tasks and responsibilities
- specify temporal arrangements

mental patients and residents of geriatric facilities may fear negative sanctions if they refuse a service. Freedom of choice may be asserted by agency and worker, but potential clients often experience it as coercion.

When services are imposed, people are not likely to welcome an organization and practitioner who would have extensive power over their lives. Social workers in mandated services need to remember that they represent a serious threat, even an obstacle, to potential clients' own aims. Some people acknowledge their need for help, finding the service to be congruent with their own definitions of life issues and aspirations. Others resent having problems attributed to them and being coerced by external authority. Some people hide their resentment by superficially cooperating in order to obtain a desired goal. Others reject the agency definition of their goal or life issue and actively resist the social worker.

Cingolani (1984:442) views the encounter of mandated client and social worker as a political process, "one that involves the socially sanctioned use of power or influence in a context of conflicting interests between the client and some part of his or her social environment." Within this context, social workers have to anticipate struggle and conflict against their power and authority (Gitterman 1989b, 1983). Many social workers in mandated settings commit one of two common practice errors. Because they are intimidated or angered by these clients, they avoid dealing with the question of legal, organizational, and professional authority or they set out to build a relationship before risking the client's anger, failing to recognize that the relationship can only emerge from effective work together. In either case, the difficulty in engaging a distrustful and angry client is increased. If the social worker also becomes angry, unnecessary confrontations may follow. Misuse of authority and power increases client distrust and resistance. The practice task is to turn formal authority into professional influence.

Effective social workers are direct and honest about the source of the mandate, their own authority and responsibility, limits on confidentiality, potential consequences of noncompliance, and definitions of noncompliance. The guiding principle is to provide the least intrusive service. Ethical practice requires social workers to use their authority to provide resources to mandated clients as they would for nonmandated clients and not impose personal standards that are not part of the mandate. And, even in mandated settings, social workers must influence employing organizations to "further a progressively constructive relationship between the individual and society" (Hutchison 1987:587). Professional directness and honesty reduce mistrust, thwarted expectations, and resistance.

The social worker also shares available information and invites the mandated client's perceptions and reactions. The worker must demonstrate warmth and caring if the person is to hear the worker's description of the service. Professional "straight talk" has to be mediated by compassion for the client's predicament and life stressors over which any semblance of control is being lost. Also, the description of service should fit the client's perception of reality (for example, "You feel the parole officer is hassling you"). The aim is to actively engage the client in an area in which a commonality of interest is greater than a conflict in interests (Cingolani 1984). At the same time, non-negotiable legal requirements and agency policies have to be separated from negotiable rights, choices, and options (Rooney 1992). In many instances, common goals can best be described as "helping you get the agency and me off your back." This includes helping neglectful or abusive parents to improve their child care so they will be free of surveillance, or helping probationers or parolees to meet the conditions for changing their status. Sequencing objectives in accordance with client priorities is frequently involved. The pressing, concrete needs of neglectful or abusive parents often have to be met before they can even think about and respond to the needs of their children. Table 3.4 summarizes the social work skills in imposed and mandated services.

Oppressed People and Their Particular Life Issues

In response to racism, attendant poverty, and powerlessness, some oppressed people react with rage. Others internalize society's rejections and turn the rage against themselves, their own families, and communities. Many, in spite of the heavy toll of oppressive social and economic conditions, maintain a positive outlook and high levels of self-valuation (Foster and Perry 1982).

The initial contact of a person of color with a social worker takes place in a racist environment in which persons of color are labeled and stereotyped, their families and life styles disparaged, and their survival strengths and adaptability ignored. To applicants or clients of color, a white social worker is likely to represent institutional power and a threat to desired goals. Clients may directly or indirectly express their resentment by hostility or exaggerated compliance. For example, an African-American adolescent mandated by the court to a residential treatment center, might respond to a white social worker with direct hostility, staring at the floor, or monosyllabic, noncommittal responses. African-American teenagers have reason to resent the poverty and racism that rob them of their adolescence and rapidly propel them into adulthood (Devore 1983). Why should they trust white social workers? African-American social workers might create powerful ambivalent feelings and so be distrusted. Both white and African-American practitioners might experience guilt, defensiveness, and resentment because their efforts are not appreciated.

The worker must anticipate some degree of distrust, and not personalize it. Trust has to be earned. A client's initial testing behaviors and resis-

Table 3.4   Skills Related to Degree of Choice: Service Mandated

- prepare to be perceived as a potential threat to client
- anticipate struggle and resistance
- be direct and honest about source of mandate, potential consequences for noncompliance, and limits of professional authority
- specify conditions for termination of mandate
- identify limits to confidentiality
- share available information
- demonstrate compassion for person's life stressors
- identify areas in which the commonality of interests is greater than the conflict in interests
- use the elaboration skills listed in table 3.2

tance have to be understood and accepted as adaptive efforts. Social workers must explore their own attitudes before they can demonstrate that they genuinely care and are committed to trying to understand the clients' pain and oppression even when it is turned against themselves, their families, or their communities. Social workers must understand their clients' dual worlds: the local community of people of color, and the institutions and mass media of white society (Logan, Freeman, McRoy 1990). Social workers need to identify and be sensitive to potential racial differences. They must avoid blaming clients for the "messes" in their lives, and connect on a human level.

George R., age 15 and black, lives in a western city with his mother and two younger brothers in a recently integrated neighborhood that they had just moved into. His mother is a registered nurse. She divorced her husband ten years ago, and George sees his father about once a year when he drifts into the city. George was referred to the mental health clinic by a probation officer. Since his arrival he had been repeatedly involved in fist fights. When he was suspended from school, he threatened to kill school personnel. Following the next fight, an "unprovoked attack" on a smaller boy, police were called and George was to be taken to juvenile hall. However, when handcuffs were used, he became so out of control and threatening that he was taken instead to the psychiatric ward of the county hospital, where he remained for ten days until his court hearing. He was diagnosed as schizophrenic, paranoid reaction, and commitment was recommended. However, disposition was delayed because his mother agreed to seek outpatient treatment for George and to take a leave of absence from work to care for him at home. He was ordered by the court to stay away from school until a second hearing in two months. The first two interviews illustrate the worker's efforts to engage George.

First Interview. In my office, George was almost ostentatiously menacing as he stood over me and glowered, fists clenched, shoulders held in such a way as to make him appear even more broad shouldered than he is. At first, he seemed to struggle against speaking, then he exploded: "I'm not coming here, I don't care what they do to me, I don't care, I'm not crazy. I'm going to sue the judge, he can't get away with this, let them send me to a state hospital, I don't care." I cut in, "OK, so sit down and let's talk about it. I don't know whether you belong here either—all I know right now is that you are very upset." (He sat down.) "Now, tell me, what's happened to you?" His story was incoherent and interspersed with threats to kill the principal, the judge, and particularly the school counselor. He insisted that the school fights were not started by him, but that everyone was against him. He told, in a particularly frightened fashion, of the arrival of the police, the handcuffs, and the days on the psychiatric ward. He repeated many times, "I don't care." I said, "Handcuffs and the psychiatric ward is no place for a 15-year-old boy. It's terribly frightening. You weren't prepared to go there, and you didn't know what would happen next." He said, "They were going to send me to state hospital. I don't want to go anywhere. I'm not crazy, I'm not coming here, I don't care what the judge's or psychiatrist's report says about me." He stood up to leave. I said, "George, I don't know what the report says about you because I don't have it, but I will in three days. Let's set up another time so I can tell you what's in the report, OK?" He reluctantly agreed.

Second Interview. George's first words were, "I'm only going to stay five minutes." He turned my clock to face him and stared at it. He did not look at me. I said, "I hope you will stay longer, but let's make the most of the time we have." George asked me if I received "those" reports. I said, "Yes, the report says that you have had a lot of hurts. When you were a little kid, first and second grade, the kids picked on you, and they would not stop no matter what you did. You wanted to but didn't know how to make them your friends. You must have been very lonely . . . That's rough on a little kid, and you were very small and thin, in a neighborhood full of bullies." He remained silent, looked at me and then said, "Five minutes is up," but he did not get up from his chair. I added, "The report also describes the hurts from your father." He stopped me and said that he wanted to talk about grade school. He described how the bigger boys would waylay him to tease him for wearing a cap and would knock it off his head. He jumped to the present, describing his loneliness. He had been kicked out of the YMCA; he was out of school; a month ago he'd been told to leave the roller rink and never come back. He added sadly, "I still got no friends, see? Nobody wants me around, but I don't care." At the end of the hour, George agreed to return next week.

The worker's high degree of empathy and acceptance helped alleviate some of George's fears and anxieties. The worker was not intimidated by

George's menacing stance, but instead recognized and responded to George's feelings at the moment and throughout the case. The social worker's approach is racially sensitive. She realizes the racist context of George's experiences: the school's lack of sensitivity to its newly transferred student; the police's harsh response; the mandated referral to the psychiatric ward of a county hospital. These experiences are more likely to be confronted by black than white adolescents.

In working with diverse populations, social work practice has to be racially and ethnically sensitive. For example, Puerto Rican, Cuban, and Mexican Americans, the largest Hispanic populations in the United States, share a common language while having distinguishing customs and folkways. Hispanic cultures do not generally support the use of social agencies. Institutional help is sought only if all other informal options have failed, i.e., family, friends, neighbors, shopkeepers, clergyman, and spiritist. Spiritism is an important belief system in many Hispanic cultures. Approximately one out of three Puerto Rican adults has used a medium for help with some problem; more than 100 million people throughout the world, primarily in Latin America and the United States, practice Santeria, a spiritist tradition (Berthold 1989). Spiritism is the belief that spirits have a powerful influence on human behavior. Since problems are primarily defined as caused by spirits, spiritists resist hospitalization and drug treatment. They believe these "external" treatments undermine people's ability to gain control over invasive spirits. For example, in Puerto Rican culture, *ataques*—hysterical reactions or seizures—are accepted as normal means of coping with pent-up stress. The medium communicates with spirits to eliminate the evil ones and replace them with protective spirits (Delgado 1988). Since the dominant culture defines these attacks as pathology, Hispanic clients are reluctant to share their spiritual lives with physicians, psychiatrists, and social workers. In addition to the spiritist, other folk healers include the *santero*, who uses rituals of song, music, and animal sacrifice; the herbalist who treats "hot" and "cold" illnesses with combinations of foods, teas, and herbs; the *santiguador* whose cure requires the will of God and various treatments such as massage, herbs, prayer; and the *curandero* who strengthens ties with the Roman Catholic church (Delgado and Humm-Delgado 1982).

Mrs. Morales, a Puerto Rican solo parent of two young children, casually informed a Hispanic settlement house worker that she is in danger of being evicted from her apartment. The worker invited her into an office.

MRS. MORALES: I got until September to move out. Next month I have to go to court again.

WORKER: What happened so far?

MRS. MORALES: Last time I went to court, the landlord tricked me. They say the receipts I have of payments are no good.

WORKER: Did you have a lawyer with you?

MRS. MORALES:	No.
WORKER:	Do you want me to help you get a lawyer from Legal Aid?
MRS. MORALES:	No, it's OK.
WORKER:	I am afraid you will lose your apartment.
MRS. MORALES:	They will have to put me into a hotel.
WORKER:	A hotel may be rough for you and the kids.
MRS. MORALES:	It is OK. I lived in a hotel before and you could cook there with a hot plate. It's OK.
WORKER:	I sense you are not pleased with your apartment.
MRS. MORALES:	There are things going on in that apartment.
WORKER:	What do you mean?
MRS. MORALES:	Last night Hector woke up and started to talk but he was really still asleep, but with his eyes open. I did not call him by his name because if you do that the child could die. Then I am half asleep and I feel this hand that grabbed me by my neck. I really had to struggle to get rid of it. The woman who was in the apartment before me also had a lot of trouble with her husband, and had to move out. You see a man died in the bedroom. I don't feel right with it—his spirit is still in the apartment. I am afraid of it. I am glad you are also Puerto Rican. White people do not believe in spirits.
WORKER:	How have you managed so far?
MRS. MORALES:	I try to stay in the street as late as possible. Sometimes, I bring the mattress into the living room. I don't get much sleep. A friend slept over one night and felt the spirit also. I bet you wouldn't sleep there one night by yourself (she began to laugh). The other night I felt this man and he was trying to touch my parts. I woke up in the morning with pains all over my body. I am a strong woman, and in the morning I have no energy to get up. I feel like someone has beaten me up.
WORKER:	This is very scary for you.
MRS. MORALES:	I went to a Santero a couple months ago. He told me to go check my parts and to be careful in the kitchen. Everything he said was true—a doctor found a cyst, and the frying pan moves in the kitchen. I am afraid to cook there.
WORKER:	I hear how difficult it is for you to stay in the apartment. Let's put our heads together and figure out what we can do. OK?

Hispanic cultures emphasize an informal, expressive style of relating, requiring "personalismo" or trust in a person. The worker needs to establish an informal atmosphere (e.g., sit in the kitchen, have a cup of coffee together, exchange observations about the children) for the prospective client to feel comfortable. The worker also has to demonstrate a willingness to be incorporated into the client's informal social system rather than remaining solely a representative of a formal bureaucracy. Without confidence in the worker's interest in developing a personalized relationship, "much time is wasted and often treatment is discontinued" (Ghali 1977:461). This Hispanic worker's knowledge of and comfort with the cultural concept of spirits helped Mrs. Morales to reveal her fears. By shifting from advocating for Mrs. Morales' legal rights to inviting her fear of evil spirits, the worker engages her. The culture-specific intervention led to an ingenious solution: inviting the spiritist to the apartment to expel the evil spirits and replace them with protective ones. The culturally sensitive intervention enabled Mrs. Morales to maintain her apartment, instead of risking homelessness.

Encouraging the client to reach out to supportive kin and kin networks to reach out to the client can be helpful. These networks can have a profound impact on people's use of institutional resources (Birkel and Reppuci 1983). Whether people apply for social work services and whether they remain connected to the agency and the worker may depend on what their networks think of applying for formal help, social workers, or of the agency itself (Mayer and Rosenblatt 1964). Burruel and Chavez (1974) report that young Chicano adults living with parents are sometimes labeled passive-dependent as though they are unable to separate from parents and home when, in fact, this is normal expected behavior, especially in Mexican families. Hence interventions directed toward emancipation from the family create guilt and stress and might lead to drop-out.

People's sexual orientation ranges along a continuum from exclusively homoerotic sexual orientation to exclusively heteroerotic. People with a homoerotic sexual orientation confront the choice of keeping their orientation secret and remaining in the "closet," and suffer from the split between their public and private lives; or being public about their orientation, and suffering discrimination and scorn (Moses and Hawkins 1982).

Two graduate students, Helen and Kaye, interned in an urban agency that provides programs for elderly homosexual people. From reviewing agency records, they learned that many elderly gays and lesbians have remained in the closet in order to survive in a homophobic culture. Some married and others continually worried about possible exposure. Now that many are retired or have lost their spouses, older gays and lesbians are contacting this agency. Yet the students observed that many older women applied for service yet failed to continue. Some welcomed telephone calls, but did not wish anyone to come to their homes. Several reported that they disliked the drop-in center because it was dominated by gay men. The students concluded that a group might best serve the psychosocial needs of isolated older lesbian women. If a mutual aid system were to develop, such a group would have the potential to universalize individual life issues, reduce isolation, and relieve feelings of stigma (Gitterman 1994). Ten women were selected from the students' caseloads, and handwritten invitations were mailed to each one followed by a phone call a week before the meeting date. Refreshments were mentioned as well as transportation for those needing it. All appeared interested and all said their attendance would depend on weather and their health. On a rainy night, four women came to the first meeting. Carolyn, 69, and Virginia, 60, both African-American, have been a couple for 35 years. Virginia is employed as a professional and Carolyn is a retired professional. Mary, also African-American, 68, is a friend of Virginia and Carolyn. Betty is white, 66, and has never married. Her lover of many years is a bisexual woman. The students are white. Kay, 40, is a lesbian and has lived with her lover for five years. Helen, 24, is heterosexual. Helen records a summary of the first meeting:

After welcoming the members to the group meeting and a period of introductions, I stated, "You have a great deal in common—as I mentioned on the phone, you are all older women who share a lesbian sexual orientation. That's being in triple jeopardy in a sexist, ageist, homophobic world. Those of you who are black also share the experiences of living in a racist society. [Since the agency had served only seven people of color in a total of 615 service units during the prior month, we were especially happy with their group attendance.] We invited you to the group because we thought you would help each other in dealing with common experiences that you have to confront because of your sexual orientation—such issues as whether to tell friends and family you are lesbian, how to deal with discrimination and prejudice." The members immediately connect with each other and begin to share life experiences. They agree to work on life issues such as their social isolation and the struggles and joys in their lives as older lesbians. They also express interest in helping recruit more members. Halfway into the meeting, the subject of work and "coming out" is brought up. Carolyn (addressing the students) inquires, "What do you think of coming out?" I responded, "I think coming out is a very personal decision that a woman makes every day. Are you thinking of a particular situation?" (My response was brief and impersonal because I felt uneasy offering an opinion on a choice that I have never had to make. I also realize that the current generation of older lesbians have had to "pass" as straight as a way of coping with their homosexual identity.)

Technically, the student moves from the general to the specific. She recognizes that Carolyn could have been asking several questions: do you think people should be out? Are you out? what do you think of gay people? She realizes that group members' coping styles have been developed and maintained for several decades and respects them by not responding with a simplistic opinion that would frame the discussion. At the same time, if she could have used her discomfort and said "I feel a little uneasy offering a decision about choice because I am not gay. What do you think about Carolyn's question?" she would have clarified her role and modeled directness. Instead her discomfort increased when her co-leader identified her own homosexual orientation. Before the initial contact, a worker must explore her own self-comfort with her sexual orientation and potential homophobic feelings.

Virginia picked up on Carolyn's question and asked, "Well, for example, what do you think about coming out on the job?" Kay responded, "It depends on the job. Many people who volunteer at this agency are in the closet at their regular jobs. I am out of the closet all the time. I just am. I know I want to work where I can be out. Of course, that limits my options for jobs." I was feeling terribly 'on the spot.' I felt all the group members were staring at me, expecting my testimony as well. Because of my unease, I redirected the attention to Virginia, asking "How about you, Virginia, are you closeted or not?"

The student's dilemma is understandable: she is white, young, and heterosexual. She decides to keep her heterosexuality in the closet. As part of her education, the student will learn to trust group members' capacity to handle difference; after all, they have been handling difference for most of their lives. Encouraging discussion of differences in sexual orientation, race and age—even in the first session—can advance the group process, build trust, and help develop mutual aid.

In reviewing this first session, Helen analyzed her reluctance: "I made the choice at this time not to tell the group members that I am not gay. I feared their rejection. I thought if I revealed myself, the group might not trust me and would be more guarded in their discussions." Fortunately, there was another opportunity at the next meeting for Helen to be more candid and to come out of her own heterosexual closet. The ensuing discussion not only helped resolve the ambiguity, but also advanced the group's development as they struggled with the inevitable issue of difference.

Later the group reminisced.

VICTORIA: Do you think it is easier to be gay now than then? [meaning Stonewall and the gay rights movement]

ANN: Oh no, it was easier for me years ago. I used to be quite popular. I was accepted in several different cliques. A bunch of us would meet at the Eastgate, it was a very popular bar then, and we'd have a great time. We'd all stay over someone's apartment and go to the park the next day and back to the Eastgate Saturday night. A whole group of us would spend the weekend together. It was so much fun.

MARLENE: Oh yes, we used to have a wild time up at that bar.

ANN: I used to be there too.

MARLENE: Yes, that was a great place. We'd have barbecues and go to the beach and meet in people's homes.

HELEN: It sounds like there were a lot of bars for lesbian women to go.

LORI: There were many more than today.

HELEN: I've heard there used to be more places for women to go out. It must be quite a loss for all of you now.

JANET: Oh yes. [Marlene and Lori nodded, Ann agreed.]

HELEN: Are you all feeling isolated?

LORI: Yes, we need a center like this in Queens where people can just sit together and talk.

JANET: A place where we could meet other gay women to be friends with.

MARLENE: Yes, we need a center for gays in Queens. I go to a senior center but most of the women there are complaining about their children. The other day a woman asked me if I had a husband because she and her husband are looking for a couple to socialize with. I just said no.

ANN: I'm "in the closet." The people in my building would never tolerate a gay person. It's a building for senior citizens. I'm friendly with the super's wife. She has me down for dinner and stuff like that. If she knew—oh boy.

HELEN: You've been forced to give up a very important and special part of your life, that's sad.

ANN: Yes, it is very depressing.

MARLENE: I have always been in the closet. That is my personal life. I have my public life and my personal life.

HELEN: How does that make you feel? Do you wish you could let people know?

MARLENE: No, that's just the way it is. I have my group of gay friends whom I socialize with, but as for everyone else, I keep it quiet.

The group members communicate feelings of loss, loneliness, and isolation. The lesbian world they belonged to and enjoyed no longer exists for them. However, the review of common life experiences connects group members and encourages mutual support. Passing through life as someone other than you are, feeling that you have to hide your sexual orientation, fearing that you might be caught and uncovered takes a heavy daily toll. The group provides a safe environment for acceptance and unconditional regard.

People with physical, intellectual, and emotional challenges also experience oppression. In the previous chapter, we presented the situation of Mrs. Richards to illustrate the life stressors experienced by a person with paranoia. The more overwhelmed and disabled a person is, the more directive and active a worker needs to be in helping the client to identify life stressors, goals, and coping skills. Mrs. Richards's social worker assumed an active, orchestrating stance in their work together.

In beginning with a chronically depressed client, the person's intense despair may well threaten the worker's own private demons. Hence, beginning practitioners must guard against a wish to simply "shake" a client out of a depression, or to detach themselves and flee from the threat of being engulfed by it. Most chronically depressed people manifest a lack of energy and bland affect; others may be agitated and even psychotic. A few will readily share the content and feelings of their depression. Practitioners must monitor their reactions to the client's depression and its manifestations in order to avoid judgments, impatience, and premature interpretations. The depressed client needs to feel the worker's acceptance, caring, and interest through helping the client confide his or her life story, express associated feelings, hew to reality, and comply with prescribed medication (Turnbull 1991).

People addicted to alcohol or drugs pervade social work caseloads. Whatever physical, emotional, and social stressors people have, alcohol abuse exacerbates their suffering and worsens their life circumstances. Alcohol abuse makes the depressed more depressed; the hyperactive more hyperactive; the spouse abuser more abusive; the homeless more likely to remain homeless; the employed more likely to become unemployed. A person who abuses alcohol presents challenges to the social worker (Hanson 1991). Our profession in general has accepted the notion that alcohol abusers must be immediately confronted with their alcoholism. However, when confronted before they are ready to accept the labels of alcoholism and alcoholic, many deny the problem and refuse to stop drinking. The belief is "I am not an alcoholic . . . I don't have to abstain from alcohol for the rest of my life." While denial is considered the core defense of the alcoholic, the denial might be a response to the practitioner's early confrontation. The more forceful the confrontation, the more intense the counterargument (Miller 1983). We suggest that workers initially avoid confrontation. At the outset people are more likely to accept only that they have some problem with drinking. Focusing on problem drinking or life issues created by the drinking is less likely to produce defensiveness. A group's first session is illustrative:

I began by stating, "It must have been hard to come in such terrible weather. I appreciate your coming. Before I ask you to introduce yourselves, let me restate what I see as the purpose of the group. I have spoken to each of you about the problems in your life and how your drinking was making them worse. You have in common a problem with drinking and the drinking is a serious stressor in your lives—with your wives, girlfriends, children, and bosses. Since you have had similar experiences and current difficulties, I thought you could offer each other a great deal of support and help with the stress in your lives. What are your reactions?" Nick suggested we begin by introducing ourselves. I asked the other group members, and they agreed.

Nick began, "My name is Nick, and I want to make it clear that I am not an alcoholic, but I do drink a lot. I used to drink a lot of V.O. and ginger ale, then I switched to wine. I used to buy two bottles of wine a day. It was costing me a lot of money. Now, I'm trying to drink less because I have big dental bills. I drink only in the apartment. I don't go to bars. I drink a bottle of wine every night before I go to sleep. I know I am not an alcoholic because I cut down with no problem. My main problem is that I don't work, I am on one-hundred-percent disability, I don't know what to do with all my free time. I get very bored and down in the dumps."

Ralph spoke next. "I'm Ralph. I don't consider myself an alcoholic because I don't really crave it. I do have problems when I drink too much. Whenever I start to drink or go to a party, I drink too much, and something happens to me. I get into fights, or am attacked, or my wife gets crazy. I would like to stop drinking but it's hard, man."

"My name is Jack, and I work at the post office. My supervisor tells me I am an alcoholic and insists I attend the postal alcoholic recovery group. My job depends on my participation in the group. Man, I know I got a problem drinking, but I ain't no alcoholic. But I don't want to lose my job. I don't know what to do."

The last member introduced himself. "Hi, my name is Gary, and I am an alcoholic. I drink on the spur of the moment, and I can't control it. I don't kid myself anymore. I drive a cab at night. I have a good night, and I say, well, before I go home I'll stop for one drink. I know that if I have that one drink, I am going to continue drinking, but I still have that one drink. I have lost some great jobs, and now my wife has moved out with the kids. I gotta find some ways to get control over my life."

The worker focuses on the stress in their lives created by drinking and avoids a struggle over their accepting the label "alcoholic." Several members assert 'for the record' that they do not accept the label, immediately describe their problem drinking, and energetically begin to share their life patterns. Focusing on life stressors created by drinking rather than on the label, we tap into the positive side of the ambivalence. This supports potential for engagement. Miller and Rollnick (1991) emphasize that people with alcohol-related problems need to be treated as responsible adults capable of making decisions, rather than as weak, inferior, diseased. Only they can decide whether to drink or not to drink. If they relapse, they can make a new decision to abstain. The social worker can only help the addicted person to struggle with life stressors and decisions, but cannot take responsibility for the drinking itself. The social worker has to convey empathy and respect for the client's struggles.

The exploitation of a child for an adult's sexual pleasure is a devastating betrayal and abuse of power. The closer the child is to the offender, the greater the hurt (Gelinas 1983). A further betrayal transpires if the child discloses the abuse and is not believed, or is insensitively treated by family or institution. Sexual abuse distorts the child's self-concept and undermines the child's sense of control over the environment. The linkage of sexuality with manipulation, force, fear, or secrecy traumatizes the child. The sexual trauma then shapes the child's behavior in inappropriate ways, including erotic relating to others, compulsive sexual play, obsessive masturbation, and withdrawal from peers. As teenagers and adults, sexually abused children will be at risk of self-destructive behaviors such as promiscuity, prostitution, anorexia, bulimia, suicide, addictions, hypervigilance or impaired judgment about others' trustworthiness, or reenactment of their own abuse (Finkelhor and Brown 1985).

In beginning with a sexually abused child, the worker must follow the child's sense of timing and pacing in discussing the trauma. Barbara is a bright, engaging, 9-year-old white youngster. She has been sexually abused by her mother's boyfriend for three years from the age of four to seven. When she turned seven she told her mother, "Bill hurt me downstairs with his finger." The accusation was investigated by Protective Services, but the matter was dropped when Bill passed a lie detector test. Barbara was not even taken for a medical examination. Six months later Barbara's mother resumed her relationship with Bill. Two years later the mother lost her job and she and Barbara left the area and moved in with Barbara's grandmother, thereby ending the relationship with Bill.

Barbara came to the attention of the community mental health center when she was found engaging in oral sex with a neighborhood friend. She was also having difficulty in adjusting to a new school and complained of nightmares and anxiety. In the first session, Barbara and the social worker agreed to work on difficulties she and her mother were having in getting along and on her own confusing memories about Bill.

The social worker hypothesized that the relationship to her mother had been affected by Barbara's likely feelings of having been left unprotected by the person she most expected to protect her. She trusted her mother and risked disclosure. Yet Bill remained an active member of the household. In fact, Barbara's mother was reluctant to believe that her Bill could be capable of such abhorrent behavior. Barbara may have blamed herself since "something unexplainable, out of the child's realm of understanding, is being done furtively or coercively, or both, so it must mean that the child is bad" (Friedrich 1990:149). Barbara turned confusion and despair against herself. She overdosed on her asthma medication and exhibits hypersexualized behaviors such as inappropriate sex play, provocative dress, and seductiveness. She also suffers anxiety and nightmares in which Bill is watching her and sneaking into her room through a window.

Barbara and the worker agreed that every week the worker would ask Barbara if she felt ready to talk about the "hard stuff" concerning Bill. This gave the child some sense of control over what and when to disclose. The social worker knows that Barbara has to be learn to trust. In an early session, while playing a game with Barbara, the worker asked if Barbara felt ready for the hard stuff:

BARBARA: But I just got here!

WORKER: I know time goes by very quickly when we are playing together and having a good time.

BARBARA: (after a short silence) Well, I did have a nightmare the other night.

WORKER: What happened in the nightmare?

BARBARA: (with heightened anxiety) Well, I was in my bed and I thought Bill was climbing in my window. I thought he was coming to get me.

WORKER: Oh, how scary!

BARBARA: Yeah, it was, and I had to get out of bed and tie my closet door and my bedroom door with a hair ribbon because that covers the window.

WORKER: It was so scary, you had to figure out some way to keep him out?

BARBARA: Yeah, because my window doesn't have a shade, and my room is so small.

WORKER: What an awful nightmare. Bill could come through your window and then you would be trapped with him in your little room and he would hurt you. (Barbara, looking worried, nods her head in agreement)

WORKER: What did you do—how did you get to feel safe?

BARBARA: I ran into mommy's room—I slept in her bed.

WORKER: And mommy helped you to feel better? (Barbara nods yes.)

WORKER: I am glad because that was a very scary dream. Do you have these dreams often?

BARBARA: Yeah, Last night I had another dream—it was more like a nightmare!

WORKER: (nodding her head to encourage her to continue) Tell me about it.

BARBARA: Well my uncle took me swimming and we were having a lot of fun in the pool, but then I turned around and couldn't find him.

WORKER: (looking concerned) What happened next?

BARBARA: I went to look for him at the bar, but he wasn't there. But when I turned around I saw Bill and then I screamed really loud.

WORKER: You must have been really shocked and scared to see him.

BARBARA: Yeah, but I don't think I could have screamed in real life. I think I would call him a bastard or something.

WORKER: Because you're so angry at him for what he did to you?

BARBARA: Yeah, and then I thought, well . . . maybe I should write this part down.

WORKER: (handing Barbara pen and paper) Okay?

BARBARA: (after writing down what she wanted, she handed the piece of paper back.)

WORKER: Is it okay if I read it aloud?

BARBARA: (nods)

WORKER: (reads) "And I was thinking he might have touched me there. I know I said it happened in his bedroom, but I think it happened more than once."

WORKER: It's terribly confusing for you.

The worker legitimizes Barbara's fear and creates a climate in which she feels safe in a supported environment to begin to discuss her fears. The worker follows Barbara's cues about how and when to proceed, pursuing suppressed traumatic material at the child's pace. She stays focused and the ongoing phase begins.

Practice Modality

Selecting the appropriate practice modality requires consideration of the advantages and disadvantages of individual, family, group, community, social network, or organizational and legislative modalities. This is a difficult area: organizational constraints and fears, rationalized by "our job is not to organize," "we're not set up to supervise work with groups or families," or "our mandate is long-term psychotherapy," inhibit a flexible response and the exercise of professional judgment. Theory and research-based criteria for selection of modality are limited. Few explicit criteria exist for the informed selection of modalities beyond custom, tradition, and the medical model. Client choice and comfort should be the most significant factors. Table 3.5 summarizes principles for selection of appropriate modality.

Table 3.5	Selection of Appropriate Practice Modality

Select practice modality responsive to client choice and comfort
Select practice modality responsive to the type and definition of life stressor
Select *individual modality* for people:

- under intensive stress, requiring frequent and immediate contacts
- in need of specific, concrete, entitlement resources
- in need of privacy
- in states of extreme anxiety and shyness
- in need of a long-term, trusting relationship
- in situations in which the family modality is inappropriate

Select *family modality* for:

- life stressors located in family relationship, communication patterns
- life stressors located in family developmental transitions, traumatic life events, and other critical life issues

Select *group modality* for people who:

- share a common set of threatening life events
- share a common set of life tasks and issues
- suffer from isolation or stigmatized status
- need to act and gain greater control and mastery over their environments

Select *community modality* for people who:

- need to work to improve community or neighborhood conditions

Certain clients are most effectively helped through use of the individual modality.

Mrs. Melvin, 55 years old, is depressed, anxious, and reports sleep and appetite disturbances. She has experienced severe losses in the past six months. Five years ago Mrs. Melvin was awarded physical custody of her two cerebral palsied granddaughters after an investigation of their mother by protective services. Last year she was granted permanent custody of the children. This year the children's mother, who had since borne three more children by her second husband, went to court to regain custody. Despite overwhelming evidence in favor of Mrs. Melvin, the court recommended that the mother be given temporary custody with weekend visitation rights for Mrs. Melvin. With little counseling or preparation, the children were removed from Mrs. Melvin's home. Six months later Mrs. Melvin's father died. Last week her sister died of breast cancer. The youngest of seven children, Mrs. Melvin was the caregiver for her aging parents and siblings. She continues to care for her mother, who lives in a nursing home a few blocks away from Mrs. Melvin.

Mrs. Melvin is motivated, resourceful, and displays good judgment. She and the social worker agree on the following goals: (a) resolution of grief; (b) new relationships with the grandchildren and their mother; (c) new sources of meaning in addition to caregiving; (d) possible employment that makes use of her strengths; (e) a new support system to replace the community and agency supports that were related to the care of children with disabilities. Mrs. Melvin and the social worker plan to meet weekly and to re-evaluate the situation in three months.

A client experiencing severe stressors may require frequent and immediate contacts. Some people are relatively private, and sharing and confiding in groups could be disconcerting and uncomfortable. Similarly, extremely anxious and shy clients usually require a period of support before they feel comfortable in a group. Clients in need of a long-term, trusting relationship in which past traumas and their effects on current functioning are explored benefit from individual work. Finally, certain situations may make the family modality unsafe for an individual. For example, if an abusive partner is violent and unmotivated to change, conjoint or family service places the abused partner at risk. If an abusing husband is mandated to enter family therapy or agrees, only to appease his wife, she risks retaliation. Unless the abusive husband identifies his abuse as the foremost marital issue to be discussed and changed, marital counseling can be contraindicated (Bogard 1984).

The definition of the life stressor can determine the choice of modality. If the stressor is located by worker and client in family relationships, communication, and structure, the living unit related by blood, marriage, or association is the natural modality of choice. Within the living unit itself the sibling, marital, or parent-child subsystems may represent an appropriate focus. A combination of family, subsystems, and individual contacts are sometimes used, depending on the nature of the issue, the rhythm and tempo of family life, and the developmental tasks of individual members.

In many agencies individual services are assumed at the outset. It would be useful to explore the relative advantages of group and family modalities with clients. The group modality provides multiple opportunities for relatedness, mutual aid, and learning coping skills. A group is particularly responsive to people who share a common set of life events such as violence, bereavement, serious illness, or common life tasks and issues. By its very nature, the group can universalize individual and family troubles, reduce isolation, and mitigate stigma. As group members share and reach out to each other, they experience a "multiplicity of helping relationships" and experience their life issues as neither unique nor deviant. Group members may receive support for definitions and perceptions of their concerns,

Table 3.6   Skills for Helping a Group Develop Common Focus

- direct and redirect member transactions to one another
- invite members to build on one another's contributions
- identify and focus on salient collective themes
- invite expression of differences
- reach for contradictory perceptions and opinions
- invite participation of all members
- establish protective ground rules

or they may be challenged to examine them further. Since they have had similar life experiences, they are apt to be more receptive to fellow members' definitions and suggestions than to those offered by professionals. The group modality also provides a force with which people can act and gain greater control and mastery over their environments. Collective action is likely to gain organizational or community attention. It reduces the risk of reprisals and also is apt to be more successful than individual action.

In developing a common purpose with groups, the social worker directs and redirects member transactions to one another and helps them to express their common and different perceptions. Members are invited to build on one another's contributions, enhancing mutual involvement. Practitioners identify and focus on salient collective themes that provide the "glue" which binds members together, and helps them with their shared concerns. They encourage respect for individual opinions, creating a culture that permits expression of difference. Family, group, or community members may not agree about definitions of needs, goals, and tasks. The social worker helps members develop understanding of one another's views by eliciting and accepting discrepant perceptions and opinions. Collective support is as strong as its capacity to tolerate differences. At times, certain members may be reluctant to participate. In a caring and supportive manner, the worker invites participation of the "outside" members. Finally, the worker establishes ground rules that facilitate open communication and allow for expression of difference without fear of recrimination. Explicit rules that bar physical violence, verbal abuse, or threats have to be established (Gitterman 1989a). Table 3.6 summarizes distinctive skills of helping a group develop common focus.

A hospital social worker had invited eleven cardiac patients to form a group. Her interventions illustrate several distinctive skills of the group modality.

After the refreshments and introductions, I said, "As I had explained to each one of you individually, you were invited to participate in a four-session group for patients with recent heart attacks. The staff believed you could be helpful to one another in dealing with your concerns about hospitalization, the heart attack, and what the future has in store for you."

Bill indicated that work worries him the most. Mario, Hector, and John agreed. In an agitated way, Bill continued, "If the doctor won't let me go back to work, what can I do? It's been twenty-seven years of my life and I always put in an honest day. Now the doctor says give it up. What kind of bullshit is that? Doesn't he realize that I have family and financial obligations?" Lenny agreed, stating angrily that the doctors don't care that a medical recommendation could destroy a man's life.

I asked if they were mostly annoyed about what their doctors said, or how they said it, or both? Hector explained that he thought it was a doctor's responsibility to make work recommendations in order to protect health, no matter the economic consequences. He has ended up on welfare and that's been hard to swallow. Bill responded with intensity that no doctor was ever going to do that to him, and he released a barrage of angry words. Mario suggested that Bill was doing what he himself has stopped doing—taking out the anger at the doctor's recommendation on his own heart. Hector understood Bill's being fighting mad because he, too, is having a hell of a time living with his "bum ticker." He is just beginning to calm down and to realize that it will never be the same. Bill shook his head in disbelief, "How can I be calm? I have a family to take care of." Lenny explained that he also has a family, but getting excited and upset will only lead to another heart attack. Andy supported Bill. Peter exclaimed, "But, shit, common sense will tell a man that health is the only important thing and everything else has to become second." Most members agreed that if they let themselves get excited or experience too much pressure, they will only hurt themselves. Bill became angry again, telling group members that they had to be as dumb as the doctors to be forgetting their problems. Bill's eyes teared as he shouted, "If the doctor says give up truck driving where I feel like a real man, what am I going to turn to? Who is going to hire me? What good am I?" Lenny suggested that Bill calm down. Mario suggested that Bill talk to his boss and ask about a light job. Bill was insulted by the suggestions and shouted that he has pride and isn't going to degrade himself and tell the boss to pity him, to give him crumbs. What kind of man did Mario think he is, anyway? Mario answered, "I think you are a good man and I respect you. I know a wounded animal has to fight for his brood, but Bill you have brains, you have to listen to your body and accept its limits. It takes a man to talk to his boss about lighter work."

I said that it seemed some of them have made peace with their hearts, while others are still fighting. Either way, I realize how much pain they are experiencing. Peter implored Bill to take it easy, to accept his heart condition. Bill insisted that his boss wouldn't give him light work because it would raise insurance rates. He feels he is no longer a man. At this point, Bill began to sob. Several members tried to change the subject, but I encouraged others to share their struggles. Walter referred to the mortgage and his family food needs. Hector talked of his pension and how it helps. In a disgusted tone, Bill wanted to know how he was going to get by with workers' compensation.

Mario spoke quietly but firmly: "Bill, I can see you are a big man, strong, and you can beat anybody here in a fight, but I'm gonna tell you something, you gotta stop crying and be a real man, that means accept what is, do what has to be done, face the facts. You want to help your family, you ain't gonna help them by killing yourself. You have to cut down on your expectations, do what the doctors say, and start to build a new life."

Everyone waited for Bill's reaction. He stared at Mario as if trying to decide what to do. After a while, he said, "I guess I could sell my home and buy a smaller one. My oldest son can go to work." Peter put his hand on Bill's back, saying that it was much better to be a live father than a dead one. Hector agreed, suggesting that they are all afraid of the same thing but handle it differently. Each man then spoke of how they changed or plan to change life styles and habits, and of their fears and common objective: "Life!" Bill said the guys had been helpful. He continued, "I'm a man, and I'll do what has to be done."

At the end, I asked what they thought of the first meeting, and many said it was helpful to see that others struggle with the same kind of problems. Mario's comment caught the essence: "It's like we are in the same boat trying to keep from drowning. Talking can help us stay afloat." We agreed on the place and time of our next meeting.

The social worker's straightforward statement of the group's purpose, her reference to their common concerns, and her interest in their feedback is all the group needed to begin developing its own processes of mutual aid. The intensity of feelings and concerns associated with heart attacks propelled the group into their common tasks of dealing with life and death fears, concern about their families' wellbeing, their ability to work, and their self-images as "whole" men.

Temporal Arrangement

In recent decades, emphasis on short-term services has increased. This shift was, in part, a response to high dropout rates (Presley 1987; Toseland 1987) in mental health and family agencies, and changes in funding and accountability arrangements. Research had demonstrated that for a wide range of life issues and client populations short-term services are more effective, or as effective, as long-term services (Koss and Butcher 1986; Parad 1971). Most clients now receive short-term services. Some are seen episodically; others are seen during periods of severe stress; still others receive planned short-term service. A small percentage of clients receives time-limited services, and an even smaller percentage receives long-term, open-ended services. Each temporal arrangement requires distinctive contracting skills.

In episodic services, the contact is brief and temporary, and the worker immediately involves clients in a rapid assessment of life issues, their nature, longevity, and severity; the availability of supports in the environment; and the level of fit between their personal and environmental resources for effective coping with the issues. Based on the assessment of issues and the resources, workers and clients develop a plan for focus and direction in service at irregular intervals as needed.

In emergency services, clients require focused and immediate services with sessions as frequent as needed. The primary goal is to restore the client's prior level of functioning. The worker takes a directive and structured approach and immediately focuses on the severe stressor, assesses precipitating factors, and whether other people are involved. The social worker assesses the client's level of functioning, particularly cognitive grasp of the situation ("What happened?"), level of anxiety and immobilization ("How are you managing?"), and potential sources of personal and environmental support ("Have you been able to discuss this with anyone else?"). By eliciting details associated with the severe stressor, the practitioner explores objective and subjective perceptions. Through empathic support, the worker conveys an understanding of the stressor and related pain. The worker specifies the issues and focuses the client on making essential immediate decisions and specifying goals. Specification, clarification, and focus help people to master stressors. The worker provides a sense of hope and confidence in the client's ability to master the stressor. The worker also actively engages and mobilizes personal, family, community, and institutional resources to help in coping with the critical life event. Throughout the focus is on personal and environmental strengths.

Research suggests that planned short-term services are associated with more positive outcomes and more positive views of the service than are open-ended temporal arrangements (Reid and Shyne 1969). Clients are also less likely to drop out of short-term services (Beck and Jones 1973). Because of the time limit, the worker assumes a more active role in the initial interview, adhering to essential professional tasks: (1) specifying one or two stressors; (2) demonstrating empathic understanding; (3) creating a sense of hope; (4) developing an agreement to work on a specific stressor; and (5) setting a clear time limit (Wells 1982). The first task should be identified in clear operational terms. For example, a woman became very depressed over a recent transfer to a new job. Contrast the following two statements: "The focus is to restore your sense of self-esteem" with "The focus is on helping you to deal with your new job pressures and the increasing strains at home with your husband and children." Identifying specific,

Table 3.7   Skills Related to Temporal Arrangement: Length of Contact

• *Episodic services require:*	Developing rapid assessment of life issues
	Developing immediate plan for focus and direction
• *Emergency services require:*	Providing rapid, focused, and immediate services with fre quent sessions as needed until the crisis is past
	Assuming a directive and structured approach
	Assessing precipitating factors and identifying significant people involved
	Assessing cognitive grasp of the situation, level of anxiety and immobilization, and potential sources of personal and environmental support
	Inviting the details associated with the crisis event
	Providing empathic support
	Specifying issues and focusing on essential, immediate decisions and specification of goals
	Providing a sense of hope and confidence
	Engaging and mobilizing personal, family, community, and institutional resources
	Identifying and working on personal and environmental strengths
• *Planned short-term services require:*	Assuming a very active role in the initial interview
	Specifying one or two stressors
	Demonstrating empathic understanding
	Creating a sense of hope
	Developing agreement to work on a specific life stressor
	Setting clear short-term time limit
• *Time limited*	Establishing termination date in the first session
	Developing agreed-on focus
	Developing pre-established time periods to evaluate progress
• *Long-term, open-ended services require:*	Providing an ongoing supportive long-term professional relationship
	Sustaining original sense of purpose and vitality
	Exploring potential impact of dependency on the relation-ship
	Introducing concept of time-limited services

concrete life issues that occur in daily human interactions helps both client and worker to be less overwhelmed and more hopeful and focused in their work. Limited time leads group and family members to focus quickly on their concerns and to maintain purpose and direction. The time limit creates a sense of immediacy and urgency for both clients and workers; it must be clearly established in the first session. A two-session post-surgical group, a four-session adoptive parents group, or an eight-session divorce group sets the time limits within which work is to be accomplished. As an individual, family, or group service nears completion, however, clients and worker may decide to begin another cycle of services or a specific number of additional sessions (Gitterman 1994).

Time-limited services utilize all the principles of planned short-term services. The termination date is clearly established in the first session and

Table 3.8   Skills Related to Temporal Arrangement: Personal Factors

- assess person's experience of time according to culture, age, physical, and psychological states
- select temporal arrangements which fit the nature of the stressor, the agreed-on goals, and the client's own temporal resources and orientations
- provide quick response to physically ill client
- communicate a sense of commitment and urgency in contracting with the elderly, avoiding delays or postponements
- provide individuals, families, and groups in crisis several sessions a week, at least until the crisis is past
- provide young children with frequent, shorter sessions

can be anywhere from six months to a year. Certain settings such as schools have a natural time calendar in the academic year. Therefore, social work services can be timed with this natural limit. We recommend the use of pre-established time periods to evaluate progress on a mutually agreed focus. Events such as Christmas/Chanukah and Easter/Passover serve as excellent benchmarks for the evaluation of the service. If client and worker agree that objectives have been met, the work comes to a natural end. If, however, client and worker agree that more time is needed, the work continues until the next natural calendar benchmark.

Long-term, open-ended services can best serve clients with chronic, intractable personal and environmental stressors who need more help than episodic or planned short-term services can provide. Clients who experienced childhood traumas such as physical and sexual abuse are unable to immediately identify and focus on these issues. Others are prone to continuous crises such as those associated with homelessness. Chronically mentally ill and developmentally challenged clients require continuous support, and they benefit from long-term, open-ended services. The long-term professional relationship becomes a lifeline for everyday functioning. However, clients may learn to depend on the relationship "rather than seek meaningful companionship in their 'real' lives" (Woods and Hollis 1990: 437). The dependency could lead to lingering self-doubts about their competence. In open-ended group services, frequent shifts in membership often result in a group's inability to move beyond an early stage of group development. Table 3.7 summarizes professional tasks and skills related to length of professional contact.

People experience time in different ways according to culture, age, physical, and psychological states (Germain 1976). Cultural orientations to time, for example, affect people's regard for punctuality, their interpretations of long waits, their attempts to prolong or to shorten interviews, and the value placed on the past, present, or future. Such variations need to be considered in developing a mutual agreement, and throughout the contact, in planning the respective responsibilities of client and worker. Stressful life events do not accommodate themselves to agencies' and institutions' temporal structures, so meeting more frequently or less frequently, for longer than an hour or less than an hour, could be helpful. Temporal arrangements agreed to by worker and client should, to the degree possible, fit the nature of the stressor, agreed-on goals, and the client's own temporal resources and orientations rather than the organization alone.

Depending on members' physical and emotional states, most adult groups, even those for the elderly, can sustain work on group tasks in sessions of one and one-half to two hours' duration. Open-ended groups with changing membership gain more from frequent meetings than do time-limited groups. Crisis groups such as those for hospitalized cardiac or post-surgery patients benefit from several sessions a week, at least until the crisis is past. The frequency and duration of sessions with children must be geared to their orientation to present time and their limited awareness of future time. In providing group services for children having difficulty with school, we discovered that weekly sessions for an hour were insufficient. During intervals between sessions, the youngsters confronted various stressors, but the group was unavailable for assistance. Consequently, meetings were restructured for greater frequency (twice or three times weekly) and for shorter duration (thirty or forty minutes). Young children usually benefit from short sessions of less than forty-five minutes. Generally, children and mentally challenged adults are responsive to more frequent and shorter sessions, while well-functioning adolescents and adults are responsive to longer, weekly sessions. Table 3.8 summarizes selection of temporal arrangements responsive to needs.

Assessing

Accurate assessment rests on the collection of relevant information, its systematic organization, and the analysis and synthesis of the data. Without information on the nature of the life issue and the social and cultural context, the practitioner is unable to determine an appropriate purpose and direction. Sources of data include the client's verbal accounts; the worker's observations of nonverbal communication; verbal and nonverbal presentations by others (obtained only with the client's informed consent); and written reports (obtained only with client's permission, except for the agency's own earlier records). One could be overwhelmed by the amount of data; therefore a schema is needed to grasp and organize data. The life stressors formulation provides a schema for grouping data and guidelines for potential professional interventions.

Inferences are drawn by inductive and deductive reasoning from the collected objective and subjective facts. Inductive reasoning uses collected and organized data to generalize: if the social worker asks a client how she feels about her job, her responses can be used to infer the degree of job satisfaction. The validity of an inference may be questionable. If the social worker observes a client's hand trembling and infers that the client is anxious, it may not be a valid inference. If the client does not respond to the worker's invitation to explore the anxiety, the client's "denial" may be perceived as strengthening the original assumption of anxiety. Yet the explanation could be cerebral palsy, recent physical exertion, or fever. Social workers need sufficient facts to support tentative inferences.

Deductive reasoning applies practice knowledge and research findings to a client's life situation. For example, depression is manifested by a combination of certain symptoms such as difficulty in sleeping, loss of appetite, internalized anger, low self-esteem, agitation, and feelings of helplessness and despair. If all or several symptoms are present, practitioners can reasonably infer depression. Consultation with other social workers or other mental health professionals can strengthen or eliminate the assumption in less clear situations.

Assessment is especially difficult for social workers in mental health services because of the dominance of the American Psychiatric Association *Diagnostic Statistical Manual* (DSM–I, –II, –III, –IV). For services to be reimbursable, clients must be assigned a clinical diagnosis from the DSM which is then registered with the state. Social workers are concerned about the implications of clinical diagnosis when a client's difficulty arises out of struggles with life issues and their effects on psychosocial functioning. Many claim that the reliability of DSM categories is questionable (Kutchins and Kirk 1986, 1988) and others believe that a diagnostic label tends to reinforce behaviors that are associated with it (Gingerich, Kleczewski, and Kirk 1982; Lind 1982).

During the late 1980s, however, a NASW chapter in California developed a Person-In-Environment (P.I.E.) Manual for describing clients' difficulties in social functioning, using the concepts and terminology of social work (Karls and Wandrel 1995). The hope was that social workers could substitute this manual for DSM. But funds were lacking for a proposed national study of the manual by the national office of NASW.

Assessing Person:Environment Fit

How well people manage stress largely depends on the fit between their internal and external resources. As mentioned in the previous chapter, the amount of physiological and emotional stress suffered by Mrs. Stein, a stroke victim confined to a wheelchair on discharge from the hospital will depend on: (a) inner resources (motivation and outlook on life, coping skills, meaning attributed to the illness); (b) family and social network (emotional and instrumental supports, geographic proximity, motivation); (c) access to organization resources (competent medical staff, nurses, homemaker, physical, occupational, and speech therapists); and (d) entitlements and financial resources for achieving flexibility of the physical environment (outside ramp, wide entrance, interior doors and corridors to accommodate the wheel chair, movable furniture, and suitable bathroom and kitchen equipment).

In assessing individual life situations, four areas need to be understood: the nature of the particular life issues; client expectations of the agency and worker; client strengths and pertinent limitations (Cowger 1994); and environmental supports and hazards. Together, these reveal the current adaptive balance or imbalance (level of person:environment fit). Discrepancies might arise between the client's and worker's expectations of how active or inactive, directive or nondirective, personal or impersonal, spontaneous or detached, each should be (Specht and Specht 1986). Based on the examination of the data, the worker and client assess the level of fit between the stressor's demands and the personal and environmental resources for meeting them. The assessment must be difference-sensitive (Congress 1994; Hess and Howard 1981; Rodwell and Blankebaker 1992).

Individual Assessment

Background data. Mrs. Ross, a 65-year-old Catholic of Italian and Scottish descent, was receiving daily homemaker service. A Medicaid patient, she was also periodically visited by a public heath nurse. Because of Mrs. Ross's increasing withdrawal and apathy, and with her consent, the nurse called the senior service division of a family agency, requesting social work service. After three home visits, the social worker (a first year student) prepared a tentative formal assessment for a case conference.

Mrs. Ross had accepted the offer of service and supplied her background. Her mother died when Mrs. Ross was four months old and her father placed her in a Catholic institution where she lived until her adoption at age 6. She remembers her adoptive mother as loving and compassionate; but she died six years later after a long illness. A year later her adoptive father married a young women four years older than Mrs. Ross. At age 17 Mrs. Ross was engaged to a man who burned to death in a car accident. A year later she married a man who was a "gentleman" until the day of their wedding, when he turned into a monster overnight. Several years into the marriage a son, Jack, was born, and five years later a daughter, Janice, was born. Her husband beat her almost daily, and he also beat both children.

One day, Mrs. Ross found Jack with a shotgun; he said he was going to kill his father. She took the children and walked out of the marriage. She moved to another town and worked at two jobs in order to support herself and the children. Some twenty years ago she married a "good man." Six months later he died of a heart attack, and since then she has lived alone. Her daughter is married and lives across the continent, and they occasionally visit by telephone. Her son lived a few blocks away from his mother, with his wife and two children. He visited often. Six months ago he was hospitalized for minor surgery, suffered a stroke, and died. Mrs. Ross did not visit him in the hospital nor did she attend his funeral, as she had no way to travel. She loves his two children, but she never felt close to her son's wife and was uncomfortable whenever she visited their home.

Fifteen years ago, Mrs. Ross developed Crohn's disease, a painful, debilitating intestinal disorder.[1] She had to stop working and has since been housebound (Freeman 1984).

1. *Definition of Life Stressors.* Initially, Mrs. Ross requested help with emotionally-charged life issues. "Losing my son, Jack, is the latest and most dreadful of the losses in my life. When he died, I couldn't stand the pain. I wanted to say the hell with it all, but five months later I'm still alive and the pain is still unbearable. I just can't handle it on my own any more." Mrs. Ross and I agreed on twelve weekly home visits, framed by my impending departure from the agency and the agency's waiting list.

After three home visits, other painful life issues emerged. Clearly, some are interrelated unresolved earlier transitions and losses reactivated by the son's death. All are now intensified by Mrs. Ross's worsening physical condition, her grief, and social and emotional isolation. Her increasing disability and dependency are additional current stressors. Her loneliness is connected to the great geographic distance between her and her daughter, to her dislike of her daughter-in-law despite the latter's frequent invitations to Mrs. Ross to visit her and her grandchildren, and to the lack of friends. Another stressor is living on the second floor and being unable to negotiate two flights of stairs. She cannot leave the apartment by herself; she is carried down by the ambulette attendants who drive her to medical appointments. Mrs. Ross says she cannot afford a move to the ground floor. Mrs. Ross needs and wants help in coping with these difficult life issues and her feelings of depression, anger, and helplessness.

2. *Client Expectations of the Agency and Worker.* Mrs. Ross expects me to provide her an opportunity to talk about her life losses and her suffering. Since she is not used to sharing and exposing her innermost thoughts and feelings, she will be sensitive to my reactions.

3. *Client's Strengths and Limitations.* When Mrs. Ross's life situation was presented to the agency's utilization review committee, several members suggested that Mrs. Ross is quite disturbed and deals in a pathological way with her stress (e.g., not getting up from her bed for three months). I believe that this assumption ignores the magnitude of her loss, gives insufficient attention to the physical disability caused by Crohn's disease and severe arthritis, and underrates Mrs. Ross's strengths and her coping efforts.

Strengths. Mrs. Ross demonstrates many strengths in coping with her losses, such as her religious faith. She finds comfort in prayer and in her belief in a life hereafter. Her God is close and personal, and she often talks to God. Several times since Jack's death, religious beliefs have deterred suicidal thoughts: "It would come into my mind that I didn't want to live any more, but I couldn't do that—it is a sin."

Her sense of humor is another strength. After Jack's death, in despair, she questioned the meaning of life. She called her church and asked to talk to a priest. When she was told, "Sorry, but they are all at bingo," she was able to laugh at life's ironies. She also finds pleasure in small things so that in the midst of her grief, she still enjoys looking at flowers or reading a letter from an overseas relative.

Mrs. Ross remembers her mother telling her to "stand straight and hold your head high." Mrs. Ross has lived by her interpretation of this message: "I rely on myself and keep going no matter what happens to me."

Courage, selfreliance, and ability to blunt emotional pain have sustained Mrs. Ross through many traumatic life events and have supported her through physical pain and emotional suffering. She is a survivor, finding ways and reasons to go on with the tasks of living.

She deals competently with various organizations and bureaucracies, initiating contacts as needed and following through on commitments.

Limitations. Self-reliance seems to mean self-control to Mrs. Ross. As she speaks of her losses, she conceals the hurt and buries the pain. The emphasis on selfreliance may have cost her dearly in the past in terms of poor health and currently in terms of isolation from her son's family. Inhibiting the grieving process, while it may help her to survive, seems to be a maladaptive coping pattern. Her stoicism in the face of trauma may be related to the belief that traumatic events are expressions of God's will.

Mrs. Ross's increasing immobility poses another serious limitation.

4. *Environmental Supports and Obstacles.* The social and physical environment have profound effects on Mrs. Ross's functioning.

Social environment. Mrs. Ross's contacts with complex organizations are generally favorable. Representatives from Social Security and Medicare are responsive to her needs. She has experienced little difficulty in maintaining daily homemaker services and the attention and responsiveness of health care systems, especially the public health nurses. In contrast, her informal network is severely depleted. She was accustomed to contacts with friends, but in the ten years since she became homebound they faded away. In spite of having lived in her apartment for nineteen years, she apparently is not involved with other residents. She says she feels close to her daughter and four grandchildren 3,000 miles away and they talk by phone every other week. But she has not seen them in seven years. No other relatives are within reach. However, a deacon from her church visits weekly; her homemaker has been with her for four years; and her doctor, physical therapist, nurse, and now I are also supportive professional resources. She has a cat, acquired as a kitten just before Jack's death. It is a pleasurable companion.

Her daughter-in-law occasionally telephones, but she and her young children have not visited since Jack's death. Mrs. Ross says she doesn't understand why, but she has neither asked why nor invited them to visit. So far she resists my offer to work with her on finding ways to connect with her daughter-in-law and grandchildren. It is hard for her even to discuss or share her feelings about this relationship, beyond insisting that she is rejected rather than rejecting. She is apparently willing to risk estrangement from her grandchildren rather than negotiate a truce with their mother.

Opportunities for making new social contacts are severely curtailed and Mrs. Ross doesn't "send out invitations." Thus her isolation is partly of her own making, perhaps because of her emotional vulnerability and her sensitivity concerning her physical disablement. For instance, she describes herself as "ugly" and "crippled."

Physical Environment. Mrs. Ross is isolated in her second floor apartment, accessible only by a narrow flight of stairs. The apartment is sparsely furnished but spotlessly clean. Rugs and doors are missing in order to allow easy access for the wheelchair. She is only able to leave her apartment to go to the hospital or the doctor.

5. *Plans.* (1) More information is needed about Mrs. Ross's relationship with family members, from their perspective as well as hers. (2) Because it takes time to build a trusting relationship, and given Mrs. Ross's severely stressful situation and my limited time with the agency, I recommend an increase to two home visits a week for the nine weeks remaining of the twelve agreed on. (3) A carefully planned termination is crucial so that Mrs. Ross has some control over the loss it will represent. I believe she is likely to be receptive to transfer to another worker. I am not sure what the agency's response will be but I shall inquire.

Life Stories

Interest in narrative theory is growing and the use of life stories in practice is replacing elaborate formalized intake histories. Because they are offered spontaneously at critical points in the work together and after trust and comfort are established between the partners, life stories appear to be more useful and usable than traditional history taken in the first two or three interviews.[2] Life stories are not coerced or prompted by the worker's probing questions, and they tend to be rich in detail. "Life histories" are usually obtained early in the work through the use of probing questions and skilled observation, but before a trusting relationship is in place. Although elaborate assessments based on life histories are said by some to be essential guides to intervention, many are often filed away and forgotten. In contrast, personal narratives immediately become part of the work together.

Bits and pieces of their life stories are told by clients to themselves and to the practitioner, and those bits and pieces become therapeutically relevant over the span of their work together. Life stories are not necessarily valued for insight into the past so much as for serving as significant therapeutic vehicles. The client tells and the social worker listens empathically. In the telling and listening, the life story gains in personal and cultural meanings, and the teller acquires a new acceptance of his or her one and only life course (Laird 1989; Saleby 1994; Stern 1985). The "truth" of life stories lies in their capacity for bringing out connections among life events that lend a sense of coherence to individual and family life (Spence 1982). Despite their subjectivity, life stories nonetheless exhibit integrity and provide continuity to a life course that is inherently unpredictable (Cohler 1982). The teller of the story is reinterpreting and reconstructing the narrative that ultimately will contain new conceptions of self and of relationships with others (Stern 1985). In a way, through the telling and listening the partners co-construct a new and more valid story. Life stories enrich assessment and are important components of the helping process in the ongoing phase.

HELPING INDIVIDUALS, FAMILIES, AND GROUPS WITH STRESSFUL LIFE TRANSITIONS AND TRAUMATIC EVENTS

Helping people manage stressful life transitions and traumatic events requires distinctive knowledge and skills.

Stressful Life Transitions

The value placed on particular biological changes varies across cultures. In traditional Asian societies old age is venerated, as it is among Native Americans. In many segments of American society, however, becoming old is frequently regarded with dread. The aging process begins at birth and continues until death. But the upper end of the life course presents universal, biologically-based life transitions with cultural and psychological components and social consequences. For some, life stressors associated with the biological transition and the change in social status may include poor health, diminished financial resources, social isolation, and losses. If such stressors exceed coping resources, aging is experienced as a difficult life stressor (Becker 1993; McNeil 1995).

Puberty is biological but adolescence is a social status. They are not the same. Adolescence has been recognized as a social category in our own society and culture only since the late nineteenth century (Kett 1977) and has slowly been extended well beyond the duration of puberty. Adolescence is not recognized in all societies: in some cultures, puberty alone marks the entry into the rights and responsibilities of adulthood, with no intervening state.

Social workers mostly meet troubled teenagers in their practice (Armstrong 1991; Williams 1995). The number of troubled teenagers may be a result of unemployment and school drop-out; unplanned pregnancies and an increase in AIDS among adolescents; abuse of illicit drugs and alcohol (associated with criminal behavior, homicide, suicide, and accidents among teenagers); and homelessness. Social workers also help adolescents deal with traumatic life events such as coping with parental divorce and physical illness or injury.

For example, Louise, a Jamaican 13 year old, is dealing simultaneously with developmental life events, social life transitions, serious illness, and traumatic life events. She was admitted to the hospital for correction of a slipped epiphysis (part of a bone that ossifies separately and then becomes attached to the main part of the bone). Since the surgery she has been in a spike cast which keeps her flat on her back. After the cast is removed she will be in traction, and following discharge she will require weeks of recuperation at home. Louise was referred to social service by the head nurse because of crying fits, tantrums, and uncooperative behavior. The worker learned the following from Louise and her family:

When Louise was five months old, her parents left Jamaica for England and better economic conditions, leaving the baby with her grandmother. Many years passed, and they had seven more children. Louise knew of her parents and siblings in England, but had no contact with them. The only mother Louise knew was her grandmother, and her first nine years were apparently happy and stable ones. Three years ago her grandmother became ill and could no longer care for her. Louise was sent to the United States to live in a large city with her aunts who were married with children of their own. The aunts accepted full responsibility for and financial support of Louise.

The aunts said that Louise adapted well to living in the city. She made friends. She is cooperative and helpful around the house and baby-sits for her young cousins. Although bright, she is lazy about studying and had to repeat the fifth grade. She is now in the sixth grade. Recently her grandmother died, and the aunts said Louise took the loss very hard. Louise's medical problem was only recently recognized. She started walking awkwardly a year ago, and the aunts urged her to lose weight (the worker noted her obesity). But her walking became worse, and they brought her to the hospital.

Her aunts told Louise's mother about the surgery, and she flew to the United States. The visit was extremely painful for Louise. In front of the aunts and Louise, her mother complained that Louise was being "spoiled." She talked of taking Louise back to England but stopped short of any action. She visited Louise three times, one of which went badly. Crying, she told Louise how homesick she was and how she wanted to go back to England. Louise told her mother that if she wanted to go she could. When her mother left, Louise began to have crying fits and temper tantrums.

This "normal" early adolescent youngster has endured many grave losses. She faced pressing tasks of adapting to a new environment, a new family, a new school, a different climate, culture, and life style, the loss of her beloved grandmother, rejection by her own mother, the medical trauma of hospitalization, pain, surgery, and the prospect of a long convalescence.

All transitions have to be understood within an ethnic or racial context. In the above illustration, for example, knowledge of Jamaican culture suggests that West Indian families are closely knit, and extended members are significant resources. Practice with these families "is rewarding because they are truly motivated to help one another" (Brice 1982: 132). This is a generalization, but it will be important to keep in mind in contacts with the aunts and with Louise. While white social workers may assume Jamaican culture is the same as African-American culture, their historic and contemporary experiences have been very different (Brice 1982; Clarke 1957). Jamaica's history of slavery began and ended much earlier. The descendants of European colonists in the West Indies now represent a mere 5% of the population. West Indian blacks have a strong sense of ethnic identity and identification with their particular island's culture, shaped by their African roots and island life.

Across the life course, human beings must cope with numerous social transitions. They must cope with stress associated with entering new experiences and relationships, or leaving familiar ones. Beginnings require a change in status and new role demands. Whether entering a new school, a new relationship or marriage, a new job, or having a child, status entries create some degree of stress. Exits from desired social statuses imposed by divorce, loss of employment, placement of a child, or widowhood, are usually more potent stressors than entry into new statuses (Esterberg, Moen, and Dempster-McCain 1994). The diagnosis of infertility for a couple can be as painful as coping with the loss of a valued relationship.

The timing of a status transition and life event affects cognition and perception. When entering into a new experience comes too early or too late in the life course, the potential for stress is increased. For example, a young adolescent who becomes a parent, a young child who is not ready for day care, a grandmother who must take on parenting tasks, may all experience intense stress because of the maladaptive timing.

Not all helping efforts are successful. Mr. Connors, age 75, was admitted to a rural hospital for below-the-knee amputation of his lower leg because of acute gangrene. His general condition showed extensive evidence of serious physical neglect. Surgery was followed by rehabilitation; later Mr.

Connors was transferred to the hospital's Intermediate Care Facility (ICF). He was exceptionally and delightfully sociable with staff and patients and was hopeful for the future. His goal was to return home as soon as possible.

Mr. Connors had lived alone in his own home for 20 years after his wife's death. His only relative was a supportive cousin in a neighboring town. Mr. Connors had retired from sales work because of arthritis some years earlier. He said he had always had an active social life, and added he liked an occasional beer. He participated regularly in ICF team meetings in which goals were set and reviewed. He needed assistance with activities of daily living (ADL). The team and Mr. Connors agreed he would have to be totally independent in ADL in order to return home. He also would have to be able to walk independently with his prosthesis and a walker. Because of poor circulation, he had many skin breakdowns that would require continued treatment after his discharge.

The social worker met weekly with Mr. Connors. With her encouragement and his strong determination he worked hard for discharge. On that first visit, after finding many empty and partially filled liquor bottles strewn around, the worker suspected that Mr. Connors had a problem that all the disciplines had ignored—alcohol abuse and its effects on his physical condition. He consistently denied to her that he drinks much. His doctor told her not to worry, "you can't change him" and, in fact, had prescribed two beers a day. Concerned, the worker discussed with Mr. Connors the danger of alcohol in light of his medications, but he continued to deny drinking. She also discussed the dangers with his cousin.

Mr. Connors began to drink heavily. He continued to deny the problem, and the worker learned the cousin was buying him beer and whiskey. Mr. Connors's appetite declined, and he said he didn't like the Meals on Wheels he received. His cousin shopped for food but Mr. Connors ate less and less, and the food spoiled. Finally, the team decided to terminate services, and the worker arranged for community health services to take up Mr. Connors's care. However, they, like the ICF, later ended service because of his continued failure to comply with regimens.

Mr. Connors's addiction to alcohol endangers his life. Yet his denial of an alcohol problem persists, despite the efforts of the social worker to help him. And his physical and emotional condition steadily declines. The worker tried to help Mr. Connors relax the rigid denial by confronting him and also by explaining the perils of drinking in view of his illnesses and medications. Only if he could acknowledge to himself that he had a problem with alcohol could he be helped to abstain and thereby save his own life. However, ICF staff (including the physician) and other institution staffs clearly engaged in maladaptive denial (probably unconscious) in the face of Mr. Connors's zest, attractive amiability, and determination. The generalized denial of Mr. Conners and the staff led to failure and adversely affected any potential of recovery or improvement.

Traumatic Life Events

Traumatic life events represent losses of the severest kind—the death of a child, rape, the diagnosis of AIDS, the birth of a genetically defective child, or a natural disaster. Such events are experienced as disastrous and overwhelming and, therefore, tend to immobilize us. While a crisis can provide opportunity for growth and mastery, inherent is the hazard of regressed functioning if the tasks in resolving the crisis are not successfully completed (Rapaport 1970). We cannot long remain in the state of extreme discomfort implied by crises.

While the state of crisis has a time limit, chronic pain and obsessional thoughts associated with the traumatic life event may last longer. The crisis caused by the death of a spouse may be limited, but the stressful process of mourning may continue. The stressful transition from husband to widower will continue long after the crisis of bereavement has subsided. A condition such as AIDS leads to progressive phases of functional impairment. Each phase of deteriorating health may precipitate its own stress (Getzel 1993; 1991). Traumatic life events can remain a significant issue throughout the life course. A 95 year old resident of a nursing home shared with her social worker for the first time that she had been sexually abused by her father. To cope with the trauma, she had repressed the experience for a lifetime, not feeling safe enough to share her secret. Although the defense of repression helped manage the pain of betrayal, it blocked her from dealing with the assault and from learning to trust and to be intimate. At 95, she took the first steps and risked asking her younger sisters whether they had also been sexually abused by their father.

Social Work Function, Modalities, Methods, and Skills

The Worker and Stressful Life Transitions and Traumatic Events

With people who are experiencing life stressors that arise from difficult developmental and social transitions and traumatic life events, the social worker helps them effectively cope with the biological, cognitive, emotional, behavioral, and social demands posed by the life issue within a particular environment and cultural context. The social worker helps people move through stressful life transitions and deal with traumatic life events in such a way that their adaptive capacities are supported and strengthened, and the environment's responsiveness increased.

Professional Methods and Skills

Helping individuals, families, and groups cope with life stressors of painful transitions and traumatic events requires a repertoire of professional modalities, methods, and skills. By enabling, exploring, mobilizing, guid-

Table 4.1   Enabling Skills

- use minimal responses to encourage
- wait out a silence
- reach for silence
- reach for facts
- verbalize feelings
- legitimize and universalize thoughts, reactions, and feelings
- reach for specific feelings
- highlight specific cues
- rephrase concerns
- use metaphors, analogies, and euphemisms
- use humor
- summarize concerns
- share thoughts and feelings

ing, and facilitating, the social worker supports and strengthens people's adaptive capacities and problem-solving abilities.

Enabling is encouraged by a professional stance of "I'm with you, and want to help you with your concerns." Enabling clients to present their concerns requires skills that include encouraging with minimal responses; waiting out silence; reaching for facts; verbalizing feelings; legitimizing and universalizing thoughts, reactions, and feelings; emphasizing and highlighting specific cues; rephrasing concerns; using figures of speech and, occasionally, humor; and sharing one's thoughts and feelings as appropriate. These skills were discussed in the previous chapter and are summarized in Table 4.1.

Through *exploring and clarifying*, focus and direction are provided to the work. Some clients confide and explore their life stressors with relative ease, others ramble without focus or direction, and still others remain painfully silent. In helping clients to confide and explore their concerns and feelings, the social worker's tasks are to help the person explore the objective and subjective facts about the life transition. The following skills are used to address these tasks:

- *Developing focus and direction.* The social worker explores and clarifies with a professional stance that conveys "I'm with you and I need your help in understanding better." By developing a clear and mutual focus in the work, client and social worker minimize the emergence of competing or overlapping concerns. Focus and attention are associated with achievement of agreed-on goals.
- *Specifying concerns.* People express their concerns in vague phrases such as "My husband is unfair" or "And I thought he had integrity." A general term may cover an important life story and also have different meanings to clients and social workers. Abstractions such as "integrity" and "unfair" require

clarification: "In what way is he unfair?" or "Can you give me an example of his being unfair?" Specifying what clients mean improves clarity in communication.

- *Reaching for the meaning of experiences.* People attribute different meanings to life experiences. The worker explores such hidden or understated meanings by direct questioning: "What does the idea of divorce mean to you?" or "Telling the truth is very important to you?" By reaching for the meaning of experiences, the social worker explores belief and value systems that influence behavior (Daly and Burton 1983; Levine and Lightburn 1989).

- *Exploring ambivalence.* In exploring ambivalence, the practitioner examines the duality of conscious feelings: "Let's identify the main reasons and feelings you have for wanting and not wanting to leave your lover." People are sometimes aware of one side of their ambivalence, but not the other. Thus gentle questions or comments are needed to bring the other side to awareness: "You say you have decided to leave your lover. Sometimes people have doubts about big decisions. What about you?" Often the ambivalence is unconscious and therefore exerts a powerful influence on behavior, without the person's awareness.

- *Identifying discrepant messages.* Mixed thoughts and feelings are communicated through contradictory messages. To explore the extent and depth of life transitional concerns, discrepancies between verbal and nonverbal behavior are identified and clarified: "You say it doesn't bother you, but I notice you are clenching your fist" or "I am confused by your saying how angry you are at your lover's coming home at 2:00 A.M., BUT THEN HAVING SEX WITH HIM."

- *Recreating experiences.* Some people intellectualize concerns; efforts to focus and specify fall short because associated emotions have been removed from content. At these times, the worker helps the client re-experience the situation by dramatizing events and episodes: "So you remember your brother sneaking into your room late at night. What were you thinking and feeling when you first saw him coming toward you?" By recreating the experience, the client's affect is more likely engaged in exploration.

- *Sharing being puzzled.* Communications are complex and difficult to follow. Practitioners should not pretend to understand when, in fact, they don't understand people's communications: "I am unclear about what you just said; could you tell me again?" Asking for help in understanding can clear up contradictions in behavior and ideas for the client as well as for the worker.

- *Patterning concerns.* In presenting stressors, people may focus on repetitive details or behaviors. Helping them to see patterns and themes encourages greater depth in exploring and clarifying, e.g., "I noticed your major battles with Billy seem to have started over his coming home and putting on the TV. Let's examine this." By observing a pattern, the person, family, or group is able to examine various isolated incidents in a new way.

- *Offering a hypothesis.* A hypothesis provides a new frame of reference for people to consider, for instance, "Do you think it is possible that a lot of your hurt and anger with your father is being transferred to your son, for exam-

Table 4.2   Exploring and Clarifying Skills

- develop focus and direction
- specify concerns
- reach for the meaning of experiences
- explore ambivalence
- identify discrepant messages
- recreate experiences
- share being unclear
- pattern concerns
- offer a hypothesis
- invite feedback
- provide feedback
- invite self-reflection

ple?" or "I wonder if your husband gains control over you through his silence?" Sufficient data and timing are essential before sharing one's inference or hypothesis. Premature interpretation could prove to be incorrect or the client might not be ready to accept it. Skilled, tentative questions can evoke a client's own recognition and acceptance.

- *Inviting feedback.* Directive interventions should be followed by inviting the client's reactions: "What's your reaction to what I suggested?" The client may directly respond whether the hypothesis is helpful or unhelpful. Other responses may be more indirect: "I guess you're right," or "Yes, but . . . !" The worker reaches for hesitation, lack of clarity, or negative reactions. Even if the advice or interpretation is perceived as unresponsive and unhelpful, the client's feedback stimulates further work. Without client feedback, the worker may sound "smart" or be insightful, but the work is not deepened.
- *Providing feedback.* People may be unaware of how others perceive them. By sharing one's own reactions to a client, the social worker provides valuable feedback. When offered out of caring and concern and not because of frustration or anger, such feedback is more likely to be accepted. After trust has been developed, the worker may share reactions directly: "When you answer only 'yes' or 'no' to my questions, I feel frustrated in understanding and I really want to understand." The worker's reaction is presented in concrete, behavioral terms and expressed calmly in a caring manner.
- *Inviting self-reflection.* self-reflection and self-discovery have more profound and lasting outcomes than giving advice and interpretation. When a client grasps the relation between current and earlier experiences, the realization is more likely to be "owned" and transferred to other situations and experiences. Encouraging clients to reflect on and to consider self-defeating patterns is initiated by tentative questions such as, "Do you sense any similarities among the last three men you have dated?" or "What happens to you when you feel out of control?" Such questions enable clients to see patterns in their life experiences. Dependence on the worker for advice and interpretations decreases and self-direction and self-regulation increase.

These exploring and clarifying skills are used in various combinations. The worker assumes the initiative in stepping out in front of the client in order to deepen their professional interchange. These interactions must be responsive to people's signals that they are ready to explore and clarify, rather than reflecting the worker's impatience or need to be in control. Helping requires the worker to follow the client's cues and signals rather than the reverse.

In *mobilizing*, the social worker strengthens people's motivation to deal with painful life stressors and manage disabling feelings and stress. For some, the support, caring, and interest they experience in elaborating their life story and the help provided in exploring their concerns are sufficient to release energy and provide a sense of wellbeing. Others, however, require more help with mobilizing their personal strengths and motivation.

- *Identifying strengths.* People who seek out (or accept the offer of) professional help may feel inadequate and insecure. Self-doubt and preoccupation with life issues and limitations can be immobilizing. The worker breaks through this by identifying the person's or group's strengths: "Raising three children as a single parent and working full time takes so much energy, determination, and skill; let's look at all the things you do to manage so effectively." Helping people to review their competencies creates a foundation for coping.
- *Offering reassurance.* At times, realistic reassurance provides important support: "The doctor told me you are undergoing a simple surgery, and she is confident there is absolutely nothing to worry about." However, if the reassurance is unrealistic the worker's credibility is seriously damaged.
- *Offering hope.* Without hope that things can improve, people despair. The social worker offers needed hope by conveying confidence that something beneficial will emerge from their work together. Specifying tasks ranging from simple to more complex provides potential for success: "I know you can be firm with Jennifer the next time she stays out all night; you can stick to your guns in the way we rehearsed."

Some people are unable to manage their feelings and resolve a life issue because they lack necessary information or are hampered by misinformation. Others have difficulty because they do not recognize their dysfunctional, possibly self-destructive, patterns. They are overwhelmed by life events despite their potential abilities to manage feelings and to solve problems. Perhaps they are immobilized by a particular life event (surgery, divorce). In these situations, the worker calls on the method of *guiding* to encourage inherent coping abilities.

- *Providing relevant information.* Information about their concerns principally flows from clients to social workers. However, clients also need and expect relevant information from their workers. For example, information about the common phases of bereavement and community resources is an essential tool

Table 4.3 Guiding Skills

- provide relevant information
- correct misinformation
- offer advice
- discuss
- present
- visualize
- participate
- specify action tasks
- prepare and plan for task completion

for effective coping with loss. If the need for information is unfulfilled, people feel frustrated.

- *Correcting misinformation.* Misinformation about physical, emotional, and social functioning is an additional stressor. For instance, adolescents who believe that crack is not addictive until used a few times, or that the rhythm method or withdrawal will prevent pregnancy, must be given accurate information.

- *Offering advice.* In seeking or in accepting an offer of social work services, people expect advice about what to do and are dissatisfied when little advice is forthcoming (Maluccio 1979). Advice is offered to encourage people to try a new approach: "I suggest you present Jessica with an 11:00 P.M. weekday curfew and enforce it by . . . ," or to discourage the use of a maladaptive behavior, "When Jessica misses dinner, I think its best if you did not reheat the food for her." The practitioner determines how direct the advice should be depending on the severity of the issue and the person's level of anxiety or impairment. The advice can range from suggesting, to urging, to warning, to insisting. In offering advice, social workers must avoid imposing their own values and coping styles. The advice should be responsive to what a client is requesting and is prepared to hear, rather than to the worker's need to demonstrate concrete help. For clients who cannot manage emotions and solve problems, the worker may become an important teacher of life skills (Whiteman, Fanshel and Grundy 1987), calling on the method of guiding to develop problem-solving strategies as needed. The worker pays attention to the differing ways in which people learn. Some learn primarily by taking action ("enactive" learners); others learn primarily by summarizing, visualizing, and organizing perceptions into patterns and images ("iconic" learners); still others, "symbolic" learners, learn primarily by abstracting and conceptualizing (Bruner 1966). The worker uses a diverse repertoire of guiding skills, depending upon individual and social factors.

- *Discussing.* Discussion helps people learn coping behaviors. By focusing discussion on the meaning of the life transition the social worker explores faulty perceptions, reasoning, and beliefs, and helps clients learn ways of restructuring maladaptive thought processes. As discussion leader, the worker (a) poses questions to stimulate clients' reflective thinking aloud; (b) supports and encourages client examination and evaluation of alternative coping responses; and (c) maintains a flexible focus to provide clients sufficient "space" to examine, explore, and try new behaviors.

- *Presenting.* Informal and brief exposition of issues and ideas by the worker can increase people's problem-solving abilities. Practitioners share what they know simply and without jargon. Parents are helped by introducing such simple ideas as ignoring a child's tantrum, praising a child for appropriate behavior, and developing their own observing and listening skills. New knowledge has a profound effect. Helping people master the steps in problem-solving is important: delaying immediate action; defining issues; developing means to deal with the life issue; evaluating means; and selecting and carrying out specific action.

- *Visualizing.* Graphic presentations can illuminate heretofore unidentified patterns of relationships and behavior. Egograms (Dussy 1977) reveal communication styles between people; genograms portray family trees over several generations, including illnesses, occupations, nicknames, and migrations (Hartman and Laird 1986). Similarly, ecomaps delineate the complexity of people's transactions with the environment (Hartman and Laird 1983; Swenson 1979). For people who are primarily visual learners, graphic representations especially enhance understanding.

- *Participating.* In work with children and severely impaired adults, games and activities facilitate comfort in interaction. For some, it is much easier to talk while doing something. Activities are also used to help people learn to manage their feelings and problems (Middleman 1978; Poynter-Berg 1994). Managing feelings is also learned by relaxation exercises as well as by systematic desensitization and cognitive behavioral interventions (Berlin 1983). Role play can prepare a survivor of incest for a conversation with her mother. Role reversal permits a person to examine her own as well as her mother's experience and reactions. By mirroring the incest survivor in a role play, the social worker demonstrates how she will be perceived by her mother. By role re-creation and dramatization the woman examines the actual conversation with her mother, analyzing its effectiveness. By role modeling and coaching, the social worker demonstrates effective communication skills. Family sculpture dramatizes interpersonal patterns in families. By sculpting, family members consider and reflect on their interpersonal roles (Hartman and Laird 1984).

- *Specifying action tasks.* People might require assistance in planning next steps. For example, with a couple planning to separate or divorce and worried about their children's reactions, the social worker might say at an appropriate time, "Let's decide when and where you want to tell the children, how you want to tell them, and what you want to tell them." The more active and specific the task, the more likely it will be put into action. Similarly, the more actively people are involved in specifying and selecting their tasks, the more likely progress will result (Reid 1992).

- *Preparing and planning for task completion.* In addition to specifying actions to be taken, clients prepare and plan for such actions. Assignments such as "During the week, how about you write down what you want to tell your father about his abuse . . . " or role play such as "I'll be your father—let's rehearse what you will say to him" are helpful in preparing clients to carry out agreed-upon tasks. Such preparation helps them to anticipate and handle possible responses, as when others remain silent, refuse to listen, or deny responsibility for their actions. When preparatory planning is completed, it is useful to review and summarize the agreed-upon approach.

Clients can be reluctant to work on painful life transitions and traumatic life events. Discomfort arises when one must reveal, share, confide, and explore one's troubles. Even the most skillful practitioner cannot easily overcome the client's tendency to avoid the vexing and painful. Avoidance is expressed by active provocation, intellectualization, interruption, verbosity, and seductiveness, or by passive withdrawal, compliance, procrastination, and extreme diffidence. Flight behaviors such as changing the subject, withholding data, and minimizing concerns are often encountered. If avoidance persists, *facilitating* encourages clients to remain committed to the work. In a supportive manner, the worker challenges and demands purposive work.

- *Identifying avoidance patterns.* Identifying the avoidance pattern is the first step (Snyder 1984). The social worker makes an explicit direct statement about the pattern and its self-defeating consequences: "I notice you have many excuses for not seeing a doctor about your diabetes when you know it's very important for you to do so" or "Every time we begin to talk about your son and his homosexuality, you change the subject; we have to find a way to talk about it because it is upsetting you very much."
- *Challenging the illusion of engagement.* When a social worker and client become too comfortable with each other, an illusion of work may develop (they may in fact collude to avoid pain). Engagement in the helping process requires focus, direction, and investment of energy and motivation. The illusion of work has to be challenged by the worker: "I sense a lack of urgency and energy in our work." Schwartz (1971:11) identified a core professional task as "continually challenging the client to address himself resolutely and with energy to what he came to do."
- *Generating anxiety.* To break through avoidance, people need to experience some discomfort: "You have to make discharge plans because the hospital will kick you out." Out of concern and caring, the social worker challenges a person's defenses and generates a degree of anxiety needed to advance the work. By demanding focus on core issues, the worker creates sufficient tension to mobilize coping efforts.
- *Responding with directness to discrepant messages.* At times, pointing out discrepancies between verbal and nonverbal messages helps to move the work ahead.

Sometimes, a more direct approach is required ("How come you tell me you stopped drinking when I can smell the alcohol on your breath?" or "Look at all these things you have done which are self-defeating, yet you tell me you're not hurt by his leaving you"). The worker makes the contradictions explicit and prods the client to deal with them.

These interventions challenge avoidance and seek to stimulate and mobilize energy for work. They work only if trust and confidence in the worker's caring have been established. Thus, these skills are used selectively and with caution. If they are used inappropriately, defenses are intensified and dropout from service is likely.

How practitioners use these diverse methods and skills depends on their individuality, creativity, and experience. In this section, we present practice materials to illustrate how social workers have helped individuals, families, and groups deal with difficult life transitions and traumatic events.

Practice Illustrations

Stressful Life Transitions

In chapter 3 we described the initial phase of the work with George R., a 15-year-old African-American. Here we pick up on the ongoing phase, starting with the third interview.

Before George's third interview a relative commented on George's coming to the clinic. This reinforced George's fear that everyone considered him crazy. He refused to return to the clinic. (Stigma is attached to mental health services by all adolescents, and many black and other minority communities also view such services with suspicion.) George's probation officer and the worker decided that George should be told that the court ordered him to continue until his next court hearing. The probation officer was a young African American who liked George and felt strongly that the precipitating factor in George's emotional upheaval was the move to a new school where he was poorly handled from the beginning. However, the probation officer exerted benign but firm authority by spelling out rules of conduct, repeating them weekly, and gradually allowing George more freedom as he seemed able to tolerate it. Mrs. R. trusted the probation officer and supported his decisions. The social worker recorded:

Third and fourth interviews. George did not bring up his earlier decision to drop out of service, and when I mentioned it, he grinned and acknowledged that it was all right as long as no one thought he came because he wanted to. In these two interviews we dealt with George's feelings about the recent traumatic events. There were some wild threats to "get" the school counselor, to sue everybody, and one or two lapses into fantasy. As George gave a detailed account of his experiences with the police, it was obvious that he could not tolerate the feelings of helplessness associated with handcuffs. His fears on the psychiatric ward were similar. He asked me about patients who were strapped down, and he was particularly concerned about a patient who suffered delirium tremens. George had been put in restraints when he first arrived. As he told of this, he groaned and was perspiring. I answered his questions and tried to underline the fact that, given a very difficult and frightening situation, he had handled some things very well. I did this to cut through some of the grandiosity and also the abject feelings of inferiority and inability to cope effectively.

He told of a second time he had been threatened with restraints. This had occurred after he had been told he could not go home prior to the court hearing, and he understood that he was considered crazy and dangerous. He then began threatening to kill ward personnel, and he behaved in a psychotic manner. As we talked, he agreed he would label as crazy someone who behaved as he had. I suggested that whenever he felt someone in authority was criticizing him, "you seem to knock yourself out proving they are right." He was amused by my choice of words and agreed. I tried to carry this further by bringing up the way he had behaved in school in an instance he brought up, but he would not accept this as he was still too angry at these people. George brought the subject back to the psychiatric ward, and said it wasn't just that he had to prove he was as bad as they thought—he was also scared. I agreed. By the end of this fourth hour, he was speaking coherently, calmly, and with surprising self-understanding.

The worker identifies George's strengths in dealing with a very frightening situation, and through clarification offers an interpretation of a dysfunctional behavioral pattern. When George agrees with the interpretation, the worker prematurely offers a second interpretation. George disagrees and returns to his primary message of concern about being scared when placed at the psychiatric ward. Timing is an essential factor in a client's ability to "hear" an interpretative comment.

Fifth interview. George's improvement was striking. He began by telling me of a new boy, his age, who had moved next door. They had swapped music tapes. (Later, his mother telephoned to tell me this was the first time George had a friend in a long time. She was extremely pleased.) After a short silence, George said he was thinking about school. He wondered if they'd let him re-enroll after the court hearing. The semester is "mostly gone, and what will I do? I don't know, but I'll get A's. They can't stop me if I try hard enough." I said, "Why do you have to get A's? Superman again?" He tried to deny that getting A's was impossible. I said, "It will be a triumph if you can pass any of your courses." He finally admitted this. I said, "So why do you set such goals? You know, I think when you do this, you are very mean to yourself." He said it was the school personnel who were mean to him. I said, "You are the one who says you have to be Superman. It's you who won't give yourself credit for doing the best you can." After a long pause, he said, "You have to get A's to be a doctor. I'm going to be a doctor, not just any doctor, I'm going to be the head doctor. My mother says they try to keep blacks from being doctors, so a black has to be better than any white doctor. I'll run the whole hospital, I'll be the one who tells the white doctors what to do." He stopped, said firmly, "And don't go talking about Superman. On TV Superman is not a doctor." We both smiled, then I said that regardless of our smiles, I felt this subject meant a great deal to him.

He said, "Ever since I was born, I guess I was going to be a doctor." He told of his mother buying him a set of encyclopedias "when I couldn't even read much at all. And I read them too. I read all the way to the M's." He sounded very depressed. I said, "Then what happened?" He said, "I just stopped, that's all. I got too tired, maybe, I don't know. It is like being tired." I asked when that was, and he said, "in junior high." As he talked, he told how hard he had tried to get good grades, but he never got better than C in junior high. I said, "And that is why you stopped reading the encyclopedia?" He said, "It wasn't any use. My brother could read all the way through them, if he tried. He doesn't even have to read them, he always gets A's. I guess he will be the doctor." Long pause, then, "I don't know what will happen to me." He sat silent for a time, then said, "It is strange here. We talk and talk and then everything is said, and there is nothing more. Only silence." I said, "Yes, that is how it can feel, when you have finally been able to tell so much about yourself."

When George informs the worker of his expectations to receive all A's, she challenges the illusion and invites him to view the unrealistic expectations in a new way. Using the metaphor of Superman helps George to connect his grandiose statements with his feelings of inferiority. The worker uses various exploration skills to invite elaboration of his feelings of inferiority to his brother.

Four days later the worker received a frantic call from George's mother. George had been picked up by the police for attempted shoplifting. The police took him home and notified the probation officer.

Sixth interview. George said he was falsely accused of stealing. He went into the store to buy a bicycle pump, had the money in his pocket, and was holding the article "in plain sight" when he decided to go out on the sidewalk to tell his brother something. He carried the pump with him. He was planning to prove in court that he had stood in the doorway rather than on the sidewalk and therefore was not guilty. He would then sue the store for false arrest. He said, "They could send me to the youth authority for nothing!"

I shared my concern that at times it seems he gets himself into precisely this kind of trouble, in which he feels both abused and innocent. I pointed out that it seemed this had happened before and referred to his telling me in an earlier hour about being falsely accused of vandalism. He finally acknowledged that maybe he had behaved in a suspicious manner.

I said that two things might have upset him this time. One was the notice of the court hearing which came the day of the attempted theft. The other was what we had talked about last time. He said, "And I wouldn't want to do something suspicious before court, that doesn't make sense. I want to go back to school." I said, "last time we talked about grades." "Oh yes, how could I forget that?" Then he said, "One other time I was out of school, and I didn't flunk. It was when I had my operation." He said in third grade he was operated on "because my navel stuck out like a pickle."

We talked of the operation in terms of how a "little kid" would have felt about it. He said, "It's when you wake up that it's bad. I saw this scar. It's long enough they could have done anything inside me. I didn't know what they could have done. They could reach just about anywhere from so big a scar." I said, "What did you worry they had done?" With great hesitation and embarrassment, he revealed his fantasy: "Is there a tube, I mean a connection, from your navel to your . . . sex parts?" He felt they had shortened or somehow badly damaged his penis, and this was why he hadn't grown. "When a little kid is the smallest in the whole school, even smaller than his brother, and he sees a midget, you know what he thinks? He thinks he's a midget too." He then asked me to tell him what had happened during the operation. I described a hernia repair as well as I could, and he said with great relief, "Only muscles? Well, then, I'm all right. My stomach muscles are all right, you use them to lift weights." (Later I learned from his mother that he had not only a hernia repair, but a circumcision and tonsillectomy during the same operation at age 6.)

I asked if he had current fears about his penis. He said, "No, I think it's OK. But you can be scared of things just the same." I then brought him back to the fears surrounding the operation and said maybe the operation had something to do with some of his current fears. I wondered, for instance, if he wasn't afraid of being helpless, tied down, handcuffed, in much the same way a boy is afraid of submitting to an operation. He thought about that very seriously, and said, "I'm always afraid of being at the mercy of someone. Like someone is going to do something terrible. That part's like an operation." I said, "So you have to pretend to yourself you are Superman, because you are afraid of being helpless. You're really not as helpless any more. In fact, I imagine you'll be able to get through court this time without being so scared and without pretending you're Superman either." He said, "I'm sort of worried about that." We decided we'd talk more about it next session, several days before the hearing.

The worker offers an interpretation about George's setting himself up to be an abused victim in relation to the forthcoming court appearance. The worker moves ahead of George's readiness to assess her interpretation. Thus, this interpretation seems premature, lacking sufficient client exploration and involvement, and possibly reflecting her own frustration with his self-defeating pattern. When George shares the trauma of his surgery at the age of six, the worker skillfully invites his major worry ("What did you worry they had done?"). This moves them into the taboo area of concerns about possible damage to his penis. The worker provides relevant information about a hernia operation, clearing up misconceptions and greatly relieving George. However after reaching for George's current concerns about his penis, the worker does not explore his tentative response, "I think it works ok. But you can be scared of things just the same." The worker changed focus, and lost an opportunity to reach for his fears and insecurities. The lengthy interpretation of George's current behavior and its relation to this childhood experience illustrates a worker regaining control over an uncomfortable situation rather than making a helpful intervention.

Seventh interview. George said he was worried about court and what the judge might do to him. The judge would never believe he hadn't tried to steal the bicycle pump. He said the probation officer was going to get a report from me to give the judge. I asked if he was wondering if I would say he hadn't tried to steal it. He asked what I would say. I said I believed him when he said he hadn't, but I also believed he had tried to make it look as if he were stealing, even though he wasn't aware of it at the time. We then discussed my perception, primarily in terms of his doing these things when he is upset and feeling not good and unable to defend himself. I related this to his feelings about court and about not being able to do as well in school as his younger brother.

For the first time he admitted that he started that final school fight by hitting a boy who called him "brainless." He said, "But I don't want to admit this in court. The judge will think I'm no good." I said, "Again, I think you are meaner to yourself than any judge could possibly be. You look at one thing you consider a failure, and you damn yourself. I think the judge will consider other things too like the fact that you have been able to go to the park and play baseball these past two weekends, have had no fights, and even with the bicycle pump business, you didn't lose control of yourself. I don't think he will find you a worthless person because you can't get the world's best grade, an A." He gave a short laugh, as if in relief. Then he asked what I was going to tell the judge. I said I was going to tell him that "you are much less upset than when I first saw you, and you seem to be doing well. In fact, I will tell him that I think you are going to be a good man." He was very touched by this, and looked as if he might weep. Instead, he stood up, said, "I have to leave early today, is that OK?" and hurried out.

The social worker's reassurance about the judge's benign behavior is risky. No one can ever safely predict how an organizational representative will behave. The worker could and should only have described her own behavior in his behalf. Telling George that she would tell the judge that he will "be a good man" is powerful, and George is obviously moved by her sensitivity and confidence in him.

In discussing the hearing with the probation officer, the worker interpreted the "stealing" episode as primarily a fearful reaction to the court appearance. George needed an incident that would allow him to feel injured, perhaps punished, and utterly innocent. The worker asked the probation officer's assistance in not allowing the episode to thwart George's progress. The probation officer said he would discuss this with the judge before court so the judge could give George an opportunity to tell of his success in meeting the terms set by the court at the first hearing. The judge was so impressed with the change in George that he allowed him to return to school. The social worker was worried that neither George nor the school was ready for this development.

Eighth interview. George described the hearing and said, "This time I had a nice judge. He was the nicest white man I ever met." I told him it was the same judge at both hearings. He was dumbfounded, and we were able to discuss how one's own upset can color one's views of other people—the hateful judge and the likable judge were the same person. In addition, we discussed his apprehension about returning to school and his hopes that he could stay out of trouble.

The worker continued seeing George for six more interviews devoted to his real and imagined difficulties at school, his feelings that his father had never "even cared enough about me to know how old I am," and a reworking of issues from earlier sessions, including fears of sexual damage and inadequacy stemming from the operation.

At the end of the school term, he recited Robert Frost's "A Road Not Taken" to me. "Had to memorize it for English," he muttered. He saw the two roads as representing good and bad, or perhaps emotional sickness and health. He said, "The trouble is, they do look alike. They don't have the right markers so you can know. Or maybe you only see one road, you never know the other is there. That's when you need someone to show you there are two roads after all."

The work was terminated over the summer vacation. In the fall, the worker telephoned George's school and learned that he was still considered a pest, a poor student, and he bragged too much, but had been in no fights. He made friends and is no longer thought to be dangerous. Probation was also ended as George had been in no further trouble.

Institutional racism and social and economic inequities and their impact on an adolescent's development must be thoroughly understood by the practitioner for ethnic-sensitive practice. While George's social worker does not refer to these factors, the work shows some implicit recognition that disruptive behaviors are defined as psychopathology more often with black than with white youth. George had been inappropriately diagnosed as schizophrenic and paranoid on the psychiatric ward of the county hospital. The worker ignored the label and elected to work with George's potential for growth and his existing strengths. Indeed, disruptive behaviors at school can mask difficulties that stem from inequities experienced in an oppressive and racist school environment (Franklin 1982).

However, there were two missed opportunities for the social worker to acknowledge and explore the impact of institutional racism on George's life. Doing so would have raised his consciousness. The first occurred in the fifth interview, when George talked of becoming a doctor: "My mother says they try to keep blacks from being doctors." The second occurred in the eighth interview when George said, "This time I had a nice judge. He was the nicest white man I ever met." The worker did well in helping George to see that how we feel can affect how we view people, but overlooked considering together some effects of racism in George's life, which would have been empowering.

Two observations about other environmental factors: first, we know less than we need to know about George's mother and their relationship. More effort was needed to engage her in a supportive partnership directed to releasing George's potentials. She is involved, she does care, but we really know too little about the nature and quality of the mother-son relationship.

Second, we need to know more about George's school. It would have been helpful had the worker, with George's permission, visited the school to talk with the guidance counselor, principal, and teachers. They could have discussed George's needs and his strengths in order to increase the school's understanding of him as a unique individual, block their continuing perception of him as pest and braggart, and ensure their supportive contact with him. Aponte (1976), for example, suggests a joint, nonblaming meeting, in which all participants (student, parents, relevant school personnel, and the agency social worker) are clearly cast as problem-solvers, not as problem-causers.

From the beginning, the social worker was candid, direct, and at ease with George. The worker conveyed hope and confidence in George's ability to change his behavior and to recognize his own actual feelings. The social worker helped George gradually to construct his own inner controls, reduce his impulsiveness, analyze possible consequences of planned or actual actions, and acquire some self-understanding.

Yet an apparently unrecognized ethical issue related to self-direction arose when George refused to return to the clinic after his relative's comment. The worker and the probation officer agreed that "George should be told that the court ordered him to continue until his next court hearing." The wording suggests that the court did not actually issue this order. If it did not, then both the worker and the probation officer acted unethically and paternalistically.

Particularly striking was the excellent work on George's fantasies about his surgical experience at age six, an important source of his insecurity about his masculinity and a possible basis of his aggressiveness. Also striking was the work done by George and the practitioner on his crippling grandiosity. The worker used the effective metaphor of Superman to connect the grandiose statements to George's deeply-felt inferiority. The worker's acceptance and empathy permitted George gradually to relinquish the defense and begin to accept the reality of both his abilities and his limitations. This freed him to cope more effectively with the life stressors.

The methods used by the worker included enabling, exploring, mobilizing, guiding, facilitating, and collaborating with the probation officer. The worker used various skills (minimal responses and nonverbal gestures, verbalizing feelings) to enable George to elaborate his concerns. In exploring and clarifying, the skillful use of focus and direction, specification, interpretation, and direct feedback enhanced George's self-awareness. Defensive grandiosity was reduced by hewing to the reality of George's actual capacities. The worker consistently responded to George's signals of distress by affirming strengths and self-worth, accepting negative feelings, legitimizing his concerns, and supporting self-awareness by the use of symbolic descriptions of what George had suffered and felt as a "little kid." In mobilizing, the worker identified George's strengths, and offered reassurance and realistic hope.

In guiding, the worker helped George to identify possible actions and their likely consequences. She gave advice as needed; and modeled relatedness and competent problem-solving. She enhanced the growth of self-direction by providing information in an appropriate cognitive mode (the metaphor of Superman; the work on the surgery) at the appropriate time and in the appropriate amount. In facilitating, when George appeared to be ready, the worker confronted the grandiosity and reframed the coping demands (e.g., "you're meaner to yourself than any judge would be"); managed episodes of regression (e.g., the shoplifting incident); and provided adequate time and metaphorical space (in accord with George's own temporal rhythms and readiness) for him to develop new ways to cope with loneliness and anxiety.

Together, the social worker and probation officer constructed a strong collaborative relationship that facilitated George's trust in them and in their caring. No doubt his trust was enhanced by the fact that the probation officer was a black male like himself and a strong role model for caring and competence. The social worker drew on the collaborating method, using skills of conferring, cooperating, and consulting with a person who represented official authority vis-à-vis George.

Status Changes

Mrs. Kenyon is a 45-year-old widow who works full time as a secretary. Her husband, Tom, died of cancer four months ago. She is extremely thin and looks ten years older than she is. She has four children: two daughters, Bernice, age 23 and Alice, age 22, who attend separate colleges and do not live at home; and two sons, David, age 22 and Bob, age 16. David is single, employed, and lives in an apartment in the same town. Bob lives at home with Mrs. Kenyon and attends a technical high school. Home is a house in a lower middle-class community.

She told her family doctor that she was nervous and upset and everyone was talking about her. At times she heard voices. Mrs. Kenyon had a history of severe emotional illness. Her doctor referred her to a psychiatrist. Dr. A saw her once. His view was that she was not coping effectively with the life stressors she was facing. He believed she had not yet mourned her husband's death. He referred her to a family agency social worker.

When the worker called to set an appointment Mrs. Kenyon spoke for half an hour describing how nervous she was and how she needed to talk with someone about it. She goes to church every lunch hour since her husband's death and repeatedly asked if this were normal. An appointment was made for three days later. However, Mrs. Kenyon called the worker the next day very upset. She had spent the day at work believing that her name had come up for promotion and that people had discussed her all day; she was not promoted and was very hurt. She added she was not even qualified for the position and did not want the job. She felt she had made a fool of herself by calling a fellow worker when she got home from work. The woman denied that Mrs. Kenyon's was mentioned, much less considered. "The woman had a big mouth and now the whole office will know I called."

Mrs. Kenyon's repeated themes in the first interview were that no one cares about her feelings, no one understands what she is going through and, with her husband gone, she has no one she can trust and to whom she can talk. The worker's major concern was to help Mrs. Kenyon begin to mourn and reach a beginning resolution. Clearly, she was feeling acute and painful stress and was unable to manage the tasks of bereavement or the associated negative feelings. The worker suggested a connection between her grief and her current feelings at being alone. Mrs. Kenyon saw the connection, and agreed to work on both.

In an early session, Mrs. Kenyon was upset because of her need to change things. She had changed her hair color and changed the way she dressed. The worker supported the difficulty of all the changes she has had to confront. She also found giving clothing and jewelry away frightened her because when she became emotionally ill "the last time," she also had begun to give things away. Because Mrs. Kenyon kept referring to that time, the worker felt it was important to discuss it with her.

Mrs. Kenyon said she had been very ill, had tried to commit suicide, has the marks on her arm. She rolled up her sleeves and showed me the scars. She said she took a bottle of pills and turned on the gas, all in one morning. "I became like a hermit, I was afraid to go anywhere. My husband worked shifts. I just felt everyone would be better off without me, because I was so sick, and I heard these voices and was haunted. It was terrible, like there was only one way out of my misery." I asked, "Are you afraid you are going back to being this disturbed?" Mrs. Kenyon said, "I think I have this fear again, now. For a long time I had Tom to talk to, and now he's gone." I replied, "That makes a difference, it is real. Tom is not around to talk with, and it is scary to lose the person you talked to the most. It must have been difficult all the three years he was sick and particularly the last 6 months when you knew his death was imminent." Mrs. K replied that it was, and she had no one to talk to. I asked if her husband knew he was dying, and she said he did but they never discussed it. I commented, "It had to be very painful for you to have to deal with his dying all by yourself." Mrs. Kenyon replied, "I used to leave work at five and cry all the way home. His room, really Bob's, was turned into a hospital room. David moved back home when I told him his father's situation, and Alice came home from college. She was stronger than I. She would get up at night with Tom and never waken me." I asked, "Did the family ever talk about his illness?" Mrs. Kenyon: "Not really. In the beginning, everyone was screaming at one another. I had a talk with each one, and I said there's a great deal of pressure, and you usually take it out on the one nearest you, and that's what we're all doing. I told them I would understand if they were cranky or abrupt but they would have to understand me too. One time I was crying, and Bernice said I just wanted someone to feel sorry for me. I really wanted her to understand me . . . If you don't have someone to talk to, you begin talking to yourself."

I believe Mrs. Kenyon has real reason to fear regression to psychiatric illness. However, if we can keep her in touch with reality, reassure her that what she is going through is normal and applies equally to those who have not had a breakdown, she may be able to stay intact. I will try to help her: 1. develop greater cognitive clarity about her situation; 2. manage her feelings through ventilation with my emotional support; and 3. seek and use social support through family, and new friends and activities. I think it is imperative that she accept and integrate the stressors generated during her husband's illness and death, and her own stress reactions. I will try to help her to allow herself to feel the grief in recognizing that she will never see him again.

The worker's empathic and supportive stance enables Mrs. Kenyon to begin to deal with her loss and the status transition. Elaboration and explorations skills helped Mrs. Kenyon to begin to unload the pain of her husband's death. The worker also developed a responsive plan of action. We note that Mrs. Kenyon is Catholic, and she could be hoping for or expecting reunion in eternal life. Indeed, it might have been supportive to ask Mrs. Kenyon if she and the children had talked with her priest or visited the grave together.

Over the next couple of weeks, Mrs. Kenyon went to church daily, and talked to her husband's picture every night. In her grief, she seemed to want to recover him, at least in fantasy. In the early phase of mourning, a person often yearns and searches for the lost figure (Bowlby 1980:85). The social worker took every opportunity over the next five sessions to refer to Mr. Kenyon in the past tense and to the fact that he is dead. She did this in a sympathetic and matter-of-fact way to help Mrs. Kenyon through the first phase of the mourning process.

Fifth session. I asked if she and her husband ever talked about what she should do after he died? Mrs. Kenyon responded, "No, we had three years. I wished sometimes that he would talk about it. He would lie in bed and just stare at me. Sometimes I would take his hand and wish I could make him well. I just miss him so (much crying). I lost my father 2 years ago and my mother 20 years ago. My only relative is my brother and he's in a state mental hospital. I always feel for him, but I think I have to straighten myself out first. He's 47 and has been there since he was 19. I had a rotten life too. Our father and mother drank. We never had Christmas. Sometimes they would start cooking a turkey and then they would get so drunk it would be the end of the turkey." I held her hand as she continued to grieve for the childhood she never had, the love and support she never received, the lost relationship with her brother, and most of all the emptiness of life without her husband.

From this session on, Mrs. Kenyon began to marshal her strengths as preparation for reorganizing her life and environment. In the next session, she talked of wanting to make new friends as she and her husband had few friends. He wanted her to take up a hobby, but she had felt her job and taking care of the home were enough. Maybe she took the wrong attitude. The worker asked, what she meant, Mrs. Kenyon responded, "I do get very depressed. I'd like to have more people around me." The worker encouraged this quest. Mrs. Kenyon soon joined a group in a neighborhood crafts store where she can work on a project either there or take it home. She reported pleasure in this.

During this period, Mrs. Kenyon also described ways in which it had been difficult to live with her husband. Sometimes he was moody and wouldn't communicate and that left her with no one to talk to. Earlier, she talked of how supportive he was, but now she referred to his coldness, how much he was away and how much of the child-rearing was left to her as the children were growing up. In the seventh interview she reported going out to dinner with a married man from her office and then going to Confession. Her priest absolved her of sin, and told her she was a very lonely woman. Grief work includes resolving anger and guilt one might feel toward the deceased, but the worker notes that, for the time being, she is touching lightly on this aspect because of Mrs. Kenyon's fragility.

The worker notes that Christmas is coming, and it is a source of much fear and insecurity for Mrs. Kenyon and the whole family. It points to the need for setting up new ways of dealing with each other and new ways of viewing themselves within the family structure. Mrs. Kenyon and the worker prepare for this together by anticipating situations or processes that could produce anxiety and depression. Their hope is that the holiday, always extremely difficult after bereavement, will bring the family members closer together if they can now at last express and share their grief, and incorporate their painful loss and mourning into their own life stories.

The next illustration demonstrates the helpfulness of group mutual aid in bereavement. The group is one of many provided by a social service agency for family members of cancer patients at all stages of the illness.

The groups provide a supportive environment in which members can share their feelings and experiences, engage in the tasks of mourning, reduce their feelings of isolation and loneliness, and learn from one another how to cope with their many life stressors.

Prior to the first session, the worker met with each person individually to describe the group's purpose and tasks and assess the person's readiness for the group and the appropriateness of this particular group. Thirteen people from the waiting list were screened for membership, allowing for expected dropouts. Nine were women (6 white, 2 Hispanic, 1 African-American) and four were white men. Their ages ranged from 38 to 73. Although the group was quite diverse, the common need to relieve pain was powerful enough for members to develop a collective identity and mutual aid system (Gitterman 1994). No one dropped out so the work was a little more difficult because of group size. As group size increases, possibilities for potential relationships increase, yet fewer opportunities and less time are available for everyone to communicate as fully as each might wish (Toseland and Rivas 1995). The group met one evening a week for ten consecutive weeks. Following the second session, the group was closed to new members. Although members were at different points in the mourning process, the group instilled hope in those at earlier points and permitted those at later points to recognize their growth. During the seventh session, members re-contracted to meet for two additional sessions.

All members expressed the difficulty of sharing their pain and sorrow with family and friends. Hence, a collective need emerged: to talk in the group about their experiences from the past, to understand their current feelings, and to figure out how to go on living. Members also agreed to share their experiences of taking care of their spouses and to express their feelings about the loss.

By the fourth meeting, members began to help each other with specific life issues. For example, Elyse described her difficulties talking with her 12-year-old daughter about death. The group helped her to explore her concerns, and members suggested alternative ways to initiate discussion with her daughter. Members developed problem-solving skills and began to balance the sessions with work on both general themes and specific concerns. At first, members were polite in entering into the discussion. By the fifth session they were interrupting others and asserting themselves. Less assertive members were consciously included in the discussions. Gradually a norm developed that permitted expression of a wide range of emotions. Use of the pronoun "we" grew as group cohesion, loyalty, and commitment increased.

In the sixth session, the discussion focused on their spouses' final days: the feelings they had as they realized their spouse was going to die, and the words which were spoken during those last precious days. Lorraine said her husband never acknowledged he was going to die, while Carol told of the intimate conversation she had with her husband about death. Diana cried for the first time since her husband's death. Tara opened up for the first time and told of feeling relief when her husband died because his suffering was over. More members shared their pain and underlying feelings in this session than in any other. The critical incident occurred when Lorraine said, "I want to tell the group something."

She looked at me. I nodded my head and encouraged her to share her thoughts.

LORRAINE: I think this discussion is very disturbing. I don't see the point of going back over the terrible details of the hospital, the doctors, and the illness. I don't think it's productive for us to dwell on this. I don't want to remember the bad times, I try to think about the happy times when my husband was well. (Elyse was almost in tears.)

CAROL: Stop! Lorraine, you are going on too long.

WORKER: Carol, can you tell the group what was going on for you as Lorraine was talking? (My intent was to help Carol to clarify and express in the group what she was feeling at this moment, to encourage the group to talk about what had just happened, and to explore the interpersonal tension.)

CAROL: OK, this might help Lorraine. I'm not a psychologist or any thing, but I am aware that there are two major breakthroughs tonight.

WORKER: (looking around the room, saying softly) Yes, there were.

CAROL: I thought tonight's discussion was very important.

JACKIE: I think it has been a significant meeting. This is what the group is all about.

ELYSE: It was very helpful to me to talk about the last few days with my husband. You see, I have such pain inside me and I don't have anyone I can talk to about this.

DIANA: It was hard for me to talk about my husband's death, but tonight the group helped me. It's the first time I've cried, and Lorraine thinks it was a waste of time. I'm hurt.

WORKER: The group is a place where you can talk about the experiences that are painful for you. You all have so many memories and feelings about your experiences in the hospital, watching your husband or wife endure treatment, and watching them die. These experiences bring up painful feelings, and yet, they are important to talk about in the group.

To realize her intent of exploring the interpersonal tensions, the social worker would have to reach for Lorraine's reactions and experiences. In the record, the worker is struggling with her reactions.

I was uncomfortable as Lorraine expressed her thoughts. I was aware that bereaved people have a strong desire to avoid experiencing the pain and emptiness of a profound loss. I was torn between wanting to acknowledge and validate her feelings and concerns and wanting to point out the meaning this session had for the others. A part of me was angry that she was negating the value of our work.

The worker struggles to control and hide her anger by becoming somewhat wordy and "sticking up" for the group. Lorraine is really saying she must forget the sad times and remember the happy ones. At 73, Lorraine is much older than the other members. Most people in their seventies value the time left. Their happier memories are boosters as they get on with the tasks of life's closure and the satisfactions that may remain despite the loneliness imposed by loss. If the worker could reach beneath her anger, she would experience the empathy she feels for group members' pain, and Lorraine's individual expression of that pain. Pain is an essential part of mourning, and is a means to feeling better. The worker is fearful that Lorraine's comments undermine an essential area of work. But, in reality, Lorraine's comments actually increase the demand for work on this painful life transition.

LORRAINE: It brings back the feelings I had while I was at the hospital with my husband. I felt nauseous and I had a headache. I could almost imagine the smell of the hospital and see all the tubes. This is how I was feeling here tonight.

WORKER: So, as other people were talking about their experiences, it was almost like reliving the awful experience you went through with your husband.

LORRAINE: Yes, and I try not to dwell on that. Now I feel terrible.

WORKER: You know, sometimes it's very hard to be in the group, and it can be uncomfortable to sit through a discussion that brings up painful feelings. You have all endured so much over the last several months. It hurts to relive all the pain of those experiences, and yet, it's part of healing. (I felt very connected to the pain of the group. My own natural instinct is to want to make everything better, but I realize that the pain is an essential part of their healing. I can identify with Lorraine's desire to move away from the pain. The group's pain brings forth my own pain about losing my husband to cancer.)

It would have been helpful to the group if the worker had shared her own loss and personal feelings with the members. Some practitioners consider self-disclosure inappropriate or unprofessional. We believe referring to the commonality of a status or experience for the client's benefit, and not for the practitioner's, deepens the work.

> CAROL: I'm sorry Lorraine for cutting you off, but I thought the discussion was helpful to many people. You know, I didn't want to come tonight because it can be so painful, but I also knew it would be helpful.
>
> WORKER: It takes a lot of courage and strength to come to the group each week.

The work seems to have been too intense for the worker because she focuses on the courage rather than on Carol's message of natural ambivalence about the group. In her analysis, the worker recognized that her intervention closed off further discussion. A more helpful response would have been, "It's been an intense session. It can be painful to come each week. It takes a lot of courage and strength. We are almost out of time, but I think it's important that we begin to talk about how we can help each other when it gets too painful." This affords support and is a facilitating demand for work at the same time.

For the following week the group agreed to share photographs of their spouses. Most had pictures of their spouses when they were healthy and happy. Lorraine brought in the "happy" pictures she displays around the house. But she also brought in some photos of her husband just before he died. She pointed to his physical deterioration and told the group how painful it was to watch this happen. She said this was the first time she had shown these pictures or shared this pain with anyone.

In the ninth session, Jackie brought a problem to the group for help. She appeared extremely agitated, and reported she was dealing with a stressful legal and financial situation that involves her husband's business. Jackie is legally responsible for running the business and feels miserable in her role. She dreamt of pursuing her ambition to be an opera singer. She recently discovered stipulations in Robert's will which tied her to the business and left her in a financial bind. (They were married only six months before his death several months ago. He had cancer and a heart condition, and died after a heart attack.)

The group began to offer suggestions and advice, but Jackie was too upset to accept their help. She said, "I'm so mad at Robert. How could he do this to me? You just don't tell someone something and then do something different." I said, "Jackie, you feel let down by Robert. You trusted him and now you're not so sure what he did or why." Jackie responded, "You're damn right." Barbara said, "He probably didn't have time to make the changes in the will that he intended to make. Look, he didn't know he was going to die. People just don't plan ahead." Jackie looked ready to explode. She said, "Look, he told me to my face that he was going to put something in the will, and he didn't. I really don't know if he loved me." Diana said, "Oh Jackie, I'm sure he loved you." By Jackie's nonverbal response it was clear that the well-meaning reassurance was not helpful. Jackie was probably thinking, "How can she know whether Robert really loved me?"

We social workers sometimes do this too out of our own anxiety, and it cuts off exploration and expression of feeling.

JACKIE: I've given up my whole life for this business. I haven't had time to sing and now I'm left with nothing. How could he do this to me? He's probably getting back at me.

WORKER: Jackie, how would he want to get back at you?

JACKIE: I wasn't there for him before he died. I was so busy taking care of the business that I didn't have time to go with him to chemotherapy. I shouldn't have let him walk up that flight of stairs. I should have known he couldn't take it.

BARBARA: Jackie, how could you have known? I kept pushing my husband to walk three days before he died. Jackie, you took care of his business because that's what he wanted you to do.

CAROL: Jackie, you didn't know he was going to die so suddenly.

JACKIE: You know, he died of a heart attack after trying to walk up that damn flight of stairs. Autopsy showed the cancer was in remission. That's just like Robert—oh, he was determined. He did such a great job getting rid of the cancer that it killed him. (She began to cry again, and I put my hand on her shoulder.)

AL: Jackie, we all probably think about things we could have done or should have done differently. My wife went to the same gynecologist for years, and she really trusted him. She complained for four years about irregular bleeding, but he insisted it was nothing to worry about. I went along with her, without questioning any further. She had cancer of the cervix. If it's detected early, it's curable. If only I had done some reading, or insisted on a second opinion, but it didn't occur to me or I would have done it.

WORKER: And yet, Al, you did the best you knew at the time. You trusted your wife's faith and that was important too.

GLADYS: Look, I still feel guilty about allowing the brain biopsy to be done on my husband. I didn't know what to do. Everyone encouraged me to sign for it. But when he was left in a semi-comatose condition his family blamed me. (She began to cry, and Elyse passed her the box of tissues.)

JACKIE: Gladys, it had to be done, you had no choice.

WORKER: Each of you was faced with difficult decisions based on so much uncertainty. It's hard to look back with the knowledge you have now.

LORRAINE: We did the best we possibly could.

AL: We all wanted our husbands and wives to live, but we couldn't do much to change that.

Jackie's anger seemed to be directed not so much at the misunderstanding in the will but at Robert for dying and leaving her alone with many dreams unfulfilled. As the group was helping Jackie, they began to express their own feelings of guilt and anger. Having heard some speak the "unspeakable," they openly express the same emotions. Bereaved people commonly go over the events leading up to the loss and find someone to blame, even oneself. For many, this is less disturbing than accepting that life is uncertain and one is helpless.

The social worker's intent was to help all members explore and express those negative feelings. She wanted them to know it was OK to have such feelings and to share them. As the group became more involved in problem-solving, the worker gave them room to provide mutual aid to one another. She felt that the emotional support of peers was a more powerful healing force than the support of the worker. This was a powerful episode for both the members and the social worker. The empathy, knowledge, exploring, mobilizing, guiding, and facilitating of this practitioner enabled all members of the group to integrate their bereavement experiences and feelings into a new and more growth-oriented life story.

Traumatic Life Events

Mary is a 25-year-old single white woman. She is well educated and works as a stockbroker in a large investment firm. She has worked very hard to reach the goals she set for herself and she spends a great deal of time at work. Until a year ago, Mary always had a roommate; she is now living alone and moved into a new apartment about a month ago.

Mary called rape victims services seeking counseling. She was raped by a coworker with whom she became friends a few months ago. She had "tried to put this behind me, and go on with my life." However, she described how things seemed to continue to get worse. Friends suggested that she speak to a counselor. She also realized that she was not coping well with what had happened and felt isolated, confused, and frustrated.

One of the first issues Mary and the worker discussed were feelings of guilt, self-blame, and distrust of her own instincts. "There must have been something that I did to invite the rape." She held herself responsible for not preventing the rape. She verbalized that the rape has defined who she is: she no longer is the person she used to be. "I should be able to get over it, stop thinking about it, and forget it." She attempts to cope by working even longer hours, keeping herself busy, fighting against flashbacks. However, after "trying to get over it" on her own, she realized that she is unable to move on and that she is still feeling many of the feelings she felt right after the rape. In fact, the feelings have intensified.

The worker realized that she had to explore with Mary the meaning of the rape before she could help her to assimilate and desensitize the traumatic event (Koss and Harvey 1987). In the first two sessions, Mary talked "around" the rape itself, discussing relationships and trust in general terms. The worker respected Mary's sense of space and timing. In the third session, Mary indicated that sufficient groundwork had been established for the more intense and painful work to come. She began by stating that she has no control over the things that have been happening in her life.

MARY: I feel like so many things that have been happening to me have happened to me in the past and are all building up to one horrible ending.

WORKER: What are some of these things that you have been focusing on?

MARY: I remember about seven or eight years ago when I lived in Washington D.C. and I passed by a construction site and one of the construction workers said to me as I passed, "You are going to die." I thought nothing of it at that time, and well, it doesn't seem like much now, but I keep thinking of that, and there are other incidents.

WORKER: What kind of other incidents?

MARY: Well, I remember coming back to this city after living in Washington and I got off the train and this homeless woman picked me out of everyone, got right in my face and yelled, "You're going to be murdered." I couldn't believe it, and I thought very little of it at the time. And there have been other things that have happened. When I am with a bunch of people for some reason an incident always happens to me, whether it is getting yelled at, a nasty comment, or being spit on which happened to me once on a subway. Someone has it in for me, it always happens to me, and the incidents just seem to get worse, and I always find myself thinking about what could be worse, what will happen if I continue along this path?

WORKER: What have some of your thoughts been about what might happen?

MARY: I really feel that all these things are leading up to a violent death, and it could happen any time. Or, this could happen to me again, and the thought of it being a stranger next time really scares me. I feel there is a greater chance of it being a stranger, although this time it was someone I knew or thought I knew.

WORKER: You feel that all these incidents are leading up to the possibility of your being raped by a stranger, is this what's most frightening to you?

MARY: What I am worried about is that I have no control over what happens. This really frightens me, but I feel that anything is possible because of all the things that have already happened.

WORKER: A lot of people feel that because they were raped once something like this could more easily happen again.

MARY: What I am worried about is I have no control over what happens. I limit myself so much already, it is not fair.

WORKER: It is not fair, and it's frightening to think of these incidents and what you think could happen.

MARY: I never felt this way before and I just want to feel the way I used to feel. I used to do things to prove to myself that I could take care of myself, that no one could hurt me. I used to take walks at midnight and not think anything of it. Now I come home from work, I have a hard time walking on my street because I pass all of the reminders of that night. I lock myself in my apartment, and even if it is 7:30 and I would like ice cream, I decide it is not that important because I do not want to leave my apartment. I do not have any control over what I do. I feel there is so much I do or not do that one incident has defined who I am and what I can do.

WORKER: The rape has defined who you are?

MARY: There are so many things I did before that I no longer do, just in my everyday routine of walking down the street or meeting people. I did not have much trust in people before this happened, and now I have even less, practically no one. I feel I have taken steps backwards; I just want to feel like myself again.

WORKER: The rape has made you feel a terrible loss of control over your life?

> MARY: Yes, I feel that before I did what I wanted and when I
>   wanted to do it. And now I feel that I can't do anything
>   except what I have to do, like go to work. It is an effort for
>   me to go out with friends because I have to be so careful
>   about when I go out with, whom, when I will be coming
>   home, at what time.
> WORKER: To feel so little control is very frustrating and scary.

In this practice excerpt, Mary conveys the intensity of her helplessness.
She is a trauma victim. Mary is also asking the social worker to make her
feel whole again, to help find her former identity, and to regain control
over her life. The worker sensitively reaches for Mary's fears ("What have
some of your thoughts been, about what might happen?" and "You feel that
all these incidents are leading up to the possibility of you being raped by a
stranger, is this what's most frightening to you?") and empathizes with her
fears ("its frightening to think of these incidents and what you think could
happen"). At one point, the worker moves too quickly to universalize and
teach about reactions to rape ("A lot of people feel that because they were
raped once that something like this could more easily happen again"). Mary
is not ready to examine universal reactions: she wants to discuss her own
distinct reactions. The worker skillfully refocuses and continues to explore
Mary's fears, "simply" listening and empathizing.

There are no easy formulas to help someone regain feelings of control.
The first step is for Mary to tell her story and to examine the experience
itself (Herman 1992). In order for the rape victim to become a rape survivor, she has to regain control over the experience (Koss and Harvey
1987). In the next session, the worker helps Mary to discuss the trauma of
the actual rape.

> MARY: I do not feel like I can trust my own instincts. I trusted them
>   with a person I thought I knew and could trust and look
>   where it got me. Why should I trust my own instincts, my
>   own judgments? There were things that happened, that he
>   said or did that I should have been clued into, but I thought
>   he was being flirtatious. He had always been so nice, and I
>   liked him so I didn't want to make him feel bad or for him not
>   to like me.
> WORKER: Sometimes it is very hard not to trust someone that you know
>   as being nice, especially if you like them and they like you.
>   What are some of the things you believe you should have
>   clued into?
> MARY: Well, first I really feel as though this all would have been
>   avoided if I hadn't called him, I feel partly responsible for
>   making the date. Maybe he thought I was being forward so I
>   wouldn't mind what happened.

WORKER: There is no reason, no excuse, why he should have believed that because you called him for a date you wanted more than just a date with him, or that you agreed to sex.

MARY: Yeah, I guess I know that but it makes me wonder. What makes me feel a little better is that I think he has done this to other women, so maybe it is not what I did.

WORKER: No, it is not what you did, it is not your fault no matter what you said, did, or didn't do. It does not give him any right to what he did to you. You are probably right that he did rape other women, but what makes you think so?

MARY: Well, it is the things he said, like after we had sex I realized I was bleeding and I told him. He responded, "Oh don't worry, that happens all the time." Well, I thought, it never happened to me before. And he didn't even make an effort to help me or to offer to bring me to a doctor. Although I do not know why I even wanted him to stay around. He left and I couldn't believe that he left me like that, as if nothing had gone wrong. It didn't hit me that anything was really wrong until after he left and I sat and thought about it. I just tried to put it out of my mind at the time. But the more I think about it now the more I feel that he has done this before to other women, and although it makes me feel awful, maybe it wasn't my fault.

WORKER: He probably has raped other women. It is not your fault. There was no way for you to know that he would rape you, and that he should not be trusted.

MARY: There are other things that should have clued me in to what he was capable of doing—what he did when we were at the bar. I can't believe I didn't do something at the time. We were talking and drinking; he had been drinking a lot. He flirtatiously said to me, "Tonight either you are going to rape me, or I am going to rape you" and then laughed. I kind of just laughed with him not knowing how to respond. I thought it was a little strange but I didn't take it seriously. Now thinking back on it I guess I should have ended the date and I definitely should not have gone to my apartment with him. There were so many signs I should have recognized and then I could have stopped it from happening. Maybe he did this, but maybe there was enough that I knew in order to have stopped this rape from happening, before it went so far. (When she started to blame herself my eyes lifted and my eyebrows raised. I paused at first because I could feel the expression on my face. Before this point I could feel my eyes were squinting and my eyebrows furrowed and I was biting my lip.)

WORKER: What happened was not your fault. He violated your trust
           and your person. He took that control against your will. It
           sounds like it really frightens you to think back to what hap-
           pened not only because of the rape but because of what you
           believe to be your role in it all.

MARY: I just don't understand it, why did this happen? It is not fair
           that this has affected my life so much, and I feel the rape has
           defined my life and who I am now. I just want to be back to
           normal.

WORKER: It is very understandable that you are having these feelings.
           It takes some time to get over the trauma of being raped.

MARY: I feel this takes up so much of my life—this is all I focus on.
           But talking about it with you does help. It not only helps me
           to hear myself say what I am feeling, but also to think about
           the incident and what happened because much of it I have to
           put in the back of my mind. It helps to talk to you and get
           feedback and to hear someone say that my feelings are not
           ridiculous, nor am I going crazy.

WORKER: Is it comforting for you to know that your feelings are nor-
           mal and that it is okay to talk about those feelings and about
           the rape?

MARY: It is great to know that it is okay to talk about my feelings
           here and I know that you do not blame me. You are more
           objective than most people I talk to about what happened
           because you did not know me when I came here, but you
           believed me and my story. But my real concern is how will I
           know how to trust others; I do not trust my own instincts.

WORKER: This is something that will take time, something that you can
           rebuild, and something we can work on together.

Mary describes her own behavior on the date, testing to see if the worker
will support her self-blame. As the worker passes each respective test, she
releases additional information. The worker repeatedly corrects misinformation regarding Mary's contribution to the rape. Mary begins to develop a new
cognition in the change in her reference from sex to rape. However, Mary
continues to struggle with assuming responsibility and self-blame in the next
session. After discussing a number of concrete issues, the worker identifies and
reaches for Mary's apparent reluctance to continue working on the rape.

MARY: I am ashamed to talk about it. I really do think at least to
           some degree that I brought this on myself, that I did not
           stand my ground with him. I acted differently than I thought
           I would act and have acted in the past. I don't know why.

WORKER: Differently, in what way?

MARY: Well, with other men, when I have told them no, I did not
feel that I needed to give them an explanation. With Jim, I
told him no, but I then gave him some lame excuse. It was so
bad, and I don't know why I felt I had to give him any excuse,
"no" always had been good enough for others (her voice
trailed off, and I nodded my head all the time she was saying
this, sitting silent for no more than two or three seconds
before she continued). I told Jim that I did not have any new
condoms; all the ones I had were old and it would not be safe
to use them. He agreed, and said he understood and that I
was being good. We would talk about something else for a
few minutes, but then he would start pressuring me again.
We must have gone through this four or five times and I
thought he really understood, he said that he did. But I do
not understand why I felt that I had to give him an excuse. I
never did before.

WORKER: Did yoo feel so much pressure from him that you felt "no"
was not enough for him to understand?

MARY: Yes, I think that is part of it, but it is still confusing. I am not
sure what I was thinking at the time before he raped me. But
I liked him and maybe he realized this, and so he did not
think that my "no" really meant no.

WORKER: Whether or not your "NO" meant *no*, it is not something for
him to decide. He should take that *no* meant *No*.

MARY: That is true and I know that I said NO.

WORKER: That should have been enough, that is all you had to say
to him. You tried to make it even more clear to him and
that did not help either. He chose to rape.

MARY: There are other things that I have started to think about that
should have clued me in.

WORKER: Can you give me an example?

MARY: Before we went out we spoke on the phone. I don't know if I
told you he has his master's in poetry. Well, anyway, we were
talking and he told me that he was going to tie me up and
read to me. That sounded weird to me, but I thought he was
just trying to be funny. However, I was really thinking about
it so I asked a few people what they thought. And I got a
range of reactions from "that's good, Mary, he's flirting with
you" to "oh, that is kind of scary, I hope that is the worst
thing he'll do to you." And there were other conversations
that now that I think about it I should have paid more attention to what he said.

WORKER: It's natural to look at a comment like "I am going to tie you
up and read to you" as something a little odd but funny, espe-

cially if you like someone and you want them to like you. He sounds like he is good at charming people, getting people to become interested in him. When you look back, suddenly things he said provide clues. But at the time, he is simply charming. So you are being real rough on yourself when you blame yourself for not knowing his intentions. It is human nature to trust, especially when you want to become romantically involved.

MARY: That is true, and I did like Jim. I even broke up with another boyfriend partly because I wanted to have the chance to start dating him.

WORKER: Is this adding to feelings of self-blame because you did like him and because up to that point he had been nice?

MARY: Yes, very much so. I feel ashamed that I could have ever liked him, and that somehow he must have known this. So I begin to think that maybe it was partly my fault for not giving him a clear message.

WORKER: The message you gave him was no and that was enough not only for him to get the message, but for him to understand it as well. This is not your fault. You are not at fault because you liked him, or because there were things said that you think should have given you a clue. The bottom line is that you said no, he violated your trust and your body, and he committed a violent crime. (Mary began to sob, thanking me for my support.)

The worker's support invites Mary to provide further details to explore her feelings of self-blame. She refers to the rapist by name for the first time. The worker creates a safe space for Mary, repeatedly emphasizing the rapist's responsibility for his actions. When Mary is able to direct her rage at Jim, she will become less depressed and can begin moving from victim to survivor.

In the next session, Mary relived the experience of the rape itself. She sobbed uncontrollably as she described the invasion of her body and self-identity. Mary referred to this session as "taking a hundred pounds off my back" and the "lifting of a huge black cloud." The worker also helped Mary to explore her fear of AIDS from the rape and mobilized her to get a blood test. Finally, she helped Mary to reconnect to family and friends, and to join a rape survivors mutual aid group. Mary is also considering pressing charges against Jim. This is the current focus of counseling.

The human capacity to create and narrate a life story and to make a healing process of it is a compelling life force available to client and practitioner in their joint work. Most practice vignettes in this chapter illustrate life stories of loneliness, despair, illness, or loss, and the search for meaning and coherence in these and other critical life stressors. With social work help, the narrators were better able to integrate difficult and traumatic events into a more positive, helpful life story.

With the empathic, active listening of the social worker in each of these case examples, each person reinterpreted and reconstructed a life story that ultimately contained new conceptions of the self and of relationships with others. As it was being reconstructed by the story teller, each life story gained increased intelligibility, consistency, and continuity (Stern 1985). The telling of the story, together with the listening, is a healing process. It is our human way of finding meaning in life events, of explaining our life experience to ourselves and others, so that we can move on. The point of origin of the person's troubling life issue may be located at any point in actual time over the life course and not necessarily at some theoretical point in very early life (Stern 1985). Stern adds that it may not be necessary to uncover memories of very early life to find a trauma that can explain the present life issue. It is enough to seek out its narrative point of origin in the remembered past, that is, the time and the circumstances under which it entered the life story. That narrative point is viewed as the first edition of the life issue, not a re-edition of earlier life events.

FIVE

HELPING INDIVIDUALS,
FAMILIES, AND GROUPS WITH
ENVIRONMENTAL STRESSORS

In this chapter, environmental stressors are limited to organizations, social networks, and built and natural settings. Organizations, social networks, and physical space can be important supports or significant life stressors.

Environmental Processes as Life Stressors

The Social Environment

Contemporary urban society is characterized by the prevalence of complex organizations in most areas of life, including health, education, and social service organizations. Such structures are themselves embedded in social and physical environments. They affect and are affected by political, economic, and cultural forces. Growing numbers of people served by social workers face such grave life issues as family and community violence and neglect; unemployment; social and physical disability and chronic illness, including AIDS, homelessness, and substance abuse (Gitterman 1991). Limited attention is given to economic stressors that arise from institutionalized blockage of access to stable and sufficient resources (Hartman and Laird 1983; Vosler 1990).

Social welfare organizations. Initially, health, education, and social service organizations are established with financial support from private or public funds. Once established, however, social service organizations must maintain a balance among pressures exerted by legislative bodies, regulatory agencies, funding sources, the community, changing definitions of social need, and new knowledge and technologies. These forces continually threaten organizational obsolescence. Once established, how an organization defines its function and boundaries has an impact on the experiences of applicants and service users (Gitterman and Miller 1989; Weissman, Epstein, and Savage 1983). A social work agency, for example, may define its function in terms of specialized services to groups, individuals, families, or communities. Applicants must fit their life stressors to the agency's single modality instead of the agency's providing varied modalities fitted to applicants' needs. Another agency may define its function in terms of helping people change, with little account taken of the complex interactions between people and social variables.

In some schools, for example, pupils are referred to social work services as disruptive or disturbed because teachers find them unmanageable. The social worker is expected to help such children passively adjust to the school environment. By acquiescing in this definition of professional purpose, the social worker overlooks the need to intervene at the classroom, family, educational policy, or community level. Yet one or all levels may be creating or sustaining the life stressors (Germain 1991a; Gitterman 1977). An unintended consequence of this definition of social work's purpose is to stigmatize service. Preventive help to all children and their families in their exchanges with the education system lies outside the boundary of social work in such a school system.

All organizations gradually develop a structure of statuses and roles for division of labor. If roles constrict professional function and negatively impact services, they increase stress for service users and providers. The function of inpatient medical/surgical social workers, for example, is severely limited by the current emphasis on rapid hospital discharge. This deprives patients and their families of social work help with the psychological and social consequences of illness and disability. The pressure of large caseloads, limited time for discharge planning, and shrinking resources create pronounced ethical dilemmas and increased stress for social workers (Abramson 1983; Blumenfield and Lowe 1987; Germain 1984).

Stress may also be created by organizational boundaries. Some agencies locate services away from those they seek to serve, thus inhibiting client use because of transportation costs, babysitting costs, or social intimidation in an unfamiliar geographic area. Agency gatekeepers such as telephone operators, receptionists, and intake personnel may be unwelcoming and gruff. Physical aspects may be unattractive and uncomfortable; long waits may be involved (Germain 1983; Seabury 1971).

Boundaries of other social service organizations may be too easily penetrated. For example, children may be taken into substitute care without sufficient effort to keep them in their own homes, or with other kin, or at least in their own neighborhoods and schools so that all social ties will not be broken.

Intraorganizational boundaries might be too loose, particularly in those interdisciplinary settings where useful role distinctions are blurred. The distinctive contribution of the social worker may be lost in the general welter of "everyone can do everything." Clients could then be confused by ambiguity in professional function, and the competitiveness among varied professionals.

Where interorganizational boundaries are drawn unrealistically or where there is a lack of linkages to ensure effective referral and service pickup, some clients become "lost" and do not receive needed service. An aged person in need of medical care may be deemed ineligible by a clinic because he is financially unable to purchase insurance to supplement Medicare. A mental patient discharged from a state hospital but lacking an aftercare program may be denied service by a family agency because of poor prognosis, weak motivation, or other personal "deficits."

An organization develops structures, policies, and procedures to manage external and internal pressures. An authority structure allocates responsibility and coordinates tasks. It provides a chain of command through which decisions are made. Some authority structures are rigid; they reward conformity, discourage innovation, and block horizontal and vertical communication. The layers of authority may become so numerous, or communication channels so clogged, that the time span in decision making discourages both practitioner and client from pursuing individualized needs or even common entitlements. In other cases, authority structures may be too flexible; allowing inappropriate discretionary power to practitioners having minimal accountability. Clients are then vulnerable to individual whim, prejudice, or narrow interpretation of service provisions.

The organization develops a set of policies and procedures to assure fair and neutral treatment for all service users regardless of personality traits, ethnicity or race, sex, age, physical or mental disabilities, sexual orientation, or social status. In some organizations, policies and procedures proliferate as circumstances change or exceptional situations arise. They assume a life of their own and take precedence over client need and the organization's avowed goals. Some organizations demand strict adherence to policies and procedures: the agency manual supersedes the applicant's or client's needs and interests. In effect, individual needs are held hostage to bureaucratic needs. Some organizations use procedures and policies to ration or deny services. A welfare agency, for example, may rely on long waits and complicated forms to discourage applicants, delay service, and block referrals. Other organizations may not formalize or codify practices, and clients are subjected to nonuniform practices and to workers' idiosyncratic judgments. When procedures or policies are either underformalized or overformalized, they are potential stressors for clients (Fischer and Siriani 1994; Hasenfeld 1992; Holland 1995; Meyers 1993; Schmidt 1992).

Informal structures also develop within organizations. These may support the organization's responsiveness to client need or subvert it. Just as formal structures socialize each organizational member to the agency's culture, the informal system socializes members to its culture (Gitterman and Miller 1989). Formal and informal sanctions influence members to accept formal and informal structures and processes as natural and immutable.

Even the informal system sometimes exerts pressure toward conformity with the organization's own norms and practice and discourages creativity or innovation. When staff dissatisfaction with personnel practices and working conditions exists, the informal system may support scornful, punitive, or uncaring attitudes toward clients as displacements of feelings aroused by the authority structure of the agency itself. For example, Anita Dorsey, age 34, requested a private child welfare agency to provide temporary placement for her expected baby, due in four months. The baby's father had left her and she had no money or job. A friend was willing to provide shelter until the baby was born. Ms. Dorsey wanted to find work, get a suitable living arrangement for herself and the baby, and find someone to mind the baby while she was at work:

> After the first interview, I felt Ms. Dorsey was confused and unrealistic about the meaning of the baby for her and her plans for herself and for the baby. Yet she is concerned about the baby's wellbeing. During the next two interviews, she continued to be uncommunicative, and was reluctant to answer my questions about her feelings, her family, her relationship with the putative father, or her past life. She felt I was overlooking her real problem, that she is expecting a baby and does not have the means to provide for it. This is the only thing that worries her. She asserted that it was useless to discuss anything else. She was obviously angry and suspicious of me, and refused to give more information because she did not see how it could help her.

This agency assumed the primacy of intrapsychic phenomena in people's needs and the informal system supported harsh attitudes toward clients. Workers rationalized their attitudes by blaming clients for their resistance.

People's transactions with the organizational environment represent a critical arena for social workers. In helping clients to secure services from an organization other than their own, workers' tasks may be difficult, but not hazardous. The task is more delicate when one seeks to influence one's own organization in order to secure services or resources required by clients and withheld by the agency. Particular skills are required so that neither client nor worker is placed in jeopardy. Issues of job security, agency loyalties, and professional reputation may be involved. Above all, the social worker's responsibility and accountability to clients, with recognition of the vulnerability inherent in the status of client, must be constant and unflinching.

Social Networks. Social support systems consisting of kin, friends, neighbors, work mates, and acquaintances are increasingly recognized as important elements of the social environment. Social networks are comprised of various circles that move outward from the innermost (which includes people with whom one lives and has most intense investment), to the next circle (which includes those whom one highly values and interacts with frequently), to the next circle of people with whom one interacts frequently but who are less important, or important people with whom one interacts less frequently, to the next circle (which includes people who are known but considered of less importance), to the final circle (which includes people who are known about or linked through significant others) (Specht 1986).

Supportive social networks serve as environmental resources. They are important sources of our self-concept and also help shape our world view (Miller and Turnbull 1986). Social networks may meet the need for human relatedness, recognition, and affirmation. Some members may consciously serve as effective informal helpers, eliminating the need to seek institutionalized services (Collins and Pancoast 1976; Kelley and Kelley 1985; Patterson, Brennan, Germain, and Memmott 1992, 1988). For these and other reasons, social networks are critical buffers against life stressors or the stress they generate (Brown and Gary 1987; Cohen and Willis 1985; de Anda and Becerr 1984; Gallo 1982; Lin, Woolfel, and Light 1985; Rene 1987). Social networks can cushion an individual through four types of support (Auslander and Levin 1987): instrumental (goods or services); emotional (nurturance, empathy, encouragement); informational (advice, feedback); and appraisal (information relevant to self-evaluation) (House 1981; Luckey 1994). Knowing that networks are available for support results in people being less anxious and more confident in dealing with new stressors (Gottlieb 1988:36).

While informal support systems may exist, some people are unable to make use of them. Background and personality affect people's perceptions and help-seeking behavior. For example, women are more likely than men to identify life issues, acknowledge the need for help, and seek help (Asser 1978; Barbarin 1983; McMullin and Gross 1983). Seeking help may threaten a person's self-esteem. For some, seeking help from social networks evokes a negative social comparison. Seeking help generates and reinforces relative feelings of inferiority and failure (Fisher, Goff, Nadler and Chinsky 1986). Self-esteem might also be threatened when help-seeking is uni-directional rather than reciprocal. Receiving without reciprocating may have negative consequences (Goodman 1984; Goodman 1985). Finally, people who attribute their life issues to internal rather than external causes are more likely to feel threatened and to avoid seeking help from significant others (Shapiro 1983).

For some, the needed degree of privacy and anonymity affects their ability to seek help. Public admission of need evokes shame and humiliation. Prior experiences in obtaining assistance from the network could have left a residue of negative feelings, inhibiting future use. A life stressor that conflicts with the network's value or moral system is yet another deterrent. In certain issues pertaining to sexuality, for example, individuals may be reluctant to turn to their network because of the network's restrictive or repressive norms. Harsh judgments or rejection anticipated by a gay person may deter him from reaching out to the network for help with such a devastating life stressor as AIDS. Cultural emphases on independence and self-reliance may inhibit some people from asking their network for help.

Loosely knit networks may be unaware of a member's stress. Lacking meaningful contacts, members' stress remains invisible. In addition, some networks do not offer their resources to members even when stressors are actually visible. When network resources are stretched out, some members may fear incurring additional pressures and burdens (Schilling and Schinke 1983; Marsden and Lin 1982) while others may fear encouraging dependency.

While it is generally assumed that social network resources are always useful and helpful, they could at times have a negative impact on members facing life stressors (Schilling 1987). Some networks are subject to internal exploitative and competitive processes that could undermine one's sense of identity and autonomy. A network with rigid boundaries could isolate the client from growth experiences outside the close-knit network (Mayer and Rosenblatt 1964). Some networks have ill-defined boundaries, and are so loosely knit that the network is actually unavailable for material or psychological support.

Other networks are maladaptive in other ways. They reinforce deviance, holding to values that contravene healthy or normative strivings of the client (Duncan-Ricks 1992; Hawkins and Fraser 1984). A member of a drug-oriented network or a delinquent network may want to end his affiliation in order to modify his values and aspirations. Yet the network may exert a strong counterforce, leading to severe stress and even danger. Some families have difficulty combating the influence of peer networks on younger members or unwanted interference by kin networks on day-to-day functioning of the family.

Life transitions such as school changes, marriage, migration, job promotion, and retirement are sometimes difficult. Critical life events such as job loss, sickness, and death, interrupt or dissolve linkages to others. The sense of self is dependent in part on involvement with others. Some of the most painful and stressful experiences of humankind are loneliness, isolation, and unwanted distance from others (Weiss 1982, 1973). In old age, friends and kin die, one's activities are curtailed, and the acquisition of new networks is limited (Whittaker and Garbarino 1983). Women appear to make greater efforts than men to establish and maintain friendships and kinship networks. For elderly men, the death of a spouse frequently means more than a lost attachment. The widower has also lost social ties which were maintained by his wife (Chiriboga 1982). This stressor might be intensified by concurrent retirement and the loss of the network created at work.[1]

The Physical Environment. The human services tend to neglect the physical settings of human behavior. The physical environment was long viewed as a static backdrop for psycho-social forces that were believed to be the only influence on human behavior and development. Our clients require a more balanced view. The physical environment is an important factor in the development and maintenance of relatedness, competence motivation, and self-concept. Trust, for example, is based on the security of stable physical arrangements, as well as on stable companionship. Children refer to *my toys, my room, my clothes* as part of themselves (Cohen and Horm-Wingerd 1993; Lindholm 1995; Susa 1994). Some adults identify the outdoors as the most significant place in their childhood. Children experience the natural world in a "deep and direct manner, not a background for events, but rather as factor and stimulator" (Sebba 1990:395). Stressors are generated from the loss of familiar and cherished places and structures that comfort and protect, and are part of one's individual and group identity. The life stressor of uprootedness is attributable, in part, to the sense of being torn from an identity base.

In order to analyze complex exchanges between people and physical settings, we distinguish between the built world and the natural world. The built world includes: personal space; semi-fixed space; and fixed space. *Personal space* refers to an invisible spatial boundary that people maintain as a buffer against unwanted physical and social contact and to protect one's privacy (Altman 1975). Some people react to intrusion into their personal space with gestures, withdrawal, or aggressive responses.

Semi-fixed space refers to movable objects and their arrangement in space. Furniture, curtains, plants, pictures, colors, and lighting provide spatial meanings and cues. People rely on environmental props (locks, labels, fences, etc.) to regulate interactions with the social environment. Too much interaction is experienced as crowding. Too little interaction is experienced as social isolation (Altman 1975; Baum and Paulus 1987; Evans and Lepore 1992; Lepore, Evans, and Schneider 1992). Both can be life stressors. Families and groups experience differing levels of fit between their interactive patterns and the physical design of their living space (Minami and Tanaka 1995). The degree of interpersonal coordination required in a limited space is often a stressor. High density limits physical movement, demands behavioral coordination, and increases the number of people with whom coordination is necessary. The close proximity, social overload, and spatial constraints lead to irritation and conflict. Laying claim to an area and defending it are difficult (Pruchno, Dempsey, Carder, and Koropeckyj-Cox 1993). Such behaviors are influenced by culture (Altman and Gavain 1981). For example, Asian cultures are strongly oriented to collective, communal use of space, whereas Western cultures emphasize private use of space.

Seabury (1971) examined the uses of semi-fixed space in six different types of social service settings. He found a significant association between arrangement of space and the social class of an agency's clients. The public welfare center and hospital social service departments were the most unattractive and uncomfortable while the private offices and private agencies were the most attractive and comfortable.

Reception areas make important symbolic statements to applicants and clients (Ornstein 1992) as described by a social work intern in an agency serving poor elderly clients:

> The Senior Service Center (ssc) is located in the basement of a two story project building entered directly from the street. The building is not conspicuous. It has two doors, one for administrative offices and the other for clients. Wire fences hidden by overgrown plants and weeds surround the two doors. A small sign is posted on the door bearing the initials ssc. A passerby could easily miss the agency.
>
> On entering, one climbs down a few steps to reach the reception/waiting room. The room is small, dimly lit, and unpretentious. The secretary's desk is located in the middle of the room. Covering one wall is a bookcase containing magazines; various pictures and diplomas hang on the other two walls. Chairs are lined up side-by-side forming a line along two walls.
>
> Most interviews are held in an office in the administration building. The office is shared by ten social workers. It contains a table and desk; two chairs are located next to the desk and two others face the desk from across the room. No lamps or pictures adorn this room. When this room is unavailable, I must use a staff office that I share with four other social workers. It contains five desks, and is sparsely decorated. The agency's drab features probably reinforces feelings of helplessness and despair in those served.

In institutional settings, the need for supervision and surveillance often leads to concentrated use of a limited portion of available space. Unchanging spatial arrangements limit residents' opportunities for privacy and spatial identity. Arrangement of open and closed spaces in institutions, treatment cottages, and schools either invites or discourages certain behaviors in children; arrangement of furniture and other objects in mental hospitals and geriatric facilities promotes or discourages social interaction among the residents (Devlin 1992; Osmond 1970). Ward "geography" in any inpatient setting either supports or inhibits patients' shifting needs for privacy or for socialization. A social worker intern reports:

When I enter a resident's room, I feel immediate discomfort as a result of the limited space shared by two people, the intrusive proximity of the beds, and the lack of adequate provision for personal objects. The organization's policy is to have nothing on the walls except the bulletin board provided each resident. The policy is aimed at keeping walls clean and without holes, and at avoiding frequent repainting. Each board provides a few square feet of space for displaying cards and pictures. The only other space the residents have access to is a small bedside table and a small space by the sink. I was struck by how unhomelike this felt.

The dayroom is located far from the nurses' station, the elevators, and the bathroom. The chairs and sofas are neatly arranged shoulder-to-shoulder around the perimeter of the room. A television is at one end and a small table piled with books and games is at the other. There are no tables for games. The room is rarely used by residents. Conversations are rare except when visitors are present. They usually arrange the furniture to make small groupings. I thought to myself: "Why can't this be arranged more like a living room?"

I observed several residents in wheelchairs lined up in the hallway and I realized that it was close to lunch time. They were waiting for someone to escort them onto the elevator and into the dining room. The wheelchairs were lined up one behind the other. Needless to say, no conversations could take place.

The answer to the student's question, "Why can't this be arranged more like a living room?" is that patients and staff who are confined to an environment for a long period of time eventually view semi-fixed, movable space as fixed and immovable. Habit and tradition become institutionalized and achieve "institutional sanctity." The absence of color, sound, and adequate light in bleak unchanging environments is stressful and coping with it is difficult.

The design of dwellings (*fixed space*) is influenced by the character of the physical setting, including climate, and by cultural styles and meanings. The structure and design of high rise, low-income public housing violate cultural and psychological aspects of the self-image. Such housing is a warehouse symbol of lost identity, rather than a personal symbol of the unique self (Germain 1978). It gives tenants no safe territory on the ground, and no defensible territory within. Vandalism and lack of care by tenants may represent their angry responses to stressful assaults on their identity and dignity, and lead to further social, psychological, and physiological stress. Other physical settings such as mental hospitals, prisons, schools, and residential facilities for the aged or the very young, reflect similar social and cultural processes which dehumanize and devalue society's "outsiders."

The *natural world*, too, influences human functioning more than most of us realize. Studies of accidents, suicides, crimes, psychiatric hospital admissions, and even rates of social interaction have revealed suggestive associations with features of the natural environment such as hours of sunlight, climate, and phases of the moon (Proshansky, Itellson, and Rivlin 1976; Retton 1993). Barometric pressure, wind, excessive temperatures and humidity, and seasonal variations in climate influence the moods and behavior of people, and contribute to stress. The influence of the natural world may be intensified in rural areas where climate, lack of public transportation, and greater distances from neighbors, friends, and relatives are more important than in urban areas.

Landscape features such as islands, mountains, coasts, deserts, lakefronts, and marshlands have different effects on lifestyles and identities. Puerto Rican migrants to a northern mainland city, for example, must contend with differences they meet when leaving a self-contained tropical island and entering a seemingly limitless continent and a city located in a temperate zone with marked seasonal changes in climate. If the migrant comes from a rural area of Puerto Rico, the impact of urban life is all the more stressful. In the United States, similar stressors may be encountered by Native Americans or by Chicanos who move to the urban centers of the north. In Canada, migrants from India and southeast Asia, and Canadian Indians who move to cities, are subjected to similar stressors.

The natural environment has a temporal texture in its alterations of day and night, seasons, and annual rhythms as the earth journeys around the sun. Such rhythmic variations have been entrained in all forms of life through adaptive processes over evolutionary time. Biological rhythms in human beings such as rapid eye movement (REM) sleep, hunger cycles, pulse, and respiratory rhythms reflect these terrestrial cycles. Temporal rhythms imposed by schools, hospitals, social agencies and even work arrangements may conflict with fundamental biological rhythms and cause physiological and psychological stress (Germain 1976).

Plants and animals may be defined by cultural values and human needs as useful, dangerous, supportive, unimportant, endearing, or symbolic. Dogs provide numerous functions and meet diverse needs. Some people desire the security and protection of a watchdog. For others, a dog or cat or bird serves as a companion. For socially isolated and shy people, pets also serve as icebreakers, acting as a social lubricant (Brickel 1986). People with severe disabilities are helped by specially trained companion monkeys. The legally blind are served by guide dogs, and the hearing impaired are aided by other animals (Hale and Polt 1985; Redfer and Goodman 1989; Valentine, Kiddoo, and Lafleur 1993). As valued companions, pets are part of a person's or family's social network.

Social Work Function, Modalities, Method, and Skills

The Social Worker and the Environment

With limited power and limited awareness of their rights, some service users become resigned to the unresponsiveness of organizations. For poor people, the environment is particularly harsh. Because of their economic position, they are unable to command needed goods and services or to exercise their rights (Orfield 1991). They are closed out of opportunities for good education, preventive health care, jobs and promotion, safe housing, neighborhood amenities. Their mobility is extremely limited. Morbidity rates are higher, infant mortality rates are high, and life expectancy is low in comparison with middle income families (Gitterman 1991). The social worker's attention and actions must be directed to helping clients make use of available resources and on influencing organizations to provide responsive services.

Agencies are a source of some power; our profession is a source of some status. Both can be used to improve people's environments and provide them with leverage for meeting their needs. While we may believe our influence is slight, our actual impact might make the difference between disintegration and survival for individuals, families, and groups who obtain needed food, shelter, medical care, and other entitlements through our advocacy on their behalf. Similarly, social workers' attention and action must be directed to the exchanges between an individual, group or family and their social network. Mobilizing or strengthening "real life" ties, finding new linkages and re-establishing old ones, enlisting the aid of natural helpers, and helping clients disengage from maladaptive affiliations help improve transactions between clients and social networks.

Practitioners must also be prepared to act upon those aspects of the physical environment that, alone or in concert with social and cultural processes, create life stressors for an individual, family, or group. For example, social work staff in a nursing home can successfully personalize resident space. Residents can be encouraged to exhibit meaningful possessions (pictures, books, and knickknacks) and to care for plants. In one home for the aged, the communal dining room now has small circular tables for interaction; television and card lounges are available on each floor; and a bar has been added. Such changes in the physical environment enrich the social environment with sites for social interaction.

Professional Methods and Skills

When clients' knowledge, experience, and physical state permit, their taking action on the environment is an important means to achieving psychological empowerment and actual power (Mondros and Wilson 1994). If social worker and client agree that client action is not feasible, thought must be given to whether the worker and client should act together or if the worker should act alone, continually apprising the client of any progress.

Helping with environmental processes is carried out by coordinating, mediating, advocating, innovating, and influencing. We again remind the reader that work with environmental issues is usually concurrent with work on difficult life transitions and maladaptive family and group patterns, so these professional methods are used in tandem with those of enabling, exploring, mobilizing, guiding, and facilitating, as well as other methods described in later chapters. All ebb and flow throughout the service contact, as circumstances and client needs and interests require.

Assessment, exploration, and agreement on focus and action usually continue in the ongoing phase. They often disclose sources of stressors between client and organization, between client and network, or between client and physical environment. The worker might use guiding, for example, if a client has insufficient knowledge of the availability of resources and services, or if a client requires help in using them; or facilitating if psychologically or culturally-based resistance to using service or seeking the resources are present, or if fear of the unknown or unrealistic concern for independence interfere with using available organizational or network resources. For example, an elderly client refused to apply for much needed food stamps. The worker encouraged him to "tell his story." His narrated experiences, behaviors, thoughts, and feelings explained his reluctance to seek the entitlement. To help this elderly man hold on to his dignity, manage his feelings, and solve his life issues, the worker used the skills discussed in chapters 3, 4, and this chapter. A routine referral would have failed.

In most instances, however, the problem is not the client's inability to use the social environment, but distorted communication between client and the organization or the social network. In coordinating services, the worker links the client to available resources. In mediating, the social worker helps client and social system connect in more realistic and reciprocal ways through intercession, persuasion, and negotiation (Berman-Rossi 1994a; Brown 1994; Schwartz 1976). The problem frequently lies within the organization. If collaborating and mediating do not accomplish the desired end, the social worker seeks to influence the organization to be more responsive by advocacy and its skills of pressure, coercion, or appeals to third party intervention. The social worker might also use the media, mobilize a group, neighborhood, or community, or involve legislative, fiscal, or regulatory agencies in the organization's environment (McGowan 1987; Mickelson 1995; Reisch 1990).

There may be unresponsive or punitive individuals within the social network whom the worker must engage on the client's behalf. Authority figures outside the network are sometimes unresponsive or punitive toward a client. A landlord, policeman, creditor, physician, or others may need to be approached in an attempt to increase their understanding of the client's needs and responses, or to secure concessions, delays, access to rights, or entitlements (Davenport and Davenport 1982; Erikson 1984; Gottlieb 1985; Swenson 1981b). When the client lacks a network, or wants to disengage from a network, the social worker might arrange an introduction to other networks of neighbors, fellow tenants, or to institutionalized sources such as parent-teacher associations, church-sponsored groups, etc. (Morrison 1991). Or worker and client may decide on referral to a self-help group such as Parents Without Partners or Alcoholics Anonymous as a network substitute or to improve coping (Katz and Bender 1990; Kurtz and Powell 1987). If the client lacks networks or network substitutes, the worker, alone or with clients and colleagues, and usually with agency support, might develop an informal network or a more structured self-help group (Coplon and Strull 1983; Powell 1990, 1987). A social worker might help the client and others with similar interests or needs form a telephone network for elderly neighbors or physically challenged people, a babysitting exchange among young mothers, or a support network in a homeless shelter (Brown 1994; Lee 1994).

Enabling, exploring and clarifying, mobilizing, guiding, and facilitating are appropriate when a client lacks information, is fearful, or is unable to use or respond to the natural and built worlds (Resnick and Jaffe 1982). Mediating and advocating are appropriate when service systems or powerful individuals in the social environment must be influenced before the physical environment can be improved. Innovating is appropriate when mobilization of group or community efforts is necessary for modifying the physical environment. Table 5.1 summarizes environmental stressors and responsive professional methods.

In *coordinating* and *connecting* clients with available organizational resources, the first task is reaching an agreement on a division of labor in dealing with environmental difficulties:

- *Obtaining informed consent and involvement.* While doing "with" a client is preferable, doing "for" is better than ignoring the problem out of misguided insistence on client participation in all situations. Differences in power relations often call for social workers to intervene on behalf of clients, with client consent and involvement. To proceed without informed consent and involvement is unethical and conveys a lack of faith in the client's abilities.
- *Defining a division of labor.* Hopeless and vulnerable clients often expect social workers to do for them; some practitioners, however, are concerned about encouraging dependence and are reluctant to intercede directly. A clear division of labor encourages client involvement and meliorates discrepant expectations: "I will make the call for you, but we need to prepare for the landlord's possible reactions and for how you want to respond." Even when doing

Table 5.1	Relation Between Sources of Environmental Stressors and Responsive Professional Methods

PEOPLE'S ENVIRONMENTAL STRESSORS	PROFESSIONAL METHODS
1. People are unwilling or unable to use available social or physical resources	enabling exploring mobilizing guiding facilitating
2. Client needs and social/physical environment resources lack sufficient fit; communications and transactions are distorted	coordinating/connecting mediating
3. Social environment is unwilling to provide available resources	advocating
4. Formal and/or informal social environment resources are unavailable	organizing innovating

"for" a client, the social worker engages the client in the process. Otherwise feelings of powerlessness and helplessness are reinforced.

- *Mobilizing client's energy and personal resources.* People need to experience some control over their lives. If that need is frustrated, motivation and self-direction suffer (Gold 1990; Seligman 1980). People can slip into victim roles, apathy, and learned helplessness (Hooker 1976). The worker must challenge this response. To mobilize an elderly client's energies and personal resources, the worker makes a direct appeal: "To stop your neighbor's verbal abuse, we have to find small things you can do to change his behavior . . . the problem will not go away, unless we take small steps." This approach to coping helps to make the stressor more manageable.

- *Lending the social worker's professional status to the client.* Although practitioners may feel relatively powerless in relation to their own and other organizations, for clients to have a professional "on their side" provides support and hope. Sitting with a client in a waiting room, telephoning on a client's behalf, and making appointments for a client, make a difference. Our presence conveys to the other person that the client is not alone. The presence of an observer or witness reduces the possibility of peremptory treatment. How we define our roles and how we engage formal and informal structures and networks can either reduce or intensify a client's vulnerability and powerlessness. Client-oriented motives must be pursued in an organizational context of other imperatives and people, if we are not to become isolated and ineffective.

To be helpful to clients with environmental stressors, the social worker must have *collaborating* and *mediating* skills.

- *Demonstrating professional competence.* Organizational effectiveness usually depends on achieving informal influence through demonstrated professional competence. Competence must be visible.
- *Developing and using informal contacts within the employing organization.* The worker who is an insider, attentive to colleagues' interests and concerns, acquires an interpersonal network. Having lunch or coffee, sharing greetings and support with colleagues, and exchanging personal and professional favors, activate a "norm of reciprocity" and provides the basis for a favor from a colleague on behalf of a client in a "special" circumstance.
- *Building and using interorganizational resource networks.* For effective contacts with other organizations, social workers need to develop and maintain an interorganizational resource file in which they log helpful (or unhelpful) personnel. Similarly, if the practitioner has been helpful to a staff member from another organization, the "norm of reciprocity" can be activated. By developing a resource file, staff are able to pool their contacts and elevate the level of fit between client need and organizational resources. Continuous updating and searching are needed. Resource files developed by the agency or published centrally within the community are useful adjuncts, but formal files are no substitute for the professional exchange of favors or for building a professional reputation as a competent practitioner.
- *Developing and using formal system contacts.* Active, skillful involvement on committees, teams, consultations, conferences, staff meetings, task forces, and community meetings provides opportunities for contacts. A staff person from another organization is more likely to respond to a social worker who has exhibited clarity, discipline, and good humor in interdisciplinary contacts.
- *Demonstrating awareness of the perspective of other staff.* Before meeting with a staff member, the social worker prepares for the encounter by anticipatory empathy with probable reactions to still another request for service. By identifying with feelings of pressure and of being harassed ("I know how terribly busy you are") and yet appealing to self-interest ("I think Mrs. Smith will become less demanding and complaining if . . . "), the social worker presents requests in a nonthreatening manner. The aim is to achieve positive rather than defensive or resentful responses.
- *Knowing and using organizational policies, procedures, and precedents.* In dealing with others in organizations, knowledge of relevant policies, rules and regulations, research findings, practices, technical procedures, and professional language is critical. In a medical setting, social workers must be familiar with medical terminology and Diagnostic Related Groups (DRGs). In psychiatric and mental health settings, practitioners must be knowledgeable about categories in DSM–IV. In a welfare setting, the policy manual rules. Being able to cite a specific policy or procedure useful to a client is most effective in securing entitlements.

Table 5.2	Coordinating/Connecting and Collaborative/Mediating Skills
• *Coordinating/Connecting Skills*	reach for informed consent establish a division of labor mobilize client's energy and personal resources lend the worker's professional status to the client

• *Collaborative/Mediating Skills*	demonstrate professional competence
	develop and use informal system contacts within the
	    employing organization
	build and use interorganizational resource networks
	develop and use formal system contacts
	demonstrate awareness of the perspective of other
	    organizational staff
	know about and use organizational policies, procedures,
	    and precedents
	demonstrate perseverance

• *Demonstrating perseverance.* Being a "charming" pain-in-the-neck is an art worth developing and is a useful collaborative intervention: "It's Louise again, I'm sure you have been waiting all day for my call." Red tape and unresponsive functionaries can certainly evoke anger, despair, and behavioral extremes. We must move past these responses and demonstrate dogged endurance: "Let's call one more time," "Let's write one more letter," "Let's try just showing up."

Collaborating and mediating are not likely to result in negative repercussions. If they fail, more *directive*, *assertive*, and *persuasive* interventions might become necessary:

• *Creating organizational tension.* Elaborate defenses develop in organizations, through which a client's life issues are minimized, avoided, or denied. Before the organization will bend an agency policy, make an exception, or stretch service boundaries, the social worker might have to generate general discomfort with the status quo and its consequences for the client. "I know our policy discourages financial assistance, but I spoke to John's aunt in Virginia. She's willing to have him stay with her, but needs our help with buying him a bus ticket. If we don't do that, he will be homeless and vulnerable to all kinds of violence."

• *Climbing the organizational hierarchy.* If a worker receives a negative response from another agency, a polite request for the name and phone number of the supervisor is advisable. In one's own organization, suggesting that a colleague or supervisor check with the respective supervisor should precede skipping a level.

• *Asserting client entitlement or need.* Disciplined assertiveness is a major means of improving the fit between client need and environmental resource. Assertive behavior requires abilities to: (a) objectively describe the concern;

(b) express associated feelings; (c) specify the desired change or outcome; and (d) explicate consequences. "I know how it is—Mrs. Jones starts to yell and it's hard to resist not yelling back at her [a], but when you yell at her, she feels totally helpless, begins to cry, and becomes unmanageable [b]. Maybe if you explain to her that if she only rings her buzzer once, you'll try to come within five minutes and won't yell at her [c]. In that way she will be a more cooperative patient [d]."

- *Arguing on behalf of the client.* Making a case includes clearly defining the issue, specifying its boundaries, and proposing possible solutions. Next, the social worker tries to anticipate potential opposition to the proposal and the expected and unexpected consequences of adopting it. Throughout the process, one respects others' opinions, but presses one's own position out of expressed concern for the client, the organization's good name, and its mission.

If mediating, asserting, and arguing fail, worker and client might consider *adversarial* actions. Professional ethics actually require such action if essential entitlements are denied or client rights are curtailed (NASW Code 1993). Before taking such action, the social worker evaluates potential consequences. In taking an adversarial position, the worker assumes a polite, respectful stance, not one of outraged righteousness. As stated in a previous chapter, it might make the outraged feel better, but it could cost the desired end. Also, client and worker could be vulnerable to retaliation so that probity and caution are always needed.

- *Implying further action.* An even-tempered assertion—"We are running out of patience. My client and agency are prepared if necessary to seek a fair hearing, or to move to a class action or both"—can, by shifting the balance of power, release a client's entitlement. Sometimes the action has to be initiated before willingness to negotiate or to concede is brought about.
- *Refusing compliance.* Social workers might sometimes be expected to take actions which conflict with established professional standards and ethics. Polite firmness can be highly effective, "I am sorry, but the client has to be informed about her legal rights and options—professional ethics requires it. I am also concerned about the negative impact upon our department's reputation if this practice became known." Unwillingness to carry out a wrongful departmental policy is a part of organizational loyalty.
- *Organizing protests.* Clients gain strength and security from joining with others in similar circumstances. Group services usually diminish client isolation and risk of reprisal, and they increase chances of success. Group action gets institutional attention. In some severe instances, the social worker helps groups to express grievances through sit-ins, vigils, marches, rent strikes, picketing, the use of mass media, and engaging the interest of political figures. These actions increase client visibility and bargaining power.

Skills with organizational issues are also applicable to network issues. Some require simple modification. "Knowing and using organizational policies, procedures, and precedents" becomes "Knowing and using network structures and processes"; "Climbing the organizational hierarchy" becomes "Traversing network boundaries" (Adams and Bleiszner 1993; Bergman 1989; Biegel, Tracy, and Corvo 1994; Galanter 1993; Lee 1994; Nakhaima 1994).

The physical environment offers the social worker an additional dimension in helping people. Improving the degree-of-fit between people and their physical environments requires distinct professional skills.

- *Responding to the client's spatial needs.* People with schizophrenia have been found to have a large personal distance and often react with flight if too closely approached, even by eye contact. In responding to their spatial needs, the social worker might sit side-by-side rather than across from them, minimizing eye contact, thereby providing greater distance. An aging client, because of declining sensory perception, or a physically challenged client, might hunger for physical nearness and the worker could respond by moving closer, touching, etc. By responding differently to clients' differing spatial needs, help is more effective.

- *Arranging professional space.* Spatial arrangement of a worker's office provides significant clues to clients and affects their comfort and interaction (Seabury 1978). Appropriate posters and plants convey welcome and receptiveness. Personal mementos such as pictures of one's children or pet conveys a willingness to be personal and involved. In working with a female adolescent group, Gitterman assumed that chairs arranged in a circle would create an intimate atmosphere and facilitate interaction. The adolescents, however, experienced self-consciousness about their hands and their miniskirts. The small circle demanded too much physical and emotional intimacy with an unknown professional.

- *Arranging agency space.* In a family agency waiting room, a social work student noticed the lack of toys or reading matter for children and organized an effort to add inexpensive ones. In a public welfare setting, another student asked staff to contribute magazines, children's toys and books, and plants to make the waiting room more attractive and welcoming. Sensitivity to arrangements of physical space reflects staff interest and caring.

- *Coordinating spatial access and use.* In families where many members share a limited amount of space, stress can result from the interpersonal coordination required to manage restricted space. Sharing a television, a closet, or a dresser places a strain on civility. Helping a family develop a schedule for morning use of a bathroom, for evening use of a television, or for planning meals, may significantly mitigate interpersonal tensions and facilitate mutual support and assistance. Sometimes a worker-initiated discussion about privacy and clearer spatial agreements is sufficient. In other cases, the worker

Table 5.3	Persuasive and Adversarial Skills

- create organizational tension
- climb the organizational hierarchy
- assert client entitlement
- argue on behalf of client
- imply further action
- refuse compliance
- organize protests

may suggest a simple environmental prop such as a lock on a bedroom, a room divider, or a screen. Living space is an important area for professional attention and intervention.

- *Encouraging and teaching clients to use the built and natural environment.* The physical environment can be overwhelming and threatening. Deinstitutionalized mental patients and developmentally challenged clients frequently lack basic skills needed for moving through and using the built environment. Some residents of inner cities are fearful of leaving their neighborhood. The worker can provide camping experiences, hikes, trips to the zoo, parks, seashore, and countryside. These refresh the spirit and renew energies as do visits to libraries, museums, and free concerts. They bring relief from urban and rural isolation as well as the stress of overcrowded living.

- *Using animals to provide companionship and unthreatening relationships.* Pets meet people's unmet needs for companionship (Cohen 1989; Hoffman 1991; Netting, Wilson, and New 1987). Animals are also used for specific therapeutic purposes, e.g., rebuilding trust in abused children (Germain 1991a:82; Mallon 1994). Pets provide people certain control over their environment. A pet provides its human companion an opportunity to be nurturing and responsible.

Practice Illustrations

Organizational Environment

In work on dysfunctional exchanges between client and service system, social workers rely on the mediating method and its collaborative skills of interceding, bargaining, and persuading. The effectiveness of these skills depends, in part, on familiarity with the client's situation, careful assessment of the organizational components in the problem, and knowledge of organizational properties and operations.

In the following illustration, a nursing home group is meeting with the social worker and the members are discussing their concerns about the food:

Mrs. Schwartz said she thought we should spend time talking about all the things that go wrong during meals. Mr. Ball agreed, saying that the food is

Table 5.4	Skills of Influencing the Physical Environment

- respect client's spatial needs
- arrange professional space
- arrange agency (department) space
- coordinate spatial access and usage
- encourage and teach clients to use the natural and built environment
- use animals to provide companionship, assistance and non-threatening relationships

lousy and the service is lousy. If he didn't have to eat to survive, he would-n't even bother going to meals. Several other members nodded. I asked the residents to say specifically what was bad about the food and service.

Mrs. Schwartz said the napkins either arrive wet on the trays or they're given out at the very end of the meal, which defeats the purpose. I said I could understand how annoying this is. Mr. Silverman added that silverware is often missing from the trays. By the time the missing pieces are brought, the food is cold. He sighed, "For all they care, we can eat with our hands." Mrs. Schwartz commented that it would be logical for the kitchen to send up extra silver, so the aides could replace the missing pieces right away. Mr. Phelps added they often get different food from what they ordered. Mrs. Schwartz confirmed this, saying she doesn't know why they put things on the menu if they have no intention of giv-ing them to the residents. They pretend to give you a choice, but in the end, they give you whatever they damn please. I acknowledged their frus-tration and asked when these substitutions occur. Mrs. Schwartz said it usually happens with things like dessert - you order ice cream and get Jell-O . . .

I said, "So, you have three specific complaints: napkins that are either wet or not given out until the meal is almost over; missing silverware; and the substitution of items that you've selected from the menu. I wonder if you have ideas about what we might do about these problems?" Mrs. Liebner asked, "Who could we speak to?" Mrs. Schwartz responded, "We could meet with Miss Jackson [the kitchen supervisor]." I asked the oth-ers what they thought. Mr. Goldstein said "Talking to the supervisor won't help." Mr. Lazar agreed, "No one will listen to us anyway, so why bother." I sensed their hopelessness but suggested it was worth a try and I would like to help them improve the situation. This led to a discussion of the advantages and disadvantages of my doing it or of a member's inviting the supervisor to a meeting. We decided that a positive response was more likely if I extended the invitation. We reviewed what I would say to her.

I then asked them how we should present their concerns to the super-visor comes. Mr. Silverman suggested we make a list and read off the items. This was agreed on, and I asked who would begin the meeting and read the list. Mr. Goldstein said that as the group leader, I should. I responded that I could, but I felt it was important for the supervisor to hear directly from them about their experiences. Mrs. Schwartz volunteered to start the meeting off. We role-played what she would say. Mr. Silverman volunteered to offer specific examples of his own experiences. Others volunteered to share theirs. We then considered possible responses and how to handle them.

Before she approaches the supervisor with the group's request for a meeting, the social worker prepared herself for the encounter. She put herself into Miss Jackson's shoes, and imagined the likely impact of still another pressure on a busy, harassed staff member, and her possible responses. She considered how best to present the request without stimulating resentment against the residents and with a view of engaging Miss Jackson in collaborative problem-solving.

I said, "The group members have been discussing their dietary problems, and they feel it will be very helpful to have your input, so they have asked me to invite you to our next meeting." She said she didn't know if she could make it. I responded that I knew she was very busy. She explained she is responsible for several floors, and it's hard to find time for everything. I acknowledged it was, but added that the group members really feel she can be helpful to them, especially since their concerns are quite specific. She asked me what their complaints are, and I mentioned several. She smiled and shook her head. I said, "I imagine you're really tired of hearing complaints, especially when you're working so hard." She responded, "You're not kidding." There was a pause, and she asked me what time the meeting would be. I told her, and she said she would come. I expressed my appreciation.

In mediating, the worker conveyed her understanding of the supervisor's perspective and commiserated with her difficulties. At the same time, she persisted in stating the clients' need for Miss Jackson's assistance and clarified their concerns. In such efforts, the worker must be willing to risk tension and even conflict while persevering. In this instance, perseverance succeeded, and Miss Jackson agreed to come.

Miss Jackson entered the meeting. As we agreed, I began by stating the general purpose of the meeting, and suggested Mrs. Schwartz describe the first concern. Mrs. Schwartz began by asking who was responsible for setting the tables. Miss Jackson said she usually oversees the preparation of the dining room. Mrs. Schwartz explained the problem with the napkins. Miss Jackson explained that staff is sometimes rushed and water spills on the napkins. She assured the group she will try to correct the problem. Group members said they would appreciate it. There was a pause, and I asked if anyone else wanted to say something about this particular problem? This was a pre-arranged cue for Mr. Silverman to ask about the pieces of silverware missing from the trays. Miss Jackson replied that she knew this was a problem and that she would have two extra sets of silverware sent up. I asked the members if they felt this was a good solution. They all agreed. Mr. Phelps said he would like to know why he gets Jell-O every day when he hates it and orders other desserts. Ms. Jackson asked him if he had dental problems. He said no. She explained that when a dessert on the menu has to be changed at the last minute, they substitute apple sauce or Jell-O. Mr. Phelps said he prefers applesauce. Ms. Jackson made a note of his request. I asked why substitutions have to be made. She explained that when menus are made up, the department assumes a certain item will be on hand. When it isn't, or they run out of a popular dish, substitutions are made. Mrs. Schwartz said she could see how these become problems. After discussing how residents could be given some choice, the meeting ended with Miss Jackson's agreement to return in a month for a review of the results.

The changes were immediately implemented and institutionalized. Members felt a sense of accomplishment, and they were now more willing to work on other environmental tasks.

In this instance, the transactions between the service system and its residents had unintentionally become distorted. The residents, fearful of asserting themselves to the appropriate authorities, had continuously but ineffectively complained to the dietary aides. This only increased their sense of powerlessness. Meanwhile, the kitchen supervisor was vaguely aware of inefficiencies, but since she already felt overburdened and no one approached her directly, she did not address these problems. After mobilizing the group's interest in taking action, the worker interceded by persistently requesting the supervisor's meeting with the residents. Had the supervisor been less willing to come, or had she or the group been antagonistic, other skills would have been brought into play. Here, the worker used the least amount of pressure needed to bring about the desired outcome. From the outset, she correctly assumed goal consensus that required direct, effective exchanges.

In mediating, a critical area to assess is how much clients can do for themselves to increase their sense of competence and self-direction. For example, Sal, a 16 year old, and his 11-year-old brother Paul, were placed in a residential treatment center before being placed with foster parents six months ago. Sal had lived until age ten with his natural mother and her husband, both heroin addicts. Five years ago, because of severe neglect, the child welfare agency placed him in a foster home where he and the other children were subjected to extensive physical and sexual abuse by both foster parents. Sal was removed to a residential treatment center, and six months ago, he was placed with other foster parents.

The supervising foster care agency decided that Sal and his brother should visit with their mother in her social worker's office. The mother has no permanent home, but stays on and off with a current lover, Jerry, who had once beaten Sal for refusing to call him *Dad*. Jerry also frequently attends the sessions with the mother's social worker, Mr. Briggs. At their last visit to Mr. Briggs's office, while they waited for their mother's late arrival, the boys were bored and acted up. Mr. Briggs threatened to send them "back to the residential treatment center." According to the foster parents, when the boys returned home that evening, they were pale and shaken, and Sal vomited. When I spoke to Sal, he exclaimed, "I am never going to see either my mother or Mr. Briggs again, because I don't need people like this. I finally live in a normal home and I intend to keep things that way." Sal asked the worker to intervene for him. However, she thought that he was capable of fulfilling this task by himself with her assistance.

SAL: Did you call Mr. Briggs?

WORKER: Remember, Sal, what we talked about before? You have the ability to call Mr. Briggs yourself. I want to help you make this call, so let's figure out what you want to say to him.

SAL: I will not go to see my mother tomorrow! My brother wants to go, but I can't go with him any more. He has to go alone and that's too bad. But I am not going!

WORKER: Tell me in more detail what you would like to say to Mr. Briggs about why you don't want to go.

SAL: I hate him. I wish he was dead. I can't believe a grown-up can behave like that—a man with schooling and a social worker, besides. He's a jerk. Because I didn't behave in his office, he actually threatened to put me in placement! Can you believe that?

WORKER: I understand your anger and hurt, Sal. Let's think about what you want to say to him so he can hear your complaints.

SAL: I'm going to say I hate him and I'm not going to see him or my mother ever again.

WORKER: Besides wanting to tell him how angry you are because he threatened you with placement, are there other things about the meetings you don't like?

SAL: I can't stand it that Jerry is there. I want to be alone with my mother. He doesn't belong to our family. And I don't want to see Mr. Briggs there either. And I also can't stand my mother being always high and always telling me that "your friends in the Bronx are always asking for you." Especially since they haven't seen me for years and years.

WORKER: I think it is very important that you tell Mr. Briggs all the things bothering you—not that you hate him, but the specific things which you hate. He needs to know exactly how you are feeling and reacting. You must tell him how deeply his threat affected you.

SAL: Mr. Briggs should really call and say he is sorry. That would be the right thing to do.

WORKER: You already know that grown-ups don't always do the right thing and are not always aware when they do things wrong. You're right—it should be different.

SAL: I hate his guts! That's what I want to tell him.

WORKER: I understand that, Sal, but do you remember how, not very long ago, you stood up against your former foster father in court? You told him in front of everybody how you felt about him and all that he had done to you. Do you remember how the judge came up to you afterwards and told you that she had never before seen so young a man do so well in court?

SAL: (After a long pause) Y-e-a- I did tell him what I thought of him in front of the whole courtroom full of people.

WORKER: You did. And you were very brave to tell the whole story, the total truth. I would like you to be brave again and continue being brave.

SAL: You're right. I can call Mr. Briggs. I'll tell him what my reactions are to everything that's been going on.

Sal called Mr. Briggs from the worker's office and told him everything he felt about his visits to the office. He added that because he was so upset, he would discontinue future visits. Mr. Briggs apologized for his threat and informed the worker, "I can hear that Sal is improving. And he does have the right to decide for himself. I will tell his mother that he will only consider seeing her if she is by herself and is not high."

The worker encouraged Sal to stand up for himself and to be self-directing. Supported by her presence and in her office, he ably confronted his mother's social worker. With his worker's support and demand, Sal demonstrated competence and self-direction. The worker's demand was a statement of confidence in his competence.

When a disparity in power exists between client and service system, the social worker must assume an active and directive role. In helping young children and clients with impaired cognitive, emotional and social functioning, the worker's active presence in the mediation process is crucial.

For example, Mrs. Simpson, a "tired" teacher in an elementary school, acted out her frustration by scapegoating 9-year-old Jill. She often singled out Jill in front of the class or wrote her name on the blackboard for mis-behavior or unfinished work. Jill worked hard to fulfill Mrs. Simpson's expectations of her, but with fussiness, interruption, and other inappropri-ate behaviors. The school social worker's helping efforts were sabotaged by Mrs. Simpson's negative reinforcement of Jill's behavior. One afternoon, Mrs. Simpson drew the worker into her inner office to begin yet another tirade against Jill.

"That kid is driving me crazy . . . she draws attention to herself in the most inappropriate ways, constantly bothers people, and doesn't do her work. . . . The nice kids in the class will not give her the time of day." (Since little progress was being made, I decided to focus Mrs. Simpson on a search for positive attributes—to try to dramatically change their ways of interacting.) After listening and empathizing with Mrs. Simpson's frustrations, I suggested the only way we can change Jill's behavior is to identify and focus on some of her strengths. "Well, she is bright," Mrs. Simpson responded, "does good atlas work and does a good job explaining things in Friday class discussions." I supported Mrs. Simpson's assessment, noting I had seen similar qualities, and also com-mented on Jill's creative imagination. I asked, "Can you think of any ways that we can use and channel Jill's abilities in imagination and theatrics (the same attributes that repeatedly get her into trouble)?" She was will-ing to try, but wanted to know, "Meanwhile, what are we going to do about her behavior?" I replied, "How about if the three of us get together and talk about your frustrations with her in light of her special abilities and things Jill has to offer?" Mrs. Simpson agreed, and I prepared both her and Jill for our three-way meeting.

Mrs. Simpson began the meeting by berating Jill for her behavior and waving a note from a volunteer art appreciation teacher about Jill's rudeness. She also emphasized her lack of cooperation on a class outing. Jill was quiet, sad, and despondent. (I began to feel that still another of my efforts was being sabotaged. But I was determined to focus on Jill's many assets.) I tried again. "You know, Jill, the other day Mrs. Simpson was telling me about some of the things she thinks are very special about you. Mrs. Simpson, I would appreciate your telling Jill what you told me." As Mrs. Simpson began, she opened herself up more, telling Jill she was a talented girl and highlighted her special qualities. She also told Jill about her frustration when Jill doesn't follow rules, how it disrupts the class and upsets her. Jill listened, and said she would try to behave better, but she doesn't like Mrs. Simpson's singling her out and yelling at her. After discussion, I suggested they might try a private signal between them when Mrs. Simpson thinks Jill is going too far—it would be their secret signal. They agreed. I also asked Mrs. Simpson if she could credit Jill more, in front of teachers and students. She agreed to try. We also decided to meet in a week to evaluate the results.

During the week, Jill represented her class in the all-school assembly. She talked about Martin Luther King, Jr., and was outstanding. Mrs. Simpson praised Jill on her articulate, informative presentation. She also received praise from classmates and the principal. Positive reinforcement increased Jill's motivation to cooperate. The following week Mrs. Simpson enthusiastically informed me of Jill's cooperation on a class project. For the project, Jill called various companies and obtained information for the class. Jill proudly showed me the mass of information she had received in the mail. She read and explained the information to the class. Jill asked Mrs. Simpson if she would send her mother a "happy note," like she sends to other kids when they have a good week. Mrs. Simpson was obviously embarrassed since she had not done this for Jill, and she readily agreed to send her mom two notes—for the last two weeks. When I saw Mrs. Simpson later, I thanked her for her efforts and praised her ingenuity. She beamed and said it was all worth it to have a week like this!

The social worker's determination to improve the fit between student and teacher was contingent on her ability to build on the strengths of both. Each needed to feel better about herself in order to feel better about the other. Jill was particularly vulnerable to scapegoating, so change had to be initiated by the more powerful teacher. While each party contributed to and had a stake in the issue, the teacher had the power to reward and punish. The worker's mediating changed the degree of reciprocity to a more favorable balance for Jill.

The worker often has to intervene on behalf of clients, guided by their involvement if possible and by the ethical principle of informed consent.

Karen, age 32, had been given alcohol by her alcoholic mother. Karen was also sexually abused by her mother's boyfriend when she was 11 years old. She stopped drinking approximately six years ago, attends AA meetings regularly, and has seen a family agency social worker for a year, trying to "get her life together." Recently, Karen had been having severe digestive distress and menstrual problems. She consistently resisted the worker's suggested medical referral: "they're all alike, those gentleman doctors." The worker referred her to a women's health service. Ulcer medication and vitamins to reduce heavy menstrual flow was prescribed. The physician also strongly recommended dilation and curettage (D and C). Karen refused to consider D and C, emphasizing that she wasn't

"going to lie down in front of a doctor and a bunch of medical students
and open my legs."

The social worker called the physician who confirmed that medical students would observe the surgery. The worker empathized with Karen's
aversion to the lack of privacy, given her history of sexual abuse, and offered
to intervene with the hospital. Karen welcomed the worker's offer:

I called the hospital's Obstetrics/Gynecology department, introduced
myself as a social worker from Family Services calling on behalf of a
client, and asked to speak to the medical director of the department. He
was unavailable and I left my phone number. A week later, I called again,
spoke to the same receptionist and left the same message. After three
days, I called again and asked to speak with a female gynecologist. That
afternoon Dr. Park returned my call. After introducing myself, I
explained Karen's background and situation, and her aversion to undergoing surgery with medical students observing. I also mentioned that
Karen would only respond to a female gynecologist. Dr. Park suggested
I send a letter to the medical director. I expressed my concern that the
letter would receive a response similar to my phone calls, and inquired
whether I could send the letter to her. She agreed to follow up my
request. I wrote the letter with a return permission form for Karen to
have a private operation with a female gynecologist, no students present.
Approximately a week later the signed permission was returned to me
with instructions for next steps.

Powerless and vulnerable clients often need workers to do "with" and "for"
them to obtain essential services. *Doing for* the client is opportune when
conflict exists between client and organization, particularly when the
client's presence may exacerbate or increase the potential for negative outcomes. Under these conditions, it is more productive for the worker to
mediate on the client's behalf.

Mrs. Johnson, a homeless client living with her 2 year old daughter in a
suburban welfare motel, had no food. She asked the social worker in a child
abuse prevention program to drive her to the district office for a required
referral card from her caseworker. The social worker called for Mrs.
Johnson and her daughter, stopped for the referral card, and drove to the
pantry. On the way Mrs. Johnson explained the procedure: the client turns
in the referral card and is assigned a number; on a first visit, the client must
see the pantry minister for a brief intake and counseling session; when the

number is called, the client must show an identity card; the amount of food needed is determined; the client returns to the waiting room until her number is again called; the client signs for food and waits in the hall until the bags are brought out.

Mrs. Johnson and I waited two hours until her number was called. I was sitting nearby and could see her engaged in heated discussion with Mrs. Folk, the coordinator. Mrs. Johnson came out and said she was refused food, and went out into the hall. I went out after her. She said the coordinator was a nasty woman who had previously banned her from the pantry. I asked how come and she said, "I was with a man who got mean and swore at Mrs. Folk." Mrs. Johnson felt that Mrs. Folk is taking it out on her even though she was not directly involved in the incident.

I suggested we figure out how to obtain some food, for it would be a shame to leave after such a long wait. She said usually a priest is around. We finally found him. Mrs. Johnson immediately explained that Mrs. Folk had banned her, even though she "did nothing wrong." The priest explained to us that Mrs. Folk was in charge and that he couldn't intervene. He volunteered to speak to her and suggested we return next week. I explained that Mrs. Johnson didn't have any food and inquired whether something could be done today. He suggested we talk to Mrs. Folk again, and walked away. I asked if she wanted to talk to Mrs. Folk again. She felt it would be no use, she won't change her mind, "I tried to apologize, but she didn't care!" I wondered if it would help if I try to talk to her? Mrs. Johnson didn't think it would make any difference, but agreed to my making the effort. I asked if we should go in together and she responded, "No way—I'm not going back in there with that bitch."

I returned to the waiting room. Mrs. Folk was seated behind a desk. I introduced myself and hunkered down in front of the desk so we would be at eye level (there were no chairs). I said, "I know you are very busy, but would you have a few minutes to discuss Mrs. Johnson's problem?" She exclaimed, "She's banned. I told her she's banned. I banned her three months ago." I explained that I really didn't know what happened. She reported that Mrs. Johnson came in three months ago with Mr. Brown. They had cards for a Mr. Smith which they had stolen from somewhere. When she informed them that Mr. Smith had just picked up his food, that he was right here, they started cursing her. I inquired whether both of them behaved this way. She replied that Mrs. Johnson was as much involved as he was: "Believe me, she was really nasty to me. And I take a lot. Believe me, it's only happened two or three times that I've had to ban someone. They were really violent." I said it sounds like they gave her a rough time and she has a big job. She replied, "Yes. It really is. For no appreciation." I asked if there was some way she might make an exception, because Mrs. Johnson and her daughter had nothing whatsoever to eat. She repeated, "But she really was nasty. And structure is important here. If I let her get away with it, there will be chaos." I responded, "I agree with you about how important structure and rules are. And I understand your concern about losing authority if you change your mind. But is there some sort of possible compromise we can come to . . . some way which will keep your authority intact and allow Mrs. Johnson some food?"

Mrs. Folk asked if Mrs. Johnson is my client. "Yes. This is the first time she has asked for my help. And even though it is a very small step, I think if we work this out, she'll start using me more for things going on in her life." Mrs. Folk exclaimed, "Do you know why she asked you? She knew she was banned. I told her caseworker that too. She's just using you!" I replied, "You may be right. But if you can think of a way out of this problem, I'd really appreciate it." She said, taking out Mrs. Johnson's card, "Look at what I have written here. You see. I'll tell you, this has happened only two or three times." I tried once again, "I can see you feel strongly about this. But I would really appreciate if you could find a way to give her some food—nobody should have to go hungry, particularly a two-year-old child." Mrs. Folk threw up her hands and replied, "I'm not going to do this for her. I don't care about her. I'm doing this for you because I see how much you care. She can get food here, but only if you come with her. Alone, she is still banned." I thanked her and said that I thought her decision was a fair one. Her last words were, "Remember— only if she's with you!"

Mrs. Folk and Mrs. Johnson saw themselves as adversaries. They both felt humiliated and angry. The worker could do little to remedy the situation. She realized that Mrs. Folk needed some appreciation for her work on behalf of homeless people. She accepted Mrs. Folk's perceptions of reality (i.e., the need for authority and structure), and Mrs. Johnson's need for food. The worker remained calm, used various arguments, and persisted. Since her relationship with Mrs. Johnson was tenuous, she did not press her to examine her part in the problem, nor to participate in the negotiation. The worker sought to get her foot in the door. And with skill and determination, she succeeded.

In exchanges with organizational personnel, the worker's knowledge of relevant laws, policies, research findings, technical procedures, and professional jargon within the field of practice is a critical source of influence (Gitterman and Miller 1989).

Case management is a rapidly growing system of community-based care for chronically mentally and physically challenged people.[2] Those suffering profound long-term or permanent mental or physical disorders often encounter difficulties in finding their way through the complex of formal services and programs. They may be unable to deal with difficult eligibility requirements and restrictive policies. Coordinating services and linking vulnerable people to entitlements and needed services such as Social Security, Supplemental Security Income (ssi), public assistance, and health care are essential. Monitoring entails regular contacts with service providers and clients to ensure that appropriate and effective services are provided in a timely way (Rothman 1994; Rubin 1987).

Mark, 42 years old, had been diagnosed with multiple sclerosis (ms) ten years ago. A family agency with a case management service assigned a worker to assess his need for homemaker services.

On the first home visit, Mark narrates that before the ms he was happily married to his high school sweetheart, adored his two children, and had a responsible and financially rewarding job. Suddenly, his life was shattered. He lost his job; and last year, his wife and children. Currently, he is wheelchair- and home-bound, and lives with his elderly mother who does the cooking. Since last year he has become incontinent. He freely describes the progression of his disease and the consequent losses. He talks movingly about his loneliness and sadness.

At Mark's invitation his sister, Jackie, entered the increasingly desperate situation. She and her teenage children are major resources in Mark's care. She told of her unsuccessful efforts to obtain a Medicaid card so that she could obtain three shifts of homemaker services for Mark. "I have a family. We all help out, but my children are in school and my husband and I both work. My mother can't do too much anymore." When I returned to the agency, I persuaded the supervisor to provide Mark with at least one shift of homecare prior to his receiving Medicaid. The agency agreed to wait to be reimbursed.

As I helped Mark follow Medicaid eligibility procedures and submit the paper work, he told of the intense pain of being abandoned by his wife. While we awaited a response from Medicaid (his Medicaid worker left on vacation, then his papers were transferred to a new department and worker), we agree to work on his loneliness and isolation. His main objective is to get out of the apartment to be with people. Because of his reluctance to make telephone calls, I called Paratransit to help Mark gain transportation, and the MS Society to learn about available programs. I discovered a local ymca with a program for the disabled that will meet Mark's interest in swimming. I connected him to a monthly conference-call book club and a bi-weekly conference-call game group sponsored by a community agency. From these phone contacts, Mark found new friends who share his loneliness and courage.

After several months, my agency began to pressure me about Medicaid reimbursement, threatening to discontinue homecare. I won an additional month. Jackie, Mark, and I developed a strategy to expedite Medicaid. Jackie wrote a letter to her congressman, describing the many delays and consequences for her brother. The Paratransit card arrived, and I connected Mark to a loosely organized social group for the physically disabled that meets three times a week. He loves his new friends and the activities.

Meanwhile, Mark received his Medicaid card. A Medicaid worker and public health nurse visited him to determine how many shifts of aides he requires. In a few weeks, he was granted three shifts.

With the worker's assistance, Mark has gone from being completely dependent and isolated to having homecare assistance, participating in a social group, conference-call groups, swimming, and a level of privacy appropriate for his age.

Occasionally the social worker needs to consider advocacy and the use of pressure, coercion, and appeals to third party intervention. The advocacy method calls for data gathering, assessment, and planning to minimize the risk of failure.

The following example illustrates a transition from mediating to advocacy. It also illustrates missteps along the way caused by the worker's neglecting to secure necessary information.

Mrs. Thomas, a 25-year-old African-American with two children, came to a community service agency requesting help in obtaining ssi benefits for her daughter, who suffers from cerebral palsy. She explained that her daughter's claim was approved, but no checks arrived. When she went back to the local Social Security office, she received an emergency grant of $200. Still no checks came. When she went back again, she was told she was not eligible. Since then, she has moved to another district but continued her efforts through the local Social Security office in the new neighborhood, again to no avail.

Mrs. Thomas and I agreed to work together: she will bring in all her documents, and I will call the Social Security office. When she returned with the documents, we went over them. Then I telephoned the local office, identified myself, and described the problem. The staff person responded that Social Security doesn't handle that kind of problem and we should try welfare. I suspected he was wrong, and I challenged his assertion. He said, "Listen, we can't help you." I asked to speak to a supervisor. She took the phone and again I described the problem. I fared even worse with the supervisor, who said that cerebral palsy does not qualify Mrs. Thomas's daughter for benefits. I said, "Are you sure?" The supervisor responded with a firm *yes*. I thanked her and hung up.

The worker made a serious error by contacting the organization before learning Social Security policies and structures. Fortunately, the social worker and Mrs. Thomas were undaunted, and they set about learning the rules regarding disability claims. The worker obtained the ssi manual and together they studied its contents. Several sections seemed to establish Mrs. Thomas's eligibility, so they decided to retrace Mrs. T's earlier attempts. The worker called the first Social Security office.

I related the problem. The staff person listened without much interest and referred me to the current office. Playing a hunch, I said I understood records of initial claims were held in the original office. He then referred me to the records representative, Mr. Ross, who turned out to be responsive. He asked for documentation, and I said that Mrs. Thomas had received an emergency grant from that office, so her claim must have been accepted. Mr. Ross agreed to look into the matter. He called back and said the application had been initially accepted and processed. He believes a large retroactive sum is due, and outlined the steps to be taken. I thanked him for his help.

I was elated and called Mrs. Thomas to tell her the good news. We talked about remaining steps, and she felt she could take them alone. I encouraged her to do so.

One month later, however, Mrs. Thomas advised the worker that she still had not received a check, and she asked the worker's help. They discussed the steps she had gone through and agreed that the worker would again telephone the first Social Security office.

Mr. Ross was not in and I spoke to another person. I informed him of the situation and asked him to find out what had happened. After a few minutes he returned, saying Mrs. Thomas's grant had not been processed because she first had to go to the welfare department and notify them of the large retroactive benefits she would receive, which she would be obliged to turn over to welfare (Mrs. Thomas had been receiving welfare for her daughter in the interim). I asked if this was agency policy, because the ssi manual did not mention formal collaboration between the two organizations. The staff person insisted it was policy, and Mrs. Thomas could not receive checks until she fulfilled the requirement. I asked him to mail me a copy of the policy and he refused to do so. I then asked to speak to his supervisor, who confirmed the policy and who also refused to forward or even to read the policy to me over the phone.

Up to this point, the worker had depended on the mediating skills of requesting, pleading, and persisting with staff members. He also used negotiating skills to the extent that the situation allowed. Still the organization withheld the daughter's entitlements. The Social Security office denied Mrs. T's rights by not informing her of the basis on which benefits were denied. After conferring with Mrs. Thomas, the worker decided that he must go beyond mediating to advocacy, utilizing adversarial skills of pressure and coercion. He began with pressure, that is, with threats and challenges.

After searching, I found a lawyer whose expertise was in welfare and Social Security legislation. He explained to me that the agency has no right to withhold payments from clients because of informal agreements with the department of welfare. The practice is clearly illegal. He offered to intervene, and I said I would first discuss the matter with Mrs. Thomas and get back to him, if necessary. I expressed our appreciation.

Mrs. Thomas decided that she and the worker should make one more effort before turning the matter over to a lawyer. She preferred to avoid legal escalation, fearing reprisals. So they prepared for another telephone contact, selecting and rehearsing the worker's approach.

I asked to speak with the supervisor [at the second office] and brought him up to date on our previous contacts with the office. I said Mrs. Thomas and my agency had retained a lawyer who informed us that the daughter is the legal recipient of the disability allowance and welfare has no claim to the retroactive payment. I informed him that we are presently prepared to seek a fair hearing, and the lawyer may wish to move to class action. I continued that this was our final effort to handle the matter ourselves, before seeking legal redress. The supervisor asked for half an hour, to look into the matter. When he called back, he apologized for the misunderstanding and announced that the claim had been processed. I asked for specific commitment, and he said that Mrs. Thomas would receive her first check and all retroactive benefits within three weeks. She did, indeed.

As frequently happens, the bureaucratic organization's formal policy is more responsive to client need than are its actual practices. What seemed to be the real lever of change in Mrs. Thomas's situation was the threat of legal challenge. It is often the case that individual members of organizations are responsive to the threat of crisis, making it unnecessary to go further. The worker's decision to move beyond collaborative strategies of interceding, persuading and placating to the adversarial strategies of pressure, challenge, and threat was effective in securing his client's entitlement. His entrance into the situation, especially as he gained knowledge and competence in the two roles, lent weight to the cause of a vulnerable client. The unfavorable balance of power was corrected in some measure. In receiving her entitlement, Mrs. Thomas experienced satisfaction in taking effective action on her own behalf.

When persuasion and negotiation are ineffective, the social worker needs to involve the client in considering adversarial strategies of pressure, challenge, and threat. In turning to the adversarial method, worker and client must understand that risks increase and consider their respective vulnerabilities.

In dealing with organizational obstacles, the problems are frequently overwhelming, the tasks complex, and the process frustrating. The client may experience despair and a sense of futility. Social workers must provide realistic support, and encouragement, and invite clients to express doubts, hesitations, fears, or resentments. In pursuing environmental objectives, social workers must not forget the person in the process. Whatever the method, workers must continuously take possible consequences for clients into account.

The Social Network. To help people suffering from loneliness and emotional isolation, practitioners work toward mobilizing or strengthening real-life ties between client and significant others, reestablishing old linkages, or helping the client find and develop new connections.[3] The worker considers various potential network units for professional interventions. For example, the worker may help a client to reach out to one significant other inside the current social network, or help a significant other to reach out to the client.

Maria, an 18-year-old single Hispanic Catholic foster child, was voluntarily admitted to a psychiatric hospital by her psychiatrist after one of a series of suicide attempts over two years left her with razor cuts on her arms and abdomen. Maria was abandoned by her mother at birth; for several years she and her sister lived with the maternal grandmother until both were placed in foster care. As a teenager, Maria ran away from several foster homes. At 16 she was sent to a residential treatment center where she made her first suicide attempt.

In two meetings with Maria, the social worker ascertained that she yearned for family and roots, having lost contact with her older sister, who had enrolled in the state university. She felt isolated, unwanted, without a sense of place. She found it increasingly difficult to interact with people. The first aim was to help Maria reestablish contact with her sister.

One day, Maria approached the social worker in the hospital corridor, on the verge of crying. Sensing her need, the social worker suggested they sit on the couch and talk.

WORKER: You look so sad right now, what's bothering you?

MARIA: (looking down) I miss my sister (tears falling down her cheeks).

WORKER: Uh huh.

MARIA: I miss her for so long. I haven't seen her since she went to college.

WORKER: And it's far away.

MARIA: Yes. We both have no money. I get $60 from the agency each month, but that's not much. So I only see her on Christmas and holidays. I wish it were the holidays.

WORKER: I sense you feel a special need for her right now.

MARIA: Yes (cries). We're close, I can talk to her, though she doesn't know what I've done or where I am. I don't even have money to call her.

WORKER: It's very lonely not to be in contact with someone you need.

MARIA: Yes. But there's no way to change it, no way (voice shaking), I'll just have to wait until Christmas.

WORKER: Well, I think there is a way to talk to her. We could go into the staff office and call her right now, if you want.

MARIA: (brightens) Could we do that?

WORKER: Sure. And perhaps you could invite your sister to visit you here. Maybe the hospital might help with the travel expenses.

MARIA: I doubt she can come. I'm sure she's busy with schoolwork and friends.

WORKER: Let's try, ok?

MARIA: I'd love to talk to her now, but how would I explain being here? I'm not sure she'll want to visit me here.

Maria discussed her worries with the worker and together they developed a plan for Maria to explain her hospitalization to her sister.

The worker successfully connected the client to the most valued member of her limited social network. Her sister is the only positive source of continuity in her life, and the reunion generated significant breakthroughs in her treatment. She engaged in counseling, followed prescribed protocols, and invested herself in developing new relationships on the ward.

Extended kin networks can also maintain effective ties, even across geographical distances. For example, Mrs. Bates is an 80-year-old white Protestant widow living alone in an apartment in a suburb. Her two daughters live across the continent. The older daughter, Margaret, and her husband, Paul, hold jobs that require travel, so they visit Mrs. Bates every two months. The younger daughter can afford to visit her mother only once a year. Mrs. Bates's lawyer called the community family agency at her daughters' request to inquire about services for the elderly. The daughters were very concerned about their mother's mental health.

The assigned worker made several calls to the lawyer and to Margaret, making an appointment with her during her next trip. Margaret said that Mrs. Bates's mental condition sharply deteriorated following a hospital stay a year before, and the doctor explained that she suffers from arteriosclerosis. The daughters were extremely concerned about their mother living alone and so far away. Margaret then asked the worker to visit her mother, assess the situation, and provide whatever services were required. Cost was not an issue.

Initially, Mrs. Bates was uncertain about meeting with the social worker. However, after several home visits, she became more comfortable and admitted to depression and distress about confusion and memory loss. Transactional issues between Mrs. Bates and her kin and others were apparent. To compensate for living far away, her daughters and son-in law frequently called, trying to manage Mrs. Bates's life from a distance and to do "for" her rather than "with" her. Their suggestions and actions clashed and increased her distress, disorientation, and confusion.

The social worker focused on helping Mrs. Bates's family be more responsive to her need to retain control over her life, while at the same time supporting and encouraging their involvement. She wanted them to understand how important it was to Mrs. Bates to feel actively involved in plans for her own care:

The first intervention was to introduce myself to the family members in order to gather data and gain acceptance of my involvement in the plan of care. After two interviews with Mrs. Bates, I called members of her support network with her informed consent. With her lawyer we discussed how she could involve Mrs. Bates in some legal decisions without causing her too much confusion. Her physician informed me of the etiology of her dementia. He said her condition was apt to progress in stages, and told of his long-standing relationship with Mrs. Bates and how much he likes her. Her cook and the accountant impressed me with their genuine concern and apparent honesty. Mrs. Bates's niece and her niece's best friend both care very much for her and want to be kept abreast of developments. They were openly critical of the daughters for "allowing" their mother to live alone (despite the fact that Mrs. Bates refuses to consider an alternative). The hospital volunteer coordinator told me that every effort is made to support Mrs. Bates and help her to feel needed. The practitioner and network members agreed to stay in touch and to exchange information.

When Margaret and Paul came to visit their mother, she had a panic attack. Pressured by their need to solve everything and tie Mrs. Bates into a neat package before their return home, they overwhelmed her with proposed changes (forming a trust fund to take control of her finances, replacing her cook and accountant with people they would hire, changing her physician to a specialist in geriatrics and dementia). I met with them, acknowledged their concern and love, but suggested that less can be more. I spoke of Mrs. Bates's comfort with and confidence in the cook, accountant, and physician. It is true that her financial situation is messy—she writes several checks for the same bills and ignores overdue notices on others. But in terms of establishing priority issues, wasn't it much more serious that she still drives her own car? The cook had told me that Mrs. Bates is losing her sense of direction, is easily distracted, and once used the accelerator instead of the brake. I suggested we need to prioritize changes and begin with her driving. They agreed, and we decided that the most appropriate person to discuss driving with her was her physician. They spoke to him, and he did talk to Mrs. Bates and she agreed to use taxis instead.

A month later, the volunteer coordinator at the hospital called to say that Mrs. Bates was in the emergency room, having fallen outside her apartment. Her wrist was broken and her ankle sprained. The coordinator also called her niece who then called Margaret to say she should come at once (she had been scheduled to leave for a business trip to Europe the next day). I immediately visited the hospital, and subsequently called Margaret, the niece, and the friend to reassure them that I was in touch and that Mrs. Bates is being well-cared for in a familiar environment, and she will be discharged in a few days. I made reassuring calls over the next few days.

Mrs. Bates was shaken by the fall but was comfortable in the hospital. My concern and that of network members was to make a plan of care for her upon discharge. I believed she must be actively involved in this planning. I began by asking her what help she will need when she returns home. She agreed to live-in help, at least for a while. She wanted her cook to be that person. With Mrs. Bates's permission, I talked with the cook. She isn't available, but her young cousin is. I spoke with the cousin to satisfy myself that she had some experience in caring for people with intellectual impairment. Then I encouraged the cook and the cousin to visit Mrs. Bates in the hospital. I wanted to keep the feeling of control in Mrs. Bates's hands. She liked the cousin and informed her daughter, niece, and friend, of what SHE had arranged. While live-in help resulted in some loss of privacy, everyone was relieved when she accepted this arrangement as permanent. It had dramatic positive impact upon Mrs. Bates's daily functioning.

The worker used the coordinating method and its skills of orchestrating and brokering. Mrs. Bates's accident was also an opportunity to make rapid use of environmental resources. The social worker thus counteracted the network's tendency to overload the telephone lines with instructions to one another and to Mrs. Bates about what ought to be done "for" her. The worker demonstrated how to manage Mrs. Bates's care without taking control of her life. Hence, when Mrs. Bates expressed dissatisfaction with her young companion, Margaret and Paul took Mrs. Bates with them to interview an older woman, and let her handle the hiring as well as the firing.

Peer and friendship networks also serve as critical units for professional intervention. While they may lack the permanence of kinship networks, they do provide diverse and relatively durable support (Fisher, Goff, Nadler, and Chinsky 1988). Friends from work, religious, social, or recreational activities can offer potential ties for effective support. The social worker might help the client to assess friendship resources and potential obstacles such as embarrassment, fear of imposing, or reluctance to risk rejection.

Neighbors, since they are usually in frequent direct contact, can help with immediate and short-term tasks (Patterson et al. 1992, 1988). Because neighbor networks have a shifting membership in our mobile society, many are helpful in immediate emergencies ranging from the trivial to the catastrophic. They might lend or provide resources (a ride to the store, use of the telephone, watching the baby, and providing information about neighborhood customs and resources). Natural networks of neighbors are often found in multiple-unit dwellings. In single-room occupancy hotels—tenanted by isolated elderly, recipients of public assistance, discharged mental patients, addicts, and alcoholics—natural helpers are not uncommon. They look after the frail, manage their checks, care for them, see that they take medications, keep clinic appointments, and report to the welfare center as required. Although sometimes functioning marginally themselves, these natural helpers enable their neighbors to cope and survive (Shapiro 1970). The social worker must be careful not to undermine the influence or role of natural helpers, which could disrupt the delicate structure of informal aid.

Being emotionally attached to at least one other person promotes and protects physical and mental health (Cohen and Syme 1985). The significant other may be part of the current social field or, if unavailable, a new tie may need to be forged. For certain situations and problems, the new tie may be linked to an organization such as Big Brothers and Big Sisters, Extend-a-Family, AA, or a volunteer "friendly visitor" to homebound elderly.

Mrs. Trask, an 83-year-old widow, reported to a doctor at a community health clinic that she felt nervous, agitated, and was unable to sleep. After examination, the doctor found no health problems as the basis for her nervousness. He suggested she might like to talk to the staff social worker.

Mrs. Trask replied that she did not know how that would help but agreed to talk with him. The social worker made a home visit to her clean, well-furnished apartment. Mrs. Trask could not identify any recent precipitating events that might account for her nervousness. She said she had no one to confide in and had little to do, which left her with too much time to worry about small things that ordinarily she would not worry about, such as her declining health.

Mrs. Trask said she was the last surviving member of her family: the last of her six sisters having died two years ago. Her second husband died seven years ago and she moved here from Florida, losing touch with her friends. She has only one friend in the apartment complex, a woman thirty years younger. While they occasionally do things together, Mrs. Trask feels she can't confide in her, and she is annoyed because her friend takes financial advantage of her. Her only relatives are a nephew who lives twenty miles away but doesn't call or visit, and a niece. She said she is angry that her nephew is uncaring and added that she terminated her relationship with her niece about six years ago after an argument. Hence, her social "network" is limited to one unsatisfactory person. Her declining health and physical capacities are a source of consternation, and Mrs. Trask finds it difficult to accept her physical limitations. Her own doctor retired two years ago, and she is unable to trust her new one completely—she wonders aloud if a thirty-year-old female physician is capable of providing quality medical care (not an unusual assumption for members of Mrs. Trask's generation).

After several visits and Mrs. Trask's positive response to empathic support, the social worker concluded that Mrs. Trask was motivated both to act for herself and to be reconnected to people. She wants to end her absorption in her fears and become active. His assessment was that she is energetic, well organized, and has a sharp mind. Her cognitive style, however, is obsessive, and she usually assumes the worst about any situation. When she is busy, Mrs. Trask is less obsessive and less agitated. Similarly, her level of self-esteem rises and falls with the availability of environmental activity and contacts. When she is inactive and isolated she feels unimportant and useless.

Together, Mrs. Trask and the worker agreed to look for a productive activity that would also provide opportunities for socialization. They decided on Retired Seniors Volunteer Program (RSVP). She was interested yet hesitant for fear that she would be unable to manage a new experience and would be a burden to the program.

I continued to point out potential benefits of activity with others and to identify her real strengths. I also encouraged her to talk of her fears about what might go wrong, and empathized with what I described as the universal fear of change. I suggested there wouldn't be dire consequences if things didn't turn out well. After several weeks, she did make an appointment with RSVP and was given a list of openings. We discussed the pros and cons of each. While the decision-making was distressing, it did enhance her sense of competence. She decided she would like to work as a card-filer in the local library.

Mrs. Trask was met her first day by the library administrator, who had not been told by RSVP that she was coming and was annoyed. Mrs. Trask felt rebuffed and returned home vowing never to return. The worker felt this was probably the outcome of an exchange between an overly sensitive, anxious elder and an undersensitive, busy, anxious person. It was not Mrs. Trask's failure as a volunteer.

I wanted to help Mrs. Trask interpret the incident as a misunderstanding (rather than her obsessing about a perceived rejection). I accepted her expressions of embarrassment and anger and also gently challenged her tendency to perceive events from a self-centered position. She was then able to consider other possible explanations for what had happened. Agreeing that it might have been a misunderstanding, she called RSVP, explained what happened, and cleared up the misunderstanding. With Mrs. Trask's permission, I intervened in the environment: I called the library administrator and explained how frightened Mrs. Trask had been of trying something so new. She again expressed her annoyance, but volunteered to reassure Mrs. Trask and to clarify for her what happened.

Mrs. Trask continued her work at the library, but during weekly interviews with the worker she fretted about not being liked because she wasn't working up to the library's expectations.

Knowing she is a perfectionist who continually underestimates her abilities, I encouraged her to ask for feedback on her performance from her coworkers. She agreed, and asked that I also call to find out how the librarian feels about her work so that we could compare notes. As anticipated, the library reported that Mrs. Trask was doing exceptionally well and seemed to prefer working by herself. I mentioned my perception that she does not feel confident in her work and could use a few "strokes" now and then, as well as some rest periods just to chat with fellow workers. This two-pronged approach resulted in a better fit, and Mrs. Trask began reporting pleasurable success in her work and enjoyment in her new friends.

The social worker and Mrs. Trask then worked on improving her relationship with the younger friend in the apartment complex by heightening Mrs. Trask's awareness of what she wanted from this friend. She stopped relating to her friend as a mother nurturing a nonreciprocating child. This triggered a change in the friend's behavior, and apparently resulted in a more satisfying relationship for both. On her own, Mrs. Trask then decided to write her nephew and to tell him of her library work. In response, he telephoned to let her know he was pleased for her.

Throughout, the worker tried to help Mrs. Trask recognize her personal and environmental resources for coping with the multiple life stressors facing her. These interventions and others through the ongoing phase helped Mrs. Trask build new relationships, reestablish former ones with relatives, find new activities, and accept her increasing physical limitations with less despair. The worker writes, "We agreed that she feels more competent and powerful because she found she is once more able to act for herself."

Built World

Sensitive practitioners have often attempted to improve aspects of the physical environment. Little such work is found in agency records or textbooks, perhaps because its importance went unrecognized. It was viewed as common sense rather than professional knowledge or skill. With the advent of concepts relating the physical environment to the social environment and to the culture, the significance of the physical environment in growth and adaptation became clear, and hastened the development of practice principles.

Shelter is a basic human need. Yet deinstitutionalization, loss of employment, eviction, displacement, intolerable conditions, natural disasters, and the lack of affordable housing leaves an increasing population homeless (Holloway 1991). The fastest growing sector of homeless people is families with small children—a national disgrace that leaves people vulnerable to brutality and exploitation and with the basic human need for shelter unmet.

When people lose their dwellings, they do not grieve for their lost home alone, but also for the lost sense of community. People are embedded in their local environment and develop a sense of "physical insideness" (Rowles 1980). They know the shortcuts, sidewalk cracks, creaky steps, the elevator's idiosyncrasies. Familiarity with physical aspects of their environment is further reinforced by "social insideness"—neighbors, community helpers, store clerks and owners, familiar teachers and school officials provide a sense of *communitas* and personal identity. Physical and social "insideness" develop from living in the same place over time and a landscape of memories that are integrated into life stories (Rowles 1983). For homeless individuals and families who live in a welfare motel, public shelter, or on the street, such physical, social, and autobiographical "insideness" is ripped away.

A community agency assigned social workers to reach out to mentally impaired homeless people, who require a great deal of assistance in obtaining needed resources. Their life stressors must be worked on in small coping tasks. Appointments must be made for them; they must be prepared for, and escorted to, appointments. They must learn how to fill out forms, manage money, and take care of themselves. The social worker has to be active, persistent, and directive. Agencies have to be pursued and persuaded to extend additional time and effort, to anticipate problems and regressions and, most of all, to "hang on." The following illustrates a social worker's struggle to help a homeless man with a mental impairment find housing.

Carmine is 59 years old. His parents were Italian immigrants. As early as he can remember, his parents beat him on the head with a wooden knife handle. He frequently ran away from home only to have the police bring him back, in spite of his many bruises. At age 7, he was taken by his parents to a municipal hospital where he was diagnosed as mentally retarded. He was institutionalized and released in his late thirties. He met a woman, and married. He inherited his parents' home when they died and moved into it with his wife. Within five years, his wife left him and their two children. Since then, "everything went down the sewer." It's unclear how he lost his house, but he has been homeless for ten years, living in abandoned cars, automobile repair shops, and parks.

Carmine initially responded to the worker's outreach because of failing health. He was losing weight, not eating, just drinking coffee and smoking cigarettes. He denied abusing alcohol (and this was later confirmed). Within several days, he arrived at the agency spitting up blood. The worker accompanied him to the hospital and stayed while he was x-rayed. When she had to leave for another appointment, Carmine bolted. Henceforth, subsequent work included escorting Carmine to his various appointments and participating in the entire process.

The mutually agreed-on goal was placement in an adult group residence. This required Carmine to complete medical and psychiatric assessments. He completed the psychiatric assessment with the worker staying throughout. Carmine was thought to have been misdiagnosed as a child.

The current psychiatric diagnosis is "borderline personality with border-line intellectual functioning." Even with the worker, he is impulsive, unpredictable, self-damaging, and often inappropriately angry. He fre-quently yells at the social worker and then storms out of the office. He con-sistently reaches out to her but then pulls away. He says, "no!" to every-thing and then shows up for appointments. His judgment is poor in most areas. He offends almost everyone, so he is socially and emotionally iso-lated. From his own perspective, Carmine is dealing with a hostile envi-ronment and he responds with equal hostility. He said he had attempted suicide at least seven times. Yet, in his own way, Carmine adapted to a phys-ical and social environment with which only a few could cope. He has remarkable tenacity and survival skills.

The social worker helped Carmine with health issues and medical care first. As they developed a relationship from this work together, the social worker next helped him with entitlements. In the past, Carmine had applied for ssi, but certain forms were never filled out. A Social Security employee with whom the practitioner had worked agreed to meet with Carmine in the social worker's office (Carmine had had an upsetting expe-rience in the Social Security office a few years ago and refused to return there).

Carmine assumed his usual position in the far corner of my office, wedged between a table and file cabinets. He could see everything that went on while remaining fairly invisible. I introduced him to Bill (I had asked and received Mr. Jackson's permission to introduce him by his first name as I observed that Carmine is more comfortable and pre-dictable in informal, relaxed encounters). To my surprise (Carmine was full of them), Carmine began speaking Italian. Whether he assumed Bill was Italian, or felt more in control speaking Italian, I wasn't sure. However, I complimented Carmine on his ability to speak Italian, and explained that Bill didn't speak Italian. Carmine feigned shock (he seemed very pleased with himself). I reminded him that Bill was here to help him with ssi and it would help if he spoke English. The rest of the meeting went smoothly. Bill asked Carmine some questions, filled out some forms for him, and so on. Carmine agreed to have the first check mailed to me and subsequent ones to a bank where we will open an account for him.

The worker structured the situation, created norms of informality, talked to Carmine respectfully and mediated the exchanges. She also made a supportive demand that Carmine not waste Bill's time but get "down to business."

Before Carmine would accept more testing, he asked to visit a group residence. The worker arranged for Jackie, a social worker she knew at Century House, to show them around and to answer Carmine's questions.

On the way, Carmine was quiet and tense. I reassured him that this was only a first meeting: he doesn't have to make a decision. He is not being interviewed, and if he doesn't like the place we will visit others. He was silent but, as always, listened to every word. On arrival, Carmine announced that he isn't going in—he will sit in the car. I sensed his growing panic and resentment. Fortunately, that signal usually tips me off to MELLOW OUT! I told Carmine that I would really appreciate his just having a look at the place. He didn't have to talk, but if he chose not to come in, I would go inside and then describe to him what I saw. Carmine followed me in.

Jackie gave us a tour, and Carmine was introduced to a benign older Italian resident. They enjoyed speaking Italian, especially since we couldn't understand what they were saying. After the tour, we sat down to talk. Carmine announced that it would take him a year to make up his mind and he would get back to me with his decision. I thought this was meant to be humorous since he had no place to live, but realized it was his pattern of rejecting before being rejected. The resident and Jackie encouraged him to think about it. Carmine and I thanked them and left. He then informed me he wants to live there. He said he was quiet and cautious because he doesn't know "those" people and he didn't feel comfortable trusting them right away. I supported his stance and credited his behavior.

The practitioner avoided a potential power struggle by leaving to Carmine the decision about entering the residence. She fought against understandable personal reactions: "after all I've done for you, how can you do this to me?" She worked at involving him, supported his decision making, and respected his style and manner of coping, thereby increasing his self-esteem and self-direction. At their next meeting, they discussed Century House.

CARMINE: I've got to think about what I wanna do.

WORKER: Well, Century House is one possibility and if that's where you want to live, there are certain things we need to work on in order for you to get in. I want to make it clear to you that you don't have to go there. If it's not what you want, then we'll work on other possibilities.

CARMINE: It's better than living in the garage or on the street. I'll tell you right now, I am getting ready to run away.

WORKER: I understand your feeling impatient and frustrated, but I don't think running away is the answer.

CARMINE: I gotta have people to talk to. I can't keep living lonely like this. It's impossible.

WORKER: And so are you thinking if maybe you go to Century House, since it is a place with lots of others, you'd be able to make some friends?

CARMINE: Well, I'd be able to live a happy life—I have no life right now.

WORKER: You know you'll have to have some tests (last time I mentioned this, he exploded—I braced myself).

CARMINE: Well, I'll tell you, forget it!

WORKER: But it's the only way we can get you into Century House.

CARMINE: Forget it!

WORKER: I have to get you to understand that it's really important for you to have these tests done. Would you be willing to pick a male or female doctor and let him or her examine you?

CARMINE: Maybe. But no needles. I am afraid of needles.

WORKER: Are you afraid that they are going to use needles on you?

CARMINE: Yeah, I don't like getting pricked.

WORKER: How did you get through it before?

CARMINE: Crabby. I was real crabby.

WORKER: I don't blame you, I don't like it either. But they often need to test our blood and it's the only way. How about if I stay with you and we can be crabby together?

CARMINE: If you stay with me, then I'll stay, but if you walk away, then I'm going to leave too.

WORKER: Let's shake—we just made a deal.

Throughout this exchange, the worker balanced support and demand: support to provide the foundation for the next step; demand to move the work and take the next step. The next step was a medical examination.

The meeting with the physician was a bit tricky. I was outside speaking to Doctor Gwynn about Carmine's fear of needles when a technician entered through another door to take blood samples from Carmine. I heard him scream that he was going to slit my throat and the technician's throat before he would have a blood test. He said a few more choice words as I ran into the room. Dr. Gwynn asked the technician to come back later and I apologized to Carmine for the mixup and emphasized that I will be with him throughout the examination. He was cooperative and remained calm, just looking over to see if I were still there.

On the return trip I credited him for his cooperation. Since he was in good spirits, I decided to introduce the next hurdle, the psychiatric examination. He initially responded that he wasn't going to go to "no head shrinker." I reminded him that in order to have all the paper work done for Century House, he needs to speak to someone about his life (as I said this, it sounded quite ridiculous). I added if he wants me to go with him, I will, and I kidded him that at least there would be no needles. After some bantering, he agreed to see a "shrink" if I accompanied him.

The worker slowly helped Carmine to plug into the various systems to obtain housing. He lacked the skills and trust to negotiate environmental systems. With the worker's presence, persistence, support and demands he gained strength and confidence in his own abilities. Each success motivated further willingness to risk and trust, and to feel competent and related. The agency had had positive experiences with a young, female psychiatrist, so the worker set up an appointment for her to meet with Carmine.

When we arrived Dr. Raimes asked to speak to me alone for a few minutes. I asked Carmine if this was OK. He threatened to leave, and then said he would wait. I told him and Dr. Raimes that if he was going to leave, I would wait till the end of their meeting to talk to Dr. Raimes. Carmine replied it was ok, and we should go ahead.

Dr. Raimes wanted some background information about Carmine and what type of an assessment Century House required. She then met with Carmine, sensitively asking for his life story. He answered all questions. When the interview was completed, Dr. Raimes informed us she would write a supportive report and wished Carmine good luck with his application. As we left the office, Carmine informed me that he felt ready to open a bank account. We set up a time to complete this next coping task.

When the worker received Carmine's first social security check, they opened his savings account and figured out a weekly budget. In the worker's company, he began literacy classes at the library and sustained the task without the worker's direct assistance. He also began to participate in the agency's support group, trips, and educational seminars. Five months later, he moved into Century House and the worker spent the first day with him.

Transportation systems are features of the built world that can be overwhelming and unsafe. Private and public transportation systems are often inaccessible to people with physical, intellectual, or emotional impairments. Discharged mental patients, especially after lengthy hospitalization, frequently lack the basic skills of moving through the physical environment.

A social work student in a program serving developmentally challenged adults was assigned to work with Andrew, a 19 year old African-American. Andrew is mildly retarded. He felt socially isolated, especially after completing a school program one year ago. Andrew does not know how to travel; he cannot navigate the bus and subway systems. He wishes he could visit former classmates who live in other parts of the city. He feels he is a burden to his mother and wishes he could shop in the downtown mall or seek a job in a store stockroom.

The student felt that helping Andrew use public transportation would broaden his horizons, make him employable, and enhance his sense of mastery and competence. Andrew was elated: "If I can learn to travel, I'll be independent. I won't have to bother my mother anymore."

The student asked Andrew where he would like to travel to first. He immediately named the shopping mall, twenty minutes away by subway. At their next appointment the student suggested they map out a plan prior to taking the trip together. She had already thought through the multiple steps involved in using the subway system. They traced a map from Andrew's apartment to the subway and discussed how to pay the fare. They thought about how to look for signs and counting the stops until his destination. The student described her own first trip and worries in taking the subway.

After they reviewed the steps several times, they agreed to meet at his home and try the trip together the next day. The student met Andrew, pointed out directional signs, tried to let him take the lead, and coached him when he looked to her for advice. The ride went smoothly and Andrew was very happy when they arrived at the mall.

They reviewed the directions home before embarking on the return trip. Andrew moved cautiously through each step and grew more confident as he mastered each step. When they got back to his home, Andrew dashed up to his mother and proudly announced his accomplishment. They showed his mother their maps so she could remind him of the steps prior to his next trip to the mall.

Such work in the physical environment requires a considerable investment of time and effort on the part of the social worker. Traditional policy and agency caseloads rarely permit such investment. Hence, social workers need to alert administrators and policy-makers to the importance of the social work function in such necessary but often overlooked areas, and its implications for preventive work.

Natural World

Caring for a pet can sustain relationship capacities and a sense of purpose and achievement. Angel, age 8, was placed in residential care for emotionally challenged children. Angel had been severely abused by his father, and saw the continuous abuse of his mother and siblings. His father used sadistic means to enforce total subservience. He demanded quiet in the apartment. Angel had a sock placed in his mouth and duct tape over his lips. He was tied up for long periods of time. After Angel was forced to hold a knife to his mother while his father raped her, he "snapped" at school, breaking furniture and windows.

Angel entered court-ordered placement with minimal language, social, and learning skills. He was withdrawn and fearful of others and always looked sad. He suffered frequent nightmares about his father escaping and killing his mother and him. His mother visited every weekend and called him several times a week. She is a stable force in his life.

The worker noticed that Angel was gentle with a child care worker's dog. When she had puppies, the social worker persuaded administration and the child care worker that if Angel were willing to assume responsibility for a puppy, the center should keep one. After receiving permission, she discussed the idea with Angel. He responded with rare enthusiasm, and immediately assumed a nurturing role. He named the puppy Beauty and took wonderful care of her. If she had an "accident" in the office, Angel cleaned it up, and gently picked her up, saying "Oh, Beauty, you are too little, you just don't know." The worker drew parallels between Beauty's and Angel's experiences.

ANGEL: Oh, Beauty don't do that. I have to watch you every minute. You need me to take care of you and protect you. You are so little, you don't know. You just don't know.

WORKER: She doesn't know?

ANGEL: No. She's just a little puppy. Little puppies don't know.

WORKER: So, I shouldn't be upset with her because she is chewing on my calendar.

ANGEL: No, no. She is little. She doesn't know. She doesn't understand. AHHHH, BEAUTY. No! See, she does things but doesn't know she's not supposed to because she's so little.

WORKER: Uh-oh. She just began to chew on a report I was preparing.

ANGEL: Important?

WORKER: Yes, but I should have put it away because I am the big person and Beauty is the little puppy; she doesn't understand.

ANGEL: Yes, Beauty. I'm the big person who will protect you. No one is going to hurt you. I'm here.

WORKER: Beauty has a big person to protect and care for her. Did Angel have big people to protect and take care of him?

ANGEL: My Mom yes; my Dad no. I told you my Dad is bad. Not my father, never.

WORKER: I remember the things you told me.

ANGEL: Yes, like when he raped my mother and had me hold a knife on her.

WORKER: Yes. Remember how I am always trying to help you under-
          stand that it wasn't your fault.

ANGEL: But, I did it.

WORKER: Yes, but you were little and you didn't know. Like Beauty.
          Beauty is little and doesn't know what she is doing, so we
          don't blame her or get mad at her. And Angel, you were too
          little and scared, and had to do what your father demanded.
          He would have hurt you if you didn't obey.

ANGEL: He would have killed me if I didn't.

WORKER: Angel, your father was very big. He did know what he was
          doing was wrong.

ANGEL: Yes, he should have kept me safe.

WORKER: Exactly! Like you are keeping Beauty safe.

ANGEL: Oh, Beauty, I won't let anyone hurt you. Come here. I won't
          hurt you, never. You're just a little baby puppy who doesn't
          know.

With Beauty's help and the social worker's skilled use of metaphor and sim-
ile, Angel began to understand that as a small child he was unable to protect his mother from his father's violence. He began to understand that he,
like his mother, was also a victim of his father in the rape incident. As he
felt more protected and less guilty, Angel told terrifying stories of his
father's sadistic abuse. He re-lived being locked in a basement for two days
while his father went out to "party." Many elements of his life story were
told with Beauty in his lap. They were painful to hear. They were told with
increasing anger and decreasing self-blame. Beauty provided a nonthreatening, secure relationship to which Angel made a deep emotional commitment. Beauty was his bridge to gradual human connections with peers,
teachers, and child care staff. Taking care of Beauty made Angel feel
responsible and valued. He received recognition for his excellent care of
her. Without minimizing the contribution of the social worker and others,
we recognize that Beauty helped Angel to transform himself from victim to
survivor.

HELPING WITH DYSFUNCTIONAL
FAMILY PROCESSES

Most families experience difficult life transitions, painful life events, and environmental pressures, and they manage the inner and outer demands of such life issues, often by developing new forms of coping with the associated stress. They need no help. For others, the demands may generate additional stress if the family does not recognize the need for change. In many such instances, family members may need only modest help in revising their usual patterns. In other instances, dysfunctional relationships and communications in the family are themselves the primary stressors.

Family Forms, Functions, and Processes

Families may be bound together not only by ties of kinship or by legal rights and responsibilities, but by self-definition. In addition to traditional nuclear families and extended families, there are growing numbers of families that are childless by choice, two-provider and two-career families,[1] commuter families (where the adult partners live and work far from each other), gay and lesbian families, solo parent families, blended families (formerly "step" families), communal families, and augmented families (composed of two or more people who may not have a sexual relationship and may be of the same or different sex and age). These families confront most of the same challenges and stressors faced by the traditional nuclear family plus additional challenges and stressors that may be unique to a particular form.

Family Functions and Forms

The traditional functions that have been ascribed to families across diverse forms, cultures, and historical eras are: (1) procreation and socialization of children; (2) providing shelter, food, and protection for survival (instrumental functions); (3) meeting members' needs for nurturing, acceptance, security, and realization of potentials (expressive functions); and (4) connecting members to the outer social and physical worlds.

In modern life, former family functions such as education, socialization, production, and health care have gradually been taken over in whole or in part by other social institutions. Thus families must also develop structural channels for connecting their members to schools, workplaces, health care services, day care and respite services, voluntary associations and, for the affiliated, religious institutions.

Nuclear families face pressures and adaptive demands that may or may not exceed adaptive limits, as when both parents must work (typical of two-provider families) or choose to do so (typical of two-career families). Geographic mobility, previously considered a strength, has become a significant strain in many middle-class families. Constant uprooting in response to corporate demands or the personal quest for achievement places stress on the adult partner and on the children. Likewise, suburban families may suffer from the long daily absence of the employed parent(s), social isolation, heavy indebtedness, and other pressures such as job loss or the fear of it in a stagnant economy. While it was responsive to the demands of industrialization and urbanization, the nuclear family is exceedingly vulnerable to the loss of one parent, since the entire system rests on the marital pair.

Families headed by women are characterized by poverty. Working women still earn less than men in comparable jobs. And more women than men are in lower-paid jobs. Some are out of the labor force altogether; they and their children are dependent on welfare. Relatively few families headed by women receive child support from fathers, whether they had been married or unmarried. Some states now have mechanisms for tracing fathers and legal measures to enforce child-support, which, if paid, is usually deducted from the family's welfare budget. The disadvantages for the millions of children living in female-headed families, including those of never-married mothers, derive more from the multiple adverse conditions associated with poverty than from the family form per se.

The situation of solo fathers is qualitatively different from that of solo mothers. Until recently little attention has been given to their plight in the literature, although it appears that they are vulnerable to special stressors that are different from those of women (Nieto 1982). Solo fathers confront role ambiguity and the lack of norms for role performance. Solo father families are frequently presumed to have resulted from the mother's pathology. And the solo father is apt to be perceived as poorly prepared by his very nature for the performance of the expressive functions in child rearing. Social workers have begun to provide support groups and educational programs for solo fathers, whose numbers are growing.

The solo parent must double for the other parent, or may need to cast an older sibling in that role. Stressors may arise in association with household management, child care, personal respite, and personal fulfillment. Society has not yet developed institutional solutions to meet these adaptive needs. If social work help is to be effective, the distinctive nature of the solo parent family must be taken into account, needed supports mobilized or constructed, and worker or agency advocacy undertaken for needed social policy, programs, and services.

Same-sex families are also markedly different from the nuclear form. In addition to the tasks and environmental opportunities and limitations that characterize nuclear families, these families must also manage additional tasks and environmental strains due to discrimination and, in rural areas, to the lack of a gay community.

Extended families who live together in the same household are prevalent around the world, but in the United States and Canada they are mainly limited to certain ethnic groups. Nevertheless, most other American and Canadian families remain close to extended kin through visiting and reciprocal care and support or, if at a distance, by telephone and letters.

Independent living on the part of young unmarried adults became the norm in the white urban middle class beginning in the 1960s. Ethnic families and families of color who still placed value on adult unmarried children (and sometimes married children, their spouses, and their offspring) remaining in the parental home, were unthinkingly defined as overly dependent. It is only recently that social workers and social scientists stopped viewing adult children in these groups who continue to live with their parents as overly dependent. The overall pattern is now beginning to change, with college graduates in some cases returning to their parents' homes for economic reasons.

Blended families have grown in number as the divorce rate and the acceptance of divorce and remarriage increased. By 1982 there were 35 million American adults living in blended families. About 1,300 new blended families with children under the age of 19 are forming every day. The Bureau of the Census estimates that 60 percent of all children born in the late 1980s and beyond will live in a blended family or a solo parent family for some part of the time before they are 18. Sometimes both partners bring children to the new marriage or only one may have children and either the other partner may be childless or the children may be in the custody of the other parent. Those children may visit the remarried family either occasionally or not at all, depending on custodial agreements, proximity, and so on. Children living in the new family not only have a new step-parent but may have step-grandparents, step-siblings, and other adult kin who may or may not accept the new parent and children as relatives. To complicate the structure and relationships even more, the new parents may have a child or children together, who are then half-siblings to all the other children. While possibilities for individual and family identity confusion, jealousy, conflict, and divided loyalties are rife, the potential exists for extended-kin support, loving relationships, a cohesive family life, and the emotional growth of all members.

For the most part, research into blended families is limited to the study of remarried families who seek services because they are troubled. Less is known of such families who are making it without professional help. What is learned about the life issues faced by the families receiving service may or may not be generalizable to families who do not ask for service (Ahrons and Rodgers 1987; Wald 1981). However, the findings of one exploratory study of 30 nonclinical remarried families (27 white, 1 African-American, and 2 Hispanic, of varying economic status) were doing better than expected. They did face life stressors arising from complex, ambiguous relationships and uncertain social expectations. But after the first year most of the 60 adults and the 37 children interviewed reported positive feelings toward their new family. Many commented that it took time and work (Dahl, Cowgill, and Asmundsson 1987).

Family Structure

From the ecological point of view, attention is also paid to family subunits, usually recognized as the marital (or unmarried) adult partners, parent-child, and sibling subunits. Social work intervention may be with one, two or all three subunits. However, sometimes practitioners deal with the parent-child subunit as though it were unrelated to the marital subunit, thus leaving the father out of the work. At the other extreme, some workers focus mainly on the adult pair on the assumption that it strongly influences the parent-children subunits. Sibling relationships are frequently overlooked altogether as a possible focus of attention.

Such practice deficiencies are being corrected as more social workers engage in family-centered practice (Hartman and Laird 1983). For example, because sibling relationships are significant elements in family life, they may be an additional site for intervention (Bank and Kahn 1982). Sibling relationships remain influential throughout the life course. In particular, sisters who were not close in childhood or adulthood often draw closer together as they grow old or outlive their husbands. Increasingly, grandparents living with or apart from the focal family are viewed as important elements in family life and may be included in social work sessions as appropriate. In augmented families, other kin or non-kin (lodgers or friends) live in the household and may provide valued instrumental functions such as child care for the working solo parent. However, some people living with or outside the family may participate in dysfunctional alliances with one or more family members.

Increasing numbers of grandmothers are raising their grandchildren, some of whom have been orphaned by AIDS. These grandmothers can experience intense economic, social, and emotional strains.

In the following example, the grandmother plays quite a different role. Mr. and Mrs. Conroy are concerned about the troublesome behavior of their only child, 10-year-old Annie. She tells lies excessively at home and at school, has no friends due to her "bossiness," and pits her parents against each other. When the parents complain about or describe Annie's behavior, they grin. Smiling, Mrs. Conroy says Annie's behavior reminds her of herself as a child, stubborn and with a fiery temper. Even now when angry she screams and throws things. She and Annie struggle endlessly about who is going to control whom. Mrs. Conroy is proud that it is she who "rules the roost," and Mr. Conroy seems quite comfortable with that. Both parents work in factories, Mr. Conroy on the night shift and Mrs. Conroy on the day shift. Mrs. Conroy says that her mother, Mrs. Kirk, who lives close by, belittles her in front of Annie by telling Mrs. Conroy that she isn't properly handling a situation. Mrs. Kirk dotes on Annie and constantly undermines the parents' authority. When Annie is angry or loses the battle with her mother she turns to grandmother, who either chastises mother or gives Annie a gift to compensate for mother's error. Boundaries between the Conroys and Mrs. Kirk appear to be nonexistent, reinforcing the turmoil and conflict. Physical boundaries are breached also as the Conroys have no hot water, so Annie and mother wash their hair and clothes at Mrs. Kirk's home. And Mrs. Kirk collects the Conroys' dirty dishes twice weekly and washes them. Mrs. Conroy feels helpless in coping with her mother on issues involving Annie and says they never have had a good relationship.

Over time, families develop a structure for dealing with role and task allocation and issues of authority and decision-making. Structure helps shape relationship and communication patterns and, in turn, is influenced by the nature and quality of those patterns. In each subunit, characteristic patterns also develop that may or may not be in conflict with those of the family as a whole or with those of other subunits. In some families there may be subunits which are long lasting, and others which are temporary and shifting, such as coalitions and alliances that cross over age and sex boundaries of the other subunits, usually in maladaptive ways. A common example is the triangulation represented by an alliance of child and one parent that closes out the other parent.

It is imperative that social workers be aware of the culture—racial, ethnic, or religious—of families with whom they work, and its influence on family structure, worldview, and functioning. In the multicultural societies of Canada and the United States, it is unlikely that all social workers can be familiar with all cultural differences within their own society. But all are professionally responsible for learning about the culture of the particular individuals, families, and groups with whom they work.

Family Processes

Social workers must familiarize themselves with family processes that can become dysfunctional, such as secrets, myths, and rituals. A maladaptive collective process sometimes seen in troubled families is a secret or a tabooed area of experience which members are skillfully coerced into keeping from spreading to outsiders or particular family members. In the following example, a family's secret is kept from outsiders, adversely affecting the emotional and social development of the 13 year old son, Tom:

Tom is the youngest of six children and the only one still at home. His teachers are concerned because he is failing most subjects, has no peer relationships, and appears to be continually angry at everyone. Initially, the school social worker thought that Tom was experiencing identity issues, having just entered middle school and its teen culture two months ago; or was mourning the loss of close siblings as they left the family, and the loss of friends at his former school (where Tom had friends and performed well academically).

As his trust in the social worker grew, Tom revealed to her the family secret that seemed to be the dominant source of his troubles. His mother is alcoholic. He was very angry at his mother for drinking and for treating him like a baby when she is drunk. He said he was afraid to make new friends because he might be tempted to divulge the secret of his mother's alcoholism. His mother's drinking problem was not a new family issue, but Tom's entrance into early adolescence might mean he is now meeting an old problem with diminished coping skills. All his energy is invested in maintaining the secrecy with left for school work or new relationships.

> Toxic events and themes in intergenerational family systems are often shrouded in secrecy, distorted by misinformation, and made even more powerful and threatening because they are cut off from the family discourse. . . . Sometimes the oppressive presence of these avoided issues interrupts the potential for clear and open communication of any kind in the family. It is almost as if communication must be tightly controlled so the secret will not emerge.
>
> Hartman and Laird 1983:248

Included in a family's implicit beliefs are the myths and rituals it develops to explain its experiences through time and across space. Family rituals are usually adaptive. They help maintain channels of communication or open closed channels, maintain relationships or restore fractured ones, and help construct or reconstruct salutary arrangements of the family's interior life. They are maladaptive if they continue destructive myths, promote illusions, maintain women's lack of power in the family, or reinforce maladaptive rules. Rituals embody the should's and ought's of the family's implicit rules. Especially important in family life are rites of passage, those rituals surrounding individual and family transitions. They include observances of biological transitions such as birth, male sexual maturation (in some cultures), and death, and of social transitions such as graduation, first job or new job, promotion, engagement, marriage, anniversaries, adoption, return from war, and retirement. Some rituals help families cope with change or discontinuity, while others support stability in family life and bind the members to one another in shared, memorable experiences (Hartman and Laird 1983). When rituals cover up distasteful facts, however, they may take on a hypocritical quality (Turner 1982). Mother's Day, a societal ritual, is such an example if it merely represents one day off a year from domestic chores that a family considers to be the mother's exclusive responsibility.

Family processes are affected by differences among birth cohorts. As the life course of a cohort proceeds, its collective lives set off social changes. For example, the cohorts of young women in the late 1960s and early 1970s—responding to feminist thought—developed new norms, values, definitions of self, and patterns of living. As a collective force, they pressed for change in social roles and social values. Cohorts of young women and some young men brought the new ideas into the open, institutionalized them, and began to seek changes in gendered roles, sexist attitudes, and power differentials in the family and the workplace. These changes led to changes in the life patterns of many of today's cohorts of young men and women, as well as the developmental experience of their children. Cohorts' patterns of living are influenced by unique sequences of social changes in the family, the school, the workplace, and the community; in ideas, values, beliefs, science, technology, and the arts; and in patterns of migration, fertility, and mortality (Riley 1985). More powerful influences on individual and family development within the cohort are differences in personality, culture, and life experiences. Nevertheless, cohort influences add important historical contexts and social dimensions to the understanding of individuals and families. Failure to take account of cohort influences in historical time can lead to the erroneous assumption that each cohort follows the same developmental pathway of our personal cohort (Riley 1978).

Also within the dimension of historical time, traditional timetables of many life transitions are disappearing:

> Ours seems to be a society that has become accustomed to 70-year old students, 30-year-old college presidents, 22-year-old mayors, 35-year-old grandmothers, 50-year-old retirees, 65-year-old fathers of preschoolers, 60-year-olds and 30-year-olds wearing the same clothing styles. Neugarten 1978:52

With increased longevity many of today's elders do not regard themselves as old until their late 70s or early 80s. We also see 65-year-old caretakers of their 85-year-old parents, as well as a particularly tragic age crossover of child-mothers rearing their infants, while some adults postpone childbearing to the last biologically possible age. Therefore, fixed age-connected times for learning, selecting sexual partners, marrying or remarrying, first-time parenting, changing one's career direction, retiring and many other life changes have become relatively independent of age.

Family Development, Paradigm, and Transformation

Family members develop simultaneously, with parents and offspring as active agents in their own and one another's development (Germain 1991a). That is, parents and children develop in tandem. Individual adaptive and maladaptive processes merge into collective processes, and collective processes lead to family development and change. Over time the family constructs a unique "family paradigm" or worldview (Reiss 1981), defined as the members' shared, implicit beliefs about themselves and their social world. The paradigm shapes the family's basic patterns in living and its experiences in the environment. A painful life event or other life stressor that causes serious discontinuity in family life requires the family to change its ways of functioning as embedded in its paradigm and structure.

Terkelsen's (1980) distinction between first- and second-order life issues clarifies how collective processes involved in family development and transformations are formed out of individual processes. First-order life issues represent individual life transitions that occur frequently and can be expected in average experience, fitting into the continuous flow of family life. They include developmental transitions of individual members, such as puberty, pregnancy, and aging processes, and social transitions such as school entry, work, marriage, retirement, and the like. Life transitions from birth to old age present both individual and family with new requirements and new opportunities for mastery and growth.

First-order life issues are perceived by most families as challenges rather than stressors, and most families manage them more or less smoothly, without serious disruption. First-order issues can lead to increased mastery and competence that yield pride and satisfaction to family members despite any frustrations involved. The family paradigm does not need to be changed. It is enough that several new behavioral sequences emerge as the family learns to manage the issue effectively. As the new behavioral sequences appear, outmoded sequences drop away.

Second-order life issues, however, are much more frequently encountered in social work with families than first-order ones. Second-order stressors consist of serious, unpredictable life events and other life issues ranging from natural catastrophes to family violence, addictions, unplanned and unwanted pregnancy, sudden and serious mental disorders, onset of disability or chronic illness, job loss, separation and divorce, and premature loss of a loved one. When such unexpected events occur they represent

severe discontinuities in the routine flow of family life. All such life stressors put the family in harm's way. They also may include any first-order
issue perceived by a particular family as a harm or threat of harm, either
because of the meaning the issue has for the members or because of the
absence of internal or external resources needed for moving through it.
Second-order issues also include such grievous harms as poverty and
oppression, which themselves generate multiple second-order life issues.

Second-order life issues require the family to go beyond the process of
simply adding new behaviors and dropping outmoded ones. Often, because
of the severe discontinuity and the greatly changed conditions imposed by
second-order life issues, many families require formal or informal help to
change the fundamental characteristics embodied in the family paradigm.
These changes include the reorganization of its structure of roles, tasks,
and routines, and redefinition of the family's values, norms, and meanings.
In some instances, a family may have to modify its goals, plans for the
future, and interpretation of its past. While these and other alterations are
going on, family members also must regulate the accompanying anxiety,
guilt, depression, resentment, shame, anger, or despair they feel so that
these feelings do not interfere with efforts to change. For example:

Mrs. Abrams, a 52-year-old, white, Jewish woman, is the mother of
three daughters, ages 27, 25, and 23. The youngest, Rebecca, was admitted to a private inpatient psychiatric facility after her attempted suicide
by Valium overdose. Rebecca had moved back home five weeks earlier.
She is now diagnosed as suffering major depression with psychotic features, including delusions and bizarre behaviors. Three years ago Mr.
Abrams had surgery for colon cancer. Currently, he receives chemotherapy and is also being treated for a heart condition. Total home care is
provided by Mrs. Abrams. The oldest daughter has two small children
and works full time. The second daughter also works, is very upset about
Rebecca, and depends on Mrs. Abrams for comfort and emotional support. Mrs. Abrams says, "Both lean on me too, it's easier to keep them
out of it."

The couple have few friends and no kin other than their daughters.
Their finances are limited. The cancer center reports that Mrs. Abrams
keeps her husband home at times when others would have sought hospitalization. Mrs. Abrams says she has come to terms with her husband's illnesses, but Rebecca's disorder "came out of the blue and is a shock to my
system. I don't know how to cope with it and I don't understand it." She
worries that somehow she is at fault for Rebecca's condition, and her
sense of competence and her self-esteem as a mother are seriously undermined. She also feels angry and cheated as a woman engaged in multiple
caregiving who hasn't yet lived for herself.

Rebecca is to be discharged to her mother's care in three weeks, and will be on medication as an outpatient.[2]

If the difficult life issues facing the Abramses are to be managed successfully and the new reality of Rebecca's psychiatric disorder incorporated into the family paradigm, a transformation of its structure of roles, tasks, coping modes, goals and expectations, and views of the environment will be required. But with the lack of resources for Mrs. Abrams, the outlook appears bleak.

Successful first- and second-order changes lead to family development. First-order developments occur frequently, so that the family experiences itself as living in a state of flux. In contrast, second-order developments occur infrequently, so that the family experiences itself as living in a state of constancy. Flux and constancy proceed together. Through successful first-order changes, the family is continually evolving and the members are continually developing (Terkelsen 1980). Through successful second-order change, the structure and the paradigm governing family life are transformed in order to be congruent with changed realities, and the family and its members develop as a consequence (Hoffman 1980).

However, should a family persist in maladaptive patterns that block needed change, it may become a troubled family. Its implicit paradigm and structure governing life together are characterized by conflicted relationships, destructive negative feelings, contradictory communications, and rigid systems of control (Reiss 1981). Failure to change can lead to other second-order stressors such as break-up of the marriage, destructive behaviors in either partner or in the children, or physical or social dysfunction.

Social Work Function, Modality, Methods, and Skills

The Social Worker and Dysfunctional Family Structures and Processes

Families which face painful life transitions, traumatic life events, or other critical life issues may find that coping with such stressors is made more difficult by dysfunctional patterns of relationships and communications. Other families may not be facing external life stressors, but their interpersonal processes are a serious life stressor. In either instance, the social worker's function is to help such families identify sources and consequences of dysfunctional interpersonal processes, communicate more openly and directly, and develop greater reciprocity and caring in family relationships. However, if coping efforts continue to be ineffective, the worker will need to help members discard some behaviors and adopt new ones. If that is not enough, the family will need to develop a new paradigm that restructures family roles, tasks, and goals and incorporates the new reality posed by the critical life issue. With the social worker's help, the family transforms itself into a more functional unit that can cope with the stressor and can better support the needs and growth of all members.

Professional Methods and Skills

Given these aims of the family modality, the social worker enables, guides, and facilitates in the ways previously discussed. In addition, in family practice the worker joins a family system, mediates its internal structures and processes, and advocates for the rights and needs of weaker members. This is internal mediation and advocacy as contrasted to the external mediation described in the previous chapter. Unfortunately, analyzing each method isolates the method from all others. In reality, various methods and their skills are called on as needed so that many sessions may present a blend.

The method of *joining* is characteristic of the first interview, but it is also remains important throughout the contact with the family. The skill of joining includes:

- *Affirming*. Seek out and affirm positives. Affirmation builds on the strengths of family members and may also help to modify some members' negative perceptions of another member.
- *Tracking*. Encourage narratives and life stories of the family and of individual members. Practitioners must track all the members and not only the most verbal. They must be aware of their own tracking processes. Worker reactions such as talking mostly to the mother or failing to ask why father did not come to the session may on reflection yield insight into the family structure.
- *Creating therapeutic contexts*. Establish a climate in the sessions that enables members to feel competent or to experience hope of change. Identify family strengths, facilitate the enactment of familiar, positive patterns, or introduce novelty by encouraging members to engage with one another in unusual exchanges (Minuchin and Fishman 1981).
- *Monitoring the family's worldview*. Social workers must learn the elements of families' paradigms in order to support the family's reality or to help members construct a new or expanded worldview. The new paradigm must incorporate a new reality, new attitudes and beliefs, and other changes. The worker must learn how family roles, tasks, routines, and goals are organized in order to help the family manage the stressor and change what needs to be changed.

To help family members change dysfunctional interpersonal processes, the social worker relies on specialized skills to encourage clear *communication*, positive relationships, and needed *behavioral change*. These skills include reframing, homework, work on rituals and myths as needed, and reflective comments:

Table 6.1	Joining Skills
• *Affirming:*	Seek out and validate strengths
• *Tracking:*	Encourage and value narrations of life stories of family and individual members
• *Creating a therapeutic context:*	Establish an emotional climate in sessions that enables members to feel competent and/or hopeful of change
• *Monitoring the family's paradigm (worldview and structure):*	learn the elements of the family's worldview, such as values norms, beliefs, assumptions about themselves and their world Learn the elements of the family's structure (organization) of roles, tasks, routines, and goals

- *Reframing.* The worker makes statements to family members designed to change their views of an event or a situation, to modify their conceptions of causality, or convert what they see as linear communication into exchanges between members (Hartman and Laird 1983:307). Reframing also includes putting a positive connotation to destructive behavior, naming it as an effort to preserve the family system; defining a problem as a solution to another problem; and using metaphors and analogies to integrate information or to intensify its meaning.
- *Assigning homework.* Homework brings the clinical work into the daily life of the family through assigned tasks to be carried out at home (Hartman and Laird 1983). Techniques used to ensure the effectiveness of an assignment include relating it to what is going on in that session's work, presenting it as serious and important and, if possible, imbuing it with a bit of drama.
- *Working on rituals and myths.* Rituals help unite families by infusing events with meaning and value and preserving family paradigms. However, a family may adhere to maladaptive rituals. For example, holiday rituals can be pleasurable and contribute to a shared identity of the members. But in some families they are dreaded for their rigidity, hypocrisy, and emptiness. The social worker may be able to help the family design new holiday rituals that are more congruent with life styles of the children, now adults. Other families may be under-ritualized. They need help in constructing beneficial rituals such as marking a divorce as a fresh start, celebrating a lesbian or gay partnership, a new achievement of a seriously disabled family member, or reuniting with estranged family members. For example, a poor family living in oppressive circumstances and without ceremonies and regularity was helped by a social worker to develop "mealtime, bedtime, and recreational rituals that served to synchronize family activity and bound the use of space and time" (Hartman and Laird 1983:321). Myths help families integrate their history and values, but some myths are dysfunctional. For example, a family explains the suicides of a father, uncle, and grandfather as deaths due to heart attacks. This myth about death is designed to protect a vulnerable child from a terrifying family secret, but it can lead to destructive consequences. The social worker may accept and support some family myths, while avoiding,

intentionally ignoring, raising a question about others, or helping the family to relinquish a dysfunctional myth and to accept the truth as part of the family's life story.

• *Offering reflective comments.* Comments by the social worker on the family's interpersonal processes help the family learn about itself and even begin to identify maladaptive communication and relationship patterns, implicit rules, and other paradigmatic elements. Comments that describe a behavioral sequence as it is happening and experienced by everyone in the session call the attention of the family to how it is functioning (Hartman and Laird 1983:309). Families may unwittingly exhibit their patterns or difficulties in the session through their seating arrangements, who always speaks first, and the like. The worker's comment on the displayed behavior brings the maladaptive pattern to members' consciousness and stimulates change. When a member talks to another member through the worker, the worker instructs the communicator to redirect the communication to the other member. Their growing awareness empowers the family to make the changes they desire.

Internal mediation and advocacy are particularly useful in helping couples to reduce chronic marital or family conflict. The skills of internal mediation and advocacy include exploring divergent views; searching for common ground; legitimizing differences in perceptions and behaviors; inviting feedback on each other's comments; lending support to each partner as needed, most often the weaker member; exploring family-of-origin issues; encouraging self-awareness and other-awareness in both partners; using agreements reached at the outset to maintain focus; and making therapeutic demands. These skills are elaborated and illustrated in this chapter (table 6.3) and chapter 7.

Practice Illustrations

Family Structure

Mr. and Mrs. Weiss, a young, white, married couple with no children, sought help from an outpatient mental health clinic. Mrs. Weiss, 24 years old, is Italian and Roman Catholic. Her family history includes harsh physical punishment by her mother, repeated rapes by her father from the age of twelve which continued for an unspecified period of time, and responsibility for caring of an infant sibling during her adolescent years while her mother worked. She graduated high school and entered a college pre-med program two years ago at the urging of her husband. She received good grades, but dropped out after a year because she felt too much pressure. Since then, she has been too depressed to seek employment or further study.

Table 6.2	Skills of Inducing Communication and Behavioral Change

• *Reframing:*	Make statements that can change the family's views of an event or situation
	Place a positive connotation on destructive behavior as an individual member's effort to preserve the family
	Define a problem as a solution to another problem
	Use metaphors and analogies to integrate information or intensify its meaning
• *Assigning Homework:*	Bring the clinical work into the family's daily life by assigning tasks to be carried out at home
	Relate the assignment to what is going on in that session's content
	Present the assignment at the end of the session and as serious and important
• *Working on Secrets, Rituals, and Myths:*	Help members to dissolve a family secret defined as blocking growth
	Support adaptive family rituals and myths
	Help members to create celebratory or other rituals when the family is underritualized
	Avoid, ignore, or raise necessary questions about maladaptive family myths
• *Reflective Commenting:*	Comment on family interpersonal processes to help the family learn about itself
	Describe behavior as it is happening and as it is experienced by everyone in the session
	Make use of enacting, such as family sculpture by the members
	Observe and comment on family-of-origin issues as family and worker analyze genograms, eco-maps, or enactments such as family sculpture

Mr. Weiss, age 30, is Jewish. He is employed as an accountant and is completing an undergraduate degree in accounting. He has attended ten colleges and has frequently shifted jobs, usually after a year. He met his wife at work. She was a clerk and he was a bookkeeper. After several years of dating, they were married. He is the younger of two children, and says he was "spoiled," always getting what he wanted. His facial expression is bland with consistently flat affect. In contrast, Mrs. Weiss is distraught, verbal, and expressive.

The primary life stressor was Mrs. Weiss's depressed feelings concerning an abortion two months earlier. The pregnancy was not planned, but Mrs. Weiss stated that she wanted the baby. She decided to abort because her husband did not want a child at this time. Mrs. Weiss complained that he always gets what he wants when they disagree. She felt that her husband was insensitive to her need to have a child and did not care about her: "Bill and I are two different people—we even have trouble talking to each other." She had a severe reaction after the abortion. Everything slowed down and she perceived people and objects in lights of different colors flashing ahead of her, felt a tingling sensation in her body, had trouble

Table 6.3	Mediating and Advocating Skills

- explore divergent views
- legitimize differences in perceptions and behaviors
- invite feedback on each other's comments
- search for common ground
- lend support to each partner as needed, most often the weaker member
- explore family-of-origin issues
- encourage self-awareness and other-awareness in both partners
- use initial agreements to maintain focus
- make therapeutic demands

sleeping and a fear of going outside. The symptoms coincided with her resumption of smoking marijuana. After the first session, Mrs. Weiss experienced a dramatic reduction and subsequent absence of symptoms.

While Mr. Weiss recognized the existence of marital issues, his initial motivation for coming to the agency was not to deal with these, but rather to "get help for my wife who has a lot of problems." After he described his wife's problems, the worker asked for Mrs. Weiss's perceptions. She is concerned that they are incompatible and probably should never have married. He probably married her only because he felt sorry for her because of her difficult family life. She complained that Mr. Weiss neither expresses emotion nor talks to her. This, coupled with his opposition to their having a child, confirmed his lack of commitment to her and their relationship. Mr. Weiss explained that there were too many problems in the marital relationship to have a child, and he is not ready. He had not even wanted to get married, preferring simply to live together, stating "marriage meant responsibility, commitment and roots." She resents his attitude, leaving her no choice but to have an abortion. The worker records the following:

I asked Mr. Weiss if he did not want to have the baby. He said he told her he didn't want a baby, but it did not have to be his way. I asked Mrs. Weiss to comment on that, and she responded that he always says, "It does not have to be that way," but he always gets his way. I asked, "How come?" She replied, "I knew Bill never wanted a child, I knew he would never let me have a baby. So when I found I was pregnant I called a doctor to set up an appointment for the abortion and then I told Bill." I said, "You told Bill after you called the doctor?" She replied angrily that she knew what he would say, "He always gets his way and doesn't care what I think. I said to myself, I might as well get it over with and I called the doctor." I replied, "It had to be a very painful call to make and to follow through on." She lowered her head and tears streamed down her cheek. I offered her a tissue, and asked him for his reactions to what his wife said. In an unemotional tone he said, "I state my opinion and Mary can state hers.

She doesn't have to go along with what I say. I just didn't want her to get pregnant." I asked if they had agreed on a birth control method. Mrs. Weiss replied that they had not planned the pregnancy, nor had they used birth control. I suggested that this seemed to be a contradiction. She replied that they could not agree on what birth control method to use. I asked what happened after she had the abortion. Mrs. Weiss scowled at her husband. He expressed guilt about leaving his wife right after the abortion (he went on a business trip for a few days), and realized that he should not have left her (expressed without emotion). I said he seemed to be genuinely sorry, but had difficulty expressing his feelings, and added, "Bill, I think you would like to, but find it difficult to do." He responded, "I have always had difficulty expressing my feelings—I don't know why." I asked what it had been like for him in his own family. He began to describe a similar pattern in his own family with his mother complaining that his father never talked.

After describing his experiences with an overbearing mother and detached father, he made the connection to his needing the freedom to pick up and get away. He doesn't even like any furniture in the apartment—it confines him. He married only to please his wife. Mrs. Weiss said she wanted the "benefits" of marriage if they were going to live together. He abruptly switched focus, stating, "Everything is meaningless. We all just exist." I said what he was saying is important, but I don't understand. He responded calmly that he is just being negative, and needs some space from the conversation. I commented that he seemed to put up a wall when he is under pressure and feels the need for space and privacy. I asked Mrs. Weiss what it is like for her to try to break through the wall. "It's totally frustrating. I try everything possible to get a response from him. The more I scream, the quieter he gets." I asked Mr. Weiss what it is like for him to see his wife become increasingly frustrated and upset. He feels good because it shows that she cared, but at the same time it invaded his privacy. I asked what he meant by "privacy." "To be able to breathe," he said.

Mrs. Weiss has experienced a deep sense of loss and is angry at her husband for his detachment and lack of empathy. The abortion has profound meaning to her. She sees her husband's problems with intimacy and his emotional defensiveness as a lack of commitment and affection. The worker empathically explores the divergent perceptions and invites feedback on each other's comments. She asks clarifying questions and points out contradictions, creating the context for fostering self-awareness, mutual understanding, and open lines of communication. She effectively joins the family system.

A rigidly defended person such as Mr. Weiss requires empathic understanding from the social worker, which the practitioner tried to give by at least controlling any negative reactions she might have felt. It is easy to empathize with Mrs. Weiss's pain at her husband's lack of caring, loving, and concern for her and her very human neediness. It is far harder to recognize underneath Mr. Weiss's defensive armor a desperately hungry but frightened child who himself seldom experienced caring, love, or parental concern for a child's neediness. Slowly, the social worker will need to tune into Mr. Weiss's feelings under the armor and help him to experience and express them to whatever degree might be possible. Once he can love himself a little, he might be better able to experience and convey loving feelings to his wife.

In family systems, the conflicts and tensions between adult partners affects children. They are innocent victims caught between adult partners' crossfire. At times, children take on the symptoms of adult partners, and become the "identified patient" in mental health services.

George and Martha Simpson, white, Protestant, in their mid-thirties, and the parents of three sons, aged 10, 7, and 3, sought help from a family agency. They had been seen before, about their "unmanageable" oldest son. After six sessions they withdrew because Mrs. Simpson felt that the worker sided with her husband. Their current concern is marital conflict which has escalated to the point where both are considering divorce. A first interview was scheduled for the couple, but Mrs. Simpson was unable to come to the interview or the next two, because of illness. Mr. Simpson was seen alone in the three sessions. He told of recently being cheated out of his business by his partners and then suffering a back injury which left him unable to work. They are rapidly going into debt, but his wife refuses to get a job or to curb her spending. According to Mr. Simpson, she is more involved with her relatives and friends than with him or the children.

The couple came to the fourth and all subsequent sessions together. Mrs. Simpson had been crying and was still visibly upset. Mr. Simpson was angry and sullen, refusing to direct anything but verbal abuse toward his wife. She said that all their disagreements ended in her "giving in after being tortured by silence or yelling, and threats of desertion." She does not want a divorce, but seriously doubts they can continue together much longer. He admitted the situation is now intolerable for the entire family. Both blamed the interaction on each other.

MR. SIMPSON: We can't even go anywhere anymore because we don't have the money. We're stuck together all day long and getting on each other's nerves.

WORKER: (to Mrs. Simpson) Is that how it is for you too?

MRS. SIMPSON: When George was working, he was gone from early morning until late at night. I'd get the kids off to school and do whatever I had to do in the apartment. Then maybe a friend would come over, and we'd have lunch and watch a soap opera. Or I'd visit a friend. I've also been a volunteer at church and the school. The kids came home in the late afternoon and kept me busy with dinner and all.

MR. SIMPSON: You also like to stay on the phone all day.

MRS. SIMPSON: (smiling) I like to talk on the phone.

WORKER: What about you, Mr. Simpson?

MR. SIMPSON: I worked ten hours a day, seven days a week. My schedule didn't allow me much time, but I used to play poker with the guys on Monday nights. Now I'm not able to play basketball and I don't have the money to gamble.

WORKER: What about your time together?

MR. SIMPSON: What time together? (both laugh)

MRS. SIMPSON: George was always so busy at the store that I guess I got used to living alone and handling things myself. Now I have no privacy. I'm embarrassed to have friends over because he joins us and monopolizes the conversation. He even stands around while I'm on the phone and comments on my conversations. I feel like a fourth child.

MR. SIMPSON: What am I supposed to do, lie in bed all day?

MRS. SIMPSON: Of course not! But you could find something to do besides watching me all day.

WORKER: Mr. Simpson's being out of work has caused some major changes in both your lives. While he was working you were apart all the time, and now you're together all the time. That's a difficult adjustment for both of you.

MR. SIMPSON: I get real bored, but I keep thinking, why start a project or anything when I might be going back to work soon.

MRS. SIMPSON: And I keep putting my friends off until George goes back to work.

WORKER: It sounds as if you've both put your lives on hold and are waiting for things to get back to normal.

MRS. SIMPSON: (thoughtfully) Yeah. That's exactly right. (Mr. Simpson nodded in agreement)

The life stressors of injury and unemployment and the stress they generate heighten existing vulnerabilities, trigger emotional reactivity and maladaptive responses (Guerin, Burden and Kautto 1987:31), and sharply lower the level of person:environment fit. The worker joins the couple and avoids taking sides. She creates a therapeutic context by validating their difficulties and lowering emotional arousal. The couple's perspective is limited; they blame each other for the state of their marriage. But by focusing on the two critical life events that beset them, rather than on the maladaptive patterns, the worker broadens their perspective and reduces their anxiety and anger. By the end of the session, and motivated by their mutual love for their children, the couple agree to work on their relationship and communication patterns in order to improve their marriage.

The Simpsons were extremely angry with each other when they arrived for the next session. He began by declaring that he was taking the children to visit his dying father in another state. He had set aside a portion of his insurance settlement for this trip, as he wanted his father to meet the children before he died. He was doing it for the children so they would have a sense of family. He was not doing it for his father—they never got along. He was angry that his wife is against the trip and said he plans to go without her. Although Mrs. Simpson agreed to go, she did so grudgingly. She objected to taking the children out of school, to the cost, and the fact that her husband had not arranged accommodations. They then bitterly argued about arrangements. Mr. Simpson accused his wife of picking a fight with his sister-in-law and making it impossible for them to stay with his brother.

MRS. SIMPSON:	You know she didn't want us there.
MR. SIMPSON:	Not now she doesn't. (Suddenly furious with his wife and shouting at her) You could give a shit. You hate my family. Bitch! You destroyed my relationship to my brother and fixed it so we can't stay with them.
MRS. SIMPSON:	(More hurt than angry) You know damn well neither he nor she wants us there, and that's not my fault.
WORKER:	(Holding hands up in a "stop" gesture) Please hold it a minute.
MR. SIMPSON:	(to the worker) She pisses me off.
WORKER:	I can see that, but I'm not sure I understand what pissed you off.
MR. SIMPSON:	All she ever does is criticize me.
MRS. SIMPSON:	It's the other way around. I can never say or do anything right. I'm too fat. I'm a lousy wife, a lousy mother. I ruined his family. (Shrugs) I don't know. I'm so used to it. He doesn't like anything I do. It's like this all the time—Martha, the punching bag.
WORKER:	Each of you feels criticized. What is so sad is that you both are in the same boat and can't seem to help each other. You're both feeling unappreciated, unloved, alone, stuck with things as they are. The longer you wait for the other to change, the more hopeless it all seems.
MR. SIMPSON:	(Halfhearted attempt at humor) I didn't think we had anything in common.
MRS. SIMPSON:	(Smiles)
WORKER:	Let's try to solve the problem without name calling and blaming. Two people in the same boat, and the boat will sink

unless you can learn to work together to resolve issues. So, about your trip?

MRS. SIMPSON: Well, we know we can't stay with your brother. The way things stand right now it looks like we're going to spend five days in the car.

WORKER: Are there other options?

MRS. SIMPSON: If we had to, we could stay in a cheap hotel.

MR. SIMPSON: I really don't want to spend the money. We could sleep on the floor at my father's place, but my stepmother is very sick.

MRS. SIMPSON: Three kids would be too much for her.

MR. SIMPSON: Why don't you ask your friend if we can stay there? (To the worker) It seems like the least she can do.

MRS. SIMPSON: (To the worker) She said it was all right, but I feel she wasn't pleased. She's one of those perfect people who never has a thing out of place. I'd never be able to relax with the kids and all. I mean, our kids aren't bad, I'd just spend the time worrying that they'd spill something or put their hands on the wall. You can't watch children all the time. I don't know—I feel it's such an imposition.

MR. SIMPSON: The woman said it was OK. SHE HAS TWO KIDS SO SHE KNOWS WHAT IT'S LIKE. I DON'T KNOW WHAT THE BIG DEAL IS.

MRS. SIMPSON: That's easy for you to say. You just tune out and leave me to do the chasing around. This isn't going to be a vacation for me.

MR. SIMPSON: And it is for me?

MRS. SIMPSON: I wouldn't mind if we were flying down and staying at one of those nice hotels.

MR. SIMPSON: (To the worker) She knows we don't have the money for that. Why does she always have to rub it in?

WORKER: Please tell her directly rather than through me.

MR. SIMPSON: Martha, don't you think I wish this was a nice vacation instead of a trip to see my father dying in the hospital?

MRS. SIMPSON: (No response)

WORKER: (To both) This isn't easy for either of you. There are a few problems but you both agree it is something you have to do. (To Mr. S) You feel this is the last chance for your children to meet your father and for you to say goodbye to him. That's a difficult thing to do alone, and you would like Mrs. Simpson to support you by accompanying you and making things as easy and as pleasant as possible.

MR. SIMPSON: Right!

WORKER: (To Mrs. S) And you understand how important this is to your husband and do support the decision. But you can't communicate that to him because you feel alone in having to

	make all the arrangements. You would like this to be more pleasant for you too.
MRS. SIMPSON:	Yes.
WORKER:	What can be done to make the trip more pleasant for every one?
MR. SIMPSON:	(Hesitating while regarding his wife's expression) We do have a few days free . . (More of a question to his wife than a statement) As long as we're in Pine City, I suppose we could see some sights. We could be out all day and just use your friend's place to sleep.
MRS. SIMPSON:	I would feel better about this trip if we had something to look forward to.

In this excerpt, the worker focuses on the maladaptive communications. By empathizing with each partner, clarifying latent concerns, and searching for common ground, she promotes cooperative problem-solving. In limiting their exchanges to perceived differences, the Simpsons lost sight of their common interests. This impairs their ability to recognize and appreciate their need for each other (Weingarten and Leas 1987). The rapid shift in emotional climate was remarkable. The worker stopped the flow of anger by taking control of the interaction and restoring emotional stability to the session. The Simpsons are locked into a win-lose pattern, and the worker suggests a win-win option in which both benefit from resolution of the conflict. After defusing the tension, the worker reframes the blaming in a way they both could accept (Beck 1987).

The Simpsons returned from Pine City and were in good spirits. Both were in a light mood, laughing and sharing funny moments from their trip. Mrs. Simpson enjoyed the visit with her friend and the sightseeing, and Mr. Simpson felt satisfied that his children now refer to "grandpa" and not to "dad's father." He repeated, "The trip was for the kids—not for me or my father."

WORKER:	It must have been very difficult for you to see your father for what might be the last time.
MR. SIMPSON:	Well, I accomplished my purpose if that's what you mean. Now that's done, I really don't give a shit what happens to him. I'm serious. He never did anything for me.
WORKER:	That's really sad. (Short pause, then he shrugs off her comment) Can you give me an example of how he disappointed you?
MR. SIMPSON:	(Thinking) Our kids . . . (pause) there were a lot of things, but the kids come to mind.
MRS. SIMPSON:	(Glances at her husband and hesitates before speaking) George was very hurt that his father never acknowledged the

children. He never sent a card or gift when they were born.
There just didn't seem to be any interest. I didn't care for
myself, but I felt bad for George because he was hurt.

The Simpsons then began to explore both families-of-origin and dysfunctional family patterns. For example, Mr. Simpson learned to mask his feelings. He dealt with parental rejection by withdrawal and feigned indifference. Later in the interview, the worker pointed out that while he declared indifference toward his father, his nonverbal expressions pointed to great pain and anger. Mrs. Simpson's empathy for her husband made it possible for the worker to help him give verbal expression to those feelings.

In subsequent sessions, the Simpsons continued to move away from blaming each other. They were increasingly able to listen to each other, act collaboratively, and accept responsibility for changing their own behaviors. Their awareness of destructive patterns increased, and they now feel more optimistic about their future as a family. Mr. Simpson's back pain is subsiding, and a possible job has appeared on the horizon. The couple gained (or regained) strengths by learning to cope with serious life issues, including their own destructive relationship, without any apparent change in structure or paradigm. Growth occurred as the worker mediated their relationship and advocated for both.

Homework assignments are often used to guide problem-solving skills. For example, Mr. and Mrs. Tucker, a young couple married two years and recently separated, wanted help on the question of divorce. In the first session it became clear that they did not know how to resolve marital conflict, and they were unable to decide whether to resume living together. The social worker sensed that they both did want to be together, but each was afraid to make the first move and each feared rejection. The social worker was impressed by their ability to talk reasonably without a lot of blaming and name-calling. Hence, the social worker proposed a homework assignment:

I suggested that over the next three weeks they meet for at least an hour each time to discuss the sole question of moving back together. They were to discuss both the pros and cons. If the discussion degenerated into argument, they were to discontinue and try again another day. They carried out the task, resisted the impulse to do battle, and moved back together in the fourth week. From then on I assigned weekly tasks aimed at the more difficult demands of coping with day-to-day grievances. Although it was not easy for them, they were increasingly able to complete the tasks and toward the end of our contact were telling me about their new abilities to solve problems (none of which had been assigned by me as tasks). Clearly, both had become more like their real selves. He, taciturn and reclusive at the start, began raising his voice and becoming mildly histrionic. Her withholding behavior diminished and she became more confident about her emotionality. At the end of nine months the Tuckers had experimented with managing conflict and were successful enough times to feel they were a competent couple. The hardest tasks for them—negotiating finances and dealing with her jealousy of his former girlfriend—became manageable and were dealt with during the last month of our work.

Homework should be assigned toward the end of the session. With some families, especially those that are easily overwhelmed, the task should not be overly demanding. But with families like the Tuckers, assignments should be difficult in order to be challenging (Hartman and Laird 1983).

Parent-child conflict is a serious and frequent life stressor. While it also occurs between parents and school-age and younger children, it is seen most often in families with adolescents.

In this solo parent family, serious conflict exists between Mrs. Calhoun and her adolescent daughters:

Mrs. Calhoun, a 35-year-old African-American, was married at age 17. She left her husband two years ago because of his alcohol and drug abuse and his involvement with other women. She placed their five children in foster care until she could send for them, and left the south to seek work in a northern city. In accord with requirements of the Department of Children's and Youth Services (DCYS) with whom she had been working on reunification for almost a year, Mrs. Calhoun had prepared for the children's arrival by obtaining a four bedroom apartment in a public housing project, which she furnished inexpensively but attractively. She has been working at two jobs as a nurses' aide. A year after working with DCYS, she applied to the local family agency as the children's arrival was imminent.

Mrs. Calhoun said she wanted to work on her relationships with the children and on how to manage the multiple demands placed on a working single mother. The oldest child, 16-year-old Margie, arrived during the summer. Betty, age 15, and the boys (ages 7, 12, and 13) arrived in time for Christmas, three weeks before the session described below. Mrs. Calhoun said she had a strict upbringing, and like her parents she believes in the right of parents to train their children, no babies before marriage, owning nice furniture and a car, and supporting one's family by work, not welfare. Her verbal and nonverbal communications suggested that as a mother she is more authoritative than nurturing. Mrs. Calhoun had said in our earlier interview that she feels competent as a strong woman and breadwinner and puts her efforts into work and making money. She said that is less risky and less difficult than trying to build relationships with Margie and Betty.

Unexpectedly, she brought the girls to this January session. They both looked older than their age. They were stylishly dressed, and Margie seemed quite fashion-conscious. Neither looked pleased to be here and, like their mother, they looked tense. I began by asking how things were going. Mrs. Calhoun gave an uncharacteristic short answer, "adjustments are being made." When I asked both girls, each merely shrugged. Trying to reduce tension, I asked if Mrs. Calhoun had been able to register the children at school. She said the boys were registered and attending school; they like it and are making friends. Betty can't register for high school until necessary papers are received from her former school. The situation is different for Margie, who was expelled a year ago and is now considered a drop-out. At this point, Mrs. Calhoun added, "There's something you should know about Margie. She's carrying a baby." I said "oh," then recovered and asked Margie how she feels about being pregnant. She said she is four months along and feels tired but okay otherwise. I asked if she has decided to raise the baby herself, or if the father was in the picture. She said she doesn't know exactly what she is going to do, but the father is out of her life. I asked if she has considered adoption, and she said, "No, I'm keeping the baby." I said she could talk to a teen pregnancy counselor at our agency or she could talk to me about it, and we could set up some separate time if she wants. Mrs. Calhoun jumped in and said, "That would be nice." Margie seemed to resent her mother's comment and said, "I don't exactly know what I want to do." I said, "Well, it's something you can think about."

Several practice errors occurred at the start of this first family interview. First, the worker should have made an empathic comment on observing the girls' apparent discomfort, to elicit their expectations and feelings about the session. Second, the purpose of the agency and of social work practice should have been stated in order to engage the sisters, elicit any erroneous perceptions, and facilitate a beginning trust in the worker. Instead of making such comments, or picking up on Mrs. Calhoun's "adjustments are being made," the worker focused on school. This had been the mother's concern in the prior session. The worker did note that she hadn't given Margie and Betty a chance "because I assumed the girls weren't ready to talk."

On hearing the surprising news of Margie's pregnancy, instead of focusing on what this means to Margie, the worker took refuge in factual, non-empathic questions regarding the baby's father and adoption. She then suggested a referral to the agency's teen pregnancy counselor, which could push Margie further away from engagement with the worker herself. Despite these errors, the worker recouped later in the session:

After a silence, Mrs. Calhoun brought up an issue that was obviously upsetting her. Her voice was raised, and her speech was fast and detailed. Margie and Betty, who don't have drivers licenses, had taken Mrs. Calhoun's car and damaged a wheel driving over a curb. She said, "Here I was, out working hard to support the family, and this is what my children do to me. This is what I have to put up with." Margie said she wanted to say something, but Betty warned her not to get into it. I suggested that Margie say what she wanted, but Mrs. Calhoun broke in with, "I can't have children in my house who won't respect rules." I said it must be real difficult for her to go to work with the fear that her children, at home without supervision, would break her rules. She recalled other rules they had broken and then switched the subject back to Margie's pregnancy. She asked Margie to tell me why a crisis counselor at the community hospital had told them to get a restraining order against the baby's father. Before Margie could begin, Mrs. Calhoun proceeded to narrate the story herself. (Here the worker might have asked Mrs. Calhoun to let Margie tell the story herself.) John had come to the house with a knife, threatening to kill Margie and himself if she wouldn't talk to him. So far, Margie had said nothing, but now she asked me, "Do you know what it's like to have someone threaten to kill himself and you, and really mean it?" I said I had never been in that situation but I could imagine that she must have been really scared. She said, "He didn't use to be like this, he was nice to me at first." She added that over the summer she spent most of the time on the streets or at friends' houses. She didn't think her mother cared about her, but cared only about work and her own boyfriend. "Now I see she was working so hard to get things together for my brothers and Betty to come live with us. I know I was wrong and did a lot of dumb things over the summer, but my mother was never home." I asked how she feels about it now, and she said that with her siblings here, she sees her mother more. Margie turned to Betty and said, "You didn't see how hard she was working to buy things for you, you didn't see how tired she was, working two jobs. That's why Momma got sick, and I know it's our fault." Betty seemed to want to say something and I invited her to speak. She said she used to get mad when she was still down south: "I would ask for things, but she'd only send them maybe two or three times a year." She was angry because her Mom didn't write to her or call her. Mrs. Calhoun broke in to say that she was always working and tired, and didn't have time to write because she was getting things ready for all of them to be together again. I told Betty that when I first met her mother, all she could talk about was how excited she was that her kids were coming home and how much she enjoyed talking with Betty on the phone. She was sorry she didn't write more.

At this point all three were crying, but the worker does not record whether she responded to their crying.

Betty said she called her worker down south last week and told her that all they do is fight. "I don't know what's wrong, but things aren't working right. I can't talk with my mother any more." I asked Betty to talk to her now. She said, 'Momma, I used to be able to talk with you, but I can't any more. That's our problem, all we do is fight, and you're always mad." She then brought up an incident when Mrs. Calhoun slapped her for not getting up to bring her a scarf. Mrs. Calhoun said she was angry because the girls were talking back to her, being disrespectful. Betty said, "But you don't listen when we try to say things, Momma." Mrs. Calhoun responded that they had said she wasn't a fit mother. Betty said, "I said that Momma, but I was mad, I didn't mean it."

The worker commented that the girls were taking some responsibility now for things they had done, and saying that they sometimes say things they don't mean when they are angry.

Mrs. Calhoun said, "This family has been falling apart since the girls were 11 or 12. I've been through so much." Betty said, "We're going through it too, Momma. It hurts us too." I said, "There is a lot of pressure on all of you and maybe if you can talk some of it out, things won't hurt so much." (The worker also needed to point out that there was love, too, and a desire to make things work.) Betty said, "Yeah, we don't talk until we're so mad that all we do is fight. This family doesn't talk." Mrs. Calhoun said she still feels like the villain and doesn't think the girls love and appreciate her. They disagreed, and I helped them express this to their Mom. Then I moved closer to Mrs. Calhoun, took her hand and said, "You have a lot of pressure on those capable shoulders of yours. You're working hard to keep the family together. With all this pressure it's hard for you to take time out to really talk to one another. Your daughters don't seem to see you as a villain. They are expressing problems they see, but they love you." By now all were exhausted. I asked if they felt it helped to talk. All said yes as they wiped away their tears. I said, "This is difficult work, but you really opened up here. Talking and trying to understand each other is the first step to solving the problems. I feel we need to set up weekly meetings with the whole family or at least with you three." I added that I saw our work together as learning how to get along as a family and to feel good about being together. "You've only been together three weeks and a lot of changes are going on." I walked them to the door. Mrs. Calhoun called the next day to say they had talked some more. She still isn't sure if the girls want to follow house rules. I said we could talk about ways to help them understand the need for some rules and some ways to make things clear to them. She said, "All right, I'll see you Tuesday."

The severely dysfunctional relationships and communication in the Calhoun family need to be understood from several vantage points. One is the typical adolescent struggle for independence from parents and conformity to peer behaviors and norms. This struggle is intensified by the sisters' uprooting. They moved from a small southern town where they had lived all their lives to a depressed and dangerous area of a large northern city. We should also consider the long separation of mother and daughters during the crucial years of the girls' puberty and early teens. This reunited family faces intense demands on a working solo mother, and a lack of social supports to make coping with all the new demands easier. And, finally, the apparent conflict between Mrs. Calhoun's relatively rigid values and the more relaxed norms of urban working-class families now encountered by the girls.

The social worker's joining skills create a therapeutic context for the sharing of family members' pain. She redirects mother and daughters to talk to each other and reframes their maladaptive communication patterns. "With all the pressure it's hard for you to take time out to really talk with one another." This situation cries out for a therapeutic ritual celebration of the family's reunion, designed by the whole family (with the help of the social worker, if needed). A celebratory ritual could help with the difficult reunion tasks. It could also be a first step in relieving serious, maladaptive interpersonal processes that emerged during this family session and to help prevent further family breakdown.

Ahead lies the practice task of helping the Calhouns construct a new paradigm as a reunited family in a new environment. This requires adaptive exchanges, new attitudes and beliefs about themselves and the family, and even new values and norms. They will also need help in developing a new structure of family roles, tasks, and new relationship and communication patterns.

A *challenged child*, intellectually, emotionally, and/or physically, often presents distinctive adaptational and coping issues for parents and siblings. Chronic disability is a persistent life stressor. The Jacob family consists of the wife, Susan, a 25-year-old son, Elliot, and a 22-year-old son, Sam, the identified patient. Mr. Jacob died five years ago. The Jacobs are white, Jewish, and of Polish descent. They live in an upper-middle-income suburb. Sam was referred to a psychiatric hospital after a short-term hospitalization for detoxification of Xanax and alcohol. (Sam self-medicated above and beyond the dosage regimen his physician prescribed.) Psychiatrists diagnosed Sam as suffering from hypochondria, generalized anxiety disorder, and obsessive-compulsive disorder (Axis I, DSM III), histrionic, narcissistic, and dependent personality disorders (Axis II). His alcohol and Xanax abuse are in remission. Mrs. Jacob admitted Sam to the psychiatric hospital because of his behavior. After admission, the social worker agreed to meet with Sam twice a week, and with Sam and his mother once a week. Mrs. Jacob also participated in a parents' psychoeducation group which Sam joined after a number of sessions. Initially, Elliot was ambivalent about attending family sessions. In his own counseling, he had been working on setting limits to protect himself from becoming overinvolved in family difficulties. Therefore, the worker and Elliot agreed to weekly telephone contacts. He was also willing to participate in monthly family sessions.

Sam was an average to above-average student until high school. Behaviorally, he did not present any problems to teachers with the exception of socializing during class and excessively interrupting to ask questions. He experienced his greatest social success during junior high school athletics, band, and a leadership position held in student government. He brought friends home. When Sam was in the eighth grade, his mother underwent several surgeries for thyroid cancer. When Sam was in the ninth grade, she had a mastectomy and chemotherapy. At this time Sam began to experience severe anxiety and panic attacks. As Sam progressed through high school, mounting anxiety interfered with his ability to perform. Twelfth grade was especially difficult, and he saw the school counselor several times a week. He entered a small liberal arts college but was homesick, calling his father every day and going home every weekend. He dropped out after the fall semester because of his father's death and mother's hysterectomy. Next year, Sam enrolled in another college and again dropped out after the first semester. Subsequently, he enrolled in three other colleges as a nonmatriculated student and held a series of jobs, unable to sustain study or work. With each move, he established an unsuccessful relationship with a therapist. He was unable to live independently and became increasingly unable to manage his own affairs.

Mourning has been difficult for the family. Mrs. Jacob was not sure she could go on as homemaker or provider and became very depressed. Elliot was a supportive listener for both his mother and brother; however, he quickly became overwhelmed and fled by returning to school for an additional semester. He is currently experiencing a delayed grief reaction. Sam is highly defended against his father's death, showing little affect. He buried deep feelings of guilt, believing that he had contributed or possibly caused his father's death. Mrs. Jacob had no time to mourn. She had to cope with her own illness as well as assume responsibility for her husband's business and the caretaking of three grandparents.

Mrs. Jacob states that her husband fostered intense dependency both in herself and the children. He dominated decisions and communications. His judgment was not to be questioned. In the tradition of second-generation parents, he wanted to give his children all the material things he did not have as a youth. He strongly advocated for his children (e.g., when Sam did not make the town's baseball team, Mr. Jacob intervened and had the decision reversed). He was unable to accept that his children had any problems, offered pep talks, and "fixed" things. As Elliot and Sam grew older, Mrs. Jacob became concerned by the children's lack of ability to follow through with commitments and assume responsibility. Mr. Jacob subverted her efforts to teach discipline and responsibility. He continued to insist that the ``kids are just fine, stop worrying." However, in the area of academics, Mr. Jacob expressed his frustrations and disappointments. He expected and demanded excellence. In this area, Mrs. Jacob became the children's protector. And when Sam began to have serious problems, she took over his thinking and feeling. She did it for him.

A grandparent and uncle suffered schizoid and schizophrenic conditions—possible genetic predisposition. Life experience, and the family paradigm, have made it extremely difficult for Sam to separate from his family. Developing separateness was the focus of the worker's helping. The following excerpt is taken from the third session. Mrs. Jacob, Elliot, and Sam are present. The family had been talking about separation for forty-five minutes, and the session was coming to an end.

MRS. JACOB: Did you talk to Carol (the worker) about getting a pass this weekend?

SAM: (Looking at the worker) No, I don't want to go on a pass this weekend.

WORKER: (Smilingly) Sam, I didn't ask the question, *share your reason.*

SAM: (Looking at his mother) I don't want to go on a pass with you this weekend. I want to do something with my friends instead.

MRS. JACOB: Well, that's fine. It is your decision. I just thought I'd ask.

SAM: I think I will enjoy myself more with my friends.

MRS. JACOB: What do you mean by that? Aren't we supposed to do things together to work out our differences? Isn't that bad for his treatment?

SAM: No, I'm supposed to do things with my friends instead of running to you all the time.

WORKER: I think it is very important for you to spend time together, but I also remember that you all agreed to work on helping Sam to separate from home. It is very important to develop supports outside the family, and one way to do that is by spending time with friends.

ELLIOT: That's true. I remember making some good friends at college and realizing for the first time that I didn't have to be exactly like my parents—always together.

SAM: Yeah, I remember when Elliot decided to go away to college. I could not believe he did that, but I was proud of him.

WORKER: *What do you mean?*

SAM: Because I could never do that. I went to the college close to home my parents picked out for me. What did you and dad think about Elliot's decision?

MRS. JACOB: We, we were disappointed—sure we were. We were very upset.

ELLIOT: I felt guilty about that.

WORKER: It seems that though Elliot felt bad about making some of his own decisions, he was still able to follow through—*that took a great deal of strength.*

MRS. JACOB: I am beginning to see what you are saying. Elliot went with what was comfortable for him, and maybe that was best because he learned to function on his own.

SAM: It's always been like that. I have never been able to say no to my parents.

MRS. JACOB: Oh Sam, that's not true.

SAM: See, she's doing it again—telling me what I think and how I feel. It seems like she knows me better than I know myself. That's the problem. I never know whether she is right or I am right.

WORKER: Sam, I suggest you ask her.

SAM: Do you think it happens a lot?

MRS. JACOB: Well yeah, I do that a lot; not only with you but also with Elliot.

WORKER: *As a family, you are all working very hard at recognizing your patterns, at becoming experts in how you behave with each other. You are a very close family—you even speak for each other as if you knew the thoughts and feelings of each other.*

ELLIOT: That's true. We all need to grow on our own. I take my phone off the hook at night, because after a number of phone calls I am no longer able to talk with Sam or Mom.

WORKER: *You are learning to take care of yourself.* Everybody has to learn to take of themselves.

SAM: I think we may be on to something here.

MRS. JACOB:	Me too. You know, I never looked at it this way before. I mean, I know that we did too much for our kids instead of teaching them how to do things for themselves.
SAM:	So, how do we get better at it?
WORKER:	Sam, you are making an important start by choosing to be with your friends; Mrs. Jacob, you by your willingness to look at the patterns; and you, Elliot, by placing some limits.
SAM:	This is scary, but it does feel like a good start.
WORKER:	*Yes, a start, and we will go slowly—it can't happen overnight, but with the love you have for each other, you can do it.*

With the social worker's *support*, Sam is able to tell his mother that he prefers to spend the weekend with his friends rather than coming home. Because the worker had *prepared* Mrs. Jacob for this objective, she did not respond with panic or guilt-inducing responses. However, when Sam devalued her importance in his life, she became defensive. The worker supports Mrs. Jacob's investment in spending time with her children, but also reminds all that they had agreed to help Sam develop additional supports. She joins with each family member as well as with the family unit, *using the agreements* to keep the work focused. The fact that Mrs. Jacob acknowledges her pattern of taking over freed Sam to state the crux of the difficulty with his mother. Mrs. Jacob became defensive again; however, when she became invalidating, Sam held his own and turned to brother and worker for support. This was the first time that Sam could intervene in his own behalf. He is working very hard to stick with the theme of struggling to express his own thoughts and feelings to his mother. The worker *reframes* their maladaptive communication and relationship patterns by crediting their ``becoming experts at recognizing how you behave with each other. You are a very close family—you even speak for each other as if you knew the thoughts and feelings of each other." Elliot makes the family fusion issue more explicit by stating how he deals with their intrusiveness by taking the telephone off the hook. The worker *credits* his ability to take care of himself, and encourages the other members to use Elliot as a role model. The session ends with the worker providing *hope* that their pain could be alleviated.

Family Processes

Differences in values, role expectations, self-definitions, and patterns of daily living can undermine a family's ability to cope with painful life transitions, traumatic life events, environmental stressors, and the attendant stress. Differing generational and cultural factors account for much of the family stress evident in the Benetti family, although neither factor is a focus of the work.

Mr. Benetti, age 65, emigrated from Italy with his parents at age 4. For 30 years he owned the shoe store where he first worked as a young man. Mrs. Benetti, age 53, emigrated from Italy as a teenager. She does not work outside the home. The oldest child, Sal, age 22, lives nearby with the maternal grandmother. The other children, Mike, age 20 and Dena, age 19, live with their parents. The grandmother, born in Italy and now 80 years old, lived with the Benettis until Dena was age 3. She continues to be an active presence in the family, doing most of their cooking and cleaning because of Mrs. Benetti's crippling anxieties. Mrs. Bendetti was hospitalized for depression after Dena's birth and is treated as an incompetent child by the family. When Dena was in her senior year of high school, Mrs. Benetti developed agoraphobia (fear of leaving the house), and her husband sold his store. He is semiretired.

The children did well until adolescence. At 17, Sal, rebelling against his father's rules, was ordered by father to leave the home. He moved in with his grandmother, and is now praised as the only child to hold a job. Mr. Benetti complains about his two "weak" children: Mike is withdrawn, and while Dena did well in school, she dropped out in her senior year and was recently discharged from a psychiatric hospital.

Neither parents nor children have friends. The outside world is perceived by several family members as unsafe and suspect. Boundaries between individuals and between subunits are blurred. Mr. Benetti regularly interrupts members during sessions and tells them what they should do. He talks at everyone but does not listen. Grandmother constantly interferes in the family and tends to infantilize Mrs. Benetti. The parents rarely interact, except for his telling her what to do or complaining about the children. Both resist freeing their children to live their own lives, partly because of a cultural norm of two, and even three, generation families living together; and partly because of realistic fears and unrealistic anxieties in the parents and the children.

The social worker met Dena at a halfway house after Dena's discharge from the psychiatric hospital. She had been in the hospital for six months' treatment of severe depression and anorexia. The worker continues to follow Dena's progress and is now working with the entire family. The following excerpts reflect serious life stressors that block the family from coping with traumatic life transitions that involve the adult children's struggle for independence. In the first excerpt (from the initial session), those present are the parents, grandmother, and Dena. Unexpectedly, the focus shifted from the "identified patient," Dena, to the "unidentified patient," Mrs. Benetti.

MRS. BENETTI: It's hard to describe. I feel panicky when I'm home alone, and I can't go out of the house alone either. I don't know why I feel like this, but it's getting worse.

MR. BENETTI:	(interrupting) She's impossible. She's like a child. (To his wife) You're afraid because we were robbed once, but the neighborhood is safe.
GRANDMOTHER:	No, she's not afraid of being mugged. I wish it were that simple.
MRS. BENETTI:	I don't know what I'm afraid of.

Mrs. Benetti is signaling for help. Her husband views his wife's phobias as unnecessary fears, and he is clearly frustrated. He is not yet ready to deal with the implications of his wife's symptoms. The grandmother knows that her daughter needs help, contradicts Mr. Benetti, and invites discussion of the family secret. The worker, having joined the family, now gives support to Mrs. Benetti as the weaker member. The worker tracks life stories, in order to gain understanding of family development and structure.

GRANDMOTHER:	I grew up in a small village. I was one of ten children, and all my relatives lived nearby. When we came to this country my daughter lived with me and my husband. When he died, we lived together until her marriage. We then went to live in her husband's apartment. I was happy when she married him. He was older, and I thought he would take care of her. After Dena was toilet trained, I remarried and moved to an apartment close by. We were happy for fifteen years together, but when he died I was so lonely that Sal came to live with me.
MR. BENETTI:	I kicked Sal out of the house because he couldn't obey my rules.
MRS. BENETTI:	It was good for everybody because my mother shouldn't live alone.
WORKER:	(Looking at the grandmother) Burying two husbands has caused you much loneliness and pain.

The worker responds to the grandmother with empathy for her losses, and wonders if the fact that grandmother and Mrs. Benetti have never lived alone as adults has something to do with the difficulties the Benetti children are having in living on their own. Grandmother wanted the worker to understand the cultural values and norms to which the family adheres. The worker pointed to how these attitudes could be keeping the children from moving ahead. This interpretation, however, ignores the deep feelings involved in culturally based expectations. The significant issue of the "normal" difference in cultural norms between the two immigrant generations and the third generation (in this family) is not brought up again. Exploration and emphasis appeared to be more on emotional components. As important as those are, they are not the total explanation. An opportunity to explore and clarify a common cultural impasse between generations in an immigrant family was missed.

In the next excerpt (second session), the worker explores the parents' marital relationship:

MR. BENETTI: It makes me angry when we're walking across the street and a car comes too fast, and she refuses to run.

MRS. BENETTI: I can run if I have to—you're too anxious.

MR. BENETTI: No you can't. You never run. You're going to be killed because you won't run. You should practice running.

DENA: There you go, telling Mom what she should do instead of listening to her.

MRS. BENETTI: I think he runs too much. He's going to fall and hurt himself.

WORKER: I hear that you are both worried about each other and that you care for each other.

MR. AND
MRS. BENETTI: Yes.

WORKER: You're in the same situation, yet you are two different people and react to it in different ways. I sense your frustration with each other, and the difficulty you have in accepting very different styles and rhythms. But I want you to know that neither of you has to be right or wrong. Your difference makes you very interesting people.

MRS. BENETTI: (beaming with pleasure) I never thought about being different, I just thought that something was wrong with me.

The worker searches for common ground, their mutual caring, and legitimizes their differences in style and the pace of life. She reframes their criticism of each other, "Your differences make you very interesting people" offering a new perspective on their relationship difficulties. Mrs. Benetti is responsive to the comment but her husband, perhaps feeling threatened, continues to berate her. The worker asks for her reaction:

MRS. BENETTI: I don't like it when he yells at me. He makes me feel very bad.

MR. BENETTI: Well, you do nothing all day long, and I have so many problems with work and money. But you can't understand that, can you?

MRS. BENETTI: Yes, but . . .

MR. BENETTI: (interrupting) But what do you do about it? Do you get a job to help the finances?

MRS. BENETTI: But how can I if I'm afraid to go out of the house alone? (pause) You always criticize me, and it makes me feel so bad.

WORKER: (to Mrs. Benetti) You feel yelled at like a child, and (to Mr. Benetti) you feel great pressure and frustration. Mr. Benetti,

	could you try to tell your wife about your pressures and frustrations without yelling at her?
MR. BENETTI:	Well, I get so mad.
WORKER:	I know it's tough when somebody is very angry to control the anger. What else could you do with it?
MR. BENETTI:	Ummm, maybe leave the room, or take a walk.
WORKER:	That would be a good start. Mrs. Benetti, if your husband forgets and starts to yell, could you remind him to go for a walk?
MRS. BENETTI:	Yes, I could do that, if he won't yell at me.
WORKER:	Mr. Benetti?
MR. BENETTI:	I will leave the room. I won't yell, but she has to try also.
WORKER:	What would you like her to do?
MR. BENETTI:	Last week, you mentioned something about a phobia clinic at the hospital. I want her to go.
WORKER:	Mrs. Benetti, if I help you make the arrangements, and your husband takes you, would you be willing to try the clinic?
MRS. BENETTI:	I'll do anything as long as Mario doesn't yell at me.

Mrs. Benetti conveys how devastated she is by her husband's constant verbal abuse. His rage immobilizes her. Mr. Benetti expresses frustration at not having an adult partner to share his life. Neither feels understood or supported by the other. The situation is maintained by his aggressiveness and her passivity. The worker wants them to empower themselves so they can change their own behaviors. Her hope is to unfreeze the rigid system of exchanges so they may themselves find new ways of relating to each other.

During the third session, Mrs. Benetti complained that her husband never talks to her. Mr. Benetti said he was so tired at night that all he wants to do is watch television. The worker then developed a homework assignment: the Benettis agreed to participate together in a planned leisure-time activity each day (without any one else present). They practiced how they would do this by discussing a TV show they had both seen. The worker notes, "This was the first time I saw this couple have a relaxed conversation, talk without complaining, arguing, or yelling, and actually laugh together."

In the next excerpt, Dena and her parents are meeting with the worker.

MRS. BENETTI:	I've been to the clinic twice now, and I think it's helping me. (brightening) Look, I have this rubber band on my wrist, and now when I feel anxious, I just do this (showing how she snaps it).
DENA:	I don't know if it's good that you go the clinic, Mom. I'm afraid you may get worse and be hospitalized and then Dad would be alone.
WORKER:	What makes you think she might get worse instead of better?

DENA: Maybe their relationship will change; they may get divorced.

WORKER: You're concerned that your mother's getting help may mean that the family may change, and that worries you because you want your parents to stay together. Mr. and Mrs. Benetti, what do you think about Dena's worry that you may get divorced and the family would fall apart?

The parents' declaration that they never would divorce seemed to reassure Dena. Suddenly, the parents shift the discussion to their own concern that the children are leaving home.

MRS. BENETTI: Mike is thinking of joining the army.

MR. BENETTI: Sal is leaving for Italy next month to work on a farm. He's crazy. I don't know why he wants to go there to work on a farm. He'll be back soon, I'm sure.

MRS. BENETTI: Well, I don't know why Mike is thinking about joining the army. He should be at home.

MR. BENETTI: Yeah, he could get a good job.

WORKER: It's hard to have your kids leave home. What worries you the most?

MRS. BENETTI: I just like my kids at home with me.

MR. BENETTI: Sal needs to be near home to help me with projects.

WORKER: I sense you're feeling abandoned?

The worker encourages them to express their shared sadness at the prospect of "losing" their children. However, she doesn't pick up on the cultural norm that the generations live together, nor does she grasp the parents' desperation. They pressured Dena to leave the halfway house and return home. Dena soon became very depressed, refused to eat, and had to be rehospitalized. In the next excerpt the worker confronts Mr. and Mrs. Benetti:

MRS. BENETTI: We are so upset that Dena is in the hospital again.

MR. BENETTI: She shouldn't be in the hospital. She's better than she ever was. I think I should bring her home.

WORKER: (after a pause) She was doing much better until she stopped eating again.

MRS. BENETTI: I think she needs to meet with you more often. You've helped her.

WORKER: Dena feels very guilty about not being home to help you. She hears from her mother and grandmother that they are lonely and from her father that he needs her help with his paper work. She feels helpless to meet your needs while she is trying so hard to get better. She needs your support and encouragement to stay where she is instead of your pressuring her

> to come home. She feels you say one thing to me in the office
> and the opposite at home. This has to stop, otherwise she will
> not get better.

The worker makes an appropriate therapeutic demand on the Benettis to
stop sabotaging their daughter's treatment. They and the worker then
agree to work on new ways of relating to their children (but still not in the
cultural context). With the parents' knowledge, the worker met several
times with the siblings. She helped them to improve their relationship and
to support one another's efforts to be more independent. Their trust in the
worker and her prior support enabled the parents to support Dena in her
decision to remain at the halfway house. Mrs. Benetti continued at the
phobia clinic and is proud of her progress. With the worker's encouragement and positive reinforcement, she assumed increasing responsibility
for household management and relies less on her mother. Mr. Benetti
joined the YMCA for exercise and to meet other people. He still has an occasional outburst of anger toward his wife but quickly leaves for a walk. Both
are talking more to each other and, for the first time in years, are going to
the movies. Dena, too, is making progress. She often chooses not to go
home on weekends but remains responsive to her parents in their daily
phone calls.

The family's caring for one another, and the parents' hopes for themselves and their children, facilitated their adaptation to the family transition
that required new relationships to the children and to each other. They
coped with several serious stressors and learned to manage negative feelings, improve interpersonal processes, and resolve stressful demands by
cooperative problem-solving. Effective coping raised the level of relatedness, competence, self-esteem, and self-direction in both partners, empowering them for continued growth. Mr. and Mrs. Benetti may be on their
way to forging a new family paradigm as a couple that incorporates the new
reality of their American-born children's transition toward independence.
They are reorganizing the family structure of roles, tasks, routines, goals
and expectations. The tasks of children, parents, and grandparents might
have been easier if the members had been helped to understand the generational and cultural aspects in their struggles.

The Dubois family, working-class, French-Canadian, and Catholic
(inactive), live in a rural area. They were referred to a family agency following the discharge of the 21-year-old daughter from a psychiatric hospital. She had been treated for a bi-polar disorder with psychotic features and
was also seriously anorexic. The youngest of four children, she is the only
one still at home. The others live nearby and visit their mother and sister
almost daily and attend the family sessions with the social worker. Mrs.
Dubois struggles with severe bouts of heavy drinking.

The worker frequently referred to her puzzlement at the family's lack of progress after more than a year of work. The family group remained resistant to change, and Mrs. Dubois and her daughter also resisted individual change. The worker decided that a likely source was their inability to mourn two significant losses suffered three years earlier: the death of the maternal grandmother, who had lived with the family from the time of the parents' marriage, and the sudden death of the father several months after the grandmother's death. Unmet tasks of grieving seemed to be one source of the family's maladaptive relationships, yet they resisted talking about it with the worker. Whenever she brought up the deaths, one or more members changed the subject.

In an effort to help Mrs. Dubois and her children recognize their grief so they could work on resolving it, the worker created a ritual for them. She suggested that Mrs. Dubois place her husband's funeral flag in a prominent place in the house a week before the upcoming anniversary of his death and keep it displayed for a week. She was asked to do the same when the anniversary of her mother's death came around. Mrs. Dubois agreed amiably to both requests. But when the time came she said she couldn't do it because it was too upsetting for one of her sons.

It may be that Mrs. Dubois rejected this prescription, at least in part, because she and other family members were not invited to participate in designing a ritual of remembrance. If therapeutic rituals are to be effective, practitioners and clients need to co-create such ceremonies, rather than the practitioner imposing them on the family (Imber-Black 1991). The rejection of the ritual may also be related, in part, to the lack of attention to the family's ethnic background.

The Dubois parents and grandmother were born in Canada. Langelier (1982) points out that many rural Franco-Americans with limited education hold values that emphasize self-control, obedience, family loyalty, and rigid family roles. Aggression and anger are not acceptable. Mistrusting outsiders because of historic discrimination, many find it hard to acknowledge a need for mental health services. In some families, problems are viewed as failures in self-management and, like family secrets, are strictly private. Hence, their members tend to be guarded and to withhold information. Some working class and rural families do not seek insight and they do not expect change (Lengelier 1982). Langelier notes, "In one case where the issue was primarily focusing on grief over the father's death, the family could not bear to talk about him, it was taboo. He had been idealized, and the distortions that they were collusively protecting prevented them from dealing with themselves." (240)

Family Development, Paradigm, and Transformation

Over time and the life course family members develop shared, implicit beliefs about themselves and their environment and their worldview (the family paradigm). A traumatic life stressor (such as death, severe injury, or illness) may require the family to change its ways of functioning, integrate the new reality into their worldview, transforming itself and creating a new paradigm. Such change is difficult and takes time and energy. Family violence or substance abuse, for example, are difficult to change.

Susan Mulligan, age 31, Catholic, Irish-American, lives in a rural, working-class, factory town. She sought counseling at a women's center in connection with three major stressors. She has filed for divorce, and her husband, Richard, is not contesting. But he is asking the court for sole custody of the three children (Seamus, age 7; Maura, age 5; and Kevin, age 3), which terrifies Susan. She lacked financial resources to obtain effective legal counsel, while Richard had no such problem.

Richard had abused Susan throughout the eight-year marriage. He abused her emotionally and physically, even raping her once when she was extremely ill and on heavy medication. During the past year, he beat her severely on three occasions. He was arrested for the most recent beating a month ago. That precipitated her divorce action.

Susan is an alcoholic who has remained sober for seven months. Susan states that Richard is an alcoholic and she asked her attorney to request a court order for an alcoholic assessment and treatment of Richard. The attorney did not do so until after four months of pressure by the social worker.

Susan and Richard were ordered by the court to remain in their jointly owned home with their children, creating a dangerous situation for Susan and the children. Susan is very upset about this as she is afraid of Richard, who continues to harass her. He owns a plumbing business, yet he has not paid the mortgage, car repair, or car insurance, nor has he helped with the daily care of the children, all of which he was ordered to do by the court. Susan works as a bookkeeper and pays for all food, heating oil, and childcare expenses.

Susan suffers from a chronic, painful gynecological condition which began after Kevin's birth. A year ago the symptoms worsened. She finally went to a gynecologist who prescribed medication. Symptoms continued and six months later Susan underwent surgery. She still must take medication, and since it does not work well when combined with alcohol she stopped drinking when the medication was prescribed.

Susan's parents and eight siblings live in a nearby town. She has no contact with her siblings, but has a warm yet distant relationship with her father. She resents her mother's continuous criticism about how she raises her children and her mother's doubts that Susan is "really" an alcoholic. Mother contends that Susan has too many meetings. Susan says that her father spends most evenings in the local pub, three of her brothers and two of her sisters also drink heavily, but "my mother, who doesn't drink at all, doesn't like to think of this." Despite her criticism, her mother does help with evening childcare as needed (both parents are employed days).

The Mulligans are awaiting the completion of a family study by the family relations officer of the county's superior court. Due to budget cuts and the backlog of cases, the study may not be completed for another eighteen months. In the meantime, Susan is clearly at risk of further violence. Her patterns of communicating with her parents, her lawyers, her alcohol counselor, and the social worker alternate between cooperativeness and blaming everyone else for her problems. Although she is consistent in maintaining sobriety and being responsible with her children, she is defensive and wary. This makes a poor impression on her attorney, the Judge, and her alcohol counselor.

The social worker records their work together:

Our immediate agreed-upon aims were to improve Susan's relationships with uncaring personnel in the justice system, and with her mother and her children; strengthen her cognitive and perceptual capacities in order to correct misperceptions and faulty interpretations; and improve problem-solving.

Susan attends Alcoholics Anonymous (AA) every day and our center's weekly group for substance-using and battered women. She sees her alcohol counselor and me every week. Her compliance with the various treatments may be fueled by fear of losing her children, but she also says that AA and the group are "my only sources of sanity these days." She was suspicious and wary with me until recently. By now, the judge and three sets of attorneys (representing Susan, Richard, and the children) view both parents as difficult. Her attorney failed to push for Richard's alcohol assessment and treatment, and the judge handled the domestic violence with arrogance and insensitivity. Susan compounds these terrible realities by rude and abrasive attitudes and responses that evoke still harsher judgments and attitudes on the part of the attorneys and judge.

Susan doesn't yet follow through on my efforts to show her that if she deals with her attorney more productively she may avoid an undesirable custody arrangement. Instead, she blames him for representing her poorly and feels victimized by him. On the other hand, the children's teachers, daycare providers, and pediatrician stated to me that Susan is a responsible parent, while Richard has not been to see any of them. The pediatrician reported that the children do not manifest fetal alcohol syndrome. They are physically healthy and of normal intelligence or better.

The children's attorney, whom Susan was forced to engage and pay for, because Richard refused to, plans to recommend joint custody. She views both parents as equally dysfunctional and adds that Susan is rude to her and wastes her time with irrelevant information. She rejects my attempts to advocate for Susan and the children, as dispassionate and tactful as I try to be, and "ordered" me to have no further meetings with the children.

Considering all this, Susan is coping well with an extremely stressful and potentially dangerous situation. She continues to hold down her job, care for her children as best she can (at least from outward signs), drive her kids and herself to all the places they need to be, and maintain the difficult relationship with her mother. She takes care of her own health by remaining sober, taking her medication, and seeing her gynecologist regularly. Relations with the children have improved, and her limit-setting is calmer and more consistent. She has also complied with every task the judge put to her and takes pride in being able to perform under such pressure.

Susan has also striven mightily to meet the terms of what we both view as a very unfair and potentially dangerous court order (continuing to live with Richard). Together, we worked out a safety plan should Richard become violent, and we taught the children how to dial 911 in an emergency. I talked with Susan's attorney and the children's attorney about the primary need for safety, described research findings about men who batter, and pressed for an alcohol assessment of Richard. After months of my continuous pressure Susan's attorney filed a motion that she and the children be allowed to live separately from Richard and that he be ordered to undergo alcohol assessment/treatment.

Coping with the attorneys and judge is still ineffective as Susan fails to see how her anger and behavior lead to their rejecting, pejorative attitudes. I am now using rehearsal, role play, and positive reinforcement to help Susan manage her negative feelings in a more constructive way, bolstered by my emotional support. We're working on correcting her false assumptions and distortions about these people through reciprocal role play. Improved cognitive and perceptual capacities are likely to empower Susan and give her more control of her own life. These tasks, however, are extraordinarily difficult for Susan in light of the abuse and neglect by her husband and the court, the attorneys (including her own), and the family relations officer.

Susan and the worker may need to undertake further work, for example, "walking" Susan through the judicial process in preparation for the court appearances that lie ahead. This could increase her tolerance of delays and decrease her open, self-destructive anger. Similarly, the worker might help her to revise "self-conversations" that she, like all of us, holds with herself, especially those in which she evaluates and interprets her unpleasant experiences. This could be done by guiding and reinforcing more positive self-statements (Meichenbaum (1977). For example, instead of telling herself that the people in authority hate her, Susan could practice repeating to herself before scheduled encounters, "No matter how unpleasant they are, I am going to be respectful and calm when I explain my difficulties to these people, because everything will be better if they like me." Assertiveness training might also help her deal more effectively with the lawyers and judge, and even with her mother.

Depending on the court's decision regarding divorce and custody, Susan and her children face several difficult life transitions that will require a new organization of family roles, tasks, rules, routines, and goals. Ultimately, a new family paradigm will need to incorporate new values and norms (e. g., sobriety, centrality of child rearing, importance of pleasurable time together) and changed beliefs and attitudes regarding interpersonal relationships both inside and outside the family. In these ways, Susan and her children could transform their abusive, addictive, nuclear family to an abuse-free, alcohol-free, healthy, solo parent family. Such an achievement will merit a celebratory ritual.

In the next example a couple seeks social work help because of escalating verbal and physical abuse. Denise Carter, age 35, and Melvin Carter, age 47, are an African-American couple living in a suburb with Denise's two adolescent daughters. They are nonpracticing Protestants. Mr. Carter is a recovering alcoholic, sober six years; Mrs. Carter is a daily beer drinker. The couple married eighteen months ago after living together for two years. Both have been married before. Mr. Carter has three grown children from his first marriage, all of whom live out of state. After their marriage, their arguing about Mrs. Carter's and her family members' drinking turned to screaming matches. Last May, after Mr. Carter lost his job (he charged the employer with racial discrimination), the constant verbal arguments escalated. Mr. Carter became violent and Mrs. Carter called the police. In September, Mrs. Carter became violent and he left home for three weeks. Mrs. Carter initiated counseling two weeks ago alarmed that the relative calm following Mr. Carter's return is now replaced by days and nights of constant verbal fighting. The couple and the student social worker contracted to meet for eight sessions to deal with their dysfunctional communication and relationship patterns. At the end of the period, they are to consider whether they want to continue to work on their relationship or whether they want help in separating.

Both Mrs. and Mr. Carter come from large families. Mrs. Carter has six siblings all living in her neighborhood. There is a history of alcoholism in her maternal grandmother's family and two of her brothers abuse drugs and alcohol. Mr. Carter's siblings live out of state. His father, who died twenty years ago, had been a recovering alcoholic for the last fifteen years of his life. Mr. Carter and one of his brothers are also recovering alcoholics. Six years ago Mr. Carter entered a one month alcohol rehabilitation program; subsequently, he lived for six months in a drug and alcohol rehabilitation halfway house. He has remained sober since then. His determination to stay sober results in a militant anti-alcohol stance. When Mr. Carter met Mrs. Carter, she was not working and, by both accounts, was living a partying lifestyle. Both Carters attribute Mrs. Carter's change in habits—cutting down on beer drinking, maintaining more regular sleep patterns, finding and holding a clerical job—to Mr. Carter's encouragement and support.

Mrs. Carter grew up in a family with fluid boundaries. Today, family members and friends sleep and eat at each others' apartments with no prior arrangement and, according to Mr. Carter, little respect for individual or marital privacy. Problems are seldom owned by individuals; the group works on them together. This lack of unit boundaries is a crucial issue in the Carters' marriage. Mr. Carter resents Mrs. Carter's siblings walking into their bedroom at 11 P.M.; he also resents the time she spends at her mother's and sister's homes. He describes his family of origin as fairly formal. Visitors to his extended family were by invitation, and friends never blended easily into family situations. He rarely interacts with his own family; his interactions with Mrs. Carter's family are mostly limited to breaking up their drinking parties in his apartment and telling them to leave.

Communication between Mrs. Carter and Mr. Carter is vituperative, driven at present by Mr. Carter's increasingly toxic reaction to Mrs. Carter's drinking. They are so intensely reactive to each other that they have difficulty effecting any nonvolatile exchange. They alternate between heated fighting and withdrawal—Mr. Carter into silence and tv—Mrs. Carter into her family, friends, and beer. Although both appear to understand the role that environmental factors (unemployment, job, and financial pressures) play in their verbal and physical violence, their animosity is so great that their focus is on blaming each other. The Carters are currently experiencing the effects of bread-winner role reversal, a reversal painful to Mr. Carter and somewhat confusing to Mrs. Carter. Just at the time Mr. Carter was fired, Mrs. Carter received a promotion. Mr. Carter spends his days driving Mrs. Carter to and from her job and looking for work.

The isolation of Mr. Carter's days is not alleviated by contact with peers. Mr. Carter and Mrs. Carter developed friendship patterns as alike as their family relationship patterns are different. They cultivated drinking buddies, people who drifted in and out of their lives, people brought together by interest in partying. Mrs. Carter still has these buddies. Mr. Carter, encouraged by his association with AA, avoids his one-time buddies and is estranged from people he and Mrs. Carter had in common.

In the first session, the Carters were fully engaged in a discussion of their perspectives on the marital issues. They agreed to devote eight sessions to work on improving their life together. When the worker went to the waiting room to greet them for the second time, they were seated at opposite ends of the room, slumped in chairs, glowering. Once in the office, Mr. Carter sat in the farthest corner and Mrs. Carter sat close to the worker.

WORKER:	You seem upset, are you having a rough time?
MR. CARTER:	Yeah.
MRS. CARTER:	We had a big argument over the TV on Saturday and Sunday because I said channel 2 was 3.
MR. CARTER:	Yeah. Not only that. She's beginning to irritate me.
MRS. CARTER:	Yeah. He's beginning to irritate me. See I said 2 was 3 on TV, and he said that I knew it all.
MR. CARTER:	No. You see, first of all you irritated me from before. You know what you did. You irritated me from Friday. You called me up and you was all fired up, and I don't like that. ["Fired up" is Mr. Carter's term for drunk.] I'm getting aggravated. I'm getting sick of it.
WORKER:	(to Mr. Carter) Last time you were here, you said that you didn't like Mrs. Carter's drinking. Is this what you are saying now?
MR. CARTER:	Yeah. Because she gets nasty, and I don't like it. She called me to get her at her sister's on Friday; and I came when she said to. I waited fifteen minutes, and she came out and says she is not ready to go. She done that on purpose. I know she did.
MRS. CARTER:	But I was gonna send my niece out, but thought (taps her head), "No, I should go myself. He won't like it if I send her." So I went out. But I don't like to always be thinking like that, walking on eggshells. That's not me.
WORKER:	Help me get a better picture of when these things happened. It was Friday when you went to pick Mrs. Carter up and Saturday you had the argument over the TV—AND SUNDAY TOO?
MR. CARTER:	Yeah. She was trying to make me look stupid in front of the kids. I was showing her the paper, just trying to explain. But you don't read. You don't even know what's going on half the time. Channel 2 is not Channel 3!
MRS. CARTER:	No! No! Channel 2 is the same as Channel 3—on the cable station—they're the same. I know that. I was right.
WORKER:	But channel 2 and 3 is not what you are really arguing about—your argument started on Friday night.
MR. CARTER:	No. I was irritated before.
MRS. CARTER:	Melvin can do whatever he wants but I have to do what he wants. I'm getting frustrated! I'm getting tired! Like I told you about not sending my niece out there—I don't like to be thinking all the time.
WORKER:	One of the things—if you're going to live more peacefully with each other—is that even if you don't like to, and you may not like to, you both have to stop and think. Especially during the time when you're trying to see if you can make

things good enough to discover if there's something still good between you. If you don't do that, nothing is ever going to change because (I snap my fingers) you trigger each other.

MRS. CARTER: Sometimes I don't feel comfortable about things.

MR. CARTER: (ignoring this) Everything starts out like that. You were wrong. Channel 2 and 3 are not the same. If you weren't all fired up all the time, you'd know that.

MRS. CARTER: You're draining me. I can't go to work, and I can't function because you're draining me.

MR. CARTER: That's always your story. That's your famous story. You better get another story. I tell you I'm sick of it! (yelling and lunging out of his chair).

WORKER: OK! (I cut the air with my hand to separate them.) We can't get anywhere if we try to deal with five things at once. We're dealing with the drinking; we're dealing with the way you argue, the way that you talk to each other; we're dealing with TV channels. You are arguing about Channel 2 and 3, but it could be about anything. Mrs. Carter, you could say, "That's a crow." And Mr. Carter, you say, "No, its a pigeon." So one of the things that's very important is to stop and say, "Hey, we're not arguing about 2 and 3." What are we really arguing about? Is it the tension about drinking? Let's get to the bottom line.

MR. CARTER: Yeah. She already knew. It's that drinking that's getting to me.

WORKER: OK. Let's talk about that.

MR. CARTER: That's the real problem. The drinking. It's making me sick. The smell of it is making me sick. Most of the things start with the drinking.

WORKER: Do you see it that way, Mrs. Carter?

MRS. CARTER: Yeah. Most of the time.

MR. CARTER: You always irritate me with that drinking.

MRS. CARTER: Yeah. You ain't so fine, always yelling at my brothers, at my sisters. You call me stupid. You're the one that's stupid.

MR. CARTER: Bitch! You can't even get up in the morning. (rising out of his chair) Bitch!

WORKER: Mr. Carter! Get back into your chair. There will be no threats! We need to take turns talking. For a while, I just want you to talk to me. (I reposition my body) Please, each of you take turns talking to me—and directly talk to me about the drinking. Please do not interrupt when the other is talking. Mrs. Carter, let's begin with you. Tell me about the drinking. Friday night, for example, describe the evening, what it was like, what happened, how much you drank, and so on.

The Carters are angry and want to continue their fights. "Their acute sensitivity to each other leads to hair-trigger reactivity. Over time the cycle wears the participants down. Husband and wife interrupt each other and do very little listening" (Burden and Gilbert 1983:27). The worker's initial efforts to develop a structure for the interview and to slow down the pace failed partly because of the Carters' rage, but also because of the student practitioner's discomfort with the intensity of their feelings. When she invites them to "help me get a better picture of when these things happened," she unwittingly invites them to refuel their television channel argument. She exhorts them "you do have to stop and think," and misses their tremendous mutual pain and confusion. In the student's analysis of this particular intervention, she wrote:

> I am aware that my nonverbal presentation is that of a preacher. I am sitting erect on the edge of my chair and speaking in a loud projecting voice, scolding. I was thinking that I had to give them an answer to their problems, and I was feeling somewhat desperate. I moved away from their frightening anger.

In the final intervention, the worker prescribed a structure to the session. This was a breakthrough, as the Carters accepted the structure and took turns in directly talking to the worker. The destructive feedback loop was broken by having the communication go through her, and they begin to listen to each other. In violent families, the partners need nurturing and expression of concern for their needs before they can use cognitive inputs. "As clients become emotionally stronger, they become more receptive to education and advice" (Contoni 1981:11).

SEVEN

HELPING WITH DYSFUNCTIONAL
GROUP PROCESSES

Mutual aid is the primary rationale for the development of group services. Dysfunctional processes emerge at different points in a group's life course and the group becomes blocked from serving as a system of support.

Group Functions, Structures, and Processes

By their very nature group mutual aid systems universalize individual issues, reduce isolation, and mitigate stigma through their powerful yet subtle interpersonal processes. A formed or natural group led by a social worker is comprised of individuals who come together under agency auspices to work on a common life issue. Schwartz (1971:7) defines a social work group as a "collection of people who need each other in order to work on certain common tasks in an agency that is hospitable to those tasks." A group's primary functions are to establish and maintain a favorable interchange with its environment and develop a mutual aid system. The same two functions present challenges to the group's survival: to manage environmentally induced stressors and interpersonally induced stressors. When successful in carrying out the twin functions and meeting the two challenges, the group is in adaptive balance.

Groups are formed with different foci:

- *educational.* Participants acquire relevant knowledge and information, such as coping with a schizophrenic child, dealing with diabetes, practicing safer sex, and preparing for surgery.

- *problem-solving.* Members help each other with common life transitional, environmental or interpersonal concerns, such as raising a developmentally challenged child, coping with divorce, dealing with the death of a parent, or confronting spousal abuse.
- *specific behavioral change.* The group serves as a context for individual change, such as eating disorders, substance abuse, and phobias.
- *task.* Members help one another to reach prescribed objectives in groups such as planning and advisory committees (Toseland and Rivas 1995).
- *social.* Members learn interactional skills, make friends, and build social connections.

As members develop a sense of purpose and commonality, they begin to share experiences and concerns. Safe or less threatening issues are raised first to test the worker's and other members' genuineness and competence. Through the testing, members begin to develop and reinforce mutual bonds and alliances as they figure out where each member and the worker belongs in the interpersonal system. When collective support and individual comfort are in place, members are willing to risk more sensitive and sometimes even taboo concerns. When they learn to share and to relate to on another, they experience a "multiplicity of helping relationships," with all members investing and participating in the helping process rather than only the social worker (Schwartz 1961:18). Since they have experienced similar life stressors, they are more receptive to others' views and suggestions. Moreover, as a microcosm of members' interpersonal self-presentations, the group is a rich arena in which members can examine their own adaptive and maladaptive perceptions and behaviors. Through their exchanges members develop and practice new interpersonal processes and environmental activities and receive feedback from the group on their efforts.

Finally, groups have the potential to be a force through which members act and gain control and mastery over their environments. A passive retreat from one's environment inevitably leads to feelings of incompetence and impotence. In contrast, being active in a group, and influencing one's environment, helps develop competence and a sense of personal empowerment (Gitterman 1994; Schopler and Galinsky 1995).

Internal Stressors in Groups

Unfortunately, not all groups experience these successful outcomes (Gitterman 1979). Even after much effort some groups never begin, others begin and then disintegrate, and still others reinforce deviant and maladaptive behaviors. Even groups that achieve an adaptive balance may experience upset in the balance at certain points in the group's development. These upsets are natural and even essential to the group's construction of a mutual aid system. When the balance is upset by internal or external stressors, the group attempts to regain balance by various coping efforts. However, while some efforts may temporarily relieve stress, in the process members might develop dysfunctional communication and relationship patterns that create further stress. Such dysfunctional interpersonal processes can also emerge from formational and structural elements.

Formational elements. Lack of clarity about group purpose is a frequent formational problem. If members' needs diverge, or the agency's agenda does not fit group interests, or the social worker's conception of group purpose is ambiguous, then members may withdraw, test incessantly, or act out. For example, for five years, a group of mildly developmentally challenged young adults had been meeting as a social club in a community center. A social work student wanted to explain her proposed short term service to group members. As the director felt that members would have difficulty sharing personal concerns in a formal group setting, he invited the student to their Saturday evening social gathering.

Arriving in a casual business suit, sweater, and scarf, the student immediately felt out of place as the members were clad in jeans. The club president, Hank, introduced her, stating that she had some services she wanted to offer the group. The student recorded that before she could present her well-rehearsed offer, she was bombarded with questions: "Are you selling something?" "Are you a doctor?" "My name is Gary, what is yours?"

WORKER:	As Hank told you, my name is Joyce, and I am a social work student.
VARIOUS MEMBERS:	Are you a therapist? I have one already. I'm already in a group in my program, I don't need another group.
WORKER:	I'm here to tell you about a group I thought some of you might be interested in, but before I explain it, maybe every one can introduce themselves, so I will know who you are. (all introduce themselves) I thought the group could discuss the jobs you have, the difficulties you may have had on the job, how it feels to be different, not only on the job, but . . .
GARY:	Oh, you mean because sometimes we're discriminated against in the job market?
WORKER:	(continuing) Yes, maybe some of you have experienced discrimination in other ways too, and the group could be a place to talk openly about experiences and to share what has been helpful for you at such times.
DANIEL:	Why do you want to focus on problems, this is Saturday night, time for rest and relaxation . . . why are you so formal, you can talk to us like you talk to anyone else, we're all human you know.
GARY:	Give the girl a break, she's just trying to help us.

WORKER: I guess I'm a little nervous, I don't know you that well and . . .

GARY: Sit down, get to know us, we don't bite. (He laughed, and other members joined in.)

WORKER: I am really interested in talking with you about some of your feelings about being labeled retarded in this society.

NANCY: I am not going to be in this group.

BARRY: I don't like that word at all, I have heard that word all my life, it was like a prison sentence for me.

JACKIE: (slamming the table) Let me tell you, I don't let anyone push me around, one time a guy started laughing at me, I let him have it. I don't let anyone push me around!

NANCY: (walking around, obviously very angry) So that's what the group is about, that word, that disgusting word? (Gary and Cynthia tried to help me and an argument broke out among the members. I tried to explain what I meant, but it was clear that I had lost the members, created an internal group conflict and put a damper on their Saturday night activity.)

At the next meeting, the student changed the focus to helping members to share information about health-related, leisure time, and housing resources available to them in the community. They appreciatively accepted the revised conception of group purpose. This focus met their desire and need to focus on the "positives."

Group composition dramatically influences interpersonal processes (Gitterman 1982, 1994). Overly homogeneous groups are apt to lack vitality. A group whose members are all depressed, for example, could find communication stifled. Also, a homogeneous group is sometimes unable to absorb a member who deviates from group norms. For instance, a group of light skinned Puerto Rican girls with one African American member or a parent's group with one father may not be able to assimilate the member who is different (Brown and Mistry 1994).

A member describes a poignant experience of being "different" in a group:

My previous social worker referred me to a group at a mental health clinic. She told me it would give me something to do and people other than my children to talk to. Then I found out it was a group for recently released mental patients, many of whom were still psychotic. They talked to themselves and sometimes lost sight of reality for moments. I was frightened by them. Look, I know I am nuts, but I'm not that nuts. Maybe someday I will be, but let me get there in my own time. When I have a nervous breakdown, I want it to be my very own and not taught to me by members of my therapy group.

(Gitterman and Schaeffer 1972)

On the other hand, groups that are too heterogeneous lack stability because members with limited interests or concerns in common find it difficult to relate to one another. In school-age groups, for example, differing personalities skew interpersonal trends as some members act out and others withdraw.

A co-ed group of eleven children was composed of subgroups (of fifth graders and sixth graders) of students who knew each other from their classrooms. Gender issues also came into play because there were relatively few boys. This created another natural sub-group within the larger group:

Jean began to speak, and Ann, Barbara, and Tracy began to fool around with one another. Richard said something quietly to them about being quiet. Tracy immediately told him to "shut up" and called him a "tub of lard." Barbara and Ann began to laugh. Jean became quiet. I looked over at Tracy, Barbara, and Ann and told them that Jean was talking and they should not interrupt. Richard looked at the group of girls and said, "See, I told you, you shouldn't be talking." All three girls told him to shut up and continued to call him names, laughing. I told the girls that there was to be no name-calling in this group, and asked them if they remembered the group rules. Tracy looked at me and said loudly that Richard had started it, and called him still another name. I asked Richard if that were true.

Before he could answer, the three girls broke in to say that it was true. I told them to please be quiet and give Richard a chance to speak. Laughing, they all looked at Richard and waited for him to speak. He hesitated and then, with a little smile, said that it was not true. Simultaneously and angrily, the girls called him a liar. I told everyone to be quiet and listen to Jean. I invited Jean to continue. She hesitated for moment, shyly smiling. The other three began to giggle. I looked at them angrily and said, "I am tired of your being rude to other members." They tried to suppress their smiles, and Tracy pulled her chair in close with exaggerated interest in what Jean was saying. I looked sternly at her, and she moved her chair back with a smile to the other two. Barbara and Ann laughed.

Jean went on to describe an interesting experience. I nodded and asked whether anyone else had experienced something similar. Frank had been drawing something with his body sideways to the group, and Richard was looking over his shoulder. Billy was also drawing, but he kept his face to the group. Frank looked up from his drawing and shared his own experience. I attempted to comment on this, but was interrupted by Tracy, Ann and Barbara who were giggling about Frank's drawing, and asking him to show his drawing. I looked at them and asked them to be quiet. Ann said loudly that Frank was drawing and he wouldn't show it to the group. I asked Frank if he would show his drawing. He shook his head with a smile and continued to draw. The girls insisted that he show the drawing to them. I told everyone to please be quiet, and asked Frank and Billy to stop drawing and turn around to be with the group. I waited until they reluctantly did so. The girls taunted them and giggled. Frank told them to shut up, and Billy joined him. I stopped and told Tracy, Barbara, and Ann that I wanted them to sit between the boys and directed them where to sit, starting with Tracy. They resisted loudly saying that they did not want to sit by those "idiots." Nevertheless I insisted.

The girls became very angry and Tracy turned her chair around and the other two followed her. I asked them to please turn their chairs around and waited. They did not. I said, "All right then, everybody leave, the meeting is over. Until you guys can start acting mature in this group and participate, I don't want you to come back." The group froze and everyone became quiet. The three girls immediately turned their chairs back around and said that they would be good now. I told them quietly to leave and that we would discuss this next week.

While the worker's behaviors certainly contributed, heterogeneous composition undermined members' ability to achieve common focus and mutuality.

Group size can also skew interpersonal processes. Groups that are too large cannot provide sufficient opportunities for individual participation. Groups that are too small make excessive demands for intimacy.

Open-ended groups with fluctuating membership tend to develop two chronic problems: members lose their original sense of purpose and vitality, and the group remains stuck in an early phase of development (Galinsky and Schopler 1985, 1989). The shifting membership "obscures and retards the development taking place" (Brabender 1985).

Structural and normative factors. Social structure and culture evolve in the group and mediate between environmental demands and group needs, and between group demands and individual needs. Social structure represents a network of roles through which responsibilities are allocated, decisions are reached, and relationship and communication patterns established. Roles may shift and change as work continues and as the group passes through phases of its development. Some structures are too loose and others are too tight for adaptive interchanges to take place within the group, and between the group and its environment. In a group that is too loosely structured, individual autonomy may be valued, but the members do not experience a sense of identity and support that comes from group solidarity. Members are not sufficiently integrated into a structure, so that patterns of relationship and communication may not permit involvement in developmental or environmental issues. In a group that is tightly structured, overinvolvement of group members with one another leads to patterns of relationship and communication that limit adaptive interchange with the social environment. The price for belonging is a reduction in individual autonomy.

As in families, subunits also evolve in groups. Subgroups are usually composed of members with similar interests and interpersonal orientations to authority and intimacy. Members who are similar on these dimensions tend to find or "drift" toward each other, seeking security together. When subgroups are fluid and responsive to the phases of group development, they provide important support to group members. When they are "frozen," inflexible, and exclusionary, however, they are frequent sources of dysfunctional interpersonal patterns (Garland, Jones, and Kolodny 1968; Berman-Rossi 1992; Berman-Rossi and Cohen 1988).

The social structure and its patterns of relationship lead to the emergence of a group culture. Members set group norms regarding rights and responsibilities, modes of work, bodily and verbal expressions of feelings, and styles of relating and communicating. These unite group members and integrate their behaviors. Norms that are rigidly defined or punitively enforced, however, pose problems for members seeking to develop and maintain individuality and a degree of autonomy. The violation of norms that prohibit certain behavior poses a serious threat to group survival and generates powerful sanctions resulting in expulsion, ostracism, or scapegoating of a member.

When group norms are ambiguous, members become anxious and may engage in continuous testing of the leader and the group in order to establish guidelines. Whether ambiguous or clear, norms may be unevenly enforced, reflecting preferential treatment and double messages and creating rivalries. Members may subscribe to discrepant personal norms of morality, logic, and attractiveness. Such discrepancies could also create dysfunctional patterns.

Both the structure and culture of the group are influenced by environmental factors including societal, community, and agency values and norms, as well as opportunities and limitations. Group members may respond to environmental limitations with apathy, which then inhibits their use of whatever resources are available within the group and environment. Others may turn inward and project their anger and frustration on to the group members. In groups composed of minority school children we observed the children's consistent tendency to internalize and to project teachers' negative judgments of their intellectual abilities and potentials on to one another.

The group service may not be adequately supported by the host agency's structures and procedures. Without administrative approval and commitment to the group service, the worker "walks on egg shells." In response to any perceived issue, such as noncooperation by a hospital patient or "noisy" children in a school or social agency, the medical or psychiatric chief, school principal, or agency director may disrupt or even terminate the group. Similarly, without interdisciplinary staff involvement, a group service is easily interrupted, undermined, or sabotaged. It may be time for the group to begin, yet nurses suddenly have to take the patients' temperatures, or teachers decide to punish children for class behavior by disallowing group participation.

Along with agency sanctions, structural supports are also essential. Children cannot participate freely if the worker's office inhibits activity or if an auditorium encourages destructive behavior. If young single mothers are to participate, child care assistance is essential to support attendance. Finally, the worker, as organizational representative, can over-identify or under-identify with the organization and create internal group problems.

A hospital group was organized to help surgical patients with their common concerns about the critical life event and discharge. The worker expected members to focus on this group purpose. Instead they raised questions about the setting itself, which the worker felt were inappropriate:

> JILL: I'd like to know why this floor is so dirty?
>
> WORKER: Have you spoken to the head nurse about it?
>
> JILL: No, it should just be improved.
>
> WORKER: I can see you are angry about this.
>
> JILL: Angry . . . I'm not angry. I'm just stating the facts.
>
> WORKER: Well, the conditions around here seem to be a real concern for you, but . . .
>
> JILL: Listen, the showers are not clean and they are clean on the other side of the hall. Why do you think that is? I shouldn't be expected to walk over there.
>
> WORKER: No, you shouldn't be expected to walk over there. These are legitimate complaints, but . . .
>
> JILL: I am not complaining, I'm just telling you I'm aware of what is going on.
>
> WORKER: OK, the things you are bringing up about the conditions of this floor should be brought up with the head nurse after this group is over. The purpose of this group is to discuss similar concerns about being here and being sick. Now I'd like the rest of the group to share their concerns.
>
> MARY: The showers are dirty though.
>
> JILL: See, I'm not the only one.

WORKER: I realize you all may be concerned about the conditions here. What I am saying is that these things can be discussed with the head nurse.

ELLEN: I don't care what we talk about.

Long periods of silence and withdrawal followed. By attempting to steer group members away from their expressed concerns, the worker mobilized their resistance.

In these varied ways, societal, community, and organizational conditions affect group life and can create dysfunctional communication and relationship processes. Interpersonal processes are also affected by phases of group development. Tension and maladaptive communication arise from discontinuities in members' personal development or in group development tasks. In a group of pubescent girls, one member might already be dealing with biological and social transitions of early adolescence that pose communication and relationship issues for her and for the group as they take one another's measure. In another group, most members may be ready for the group's developmental phase of interpersonal intimacy, but their relationships and communications are already inhibited by one member's continuing preoccupation with testing the worker's authority. Thus, group developmental factors are potential interpersonal stressors and sources of dysfunctional behaviors.

Behavioral Expressions of Internal Group Difficulties

Dysfunctional interpersonal patterns in formed groups are often expressed in factionalism, monopolism, scapegoating, withdrawal, and ambiguous communications. While these processes are usually dysfunctional for most members, they can also serve an unrecognized and unintended function of maintaining the group's equilibrium. Thus, they are best understood by focusing on the functions they serve for the individual and for the group.

When factionalism becomes a fixed pattern of relations, a clique or alliance provides its members with greater satisfaction and a sense of identification than are experienced by the total group. This is desirable for the clique, but it isolates and rejects the other group members. This is dysfunctional for them and threatens the constancy of the group. Autocratic leadership promotes factions as a way to obtain security and protection from punitive interaction with the leader. The members then compete for the leader's attention and for improved status for themselves at the cost of unaffiliated members, undermining their status and security.

In monopolism, one member produces overwhelming detail in describing ideas, feelings, and experiences. At the manifest level, this gives the monopolist control over his anxiety and the group process and its content with positive consequences for him (Yalom 1985). The other group members tolerate and even encourage such communication because monopolist behavior protects them from self-disclosure and personal involvement. At the latent level, however, the behavior has negative consequences for all group members, including the monopolist, by preventing the group from fulfilling its purpose and successfully completing tasks.

In a day treatment program, a new worker was assigned to an adult group (ages 27 to 45) composed of members with a psychiatric diagnosis. The group had been meeting for over a year. The current main theme is dealing with parents and agency staff members. The members justifiably feel that they are not treated as adults in spite of their chronological age. From the first meeting Mr. Marcotti monopolized group interaction. Whereas in the day treatment center and in individual sessions he was quiet and withdrawn, in the group he has always been the "talker." One could depend on him to keep the session going. Through the group, he learned to assert himself, experienced how good it feels to talk, and to have attention and power. The worker began to view the monopolization as a hindrance to the group's growth and tried to reduce his participation. He experienced the worker's efforts as discrediting his role and fought to hold on to it. The worker recorded:

Mr. Marcotti was talking for a period of time about his sister's death. I stated that it must be very painful to lose a family member, and inquired if anyone else experienced it.

MS. RAINES:	I had a cousin who died last year and I felt sad
MR. MARCOTTI:	(interrupting) I didn't even know my sister was sick. (I asked him what he meant) Well my Mom told me one day that my sister was in the hospital and then the next day she died.
WORKER:	This seems like a very painful experience for you, but could you hold it until Ms. Raines finished?
MR. MARCOTTI:	Yeah, I guess so.
MS. RAINES:	(I encouraged Ms. Raines to continue.) Well, Mr. Marcotti can keep talking, I can wait.
WORKER:	I think it would be a good idea if you each had a chance to talk and if we waited for one person to finish before another starts. What do each of you think about this? (While they nodded in agreement, the group sat in silence.)
MS. SATZMAN:	One time I told my mother I didn't want to have my hair cut and I would tell her when I did, but she didn't even listen to me.

WORKER:	It sounds like you were very frustrated and possibly annoyed because your opinion wasn't respected.
MS. SATZMAN:	That's right. I don't see why my mother doesn't ever listen to me. I'm not dumb you know.
MR. MARCOTTI:	Yeah, my mom didn't even tell me when my sister was sick and put into the hospital.
WORKER:	Uh huh, I see. So, Ms. Satzman you are saying that you would be like to treated like everyone else.
MS. SATZMAN:	Yeah, I'm not a little kid anymore.
MR. MARCOTTI:	I don't know why my mom didn't tell me that my sister was sick. I have a right to know what's going on too.
WORKER:	It seems you both are upset about not being treated like adults. Has anyone else had similar experiences?
MR. MARCOTTI:	I have another experience of when I wasn't listened to. One time . . . (After a couple of minutes, I interrupted him)
WORKER:	Mr. Marcotti, I appreciate your contributions, but maybe we could hear from other members and then we'll get back to you, OK? (This pattern continued and I found myself increasingly annoyed.)

As we shall discuss later, the worker's feelings and reactions become part of the group system's pattern of maladaptive communications and relationships.

Scapegoating in formed groups is similar to the process in families. The scapegoat status serves important latent functions for both the individual member and the group. At the group level, deviance helps clarify behavioral norms, sharpens group boundaries, and promotes solidarity. For the individual members, the contrast between self and the scapegoat member is reassuring and offers protection against the fear of similar behavior or attributes in the self. For the scapegoated member, the status provides satisfaction as well as pain. The scapegoat is often at the center of attention and may also partake of secondary gains in the sense of martyrdom, helplessness, and enslavement in the service of others (Antsey 1982; Shulman 1967).

Usually the scapegoat is the most vulnerable member of the group. A school group of African American youngsters might scapegoat the lone Latina member. Her responses to the members' provocations may lead to the institutionalization of the scapegoating role. If an adolescent males' group is threatened by the behavior of an effeminate member, their communications could be replete with ridicule and hostility. Reciprocally, his responses influence the scope and intensity of members' reactions and will determine his acceptance by the group or his exclusion through scapegoating. In geriatric facilities, the least lucid member tends to evoke hostility from the others. She represents a safe target for the displacement of members' feelings of despair, impotence, confusion, and anger. The disoriented member's inability to fight back only frightens the other members and triggers their further acting out.

While scapegoating controls and suppresses serious group issues at the manifest level, it has negative consequences at the latent level that entrap the group and the scapegoated member. To the extent that a group permits its members to exploit one member in order to maintain their own functioning, all members become vulnerable to stress from personal, group, or environmental processes. The scapegoated individual suffers grave harm, internalizing the negative perceptions of others as self-contempt. The group members develop dysfunctional interpersonal processes that reflect their evasion, negation, guilt, and projections.

Frank is a mildly retarded member of a "truancy group." He exhibits poor self-control and occasional bizarre clowning. In an early meeting, Stanley was describing how the teacher makes school impossible for him. The work is too hard, and the teacher calls on him when he doesn't know the answers. As all the boys began to laugh, Angel asked Frank, "What're you laughing about?" I asked if anyone else had a similar experience. Frank replied, "Yeah, in dancing class, all the kids laugh at me." He demonstrated his dancing, and explained that the teacher made him stand in the corner because he made mistakes. Billy, said, "Frank you are so damn stupid anyway." Angel added, "You don't even know how to read, write, or the multiplication table." All the boys laughed and joined the attack.

Frank performs a critical function for the group, permitting members to evade necessary work on painful life stressors and to displace frustration and anger. The youngsters' hostilities are managed by focusing attention on one member,the clown, who mediates conflict by providing the group with comic relief. For Frank, the positive consequence is the momentary glow of attention. The fact that both the "deviant" and the group benefit from the scapegoating underscores the transactional nature of scapegoating. But in the long run, the process has negative consequences for the individual and for the group. It further isolates the scapegoated member, nor do the members grow and develop their full potential. Thus, the social worker must understand not only what group and environment processes make scapegoating necessary, but also what processes in the scapegoat lead to his inviting and accepting the maladaptive communications and relationships.

Social Work Function, Modality, Methods and Skills

The Social Worker and Dysfunctional Group Processes

With groups whose maladaptive interpersonal processes interfere with their efforts to deal with stressful life transitions, traumatic life events, and environmental stressors, the social work function is to help members to communicate openly and directly as they work on common life issues and to develop greater mutuality and reciprocity in their relationships. The worker relies on the enabling, exploring, mobilizing, guiding, and facilitating methods described earlier and also mediates to improve a group's interpersonal processes and the internal forces that generate them. Internal mediation is different from the external mediation directed to the environment.

Professional Methods and Skills

Mutual aid groups are organized around common concerns, interests, or tasks. These groups can universalize individual life issues, reduce isolation, and ameliorate stigma. Skillful group formation mitigates internal stressors.

1. *Beginning a group service.* Support groups emerge from a common life issue or interest. Life transition groups focus on (a) stressful developmental struggles and status changes; (b) painful life issues; (c) difficult status changes; and (d) traumatic life events. Environmental groups relate to a lack of community resources; problems within an organization; and consumer involvement within an agency. Interpersonal groups focus on natural units (patients on wards; students in classrooms; residential cottages) and forming groups to deal with maladaptive patterns (couple groups; family groups).

2. *Obtaining organizational consent and support.* A clear presentation increases the likelihood of achieving organizational approval and support important to the development and institutionalization of group services.

3. *Composing the social support group.* Group composition influences development and direction. Groups require both the stability of homogeneity and the diversity of heterogeneity. For example, in developing support groups for pregnant adolescents, the social worker identifies their common concerns about birthing; relationships with parents, boyfriends, peers, school representatives; and future plans for babies. The social worker then considers the relative advantages and disadvantages of commonalities and differences in age, first pregnancy, religion, race or ethnicity, stage of pregnancy. Members usually tolerate and even come to enjoy diversity when common interests and concerns are intensely felt. The practitioner assumes professional responsibility for group composition.

4. *Structuring the support group.* Some groups are long-term and open-ended with departing members replaced by newcomers. If a membership core remains intact, these groups provide long-lasting emotional support, social contact, and instrumental assistance. But if membership fluctuates, these groups develop two chronic problems: members and worker lose the original vitality and sense of purpose; and the group remains stuck in an

early phase of group development. In contrast, planned short-term and time-limited mutual aid groups help members focus quickly, maintaining purpose and a sense of urgency. Group size should be determined by group objectives and member needs. The larger the group the more formalized it becomes, thus limiting the opportunity for individual attention, intimacy, and spontaneity. Yet the large group provides greater community and organizational visibility, influence, and opportunities for individual anonymity. Smaller groups become informal and intimate but also vulnerable to disintegration if insufficient membership limits the strengths of diverse perspectives.

5. *Recruiting group members*. Random invitation is one form of group recruitment. This includes using a card file with common criteria for sending invitations; putting up signs; and inserting notices in a union newsletter or community newspaper. Random methods invite voluntary participation and avert pressure for involvement. However, the social worker maintains limited control over group composition. Referral is a second common recruitment method. Referrals will not be forthcoming unless the social worker has organizational or community standing and a reservoir of "favors receivable" to draw on. Appropriate referrals are more likely when group purpose and membership criteria have been clearly stated. Lastly, natural group clusters can be recruited such as isolated elderly in a building, patients on a hospital ward, vulnerable youngsters in a residential cottage. Natural clusters often develop into effective social networks.

Support is central to the group modality (Gitterman 1989a; Nelsen 1980). Support can be metaphorically viewed as the engine propelling the group process just as electric energy runs machinery. Without exchange of support groups lose drive and momentum. For members to feel supported and to be experienced by others as supportive, they must demonstrate certain behaviors to one another. These behaviors include acceptance and the experience of being accepted. Offering hope also demonstrates support. When members sense that situations can improve and become less stressful, they more readily invest themselves in the group.[1]

The social worker helps build a mutual support system by *integrating* members through various skills.

- *Scanning*. The social worker scans the group by focusing "on all the members beyond any one person who is talking at the moment" (Glassman and Kates 1986).
- *Directing members' transactions toward one another*. In the early phases of group development, members often communicate through the worker. The practitioner asks members to talk to each other.
- *Inviting members to build on one another's contributions*. The practitioner encourages members to interact by linking their comments to those of

Table 7.1	Skills of Organizing Mutual Aid Groups

- establish a group service
- obtain organizational consent and support
- compose the mutual aid group
- structure the support group
- recruit group members

others ("Bill's idea is very close to George's. What do the rest of you think about their idea?").

- *Encouraging and reinforcing cooperation, norms of mutual support, rights, and responsibilities.* Group members develop collective norms about rights and responsibilities, modes of work, and styles of relating and communicating. Dysfunctional group patterns such as competition, withdrawal, and exploitation impede the development of mutual aid. To influence these dysfunctional patterns, the social worker supports and guides members to work together supportively and collaboratively ("I hope you feel great about how you solved this problem—no one yelled or threatened—you really helped one another").
- *Examining members' expressions of approval and disapproval.* Group members verbally and nonverbally approve or disapprove of certain behaviors. Approval is expressed through mild praise to more intense acclaim; disapproval through mild rebukes and teasing to more severe scapegoating and ostracism. The social worker helps members become aware of both their dysfunctional and adaptive patterns.
- *Encouraging members' participation in activities and collective action.* Activities require planning and decision making, interaction and communication, specification of roles and tasks, and negotiating the social and physical environments. When members accomplish these, the group becomes a source of mutual support and satisfaction.
- *Identifying and focusing on common themes in members' discussions.* At times, a group theme is readily evident. Other times, a group theme is more elusive and expressed in disparate behaviors. For example, some members may cope with termination by withdrawing, others by acting-out, or by questioning the worker's caring. The social worker actively searches, identifies, and focuses on common themes: "Everybody is reacting to the group's ending— John, you're running in and out of the room; Bill, you have stopped talking to me; Jack, you have put your head down and closed your eyes; and I'm acting like the group is not ending in two weeks." The common themes are the "glue" that binds members together and develops their mutual concerns and skills.

Common themes and activities strengthen collective functioning and foster mutual support. The worker should also help group members to nego-

Tablee 7.2	Skills of Building Group Mutual Aid

- scan
- direct members transactions toward one another
- invite members to build on one another's contributions
- encourage and reinforce cooperative mutual support norms
- examine members' expressions of approval and disapproval
- encourage members to participate in activities
- identify and focus on common themes

tiate their needs for being *different* and *separate* by developing a satisfactory balance between the demands for integration and individuality.

- *Inviting individual members to disagree and supporting differing opinions and perceptions.* To help group members to tolerate differences, the social worker discourages premature consensus and the stifling of divergent perceptions and opinions. The worker invites individual members to disagree and supports differing opinions and perceptions ("Jane, you don't seem to agree. I'm very interested in your ideas"), the social worker encourages expression of individual differences.
- *Inviting participation of reluctant or marginal group member.* In any group, some members may have difficulty in participating, and they may withdraw or engage in parallel activities. With caring and support, the worker invites the participation of the "outside" member. More than one invitation might be necessary.
- *Creating emotional and physical space for individual group members.* Members have different needs for intimacy and distance. Some members are not as ready to trust and expose as are others. Hence, the practitioner helps members to respect one another's needs ("I think Phyllis is saying she need more time before she can talk about the rape. Am I right, Phyllis?").

The social worker helps members to balance individual needs with group needs.

Groups develop dysfunctional group processes for many reasons. To help members deal with dysfunctional patterns, the social worker calls on the internal *mediating* method and its various skills.

- *Developing a transactional definition of the interpersonal stressor.* A worker is curious about a dysfunctional pattern and asks herself, "What is keeping this group structure frozen so that it can't move away from this way of communicating and relating?" "What are the primary sources of this pattern?" "What positive and negative consequences, both manifest and latent, does the pattern have for the collective as well as for the individual members?," and "Am I caught up in it and unwittingly contributing to the pattern?" Social workers must consider the effects of their own interventions and take into account

Table 7.3   Skills of Mediating Individual Members' Needs

- invite individual members to disagree and support differing opinions and perceptions
- invite participation of reluctant or marginal group member
- create emotional and physical space for individual group members

---

the members' disparate views of the maladaptive pattern. The worker regards the problematic pattern in transactional terms, namely as lodged in the collective or subunit structures rather than in an individual.

- *Identifying dysfunctional patterns for the group.* Members are often unaware of transactional obstacles. Identifying the dysfunctional pattern is often the first step to consciousness raising: "I have noticed every time someone brings up a painful subject like graduating or cheating boyfriends, someone picks on Yolanda and changes our focus."
- *Re-identifying dysfunctional patterns for the group.* Since dysfunctional processes are often repetitive, the social worker reminds the group of prior incidents ("OK, here we go again, it's happening right now. Carmen, you started in on Yolanda when we began talking about fathers. . . . Let's take a look at what's happening right now.").
- *Holding members to their agreed on focus and challenging their resistance.* Giving up an entrenched pattern is not easy. Member resistance should be anticipated. The worker holds members to the work: "Everybody's fuming but not talking, what's going on?" Firmness and persistence convey strength and caring which in turn can help members face dysfunctional processes.
- *Inviting and sustaining the expression of strong feelings.* Suppressed feelings such as anger or frustration block communication. The social worker invites the expression of these feelings and the attendant content: "I would like each one to put your silence into words" or "You are furious at each other. What happened?" By inviting the expression of strong feelings, the practitioner conveys faith in the members' ability to deal with interpersonal stressors and in their capacity for mutual aid.
- *Establishing protective ground rules.* Members require an atmosphere in which differing opinions and feelings can be expressed without threat or fear of recrimination. Protective ground rules barring physical violence, or verbal abuse facilitate open and direct communication ("This is going to be a difficult conversation. Remember, there can be no bullying, threats, or hitting.").
- *Identifying common definitions and perceptions.* As members explore interpersonal stressors, the social worker listens carefully for potential commonalities. For example, in a group for parents and their foster adolescents, the social worker clarifies youngsters' struggles for gaining greater freedom and autonomy and parents' desires for maintaining some control and direction. In helping the arguments unfold, the worker searches for possible common ground: the parents' stake in their children making positive transitions into young adulthood; the adolescents' stake in their parents providing security

Table 7.4	Skills of Mediating Internal Group Stressors

- develop a transactional definition of the interpersonal stressor
- identify dysfunctional patterns
- re-identify dysfunctional patterns
- hold members to their agreed on focus and challenge their resistance
- invite and sustain the expression of strong feelings
- establish protective ground rules
- identify common definitions and perceptions
- credit members' work
- use activities and programs to facilitate work

and some structure. The social worker might suggest, "You are all struggling to find the right balance between age appropriate freedom and limits."

- *Crediting members' work.* Members struggle and deal with painful issues. By crediting their efforts, the social worker encourages continued open and direct communication: "The important thing is that as mad as you were with one another, you talked about it. It was hard to do, but you've done it real well."

- *Using activities and programs to facilitate work.* When members are unable to discuss their difficulties, the practitioner uses action, such as working on a craft project or playing a sit-down game, to facilitate communication (Middleman 1980).

Table 7.4 summarizes the skills of mediating internal group stressors.

Practice Illustrations

Dysfunctional Group Processes

A social work student named Jackie was assigned to an ongoing open-ended group on the adolescent unit of a psychiatric hospital (Malekoff 1994). The group consisted of Dick (white), Ralph (Hispanic), and Bill (white). Each had been in trouble with the law, with significant histories of fighting, suicidal thoughts, or gestures. In the last few sessions, the boys had worked on issues related to lying, betrayal, trust, loss of hospital friends, and the departure of a favorite psychiatric resident. Bill, the newest member, was quickly assigned the role of scapegoat, which he readily accepted.

In the next meeting, the pattern continued. Bill was complaining about a youngster who had been discharged from the unit when the other members vented their anger on him:

> BILL: He was just a big bunch of hot air! God! He would make stuff up! Do you know what he said? Man, he said . . .

DICK: Well what about you? You do the same thing. Can't tell you anything.

BILL: (sighs) I don't mean to.

DICK: (glares at Bill, says something under his breath to him)

BILL: (softly) I already apologized for that. I told you I was sorry. (he looks close to tears)

RALPH: (squirms in his seat, glancing sideways from Dick and Bill to me.)

JACKIE: Ralph, do you know what they are talking about?

RALPH: (smiles, looks away) Yeah.

JACKIE: Dick, what's up?

DICK: Bill is a liar. He invents stories and no one can believe him. He doesn't know how to stop it. Who wants to hang around someone like that? He's immature.

BILL: Augh! Jeeze! I do not. I told you about my dad for real. He ran out on us. (said with head hung low) OK? And I'll tell you something else, but I don't want this to get outside of the room. I mean it. I have an older brother, honest, and he had to go back to Germany because he was in trouble with the law—drugs—he's in the army now . . . (tells more of this tale which I hadn't heard either from his mother or from him)

JACKIE: (I remained silent; not a purposeful silence, but a confused one.)

RALPH AND DICK: Liar . . . liar . . . liar . . . liar . . . (Ralph and Dick begin to whisper to each other)

JACKIE: Yo! (all three look at me) Let's get back to the whole group. This isn't the place for private conversations. Remember last time we talked about lying . . . that everyone lies sometimes and there are a whole bunch of reasons why people lie? What are some of the reasons why people lie?

DICK: See, even Jackie thinks you lied.

RALPH: Some of the reasons people lie are . . .

JACKIE: (after a brief silence) What can we do as a group to help keep each other from lying? (more silence)

BILL: (fights back tears)

The meeting ended with long periods of silence and discomfort. Three sessions later Dick and Ralph are "trying to help" Bill by giving him advice on how to act more mature and stop lying.

JACKIE: I notice everyone is sinking lower and lower into their chairs and turning away from Bill. I get the feeling that you guys are pissed off at him. Am I right?

DICK: He's not listening to us. Why bother?

RALPH: How long have we talked about this and he keeps doin' the same thing.

BILL: (sulks, looking away from under heavy lids, hugging chest protectively.)

JACKIE: Bill, you have been pretty quiet so far today. It's hard to tell if you've been listening. I'm wondering if you've heard what Dick and Ralph have been saying?

BILL: I have been too!

JACKIE: (nudges Bill in a friendly way) Tell us what they have been talking about?

BILL: (repeats verbatim, beginning to straighten up and look around the circle, less rigid, half-smile)

GROUP: Laughter from everyone.

DICK: So why didn't you say so, you little twerp.

JACKIE: I'm kind of confused here, Dick. You come down on Bill and say all this negative stuff, like you don't like him, but earlier you said you wanted to help him.

RALPH: We like him. But it's hard sometimes . . . 'cuz he don't tell the truth. Man, we talk to him and stuff during the day. I am just tired of it. He doesn't listen.

DICK: He is like a little brother to me. He just needs to learn to act . . . be mature. I talk to him a lot and give him advice.

JACKIE: I'd like to know what Bill thinks about this. What do you think, do you agree?

BILL: (silence)

DICK: Answer, Bill. Don't just sit there.

BILL: (silence)

JACKIE: Dick, you've been giving a lot of advice about how Bill should change.

DICK: I feel I can help him. I know a lot about psychological testing and stuff and can coach him to act more mature.

JACKIE: Yeah, you've been a friend here on the unit, but your advice seems to have a lot of negatives. You've pointed out a lot of Bill's problems. Can you tell him some of his positive qualities?

DICK: He hasn't fought . . .

JACKIE: (pointing) Tell Bill.

DICK: You haven't fought here, but you've tried to pick on others. You're funny, but sometimes you don't know when to shut up.

After this meeting, the student attempted to assess the group's scapegoating pattern. She remembered that after another group member, John, had been discharged, Bill joined the group and assumed the scapegoat role. Bill was even accused of the same faults as John. Bill and the other members seemed to perpetuate the scapegoating role over the next few sessions. Dick and Ralph maintained that they did not have problems any more, that they are merely waiting for placement, whereas Bill needed to mature and learn how to stop lying. They took great interest in "helping" Bill with his problems. What the worker had not realized was that the processes of both helping and scapegoating Bill served a similar function: namely, to divert focus from their own concerns and issues. Dick had great trouble with intimacy and self-image and is defended with a high intellect. His coping efforts blocked the development of mutual aid in the group.

Bill fit into the scapegoating role, having set himself up as victim on the unit and in the therapeutic community. His lying represents a dysfunctional effort to gain attention and avoid painful or unresolved issues. Ralph wavers, unsure of his loyalty, and preoccupied with his own discharge plans. Transactionally, scapegoating gives Bill the attention he craves; Dick feels empowered and more competent than the others; Ralph is reassured of not being the "dummy" and of having some control over his environment.

Beginning social workers quite understandably find it hard to manage conflict. When Bill informed the group about his brother, the worker was skeptical but she was at a loss how to intervene:

Bill blurted out the story about his brother (which I suspected was fantasy) so quickly that I was unsure how to respond. I felt bombarded. I knew his story would invite a round of scapegoating. I wanted to protect him; at the same time, I realize that I was very annoyed with him. So I vacillated between a retreat into silence and a retreat from the specifics of the exchange. I changed the subject to "reasons for lying," moving to a topic that I thought would be safer and easier to control. And it was. However, by keeping the discussion on a broad, general level, I didn't help them struggle with important common concerns. Moreover, "lying" was still closely connected to Bill (it was HIS problem), and therefore I unwittingly reinforced his negative status. I struggled to not take sides, but now I see a pattern in which I choose sides and put members on the spot. I am beginning to get in touch with my own vulnerability and anger at being put on the spot. I realize this is what we all had in common—a feeling of being on the spot and vulnerable.

Members are often unaware of their transactional patterns. Identifying a maladaptive pattern ("I've noticed every time someone introduces a painful or scary concern like leaving the hospital, someone picks on Bill and our focus changes") is often the first step to consciousness raising. A social worker's identification of, and invitation to examine, an internal stressor is at times all that a group requires to begin modifying a maladaptive pattern.

For example, a student formed a task group of elderly members, with interest in horticulture, to consider uses of a newly built greenhouse. Commonality existed in their love of growing things. Because the agency wanted the greenhouse to serve as a showcase, the staff consistently increased their expectations, assigning the group primary responsibility for its development and care. The student was also pressured by her practice teacher, who emphasized task accomplishment over process. Even though group members felt increasingly overwhelmed and withdrawn, she found it more comfortable and safer to ignore the static underlying group discussions. On her field instructor's advice, she planned a series of horticultural workshops. After the second workshop, she realized she would have to change her approach and invite the members to explain their apparent lassitude and disinterest.[2]

STUDENT: That was a long workshop, you seem pretty tired.

FAY: Well, it was very interesting, but maybe next time we don't need to have slides.

STUDENT: You feel the meeting was too long.

DANIEL: (interrupting) Slides are better, they are infinitely better than listening to people.

MARY: (blurted out) Well, maybe I'm just dumb, but these lectures are getting too high falutin' for me, too—what's the word—technical.

STUDENT: So, the workshops are too technical and boring Is there any thing else about them that you don't like?

GROUP: (silence)

LUCY: Yeah, I'll tell you what's going on. I'm sick and tired of these here experts coming in and telling us what to do. Who needs it! What are they trying to prove, anyhow?

STUDENT: I had a feeling something was wrong, and I'm really glad you shared your reactions with me.

LUCY: Well, you know, I like to say it like it is.

STUDENT: I like to hear it like it is, so please go on.

LUCY: We've been knocking ourselves out with all these people coming in to give us these talks. What for? We don't want to be experts.

NANCY: Yeah, we feel like we are really being pushed around. They tell us the greenhouse is for us, but they want to do it their way.

SARAH: Nancy's right. We want to have fun, to learn from our mis takes; they want a perfect garden to show off.

The student's willingness to "hear it like it is" releases the members' mounting frustration and anger. She demonstrates courage, risking being perceived as disloyal to the agency and as failing to follow classroom pre-scriptions. She becomes curious about the members' experience and moves into the unknown, forgoing a clear and comfortable prescribed script.

Often, however, a single invitation may not be sufficient to break through the group's (and the worker's) resistance to relinquishing an established and comfortable pattern. As the pattern repeats itself, the worker can reflect on prior interventions ("OK, here we go again, it's hap-pening right now"). For example, in the prior illustration, the social worker could have commented, "Dick, you just started in on Bill when we began talking about your being discharged from the hospital." The worker could also encourage members to give up a pattern, even if slowly, by sug-gesting, "Come on, let's not start on Bill. Dick are you worried about going home?," or to examine the pattern directly, "Let's talk about what's happening right now."

Often group members cannot or do not accept a worker's identification of dysfunctional transactional pattern. Giving up entrenched processes is far from easy: avoiding conflict, painful material, intimacy, threatening changes, or escaping into an "illusion of work" may initially be an easier and understandable maneuver. For the group to progress, however, the worker has to attend to dysfunctional patterns and hold members to their agreed on focus. To illustrate, a social worker formed a group of pregnant adolescents. The group's purpose was for members to help one another with the effects of pregnancy on their relationships with boyfriends, par-ents, relatives, friends, and institutions. The group members struggled to avoid dealing with common concerns.

The worker inquired about the "boyfriend situation":

Sally began talking about her boyfriend at great length. I allowed her to continue for a while and then said, "Have any of you had similar diffi-culties with your boyfriends?" Sally stopped for a second, but proceeded with her story. I waited for a minute again, unsure of how to deal with the other members' lack of involvement, and asked Linda, "Did your boyfriend react the same way as Sally's?" Linda sighed and said nothing. I waited for her to respond, but immediately Karen started saying, "My boyfriend is wonderful, he started out as a creepo, but I blew him away." She then told the group all the fun things they had done together. I returned to Linda, and asked, "What are you thinking?" Linda began to say, "Well he doesn't even call me anymore." Sally, Susan, and Karen started a private conversation about their male conquests. (At this moment I over-identified with Linda instead of reaching underneath the bravado for the common fear.) I turned my attention to the trio and stated firmly, possibly harshly, "Let's give Linda a chance, and then you'll have your chance to share your experiences. It's only fair to give everybody a chance to talk." Sally ignored me, saying, "Oh, but listen to this" and continued with her up-beat story. I put myself in their shoes and realized they were attempting to evade and avoid their pain. I commented, "I know talking about some of the difficulties related to being pregnant can really be uncomfortable and hard to talk about." Sally broke in, "I know, but listen to this" and continued her recital of partying, staying up all night, etc. After a couple of minutes (in which I was thinking how to deal with the collective avoidance), I said, "I really feel bad. You girls have so much pain and you could help each other so much with things going on in your life, but you are choosing to act as if you aren't pregnant, as if life is wonderful, when you and I know it ain't no fun." Karen began to relate how her mother hassles her; Sally and Susan immediately began to talk and to laugh. I was moved by the intensity of their resistance, their fear of dealing with such an overwhelming and powerful reality and said, "I am sure you have noticed that every time one of you begins to talk about being pregnant and its consequences, you find something else more cheerful to talk about." Silence. "I know you are feeling badly inside, can you try to share what's happened since you and others found out that you were pregnant?" Linda started to cry. Susan said, "It's OK, Linda, I cry a lot. My father thinks I am a slut (tears came to her eyes)." Sally added, "It's no big deal, yeah, I cry too." I broke in and said, "Sally, what's happening to you right now?" Sally blurted out with rage in her voice, "OK, you wanna know, I'll tell you—my mother kicked me out of the apartment, she wants nothing to do with me." As I put my arm around her, she began to cry, sobbing hysterically.

Challenging dysfunctional patterns can induce a momentary crisis or explosion which loosens entrenched processes and structures, allowing communication and relational patterns to improve. Anger and open conflict in a formed or natural group is particularly difficult for many beginning practitioners. They experience anxiety, feel powerless, and fear members' anger and their own reactions. To cope with these own feelings, they detach themselves from the conflict and thus are unable to help members deal with the interfering interpersonal processes.

Workers must deal with their feelings toward a group member, or risk withdrawing, intervening preemptively, or acting out (Albert 1994). A student, for example, was assigned to a pre-discharge group in a mental hospital. After several meetings a new member was added. She refused to accept the client role: instead she assumed the role of helper, which threatened the student.

WORKER: Mrs. Palmer is joining our group today, and I told her this morning what the group was about.

MRS. PALMER: (interrupting) I'm quite aware of the purpose of a discharge group. I was in one last year and I contributed all I could. I finally resigned because I felt a less fortunate person should have a chance to be in it.

WORKER: What about yourself, Mrs. Palmer, do you think you can also be helped by being in the group?

MRS. PALMER: (smiling) I do not think so, I have no problems, but I will be able to help other members.

By attempting to get Mrs. Palmer to say that she could be helped in the group, the worker focused on the most frightening area for her—leaving the hospital. Mrs. Palmer might have been asked instead to describe her previous group experience. Other members could have been asked to describe the current group. Together, they might have searched for connections in order to ease her entry. The worker's confrontation with Mrs. Palmer in subsequent sessions continued:

WORKER: It's so quiet today, why do you think that is?

MRS. GREENBERG: Yes, we have been talking about some of the things that are scary about leaving here.

MRS. PALMER: I am sure you are afraid. You are always in a daze —you can't go anywhere. (Mrs. Jackson turned to Mrs. Palmer and made a face.)

MRS. GREENBERG: (after a brief pause) I don't need a spokesman to talk for me.

MRS. PALMER: Well, I think you do—you certainly don't say anything on your own.

MRS. GREENBERG: She knows everything, doesn't she?

After this remark there was another long silence. Ms. Phillips broke it by suggesting that Mrs. Palmer can be helpful to the group because she has been in a pre-discharge group before. She asked specifically about proprietary homes. Mrs. Palmer said negative things about the homes. Members' faces registered confusion and sadness. My anger was ready to burst through, and I said, "Mrs. Palmer is making you all a little uncomfortable." Mrs. Greenberg said, "Well, there is a lot of truth in what she is saying." And Mrs. Burgio added, "Yeah, I'd better get an apartment." I asked, "How else are you feeling about what Mrs. Palmer said?" There was no response, and the meeting ended in silence.

The student was immobilized by anger and withdrew from the interaction. While he struggles with his feelings, the group members feel abandoned. Finally, Ms. Phillips searches for connections between the new member and the group. The group needed to examine the specific content of Mrs. Palmer's comments. But the worker's fear that he had lost control of the group inhibited him. The group members sense that he wants them to take on Mrs. Palmer for him. They shy away.

Mrs. Palmer dominated the next two meetings. Her anxiety about leaving the hospital trapped not only her but the group and the worker. The worker felt he had lost the group. He became less active, and the group floundered.

> WORKER: Lately, it has been difficult for all of you to talk in the group.
> MRS. PALMER: It's not difficult, I have been talking.
> WORKER: For the last two weeks, you have taken us off the group focus and on to topics that have little to do with concerns about discharge.
> MRS. PALMER: Oh, no! You are so wrong. I think I have been right on the point.

This particular meeting ended on a bitter note:

> WORKER: Mrs. Palmer, I think it must be hard for you as a new member in this group.
> MRS. PALMER: It isn't difficult for me at all.
> WORKER: I think it is hard; every week you talk about anything but what we are supposed to be working on. How do you feel about being a new member in the group?
> MRS. PALMER: I am not new. I know everyone, we live on the ward. You are new! And besides, I have been through this already in the other group.

The worker responded to the provocations as though he were a group member. He located the problem in the client and her psychological difficulties, and his vacillation between withdrawal and confrontation resulted in a welter of maladaptive communications. Before work could begin on the group's structure and interpersonal processes, the worker had to recognize and accept his fears and vulnerability. In the next meeting, he acknowledged his mistakes and succeeded in placing the interpersonal issue on the group's agenda:

WORKER: I have been thinking about something that Ms. Jackson said about taking a trip. I think it's a good idea. What do the rest of you think?

MRS. PALMER: I think it's a very good idea. I said so when she first mentioned it.

WORKER: Mrs. Palmer, when Ms. Jackson made the suggestion, I was so angry and hurt by you that I didn't even respond to it or to your support for the idea—I'm sorry. (She smiled, but said nothing)

MS. JACKSON: I think trips would be fine. Like I said, it will give us some practice in leaving. (Mrs. Greenberg began to speak, but was immediately cut off by Mrs. Palmer and withdrew.)

WORKER: Mrs. Greenberg, you wanted to say something, but I think you got a little frightened by Mrs. Palmer. I can understand that—sometimes I am a little scared of her—but I don't think she means to come on that strong.

MRS. BERGIO: (lifted herself out of her chair) You, you are afraid, you are afraid of her also—it's not because we are crazy?

WORKER: (smiling) Yes, I think we are all a little afraid of her—and I think she is a little afraid of us—we each handle being afraid differently. (Mrs. Palmer returned my smile)

The student, by expressing his concerns and feelings instead of acting them out, lifts a heavy burden from the group. Their fears are legitimized, and their energies released for work.

When anger is unexpressed, denied, or avoided, members and worker often develop a reservoir of negative feelings which block communications. Thus, it is essential for the worker to elicit these feelings and the associated content. By inviting the expression of feelings, workers convey care and respect for the group members and faith in their ability to communicate and to work on interpersonal issues. When group members act out their anger and frustrations, workers must explore what underlies the interpersonal process rather than negatively judging the behavior or protecting weaker members.

I have observed members' rejection of certain men in my group at the nursing home. The more active members show a dislike of the less lucid men. Occasionally, a member will point to an individual who appears to be out of contact and say, "Look at the vegetable. You wonder why there's

no action on this ward. Look at him, he doesn't even know where he is."
The lack of response by the victim of these attacks increases the vehe-
mence of the attacker and elicits open or silent approval of the attack by
others members. Initially, I attempted to eliminate the hostility by
defending the frailer member. But the behavior continued. The next
time, I asked the attacking member what he saw when he looked at the
other man. He responded, "The hospital staff think we are all like that.
They think we have no feelings, nothing to say about anything. Like we
are a bunch of cattle, a bunch of bums." As he said this, other members
expressed their discomforts: "Yeah, bums, like we didn't work all our
lives, liked we lived off social security and welfare all our lives. We
worked until we couldn't anymore." One member pointed at the disoriented man and said, "Even him, don't you think he worked hard? He
can't help what happened to him."

The men's fears of being identified with the more impaired patients—
their feelings of impotence, confusion, and anger—would have remained
latent, sustaining the maladaptive interpersonal patterns and interfering
with the group's tasks had the worker continued to defend the symbolic
scapegoats and herself. She moved beyond her initial preemptive interventions and examined the fears underlying the scapegoating. This helped
the members move ahead on their tasks related to transitional and environmental issues.

Exchanges among members provide the means by which the group can
examine its communication and relationship patterns. The social worker
encourages each member's participation in the discussion of discrepant
perceptions, disagreements and conflicts. This requires a secure atmosphere in which differences can be examined without threat or recrimination. Thus, the worker has to establish protective ground rules which
facilitate rather than subvert open and direct communication. Explicit
rules barring physical abuse, threat, or negative sanctions against the
expression of feelings, opinions, or facts are set forth. These provide
structural and normative supports for weaker, lower ranking members.
The social worker encourages the group to abide by the agreed-on conditions to avoid situations in which the weaker member has to be protected or rescued.

A social worker developed a group service for five girls, ages 9 to 11,
in a school for learning-disabled youngsters. There are 42 students in the
school, only ten of which are girls. Maintaining control and managing
frustration are difficult for several of the girls. In the first meeting, the
worker emphasized that she would not permit fighting nor would she let
anyone get hurt. Several dyads developed in the group. Since Carmen was

the newest student, the youngest group member, and the least able to express herself verbally and control her frustration, she attempted to pair herself with the worker. She constantly sought the worker's attention and assistance. She kept her chair close to the worker or leaned on her when they sat on the floor. In contrast, Jean is more self-assured, but highly provocative. She also has low tolerance for frustration. In two consecutive meetings, the two girls got into fights with each other. Carmen is Puerto Rican and Jean is African-American. Carmen uses Spanish for teasing and name calling. Jean is the only group member who doesn't understand Spanish. This gives Carmen power over her and makes the insults even worse. Early in the first meeting, Carmen and Jean started their first fight. The worker had selected an activity to help members to know each other.

Jean stated, "I know Barbara and her (pointing at Carmen)." She continued to look at me and said angrily, "You know what she does . . . she gives out candy and then takes it back." Carmen pushed her chair back from the circle and put her hands in her pockets. She looked extremely threatened. I said, "It looked like you are really mad at Carmen right now. Why don't you tell her about it?" Jean repeated her complaint. Carmen tried to defend herself but became tongue tied. To my total amazement, Carmen jumped up and hit Jean. They began to wrestle. I pulled them apart and said loudly, "O.K. stop it, sit down!" Members started talking loudly among themselves. I remained standing to get their attention and said, "You two aren't getting along right now. Maybe you can use the group to learn to get along better. This is a good time for us to talk about group rules." Sitting down, I asked the members to develop some rules. Terry volunteered, "No fighting." I said, "That's a good rule—we will not fight in this group. We can talk to each other without hitting." Jean shouted that she was going to hurt Carmen's face. Carmen muttered something back. I interrupted them and said, "Nobody will be allowed to hurt anyone here anymore!" Carmen slid her chair close to mine and held my hand. I repeated, "I am not going to let you hurt each other."

The worker's initial intervention primarily focused on Jean's concerns. She thought the youngster was asking for help with an interpersonal conflict. She addressed the conflict from Jean's perspective by encouraging her to tell Carmen how she felt. In doing this, the worker neglected Carmen's fears of being attacked. When the worker directed the interaction between Jean and Carmen, she neglected the other group members, inadvertently set up a fight, and provided an audience. Had she made the issue more group relevant, members might have participated rather than just watching the fight. However, the worker's firm explanation that she would not permit fighting or let any one get hurt related to all the members' concerns. The worker's use of the situation to develop "ground rules" was responsive to the needs of the group, but it was not well-timed.

The establishment of protective norms is essential to a group's ability to develop their common purpose and pursue the associated goals. A group composed of poorly functioning members immediately requires structure and guidelines. Loose structure and lack of guidelines encourage loss of control. In school, youngsters are used to classroom structure and clearly defined rules. The unstructured atmosphere in this first meeting was probably too much change for these girls. Learning-disabled children often react to any small change in their environment or routine with confusion, disorganization, and loss of control.

Even with protective "ground rules" in place, conflict between Carmen and Jean resurfaced near the beginning of the fourth meeting, when Carmen said something about a retarded boy liking Barbara.

I began by asking what everyone thought retarded meant, but Jean interrupted and accused Carmen of being the retarded one. Terry joined in and agreed with Jean. They both shouted that Carmen was retarded because she takes medication (Ritalin for hyperactivity). I tried to explain that being retarded and taking medication were two different things. Jean and Carmen were standing, yelling and insulting each other. Carmen insulted Jean in Spanish. Both seemed to be saying that the other was crazy. From the start the group supported Jean in the argument, possibly because Carmen attacked Barbara, the most popular member.

When I raised my voice and said, "Stop! Time out!" they did not respond. I stood between the two girls to keep them from hitting each other. Terry said, "Oh. She's mad. You're going to get in trouble. She's going to tell our teacher." I said, "I am getting mad because this fighting messes up the group, gets in the way of your being able to help each other, but I am not going to tell your teacher. What happens here is between us." I put one hand on each girl's shoulder to separate them and said, "I am not going to let you hurt each other." The girls seated themselves on the floor. As I took my seat I asked someone to sit between Jean and Carmen so they would be separated. Barbara volunteered to sit between them. I said, "We can see that Carmen and Jean aren't getting along too well. The same thing happened in our first

meeting." Before I could lead them into a group discussion about fighting, Jean said, "I'm sorry. I didn't mean nothing." I suggested she
directly tell Carmen. Jean turned to Carmen and reluctantly repeated
her apology. Carmen did not reply. I said, "Carmen, what do you think
about what Jean just said?" Carmen muttered that she was going to
deck Jean, and something else in Spanish, which made Jean mad all over
again. Barbara translated the insult. Before I knew it, Jean picked up a
chair and was moving toward Carmen with it. The other members cho-
rused, " She said she was sorry, Carmen." I stood up again, took the
chair out of Jean's hands, separated them, and pointed separate corners
of the room where each would have to sit. I asked the other group
members what they thought was going on and what we could do about
it. The members began to express how annoyed they were becoming
with these disruptions and suggested that in the future the provoker
should be asked to leave that particular meeting. With both Jean and
Carmen participating, the group developed several consecutive steps in
dealing with group disruptions i.e., initial warning by the worker,
group intervention, and member asked to leave.

By the fourth meeting the worker was prepared for the conflict and made
the incident group-relevant. She identified fighting as a group issue, asked
members to sit between the fighting members, and engaged the youngsters
in developing ways to solve the problem. While she moved too quickly for
reciprocal apologies rather than exploring common hurts and vulnerabilities, she clearly established rules and their enforcement as group issues. She
was prepared to help them, but not to accept the policing function by herself. It was a shared issue.

A natural friendship adolescent girls' group valued interpersonal loyalty.
One member, Gladys, violated this by flirting with and kissing another
member's boyfriend. The group issue was exacerbated by the worker's tendency to shy away from conflict and anger. She used a theoretical orientation to explain and to rationalize her passivity while being too frightened
to deal with the intensity of the members' emotions and her own. In an
extremely difficult meeting, she ventured new ways of coping and managing group conflict:

Gladys was first to arrive, followed by several others. When Rita arrived,
she said hello, slugged Gladys hard on the side of her face, and continued walking to an empty chair, casually greeting everyone on the way. At
first, there was no response or acknowledgment of the action by anyone
(this was the first time a member physically attacked another). The girls

(except Gladys) began planning for an upcoming party as though nothing had happened. I was stunned. Soon a few members began to giggle. I said, "Hey what's going on? What just happened?" Rita responded that it was a personal matter between her and Gladys, and continued to plan the party.

I put my hand on Rita's arm and asked again more firmly what happened between her and Gladys. She said, "Nothing, it's all settled now, everything is over." I said, "Bullshit! Everything is not over! Gladys is very upset and so are you!" Rita said she was not upset. I was determined not to withdraw and replied, "Come on, Rita, you're still furious, what happened?" Rita began to rant at Gladys, bawling her out for kissing her boyfriend, Reggie, at a party over the weekend. Everyone else joined the attack. It seemed Rita's boyfriend flirtatiously asked Gladys for a kiss and she kissed him, twice. Rita continued her angry tirade as Gladys attempted first to deny and then to excuse her behavior. The other girls began to rant at Gladys. When I asked for their reactions, Sue responded that she was telling Gladys for her own good that she better leave other people's boyfriends alone. She said there had been an incident with her own boyfriend which she had found out about, and Gladys was lucky she hadn't said anything about it. There was a tense silence followed by Rita talking to everyone, with Gladys sitting quietly.

After a few minutes, I said, "I can't stand this atmosphere! You and Gladys are not talking to each other." Rita responded, "Everything is settled—it was settled when I did what I did." I said she was still fuming and I was still upset about what had happened. This started a second and calmer round. I asked Gladys what she thought of what Rita was saying. She said she hadn't kissed Reggie twice, and Rita should tell Reggie not to mess with her again. I suggested she tell this to Rita. Rita said, looking at me, "All the boys play around like that." I suggested she tell this to Gladys, which she did. I asked Rita if she was saying she wouldn't say anything to Reggie about messing around with Gladys. Rita said no, she was going to take care of Reggie later, but Gladys could not expect boys to not mess around. I said, "So when the boys play around, Gladys should. . . . ?" Rita and Sue said, "She should say 'No! Leave me alone!' " I asked Gladys, and she said, "I said, 'No, come on, Reggie.' " (The *no* was very soft.) I asked the girls, "What would you think if you were the boys messing around with Gladys and she said that?" Sue said she'd push Gladys right into the bedroom. I said, "So Gladys doesn't say it like she means it, doesn't say it firmly—right?" They agreed.

The girls role-played with Gladys different situations and how they should be handled. The discussion ended with some criticism of Rita's slugging Gladys. Rita said it was a spontaneous thing—she just walked in and let Gladys have it; and anyway, Gladys should have said something to her first. Gladys said she had been going to but she hadn't had a chance.

I said as mad as they were at each other, the important thing was they were able to talk about it. It was hard to do, and they did well.

The worker facilitated the group's work on successfully managing interpersonal conflict. She held the members to the work, and did not allow them to avoid the painful encounter. She communicates faith in the process by demanding they work and by investing herself in the process. She risked her emotions, trusting that she can use her anger rather than acting out. To her credit, she risked personal spontaneity. She confronted the complexities and challenges rather than retreating behind a personal and professional mask. Her firmness and persistence conveyed a strength and genuine concern which in turn released members' energies to confront the maladaptive process. She used her own feelings to reflect the group members' anger, and she invited each member's perceptions of the situation. After pulling together the facts, she directed members to talk to one another rather than through her and to examine the situation in a new way. As members considered their differences, the worker listened carefully for possible common definitions and perceptions.

Staying with conflict and searching for common ground requires open and direct communication. Group members need support and credit for their willingness to struggle and risk themselves. There is, however, a subtle distinction between rewarding members' efforts to deal with difficult issues, and praising them for meeting the worker's values and expectations. The first is responsive to members' needs; the second reflects an imposition of the worker's own needs. Members need social workers' support, but not the burden of pleasing them. In helping groups with maladaptive interpersonal processes, the worker often assumes an active and directive role. This is illustrated by Gitterman's experience with a group of disadvantaged older African-American adolescent boys who were consistently unable to plan or engage in problem solving in a simple, focused discussion.[3] A member's comment would be immediately punctuated by another member's slur or epithet about a girlfriend, mother, and so on. Chaos invariably followed.

As I struggled to help the group with these dysfunctional processes, I drew on certain concepts. The concept of social structure was particularly significant. This group's structure was too loose, with ill-defined roles and undifferentiated communication patterns. I attempted to tighten the group's structure by assigning specific roles and responsibilities. This met with limited success and was rarely transferred from one activity to another. I then redefined the issue, focused on the group's interpersonal obstacles, and invited members to examine their communication difficulties rather than continue my attempts to orchestrate a more integrated structure. When disruptions took place, I "froze" their interactions and asked the members to examine their exchanges. Unfortunately, this approach further intensified their difficulties and our mounting frustration.

During our first basketball game, I realized the issue was incorrectly defined. To them, basketball is a game of one on one moves: a pass is an alien concept; arguments and fights disrupted the game. The game dramatically enlarged my own vision. The issue was not so much a loose social structure or maladaptive interpersonal processes as it was a gap in learning the value and skill of team work. How could they be expected to collaborate in planning and decision making?

I related my observations to the members and proposed a sequence of steps we could use in planning programs or making decisions: 1. each member silently thinks through specific suggestions; 2. in round robin fashion, each member presents one idea at a time, which is then recorded on a master list (during this step no comments or alternative suggestions are allowed, in order to prevent premature closure and unfair criticisms); 3. discussion of each alternative is limited to clarification and identification of potential negative outcomes; 4. after duplicate ideas are eliminated and impractical alternatives voluntarily withdrawn, the group votes for the preferred decision and plan. These steps provided a structure for collaboration and eliminated disabling criticism. The positive results reinforced interest; motivation to cooperate and collaborative activity were gradually internalized. After several months, the boys voted to eliminate the schema as no longer needed.

This experience shows once again that different definitions of maladaptive processes lead to correspondingly different interventions. Being open to one's practice experiences, instead of blocking them out, requires keeping oneself from holding to rigid definitions. Many practice experiences fall between or outside anticipated definitions. One must tolerate ambiguities and uncertainties while acting with optimism and confidence. In the above illustration, guiding was used to replace chaos with order, and conflictual, parasitic behaviors with collaborative mutually supportive behaviors. The guiding method is also important in work with withdrawn, passive and apathetic members (Gitterman 1988).

A social worker was struck by how the environment reinforced the sense of helplessness among an inpatient group of depressed members. Hospital research staff regularly recruit patients for research protocols: at a time convenient to the staff, the patient is tested. No prior notice is given the patient regarding the type or timing of the testing, creating anxiety and inconvenience for the patient. The worker felt the group needed to learn how to deal with the outside world. She used desensitization exercises and assertiveness training techniques to teach members the interpersonal skills essential to gain mastery of their environment. As their external reality was accepted, respected and dealt with seriously, members increasingly shared their experiences and invested themselves in the discussions.

MRS. KING:	(rushing into the room out of breath and exasperated) I'm sorry I'm late—the research people asked me if I would be willing to take more tests, so I was upstairs—AGAIN!
MRS. SIMMONS:	They really upset me. Last Friday—Good Friday—actually it ended up being BAD FRIDAY—those research people asked me to do a few studies. They kept me over two hours. In the meantime, my friend Gloria came to accompany me to Good Friday Mass. I can't get out of this place without a chaperone. She left after an hour and I missed Mass.
WORKER:	Ouch—is this testing mandatory?
MRS. KING:	Well, it helps them with research that might help someone else someday.
WORKER:	How is it actually helping you?
MRS. THOMAS:	It isn't helping me, it's just easier to go along with it than put up a stink.
WORKER:	Mrs. King, is that the way you also experience it?
MRS. KING:	Yes.
MRS. MARTIN:	Well, I don't think we should go along with it!
WORKER:	Okay—how could you respond differently to them?
MRS. MARTIN:	Oh, gosh, I don't know, but we shouldn't let people test us if we don't want to.
MRS. FRANKOS:	I can't even say 'no' to my two year old, how am I going to say 'no' to a doctor?
MRS. SIMMONS:	You too? Wait until they're fifteen and you still can't refuse them!
WORKER:	I think we have a theme song, ladies: I'm a Girl Who Can't Say No! (we all laughed and Mrs. Martin went on to complete the second line, "I'm in a terrible fix.")

The worker's gentle tone, manner, and sense of humor encouraged members to share their experiences. She invited members to prepare for future encounters with research staff and to rehearse alternative responses. Using an assertiveness sequence (describe behavior, express associated feelings, request specified change, identify positive consequences), she guided members in how to complain effectively. Group members showed dra-

matic improvement in communication skills. Mrs. King, however, continued to find it difficult. After four more sessions, she once again raised her
concern.

Our discussion led us to identify outside forces to which they acquiesced.
Mrs. King voiced concern about resuming her outside therapy with her
psychiatrist.

MRS. KING: I'm a little afraid of my contact with my doctor. I know so
much more now about my illness and my medication thanks
to you helping me ask the questions. I don't agree with the
way he prescribes new medication, a hundred pills at a time.
Then if I have any side effects and we have to change the
medication I have all these pills left and wasted money.

MRS. SIMMONS: Why don't you just ask him to prescribe smaller doses?

MRS. THOMAS: He'd probably tell her he was the doctor and knew best.

WORKER: Is that how you think he would respond? (Mrs. King was
unsure what the doctor would say. I asked how she thought
she might approach him about this.)

MRS. KING: Well, I'd tell him (she looked down) "no." . . I'd ask him (she
looked at me and smiled)—"no"—I'd tell him (she was look-
ing down again) I'd rather you give me fewer pills at one time
so if they had side effects it won't end up costing me so much
money.

WORKER: Could you close your eyes and visualize your doctor's
office—how he would look, and how you would feel saying
those words to him?

MRS. KING: (she looked down for a long time silently, then looked up)
"No!" (everyone applauded and laughed, and Mrs. Simmons
congratulated her and Mrs. Martin began to sing, "We're
Just the Girls who CAN Say No.")

Role play helps members develop greater interpersonal empathy (role
reversal); to verbalize pain (role soliloquy); or to dramatize a particular
incident (role enactment) (Duffy 1990). Social workers can also provide
group members with cognitive tools to examine their communication and
relational patterns. Between sessions, behavioral assignments or tasks
such as shared activities or monitoring behavior can improve interpersonal patterns. Activities and program skills provide another means for
changing maladaptive processes (Middleman 1980; Vinter 1985; Waite

1993). For example, a member of a developmentally challenged young adult group was isolated and occasionally scapegoated. The worker's creative use of dance was an effective step in integrating the member into the group's life:

While the others were dancing, I noted a spark in Barbara's eyes, especially when Sheila danced with her boyfriend. I sat down next to Barbara and asked if she knew how to dance. She was quiet. I asked if she enjoyed dancing, but still she didn't respond. I said maybe she felt that she couldn't dance as well as Sheila. She nodded and said, "And I don't feel like it." I commented that her eyes said she wanted to dance. She smiled. After we watched together for a while, I took her hand to see if she would like to dance. She responded and joined the group briefly. She danced rather stiffly, standing in place and moving her arms around. She seemed pleased, and after a while sat down. I said, "You like to dance" and she nodded.

In a subsequent meeting, Barbara brought her own records, but she wouldn't leave her seat. The worker did not pressure her, but let her know that she was available to dance with her whenever she would like.

In a later meeting, I noticed Barbara watched me dance with others. I danced her step, precisely as I could, and told the group that I was doing Barbara's step. She smiled in response. In a circle dance, I continued to dance her step and reached for her hand to join me. She did, saying that her step didn't fit this dance so she couldn't do it right. I made an adaptation of her step and she said she still couldn't do it. I held her hand and did it over and over again. She tried and got it. She joined the circle dance, smiling at me. I said enthusiastically, "You're doing great!" Together we taught "the Barbara" to the group and she tried some steps the others were doing.

During the next meeting, she danced spontaneously with Earl. After the meeting, I credited her progress. She laughed, obviously happy with herself.

Barbara is on the way to being integrated into the group and to participating in its activities and relationships. By differential use of various techniques—which require activity, engagement, involvement—social workers can help group members to view a situation or a process in new ways and develop relationships and communications that support development and adaptive functioning.

Groups are a powerful healing force for people who share common needs, concerns, and aspirations. For this potential to be realized, social workers must help groups deal with dysfunctional interpersonal processes that might emerge at any point in a group's life course. Similar maladaptive interpersonal processes can appear between workers and members. These maladaptive processes impede communications and the formation of trusting relationships. Hence, the next chapter takes up dysfunctional patterns that develop between workers and those who are served.

EIGHT

REDUCING INTERPERSONAL STRESS
BETWEEN WORKER AND CLIENT

Dysfunctional patterns similar to those in families and groups arise between service recipients and social workers.

Sources of Dysfunctional Interpersonal Patterns

Resistance grows out of strains in the encounter between service recipient, worker, and agency and their respective efforts to maximize their own control over the situation and the process.[1] Agencies may try to control worker-client encounters with rigid policies and procedures. Workers may try to control the encounter through premature reassurance and interpretation, imposition of values and solutions, impatience with process, avoidance of relevant content and feelings, or inadequate exploration. Service recipients may try to control the content and focus of the interview and the worker, by (a) active behaviors such as provocation, intellectualization, interruption, projection, verbosity, and seductiveness; (b) passive withdrawal, compliance, martyrdom, and nonverbalness; (c) flight behaviors such as instant recovery, canceled appointments, and precipitous termination; or (d) avoidance behaviors such as changing the subject, withholding data, minimizing concerns, and forgetting appointments.

Numerous diverse and interrelated factors account for dysfunctional interpersonal patterns. These factors need to be understood as they pose difficult challenges and painful experiences both for clients and social workers.

Agency Authority and Sanction Structures

Agency authority and sanctions form the context and role-defining framework for client-worker relationships. The agency expects practitioners to carry out its mission and mandates. In chapter 3, distinctions were drawn among services sought, offered, or mandated. Each can be associated with difficulties due to agency authority, sanctions, policies, or procedures. Such agency operations can adversely affect clients and workers and their relationship. For example, Mrs. Chambers's children were removed from her home two years ago, following the detection of gonorrhea in her 5-year-old daughter and the discovery of physical abuse inflicted on her two sons, ages 14 and 7. Her boyfriend was the suspected perpetrator. She was referred by the court to agency services as a condition for the return of her children. For the past two years, Mrs. Chambers has denied that her children had been abused and resisted all court referrals. When it became clear to her that completing the court-mandated counseling program was the only way to regain custody, she reluctantly came to the agency. After missing her first four appointments, she arrived thirty minutes late, nonchalantly entered the office, and threw herself into a chair.

MRS. CHAMBERS: (momentarily stopped snapping her gum to say, in a monotonous voice) Hi.

WORKER: (after remaining silent for a few moments to see if anything else was forthcoming) I am sorry that we won't have much time.

MRS. CHAMBERS: (irritated) I'm late cause my bus was late!

WORKER: (after a minute's silence as she stared out the window) I understand you're without your children?

MRS. CHAMBERS: Ya.

WORKER: Tell me about the situation.

MRS. CHAMBERS: What's to tell—they took my children way from me. They said my daughter had 'gangorrhea.'

WORKER: (after a brief silence) You sound pretty upset—

MRS. CHAMBERS: (interrupting) You're damned right I'm upset!

WORKER: Do you believe your daughter had gonorrhea?

MRS. CHAMBERS: (in a calmer tone) No I don't think she had it, at least I know she didn't get it from my boyfriend like they're saying, because I tested negative. Now, if he gave it to her, he'd have it, and so would I.

WORKER: Does your boyfriend still live with you?

MRS. CHAMBERS: (again looking toward the window) I can't say. Somebody told me not to say anything.

Since time was up, I decided not to challenge her, and instead we negotiated our next appointment time. Before she left, I asked her what she thought about coming to the agency. She responded, "I think you people are really nosy, that's what I think"(she laughed nervously).

Mrs. Chambers is angry at the mandate and angry at her loss of autonomy. Her past experiences with social agencies were negative and, understandably, she conveys suspicion, mistrust, and rage. The social worker personalizes Mrs. Chambers's resistance and opens the interview with a hostile question, "I understand you are without your children?" She has internalized institutional stereotypes and biases and lacks empathy. To Mrs. Chambers, the worker is yet another threatening representative of an oppressive system. No wonder Mrs. Chambers is defensive and resistant.

In unwanted mandated services rife with ambiguity, conflict, and pain, workers must fulfill several simultaneous roles: (1) as an organizational representative accountable to agency mission and mandate; (2) as a colleague aware of peer perceptions and definitions; (3) as a professional identified with the profession's values and ethics; and (4) as a staff member legally or institutionally responsible for supervising and reporting on the client's progress or lack thereof. Unless these various roles are managed well, they create dysfunctional interpersonal processes that could be intractable. Managing these organizational and professional roles well requires empathic skills to hear the client's voice.

A residential treatment center required children awaiting adoption to prepare a "life book" as emotional preparation for this critical transition. Writing and illustrating their life stories was expected to help children develop a sense of continuity and positive self-concept.

A social worker was assigned to help 14-year-old Pedro, who was being adopted by a member of the child care staff. His biological parents relinquished parental rights a few years ago. The case was assigned with the hope that the social worker could help Pedro work on abandonment issues and behavioral outbursts. Pedro didn't want to meet still another social worker, but the service was mandated. While seeking agreement on focus and plans, the worker was unable to arouse his interest or energy. But the "life book" did engage his interest. However, he was unaware of the agency's and worker's hidden intent to discuss his feelings of abandonment and loss. He expected the book to be a photograph album of his loved ones and his accomplishments. He didn't want "bad stuff" in his book and he excluded his biological family. The agency and worker rationalized their unethical paternalism as fear that Pedro would not agree to the project. However, such professional dishonesty is a violation of professional ethics.

During their first meeting, the worker mentioned his "other family." He stopped her in mid-sentence with "I never will discuss that with you." He was defensive, stern, and seemingly practiced in setting this limit with past social workers. After a few sessions in which Pedro developed a "life book" that excluded his biological parents, the social worker brought in a picture of his parents to include in the book. Pedro jumped up, started going through her desk drawers, ripped up some papers, and ran out of the room. After the "life book" failed, the worker suggested a trip to his old neighborhood. Pedro looked up at the ceiling and turned his back to her. When she persisted, Pedro shouted, "NO! I don't want to talk about them, I don't want to go there" and stormed out of the office. That night he went AWOL.

The worker felt pressure from the agency's demand to carry out its new policy. The agency voice intimidated and drowned out Pedro's pain. In yielding, however, she alienated Pedro and added to his distrust of social workers.

Worker Authority and Power

The worker's authority and power are a potential source of interpersonal obstacles (Hasenfeld 1987). As organizational representatives, workers are vested with authority (Palmer 1983). They embody the organization and people have to test which side workers are on, mistrusting them if they are totally aligned with the agency. As a representative of a profession, the worker has additional authority apart from the organization. Professional status lends an aura of expertise and competence. Over time, people test the extent to which the status is deserved and merits respect. If the worker personalizes such testing and responds inappropriately, a dysfunctional pattern becomes entrenched.

Twenty-eight-year-old Mrs. Taub sought services from a family agency. She could not decide whether to seek marital counseling or a divorce. Ambivalence and consequent immobilization propelled her to seek help. Ambivalence toward her husband was transferred to the worker. She immediately questioned the social worker's competence, sincerity, and depth of understanding. A new and youthful practitioner was threatened by the testing in the first interview.

MRS. TAUB: I am not really sure how much therapy is going to do for me. I mean I've been through this before—about six months' worth of therapy and I really don't think I got much better.

WORKER: Well, I certainly do hope that our work together will be more beneficial to you. (I started to get a sinking feeling in my stomach.)

MRS. TAUB: I don't know, maybe I just don't trust the whole therapeutic process. I mean, here you have a stranger meeting another stranger, a perfectly artificial meeting. One person doesn't really give a damn about the other and one person is supposed to help the other. I mean it really seems absurd and cold to me.

WORKER: I can understand how you'd feel that way, but even in this situation some real change can happen. (I wish I said this with more confidence).

Because the worker is threatened, she doesn't respond to Mrs. Taub's core concern: "Do you really care about me as much as I need to be cared for?" Mrs. Taub missed the second appointment without calling. In response to the worker's telephone call, she attended the next session and introduced a further test.

MRS. TAUB: (looking away from me) I'm sorry I missed last week's appointment.

WORKER: What happened?

MRS. TAUB: I felt really ill (stated in a matter-of-fact way).

WORKER: Why didn't you call to cancel?

MRS. TAUB: I just felt too ill. Are you going to charge me for the visit?

WORKER: I'm afraid that's our policy.

MRS. TAUB: I feel that if you cared about me—which I really don't under stand how you can—I mean, you've only seen me for a total of two hours. But anyway, if you really cared about me you'd be more concerned about my health than about the dumb fee.

WORKER: Mrs. Taub, I am concerned about your health, but we also have a contract that we will meet weekly and that if one of us needs to cancel, we'll call 24 hours in advance.

Mrs. Taub tests the worker's caring and competence and the worker reacts with frustration and a bureaucratic explanation. By focusing on organizational policy, the worker distances herself from a direct conversation about the meaning of Mrs. Taub's behavior. In contrast, focusing on Mrs. Taub's actual behavior could have made it difficult for her to continue in an unself-conscious way (Germain 1982b; Nelsen 1975). In the fourth interview, Mrs. Taub talks of the pain of her older brother's suicide. She used this to pose another test.

MRS. TAUB: I'm not really sure you can understand how much I really loved Ted. Our love was really special. There was something almost spiritual about our relationship.

WORKER: Tell me what was special about the relationship?

MRS. TAUB: I don't know if I can really describe our relationship. And I am not sure you'd really understand it.

WORKER: Mrs. Taub, I get upset when you make comments which suggest that I don't have the capacity to understand you. What makes you distrust me?

MRS. TAUB: (pauses and responds defensively) Well, maybe I am saying something like that. I mean how are you supposed to under stand how much Ted and I shared? I don't know anything about you. I don't even know if you ever had a relationship, let alone been in love.

WORKER: It sounds as though you don't trust me.

MRS. TAUB: Why should I trust you?

WORKER: What would it take for you to trust me?

MRS. TAUB: Well, I guess I want you to tell me a bit about your life. Have you ever suffered losses? Have you ever loved anyone? Have you ever felt pain?

WORKER: The answer is yes to all your questions, but how will this help you to trust me?

Mrs. Taub continues to challenge the worker, becoming more explicit about her concerns. The social worker is threatened, defensive, and unable to deal with or use what was triggering her disconnected, unempathic responses. Interestingly, how a social worker deals with the testing behavior is a significant measure of professional competence.

Professional Socialization

Like other professionals, social workers are socialized to their profession. We take on preferred philosophical and theoretical assumptions about the behaviors and situations of those we serve. Such assumptions provide a frame of reference and a sense of order and predictability. Favorite theories and assumptions may become overly cherished so one is tempted to fit people into them. A need for certainty, constancy, and stability can compromise professional curiosity about a person's uniqueness and distinctiveness. Professional socialization can formalize the work and stiffen one's approach. Ambiguity threatens when it ought to challenge us. We then might become cautious, avoid risks, develop rigid and mechanical responses, and seek comfort in prescriptions and symmetries. The result can be our detachment from those we serve (Gitterman 1992).

Workers' assumptions, accurate or inaccurate, may color client-worker relationships. We may unwittingly select and hear those communications that confirm our assumptions. Elements of the communications that do not fit our assumptions may elude us. For example, social workers committed to advocacy practice may primarily direct people to environmental issues, fracturing life transitional and environmental stressors. A social worker committed to clinical practice may direct people to life transitional issues, fracturing environmental and life transitional stressors. In response to the worker's subtle or unabashed efforts to influence and direct, the service recipient has the choice between satisfying or resisting the worker's preoccupations. When people resist being fit into the practitioner's assumptions, they are often labeled as "unmotivated," "nonverbal," or "resistant." Rigid belief systems may blind us to the ordinary details and realities of people's lives and their aspirations, anxieties, and daily hassles.

Differences

Conflicting expectations are associated with mutual dissatisfaction. Poor clients need help with immediate and current life issues, but a worker might concentrate on past experiences to uncover underlying problems. A client may seek advice and direction, while a worker may seek psychodynamic explanations and insights. Similarly, poor clients may view themselves as being "in charge" and competent, while a worker views them as reactive, burdened by recurring troubles, underlying handicaps, and limited potential for change. In one study, most clients rated social work help as satisfactory, while most social workers were either dissatisfied or ambivalent about the work done (Maluccio 1979a; 1979b). Differences in age (Sprung 1989), social class (Hardman 1977), ethnicity and race (Berg and Miller 1992; Cooper 1973; Dore and Dumois 1990; Franklin 1992), religion (Wikler 1986), gender (Duhl 1976; Sherman 1976; Rauch 1978), or sexual orientation (Moses and Hawkins 1982) may also affect worker-client interaction by giving rise to incongruent perceptions and expectations. When clients' life styles, adaptive patterns, values, and perspectives are not respected, client testing and resistance become methods of coping.

Mrs. Cooper, a 32-year-old African-American woman, placed her 11-year-old son, James, in a residential treatment center. He is truant, constantly fights, and frequently insults his teachers. The white worker felt that Mrs. Cooper was not a good mother, and wanted to teach her to be a better mother. Mrs. Cooper and the worker had been discussing the fact that James is telling lies and Mrs. Cooper attributes it to his father's example.

MRS. COOPER: It seems pretty obvious to me! It's his father. He just keeps calling up James and promising him all these things and never comes through with them. James sees his father lying and getting away with it and figures he can do the same thing!

WORKER: Mrs. Cooper, how does it make you feel when Jimmy lies?

Mrs. Cooper wanted the worker to know her intense anger toward her husband: she had told of how he broke up the family, physically abused her, and neglected their children. After the first few years of marriage, he began using and selling drugs. He gradually sold their possessions, and ultimately they had to leave their apartment. He pushed her down the stairs in view of the children. Her leg was broken, and she left him. She couldn't provide for her son and left him for periods of time with her husband. Because of serious neglect, she brought him back to live with her. The worker wanted to focus on her son and his problems, not on her and her life stressors and issues. She wanted to use the interview to begin to teach her to be a better mother. After the first session, Mrs. Cooper canceled the next four appointments. With each cancellation, the worker's negative feelings toward Mrs. Cooper's concern for her son intensified: "if she didn't care enough to come to sessions, then how much could she care about her son?" In spite of the worker's objection, the treatment team sent James home for a week as a ploy to engage Mrs. Cooper. The following excerpt is taken from the second interview, which occurred three months after the first. The worker continued with her agenda of teaching Mrs. Cooper.

WORKER: What would Jimmy say about his father?

MRS. COOPER: Jimmy would say that he loved his father.

WORKER: Uh-huh. So, if you love somebody do you think you can say you don't want to see them or talk to them even if they hurt you or even if it's obvious to others that they may be doing something wrong?

MRS. COOPER: No—I guess not.

WORKER: Yeah, you're right. I think that as adults it's important for us, in order to understand children, to try standing in their shoes once in a while to see how it feels.

MRS. COOPER: I know I have to understand Jimmy, but my shoes have a whole lot of stuff that come with them.

WORKER: What do you mean by "stuff?"

MRS. COOPER: Oh, you know all that bullshit I went through with Jimmy's father.

WORKER: I understand how angry you are at Jimmy's father, but I think it's important, if we're to understand and help Jimmy, that we try to keep your anger toward his father separated from Jimmy.

An important practice principle is to relate to the person one is with rather than to an absent third person. For example, Mrs. Cooper has pain she wants to share with the worker. Ironically, the worker who wants to teach

Mrs. Cooper to listen more to Jimmy is not listening to Mrs. Cooper. The social worker ignores the life circumstances of an African-American low-income woman who has spent much of her life struggling to survive. Mrs. Cooper pleads for empathy, "my shoes have a whole lot of stuff that come with them" but the worker, insensitive to racial and class themes, ignores her moving plea.

An inexperienced young student began working in a nursing home with an "experienced" elderly resident who had feelings about receiving help from a much younger person.

> MRS. GOLD: How is it going? How do you like your new job?
>
> STUDENT: I was concerned when you canceled our appointment last week. Let's talk about it.
>
> MRS. GOLD: So tell me, what are your days like here?
>
> STUDENT: Rather than doing that, why don't we look at how I can be helpful to you.

This pattern continued for several sessions. At a later meeting, Mrs. Gold introduces the age factor.

> MRS. GOLD: You youngsters look at things differently.
>
> STUDENT: Does my being young affect our working together?
>
> MRS. GOLD: Well, for example, Mr. Hall (another new worker), who runs our meetings here—everyone likes him, but they feel he is young. All the residents like new workers and students but feel they haven't experienced many things.
>
> STUDENT: How do you feel about my being young and new?
>
> MRS. GOLD: To tell you the truth, I think of you as being young. I feel that you haven't had many of the experiences which I've had.
>
> STUDENT: Do you think it would be more helpful for you to see one of the older and more experienced social workers?
>
> MRS. GOLD: (silence)

While the student invites discussion about the age difference, she is unable to struggle with the difference. In an institutional setting, a resident's struggle for self-dignity and autonomy is particularly poignant. This student, however, is threatened by Mrs. Gold's effort to decrease their status differences. She becomes defensive and refers the "uncooperative" Mrs. Gold to a more experienced worker.

Interpersonal Control

Struggles for interpersonal control can also lead to interpersonal issues between worker and client. Workers possess needed information, concrete resources, and procedures for referrals. They gain further influence from such personal qualities as friendliness, articulateness, assertiveness, and gentleness. People may become dependent upon approval and sensitive to subtle disapproval or judgmental statements. Whatever the source of workers' interpersonal influence, those served are likely to experience ambivalence and anxiety about gaining or losing interpersonal control within the relationship (Specht 1985).

Clients too have means of interpersonal influence. They may try to control the focus and content of the interview or the relationship by various active, passive, flight, or avoidance behaviors. They can overwhelm social workers by the magnitude of life stressors and demands, creating in workers a parallel sense of vulnerability and impotence. This can result in expressions of impatience, inadequate exploration of client perceptions and experiences, or premature interpretation and reassurance.

Mrs. Charles, age 23, married with two young children, had been hospitalized three times within the last two months for ovarian cysts and treatment complications. Her hospitalizations resulted in the removal of a large cyst, one ovary, and, finally, a hysterectomy and salpingo-oophorectomy. At the end of her medical ordeal, she commented, "I have nothing left inside me to cause these problems again." The family was unable to cope with the medical expenses and her lost salary. The social work intern helped her apply for welfare, food stamps, and Medicaid for catastrophic coverage. She was approved for catastrophic coverage, but was responsible for $6,000 of her medical expenses. In dealing with the social work intern and other professionals, her frustration and bitterness were manifested in a combative and unappreciative style. While this helped her to exert more situational and emotional control, it decreased the motivation of the student and other professionals to help. During her second hospitalization, Mrs. Charles asked a nurse to notify the social work department that she wanted to see a social worker. The receptionist notified the student that Mrs. Charles was highly agitated and sounded "nasty." When the student worker entered Mrs. Charles's room, her "stare was strong and cold." The student was cut off in mid-sentence:

MRS. CHARLES: I'm glad you're finally here. I called your office just a few minutes ago to be sure someone was coming up.

STUDENT: Yes, Mrs. Charles, your nurse phoned the office about a half hour ago, but we were in a meeting so I didn't get the message until the meeting was over. Is there something I can help you with? (I immediately felt on the defensive and found myself somewhat annoyed)

MRS. CHARLES: I wouldn't have called you if there wasn't something I needed. I can't pay my hospital bill. I have two small children at home. My husband is between jobs and working at night. He hardly makes enough money to support us, and the bills are out of sight. I've applied to Medicaid and I don't know where I stand. Those people over there are so stupid, they don't know what's going on.

STUDENT: How can I help you with Medicaid? (I found myself reacting to her anger rather than her desperation. She almost hissed as she spoke. I snapped back the above response.)

MRS. CHARLES: You're a social worker, don't you deal with them?

STUDENT: Well, billing problems are handled by the accounts depart ment, so they are the ones to contact Medicaid to get your number. But, if you'd like me to give them a call to check on the status of your case, I'd be glad to. I'll get back to you in an hour or so. (My back up, I became preoccupied with regaining control and being in charge. She slumped on the bed and practically whispered for me to do what I could.)

Throughout the brief session, the student was overwhelmed by Mrs. Charles's intense feelings, and was unable to see beyond her tone of voice, glaring look, and combative style. The student became caught up in an emotional power struggle, fueling the confrontation rather than reaching beneath the anger and connecting to the despair. The next session came after a subsequent hospitalization. The student saw Mrs. Charles's name on the admission's chart, and went to see her.

MRS. CHARLES: (in a panicky voice) My husband received a letter from Medicaid saying we're responsible for $6,000 of my hospital costs. I just can't believe I'll have to pay it. I can't do it. I'll go crazy.

STUDENT: God, Mrs. Charles, I'm also beginning to feel overwhelmed. Let's slow down. I need to get this clearly.

Throughout this session, Mrs. Charles wanted to ventilate and the student wanted to gather facts. They had discrepant agenda: Mrs. Charles wanted a sympathetic and patient ear; the student wanted to prepare for her conversation with Medicaid. Mrs. Charles became increasingly agitated and the student became increasingly frustrated. Within two hours, Mrs. Charles called the office twice asking for her. When the student called back, the following exchange took place:

MRS. CHARLES: (in a sweet, apologetic tone of voice) Hi, did you talk to the worker?

STUDENT: (in an abrupt and matter of fact voice) Yes, she told me that

since you and your husband are employed and will be earning $30,000, Medicaid policy states you are responsible for
all medical expenses up to $6,000, or approximately 25% of
your annual income. There seems to be no way around it.
(This was my worst intervention. I reacted to her as a terrible pain in the neck. She took up a great deal of time; she
annoys everyone in the office and the nurses on the floor. In
turn, they are on my back, constantly complaining about her.
Moreover, I didn't think I could help her. She and the whole
situation made me feel incompetent.)

MRS. CHARLES: (began to sob) Then I'll quit my job and my husband will
have to quit his . . . (she continued to sob)

STUDENT: Listen, sorry about this whole thing—I'll be right up. . . .

MRS. CHARLES: I'm sorry about our telephone conversation. I didn't mean to
cry. You didn't have to run up.

STUDENT: I wanted to come up. I know you are very fed up and upset
with this, I really would like to try to help.

When Mrs. Charles began to cry, the student felt less threatened and
defensive. She felt more empathic and, simultaneously, in greater control
of the interview and the interpersonal relationship. If a worker personalizes a client's struggle for control, the result is passive and aggressive
behaviors and becoming caught in a power struggle. Interpersonal obstacles simmer as the worker concentrates on self-justification. Depersonalizing tensions and recognizing that they are rooted in a reciprocal struggle
for control is the first step in meeting the challenge and converting threat
into opportunity.

In professional relationships, workers may re-enact parental and sibling
experiences, transferring impulses, thoughts, and feelings to the client
(Dunkel and Hatfield 1986; Greene 1986; Schwartz 1978). Inexperienced
social workers, like other professionals, are affected by client personalities
and behaviors and might respond poorly to some. Their own personalities
also have an impact upon clients. Lack of self-awareness and not managing this reality encourages and intensifies interpersonal barriers. Counter-
feelings and responses give rise to power struggles in which client and
worker both feel misunderstood and put upon. But when social workers
carefully monitor their own reactions, they are more likely to respond
appropriately.

In this example, Greta, age 50, sought help from an outpatient mental
health clinic because of feeling "extremely sad, hopeless, and powerless
about my marriage." Greta described her inability to assert her needs and
wants to Steven, her husband, and to her 27-year-old daughter; prolonged
sleeping in the middle of the day during weekends; alcohol abuse; and

uncontrolled verbal outbursts. Greta repeatedly described her helplessness, despair, and anger, her views of others as tyrants, oppressors, and abusers, and herself as a powerless victim. The social work student, Michael, became frustrated and he panicked. He felt that somehow he should have immediate solutions. His experience mirrored Greta's: both felt vulnerable and out of control. Unfortunately, he acted out his feelings by confrontation, impatience, and anger. Exchanges from the eleventh interview illustrate the dysfunctional interpersonal pattern:

GRETA: Steven did go to Pennsylvania with me. He was in an awful mood most of the time. He behaved even worse with his parents, abusing and torturing me in front of them. You know when he does this in front of his parents I'm tempted to defend myself and explain to them that his complaints about me aren't true. But I stopped myself. I couldn't stand there and fight in front of his parents. One day I wanted to go to the movies and Steven jumped up from his seat and started screaming, "What! You say you are going to the movies and screw me, right?" He jumped up and grabbed the car keys. There was nothing I could do. There was no other way but to go over and kick or hit him or do anything. So I did nothing.

MICHAEL: Why didn't you say anything?

GRETA: It's always been the same. It's always feeling powerless. It's absurd. You end up in the same situation and say, "I don't deserve this." And yet you end up with the same situation. There is always a bizarre order to Steven's behavior. So why should I get upset any longer?

MICHAEL: You need to learn to assert yourself.

GRETA: With Steven there is no assertion. I'm in the car on the road, and I get abused. Or I say I want to go to the movies and he takes the car keys away, which I can only retrieve by physical force, causing a major fight. There's nothing I can do!

MICHAEL: Why didn't you ask him for the car keys?

GRETA: Because he wouldn't give them to me!

MICHAEL: But it sounds like you gave in to him as soon as he started yelling.

GRETA: I would be a fool to insist on something that would bring about a battle, especially in front of his parents. I can't do that, Mike.

MICHAEL: But he shouldn't be allowed to act like a child.

GRETA: But he is. That's the way it is. What should I do? I better not get so upset that I say, "Give me the keys, or else" because it

would be "or else." There's nothing you can do and I know
that most people don't believe me.

MICHAEL: (in exasperation) What is it that keeps you in this marriage?

Greta seeks the student social worker's affirmation and understanding of her difficult, stressful, and painful experience. She lacked the support and strength to deal with the overwhelming misery that fills her life. She needs support and encouragement to cope with an abusive relationship. She needs help in sorting out priorities so that the issues become less overwhelming and more manageable for her. She needs to learn the steps in problem-solving. Issues should be reframed in a way that points to possible changes. Instead, Michael approached her with disbelief and confrontation. In evaluating his intervention he realized that interpersonal conflict between Greta and himself was triggered by her life issues, which called up pain he had known in his own family during the prolonged, conflictual divorce of his parents. His mother occupied a similar role to Greta's and when he asked why Greta stayed in the marriage, it might have been a question for his mother. He wrote: "my impatience and frustration with Greta's passivity was in part coming from my own unresolved anger at my mother, who was unable to protect herself and her children from an abusive father and husband." For this student, Greta was a powerful teacher.

Taboo Content

Taboo areas such as sexuality, incest, violence, and death and dying—and practitioners' difficulties with such material—are significant sources of interpersonal stress (Anderson and Henderson 1985; Googins 1984; Moore 1984). Many beginning workers find it difficult to invite people to tell their story and to explore and clarify particular details. A tendency to avoid direct discussion of intimate or painful material is understandable. The content easily triggers suppressed personal experiences and associated feelings. The pain inherent in the content may overwhelm social work beginners, generating anxiety and fear of losing control of the interview.

Seventy-four-year-old Mrs. Plante's husband recently died, and she was discharged from a psychiatric hospital after treatment of reactive depression. Following discharge she moved into protective and supportive housing for the elderly. A social worker, skilled in case management, was assigned at her daughter's request. The worker and Mrs. Plante agreed to the goal of successful transition in the new living arrangement. The social worker focused on connecting Mrs. Plante to supports in her new environment, applying for Social Security Insurance/Medicare, joining the local senior center, becoming acquainted with the new community and its offerings, etc. While the worker was comfortable and competent in case management functions, she was uncomfortable with and awkward in responding to Mrs. Plante's need to express the grief and pain of her loss. When Mrs. Plante introduced this taboo area, the worker was uncomfortable and mechanical in her responses. She lacked confidence in helping with traumatic life transitions and the associated intense stress. Several exchanges follow:

MRS. PLANTE: The move here has been difficult, but I know that being around people will be good for me.

WORKER: So your initial response to moving here has been a positive one?

MRS. PLANTE: Oh, yes, everyone has been really nice. (pause) You know, Janice, one of the reasons I was brought here by my daughter was because I just couldn't accept that my husband's time had come. Even when he collapsed at home and had to be taken to the hospital by ambulance, I kept insisting that he would come back home again. My denial that he was dying was so strong.

WORKER: You must have loved your husband very much, and I hope you will get to like it here.

. . . .

MRS. PLANTE: I am relieved to be living here, I really am. It's just that it takes time getting used to. It takes time (her voice trailed off).

WORKER: You mean it takes time getting used to living in a new apartment and in a new community?

MRS. PLANTE: It takes time getting used to being alone. It was 55 years of my life with my husband, taking care of him many of those years. You know, Janice, it's not just the same being alone in this world without your husband.

WORKER: That's one of the reasons we are meeting together, to help you feel less alone.

Mrs. Plante describes her inability to deal with her husband's death. The worker tries to keep Mrs. Plante from expressing her devastating pain at the loss of her husband. The worker can't allow herself to hear this pain, and instead hopes that she "will get to like it here." Mrs. Plante's grief is so profound that it overwhelms the worker, who is experienced in environmental work, but inexperienced in work with powerful emotions. She felt the intensity of Mrs. Plante's sadness, pain, and fear, but was unable to accept these feelings in herself. A worker's emotional response is a critical barometer of the client's feelings; and investing oneself in a painful experience requires trusting and using one's own thoughts and feelings. Clients are quick to forgive genuine and caring mistakes; playing it safe and being mechanical cannot move the work forward. Table 8.1 summarizes the sources of interpersonal obstacles.

Table 8.1	Sources of Interpersonal Obstacles

- agency authority and sanctions
- practitioner authority and power
- professional socialization
- differences in social class, race, ethnicity, gender, age, physical and mental status, and sexual orientation
- attempts to control
- taboo content

Social Work Function, Modalitiy, Methods, and Skills

When dysfunctional client-worker interpersonal processes interfere with ability to help, the social worker invites open and direct communications, establishes common stressor definitions, and develops greater mutuality and reciprocity in their relationships. Practitioners rely on the methods of enabling, exploring, mobilizing, guiding, facilitating, and mediating to achieve these aims. Social workers must take a transactional view of the interpersonal issue and be willing to examine their contribution. Taking responsibility for engagement with, and easing barriers to, the relationship (often mislabeled "resistance") is an essential professional function.

Professional Methods and Skills and Practice Illustrations

Social workers must examine the source of interpersonal obstacles and acknowledge their own contributions. Unless we to do this, we will be unable to reverse a dysfunctional pattern of communicating and relating. If the pattern continues, the client is likely to intensify resistance and testing behaviors or to precipitously terminate service. When obstacles appear, as they invariably do, ecological thinking about the obstacle is essential. Ecological thinking is shown by workers and students who struggle to resolve the troubling issues noted in several vignettes:

I am struggling with Mrs. Charles's open anger, frustration, and bitterness in regard to my ability or inability to understand and work through her strong feelings about the hospitalizations and mounting financial burdens. The feelings are manifest in a combative style. Her tone of voice is accusatory. Her annoying persistence in repeatedly contacting the social work department, nurses, department of welfare, and doctors—and expecting immediate service—has taken its toll. The medical and social service staffs view her negatively. She is frequently described as having an "attitude problem" and being a "pain in the neck." From Mrs. Charles's perspective, she might describe our interpersonal difficulties as: "I cannot pay these bills, there's just no way. And you are just part of the big system that keeps making me feel like scum asking for help, and then, after it's all over and I do everything you ask, you screw me again. I'm not asking for much, and I'm furious that I have to go through all this for a little help." In fact, Mrs. Charles does exactly what needs to be done in going through the system. She keeps appointments, gives information and documents requested of her, answers questions, and tries to obey rules and guidelines. In return, Mrs. Charles expects to get what she is asking for, immediately. When she is made to wait or is inconvenienced by the system, she is quick to show her anger. Her displays turn people against her.

My view of our exchanges is that her anger, frustration, and bitterness make it difficult for me to WANT to help her. I do not want to be made a representative of the system that screwed her, nor do I wish to be thrown into that category so arbitrarily. She has not even inquired to see how I am different and how I might be able to help her negotiate the systems she confronts. I react to being blamed, become angry and unsympathetic. I become overwhelmed, self-doubting, and defensive. It's like a mechanism gets triggered—I get ready for battle, for self-defense. And when I react (actually overreact), I later feel terrible about my lack of empathy and occasional insensitivity. She makes me feel incompetent and guilty. I am struggling not to act out these feelings.

This student's self-esteem is threatened by Mrs. Charles's efforts to cope. She feels misunderstood and challenged and responds with antagonism. Belatedly the student takes the critical first step in reversing this maladaptive pattern by examining her contribution to the interpersonal problem.

In much the same way, Stephen reflected on his work with Greta:

When Greta started to talk about her helplessness, despair, and anger and casts herself as the victim, I became frustrated. I thought I should have immediate solutions, and I felt powerless. I turned off the feeling and latent content of her statements and many times only responded to the manifest and cognitive aspects of her message. I was accusatory about her allowing her husband to verbally abuse her. During other exchanges, I changed the subject and tried to uncover historical data, or I made ill-timed interpretations of what she was feeling and experiencing now as connected to what she had felt and experienced in the past. All this only served to intensify her feelings of anger, sadness, and helplessness. She looked as if she would explode. Her voice, though low, was intense and desperate. Other times when I confronted her in an impatient and irritated tone she became compliant and in low, sad voice said she would try to do whatever it was I wanted her to do. Sometimes she became silent, withdrawn, sighed heavily, and exclaimed that her situation with her husband was hopeless.

From Greta's perspective, she perhaps felt that I as a much younger inexperienced student could not understand her many stressors, much less help her cope effectively with them. I think it was clear to Greta that I was not 'hearing' her desperation and plea for help and I was becoming increasingly impatient and frustrated. She may have thought that I believed things were not as bad as she thought them to be or sensed that I too was overwhelmed by her misery. Towards the end of our work together, I think she experienced me as another uncaring, insensitive man who was not only unable to care for her, but angry at her pain, over which she felt she had no control. My behavior was just another example of how nobody understood her struggle to live. She may have taken my responses to mean that her worst fears of being beyond help were true.

The interpersonal problem between us intensified. The more she presented herself as incompetent and helpless, the more impatient and confrontational I became. She in turn became angrier (and I believe felt more helpless) and more insistent that as a victim who was oppressed and abused not only by her husband, daughter, sister; but by the agency and me. Unfortunately, I fell in with all the others and became abusing. It is hard for me to believe how I fell into the oppressor role.

Greta's life story is re-enacted in the helping process. She seeks help with abusive relationships and the student's "help" is still another such relationship. Inexperienced, overwhelmed, and threatened by a client's stressors and coping patterns, a social worker may unwittingly blame a client for being difficult. The beginning professional must view the helping encounter as a microcosm of the client's own interpersonal issues. The encounter provides firsthand data regarding people's interpersonal relational and communication style, while the worker's own reactions yield data regarding clients' reactions to them. The professional tasks are to use one's reactions rather than act them out, to be self-monitoring and self-critical, and to learn from one's errors. These tasks replace any tendency toward using theoretical and personal rationales to justify practice disconnections. Greta was a powerful teacher for this student. He examined his own reactions and will be better prepared to empathize:

If I had another opportunity, I would make a new agreement with Greta on the most pressing concerns she wanted to work on. From there, I would help her set priorities to make the stressors more manageable. We would then discuss our expectations of what the work would look like. I would explore how she envisions our work together and reach mutual understanding. I would point out that people often want and even may expect quick, simple answers to complex, difficult troubles. Some can be quickly and easily eliminated; others take longer. I would also explore her reactions to our gender and age differences. I would explain that many people wonder about their social worker's level of experience, and gender and age (and ethnic/racial when appropriate) differences and we can talk about that too.

In the case of Pedro, the agency subscribes to the philosophy that many children are not properly emotionally prepared for the transition to adoption, causing disruption and possible disintegration of the adoptive placement; therefore, preparation is an integral part of the adoption process (Elbow 1986).

While I agree with this philosophy, the agency does not deal with the reality that our services are mandated. My progress with Pedro on the "life book" was reviewed every three months at team conferences, and I felt a tremendous pressure from the agency to focus on the "outcome" of our work rather than the "process." My effectiveness was compromised by this external pressure from the agency. At times, I forced the issue and did not work from Pedro's felt need and sense of timing, which led to his refusal to continue the project.

Pedro's view of our interpersonal difficulty was that I continually bothered him with painful topics, which he had never agreed to work on. When he did bring up his anxiety or his unclear feelings, he wanted me to "make it all better" quickly. He did not want to sit with his painful feelings, nor explore and clarify them; he wanted concrete solutions to what he viewed as environmental issues. For example, Pedro would be angry at his adoptive parents and would come to me to request another family. He would speak of nothing but his concrete plan of action to escape the situation. He would became angry with those who chose not to relieve his feelings. Therefore, I was constantly disappointing him because I could not make the pain go away.

Often, I complied with his request for immediate relief, thus maintaining an alliance built on avoidance and the fantasy that the avoidance will wash away the past. Initially, my perception of the problem was clear: Pedro was uncooperative in a therapeutic relationship and I had no recourse but to continually attempt to engage him. I blamed him as he blamed me. As I reviewed my work, I began to realize that each of us had a significant part to play in the dysfunction. In addition to the agency's

implicit pressure to confront Pedro no matter how ineffective that intervention might be, I found powerful forces within myself that affected my
interventions.

Viewing Pedro as a survivor of an emotionally abusive childhood, I
desired to help him maintain his "fortress" rather than risk breaking it
down, being unsure of what I would do with the pieces. I identified with
Pedro's avoidance of hurt and disappointment, in that they reminded me
of my own early self-protective avoidance. Within my internal desire to
protect Pedro is my desire to protect myself. Our time together was in
large part spent in our mutual avoidance of his feelings about either family. When the balance was disrupted by my initiating these painful topics, a period of intense discomfort or conflict followed, which then led us
back to the safety of avoidance.

Specifically, I have observed two distinct dysfunctional transactional
patterns. First, I would initiate the subject of Pedro's feelings about either
his biological family or his adoptive family and talk to him in an unchar-
acteristically cold, calm, and serious way. Discomfort in discussing his
loss contributed to my fear of his inevitable reaction. Once confronted he
would immediately disengage with exasperation and no response to questions or react by aggressively disrupting my desk, cursing, or leaving the
room. Pedro frequently told me he would never cooperate, and I was
wasting my time by trying. I would then change the subject. Once the
balance was regained, exchanges became smooth. The less frequent second pattern is reflected in my inability to explore Pedro's feelings. A
painful event would happen in Pedro's life, he would come into my office
and express his anxiety by crying or by pleading for my immediate solution. I felt his pain intensely but was paralyzed with anxiety at the responsibility he was giving me, so I responded to his emotions and expectations
with rational explanations. I tried to be empathic, but I falsely reassured
him that everything would turn out all right one day, and gave him no
tools to cope with the immediate issue. Although my emotions overwhelmed me, my external affect became logical and rational. My patterned reaction was to ask him factual, closed ended questions and slowly
re-focus the interview on concrete, less threatening topics. Thus, we col-
luded to avoid emotional issues.

Discrepant views of the situation and focus often lead to chronic challenges
and resistance (Hartman and Reynolds 1987). After a while patterns are set
and the chance for engagement becomes increasingly difficult. To help
with client-worker maladaptive patterns, the worker takes responsibility
for reversing them by disengaging from power struggles and reaching
beyond the static. Table 8.2 summarizes how social workers prepare themselves for work with dysfunctional interpersonal patterns.

Table 8.2   Professional Preparatory Tasks

- develop transactional perspective and define interpersonal obstacle
- examine potential sources of the interpersonal obstacle
- acknowledge own contribution to the obstacle
- accept professional responsibility for dealing with and reversing dysfunctional patterns
- take responsibility for disengaging from power struggles
- tune in to own feelings and use them rather than act them out
- tune in to client's perceptions of self and situation
- develop empathy for client suffering

Barry, a young adult diagnosed with schizophrenia and recently released from a mental hospital, moved into a halfway house. He chose a low-demand day hospital program. After three months, agency policy required that he take another step towards his goal of full-time employment. This meant doing something more demanding in addition to or instead of the day hospital. Shortly after he received this information, staff and residents noticed that Barry spent increasing time away from the halfway house and seldom slept there at night. Because regular attendance at various house functions was a requirement, his absences were seriously jeopardizing residency. The social worker was instructed by the team to confront Barry about his almost total absence.

BARRY: (looking at the floor, head down, shoulders sagging) What is it you wanted to talk to me about?

WORKER: You didn't make your coffee hours last week.

BARRY: Yeah, I suppose I didn't.

WORKER: One of the conditions for living here, Barry, is that you attend coffee hours. (I handed him a copy of this rule)

BARRY: (glancing at what I handed him) Well, I'll try to make them next week.

WORKER: Actually that isn't all. The house counselors said that at rounds this week, it looked like you hadn't slept in your bed, and quite a few residents are saying they haven't seen you around much lately.

BARRY: That's MY business! I've been seeing the folks a lot.

WORKER: Is there trouble at home?

BARRY: Yeah. Quite a bit.

WORKER: What's been happening?

BARRY: Dad went on one of his drinking binges; God, I swear they are getting worse—and took a bunch of pills. Scared the hell out of Mom. I've been trying to help out over there. My Dad is OK, BUT HE IS PRETTY SHAKY.

WORKER: This has been a real rough week for you.

The worker begins the interview in a confrontational mode. One can be intimidated by organizational pressures and incorporate them into one's professional approach rather than mediating to improve the fit between agency demands and service recipient needs. This practitioner was able to reverse gears, place herself in Barry's shoes, and invite his perceptions and life issues ("Is there trouble at home?"). This avoided a power struggle which both would have lost. She engaged Barry in productive work on the debilitating crossfire of pressures emanating from home and agency.

Workers may overidentify with clients, their concerns and perceptions. Social workers are sometimes caught between clients' needs and needs experienced by significant people in clients' lives.

Mr. French, a 45-year-old, single, white, Protestant male, was admitted to a psychiatric hospital a month after suffering from decompensation (the loss of appropriate psychological defenses). He had been evicted from his boarding house after neighbors, employees, and relatives reported his bizarre behavior. Mrs. Houghton, his sister, helped him move out of the boarding house and brought him to the hospital. After six weeks, the treatment plan focused on encouraging his return to the community, return to his job, independent living, and outpatient treatment. The worker met twice with Mrs. Houghton to engage her in the discharge plan. In the first meeting, she met alone with Mr. and Mrs. Houghton and Mr. French; in the second meeting the psychiatrist joined them. Mobilizing coping resources for Mr. French was discussed, and Mrs. Houghton expressed her feelings evoked by the responsibility for her brother. The more worker and psychiatrist pushed, the more she resisted. By the third interview, the worker was more attentive to her concerns and anxieties:

MRS. HOUGHTON: I hope your plan works, otherwise you and Dr. Knight will have to think of something else for my brother. He's YOUR patient!

WORKER: Mr. French was not able to go to Byetown and perhaps it was an overwhelming initial task. We are still working on the plan as discussed. We should also think about the possibility of your accompanying him to town to look for an apartment.

MRS. HOUGHTON: I won't do it. I have leg trouble. I also don't like to drive that far. I finally have my kids out of the house, my own job, my own money from that job. I'm at the point in my life that I only want to take care of my husband and myself.

WORKER: I can appreciate the fact that you should have less responsibility for others and not more. Do you think we can explore ways that you can help your brother and still set limits on your responsibility for him?

MRS. HOUGHTON: I'm concerned about my own mental health and I need to take care of myself (in the prior session she discussed her previous psychiatric outpatient treatment for depression).

WORKER: Although Mr. French is our patient, I am also concerned about your wellbeing. I realize you are currently under great pressure due to your brother's hospitalization.

MRS. HOUGHTON: Thank you for your concern. I really do appreciate it. I am under a lot of pressure and it concerns me.

WORKER: Do you think you would feel comfortable seeking help if you felt you needed it?

MRS. HOUGHTON: Yes. I will contact someone if I feel I need it, because I know it can help. I have the names of several psychiatrists. And I may have to do it if I let my brother deplete me.

WORKER: How do you see your role in regard to your brother? That is, ideally, how do you envision it?

MRS. HOUGHTON: I would like to invite him for holidays and occasional weekends to my home, but I don't want to go see him and have to check on him. If it comes to that, I would want him to go to one of the halfway homes that my cousin operates in Florida.

WORKER: That is an alternative, but the fact is that Mr. French has invested most of his life in Byetown and his job which was meaningful to him. To remove him from what he knows might not be the most helpful option.

MRS. HOUGHTON: I see what you mean, but we will have to see if this plan works and if he can find an apartment.

WORKER: You are absolutely right. Let's see how the next couple of weeks go and plan to meet again with your brother.

In this session as in the prior ones, Mrs. Houghton is letting the worker know that she feels overwhelmed by responsibility for her brother's care. Initially, the worker ignores Mrs. Houghton's message and perpetuates the pattern of trying to convince her and "sell" the agency's treatment plan. While family members can become an effective extension of the clinical team, they must want to be included in the aftercare and must know what and how to do it (Mechanic 1980). To move beyond the emerging interpersonal obstacle, the worker had to become attentive to Mrs. Houghton's needs by inviting her to talk of her pain, anger, and associated guilt. In pursuing a desired task or outcome, family members' feelings and perceptions must be obtained and not bypassed (Anderson and Hagarty 1986). When social workers empathize and respect family members' autonomy and separate their needs from the patient's needs, the power struggle subsides.

Initial denial or negation can aid coping and therefore is adaptive until it becomes an obstacle to growth and change. Practitioners find it difficult to assess and respond to unconscious denial or conscious negation. Some are fearful and join the denial or the negation. Others seek to break down the defense, thinking that this will resolve the problem. Either response is dysfunctional, distancing the service recipient from the worker and creating a serious communication barrier. The social worker then has to struggle to reverse this pattern and engage the coping dimensions of the denial or negation. A person is more likely to examine and relinquish a contradictory reality when she feels the worker's effort is motivated by genuine concern, warmth, and care than when she feels it is motivated by frustration, impatience, or annoyance.

For example, a social worker was assigned to 14-year-old Denise in her third month of pregnancy. Two weeks before discovering her pregnancy, she was placed in foster care after reporting her mother for child abuse. Denise views her pregnancy through the rosy perceptions of an adolescent. She envisions her baby as perfect and doll-like, who will provide her with all the love and affection she has been denied. She has no realistic plan for herself or her child. She merely hopes that a solution will magically appear, allowing her to live happily ever after. She provides herself with a companion who will need her love and love her, rather than face loneliness. "Adoption" is a provocative word, met with negation and obstinacy. She is determined to keep her child. The worker, a recent graduate, is concerned about Denise's unrealistic planning: neither her natural nor foster mother will accept the infant into their homes. The worker tries to collect sufficient data in order to convince Denise that her plans are unrealistic.

DENISE: (shouting) I don't know what people are telling you about me. But I ain't going to listen to you either. Nobody is going to tell me what to do!

WORKER: I have no intention of forcing my opinion on you. Whether you decide to keep your baby, abort it, or place it for adoption is entirely up to you. My purpose is to help you make the decision that is best for you. I want to listen, and help and support you.

DENISE: (looking at me skeptically) Why?

WORKER: I realize what a difficult decision you're facing, and it could be helpful to have someone to talk to and listen to your ideas.

DENISE: I guess so.

WORKER: When did you discover you were pregnant?

DENISE: About 3 weeks ago.

WORKER: How did you feel then?

DENISE: Very happy.

WORKER: Were you surprised?

DENISE: No.

WORKER: Why didn't you use contraception?

DENISE: My boyfriend said that men can control themselves.

WORKER: Have you been dating him for a while?

DENISE: I've dated Marvin for a couple of years on and off.

WORKER: How did he view your pregnancy?

DENISE: He was upset at first but now he is happy.

WORKER: Do you feel he will be supportive throughout your pregnancy?

DENISE: He'll be a good father.

WORKER: Have you given any thought to what your decision might be regarding the baby?

DENISE: I'm going to have my baby and keep it.

WORKER: Are you certain this is the right decision for you and the baby?

DENISE: (yelling) I AM GOING TO KEEP THE BABY!

WORKER: Are you planning to continue school when the baby begins to show?

DENISE: I'll stay in school until I deliver.

Denise's hidden message is loud and clear: "If you are just another person who is going to tell me what to do with my baby, I want no part of it! This is my decision. All my life I've been pushed around, and things are going to be different now! This is my baby! Finally something that is all mine! I have a chance to be happy, to have love! You can't brainwash me lady, I know what I want! I'm tough, I can do it—oh, but God I'm scared!" While the social worker relates to some of Denise's concerns, she limits herself to a superficial level. She struggles to not impose her agenda; yet she feels that Denise's plans are totally unrealistic. These conflicting pressures ("How can I support her decision, when I know adoption is probably the best thing for Denise and the baby? But if I don't support her she will reject my help. She has rights too") immobilizes the worker and blocks her natural empathy. Her own battle absorbs the worker's energies ("the fog around me was growing so thick that it nearly engulfed me") and prevents her from responding to Denise's latent messages. She vacillates between trying to convince Denise that her plans are unrealistic and focusing on safe concrete items. And the work is at a stalemate.

DENISE: My baby will be born in November, I can't wait!

WORKER: Having a baby would dramatically change your whole life.

DENISE: I know it won't be easy, but it'll be fun.

WORKER: When all your friends are going to parties or movies, you'll be home warming bottles and changing diapers.

DENISE: I don't go for that kid stuff anyway. Besides, I stay home at night a lot with my younger brothers and sisters.

WORKER: It will be a different ball game when you're caring for an infant who is totally your responsibility.

DENISE: I said I can handle it.

WORKER: People often don't realize how demanding a baby is until they have one of their own.

DENISE: I know babies are a lot of work, but as long as I have my baby I'm going to be happy.

WORKER: There will surely be times when you'll be pleased and proud, but I am also certain there will be times you will long for peace and quiet and freedom. Babies are extremely self-centered. All they understand is "I'm hungry! I'm wet! I'm tired and I want to be held!"

DENISE: (weakly) I guess so.

WORKER: The baby will not be capable of understanding that mommy also has needs. Sometimes you will get to a point where you will give anything for sleep. And the baby will keep crying and crying.

DENISE: I'm sure that happens to some people, but my baby will be well behaved.

WORKER: Why do you feel your baby will be different?

DENISE: I was a quiet baby so my child will be well behaved also.

WORKER: I hope you're right, but it doesn't always work that way. No baby can be a perfect angel.

Denise expresses an overwhelming desire to fill the void in her empty, unfulfilled life. She longs to have a role, a place, a purpose. She associates power and meaning with motherhood. Despite the social worker's efforts to change her mind, Denise holds firm, essentially saying: "I can handle anything that comes my way—this baby is my salvation!" The worker confronts the youngster's denial and negation. Without a relationship, however, Denise is unprepared to listen to the worker's version of reality and determines that she cannot or will not be helpful. Practitioners must not attack a person's defenses. They must demonstrate an understanding and appreciation of the client's perception of reality before the client can explore an alternative reality.

Social workers have to earn a person's trust; empathy is essential to earning trust. With people who face painful life stressors, trust and relationship are often released by mobilizing environmental resources. Denise's social worker identified and assessed the interpersonal obstacle to the work and committed herself to connecting to Denise more effectively. After several missed appointments and subsequent phone calls, Denise arrived quite agitated:

DENISE: Mrs. Peterson (her foster mother) and Mrs. Thomas (foster care worker) are planning to send me to Isaac House (a home for unwed mothers). I won't go there! If they make me go, I'll run away for good!

WORKER: What bothers you about Isaac House?

DENISE: I don't want to talk about it, but I'm not going there.

WORKER: If you don't want to go to Isaac House, you have to develop an alternative plan. You'll need a place to live and a means of supporting your baby.

DENISE: I agree. Will you help me?

WORKER: Let's deal with one task at a time. First, to find a place for you and your baby to live. Can you think of any place where you might stay?

DENISE: I haven't thought about it.

WORKER: Will your foster mother allow you to remain if you decide to keep the baby?

DENISE: Mrs. Peterson told me I could stay until the baby is born. After that I'm no longer be welcome.

WORKER: Are there any possibilities for you to stay with your grand-parents, father, aunts, uncles, or cousins?

DENISE: I've never met my father or anyone on his side of the family; my mother was the black sheep of my family and I'm not on speaking terms with any relatives. I don't trust any of them after what they did to my mom.

WORKER: Would you ever consider moving back in with your mother?

DENISE: I might if she agrees to counseling.

WORKER: Are you scared your mother might abuse your baby, the way she abused you?

DENISE: This is the main reason why I will not go home unless I have no other option. I feel I can handle being abused myself, but I can't have my own child abused.

WORKER: I can understand your feeling this way, and having a bottom line. Let's examine other possible options. How about your boyfriend's family?

DENISE: That's a great idea! Marvin's parents love me and will want their grandchild.

WORKER: Have they ever discussed the possibility of your moving in?

DENISE: It'll be all right with them.

WORKER: Let's discuss how you might ask them.

The worker should have explored the youngster's intense negative reactions to being sent to a home for unwed mothers. The worker did not explore possible fears and objections. However, in contrast to previous exchanges, she did focus on Denise's agenda and tried to be responsive. Beginning with the client's definition of the issue and perception of the situation is essential to establishing mutuality and rapport.

Focusing on the client's definition and perceptions of the stressor and the situation is sometimes enough to reverse a maladaptive pattern. At other times, the worker needs to invite the client to examine the barriers. The social worker must persist in exploring and inviting discussion of the tensions between them. This communicates faith in the helping process and demonstrates caring.

Some workers are able to defuse client-worker tensions with appropriate, timely humor. In certain instances, a light touch can relieve anxiety and expedite the work:

Mr. Kennedy, a 62-year-old Irish-American widower, was forced to retire on complete disability because of severe diabetes. One leg was broken in a fall at a local city hospital when he tried to get off an examining table where he had been left unattended. Mr. Kennedy was then placed at a welfare hotel after a fire destroyed most of his home and all of his clothing. He was in the hotel two weeks when the welfare worker informed him that in another week he would have to attend a hearing to determine whether he would receive an extension. She found him abrasive and uncooperative: he was angry, cursed and yelled that he didn't intend to go to any hearing. He screamed, "if Black and Puerto Rican welfare bums can stay in this hotel, you better let me stay. I've worked hard all my life, paid my taxes." He also threatened to "bash in the hotel manager's head with one of my crutches." After this outburst, he asked if the hotel had "a social worker woman like there was at the hospital." He wanted to see her and see what she could do to "help me with all these damned people."

The assigned social worker, also Irish-American, agreed to help him stay at the hotel while he was on crutches and unable to look for an apartment. She agreed it must be hard to go up and down the stairs on crutches and told him that she would call the hearing office to request a hearing at the hotel because of Mr. Kennedy's physical condition. They agreed to conduct the hearing in an office located on the same street as the hotel. She called and gave Mr. Kennedy the time and date. Three days before the hearing, the hearing officer called to say that he had to move the hearing ahead one day. Because the worker couldn't reach Mr. Kennedy by phone, she left a note in his mailbox telling him of the new date. When the day came, Mr. Kennedy did not arrive. She called him, but there was no answer. The following morning Mr. Kennedy arrived at the worker's office for the first scheduled interview. She recorded:

When I asked why he had not come the previous day, he looked puzzled, pulled out a calendar with the date circled, and told me he was sure I had told him Friday. I explained about the change to Thursday, my effort to reach him by phone, and the note I left. I asked him if he received my note. He said he had gotten some paper in his box, but didn't know what it was about. I asked if he had read it. He said he didn't have his glasses with him that morning. I kept asking if he had read the note later that day.

Mr. Kennedy became fidgety and looked quite uncomfortable. His face was red, he looked angry, and started yelling, "I am sick and tired of this bullshit. You are just like all the others, asking me to do things I can't do for myself." Thinking that he was referring to arranging the hearing, I pointed out that I had found an easier way for him, and all I asked him to do was to get himself to the hearing on the right day. Mr. Kennedy grabbed his crutches, stood up, glared at me and blurted, "Look, you dumb S.O.B. I've been trying to tell you—I CAN'T READ!" As he walked out he yelled back, "I don't give a . . . about the hearing, you can all go to hell!"

The worker was angry at Mr. Kennedy for making her look bad. She assumed he was refusing to take minimal responsibility for his life. Moreover, as she struggled to control her anger, she became preoccupied with her own feelings, stifling her ability to be curious and to listen. Consequently, she was unable to pick up Mr. Kennedy's clues about his illiteracy. Mr. Kennedy's frustration and anger is understandable: he was being held accountable for taking charge of his life, when he could not read a simple note. From this interview, the worker became aware that Mr. Kennedy's difficulties with agency personnel are not due to temper or hostility but to his frustration, insecurity, and feelings of inadequacy. He used bravado to cover his insecurities.

The social worker realized Mr. Kennedy probably would not come back to see her. She wondered how to recover the contact and re-start the dialogue, and what point of entry would mobilize his resistance the least. She remembered from their first contact that he had made numerous references to being Irish, and she decided their common ethnic background might provide a necessary bridge.

When he asked who it was in response to my knock, I told him my name and that I wanted to talk to him. He yelled, "Go back to your office before you freeze out there." I asked if he could hear me and he didn't respond. I said, "Look, Billy, there's a mick on the outside of this door who can be just as stubborn as the one on the inside. So, you better open the door before the two of us make a holy show of ourselves." With that the door opened wide and Mr. Kennedy stood there laughing. "Well now," he said, "I guess there's still a little of the old sod in you after all." "Well now," I said, mimicking him, "I guess you are not the only Irishman who kissed the Blarney Stone either." We both laughed and he invited me to sit down and have a "good cup of tea." As we drank the tea, both of us were quiet. I broke the silence by saying, "I am sorry about the other day, sorry that I didn't listen to you and hear what you were saying, and sorry that I was angry at you without understanding how things really are for you. I really want to try to help you and hope you will give me another chance." He immediately answered that if anyone should be sorry it should be him with his "trashy mouth and rotten temper." He apologized for cursing at me and explained he was so upset because it is hard for him to let anyone know that he can't read. He told me he is very ashamed and feels like a "dummy."

The worker effectively uses their common ethnicity as a point of entry into their interpersonal obstacle. Humor eased the tension and provided a boost to their working relationship. By apologizing to Mr. Kennedy for her insensitivity, she conveys a willingness to risk further rejection. A transactional obstacle is best engaged when the interaction is between real people who have strengths and weaknesses, and struggle to come to grips with them and with each other. With Mr. Kennedy, the encounter led to a major breakthrough in the quality and the depth of their ongoing work.

Mr. Kennedy spoke of having lost everything last year. I asked if he was referring to his wife's death. He said when she died he had nothing more to live for . . . he wanted to die too . . . he felt he couldn't go on living without her. I asked him what got him through the worst days. He said he really didn't know how he managed, but he just went through the motions of living; taking his insulin, preparing his meals, and trying to rest as the doctor ordered. He did all the same things he did when she was with him. At first, she seemed to still be in the house and he found that as the days went on he gradually realized she wasn't there. Then he hit on the idea that if he didn't talk about it, and didn't mention her name, it would seem like nothing had happened, that he could somehow keep her with him. He refused to talk to anyone about his wife, or about the circumstances of her death, or anything concerning her. I remarked that never talking about the one person who was in on his mind, so uppermost in his thoughts, must have been extremely difficult for him. He looked very dejected, his head sunk low; and he cried softly, "I can't keep her with me, no matter how I try. She is gone. She is never coming back from the grocery store. I can't make her come back." I answered softly, "No, you can't Billy, but maybe you can begin to talk about her."

When I asked him if he had ever tried to learn to read when he got older, he told me his wife was the only one who knew, and he was too ashamed to tell anyone else who might help. He told me that all his life, he had been afraid to take a chance. When he was a child, he never knew where the next meal was coming from or whether there would be a next

Table 8.3	Skills of Dealing with Interpersonal Obstacles

- reach beneath manifest behaviors and verbalizations
- invite and explore perceptions, content, and related feelings
- engage coping aspects of defenses
- demonstrate genuine concern, warmth, and caring
- demonstrate understanding of client's perceptions of self and situation
- identify tension and obstacles in relationship and communication
- invite perceptions of client-worker relationship and communication patterns
- acknowledge potential discomfort in work on tensions and obstacles
- make supportive and persistent demands that issues in the work be addressed
- use appropriate and timely humor to defuse tensions
- demonstrate own stake in the work and in the relationship
- pursue client's stake in the work and in the relationship

meal. He thought this had made him cautious about everything until now, when he had lost his wife and everything he owned. He had nothing else to lose. I asked, if he had nothing to lose, would he take a chance with me? I would like to help him learn to read. At first he was cautious, even resistant, "I don't think you can teach me to read—I mean it's not your job and what would you know about how to go about it?" Sensing his tension, I said that I had a sense he was about to call me a dumb S.O.B. again. We both laughed and that relieved the tension. I told him he was right, it takes special skills and I knew a teacher with remarkable talent in teaching adults how to read. Before I could finish, he said he didn't want a teacher treating him like he was a six year old and teaching him to read. I explained to him who this person was (a retired teacher who had taught reading and English to immigrants applying to become citizens). "You mean she could teach those foreigners who didn't know anything?" I added, "And she didn't treat them like six year olds." He agreed to give the idea some thought.

The next time I saw him we talked about housing. As we ended, I asked if he had given any more thought to my suggestion about his learning to read. He grinned at me and said, "Well you better call that old lady before we both get too old for her to teach me to read."

With the social worker's support, Mr. Kennedy took lessons and quickly progressed to a fourth grade reading level. He seemed increasingly self-confident, smiling easily, getting along with his landlord, traveling independently, trying new foods. Clearly, being able to read has opened a new world and imparted a sense of mastery. The social worker's progress with Mr. Kennedy is associated with her ecological thinking, an astute definition of the interpersonal obstacle, and total empathy. Without these, Mr.

Kennedy might have been dismissed as "resistant" and "unmotivated." With ecological thinking, the worker defined the obstacle as being within her professional function. She owned her contribution to the obstacle, apologized, used humor to reduce tensions, and pursued Mr. Kennedy's stake in working on his longstanding life issue.

When client and social worker work effectively on their maladaptive interpersonal patterns, they grow in confidence and mutual trust. Hence, practitioners need to view such obstacles as inherent in the helping process and struggle against discouragement and self-blame. The work together gives the opportunity for both participants to meet and master a difficult challenge with creativity.

NINE

ENDINGS:
Auspice, Modalities, Methods, and Skills

The decision to end can occur in several ways. It could be made jointly by the client and worker (Fortune, Pearlingi, and Rochelle 1991; Fortune 1987); it could be imposed by the nature of the setting, as at the end of the school year or at the end of hospitalization; or it might have been settled in advance, as in planned short-term service. Occasionally, the decision to end comes about through an unexpected event involving either worker or client, such as illness, a move, or a job change. However the decision is made, the ending phase makes specific demands of both worker and client. These include: (a) managing feelings aroused by the ending; (b) reviewing accomplishments and what remains to be achieved; (c) planning for the future including, where indicated, transfer to another worker or referral to another agency; and (d) evaluating the service provided. Like the initial and ongoing phases of practice, the ending phase requires social workers' sensitivity, knowledge, careful planning, and a range of skills.

Preparation

Separation is painful; even the termination of a brief relationship or one that was fraught with ambivalence can reawaken distressing feelings connected to earlier losses. The termination of a professional relationship can have a similar impact. If the experience of termination and its meaning to the particular client are ignored or mishandled, any gains achieved in the work together can be lost. Future involvement with social work services could also be jeopardized. When the ending phase is handled well, however, termination results in growth for both client and worker.

Ending is a mutual experience. The client needs to separate from the worker and the agency; the worker needs to separate from the client. In preparing to help individuals, families, and groups move through termination, social workers consider organizational, temporal, and relational factors and anticipate their likely impact on the client and on themselves.

Organizational, Temporal, and Modality Factors

The agency itself influences the content and process of ending, particularly in respect to temporal features. Organizations differ in how they structure and use time. A public school, for example, has a natural temporal structure that fits well with both temporary separations and permanent endings. During holidays and vacation periods, temporary separations reflect natural pauses: the building is closed, family and friends may be more accessible, time is available for other activities. A temporary separation is less likely to stimulate feelings of abandonment and rejection than separation in other organizational contexts (Hartman 1960). Similarly, completion of the academic year carries intimations of graduation. A permanent ending at this time meshes with the temporal structure. It may be readily connected to a sense of progress and achievement, minimizing the sense of loss.

Long-term treatment facilities for the chronically ill, the elderly, and children provide different temporal structures. Holidays and worker vacations are painful for these clients, who already feel isolated and abandoned. The social worker's absence could intensify that sense of desertion and arouse depressed feelings (Schaffer and Pollak 1987). No natural point of "graduation" coincides with ending. Client or worker might leave at any time. The client may be suddenly transferred or discharged, and the worker finds the bed empty. Workers may be transferred or leave (Moss and Moss 1967). These aspects also characterize short-term institutional facilities, making endings difficult. They require careful attention in preparing for termination.

The agency's definition of the status of social work student has consequences for termination. When agencies present students to their clientele as regular staff and discourage students from disclosing their real status, unique problems in termination are generated. Beyond important ethical issues, students feel they must devise reasons for departure. They fear being found out and suffer discomfort and self-consciousness throughout the ending phase. The client, in turn, senses the lack of authenticity, and may begin to question the student's credibility, caring, and commitment.

When agencies are open and direct about their training function and present their students as supervised learners, clients expect the student's departure at the end of the academic year, and termination and transfer are likely to be viewed as legitimate (though some people do "forget" they were told at the start). Some clients are pleased to know that they contributed to student learning in return for a valued service. In settlement house programs, members often joke about "breaking in" another student. In university-affiliated hospitals, patients are keenly aware of the rotation of medical interns, residents, nursing students, and social work students, and accept the arrangement as natural. This is not to say that termination may not be distressing in these settings, but only that honesty about the student status from the outset decreases unnecessary guilt on the part of the student and unnecessary resentment on the part of the client. Ethical practice demands no less.

The temporal nature of the service itself also affects the ending phase. By definition, open-ended services carry no time limit or ending date. The relationship intensifies over time, perhaps even carrying a freight of ambivalence and maladaptive dependency along with positive feelings. In long-term services, much time and energy is invested in maintaining and sustaining the therapeutic relationship. When the worker introduces termination for whatever reason, some people may experience shock and disbelief and perceive the ending as personal rejection.

Planned short-term services have a specified duration with an ending date clearly stated at the outset (Epstein 1988; Reid 1992). The dynamics of termination in planned short-term service are therefore very different from those of open-ended services. Clients are more likely to perceive the ending as an integral aspect of the service. Both client and worker mobilize their energies to accomplish specific objectives within the designated time period, and termination is an expected and therefore neutral event. Similarly, in work on sudden, acute, overwhelming life stressors, the steps toward resolution serve as a natural temporal structure (Webb 1985).

The modality (individual, family, group, and community) of service influences the ending phase in important ways. For the individual, termination can mean a loss that has both realistic and unrealistic features (Fortune, Pearlingi, and Rochelle 1992). The person may experience anger, sadness, and perhaps a resurgence of helplessness. Such feelings are especially intense among those who are most dependent upon their environment because of age and physical factors that affect their competence and self-direction—children, elders, and disabled or chronically ill people.

In families and groups that remain intact, members will have one another as a mutual aid or support system. Less intensity exists in the relationship with the social worker, especially when the work opens communication channels and strengthens relationships. Termination of the professional relationship may therefore be less stressful for a collectivity than for an individual. If, however, the family or group faces separation from one another along with separation from the worker, as in divorce or a move away from the family, or the breakup of a school or camp group, the combined losses may be even more painful and difficult to manage (Garvin and Seabury 1984; Hartman and Laird 1983; Shulman 1992; Toseland and Rivas 1984).

Relational Factors

A social worker had been working with 10-year-old Carlos in residential treatment. The youngster avoided discussing the termination by talking to himself, singing in rhymes, and jumping up and down in his chair. The sheer energy required of the worker simply to stay with the youngster was a severe drain. Carlos maintained control during this time by not responding to questions or participating in conversation. When the social worker attempted to gently break through the negation by reminding him how many sessions remained, he withdrew into rhymes. The worker responded to his regression by assuring him of her affection and caring for him. However, promises of affection had accompanied the abandonment and betrayal of all the other "mothers" he had loved. Carlos's response was to withdraw and protect himself from yet another loss. The social worker, like the youngster, felt powerless. Her responses were often triggered by intense feelings of guilt for abandoning him. She attempted to take herself out of the line of fire by stressing that it was not her wish to leave. Her responses made it even more difficult for Carlos to express his anger at her.

The vignette illustrates that the intense emotions associated with ending depend on earlier experiences with relationship and loss and the meaning attached to the relationship with the worker. The more sudden and unexpected the loss, the more difficult is the management of realities and feelings of sadness, abandonment, or anger. Without adequate opportunity to work together on ending, the experience can be devastating (Kupers 1988; Northen 1982; Palumbo 1982).

Social workers prepare for the ending phase by reviewing what is known about the person's previous experiences with loss and means of coping with it. Through anticipatory empathy, the practitioner considers the potential impact of termination of this relationship on this person, and anticipates likely responses. With families and groups, potential reactions of each member must be considered as well as the likely collective response. For example:

I had been working with a youth group in a group home, helping the members prepare for discharge and independent living. In trying to anticipate their possible reactions to my own departure, I immediately thought of the deprivations, losses, and separations in their lives. I felt that I would be one more in a series of females who had left or abandoned them. The experience may be more difficult because of life transitional tasks involved in their impending separation from the group home. I anticipated some regression and tried to imagine how each member might deal with my leaving. Bill might reject me; Tony will probably show how much he needs me; Sam will most likely withdraw. I thought the group itself might avoid the idea at first, and then become disruptive. This might be followed in later meetings by absences or lateness. I planned to deal with avoidance of my leaving by persistently presenting the reality, impede flight by "chasing" absent or withdrawn members, and help regulate depression and anger by inviting and empathically acknowledging the intense feelings.

Social workers, too, are subject to painful feelings and reactions (Siebold 1991). We must therefore examine our own feelings about separating from a particular person, family, or group and our own patterns of coping with the stress of loss. We must especially consider the potential for guilt about leaving and the consequent difficulty in letting the client go. Without such examination, workers might deny the experience themselves. One worker might postpone announcing the ending date so there is no time left for being helpful. Another might express ambivalence toward the relationship through indirect communications, double messages, or repeated postponements of the ending date. The social worker in the preceding example continues:

I didn't have to go far within myself to touch my own feelings. I am aware that I don't cope with separations or endings easily. I know I tend to postpone the inevitable and to become detached. With these youngsters, I feel guilty about leaving them just when they are already confronting a major separation. I find myself wanting to avoid the issue, even blaming the agency, and needing to falsely reassure the group. Nevertheless, now that I am aware of these possible therapeutic errors, I am determined to invite the boys to express their feelings. I hope that if I do become defensive, I can still reverse myself and allow them to explore and express possible feelings of sadness, disappointment, anger.

By being in touch with their own pattern of coping with loss, social workers are better prepared to deal with their own feelings and will therefore be freer to help clients deal with theirs.

Table 9.1	Factors Influencing Reactions to Termination

- agency context
- professional status
- temporal nature of service
- modality of service
- relational factors
- client and worker backgrounds

Phases in Separation

While responses to termination are unique, most of us seem to go through recognizable phases in ending a relationship. However individual styles and pacing may vary, it is useful to consider four phases that might be involved in ending. The phases are analogous to those observed in dealing with death, though obviously they are not of the same quality or degree (Nuland 1994).[1] In general, the phases of termination are: negation and avoidance; negative feelings; sadness; and release. Each phase has its own tasks, although not everyone goes through every phase or in the so-called order. Some people may not experience any of these phases.

Preparation for ending the work involves anticipating which coping demands require exploration and support. The social worker must be responsive to coping processes and resources involved in termination by providing the time needed for their development. Time is critical. In abrupt ending, no time is available for the expression of feelings, review of meaning, or planning ahead. Before a client can engage in coping with the tasks, the reality of the ending must be presented. Even when the ending date was agreed on at the outset in planned short-term service, or mentioned at stated intervals in open-ended service, the actual presentation of the ending date is often met by negation.

Negation and Avoidance

The more satisfactory the relationship, the more likely people are to ward off separation anxiety by negating and avoiding its reality. Initially, some people "forget" that termination was mentioned earlier and try to avoid discussing it by changing the subject, excessive activity, or regression. Avoidance can be adaptive when it provides time to absorb the meaning of the imminent loss and to develop means of coping with it.

A social worker in a mental hospital had been working with Mrs. Miller, a deaf patient in medical isolation because of suspected tuberculosis. He was the first person to engage her in a long while. She became dependent on him for concrete assistance and now that he is leaving, she is unable to accept the reality of his departure. For a month she did not "hear" his statements about leaving or about his interest in helping her to become more self-reliant and to use other resources.

Mrs. Miller greeted me with, "Where's my toothpaste?" I wrote a note reminding her we had agreed she would ask an aide for this. After pouting, she said she liked having me help her more than anyone else. I wrote, "Because I'm leaving, it is very important for you to learn to use others, and I know how difficult that is to do. I want to help you with it." She then placed a dollar on the table and asked me to buy her a Sunday paper on Monday. She was holding on, struggling to keep our relationship intact. I wrote suggesting she ask the nurse to buy the paper, because I will soon be leaving, and she must get used to dealing with other staff. She began to pout again. I wrote, "I like you, and this isn't easy for me either, but I know you can do this for yourself." She looked at me with a smile, and said she will ask the nurse. I wrote, "Maybe you can ask her on Sunday night?" She said she will ask her on Saturday so that she can have the paper on Sunday. I credited the idea, and suddenly she began to cry.

The worker's persistence and assurance of caring helped Mrs. Miller begin to cope with the stress of an inevitable ending. His ability to do this rested on his empathy and his awareness of his own difficulty in leaving her with so many helping tasks still undone.

By contrast, another worker in a long-term chronic-care facility was unable to help her group with termination because she could not handle her own guilt feelings. She had successfully engaged a group of elderly, brain damaged, socially isolated men with one another and with her. When she decided to leave the hospital, she could not tell her group.

My plan for this meeting was to begin with my leaving, and we got onto the subject of loss. It would have been natural for me to introduce termination, but I didn't—I couldn't. Mr. Jones was verbally rambling and suddenly brought out his pipe, which was broken in two pieces, and sadly said, "Look at that—that's my only pleasure." It took a while to establish that what was upsetting him was that no one could help him get a new pipe, though he had asked several aides. He exclaimed, "It isn't too much for a man to ask, to have a smoke, there's not much else." After we established that I would help him get a pipe after the meeting, I asked if Mr. Kley and Mr. Dobbs had similar feelings about something they had lost and were sad about. They didn't respond. I said that one thing that they all had in common was that they had lost part of their health. There was much nodding. Mr. Kley agreed, "Yeah—we all got sick." I added they all live in the hospital as home. Mr. Jones said they were all together in this, like neighbors. I noted that the men hadn't known each other, even after many years—not even each others' names sometimes. Mr. Kley said, "Everyone has his own problems." Mr. Jones said he and the others couldn't remember. I asked why they thought we were getting together. Mr. Jones grinned and said, "The neighbors get together." We all laughed.

Literally and symbolically, the worker moved back to the initial phase of agreement on help—to the beginning instead of the ending. Immobilized by her own feelings, she avoided introducing and dealing with termination. She tried again the next week but, still unaware of her own feelings, she failed to anticipate individual and group responses to her announcement.

I said that by the middle of next month I wouldn't be able to meet with the group anymore as I am leaving the hospital. There were nods. Everyone looked at me blankly. I said we talked last week about having things we like break or taken away. I asked if they remembered. No one responded. After several efforts, there still were no responses. I said this is hard to talk about, or at least I find it hard. More nods, but the men just looked at me. I asked if it were on their minds that I will be leaving. Still no response. I asked Mr. Jones if it is on his mind. He smiled and said, "That's nice." I was getting uptight. I asked if the men would like to continue meeting with another worker after I leave. They remained expressionless. I asked if they wanted to close the meeting, and they nodded affirmatively.

The worker's avoidance of the meaning of the relationship evoked a reciprocal avoidance in the group members. They withdraw not only from her but from one another as well. To be helpful the worker must refer to her own feelings about ending a significant relationship. This enables the worker to persist in the reality of termination, as the worker did with Mrs. Miller. Frequent reminders are often necessary so that the painful reality remains on the agenda. With children, a calendar is helpful, crossing out each completed session and specifying the remaining number. But whatever the means, the worker needs to focus on the issue, risk confrontation with pain, and elicit expressions of negative feelings. This process of working through negation is illustrated in a practice vignette from a twelve-session school group of eighth-grade African-American and Hispanic girls.

Keika reminded the group that next week was the last time we were going to meet before the holiday and asked if we could have a party during the last half of the meeting. I agreed that it would be fun and pointed out that today marks the halfway mark for the group. Perhaps they would like to spend some time at the beginning of the next session to take stock and decide the focus for the remaining meetings. Within a few seconds, the entire ambiance completely changed. Although a few registered no visible reactions, most seemed puzzled as they glanced around the room. Alice, Helen, and Maria, who were seldom at a loss for words, looked absolutely thunderstruck. All were quiet. I waited several minutes, then observed that they were awfully quiet all of a sudden, and I was wondering if my comment about having only five more sessions had taken them off guard.

The silence just got louder. For a few minutes I had the sinking feeling that the session might end in silence. Finally, Ivory found her voice and demanded to know why I was cutting the group short when they hadn't done anything "nasty." Then she looked more closely at me and reminded me that I had said I was going to be here until May, so what was the problem? Matilda chirped in a "told you so" tone of voice that I just did not like them—that was the problem. I became flustered and defensive. I mentioned that in individual interviews and at the first meeting I had emphasized the group would meet for twelve weeks. Ivory retorted that when I had first talked to their class I had said the group would meet for the entire school year, just like last year's group.

Irene shook her head and corrected her by pointing out that it had been changed to twelve weeks because too many people signed up. Ivory indignantly declared this was the first she had heard of it. But even if that was the case why couldn't I just have a second group for the other class? I explained that if they remembered, I had informed them right away that my schedule did not allow me to have two groups, and the agency could not assign another worker. Dramatically, Ivory looked around the group and said in exaggerated disbelief that "I just want to get this straight . . . you are going to give our group to those bimbos?" I responded this was very hard for all of us. There was a tense lull, and finally Maria said quietly that it seemed like we had just started and now we only had a short time left. I agreed, saying that we had come such a long way in such a short time and it's hard to make peace with only five more meetings. Keika responded that she was upset, but if I had taken the other group first, she would expect them to finish on time so her group would have a turn. Alice was animated again and informed me I was going to need a bigger room to have a group with "those ho's" because the only way they know how to talk is when they are lying down.

Persistence and assurance of caring helps the group begin to accept the reality that it will end after five more sessions. By demanding that they confront the reality of termination, the worker helps the group to move into the next phase, expression of negative feelings.

Negative Feelings

Negation and avoidance gradually gives way to the reality of the ending through the social worker's empathic support. Still, a period of intense reaction may follow. People express their hurt in many different ways, some through direct anger at the worker.

Walking back from the bus I noticed again what had been happening lately; the girls were very busy talking to themselves and teasing each other. Although it looked as if we were together, I was quite obviously apart. At one point, they actually walked in front of me, laughing over some joke, while I walked alone and behind them.

Once again, I felt isolated. It made me sad, which must have reflected in my face, for suddenly Judy noticed I was walking alone, and came and took my arm condescendingly. Tata's response was, "Shit on her." She and Judy, Carmen, and Kathy laughed hysterically. I said I thought they seemed unhappy with me lately and asked if they wanted to talk about it. Kathy said they weren't unhappy about anything. I asked, "Even about my leaving in the summer?" Tata jumped up and shouted, "Nobody gives a shit about your leaving. Go ahead and leave now if you want to." There were tears in her eyes as she spoke (Irizarry and Appel 1994).

Some people express anger in a subtler, more symbolic manner. For instance, a physically challenged social worker student had seen John, who is seriously addicted, for nine months. They worked hard and achieved much. In her office she has a footstool she uses to help ease the discomfort of her disability. John usually sits down and hooks the footstool around so he can use it too. The sharing of the stool symbolized the kind of shared work they did together. However, in the session in which the student began termination work with John, he kept the footstool all to himself. The student commented on that, and it led to an exploration of his feelings about ending their work.

Others turn their feelings inward and experience the ending as a reflection of their unworthiness or the worker's disappointment with them. They may also develop physical symptoms or engage in self-destructive behavior. For Phyllis, a twice-divorced, depressed, battered woman, the social worker's impending departure triggered unresolved grief related to other losses, particularly the recent death of a close girlfriend from AIDS. Phyllis developed pneumonia. The worker records her session with Phyllis in the hospital.

Phyllis began the session about being distressed over her forgetfulness and asked if her medication could be causing it. I asked what she meant, and she said she knew I had told her, but she couldn't remember why I was leaving. I reminded her of our previous conversations. Then I asked, "What ran through your mind when you tried to remember the reasons I was leaving the agency?" She said she had thought that once in a while staff decide to switch cases. I asked how come she thought that. She said, "If it wasn't working out." I asked what she meant. Phyllis said if staff get tired of working with a person, if the person isn't making enough progress, they let someone else try. I asked if she is concerned that I am tired of working with her and feel she had made insufficient progress. She said, "Yes, I think I was assigned to you with the expectation that I'd be cured in a certain amount of time." I suggested it sounded like she thought she was "just another case" to me, an assignment, and maybe she wondered if I really cared about her. She replied she wasn't sure at all. I responded, "Phyllis, ending with you is also very hard for me. Our relationship has meant a great deal to me also." She said that she had learned a lot from me and would miss me. I said I had learned a lot from her also— about a person's courage to deal with grief and pain, to raise children without the help of a husband, to not allow men to batter her anymore. She said from our work together she felt "like a fog has been lifted from me."

Some people may try to re-introduce needs or tasks which had been resolved or completed (Barton and Marshall 1986). They may regress, become excessively dependent, or in other ways attempt to demonstrate their need for continued service. Still others turn their feelings outward and experience the ending as a reflection of the worker's incompetence and lack of commitment. They may confront the social worker directly with accusations of lack of concern, or indirectly with silence, repeated tardiness, or absence. The intended message is, "I'll leave you before you leave me." The behavior attempts to lessen the pain of the perceived abandonment and, simultaneously, to provoke responses from the worker that will further justify the distancing.

> CARLOS: Do you remember when I brought a snowball in here?
>
> WORKER: How can I forget? You and I got into a pretty big fight that day.
>
> CARLOS: (running around the room, looking up, avoiding eye contact, yelling) I'm bringing the snowball back in here. I'm gonna

> throw it all over your office! And I'm gonna hurt you real
> bad. (smiles)

WORKER: I know you want to hurt me cause I hurt you by leaving you
in three weeks. You're real mad at me because I'm leaving.

CARLOS: (moving to the furthest corner in the room and yelling)
YOU!! NEVER! I couldn't give a shit about you. You don't
mean anything to me. I'm mad at you, but not cause you're
leaving. I'm angry cause you're a bad social worker and I'm
bored. Can I go now? I'm never coming back even if you
come trying to find me. I want a new social worker—one
that's nice. Would you come looking for me if I didn't show
up? Because I'm warning you, I'll run away!

WORKER: You bet I will. I'm not letting you slip out of my life so
quickly (I smiled at him). I won't give up on you even if you
think I am a terrible social worker. You have every right to be
angry at me and if you want you can yell at me for the next
few weeks. But I won't let you just not show up. I care too
much about you.

Carlos wants to hurt the worker where she is most vulnerable—her professional competence. He wants to reject her before she can reject him. His
anger has an important coping function: he is fighting back rather than giving up in despair. Anger is a form of engagement, a ticket into termination
work.

When such angry and rejecting responses occur, the ending phase is difficult for both worker and client. Social workers must be both empathic and
sufficiently detached. That is, we must maintain sufficient identification
with our clients to understand the feelings that have been aroused and at
the same time we must be free to invite and pursue the expression of negative ideas and feelings about ourselves and the service. Feelings must be
accepted as real for the person. Inappropriate reassurance by sugarcoating
the feelings must be avoided.

In families and groups, the social worker must be sensitive to individual
perceptions and experiences which create disparate behaviors and
responses to termination. A session with a group of older adolescent residents of a group home illustrates the complexities involved.

I said it was hard to talk about my leaving. John said he was tired. He
arranged three chairs together and lay down across them. He talked of
how close he is to his siblings, and said they are the most important
people to him since his mother died. Nobody else matters. He
described how hard growing up had been for him, and he emphasized
his ability to make it by himself. Bill was watchful and restless, and I

asked what he was feeling. He said nothing but got up and left the room. Sam cursed at me and followed Bill out. I went after them, and they returned. I said it's difficult for us to talk about my leaving, but we have worked too hard to run away from each other. Sam screamed that I had a nerve to "open us up" and then leave. Bill yelled that he always knew I didn't care. "We are just a job." I'm just like all the other social workers they knew—"phony." I said I knew how much they're hurting, and I'm hurting, too.

In lying down, John expressed his fatigue and depression; in talking of important memories in his life, he attempted to negate the worker's importance. In contrast, Bill withdrew, and Sam acted out. The worker stayed with them, pursued Sam and Bill, and helped the members explore their shared feelings of resentment. In these ways, she demonstrated her caring about them and her faith in their ability to work together despite their negative reactions. Endings often call for the social worker to reestablish credibility, skill, and commitment. A common error is a too early expression of one's own sense of loss, which can shut off the expression of members' negative reactions.

Sadness

As the reality of ending and resentment about it are successfully confronted, clients and workers are freed to experience shared feelings of sadness at separating. Social workers encourage and support client expressions and respond to them by sharing their own sense of intimacy and loss. They now can disclose the personal meaning of the experience and invite clients to do the same. People have varying capacities for such expression; and for some the practitioner's recognition of their unexpressed feeling may be relief enough. Some clients (mostly males) express their intense sadness over the loss of intimacy by sexualizing the therapeutic relationship. For example, during termination a young adult client, Alvin, informed his female worker:

"I guess I love you." When I pointed out that caring and love can easily become confused when two people work hard together, Alvin said he must be oversexed and is ashamed for fantasizing about me. I examined his feelings of love, and he then identified "gratitude, respect, honesty, and affection." He explained, "I never let a woman get so close to me before. Jesus, we've never even shaken hands, and yet I feel we are so close." "Yes," I replied, "our minds have touched, our hearts have touched, and even our souls have touched, that's made our work very special."

Many clients will not feel anything as intense as sadness but only a mild regret, perhaps, that the relationship is ending. The worker must guard against the projection that results in overemphasis and overintensity. At the same time, the worker must be aware of attempts to cover up feelings and to avoid the embarrassment often associated with the expression of positive affect.

Both client and worker may attempt to escape into happy activities. Camp staffs, aware of the intensity of relationships that develop, structure end-of-the-season rituals that help assuage the pain of separation: special campfires and other traditional ceremonies that serve to review achievements and to reaffirm the ties of comradeship. By contrast, an emphasis on farewell parties alone may interfere with the campers' experiencing the reality of separating. Alone on the bus, or back at home, the full measure of their grief spills out, to the dismay of parents.

The worker with the group of elderly men in the chronic-care facility helped the group experience together the sadness of leaving, instead of continuing to withdraw from one another and from her:

As I reintroduced my leaving, Mr. Dobbs burst into tears. He looked at me, then down, and shook his head. I reached across the table and put my hand on his; he continued to weep. I said I knew this is rough. He wept harder, and Mr. Lawrence reached across the table and patted his arm. Mr. Andrews, immobile, watched with a blank expression. Mr. Jones's eyes filled, and he said, "'There'll be nobody left for us. Men will watch TV." I asked if he is worried there will be no more activities. He said, "Yes, ma'am, that's what I mean. You need to get up from sitting in front of that thing. You need to do things." Mr. Andrews and Mr. Kley nodded. As I mentioned the plans for another worker, Mr. Dobbs began to weep again, and couldn't talk. I said, "Mr. Dobbs, we got close this year, didn't we?" He nodded. I said I knew he and the others would miss me very much, just as I would miss them. They all nodded. I continued that sometimes when people have to say goodbye, like us, they feel very much alone. Mr. Dobbs said, "Yeah," and pointed to himself. I said I hoped they won't shut each other out. They learned to care for each other, and they still have that. They looked at each other and nodded. I looked at Mr. Dobbs, and he responded clearly, "I understand, I'm with you."

The worker recognized with the members how difficult the subject of her leaving is. She responded to their feelings verbally and with the intimacy of physical contact, which is as important to the elderly as it is to children. She disclosed her own feelings of sadness. Together, members and worker feel the sadness and the closeness, and the members struggle to identify what the group experience has meant to them. The worker locates the strength in their situation: they have each other.

Moving past negative feelings to sadness requires time. In the same way, moving through sadness to letting go of the relationship, to acceptance, also requires time. The worker with the group of preadolescent girls described earlier, provided them with ample time for them to deal with separation. Without that time, it is doubtful they could have reached the degree of acceptance demonstrated in the following excerpts.

As soon as I mentioned my leaving, Nilda turned away and started looking at pictures on the bulletin board. She asked, "Who's Joanne?" I reminded her Joanne is the social worker who will be taking my place. Nilda turned from the board, insisting, "We don't talk about her!"

For several weeks, the girls refused to refer to the new worker by name, and they avoided any discussion of her coming. But their curiosity and beginning acceptance finally generated some discussion.

Lydia said she was wondering what will happen when I leave. I said Joanne is coming in to take my place. Lydia said, "But I may not like her." I nodded, and she went on to say that if she doesn't like her, she won't come back to the club. I thought most of the girls feel this way but they will have time to see what they think of her. I reminded them they hadn't been too sure of me in the beginning, either; they hadn't liked to talk with me much and whispered together instead. Lydia roared with laughter.

With acceptance growing, more open curiosity appeared the next week.

Suddenly, Tata blurted out, "When is that other girl coming, anyway?" I said she would arrive in the beginning of August. She shouted, "We are going to kick her ass!" I said that didn't surprise me. She added, "Well, you'd better tell her about us!" Nilda asked me if I had seen her and talked to her. I said I'd seen her a few times. Tata asked if I'd told her about them. Kathy said immediately, "Of course! What do you think they talk about?" I agreed, saying Joanne had asked me about them, and I'd said they might feel like kicking her ass at first but this didn't mean they wouldn't get to like her. Everyone laughed and I said I was serious, that

Table 9.2	Phases of Separation: Negation and Avoidance, Negative Feelings, Sadness

• *Helping with negation and avoidance:*	Sort out own feelings
	Provide sufficient time to allow for period of avoidance
	Offer frequent and persistent reminders
	Refer to one's own feelings
	Use visual aids such as a calendar
	Provide support and assurance of caring
• *Helping with negative feelings:*	Sort out own feelings
	Invite and pursue negative feelings
	Accept expression of negative feelings
	Sustain expression of client anger
	Avoid premature reassurance and power struggle
	Connect client behaviors and actions to unexpressed feelings
	Convey faith in the client and the professional relationship
• *Helping with feelings of sadness:*	Sort out own feelings
	Encourage and support expression of sadness and regret
	Share own sadness and regret
	Avoid escape into happy activities

this was just what I had told her. Judy asked me how tall Joanne is, and I said she was a little taller than me. Nilda exclaimed, "My God, another tall one," and asked if she is older than me. I said, "No, younger." Tata said she'd be too young to take care of them (Irizarry and Appel 1994).

Little by little, over time, the new worker became a real person, with personal attributes and an interest in knowing the members. Table 9.2 summarizes the helping skills of dealing with the phases of avoidance and negation, negative feelings, and feelings of sadness.

Release

Having faced and shared the pain of separating, worker and client may now feel that the tasks of termination are completed. Yet, the most important ones lie ahead, for it is the next set of coping tasks that provides the client with the opportunity to integrate the whole of her experience, and to find the meaning in it. The three tasks are: (1) recognizing gains and specifying remaining work; (2) developing plans for the future such as transfer, referral, or self-directed tasks; and (3) final goodbyes and disengaging.

Earlier phases of separation, if completed successfully, stimulate renewed energy for the sequence in release. Where this is not so, however, the worker can provide energy by initiating and focusing the discussion. Joint consideration of where the agreed-upon goals and action now stand might be a starting point. "Let's examine together what has and has not been accomplished." Throughout the discussion, the worker emphasizes the client's strengths and the gains made, but also elicits discussion of any areas of remaining difficulty. Mrs. Felstein, a seventy-five year old resident in a nursing home, had severe difficulty in adapting to institutional life. A social work intern met with her for thirty weeks and helped her to cope with the stress of unresolved life transitions and to make new environmental connections. In the next to last session, they review their work together:

WORKER: What were some of the things you found most helpful?

MRS. FELSTEIN: You've helped me a great deal. I used to think you were too young and only a student, but I feel differently now.

WORKER: I think it will be helpful to review our work together.

MRS. FELSTEIN: We've talked about so many things and I've come so far since the beginning.

WORKER: When we first started you talked a lot about your sister's death and your guilt feelings.

MRS. FELSTEIN: Yes, I still feel badly about that, but I no longer have that terrible feeling of it being my fault.

WORKER: At that time you also felt pretty bad about the situation with your friend Dora.

MRS. FELSTEIN: (quickly boasting) You know, she doesn't mean a darn thing to me now. I see her and she doesn't affect me at all.

WORKER: I also remember how you felt you made the wrong choice in coming into the home.

MRS. FELSTEIN: (disappointed voice) I realize now I have to be here. It's just not what I expected it to be, but I guess I expected too much.

WORKER: I remember we talked a lot about this, and that most recently, we talked about your role here, and your trying to find a more comfortable role.

MRS. FELSTEIN: I don't know if I can ever fully adjust to being in a home. I try to read more, watch the news, and do things I like. It will be very hard for me to get along without you. You've been a great help to me.

WORKER: I know it will be hard because we have become very close. (She asked if she had ever told me about the community social worker who had originally developed the plan for her to come here. At first she thought the girl wouldn't be able to help her because she was so young—she thought she'd never understand her problems, but then she turned out to be very dedicated.)

WORKER: You thought of her in the same way you initially thought about me.

MRS. FELSTEIN: (smiling) Yes.

WORKER:	(taking her hand) I am sure you will feel the same way about the new intern in September.
MRS. FELSTEIN:	I sure will if they give me another young one. (We ended our conversation about how my supervisor will be available to her in the summer and will help her with the transition to the new social worker. I asked if she has some ideas of what she would like to work on in the fall. She said she has been thinking about getting involved with the senior center across the street and would like help in getting connected.)

Plans for carrying on with the work, encouragement in the tasks, and the expression of confidence in the client's ability to cope with life stressors can be combined with conveying the agency's availability for future services as needed.

In a situation of a worker leaving an agency, a group of five adolescent girls lived in the same cottage in a residential treatment center had met with the worker for over a year and in individual and family sessions as well. The following excerpt is from the group meeting that took place three days after it was announced in the cottage that the social worker will be leaving the agency in several months. Three girls came in together and seemed in a happy mood. They said they'd had a good week in school. Beth arrived, singing "Everything is Beautiful." She took her seat and was laughing with everyone.

WORKER:	Hey, it's great to see everybody in such a good mood and I hate to be a party pooper, but you know that I'm leaving and a lot of things between you and me will be drawing to an end.
MARGIE:	You have a hell of a nerve.
WORKER:	You mean about my leaving?
MARGIE:	Yeah, that and a whole lot of things.
WORKER:	OK, let's hear them. I am sure that my leaving and the ending of the group has caused a lot of reactions in all of you (no one picked up on that).
MARGIE:	Are we going to have a group next year?
GIRLS:	Yeah, we want to have another group next year.
BETH:	Let's have a party in honor of your leaving. (she began talking about a party that they had been to, and all of a sudden turned to me) You're leaving, you God damn fink. (everybody stopped and looked at me)
WORKER:	I'm leaving and that makes me a fink.
GIRLS:	Why are you leaving? Why do you have to leave us? Why can't you stay?
JILL:	Why are you leaving?

WORKER: I don't know if it's the reason that really matters, it's more how you feel knowing that I'm leaving, for whatever the reason.

GIRLS: No, no, we want to hear the reasons, we don't understand.

WORKER: OK, let me try to explain. I'm leaving because I've been here for a number of years. Working here has meant a lot to me and you have all meant a lot to me. Yet a combination of things, the long traveling and working nights, have become hard for me, and I want to work nearer to where I live. That's pretty much the reason. If there's anything you don't under stand, ask me and I'll try to explain more.

BETH: (crying) You can't leave. We need you.

WORKER: You mean you won't be able to make it without me?

MARGIE: You're the best social worker I ever had. I won't be able to talk to anybody else.

WORKER: We've all been real close, and I guess the thought of starting over with somebody else is scary. What do you think it was about me that made it easier to talk to me?

BETH: It's because you cared about us. We knew that even when you were mad at us you were really sticking up for us, and you were really with us.

DONNA: Yeah, but if you cared so much you wouldn't be leaving.

WORKER: That's the thing, isn't it? How could I leave you if I really care for you?

GLADYS: We know you care for us. We know you're leaving because you really feel that you have to.

WORKER: But the words don't help very much, huh? They don't take away the bad feeling.

BETH: That's right, what good does it do me to know that you care if you're not here?

JILL: Yeah, you've been my social worker for a whole year. I don't want anybody else.

WORKER: You're upset with me, you have a right to be, but it's also hard for me to leave you.

BETH: If it's hard for you to leave us then you wouldn't leave us.

MARGIE: No, Beth, that's just not the truth. It was hard for me to leave home. (Gladys put her head down and began to cry, and one of the kids hollered, "Oh, cut it out. This hurts us as much as it hurts you.")

WORKER: Maybe it hurts each of you in a different way, and this is how Gladys is reacting.

GLADYS: Oh, leave me alone. None of you care about me.

MARGIE: Yes we do. You don't want help. You just want to feel sorry for yourself.

WORKER:	You're all getting angry at Gladys, yet she's acting out how you feel. Is it that you hurt so much that you don't have room for anybody else's hurt?
JILL:	She cries all the time. Who gives a damn about her?
DONNA:	I care about her, but I don't know what to do.
BETH:	(to Gladys, who was sitting alone) Gladys, why don't you come over here? (Gladys just shrugged, and one of the other kids said, "Aw, leave her alone." There was an uncomfortable quiet in the room.)
WORKER:	I don't think that you feel right leaving her alone.
BETH:	Well, what can we do?
WORKER:	What do you feel like doing?
BETH:	(walked over to Gladys and put her arms around her) You're scared, right? (Gladys nodded)
DONNA:	We're all in that situation, too. Not only you.
BETH:	But maybe it is different for Gladys.
GLADYS:	You have a mother and father. Every one of you has at least a mother or a father. Who do I have?
BETH:	You have foster parents.
GLADYS:	Big deal. They don't want me.
BETH:	I think I know how it feels. I think I know how bad it feels. And if you want to cry, that's OK, but you gotta live. You got to pick yourself up. You gotta face it.
GLADYS:	No, I can't.
DONNA:	Even when you're alone you have to trust yourself.
MARGIE:	That's pretty hard to do.
BETH:	But you're not all alone, Gladys, you have us. We'll help you, and sometimes you'll help us.
MARGIE:	You gotta have confidence in yourself.
WORKER:	How do you do that, Margie? Can you tell her?
MARGIE:	You gotta think of the things that you do right, not only the bad things. Even when people leave you, you gotta think of what you did have with them, and all that was good. And then you got to believe that you're going to have somebody else, too.
BETH:	You gotta learn to stand on your own feet. You gotta learn how to make friends.
JILL:	You gotta take responsibility for what you do, even when it's hard.
WORKER:	It sounds like you feel that Gladys can do these things, even though now she doesn't think that she can.
BETH:	That's right, and I mean it even coming from me. Lots of times I hate her, but other times I really like her and I remember when she was nice to me, and when she helped

me, and I do believe in her, and I believe she can pick herself up.

GLADYS: I feel real, real bad. Miss S's leaving hurts me more than anybody can know, but you've helped me and I want to thank you.

WORKER: This is what it's about. This beautiful thing that you can do in helping each other, and you've got that now. You own that. And no matter who leaves, no matter how much it hurts, you can't lose that.

BETH: I hate you for leaving, but I know what you mean. I know you're right.

WORKER: Go ahead, Margie, what do you want to say?

MARGIE: I know what Beth means, and I want to feel that I can go on also, and we can even have a group without you and we can keep helping each other just like we do in the group. I'm scared.

WORKER: Sure, it's a scary thing. Can you talk a little more about what you're scared about?

MARGIE: I'm scared that we won't be able to do it alone, that we need you to help us.

BETH: Well, maybe we'll have somebody else who can help us.

DONNA: And maybe we'll have to help ourselves.

GLADYS: I know what you mean. I know that in the end I do have to help myself.

BETH: We'll help you, too. Just like we did here this morning.

WORKER: Wow, you kids are fantastic. (they all kind of laughed and somebody said, "Maybe we'll become social workers, too," and that broke the tension) (Nadelman 1994)

The social worker helped the members to express their feelings, and she accepted the legitimacy of their resentment. As members and worker experienced their sadness together, energy was released to reach out to Gladys. The worker supported their sense of mutual aid and enabled them to reaffirm their affection and need for each other. They could then contemplate a future without the worker but with one another. They expressed their appreciation and devotion by identifying with her.

In work with children and elders, or when agreements are more implicit than explicit, the social worker helps people find release by recalling together their shared experiences. This helps clarify where client and practitioner were when they started, where they are now, and even what new goals might be considered for the future. Work on release helps to consolidate gains, complete any unfinished work, and make plans for the future. It is also the time when people are helped to see the personal resources they have rediscovered for coping with the environment, managing life stresses, and making decisions about the use of community resources and other important areas of life. In the case of the group in the chronic care facility, the worker writes:

We began to discuss the things the group had done, reliving their activities together—bingo and horseshoes. I asked what they liked and hadn't liked about each activity. As they did this, I pointed to something positive each had accomplished in the group. "Mr. Jones, remember how hard horseshoes was in the beginning?" He nodded. "You got so good at it you made the highest points last time we played." He grinned. I remembered with Mr. Dobbs how he had struggled to stand up in his wheelchair to play horseshoes, and now he was really good at it. He and several others nodded excitedly. I remembered how Mr. Kley had given us the idea to make collages, how Mr. Calagieri became so good at puzzles that he could help everyone else, and so on with each one. Each time there was pleased acknowledgment.

The social worker helped the men credit their strengths and achievements. The directive approach to eliciting their shared memories was appropriate in light of their mental disabilities.

The worker also helps clients consider options: transfer to another worker, referral to another agency, or termination. If the decision is to terminate service, practitioner and client plan the phasing out of their work together. They may decrease frequency and duration of sessions. They may arrange for a follow-up and review after a few months. Whatever the arrangement, the social worker prepares them to continue to work on any remaining tasks, and to cope with expected and unexpected life events.

When transfer is accepted or mandated, the social worker involves the client in planning the meeting with the new worker. Together they may decide to have the new worker observe one session, followed by another in which they summarize their work and specify future objectives. In the final transitional session, the new worker may assume primary responsibility. Gradual transition helps minimize the discouragement in having to begin again (Super 1982).

When needed referral to another agency is accepted or mandated, the worker helps the client plan for the initial contact with the selected service. If clients are to initiate contact, workers prepare them to deal with procedures and to anticipate complications. If workers are to initiate contact, they establish client eligibility and agency receptivity. When referral is accepted by both client and agency, the worker prepares the new agency worker to receive the client. One helps the client to think about presenting his needs and priorities to the new worker. The social worker may even participate in the first meeting, but, in any case, it is imperative that the social worker follow up to make sure linkage is successfully joined.

When planning is completed, client and worker are ready for disengagement. Some clients may ask that the relationship continue on a personal basis; some may show appreciation through a gift to the worker; others may ask for the worker's telephone number or for a promise to correspond. This natural interest need to be respected and handled with sensitivity. In our judgment, there are no hard and fast rules for handling this interest, although some agencies prohibit the acceptance of gifts or the continuation of contact. Most people want to give as well as to receive, wish to continue a rewarding human relationship, and hope for some assurance they will not be forgotten. These needs are not to be regarded as problematic, but should be responded to with an understanding of their meaning for each individual. One's own human need for appreciation and continued involvement in the life of another should play no part in worker responses. The following excerpt illustrates the pressures for continued involvement as a school social worker attempts to help a young girl achieve release and a readiness to move on to new relationships.

Sandy, age 17, lost both parents the year before. Her mother died of cirrhosis of the liver and her father of spinal cancer. She now lives in the home of relatives, who are heavy drinkers. Sandy and the social worker worked together on Sandy's anger, guilt, and grief over her losses, conflicts with her relatives, the stormy relationship with her boyfriend and his subsequent rejection, and her own future plans. Sandy knew from the beginning the worker would leave at the end of the school year. Nevertheless, when the subject was introduced six weeks in advance, Sandy was devastated. Although unable to express her feelings about ending, she did use the remaining time to work productively on other areas of her life. The social worker and Sandy decided on a noon picnic for their last meeting.

***

Sandy got into my car, and I immediately sensed she was in an uncharacteristic "up" mood. She spoke animatedly of a recent humorous incident. We both laughed and then became suddenly quiet. Then we began to chat in a casual way. Finally, I said that it was pretty hard to talk about this being our last day together. Sandy said, "Yeah, but I really don't feel bad because I know I can see you again. I know you will be living in Center City, and you can become my friend. I don't care what you say, I can take a train there to visit you. I can also get your number and call you, so I don't really think of this as goodbye." I knew it was not helpful to leave Sandy with these fantasies. I acknowledged that her wishes reveal her caring. And then, to help her face reality, "You know, Sandy, this really is the end. We won't meet every week like we did, things can't be the same." Understandably, Sandy countered, "You talk like you don't want to see me or hear from me." Gently, I said, "I guess it sounds as if I don't care, but that isn't so. I care for you very much. We shared a great deal this year and have talked about so many important things. Now that it's time to say goodbye, it's especially hard." She quietly agreed.

Sandy had found it hard to express anger and loss, so I said, "Sandy, I think I would be pretty upset if people close to me were splitting." She gritted her teeth, "Yeah, everybody, and I don't have a darn thing to do with it. My mother, she had no excuse. She didn't have to drink. My father couldn't help it. It's not fair." I said softly, "It does seem very unfair, Sandy." She responded, "You're darn right, and now you. You know, you keep asking me if I'm upset with you and what do I think. I'm thinking that you really don't care. You just saw me each week because you had to, that's all. You don't care, because if you did, you would see me again." I told her, "You know it's easy to think that people—your parents, your boyfriend, your former social worker—come and go, and you have no control over it." She added quickly, "Yes, you're right. What would you do if I telephoned you? Hang up?" I said, "No, I would feel torn also. I would be pleased and happy to hear from you, but I also know it is hard to say goodbye. That's what's hard to face, isn't it?" She agreed. I said, "So, even though deep inside we know we won't see a person again, we say, 'Oh, I'll see you.' It makes it easier for the moment." Sandy remarked that was true. I then reminded her how she felt when her former worker left. She hadn't wanted to meet with me at first. But then she made a choice, and in spite of her sorrow last year, she tried again. We talked of how much she accomplished this year and what starting with a new social worker would be like. Now that I am leaving, there isn't much either of us can do. I gently told her that she might not see me again. But what we had together and what she learned was something she would always have with her. No can take away her special feeling and the accomplishments.

As we drove back to school, we both sat very still and quiet. Finally, I said, "Sandy, I don't want you to leave until you have a chance to tell me what you are thinking. Try to say it now, rather than saying to yourself later, 'I should have told her.' " Sandy turned to me and said, "I'm going to miss you a lot. I just don't know what it will be like not seeing you every week. I really liked you a lot." She held back her tears. I said I felt the same way about her and added, "I know it's hard for you. We'll both feel very sad later as you go back to school and I go back to my office, and we think about each other." Sandy said, "I know," and we hugged each other. Then she left.

As Sandy attempts to avoid the permanence of ending, the worker helps her to confront the reality. She affirms Sandy's feelings of abandonment and anger and responds undefensively and sensitively to questions about the

Table 9.3	Skills of Helping Client to Release

- invite review of work together
- emphasize strengths and gains
- elicit discussion of remaining areas of difficulty
- review work and experience
- consider next steps: transfer, referral, or termination
- develop plans to carry out next step:
    for transfer, connect to new worker
    for referral, find and link to new resource
    for termination, phase out work
- provide opportunity for final goodbye

genuineness of her caring. She helps Sandy evaluate her accomplishments and prepare for a new social worker. Her final invitation, "Try to say it now," enables Sandy to express her affection and to disengage with a sense of shared intimacy. Table 9.3 summarizes the skills of helping clients to release.

Evaluation of Practice and Contribution to Knowledge

As our profession assumes increased accountability, one consequence is a preoccupation with practice outcomes; another is a tendency to evaluate professional competence and skills primarily on a priori based outcomes. Progress or lack of progress in the work is attributed to the worker's skills or lack of skills (Gitterman and Miller 1992). These assumptions could lead us to work only with motivated people. Such confusion of ends with means negates the reality of the helping process: a worker is trying to be helpful, and an individual, family, or group is deciding whether and how to use the help from this particular practitioner at this particular time. Workers might be skillful yet clients may not progress or even regress. Workers might be unskillful yet clients make progress. Hence, professional skills must be evaluated on their own terms, as well as in terms of specific outcomes. People make progress because of, in spite of, or without our help. That is why lawyers who lose a case may be justly praised for their fine work. In these instances the question is, was the right thing done under the circumstances given the state of the art and available options? Similarly in social work, helping must be both separated from and related to its use.

Endings are especially valuable in building professional knowledge and refining skill. Joint assessment of outcomes with clients, identifying what was helpful and what was not, and why, can be gradually generalized to practice principles. Much of what is considered intuition in a gifted worker is actually practice expertise and wisdom, seldom raised to an explicit practice principle. As experience expands, one notes patterns of responses across cases and tests one's hypotheses of what works with particular groups of people, needs, or situations.

Most agencies require workers to complete statistical forms for use by the agency, regulatory bodies, or funding sources. The client's responses to questions concerning quality yield a measure of worker accountability. Accountability is not complete, however, until those served have the opportunity to evaluate their experiences with the agency and social worker during the ending phase. When evaluation is taken seriously by practitioner and agency, practice becomes more effective, services more responsive to need, and accountability to those served more assured.

Creating a climate that permits people to be candid in assessing service is a measure of worker skill. Many workers and agencies, however, go beyond the ending phase in order to assure accountability. Hospital social service departments are usually included in the hospital's questionnaire about total patient care. Many social agencies use questionnaires mailed after termination to tap client responses to the service. These are valuable as they can reveal attitudes and responses that the person hesitated to share with the worker. Workers themselves often follow up some time after termination to ascertain the individual's or group's current situation and to determine if gains continue. Even though some suggest that this creates or prolongs dependency, we strongly believe that follow-up demonstrates the continuing interest and good will of the agency and its concern for quality service. (See Appendix B for discussion about social work research traditions.)

PART THREE

LIFE-MODELED PRACTICE AT COMMUNITY, ORGANIZATION, AND POLITICAL LEVELS

Part III examines life-modeled practice designed to influence the quality of community life through engaging residents; to advocate for needed policy and program changes in human service organizations; and the use of political methods and skills by social workers to advance the cause of social justice. Porter Lee, in his 1929 presidential address to the National Conference of Social Work, noted that social work was moving away from a concern with a cause (social reform) and was assuming the character of a function (direct services). In Lee's view, both cause and function are valuable and essential for social welfare: a cause once won depends on organization, methods, and skills for its implementation. But a tendency to become overly preoccupied with methods and skills can lead to a blunting of commitment. Lee envisioned a synthesis in which social work would develop its service as a function of well organized community life without sacrificing it capacity to inspire enthusiasm for a cause.

His conception made only a minor ripple in the profession at that time, probably because the dominant practice approach, casework, was busily engaged in defining and refining its processes of diagnosis and treatment. Group work and community organization were relative newcomers. Group work, with its origin in the settlement movement, did maintain a concern for cause. But community organization, with its origin in the charity organization movement, had its institutional base in community chests and councils, which saw their function as coordinating services and establishing central information and statistical services for all member agencies. Social action and social reform were largely missing.

In the 1960s community organization specialization in social work came to view social problems as the proper focus of its practice. Yet it lacked the means to implement its aspirations. By the 1970s interventions related to concepts of power, conflict, and social change were developed. Acceptance and even enthusiasm for the new approach spread to many group work and casework practitioners who daily witnessed the impact of poverty, discrimination, and oppression on powerless and vulnerable populations. They understood that function depends on a professional vision and commitment to social justice, and cause requires organization and means for carrying it forward. Both are necessary for effective practice.

TEN

INFLUENCING COMMUNITY AND NEIGHBORHOOD LIFE

The lack of community resources, problems in the coordination of community resources, or people's difficulty in gaining access to available resources may cause or exacerbate life stressors. To enhance the quality of community and neighborhood life, all social workers in life-modeled practice must acquire certain knowledge and skills of community work. Generally, the social worker in life-modeled practice moves to the community modality because a significant community issue has arisen during work with an individual, family, or group, and affects other community residents as well. Occasionally, the community modality is used when the social worker recognizes a need and canvasses the neighborhood or community to determine if the members agree about the seriousness of the need. When the service recipient and other residents believe that change is needed to improve the quality of community life, the practitioner helps them to achieve their objective.[1]

Community and Neighborhood

Definitions of community and of neighborhood are many and occasionally conflicting. The community is most often defined as a geographically-bounded locale that performs certain necessary functions for its residents. These include the production, distribution, and consumption of goods and services; transmission of prevailing knowledge, social values, customs, and behavior patterns that contribute to the socialization of individual residents; social control to maintain conformity to community norms; and social participation through formal and informal groups (Warren 1963). These functions are carried out by a wide range of public and private organizations, institutions and services and informal means by individuals and groups.

Non-locale communities are groups of people with a common interest who do not necessarily live in the same area. These include gay and lesbian communities and non-locale ethnic communities, professional communities, the arts community, and spiritual communities.

The community is the main conduit through which resources, formal and informal systems, and political, social, and economic forces exert major influences on individuals, families, and neighborhoods. The distinctive elements of any community's influence on the development and functioning of residents consist of its demographic characteristics, mobility patterns, systems of transportation, sanitation, fire and police protection, formal and informal networks, and the accessibility, equity, and quality of its health, educational, and social services.

Neighborhoods are smaller geographic components of a larger community. A neighborhood's size is subjective. A neighborhood-based social agency might define it as consisting of several thousand people. Residents might define it spatially, depending on whether one can walk from end to end, which could depend on age and physical capacity. If one is able to walk past only a few buildings on either side of one's home, the neighborhood is apt to be defined as small indeed. Studies usually produce as many different assertions of a neighborhood's size as the number of those interviewed.

However, a neighborhood is more than its geography (Warren 1980: 64–68) or its numbers. Some definitions of neighborhood refer to even smaller units termed *social blocks*, with interaction more prominent at the block level. How many social blocks constitute a neighborhood depends again on how size is defined. Also, some residents may live in congregate units such as housing projects, single-room-occupancy hotels, residential treatment centers, nursing homes, group homes, and the like. Congregates are frequently viewed by their own residents and by neighbors as separate "communities" that are not part of the surrounding neighborhood.

The immediate neighborhood is a potential site for intimate personal interchanges and informal support systems. It also often serves as:

• a center for overt and subtle interpersonal influence (e.g., norms of child-rearing)
• a source of mutual aid (exchange of goods and services)
• an organizational base for formal and informal organizations (e.g., churches, temples, mosques, block clubs, PTA's)
• a base for identity and social norms
• a status arena

Contemporary Community and Neighborhood Stressors

Community and neighborhood stressors are often embedded in contexts of poverty and discrimination, which are themselves major stressors. Poverty and discrimination create an unsafe habitat for residents and a preponderance of stigmatized niches which undermine community and neighborhood formal and informal structures and the health, emotional wellbeing, and social functioning of its residents.

Kozol (1991) describes schools throughout the United States that are falling apart, starving the minds of poor children, and blighting their futures. Because of inequitable financing, the poorer the community, the less money is expended for each child; the more affluent the community, the greater that expenditure. Children in poor communities and neighborhoods receive inadequate education; consequently, they have less opportunities for employment. Lack of employment opportunities institutionalizes poverty. Physical, psychological, and social consequences follows upon poverty. Among poor families, morbidity and mortality rates are strikingly higher than among those of sufficient economic means. Poverty also breeds crime and violence.

> Women, children, and the elderly, especially those living in poor communities, are at highest risk of victimization by crime. They simply are easier prey. The perpetrators tend to be caught in a cycle of family poverty, illiteracy, drugs, racism, child abuse, and family violence. When they are incarcerated, they usually return to their community furthered damaged, hardened, and embittered. They often become socialized to a lifetime of crime and intermittent incarceration. In poor communities, both the victim and the perpetrator are trapped in a mire of despair.
> (Gitterman 1991:5)

In some neighborhoods, residents have little or no contact with their neighbors because of pervasive violence. Many poor people, young and old, are less mobile than wealthier people, who find a satisfying social life outside their neighborhood or community. Some poor people live in a cohesive, ethnically homogeneous neighborhood that provides social integration. But others have no way out of what is a noncohesive neighborhood despite their constant and realistic fear of neighbors and of neighborhood conflict and violence. Many low-income community residents feel powerless and alienated.

Life stressors afflicting a poor community include: shortage of affordable, safe housing; hospital closings; business and factory closings or moves of businesses out of the community; asbestos and lead paint contamination in schools and dwellings; hazardous waste dumps and toxic emanations from workplaces; and growing prevalence of AIDS and other chronic illnesses. Other life stressors are generated by inadequate systems of public sanitation and transportation (especially in rural communities); inadequate health and mental health care; and unresponsive public and corporate bureaucracies. Corporate relocation, zoning, banking and realty trends, and availability and accessibility of public services conspire to create demographic changes. Some communities and neighborhoods are subject to periodic traumatic natural catastrophes including earthquakes, hurricanes, floods, and fires.

Social workers can help impoverished and vulnerable neighborhoods or communities to meliorate some of these effects. But the responsibility for their ultimate elimination rests with society itself. This reality underlies our emphasis on community, organizational, and political advocacy to influence social legislation in conjunction with life-modeled practice.

Social Work Function, Modality, Methods, and Skills

The Social Worker and Life-Modeled Community Practice

The lack of essential and desired community and neighborhood resources in poor communities provides the life-modeled social worker with the social purpose of helping to influence the quality of community and neighborhood life of residents. The purpose is fulfilled by (1) helping community and neighborhood residents to undertake action to improve the fit between available and desired formal and informal resources; (2) developing community programs and services to meet residents' needs; (3) building informal community support systems of relatedness; and (4) improving the coordination of community services. In all areas of community work, the social worker also provides formal and informal consultation to community-based service providers, other professionals, and community members.

Helping community and neighborhood residents undertake action to improve the fit between available and desired formal and informal resources. Engaging impoverished and vulnerable neighborhood or community residents in a collective effort to empower themselves and to achieve their desire for social change is a significant professional goal for the life-modeled social worker. Community and neighborhood social action aims at assisting a vulnerable or powerless community, or an oppressed segment of its population, to demand and secure needed resources or services (Germain *1985*a, *1985*b; Grosser and Mondros *1985*; Mondros and Wilson *1994*; Rothman *1979*). Taking action to improve the quality of community and neighborhood life is essential to collective and individual mental health.

In helping community and neighborhood residents undertake action on their own behalf, the social worker carries out several tasks. Community and neighborhood residents are more likely to become involved and take action when they have identified an issue of immediate concern and importance to them. Thus, a fundamental principle of life-modeled community practice is that issues either must arise from community and neighborhood residents (including their interest in a social worker's proposal).

> If people want their windows fixed and the welfare check increased, the [social worker] helps them to begin to act on these problems even though he may privately believe they would be better off working to open up additional jobs.
>
> (Haggstrom 1987:406)

To this end, the social worker undertakes a community or neighborhood needs assessment (equally important for developing new programs and support systems of relatedness). The practitioner must learn about the physical layout of the community and neighborhood; demographic composition; discontents and intergroup tensions; formal and informal leaders; organizations and services; values and norms; political structure; financial and other resources; and the community's history. All this and more is gathered by studying pertinent documents, talking to key community and neighborhood "gatekeepers," and conducting a formal survey. By developing an initial understanding of community and neighborhood dynamics, the social worker gains information on critical existing and potential issues, turf boundaries, demographic trends and characteristics, key governmental and private institutions, informal organizations, and powerful actors in community life (Staples 1987).

The social worker develops a list of residents who might be interested in taking action in regard to a particular issue and selects the most effective recruitment method. In identifying a pool of potential members, Mondros and Wilson (1994:43–49) suggest three characteristics of effective recruitment: (1) natural networks; (2) representativeness; (3) special individual attributes.

Tapping into natural networks is an expedient method for recruiting community and neighborhood residents. A social worker might consult with a key resident who then contacts or introduces the worker to relatives, friends, and neighbors. Or a social worker might reach out to local churches, synagogues, or mosques. For many people, the trust, familiarity, and support provided by natural networks help them to become involved. However, the social worker must not settle for a convenient homogeneous pool of residents at the expense of excluding or alienating potentially significant contributors.

If a diverse constituency is required for successful action, representatives of each element of the community's heterogeneity are desirable. In this situation, the social worker purposively recruits members who represent diverse formal and informal community systems. The broader the representation, the greater the chance for legitimacy and influence.

In some situations, a community action group could be composed on the basis of special personal attributes. Residents with special leadership abilities or with an intense commitment to an issue (the need for child care, services for developmentally challenged children) could be more effective than action groups composed of natural networks or representatives of different constituencies. Social workers must avoid a common error of recruiting potential leaders solely on the basis of their articulateness. They may, for example, be actively disliked by their neighbors. Failure to carefully evaluate their actual commitment to the issues and how other members view them could lead to chronic lack of participation by neighborhood or community residents.

The next important task for the social worker in life-modeled practice is to gain community residents' initial willingness to participate in undertaking action on their own behalf.[2] Brager, Specht, and Torczyner (1987:63) define participation as "the means by which people who are not elected or appointed officials of agencies and of government influence decisions about programs and policies that affect their lives." In their view, "the participation of service users in institutional decision making is one means of promoting consumer needs and protecting consumer interests" (62). Participation educates residents and increases their competence, ensures responsiveness and accountability of services to consumers, and influences decisions that affects their lives. Increasing accountability to service users requires a transfer of power insofar as the poor "exercise a relatively low degree of influence in or control over organizations" (66) on which they depend. The authors continue:

> This view of participation turns the problem around in an important way. Instead of asking, "Why don't the poor participate like those others [middle class participants in voluntary associations]?," the question becomes, "How do the poor participate, and how can their participation be made of greatest use to them?" The issue, then, is not merely how to get the poor to participate more actively, but how to make their already active and nonvoluntary participation more beneficial and meaningful to them. (67)

In our view both questions are equally important: "How to get people to attend, join up, speak out, work on a committee, or lend support" (Rothman, Erlich, and Teresa 1979) and "How to make their participation beneficial to them." The practitioner's initial contact with community residents often determines whether they decide to become involved and the extent of their involvement. The social worker must give careful consideration and preparation to what will be said to potential recruits, and their possible reactions. Initial distrust, fear, reluctance, ambivalence must be anticipated, invited, and explored. The social worker's clarity in explaining purpose and role is critical to obtaining effective community participation. The statement should be clear, direct, and responsive to the interests and motivations of potential members. The opening statement should be responsive to the following questions: "What do we want to say in this message?" "What's in it for the joiner?" "What can the recruit contribute?" "What can I say the efforts will produce?" (Mondros and Wilson 1994:50). First contacts are important in ensuring participation.

In the first meeting, the social worker identifies a common focus and interests and explores fears, doubts, and hesitations. The worker must avoid slipping into "selling" rather than inviting, exploring, and developing mutual focus. Practitioners "incorrectly . . . prepare themselves to discuss only the issues and desired ends. Consequently they may fail to detect cues about the secondary expressive concerns of members. . . . New recruits may shrink from the overly eager approach." (Mondros and Berman-Rossi 1991:204)

Successful recruitment and effective description of purpose and the professional role generate initial interest in dealing with a community issue. Active participation is also supported by refreshments, occasional nonworking, social meetings or events, and icebreakers at meetings so that participants feel more at ease with one another. The next professional task is gaining commitment to a membership structure and to democratic participation in its activities. For community residents to sustain structured participation, they must feel that the process is democratic, i.e., rules for their participation are explicit and fairly applied. In a large group a structure of officers and specification of responsibilities integrates membership. When membership and group roles are new to community residents, the social worker is more active in guiding structured participation and decision-making processes.

For example, a social worker (Glaser 1972) found that severe interpersonal stress being experienced by families in a large housing project was generated at the stairwell level. Each highrise building had a number of stairwells. Each stairwell was shared by twelve families. Glaser hypothesized that positive change at stairwell levels could produce positive change in the building and ultimately in the total project-as-community. Over several years of stairwell meetings, Glaser and his colleagues used social work knowledge of groups and families to deal with conflicts among the stairwell families and to elicit their shared concerns about their physical environment. They also gathered individual data during home visits. At the same time, the visits strengthened participation in the stairwell meetings. They used their knowledge of communities to encourage all stairwell members to identify their common stressors and environmental needs, plan for and take action to achieve goals such as improve maintenance, develop recreational facilities, improve relations with the school, and the like. Glaser and his colleagues laid the base for what became a tenants' association that later worked on the shared life issues of the total "project-as-community." Association members addressed the power structure (the housing authority) about required improvements with confidence and competence.

Participants will often need a social worker's guidance and consultation in learning to conduct their own meetings; to engage in democratic group decision-making; to reach out and build constituencies; to deal with differences, and to build a consensus. The development of these skills becomes a source of constituency power in later, more complex efforts.

Conflict management is an indispensable skill in forming groups, developing and sustaining mutual support, and dealing with internal and external conflict. Conflict between members of a constituency or between the community and the power structure often arise. Conflict is neither bad or good in itself: engaging and successfully resolving conflict is what is important, whether conflict among community or neighborhood sub-groups of constituents or between the constituency and a decision-making body.

The social worker must expect that in most groups legitimate instrumental and expressive differences, competition for power among natural leaders, and testing whether the worker's willingness to share power is genuine are likely to emerge. Members may tend to avoid or control differences. But if difference and conflict are submerged, positions harden, and the conflict persists or is driven underground only to reappear and drain group energy. Premature consensus should be challenged and difference and conflict welcomed and invited. The social worker supports and guides the group's leaders to recognize conflict early and to invite members to discuss it. The social worker must model comfort with difference and convey a faith in the democratic processes to achieve conflict resolution. Resolving internal differences strengthens the group structure and members' ability and willingness to engage with external conflict.

Community residents may find themselves in conflict with institutional power structures. Haggstrom (1987:406) captures the centrality of conflict in social action:

> When [the practitioner] helps people to begin to act on central problems, that is, to make their own decisions about resolving their own problems and to begin to implement those decisions, by that very fact the [practitioner] deliberately creates conflict since the problems of low-income areas cannot be resolved without negative consequences for the self-perceived self-interest and traditional ways of thinking and acting of various advantaged minorities.

Although dominant groups and power structures can be expected to resist efforts at social change, the community residents and social worker are not limited to conflict-oriented interventions. Other methods need to be tried first.

For example, Mrs. Rosen, a 69-year-old, mentally frail woman living in a small apartment in a poor and crime-ridden community, was referred by the building's superintendant to a community-based social agency because of her disruptive behavior. A direct service student was assigned. The building, housing 40 elderly people, was run by the city's public housing authority. Mrs. Rosen complained to the student of feeling friendless and fearful because the emergency alarm system, intercom, and front door buzzer had been broken for almost a year and the housing authority had not responded despite the high crime rate in the neighborhood.

During her weekly visits to Mrs. Rosen, the student observed that the tenants came together only while they waited in the lobby for the mail delivery, with little or no social interchange. For several weeks, she made a point of introducing herself to those in the lobby, and many told her of loneliness and fears similar to those of Mrs. Rosen. Some expressed a wish for social activities in the building's lounge "which is hardly ever used." Most despaired of ever having their requests met by the housing authority. She came to view the residents as a "community," a congregate whose members had common needs and concerns. Her brief initial assessment of the building-as-a-community included the following:

1. *Strengths.* The super, who is also frustrated with the housing authority's red tape, is a potential ally. Also, one resident is a natural helper who has given holiday parties for the other residents, is active in community affairs, and knowledgeable about resources.
2. *Obstacles.* An unresponsive bureaucracy; physical and mental impairment of many of the elderly tenants; and the lack of a cohesive, organized group structure.

She inquired into their interest in meeting together. Some were interested in social gatherings, others desired informational meetings, and several thought they should work together to influence the housing authority. Next, the worker canvassed the group for volunteers to plan the first meeting.

Announcements of meeting dates and topics were prepared by several tenants. The first two meetings were given over to socializing, information gathered by several tenants on comparative drug prices in neighborhood pharmacies, and an outside speaker on elder health. The group decided next to hold a planning session to discuss needed repairs. Twelve residents attended. Plans were worked out, an agenda developed, and individual presentations rehearsed. An invitation to attend was sent by the planning group to the authority's director, and that meeting drew 30 residents. The director was unable to attend but he sent three representatives. The agenda was followed, and the residents' presentations were clearly and firmly stated. The group then formally requested that the needed repairs be started within two weeks. The three representatives stated that would need a few months to initiate the repairs. Members were prepared to negotiate and settled on a six-week period. The members scheduled a follow-up session with the representatives in two months to evaluate the results of their efforts and to plan next steps. The repairs actually began before the end of the month.

At the end of her placement, the student concluded,

The educational programs and social activities the tenants requested facilitated their active engagement with one another. This, in turn, led to increased social skills, enhanced confidence and self-esteem, and a beginning development of a social network. This was possible because of residents' growing interest in organizing themselves as a cohesive group to do something about the serious problems in their shared physical and social environment. I hope their new experience in mutual aid and advocacy will continue to flourish after my departure.

This vignette reveals what can happen when a practitioner helps community residents achieve their desired goals. The student's personal contacts with the elderly residents engaged their interest and resulted in active participation. In this situation, mild confrontation was sufficient to achieve housing repairs. These impoverished elderly residents also developed a new sense of themselves as a social congregate within their surrounding neighborhood. They became more self-directed with an increased sense of competence in dealing with common life issues generated by their shared environment, an increased sense of collective empowerment, enhanced self-esteem, and beginning relatedness to one another.

When community members feel ready for self-directed, ongoing community action, or when the worker has to leave, together they evaluate their social action experiences, examine reasons for successes and failures, and consider next steps. The practitioner withdraws from continuing contact, perhaps with an offer to be available (or to have a colleague available) if needed in the future. Ideally, community action itself will continue if interest continues and group leaders are in place. New activities may develop as new needs emerge.

As part of ending, the practitioner underscores with members their new skills and capacities for self-directed efforts, including the presence of self-maintaining structures for problem-solving. Where appropriate, the social worker reviews with the community's agencies or institutions the successes experienced in their coalition for social or political action efforts while specifying remaining needs for advocacy; and underscores with informal support systems the contributions they have made and can continue to make in the community. In the case of Mrs. Rosen, a last step for the student before leaving was to enlist and prepare the natural helper and one other tenant as group leaders to encourage and support the continued participation of the residents in planning and carrying out their desired social,

Table 10.1	Professional Tasks and Skills of Helping Community and Neighborhood Residents to Undertake Social Change
Construct a community or neighborhood needs assessment in order to identify residents' immediate concerns:	Study pertinent documents "Hang out" Talk to key community or neighborhood "gatekeepers" Conduct formal surveys
Select most effective membership recruitment method:	Tap into natural networks Recruit representatives of diverse constituencies Recruit on basis of personal characteristics
Gain initial willingness of community or neighborhood residents to: participate in undertaking social change on their own behalf by:	Anticipatory preparation Clear and direct statement that is responsive to potential members' interests and motivations Inviting and exploring reactions, including doubts, hesitations, ambivalence, fears Developing shared focus
Develop commitment to a membership structure and democratic participation in activities by:	Developing explicit rules for membership and their even application In large groups, developing structure of officers and responsibilities Active initial role in guiding structured participation and decision-making
Develop and sustain mutual membership support:	Challenging premature consensus Welcoming and inviting differences and conflict
Help manage internal membership conflict by:	Modeling comfort with difference Conveying faith in democratic process
Help members to manage external conflict with dominant groups and power structures:	
Evaluate social change experiences, including successes and failures, by:	Underscoring members' new skills and capacities for self-directed efforts dealing with any changes in group leadership Planning next steps

educational, and advocacy activities. In community or neighborhood groups, members might decide on a formal structure with responsibilities for group tasks spread among elected officers and voluntary committees. A selfmaintaining structure is to be firmly in place when a practitioner terminates or continues on a consultative basis. Table 10.1 summarizes the professional tasks and skills associated with helping community and neighborhood residents engage in efforts at social change.

Developing community programs and services to meet residents' needs. Successful engagement of neighborhood or community residents in developing and implementing new programs to meet collective needs simultaneously improves the fit between available and desired resources and is empowering. Programs involve planning, funding, staffing, physical facilities, and support for needed new services. All new programs require financial resources, staffing, and physical facilities (Kurzman *1985*).

We limit our discussion to (1) developing programs to improve community social conditions; and (2) developing programs to promote physical and mental health for all community residents or selected subgroups. Development of both types of community programming requires assessing needs, gaining residents' involvement and participation, guiding group process, and managing conflict. For example, identification and assessment of need includes recognizing a pattern in one's own caseload of unmet need; checking with colleagues whether a pattern is evident in their caseloads; determining who is served by community agencies and through what type of services; determining gaps in the service delivery systems found by other staff; engaging community groups and natural helpers in discussions of needs and priorities; and developing a more formal needs survey. The data gathering and assessment process in itself also heightens institutional and community awareness of the need.

As in community social change activity, community program development includes the active participation of the constituency in identifying need and planning and carrying out programs. "It is extremely difficult to develop a new program without the existence and active support of a group in the community that is highly committed to its development" (Hasenfeld 1987:455).

Improving community social conditions. Using the needs assessment, social workers help community residents improve social conditions by developing needed programs or services. To improve community social conditions, local leadership and organizational structure have to be established and residents' participation and involvement sustained (Lappin 1985). For example, an experienced work-study student at a northeastern state welfare department who served individuals and families in several rural counties provided this vignette of her life-modeled practice with a community of some 2,600 residents.

This rural town had one of the highest percentages of low income and AFDC families in its county, one of the highest referral rates for child abuse and neglect, and the highest rate of teenage pregnancy. Yet no support services were available except for a monthly well-child clinic conducted by the Visiting Nurse Association (VNA). All other formal services were twenty miles away in the nearest small city, but the lack of transportation was a formidable barrier. The social worker and her social work and nursing colleagues on the interdisciplinary Suspected Child Abuse and Neglect (SCAN) team decided to work on mobilizing and strengthening natural or informal helping systems. Interested members of SCAN formed an independent task force, the Rural Community Resources Group (RCRG) to begin a community process of developing its own informal resources (Germain 1985b).

A needs assessment gathered data needed for engaging the support and participation of influential members of the community and for seeking grant assistance. The social worker familiarized herself with the physical layout of the community, its social structure, demographic composition, and norms and values. She called on prominent residents, spoke at meetings, and met regularly with the mothers' group and with other members of RCRG. She also obtained data pertaining to teenage pregnancy, child abuse, and neglect. Almost all town residents participated in the needs assessment, which was carried out by volunteer mothers in door-to-door canvassing of residents' responses to the proposed project and their ideas for it.

Ten mothers, including some from the Visiting Nurse Association group, and some protective service clients, met weekly with the RCRG during May and June. There was immediate agreement on the goal: a drop-in parent-child center, perhaps a cooperative, where children could be cared for a few hours a day or week and where mothers could seek information and find a sympathetic ear. Both respite and improved parental functioning were seen as desired outcomes (Fraser in Germain 1985b).

The mothers and other residents canvassed all residents door-to-door, using a questionnaire. Additional questionnaires were left at the two grocery stores, the free swimming pool, and the physician's office. The mothers made and distributed posters, and a news article was written and published in the local free newspaper. The overall aim was to plan with the community residents, not for them, and to identify and support natural leaders.

The town's director of Community Development assisted us in locating four vacant sites. We hoped to make final arrangements on a visible and

accessible site by September so that the program could begin. We under-
took a search for seed money. Various community residents were helping
with this task, some approaching the trustees of a local trust fund, others
approaching the officers of the local bank, businesses, and civic clubs for
donations. I approached the State Welfare Division which has a new
grant for direct services in rural areas, and administrators agreed to
accept a proposal from us (Fraser in Germain 1985b).

The center for mothers and their preschool children opened in September
and was located in the fellowship hall of a local church. A grant of $25,000
from the governor's comprehensive children's and youth project supported
this center and one in another rural town. Both centers were open one
morning a week, providing self-planned programs and discussions for parents, child care, and transportation services. The programs were later
extended to two mornings a week as interest grew.

An inevitable question is how can an already overburdened social worker
spare the time that program development in a community requires? Fraser
commented,

The first problem I encountered was how to convince my immediate
superiors that any time involved would eventually be worthwhile for our
clients. There has only been intervention on one level, after the fact of
abuse or neglect, and preventive services are nonexistent. The Department of Welfare has never hired a community worker nor moved into
group services, and any deviation in traditional services would require a
series of administrative approvals. However, my student status, requiring
new learning experiences, won the day (Fraser in Germain 1985b).

Many agencies now view the community modality as part of their practitioners' responsibilities. In an agency that has not yet embraced this view,
however, it is important that life-modeled practitioners gain the approval
of the person to whom they are accountable for time spent in community
work. The knowledge and skills involved in influencing one's agency and
its decision-makers in such matters are discussed in the next chapter.

*Promoting physical and mental health for all community residents or selected
subgroups.* Dubos (1965) pointed out that the ancient Chinese paid their
personal physicians to keep them healthy. The really good doctors were
believed to be not those who treated the sick, but rather those who
instructed people on how to not become ill. This is a position analogous to
life-modeled social workers' interest in developing programs to promote

community physical and mental health for all residents or for a selected subpopulation.

Common life issues such as expectable life transitions, the assumption of new or altered social statuses and roles, and interpersonal processes in family, work, and community life are the major arenas in which human development and adaptive functioning take place. Therefore, programs in these three areas can forestall difficulties that some people might experience because of life circumstances or because of demands that exceed their coping resources.

Developing community programs that promote physical and mental health requires the participation of community residents in planning and carrying out such programs. If community-and neighborhood-based programs are to be successful, the residents or their representatives must participate in identifying areas of mental, physical, or social functioning that are important to them. Drawing on the practitioner's consultation as needed, community members specify the need that is not being met; set priorities and program goals; plan the program and strategies; carry out the program; and evaluate its effectiveness. "Graduates" of former programs often become conveners, coaches, leaders, or trainers in subsequent rounds of the program.

Community programs are developed for the general public and for defined populations such as teenage mothers, in which young mothers learn about infant and child development. As in all life-modeled practice, emphasis from the beginning is on strengths, not on deficits.

Hollister's (1977) classification of prevention and growth promotion programs is related to life stressors, the associated stress, and coping tasks. We use it here to present varied types of potential community programs that can promote physical and mental health.

1. Building resistance to life stress involves learning to cope effectively with common, expectable life issues people experience or are about to experience. This requires the identification of the skills, capacities, and information needed to deal with the particular life issue. Learning and emotional growth experiences, anticipatory guidance, and environmental supports are required to enhance capacities and skills.

   Community programs for populations facing new statuses and new role demands include groups for new and expectant parents, adoptive parents, foster parents, solo fathers or mothers, people approaching retirement, newly separated, divorced, or remarried people, drug/alcohol/tobacco education, and programs to increase understanding and acceptance of human and cultural diversity.

   An exemplary community program carried out by the Children's Aid Society of New York aimed at promoting personal growth and preventing teenage pregnancy. The program started in 1985 in central Harlem with 51 teenagers and 30 parents. Weekly sessions focused on sex education and healthcare services including contraception; instruction in sports and the performing arts; help with homework; and a job readiness program (Johnson 1986). In 1987, the program promoted and supported efforts to avoid intemperate sexual activity and untimely pregnancy, serving 170 teens at three Harlem community centers (Gross 1987). By 1988, 220 teens were being served and only two teenagers had become pregnant and only one had fathered a child (*New York Times* November 5, 1988).

2. In the case of unexpected, severe, and unavoidable stressors, management of life stress reactions refers to organizing informational, anticipatory guidance activities or group experiences to (a) prevent or diminish stress responses that would intensify the difficulty and make effective coping more difficult, and (b) supplant them with positive behaviors that will strengthen coping. Such programs range from inviting young children awaiting hospitalization to visit the hospital, view the equipment, and meet the staff, to groups for the newly unemployed, or for family members caring for patients with severe chronic illness. In grave emergencies such as a fatal school bus accident, a neighborhood murder, or a cluster of adolescent suicides, school and social agency support programs are designed to help children, youth, and adults to cope effectively with the associated stress, grief, and fear.

   For example, the U.S. Navy Family Center at Pearl Harbor provided a program for families experiencing deployment—sea duty that separates families for five to six months. Aimed at informing husbands and wives of the emotional, practical, and social role changes that frequently occur during deployment, the program, taught by clinical social workers, covers all phases of the separation experience from predeployment, through the months of sea duty, and the reunion process. Although the program consists largely of lectures, it provides opportunities for discussion between husbands and wives, informal meetings and talk between wives to decrease social isolation, and availability of social workers for personal questions (Gerard 1985:84).

3. Managing the life stressor to reduce its impact or even to eliminate it. When classrooms are viewed as communities, some school social workers conduct regular classroom meetings through which the children learn cooperative skills and how to manage interpersonal relationships with classroom peers (Winters and Easton 1983). During the Gulf War, community support groups for families of service women and men were provided by social workers to aid in the coping tasks and the management of the attendant fear and feelings of loss and helplessness.

4. In instances where reduction or elimination of a life stressor is not feasible but protection from its impact is possible, life stressor avoidance is a useful approach. For example, several programs across the country sponsored by the Urban League and other organizations aim to promote competence and a strong self-concept among adolescent African-American males. These programs emphasize African cultural values, rites of passage to young manhood, and the history and achievements of African-Americans in the United

Table 10.2   Types of Community Programs as they Relate to Life
                    Stressors, Stress, and Coping

• **Building Resistance to Potential Stressors:**	Programs build resistance to potential stress associated with expectable life stressors by identifying and imparting the skills, capacities, and information needed to deal effectively with the life stressor.
• **Managing Severe Life Stressors:**	Programs lead to management of severe life stressors by organizing informational, anticipatory, guidance activities, or group experience to prevent or diminish difficult stress responses and replace them with positive behaviors that will strengthen coping with unexpectable, unavoidable stressors.
• **Reducing or Eliminating Impact of Life Stressor:**	Programs aid in instrumental coping tasks and the management of negative, disabling feelings.
• **Avoiding an Anticipated Life Stressor:**	Programs protect the exposed person from the stressor's impact when its reduction or elimination is not feasible.

(Adapted from Hollister 1977)

States since the first slaves' arrival in 1619. Several programs also emphasize group activities and community service. And all are concerned with countering stressors and the associated stress experienced by African-American youth (Smothers 1989).

Table 10.2 summarizes the types of programs that promote physical and mental health of community residents as they relate to life stressors, stress, and coping.

When these overlapping types of community physical and mental health promotion programs are effective, they promote and enhance the competence, relatedness, self-esteem, and self-direction of the participants.

A "health promotion" strategy attempts to improve the quality of life and foster optimal health in the population. It focuses on "wellness" and maintaining health rather than mitigating "sickness" and restoring health. Services based upon a developmental scheme emphasize access to education, recreation, socialization, and cultural resources. These programs attempt to engage social competence, cognitive and emotional coping, and achievement. (Gitterman 1987).

In the Navy program, the situation was defined as a potential life stressor that might give rise to difficult life issues. The programs built resistance to stress generated by the stressor while contributing to growth and learning among the participants and probably enhancing their competence, relatedness, self-esteem, and self-direction.

For purposes of funding, accountability, and improving service delivery, programs need to be evaluated. An outcome evaluation attempts to answer the following question: "If a given program successfully achieves its goals, how will the recipient be different after receiving services?" (Cain 1990:62–63). The answer to this question depends on the clarity of program objectives and the criteria for measuring success. Process evaluations examine the internal operations of a program. Program implementation processes are analyzed to determine: "What is being done? How well is it being done? Is it what was intended to be done?" (Cain 1990:62). By paying attention to the details of program implementation, the worker improves the chances for its success and replication.

The effectiveness of community programs is difficult to evaluate (Reagh 1994). How do you prove that what you did prevented something that didn't happen? In the Navy program, "fewer family breakups, incidents of financial crisis, and visits to physicians for stress-related symptoms, as well as improved mission effectiveness due to decreased family stress and emergency returns home for military personnel, and greater subjective appraisal of family solidarity [were] used as indicators of program success" (Gerard 1985:88). Accurate baseline data did not exist, however, so staff relied on the subjective impressions of command personnel, the ombudsman, and health facilities staff.

Building informal community support systems of relatedness. Informal systems of relatedness are built by establishing relationships with individual natural helpers and validating the importance of natural helping in the community; helping to establish self-help groups; and recruiting, training, and supervising volunteers.

Shaped in part by the neighborhood, community, or congregate in which they are embedded, informal support systems of relatedness in turn help shape the community and its collective life. They are important bases of empowerment through which individuals and communities take greater control of their own and the community's destiny by joint decision-making, action, and social and emotional supports. These informal systems contribute to community pride and individual self-esteem, relatedness, and selfdirection. Each informal system can even be viewed as a "personal community" that helps facilitate residents' meaningful participation in their larger community, the society, and culture (Hirsch 1981).

Natural helpers. Natural helpers who function well in their own lives and whose life circumstances are similar to those of their neighbors are often known in the neighborhood for their resourcefulness and their ability to give advice, provide information and empathic support, and to connect others to needed informal and formal resources (Lewis and Suarez 1995; Pancoast 1980; Collins and Pancoast 1976). They may or may not know those who come to them for help or advice. In addition to urban communities and neighborhoods, natural helpers are found in congregates such as housing projects (Lee and Swenson 1978), some workplaces (Weiner, Akabas, and Sommers 1973), churches (Joseph 1980), and they are usually strong in rural areas (Patterson et al., 1992, 1988). Even some children and teenagers are natural helpers to their peers.

Other natural helpers include beauticians, bartenders, storekeepers, pharmacists, building superintendents, gas station owners, waitresses, and restaurant operators who are alert to the well-being of their elderly, physically challenged, mentally impaired, or depressed and anxious customers. They listen, empathize, offer concrete advice, and reassurance. Swenson (1981) found a postmistress in a neighborhood post office who was known for weighing babies on her postal scale. Many young mothers stopped by to see this grandmotherly woman and received her support and advice.

The presence of natural helpers represents a neighborhood/community strength that could be extended to others in the community who lack such resources. Social workers can readily engage the interest and help of a known natural helper in an individual or family situation, always with the individual's or family's agreement and interest. Natural helpers enlisted in this way serve as consultants and resource people as needed. The worker can also affirm their helpfulness and their value and offer them encouragement and realistic praise. Neighborhood-oriented social workers interested in drawing on or strengthening sources of natural helping can locate natural helpers by talking with colleagues, school personnel, clergy, physicians, shopkeepers, and members of voluntary associations in the neighborhood. Natural helpers could be encouraged to talk about their helping activities and be asked if they are interested in having contact with individuals or families who lack helpful friends and relatives in the face of difficult situations and wish for such a relationship.

Linking individuals to enlisted natural helpers requires the motivation, interest, and agreement of both parties. Helpers should be evaluated on the basis of how helpful they are, not on whether their values and attitudes are congruent with professional ones. Ethnic, racial, or religious matches may be desirable depending on the needs and circumstances. Many practitioners engaged with natural helpers believe that the professional's role should be limited to that of consultant or resource person. Thus the relationship is viewed as a partnership of equals, and not as one of expert and learner (Pancoast and Collins 1987:180), as shown in the following example:

In a rural good neighbor project, social work students located natural helpers in three small towns by "hanging out around lunch counters, parks, laundromats, and gas stations, [talking] to as many townspeople as possible" (*Practice Digest* 1980:5), asking who had helped them the last time they needed help. Sometimes a good neighbor was found by chance: one student lost her car keys and a shopkeeper called various people, looked in a jar of old keys to see if one would fit, and finally found a person who could open the car. After conversing with her, the student realized that the shopkeeper was indeed a natural helper.

In this project, twenty-three helpers were located and paired with social workers, nurses, and others who had undergone training and had volunteered to be resource people for the helpers. They were expected to form easy, personal relationships with the natural helpers, to visit their helper three or four times over several months, and after that to keep in touch by telephone or casual drop-in visits when in the neighborhood. Examples of natural helping included the following:

A helper put two women in touch with a day-care training program that she learned about from the volunteer professional. Another helper stayed up all night with an acquaintance who threatened suicide. She telephoned the volunteer professional for reassurance that she had handled the situation well, and indeed she had. The suicidal acquaintance was then referred to the mental health center for help.

In contrast to volunteers and paraprofessional helpers, natural helpers are not trained for their tasks. However, it is always necessary for the social worker to assess the quality of helping provided by natural helpers and social networks (McFarlane, Norman, Streiner, and Roy 1984).

Establishing a self-help group. Life-modeled social workers can also help initiate (and serve as consultant to) a community self-help group. Mutual aid through self-help groups (and telephone networks) has taken on the character of a fast-growing social movement over the past several decades. Groups of people facing a shared need or condition band together to give and receive emotional and social support and to learn effective means of managing the shared concern. It is believed that millions of Canadians and Americans are members of rapidly growing numbers of such mutual aid systems (Black and Weiss 1990; Gitterman and Shulman 1994; Salem, Seidman, and Rappaport 1988; Romeder 1981; Farquharson 1978).[3]

Developing a self-help group requires: assessing and identifying an unmet need in a community and neighborhood; obtaining information about similar groups in other communities; contacting community leaders, natural helpers, and agency staff about need and methods for reaching potential members; speaking to potential members and engaging their interest; publicizing the proposed self-help group through social agency, health, education, and religious bulletin boards, community newsletters, flyers, and newspapers; leading the first meeting with an emphasis on focus and ground-rules; and beginning development of group leader roles (Harris 1981).

Self-help groups and mutual aid systems not only fit the worldview of various cultural groups in multicultural North American society but are also a significant force for empowering impoverished or devalued communities. No matter what the groups may later accomplish, most start from a powerless position. They lack needed resources, social respect, or opportunity to be in control of their situations. Through group processes, members gradually empower themselves as they gain information, develop some control over their need or condition, and rediscover their own capacities. As the self-help group is empowered, the community itself gains in power in an upward spiral of adaptive exchanges, a reversal of disempowerment generated by a downward cycle of community–family–individual maladaptive exchanges (Pinderhughes 1983).

Recruiting, training, and supervising role-related volunteers. As Manser (1987) observed, "the volunteer community is complex, extensive, and not yet fully mapped." Growth in numbers and diversity of service have been rapid through the 1980s and 1990s and continuing. Factors include the growing numbers of elderly who are able and eager to perform volunteer services, a rebirth of the ethos of caring among some segments of the population, and a response to cutbacks in social and health care services. Some social workers volunteer their free time as board members or in disaster work, community action/advocacy activities, programs for the homeless and for AIDS patients. However, danger lies in any assumption that voluntary activities are cost-cutting substitutes for public responsibility. The need is greater then ever for professional services and adequately supported health, education, and social welfare programs, especially in areas where informal help is missing and cannot be generated.

All the informal helpers so far discussed here and in chapter 5 are actually volunteers. They receive no pay, although some may receive reciprocal help when needed. We confine our discussion here to role-related volunteers, those who are formally attached to social work services as collaborators, service extenders, or supervised assistants. For example, social workers in a large private voluntary hospital recruit, train, and supervise volunteers in several different services. One group visits lonely elderly patients while they are in the hospital and continues the visiting (and outings, if feasible) after discharge, with ongoing access to the social worker supervisor for consultation, affirmation, and encouragement.

The most successful volunteer programs are those which provide opportunities for giving service that is useful, respected by the staff, personally rewarding, and in some instances could lead to skills acquisition pertinent to a future career goal. Essential to success are training, professional supervision, and a collegial, reciprocally respectful relationship. Yet few programs of social work education provide content on voluntarism, its history and significance, the nature of social worker–volunteer relationships and activities, and how to make use of trained volunteer service wisely and well.

Increased child abuse and neglect have spurred the development of volunteer parent aide programs of varied types to supplement and complement professional services of child welfare and family agencies. One such program is built on principles of natural friendship and informal helping. The aide is committed to at least a year of service, visits the family regularly, and is available by telephone. She (90% of the aides in this program are women) models life skills and provides practical assistance in managing household and childrearing tasks. Thus the aide's function with the family is very different from the function of the social worker. Such programs benefit the family served, the trained volunteer, the social worker, the agency, and the community. Experience so far suggests that past and current parent aides form a cadre of community people whose talents and good will have been expanded and who become available as "specialists" to serve many people in their community in areas of family functioning, parenting, and child abuse and neglect. Aides acquire broadened knowledge of the community's formal systems and can connect people to formal resources when needed.

Table 10.3 summarizes some characteristics of building informal community systems of relatedness.

Improving the coordination of community services. Improving service coordination is an important objective in community practice. Service coordination refers to collaborative planning among agencies, joint fund-raising, and other general social welfare activities. At the direct practice level, however, community-based case management is an example of effective service coordination (Rothman *1994*).

The growth of community systems of care was largely sparked by the deinstitutionalization of chronically mentally ill people that began in the 1970s following the development of drugs that help control symptoms. The movement assumed that communities would provide a less restrictive, more humane, environment. Since many if not most communities were (and still are) unable to furnish group housing to people with serious chronic mental disorders, many former patients ended up on the streets or in board-and-care homes, sRO hotels (Shapiro 1970), or homeless shelters.

In the 1990s and probably into the new century, case management is a rapidly growing system of community-based care for defined populations who suffer profound, long-term, or permanent disabilities (Rothman 1994). The chronically mentally challenged are the largest population served, followed by the physically and developmentally challenged.[4] A growing population of older people who are unable to provide adequately for their health, social, and economic needs without in-home services, are also maintained in the community through public and private case management agencies staffed by social workers. Similarly, physically challenged people in the community who require multiple social and health services in order to maintain independent living are served by case managers attached to rehabilitation agencies or provided by case management and community-based agencies.

Table 10.3   Characteristics of Informal Community Systems of Relatedness

• *Characteristics of Natural Helpers:*	Function well in their own lives
	Life circumstances similar to those of their neighbors whom they help
	Known in the neighborhood for resourcefulness and ability to give advice, provide information and empathic support, and to connect others to needed informal and formal resources found in workplaces, housing projects, churches, and in certain occupations such as beauticians and barbers, bartenders, storekeepers, building superintendents, waitresses
	May or may not know those who come for help or advice
	Usually not trained
	Some school children and teenagers are natural helpers to their peers
• *Characteristics of Community Self-Help Groups:*	People band together to give and receive emotional and social support
	Members gain information, develop some control over their need or condition, and rediscover their own capacities
	Empower impoverished or devalued communities
• *Characteristics of Role-Related Volunteers:*	Formally attached to social work services in social agencies and hospitals as collaborators, service extenders, and supervised assistants
	Recruited, trained, and supervised by staff social workers
	The social worker–volunteer relationship is collegial and mutually respectful
	Successful programs provide opportunities for giving service that is useful, respected by staff, personally rewarding, and in some instances lead to skills acquisition pertinent to future career goals

Case managers serve individual clients and the community in a special way. For example, the community is always part of the case manager's direct responsibility in addition to its being an influential environment in which all resident individuals and collectivities are embedded. The NASW Standards (1992:16) state:

> The case manager has a responsibility to participate in community needs assessments, community organization, and resource development to see that the needs of clients are identified and understood and that community action—public, private, or voluntary—is initiated to meet particular needs. It is also the case manager's responsibility to present agency executives, community leaders, and government and consumer representatives with documented information about resource limitations and other major case management problems, and recommend solutions.

Providing Social Work Consultation

Social workers are frequently called on to provide formal or informal social work consultation to community-based service providers, other professionals, and community residents. For many decades, interprofessional consultation was mainly a oneway process, with social workers receiving consultation from psychiatrists, physicians and, to a lesser extent, from lawyers. Psychiatric consultation often took on the character of supervision, as though social work knowledge, skill, and experience were inferior to those of the psychiatrist in spite of differences in professional function. As the social work profession matured its practitioners themselves became consultants, not only to other social workers but, increasingly, to other professionals in the community including teachers, nurses, administrators, and less extensively to lawyers, psychiatrists, physicians, ministers, and judges; and to paraprofessional or nonprofessional personnel such as institutional child care staffs, law enforcement personnel, group home operators, nursing home and day care staffs, and other community caregivers.

Social work consultants may be locally recognized experts in a field of practice, a community agency, or a BSW or MSW educational program, or they may hold positions as consultants in public health, mental health, and other community facilities, or they become known through their work in the community. School social work practitioners and students often provide individual consultation to teachers pertinent to a classroom situation or the behavior of particular children. They also provide group consultation in the form of workshops on such topics as children with chronic illness or working with parents. In family and child welfare agencies social workers provide consultation to natural helpers, foster parents, and parent aides. Rural social workers, because of lack of services, almost inevitably serve as consultants on a range of community concerns.

Shulman (1987) distinguishes between formal case consultation, program consultation, and a blend of the two. Case consultation is client focused: a particular individual, family, group, or community being served with the intent of helping the worker solve problematic elements in the situation. Program consultation might focus on the design of new services or on needed staff development such as introducing the use of group services in a family agency. The blended type of consultation usually starts with case consultation to agency staff and subsequently moves to organizational issues that are revealed in the case situations and that affect the quality of services adversely or increase the difficulties faced by the social work staff. It is designed to help resolve problematic issues in organizational functioning and might include line, supervisory, and administrative staff.

In working with community residents, consultation tends to be less formal and more egalitarian. Community residents are experts about their community; the social worker is expert about professional practice in the community. Community residents might provide consultation to a social worker about various community resources such as natural leaders, natural helpers, and historical benchmarks. In turn, a social worker might provide consultation to community residents about community assessment tools, procedures and processes for conducting a meeting, and finding resources.

In programmatic and organizational consultation, consultants must determine if they have knowledge and skills needed in the situation; sanction by administration if the invitation did not come from administration; time to learn as much as possible about the consultee and the particular setting before consultation begins. They must also assess the reality of including consultee expectations, objectives, respective roles, and evaluation of effectiveness. In the case of external organizations, the same clarity and contracting are carried out with the agency's administrator as well, including confidentiality regarding the consultee's statements (Collins, Pancoast, and Dunn 1977).

In offering advice to other professionals, paraprofessionals, volunteers, and community leaders, the social worker must avoid creating an image as a superior expert who has instant answers to a problem that the consultee (such as a teacher, nurse, or community caregiver) has struggled with for some time. Instead, it is usually better to suggest a second session to continue the discussion, adding that the consultant will give further thought to what has been said in the light of past experience with similar situations. When the consultant is ready to present several alternative ideas—even in the initial session, if that is to be the only one—the ideas should be presented only as possibilities to consider (Collins, Pancoast, and Dunn 1977). The emphasis is on assisting the consultee to describe the situation, consider associated or contributing factors, and examine alternate solutions and their consequences. In formal and informal consulting, presenting one's view as the right solution must be avoided in order to support the ultimate goal: to increase consultees' capacity for clear thinking, problem-solving, and decision-making in their own realm.

If the social worker is white and the consultees are persons of color, Gibbs (1980) suggested that an interpersonal orientation in the consultation relationship is more useful than an instrumental one.[5] An interpersonal orientation emphasizes mutual rapport and trust in the beginning phase of community consultation. Different perceptions of values, role expectations, resource and reward allocation, and feelings about the control of dependency are apt to exist during the early phase. In consulting, the social worker must be knowledgeable about cultural differences and social class variations. According to the author, African-Americans, for example, typically evaluate professional interactions in terms of the interpersonal skills demonstrated in early encounters, while whites typically evaluate the interactions in terms of instrumental skills. Gibbs (1980) believes that this interpersonal orientation can be generalized to other racial minority groups, "particularly those who share with Black people a relatively disad-

Table 10.4	Some Skills of Community Consultation

- ask for specific information about issues: what has been done, and how is it similar or different from usual experiences
- assess associated or contributing factors
- examine alternative solutions and their consequences
- present possible strategies for consideration
- emphasize mutual rapport and trust

vantaged position in American society and have developed adaptive strategies to cope with their lower status" (205).

An example of culturally congruent consultation activity with Canadian Indians in northern Ontario is provided by Kelley, McKay, and Nelson (1985). The setting was an Indian-staffed crisis house and the authors (as practitioners, researchers, and consultants) were faculty of the Lakehead University Department of Social Work. The goal was agency development, and the consultants conceived their role as facilitators and mentors, particularly since the agency's Indian administrator called them her "elders." The designation was apt, as they provided information and instrumental and emotional support, shared experiences with staff, and modeled problem-solving behavior without imposing solutions. The role was carried out through the use of four practice principles: mutuality in relationships; maximizing understanding of cultural differences; empowerment; and a structural approach.

Early contacts were at the Indian agency where staff would feel safe in their own territory. Later sessions were held at the university, the first such experience for the staff, who delighted in viewing themselves as "university students." The consultants emphasized their own personal values rather than their professional selves, as Indian staff members differentiate very little between personal and work activities. Hence, the consultants were more person-oriented than task-oriented.

Cultural differences were brought to the surface and explored to maximize mutual understanding and self-awareness of both staff and consultants and to minimize cultural barriers in the helping process. The authors describe common value differences between Indians and non-Indians in eight dimensions, and they suggest that mutual trust and understanding are best generated by immediately acknowledging the limited ground shared by Indian consultees and non-Indian consultants.

The power differential was minimized by avoiding the expert role, validating the competence and self-directedness of the staff, and implementing the transfer of power from consultants to staff.

At the beginning the agency staff, at all levels, felt inadequate and powerless in their relationships to each other and with the external environment. Rather than directly mediating conflicts, solving problems, or advocating on behalf of the agency, the consultants assumed a nondirective position and saw their primary task as helping agency staff act on its own behalf.

(Kelley, McKay, and Nelson 1985:599)

A primary focus was on the structural aspects of the agency's internal and external transactions. "Some of these structures are accountability and information-gathering methods, records, job descriptions, and agency policies and procedures" (600). For example, the Indian resident counselors viewed themselves as house maintenance workers, while the administrator wanted to help them realize that their helping role included responding to client needs affectively and not just instrumentally. Transactions between clients and counselors were modified by new structures (e.g., a case management perspective and daily log-recording) developed jointly by the Indian workers and the consultants.

> This recording format facilitated client assessment for staff and provided intervention guidelines. It also required staff to deal with clients differently. The new demands on staff for increased knowledge and skill led to staff requests for more staff development in the areas of assessment, goal-setting, and intervention. (601)

The authors emphasize that a structural approach can only be successful when used in combination with the other three principles—mutuality, maximizing understanding of differences, and empowerment. If a structural instrument is developed by consultants and imposed on staff, their self-direction, competence, and motivation is undermined. Table 10.4 summarizes some skills of community consultation.

The common ultimate goal of all life-modeled community practice is that the community or neighborhood becomes more competent and self-directed, begins to be laced with systems of relatedness, and experiences a growing sense of community pride (Germain 1985a). These community attributes are developed or enhanced by the participants as they work together toward their avowed objectives with the guidance of the social worker, as needed. In the process, the constituents' personal competence, self-direction, relatedness, and self-esteem are regained or enhanced.

ELEVEN

INFLUENCING THE PRACTITIONER'S ORGANIZATION

The life model broadens the conception of professional function to include influencing the worker's own organization to improve services, correct dysfunctional processes, and increase responsiveness to the needs of the population it serves or is expected to serve. Within this expanded function, social workers must take account of their employing organization's presence in the lives of all actual and potential clients and seek always to improve the fit between needs and services.[1] The broader function requires practitioners to move beyond prescribed organizational roles.

External and Internal Organizational Stressors

Societal, Professional, and Bureaucratic Forces

Social needs and injustices are often brought to public attention through the vision and zeal of social reformers who make the problem more visible, support is mobilized and public or private monies are made available. In attempting to carry out its mission, the organization, or a department within it, confronts its own structural or functional imperatives as well as various societal and professional forces affecting its practices (Banner and Gagne 1994).

Society makes financial assistance and service available to those in need. However, the historic ideological distinction between worthy and unworthy poor, the work ethic, and current public reaction to the tax burden have led to stigmatizing and stereotyping recipients. Financial aid is provided in a punitive, demeaning manner, demonstrated by inadequate allowances, deteriorated and uncomfortable physical facilities, long waiting lines, and negative attitudes and behavior of some personnel in many urban welfare offices. Such conditions attest to the impact on service delivery of budget stringencies that are supported by societal values and norms. Human service organizations are provided with "conflicting mandates to cure but nor to coddle, to proffer services but not to overspend" (Holloway 1987:731). Political and economic pressures place significant constraints on human service organizations compromising their ability to fulfill social mandates.

Organizations depend upon public and private support and so are shaped by funding trends and regulatory and accountability mechanisms. Funding becomes available and agencies respond with new programs that replace other programs. Some services receive as much or more than is required; others receive less than is required. A hospital patient in one department receives excellent care, while a patient in another department of the same hospital receives substandard care. The needs of rural areas receive less than proportionate attention than those of urban areas. From time to time, certain problems and needs receive national attention while others are overlooked. When one problem increases in visibility and another recedes in the public's attention, financing shifts. Some agencies, unable to initiate new programs, hold on desperately to familiar services and processes. Others, unable to define a clear function, change with each new trend in financing.

Human service organizations are confronted by an increasing emphasis on accountability, encouraging confusion about what is efficiency and effectiveness in human service organizations as compared to other organizations (Lewis 1975; O'Looney 1991; Scott and Meyer 1994). In hospitals, for example, financial accountability demands rapid discharge, which raises a question for social workers of whose interests are being served. "Timely" assessment and "timely" discharge planning have become central tasks for social workers assigned to medical or surgical services. As Gitterman and Miller (1989:152) point out:

> The word "timely" however is the official euphemism in reimbursement regulations. It does not mean the right or the opportune time, but often foretells hurried and inadequate assessment and premature discharge. Because failure to conform with regulations would imperil the already strained financial position of the organization, we accept and condone actions which are not necessarily in the best interest of the client.

Similarly, child welfare workers are bombarded with statistical forms that have become ends in themselves.

Organizations require a chain of command or levels of authority to coordinate the various subunits and personnel; to specify responsibility and accountability; and to provide leadership in decision-making. While the authority structure serves these and other functions, it also can produce contradictions and problems; decisions may be made with distorted information. Different positions in the hierarchy develop different priorities and have different interest groups to please, which can create tensions and turf struggles. The social worker has limited ascribed authority, insufficient information, and inadequate structural opportunities to influence organizational processes. Rigid authority structures further intensify the disadvantage and stifle initiative and creativity, while ambiguous authority structures discourage coordination and accountability (Schmidt 1992).

Organizations also require a division of labor to integrate service activities. However, specialized role assignments encourage preoccupation with developing and maintaining one's turf. Organizational and client needs are often held hostage to turf interests.

As knowledge and technology proliferates and specialized competence is required to perform complex tasks, professional services are essential. Organizations that employ professionals benefit from both their competence and the associated status. But professionals can also generate problems for the organization and clients. Professionals require autonomy and often resist bureaucratic processes. Similarly, professional interests do not always match client interests. To achieve their interests, professionals and organizational administrators institute certain tradeoffs. Low salaries, for example, may be accepted in exchange for professional autonomy and limited accountability; or, undesirable work conditions and practice requirements may be accepted for high salaries or job security. These tacit agreements often lead to identification with the organization, its practices, and procedures (Perrow and Guillen 1990; Specht 1985; Weissman, Epstein, and Savage 1983; Woodrow 1987). Socialization of the social work student within a tutorial pattern of master-apprentice field instruction, where power and authority is vested in one person, may encourage organizational docility and discourage risk taking. Bureaucratic structures and tradeoffs preserve the status quo. As a consequence, client interests are too often ignored.

In one family agency intake records revealed that 75 percent of outreach clients had more than a seven week wait for intake, while 90 percent of clients seeking services were seen within three weeks. Further analysis showed that a high proportion of the outreach clients were people of color. The second group of clients received services; the first group were in effect denied service. Those 25 percent who did endure the seven week delay were frequently defined at intake as mistrustful. Barriers to service produce a pool of "preferred" clients, who are able to wait, whose lives are not in crisis, whose employment and child care responsibilities are manageable. The remaining applicants are then defined as "unmotivated" and "resistant" to service. Not only are they denied service, but to justify their exclusion we blame them. Agency and professional contributions to resistance and lack of motivation remain unnoticed. Such labels are self-fulfilling and provide a rationale for administrators' and practitioners' neglect. Examination of organizational and professional interests are avoided.[2]

In attempting to cope with practice ambiguities and clients' overwhelming conditions, social workers may try to fit people and their situations into comfortable belief systems or preferred categories. The need to fit people into a preferred orientation hinders professional curiosity about which theory or concept best facilitates our understanding and ability to help an individual, family, group, or community in a particular situation at a particular time. Some embrace a deterministic view of human behavior in which either psychic or environmental forces are thought to be outside people's control. Clients are then perceived to be adrift in a turbulent sea where survival is dependent upon the velocity of the wind, the power of the waves, and the design of the ship. Other social workers incorporate a phenomenological, existential view of human behavior in which life forces are considered to be within people's control. Clients are then perceived to be steering a craft in a turbulent sea where survival is dependent upon their will, motivation, and skill. Social workers hear those dimensions of a client's experience that confirm their beliefs and ignore those that do not.

Finally, agency and professional definitions of social work purpose also have a strong impact on clients. When an agency is characterized by divergent professional orientations, clients may be held hostage to competitive interests, struggles and discrepant practices. Yet, when an agency adheres to a single orientation, clients are often expected to fit that approach.

Organizational Issues and Problems in Service Provision

Societal, professional and bureaucratic forces can create practices that serve societal, professional, or organizational interests at the expense of client interests (Hasenfeld 1983). In general, organizational problems for users of services grow out of three interrelated areas: the agency's definition of its purposes and services; structures and procedures used to coordinate and integrate organizational operations; and service arrangements.

If agencies define a client's life issue as located in the person, external forces are likely to receive insufficient attention:

- At the Midchester Family Service, all applicants are channeled into open ended individual psychotherapy. Crisis intervention, group work, or family services are rarely offered. Dropout rates are high. Efforts to reduce dropouts must deal with the psychoanalytic orientation of clinic administrators; staff interest in long-term psychotherapy; the private practice model, in which each worker provides her own service; and other features of the service conflict with needs and expectations of the clientele.

In such an agency, the definition of social work purpose reflects professional preferences and results in service definitions and styles that are unresponsive to client needs. When agencies rigidly define their purpose and services, people may become lost in the service network. When agencies' purposes and services are ambiguous, people may fall between the cracks because no agency appears responsive to their particular situation.

To cope with community and bureaucratic pressures and forces, an agency develops structures and procedures to coordinate and integrate the varied activities of its participants. Such procedures sometimes create unintended difficulties for clients. An authority structure, for example, may discourage staff differentiation and specialization. Hence, it stifles initiative and creative programming.

- In the Ridgeway Settlement House, the director is unable or unwilling to delegate tasks and responsibilities to staff. He is involved in so many activities and projects that he cannot handle them all properly. At the same time, staff have inadequate information for performing their function and require approval for every detail. Settlement members are affected by the agency's general inertia and the staff's diminished investment in the program.

In contrast, an authority structure may delegate too much, providing staff with limited leadership and accountability. Services remain uncoordinated, and each worker practices privately. In this pattern, professional role definitions and expectations are either specialized and narrow, encouraging isolation, or they are ambiguous and overlapping, encouraging competition. Similarly, agency policies and procedures may be overformalized or underformalized. Outdated rules may be imposed in new situations. Rules favorable to client needs may be systematically ignored. Service arrangements may be inadequate or inaccessible because of the agency's definition of its purpose and service and its related internal structures:

- In the Eastern Community Mental Health Center, adaptive tasks required by day patients' transition from hospitalization to community reintegration are ignored. They fit into neither the inpatient nor outpatient departments. What is needed in the cachement area is a transitional service or a day hospital program for recently released hospital patients.

In other instances, services might be available, but methods and style of delivery discourage their use:

- Jackson Adolescent Health Center experiences a 44 percent no-show rate for applicants scheduled for intake interviews. No systematic attempt is made to "capture" this applicant pool, although an informal follow-up procedure based on professional judgment is conducted on a case-by-case basis. The procedure is largely limited to informing a referral source that an applicant did not appear for an intake and is directed to an estimated one percent of applicants.

• Longshore Community Services, a sectarian family agency, limits its intake to self-referrals. The agency does not attempt to make itself visible or accessible to the community. Since the agency offers no outreach services, many clients who would make use of the agency's services do not know it exists.

When organizational processes and structural arrangements place additional stress on users of services, social work function broadens to include tasks of influencing the agency to change.

Social Work Function, Modality, Methods, and Skills

Some social workers maintain a distance from their organization as if they are in private practice. They see clients and that's it. Such isolation fails to serve client interests. Other workers identify completely with their organization. Their overidentification also fails to serve clients' interests. And yet others identify consistently with the client, as if the agency were their mutual enemy. While circumstances sometimes justify this stance, it is sustained at the risk of dismissal. In this way clients again lose. We propose that social workers must identify simultaneously with their organization, their clients, and the profession, in a three-way mediation among clients' needs, organizational requirements, and professional purpose (Schwartz 1976).

Social workers must maintain a vigilant stance towards organizational processes that bear on client services. When such processes become problematic, ethical practice seeks modification of the maladaptive practices, procedures, or programs (McGowan 1978).

Next, we discuss and illustrate the methods and skills of influencing employing organizations through preparation, initial organizational analysis, entry, engagement, implementation, and institutionalization.

Preparation Phase

Preparation for influencing the practitioner's organization begins with the identification of a problem. Users of service are the primary point of reference. Workers obtain data about problematic organizational arrangements and practices through careful attention to clients' direct and indirect expressions, and review of records, and other data. They are open to potential organizational issues reflected in clients' troubles. Colleagues are another resource. By attentive listening in staff meetings, in-service training programs, group supervision, and in informal conversations, the worker learns of problematic patterns. Specification and documentation of where and how the problem manifests itself is achieved through systematic observation, formal data collection, and informal conversations. Practitioners then assess the problem's salience and relevance to client service. Once the problem is identified and documented, alternative solutions or objectives and the specific means for achieving them are considered. Advantages, potential consequences, and feasibility of each potential solution is carefully examined. Based on the initial appraisal, a tentative objective and specific means for achieving it are determined. The following vignettes illustrate the preparation phase.

---

1. *Medical Hospital–Surgical Floor*

Problem: Definition of Social Work Function: Social work practice is limited to discharge planning. All other patients, regardless of their need for social work services, are overlooked.

Documentation: One woman, distraught over a planned amputation, was not referred because the family could take her home after surgery. Another woman in the terminal stages of cancer and severely depressed was not referred because her sons were making discharge arrangements.

Desired Outcome: Expand the social work function to include high risk situations.

Means of Implementation: Try to broaden the content of team meetings to include identifying high risk patients.

2. *Halfway House*

Problem: Coordination and Integration Structures and Procedures: Insufficient coordination among staff.

Documentation: Residents constantly complain about lateness, service and quality of meals, inequities in house assignments, inadequate protection from residents who steal or are physically abusive, and hostile and demeaning behavior by staff. Staff complaints include residents' failure to cooperate, administration's insensitivity to staff needs, and ineffective coordination of services. Lack of enforcement of house rules and regulations is also a staff complaint. The director, on the other hand, locates the problem in the lack of staff initiative, creativity, and assertiveness in carrying out programs and policies.

Desired Outcome: Improve internal operations of the house and communications among the three groups.

Means for Implementation: My initial and tentative plan is to obtain commitment to and approval for creating an advisory staff group to the director. Once the advisory group is in place, I will try to have residents added and redefine the group as a house council.

The means for implementation in this instance is a feasible structural innovation which can lead to permanent change. The worker defined the problem as lack of structure and procedures for coordination, and devised a means for integrating the various parts of the house system. If the director's problem definition remained in place, the worker might then have sought improved staff performance through in-service training. But when problems generated by missing structures and procedures are located in the staff and call for in-service training, the dysfunctional structures and procedures escape attention. They continue to affect service adversely.

3. *Hospital Adolescent Health Clinic*

Problem: Services Provided: Clinic's intake practices discourage many adolescent applicants from using services.

Documentation: Review of the intake log over a six-month period was conducted. Monthly data were compiled that demonstrated actual numbers of intakes scheduled and no-shows. No-shows were further analyzed for the number of rescheduled appointments. In the six-month period, 465 adolescents had intake appointments and 208 (45%) failed to appear. For the first rescheduled intake appointment, 133 (28%) failed to appear. Only 38 (8%) called to cancel or reschedule their appointments. They will not be part of the targeted change which focuses on applicants who make no attempt to communicate on their own.

Desired Outcome: The objective is to increase professional staff involvement with applicants which may increase the number of applicants who become clients (Alcabes and Jones 1985).

Means for Implementation: Professional staff will be involved by initiating a call to remind applicant of appointment and a follow-up call to each no-show applicant (if self-referred), or the applicant's referral source. Such phone calls may provide a bridge into the clinic.

4. *Union Setting*

Problem: Services Arrangements: The social program for retired members is poorly planned and carried out.

Documentation: Members complain that programs are canceled, guest speakers do not arrive for announced lectures, and most activities are dull. My observations are similar. The program is losing members and is not attracting new ones.

Desired Outcome: Improve the quality of the social program.

Means for Implementation: Obtain approval for and organize a steering committee of retirees, union program personnel, and myself to plan programs.

In this setting, a steering committee is congruent with organizational norms. It is not a radical innovation, and it invites a broad representation of participants, particularly the lower ranking retirees. As union members, the retirees are entitled to services: when they become involved, their potential power will assure accountability to their interests. The new arrangement is likely to have permanent impact.

5. *Community Social Services*

Problem: Services Provided: The agency's intake practices discourage many applicants from using services.

Documentation: Telephone calls to a small random sample of people who had failed to show up for their appointments, or refused to make an appointment after intake, yielded initial data. Complaints included lack of evening hours; lapse of several weeks between intake and assignment to a social worker; demand to fill out numerous research forms; and adolescents' discomfort with the psychiatrist's detailed questions concerning sexuality.

Desired Outcome: Increase responsiveness and relevance of intake service to client needs.

Means for Implementation: An ad hoc committee to study the high drop-out rate.

Ad hoc committees are important structures for revising agency practices and programs. A direct assault on the agency's intake services can generate resistance. The agency prides itself on its scientific approach and has a full-time researcher, so the proposed research committee is consistent with formal and informal norms. Composition of the ad hoc committee will be important if change is to occur. Committee members must enjoy sufficient flexibility to entertain proposed changes in intake arrangements and sufficient respect to influence their colleagues.

Table 11.1 summarizes preparation skills used to influence an organization.

Initial Organizational Analysis

Having tentatively identified and documented an organizational problem and selected an objective and means for achieving it, the worker now undertakes a formal organizational analysis. Lewin (1952) characterized the status quo in any social system as the balanced result of countervailing forces toward and against change. A force field analysis helps the practitioner to identify and visualize the specific forces promoting and resisting change. The worker assesses which environmental, organizational, and interpersonal forces are apt to support the proposed change and which are apt to resist change (Berger 1990; Brager and Holloway 1992).

Environmental forces. The social worker must evaluate features in the environment that may support and those that may frustrate the change effort, such as societal trends and available funding. Even fiscal constraints can induce and promote creative organizational change. A financially troubled agency, for example, may be receptive to changes in intake policies and procedures that reduce costs or expand the fee base even though such changes are contrary to its ideological orientations.

The extent to which the agency is held accountable for services and practices by community groups is also important. Such groups include the

Table 11.1	Preparation Skills

OBTAIN DATA TO IDENTIFY AND DOCUMENT ORGANIZATIONAL PROBLEM FROM:
- clients' direct and indirect expressions
- review of agency records
- informal conversations with colleagues
- formal participation in staff meetings
- systematic data collection

EXAMINE ALTERNATIVE SOLUTIONS AND SPECIFY DESIRED OUTCOME
IDENTIFY TENTATIVE MEANS FOR DESIRED OUTCOME WHILE:
- avoiding mobilizing the organization's defenses
- identifying staff's self-interest

board of directors, other organizations on which the agency depends for referrals and evaluation, and public and private standard-setting bodies. Even the agency's location, condition, and size affect relations with its neighborhood. Data on environmental forces are collected from written materials, informal conversations, and focused observations. From the data, the social worker develops preliminary indicators of environmental forces likely to promote or inhibit the proposed change.

Organizational forces. Internal characteristics of the agency also affect change processes. Complex organizations with a number of professional disciplines and staff with advanced training are thought to have a higher rate of innovation. Such agencies are characterized by diversity, openness to new methods and technologies, and competing interest groups. Organizations that are highly centralized with power located in few elites, or are highly formalized with a large number of codified rules, are thought to demonstrate lower rates of innovation. Knowledge of such organizational properties is used as gross predictors for determining a feasible objective and the means for achieving it (Haig and Akins 1970; Holloway 1987). Figure 11.1 protrays the combined impact of organizational complexity and formalization on receptivity to change.

Figure 11.1	Impact of Organizational Complexity and Formalization Upon Change

(+) = Property Increasing Feasibility
(-) = Property Decreasing Feasibility

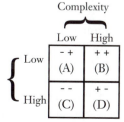

In agencies characterized by a low degree of complexity and a high degree of formalization (C), the worker has to formulate limited objectives, often limiting desired outcomes to procedural changes such as enforcement of existing rules favorable to clients or suggestions of new procedures to replace outdated ones. Modification of organizational purpose or basic programs is quite unlikely in a department of welfare or social security office. In contrast, a worker employed by a highly complex and informal agency (B) may aspire to greater functional, structural, or programmatic changes. In community mental health centers, the worker can often undertake more ambitious influence efforts. While a particular organization may have overall features of high complexity and low formalization, a department within it may not share those characteristics. For this reason the organizational analysis must include the subsystem and its relation to the larger system.

Less definitive statements can be made about agencies characterized by low complexity and low formalization (A) or by high complexity and high formalization (D). In a relatively undifferentiated community agency, for example, services may suffer from a lack of staff diversity and narrow ideological commitments. While the worker may be unable directly to influence the purpose and program of an organization that is low on complexity, he may have sufficient support and resources for indirect influence. A family or group consultant, for example, might be used to expose staff to new knowledge and technology. Determining whether sufficient organizational supports and resources are available for the change effort requires an assessment of the staff's status-role system, norms, and interests.

Interpersonal forces. Practitioners need to identify key participants who will affect and be affected by the proposed change. They then estimate each participant's likely response to the proposed change and evaluate its probable impact on their job performance and satisfaction. If the desired outcome and means support participants' self-interest by increasing their prestige, autonomy, influence or authority, their support is more likely. Conversely, if the desired outcome and means threaten participant self-interest, then resistance may be anticipated (Brager and Holloway 1978; Holloway 1987). Although people usually act in their own selfinterest with fairly predictable responses, the complexities, subtleties, and idiosyncrasies of human behavior require careful attention and preparation for the unexpected. Such attention includes observation of behaviors during formal and informal contacts with key participants—looking at patterns (risk taking, conformists, "closet" advocates); norms (work group pressures, individual and collective values); activities (job responsibilities, outside interests); and motivation (what constitutes satisfaction and stress for each person).

Worker influence. Social workers next evaluate their own position in the organization and their structural and personal resources for influence. Their structural location may or may not provide opportunities for interacting with key participants and obtaining essential data. Doctoral students, for example, quickly learn the importance of developing a relationship with the department secretary, who controls access to a critical faculty member. To most students and staff social workers, the agency secretary represents a source of influence to be cultivated. While a baccalaureate or master's social work student has a relatively limited structural position in the agency, access to influential people and opportunities to experiment may be given just because of student status.

Social workers interested in social change must also assess how they are viewed by others in the organization. In developing organizational self-awareness, practitioners must try to see themselves as others do rather than how they would like to be seen. They need to evaluate the extent to which they are viewed as competent, valuable colleagues whose advice and favor are sought and whose committee work is respected. Finally, workers must consider their time and energy: for the tasks involved in seeking change, time and energy are essential.

Through analysis of organizational forces, one can then evaluate feasibility, that is, the potential for success. When supports are strong and opposition is weak, feasibility is high. When support is weak and opposition is strong, feasibility is low. Often, a change in the means for attaining the desired outcome creates feasibility without compromising the objective. In the earlier example of the union's inadequate retiree program, the worker initially had intended to have a professional hired. The analysis, however, revealed powerful constraints which mobilized resistance by the department. The less threatening strategy of a steering committee diminished resistance and heightened feasibility. When supports and opposition are both weak, an open situation exists suggesting that supportive elements have to be mobilized. And finally, strong support and strong opposition indicate potential conflict. The outcome is unpredictable and a low keyed approach is indicated. Table 11.2 presents an organizational analysis of a branch office of a sectarian family agency where intake was limited to self-referral. The worker wants to reach out to the community.

The overall pattern and direction reflects strong supports and moderate to weak opposition. This suggests feasibility and points to entry actions to mobilize supports and decrease resistance. This outreach program can also be readily connected to agency financial pressures. Table 11.3 summarizes the initial organizational analysis skills.

Entry Phase

After determining feasibility, the next step is to develop an receptive organizational climate. For instance, in the sectarian family agency, the social worker observes,

---

I was aware of staff concerns about declining intakes and their fears of cutbacks in funding, and staff cutbacks. During my informal discussions with staff members, I encouraged conversation on the decline in intakes

Table 11.2   Organizational Analysis

- *Agency*: Branch office, sectarian family agency
- *Problem*: Intake limited to self-referral, excluding many potential clients from service
- *Desired Outcome*: To reach more clients
- *Means for Implementation*: Community outreach demonstration

SUPPORTS	ENVIRONMENTAL FORCES		OPPOSITION
	Intensity	Intensity	
Coordinating agency's threat of funding loss	High	Low	Coordinating agency's loss of some control over accountability
Threat to staff's job security	High	Low	Undeveloped community relationships
Interest and availability religiously affiliated community agencies for collaboration	High	Moderate	Present collaboration arrangements (e.g., co-leadership, fee splitting)
	ORGANIZATIONAL FORCES		
	Intensity	Intensity	
Complexity: employs variety of professionals, historically has been somewhat unorthodox	High	High	Decentralization and Formalization: staff given wide latitude, with limited accountability
Decentralized: in competition with other branches	High		
Formalization: modest number of rules, but not rigidly enforced, often left ambiguous (e.g., job descriptions not defined, leaving opportunity for community work)	High		
	INTERPERSONAL FORCES		
	Intensity	Intensity	
Administrator is experiencing environmental pressures, is liberal in views, and active	High	Low	Administrator sometimes doesn't follow up
Psychologist is service-minded, concerned about decline in number of clients served	Moderate	Moderate	Psychologist is inactive in decision-making process
The social workers are quite liberal and client-oriented	High	Moderate	The social workers have relatively low status, limited influence
Psychiatrist is relatively uninvolved, follows administrator	Mod.	Low	Psychiatrist may be threatened by outreach
Educational consultant is invested only in school collaboration and will not restrain my efforts	Low	Low	Educational consultant may be threatened; however, he has the lowest organizational status
Total work group: high identification with branch, and perception of	High	High	Total work group: outreach could potentially mean more work, travel,

themselves as innovative
creative, and committed
to serving their population

uncertainties, and
contact with less
motivated clients

WORKER INFLUENCE

	Intensity	Intensity	
Supervised by administrator, therefore has easy accessibility to critical participants	High	Low	New-worker status limits right to undertake a new project
Recent-graduate status provides legitimacy to experiment	Moderate	Low	Motivation might be suspect
Personal positioning includes excellent informal relationships, and is perceived as a highly motivated worker; on several occasions has demonstrated competence in community contacts	High		
Highly motivated and has time and energy to undertake this influence,			

and the effect on the agency. I felt out their attitudes and thinking on the subject and their possible reactions to alternative solutions. Where appropriate, I dropped hints about possible outreach to the community. I mentioned a suggestion made by a respected administrator at a central office meeting to offer premarital counseling groups. I also invited their thinking about active case finding and collaborative projects to increase the agency's visibility in the community.

The worker begins informal discussions with organizational friends, testing out possible reactions and inviting their ideas in collaborative problem solving (Gentry 1987).

In contrast, an attempt by a social worker on a psychiatric impatient service to have patients decide on their own passes failed at the outset. Without informal scouting or positioning in advance, this practitioner raised the issue at a general staff meeting.

At the conclusion of the discussion, I brought up the issue of patients' passes. The nurses immediately voiced their disagreement. The floor doctor identified the multidisciplinary conference structure as the appropriate mechanism. The meeting ended without any support for my idea.

Table 11.3	Initial Organizational Analysis Skills
• *Assess environmental forces likely to support or constrain proposed change:*	Examine impact of societal, technological, legislative, community, and physical contexts
• *Assess organizational forces likely to support or constrain proposed change:*	Examine extent of complexity, centralization, formalization of total organization or specific department
	Evaluate combined effect of organizational forces
• *Assess interpersonal forces likely to support or constrain proposed change:*	Identify key participants
	Evaluate effect of proposed change on key participants' job performance and satisfaction (prestige, self-esteem, autonomy, influence)
	Evaluate key participants' interactional patterns and organizational activities
• *Assess elements of worker influence likely to support or constrain proposed change:*	Evaluate one's formal position in the organization
	Evaluate one's personal position in the organization
	Evaluate one's resources of time and energy
• *Assess feasibility, potential for success:*	Strong supports and weak opposition suggest high feasibility
	Weak supports and strong opposition suggest low feasibility
	Weak supports and weak opposition suggest an open situation
	Strong support and strong opposition suggest potential conflict

The worker took premature action in the formal system. Resistance was mobilized and precipitated immediate rejection. Support for proposed innovation or change must be developed and cultivated before going public.

Brager and Holloway (1978) suggest three methods of preparing a system: Personal positioning, structural positioning, and management of stress. *Personal positioning* is essential for the social work practitioner. Since practitioners usually have limited formal authority, their organizational effectiveness depends upon achieving influence by other legitimate means. Professional competence is a major resource and "immediately precludes or mitigates easy dismissal of one's ideas and opinions" (Gitterman and Miller 1987:160). The first positioning task is illustrated by a social worker's effort to achieve visibility:

I had been prompt and attentive in doing weekly intakes for several months. I involved Mr. Phillips, director of intake, whenever I had a question about procedure. I recently completed an intake on behalf of the husband of a client in treatment with an experienced worker. I consulted with her to gain a better understanding and assessment of the case. She complimented my work and apparently discussed it with the director of intake and the agency director.

Being competent is not enough in itself; competence must be visible. Recognized knowledge and expertise gain respect, credibility and influence. An effective presence in the agency's informal system is indispensable to professional influence (Holloway and Brager 1985). The social worker who is an insider, attentive to colleagues' interests and concerns, and who possesses interpersonal skills will acquire a support system and organizational allies. An isolated practitioner who deviates from informal norms will have limited resources for influencing organizational practice.

In evaluating group composition, the worker considers the driving and restraining forces represented by people, jurisdictional factors, and decision-making patterns. After selecting the appropriate *structure*, the social worker considers which formal and informal processes may facilitate or retard movement and then settles on the most effective person, oneself or another, to introduce the idea. The practitioner is quite prepared to give up any claims to ownership of the idea.

Involvement of service users is critical. Their evaluative feedback and anecdotal material are vital data for both personal and structural positioning. Segments of the actual or potential clientele may welcome opportunities to be involved in efforts at change. Their opinions can be secured through questionnaires. A social worker in a child guidance clinic was interested in working with adolescents. She soon discovered, however, that few adolescents or parents sought services, perhaps because of the agency's name, lack of publicity and outreach, and the reluctance of staff to get involved with "difficult teenagers." Her first step in influencing her agency to live up to its objective was to interest the director in forging links to the local junior high school as a way of increasing agency income. With his permission, she approached the principal and guidance counselor with an offer of group services to interested students. Together they designed a questionnaire which was distributed to the students in their social science class. Responses were almost totally positive. Armed with this data, the worker and the clinic director planned staff involvement, collaboration with school personnel, parental permission. Their objective was to provide group services in the school and eventually to provide individual youth services as an integral part of the agency.

Hospital social service departments often ask patients and families to evaluate the service received. These data are important sources of support for change efforts. In addition, the process communicates to clients that their opinions are valued and used. In some instances, clients are involved in later steps of a change process. For example, a children's developmental disability clinic was threatened with closing when a new director changed the hospital's fiscal and service priorities. The clinic had been providing group services to parents of disabled children, and each group was eager to contribute to staff efforts to sustain the clinic. Members mobilized a telephone and mail campaign among their friends and neighbors, and they interested a local radio station and a neighborhood newspaper in their plight. Staff drew up proposals for funding. The administrator agreed to withdraw his plan to dismantle the clinic. Services to the needy children and their parents were safeguarded. In addition, these parents felt empowered, having gained actual power to bring about a significant change in their lives.

A family agency social worker was concerned that no evening hours were offered by the agency. She obtained the director's permission to invite several interested clients to a staff meeting, and later, to a board meeting. In such instances, clients' own presentation of their needs is more forcible in influencing staff and policy-makers than the worker's presentation. Similarly, a child welfare agency that had been reluctant to offer group meetings to foster parents was influenced to do so by a worker's carefully thought out proposal of content for the meetings and her mobilization of the eager support of many foster parents who then called and wrote to the director about their interest.

Users of the service must be fully informed of all that is at stake in their active participation, or even in their passive support of an influencing effort. The positives inherent in successful influencing are be easy to identify and share. Possible negative consequences for clients must nevertheless be considered and shared with them, so they may make an informed decision to participate or not.

Organizations can erect elaborate defenses by which the problem is rationalized, minimized, avoided, or denied. Before there can be motivation to examine and modify dysfunctional practices and procedures, some *stress* has to be experienced by organizational participants (Dalton 1970). An important positioning task is to bring the problem and its consequences to the participants' consciousness by increasing its visibility and consequences. A worker in a union setting recorded:

I made sure the director knew about the problems all staff were having with the scheduling of psychiatric consultations. I dramatized a recent experience I had with a member who waited two hours and then wasn't seen. The director was disturbed by this incident.

I also exchanged experiences with other staff members, and this created and maintained anxiety about the issue. Before long, several workers asked that the issue be placed on the agenda for a staff meeting.

In informal contacts, the worker listens to others' dissatisfactions and encourages conversations about the problem. Heightened stress is often an impetus to action.

At times, data are sufficiently compelling to create organizational discomfort. In the adolescent health clinic in which intake practices discourage many adolescent applicants from using services, the worker analyzed the 45% no-show data by referral source. Self-referred applicants had the highest (69%) and community agencies the lowest (32%) rates of no-show for the initial appointment. Self-referral usually implies recognition of a problem and motivation to seek help. Why this subgroup should have the highest no-show rate requires the agency to examine its intake structures and processes (Neinstein 1982). These data created stress for agency administrators and staff and prompted an examination of factors involved.

If stress is excessive, an agency or department staff could be overwhelmed by conflict or hopelessness. The stress itself is a constraining force. The worker needs to specify the problems and help staff mobilize. A hospital team, for example, was locked in battle and the hostility immobilized them from work on common goals. The worker attempted to reduce stress by suggesting that the source of the problem was organizational rather than interpersonal. She began with nonmedical staff, the most despairing group, affirming their value to the team and strengthening their respect for their professional and organizational roles. Three excerpts from the worker's log are presented:

We were sitting around shooting the breeze when Phyllis asked me what I thought of the new batch of residents. I said they weren't so new any more but like everyone else, I missed the old ones. Jean agreed wholeheartedly and added that the new ones "don't seem to care what anyone else has to say. Half the time they don't know what's going on with their patients." I asked if that's why she stopped coming to rounds. Phyllis replied that there's no point going. Jean added that no one wants to hear what they have to say. I said it was a sad state of affairs when staff didn't communicate with one another because "how else would I have known that Mrs. S. was thinking about signing out because she was worried about her kids and needed help, if you hadn't told me? You know more about patients in some ways than we do because you spend the most time with them." Jean responded, "You know that, but they [residents] don't." I said not coming to rounds isn't the answer because then no one can talk to each other, and patients will suffer. Phyllis said that was the pity of it all.

Alice seemed quite despondent. She said her impression is that no one is interested in occupational therapy, and she questions the value of her program to patients. I said her feelings had changed dramatically in the

Table 11.4	Entry Phase Skills
• *Create receptive organizational climate*:	Informally discuss problem with friends in the organization Develop informal support for problem identification
• *Achieve influence through personal positioning*:	Demonstrate professional competence Actively participate in interpersonal networks
• *Achieve influence through structural positioning:*	Actively participate in formal organizational structures Engage service users
• *Bring the problem to the awareness of organizational participants*:	Increase visibility of problem and its consequences Decrease excessive stress by specifying the problem Help staff to mobilize

last three months. She described how the residents ignore her, and devalue her program. I praised her program and skills, offering specific examples of impact she had made. I also pointed out that she isn't the only one feeling this way. It seems that all disciplines are questioning their value in rounds, citing social work as a case in point. Alice thought about this and agreed there did seem to be a general problem; no one talks except the residents.

Jackie suggested that people's anger with one another had developed into personality clashes which are better left alone. I responded that while this was the result, it seemed to me the problem was basically one of communication among the team members. Jackie asked me to spell it out further. I said things are not going to get better unless we talk about the problem. "I understand staff's not wanting to discuss personality conflicts which would get us no place. Perhaps there is another way to approach it, through improving communication in rounds—that really is the problem." Jackie thought about this and then said that this approach certainly might defuse the problem, and it was worth a try.

As staff depersonalized the struggle, they began to function with greater energy and resourcefulness. The positioning task was to reduce the stress so that the overwhelming problem could be confronted. In the process of redefining the problem, the social worker gained important allies in dealing with the organizational problem (Mechanic 1964). Table 11.4 outlines skills used in the entry phase.

Engagement

After establishing a receptive organizational climate for the formal introduction of the identified issue and the proposed solution, the worker must decide on methods from among demonstrating, collaborating, persuading, and creating conflict (Brager and Holloway 1978; Patti and Resnick 1972). The action taken depends on the type of issue, the degree of goal consensus between worker and critical participants, and the worker's resources for influence.

Demonstrating is especially effective with issues associated with professional practice and program gaps. Broadening the conception of an agency's or department's social work function or introducing a new modality, for example, is best achieved by demonstrating. By persistently and skillfully showing through action the value of group services, a social worker with limited organizational resources (rank), but sufficient personal resources (competence and energy), may neutralize rather than mobilize.

A recent graduate began professional employment in Rainbow House, a residential facility serving twenty adolescents and young adults. Its objective is to prepare the residents for independent living at age 18 when they are no longer eligible for substitute care. The residents have spent most of their lives in foster care. Like many of their peers, residents of Rainbow House are cynical and resentful of having been bounced from foster home to foster home and from group home to residential treatment institution. Rainbow House reinforces their sense of powerlessness by excluding them from decision-making. Although the agency emphasizes "empowerment," it limits this to individual treatment of early narcissistic injuries, separation, and loss. Being denied a voice in decision-making replicates a life pattern of institutionalized helplessness and dependency and sabotages the agency goal of preparation for independent living. A frequently heard statement, "I just want to do what I got to do and get out of this place," conceals the terror of residents of final discharge and independent living. When they do complain about unfair practices such as too many or inconsistent structures, policies and processes, they focus on the issue at hand, and not on the fact that staff make all decisions. Professional staff attribute many of residents' complaints to their narcissistic wounds and other pathologies, ("Regrettably, his defenses are too primitive for him to make mature governance decisions"; "We do not want to set them up to fail"). Child care staff attribute complaints to general immaturity and a distorted sense of entitlement.

> False assumptions, taken-for-granted beliefs, unquestioned operating rules, and numerous other premises and practices can combine to create self-contained views of the world that provide both a resource for and a constraint on organized action. While they create a way of seeing, and suggest a way of acting, they also tend to create ways of not seeing, and eliminate the possibility of actions associated with alternative views of the world.   (Morgan 1986:202)

The worker's desired outcome was to develop a youth council of residents to plan programs and discuss concerns with staff. As a new worker, she cautiously broached the idea with a few influential staff. Their response was unenthusiastic. However, within a few months Rainbow House experienced several traumatic events that seriously threatened the program. A staff member's increased disability from AIDS prevented his continued employment. A skillful senior child care worker was provoked into a fight with a resident, and his employment was terminated. A resident charged an administrator with sexual abuse. A respected professional staff member left for a new position. These changes were devastating to staff and residents. The social worker used the organizational crisis to gain staff and resident approval for weekly meetings of the youth council in a six month demonstration. He designated six months to reassure the director that the members would act responsibly. He carefully listened to the director's concern: "The one saving grace of our residents is that they never act in concert with each other. The day they stage a coup d'état is the day I retire." Staff and residents found a common ground: all parties expected the project to fail. Staff lacked confidence in residents' ability to act responsibly; residents lacked trust in staff's willingness to listen to them.

The worker acted quickly to hold Rainbow House's first resident election of members to the youth council. Of the eight elected, two missed the first three meetings and the residents selected two additional members to replace them. The social worker invited a high status child care worker to co-lead the council. This ensured child care staff cooperation with the project. The weekly house meeting structure was used to present their issues and concerns to the staff. The worker carefully prepared members to present and discuss selected issues, guiding them in how to prepare and keep to an agenda; gain maximum participation; divide up tasks and responsibilities; and keep other residents involved. The youth council also worked on rules to govern its operation. For example, after two residents asked to join the council, the members decided that nonelected members could become members with approval of two-thirds of the council. The director and child care staff were impressed by the members' articulateness and seriousness. The director increased his support by providing the council with a small budget. When invited, he attends meetings. The youth council has: effected new policies and procedures; and promoted a greater sense of community. The worker proved the youth council's value to the organization by devoting equal attention to organizational as well as council processes and disciplined completion of tasks. After the initial six months, the youth council was an integral part of Rainbow House.

Collaborating is effective in relatively open organizations where goal consensus exists and there is either equitable resource distribution or the presence of close interpersonal relationships (Brager and Holloway 1978). The social worker engages key participants in collaborative problem-solving through a shared search for data, possible solutions, and resources. Activity is limited to providing relevant information and mild persuasion, without attempts to convince or to change another's position. For instance, a worker in a children's residential treatment center was concerned about poor handling of the children's bedtime. Children were ordered to bed by child-care staff, and some were assigned early bed times as punishment for misdeeds. At the same time, the worker had a genuine appreciation for staff's concerns such as management issues, low pay, overwork, and lack of appreciation. Because of good relationships with staff and a similar organizational status, the social worker selected the method of collaborating.

1. *Psychiatrist:* During a recent treatment conference, I encouraged a parent to discuss her daughter's complaint about being put to bed early. The psychiatrist agreed to look into the matter. At a subsequent clinical meeting, I presented my observations and concerns and received a commitment that the issue will be placed on a staff meeting agenda.

2. *Child care supervisor:* I shared my concerns and engaged him in thinking of ways to resolve the problem. He welcomed knowledge about the uses and effects of punishment. For example, since children are punished with an early bed time for infractions that occurred in the morning or previous days, I brought in behavioral studies on the lack of effectiveness of delayed responses to misbehavior. I made no suggestions about this material.

3. *Child care staff:* In an informal conversations, I defined bed time as a troubling time for them to manage since many of the children were particularly difficult during this period, and I encouraged them to seek solutions to the problem.

As a result of these collaborative efforts, the supervisor raised the concern in the child care staff meeting. A respected staff member, with whom I had developed a close relationship, said that whenever she had time to tuck some of the children into bed, their management was easier. A second staff member stated that telling stories was sometimes calming. They all complained about little time for these activities. The supervisor suggested they bring unmanageable children to him. Staff was pleased with this structural change, and, in turn, agreed to tuck the children in. At the next meeting of the clinical and child care staff, my supervisor inquired about a particular child. A child care staff member reported that the child was sent twice to the supervisor at bed time, and this had calmed her as well as the other children. I suggested we spend a few minutes on additional suggestions for easing the problem further. One child care staff person suggested that the recreation department could be useful in story telling or singing before bedtime. The child care supervisors and other staff agreed, and a meeting was arranged with the head of the recreation department. A program for this was developed. At this same meeting, the psychiatrist referred to the use of early bed times as punishment and to the research I had provided him. The staff was asked to consider alternatives for discussion next week, and I agreed to inquire how other institutions handle punishment.

Here the worker used facilitating and guiding methods to engage key participants in collaborative evaluation, goal consensus, and problem solving.

Persuading is effective in situations characterized by goal dissent and disparate power. The existence of a problem must be brought home to key participants who then must be persuaded that solving the problem is necessary and feasible. To influence opinions and ideas of others, the worker requires specific skills in developing and presenting the case for change and participating in debate.

The burden of proof is on the worker as proponent for change. Issue definition is the important first task. To a large extent, how a problem and proposed solution are defined determines the grounds on which arguments will be based. The social worker has to develop arguments that demonstrate the existence of the problem, its seriousness, and the effectiveness of the plan to deal with it.

Problem definition must be clear and supported by facts, illustrative material, and if possible, by testimony of colleagues and clients. If a problem remains unrecognized, key participants will easily defeat or simply ignore the argument. A social worker student in a union setting, for example, attempted to persuade an administrator of an union local to change procedures because retirees were not informed about the termination of their medical insurance. She reflected on her mistakes:

First, I assumed Mr. Johnson knew what I was talking about when I referred to "Senior Care." I failed to review briefly the terms of this insurance coverage and to connect it to the union's responsibility for informing members of changed coverage.

Second, I failed to discuss the clients' situation adequately. I did not take advantage of the administrator's commitment to the service ethic by presenting large medical bills, describing complications in applying for Medicaid, or relating relatives' threats to sue the local.

Third, I failed to provide convincing statistics such as the percentage of all eligible members who have Senior Care and the negligible cost of my proposal.

At the end of my presentation Mr. Johnson said, "Although this seems like a worthwhile proposal, it may be a luxury, and we really can't be responsible for the members' not reading their newsletter." As I began to object, he thanked me for my interest, and we were dismissed. I tried to present my plan to get insurance information to the members, but I didn't take the first step in the persuasion process: establish the need for the change.

Forces committed to the status quo attack the problem either by denying its existence or minimizing its seriousness. The worker must possess supporting data to establish need.

When the problem is documented, argued, and established, opposition may turn on the proposed solution and potential negative consequences. The worker must be prepared to manage such attacks. If resistance is anticipated, the two-sided argument (one's own and the probable counter-position) can to some extent dissipate opposition (Karlins and Abelson 1970). Humor and role play are effective in deflecting expected resistance or rebuttal. Also, the worker should describe the proposal "in language that is compatible with the values of the audience . . . and that will address their major concerns" (Frey 1990). If a positive response is expected, however, one-sided argument is more effective since a reference to counter-perspectives could create doubts and resistance. The one-sided argument should appeal to the self-interests and value systems of key participants. If anxiety needs to be aroused about the consequences of failure to act, it is done so out of concern, loyalty, and identification with the organization, not out of dissent.

Throughout the persuasion process, practitioners must assess reactions, and determine which positions are fixed and which are flexible. They may need to change problem definition, proposed solutions, or the content and method of presentation in response to their continuing appraisal. They may, for example, broaden the proposed solution to encompass the interests of neutral participants. Conversely, they may narrow the proposal in order to eliminate the objections of a powerful participant. Implicit in effective persuasion is skillful negotiation and bargaining (Brager, Specht, and Torezyner 1987).

Smithdale High School is situated in one of the poorest cities in the state and suffers a high incidence of adolescent pregnancy and excessive rates of school truancy and drop-out. Violent encounters among students have increased significantly in the past three years. In response, the superintendent of schools created a task force to study the problem and make recommendations. Sharply divergent perspectives developed among the task force members. The school social worker argued against a proposed program that focused on punishment and advocated involving students in problem identification and resolution. She explained that without student involvement any intervention will be sabotaged. Other members disagreed. After considerable debate, the task force recommended and the principal implemented a discipline-management program of unilateral, non-negotiable interventions with students who engage in violent conflict. Administrators dictate the terms of conflict resolution and students are expected to comply.

Table 11.5	Engagement Methods and Skills

• *Select appropriate engagement method:*	Demonstrating method is responsive to problems associated with professional function and program gaps
	Collaborating method is responsive in open organizations where goal consensus exists and either equity in resource distribution or presence of close interpersonal relationships
	Persuading method is responsive in organizations characterized by goal dissent and disparity of power
	Creating conflict method is used only in situations where a more extreme form of pressure is required as in violations of client rights
• *Demonstrate through action and proposed change:*	Persistent and skillful doing
• *Collaborate with colleagues in identifying problem and effective solution:*	Invite common search for data, possible solutions, and resources
• *Persuade colleagues of problem and solution:*	Clearly define problem
	Illustrate the problem's seriousness with facts, case material, and testimony of colleagues and/or clients
	Present case of the effectiveness of the plan for solution
	Provide evidence for feasibility and desirability of proposed solution
	Use two-sided argument when resistance is anticipated
	Use one-sided argument when positive response is expected
	Use humor and role-play to deflect resistance
	Use language compatible with the values of the audience
	Arouse anxiety out of concern, loyalty, and identification with organization
	Propose alternative solutions and involve staff in process
	Prepare extreme solution and pursue a reasonable compromise
• *Engage in conflict to resolve problem:*	Evaluate potential organization responses and personal/structural resources
	Assume stance of organizational loyalty rather than moral indignation
	Reduce individual risk through collectiveaction
	Develop public commitment for each member

The social worker viewed violence in part as a response to powerlessness and oppression. As the lone voice representing the rich social work tradition of citizen participation and self-determination, she believed that the authoritarian program would not address the problem and might even increase the violence.

Education has its own traditions and mandates. Its institutions often preach democratic principles and values, but practice autocracy (Moriarty and McDonald 1991). Students are alienated by the discrepancy between philosophy and practice. As the social worker anticipated, the emphasis on unilateral decision-making and punishment led to the program's failure. The program instructed students about unacceptable activities and behaviors and the consequences for noncompliance, but it did not provide alternate means for dealing with conflict. Even the teachers were frustrated and ceased to carry out the program.

Ironically, the program's deficits increased the social worker's stature. She was asked to chair a committee to explore other alternatives and was given permission to invite the president of student government to attend. After extensive review, the committee selected a program with two important components: (1) teachers will be trained to resolve conflicts in the classroom and to incorporate a conflict-resolution curriculum into regular lessons and (2) teachers will be taught group process skills and undertake self-exploration to expand awareness of their own conflict-resolution styles. Students are to observe teachers instructing and modeling alternate conflict-resolution strategies. Other high schools have reported dramatic success in decreasing the incidence of school violence through this comprehensive program involving new curriculum content and increased ease and skills experienced by teachers.

The committee's recommendations were approved by the superintendent, the principal, the teacher's union, and the student government. The superintendent secured private funding for the training program. However, before the program could be implemented, an unrelated controversy erupted. A group of teachers was concerned about severe depressive symptoms affecting a Latino colleague. Her depression had a negative impact on the students. These teachers could no longer ignore the problem and asked the principal, a Latino male, to furnish a medical leave of absence. The principal denied the request. Some teachers wanted to appeal to the superintendent, a non-Latino. At this point, the teachers split along ethnic and racial lines. The Latino and African-American teachers refused to go over the principal's head and warned the white teachers not to do so. A severe rift ensued when the white teachers met with the superintendent. Racial polarization replaced a cooperative faculty climate.

In many school districts, administrators and teachers "dictate the role social workers will play in the educational setting" (Williams 1990:240), but in this instance, the social worker maintained a proactive stance in the school system. Although aware of her professional status as a "resident guest" in a host setting (Dane and Simon 1991), she persisted in urging the racially divided factions to deal with their conflict for the sake of the students. After much pleading and informal networking, agreement was reached to use this discord as a case example for training in conflict resolution. In preparing to undertake the teacher training program, the social worker contacted the trainers to alert them to the specific issues confronting the school's faculty. In her final report, she noted, "I hope a collective concern for the student body will sustain the training effort—now all I can do is hope."

Conflict is a method rarely used by low-ranking participants in dealing with organizational problems. The low-ranking practitioner is vulnerable to reprisals, and caution is necessary. At the same time, certain situations, such as violations of clients' rights, do require more adversarial actions, especially in the face of marked dissent over goals and methods. Before engaging in organizational conflict, however, practitioners must evaluate possible responses and their own resources. If either their job or personal credibility is at stake, only severe injustices and unethical practices should require such risks and sacrifices. If ambiguity about organizational response or worker resources exists, accommodation is only achieved through a test of respective strengths (Fisher 1994).

In undertaking individual adversarial action, the worker holds to a stance of organizational loyalty rather than one of moral indignation. Polite, respectful disobedience can be highly effective. For example, a family agency required workers to submit confidential data to the state department of social services. After several unsuccessful efforts by a practitioner to have the policy changed, the supervisor demanded her confidential data. The social worker politely refused the request, citing the ethical principle of client confidentiality. The worker also expressed concern about the negative impact on the agency and its reputation, "should the practice become public." The agency retreated and renegotiated the arrangement with the department of social services. Had this practitioner escalated the issue, an unnecessary crisis would have been precipitated. Calling attention to negative consequences was successful because it provided leverage for testing relative power.

Group action can diminish the risk of reprisal. Collective positions, manifestos, petitions, or demonstrations are effective methods in dealing with powerful harmful practices and organizational participants. The alliance or coalition must be firmly unified and committed (Burghard 1982; Haggstrom 1984; Kahn 1992). If members are intimidated and become mutually exploitative, a long period of powerlessness and despair will result. In undertaking collective action, workers must first be sure each member is publicly committed to the cause in order to avoid finding themselves with a group of "closet advocates" whose barks are ferocious, but whose bites are mild. Methods and skills of the engagement phase are listed in Table 11.5.

Implementation and Institutionalization

After a desired outcome is adopted, it needs to be put into action. Initial acceptance does not insure implementation. For the practitioner, much work and frustration may still lie ahead. An adopted change can be negated by a delay in execution. It can be distorted, undermined, or scaled down by executive participants, organizational processes, or personnel responsible for the change (Holloway 1987).

Executive staff uncommitted or opposed to the adopted change may interfere with implementation. They might simply be preoccupied with other issues, or pay insufficient attention to necessary follow-up, postpone implementation, or provide inadequate personnel and financial resources.

In the implementation phase, informal and formal structures can be used to reduce stress associated with the change. To maintain administrators' cooperation, the innovation has to be experienced as being in their self-interest. After a worker influenced a union local to establish a steering committee to improve retiree programs, the local's director changed the meeting time to discourage attendance. His ambivalence was evident. The worker came to this conclusion:

I realized our failure to take the interests of the director into account. To repair the damage, I invited him out for lunch and discovered he had long been interested in holding a reunion of the local's membership. I asked him to bring his idea to the steering committee, and I guaranteed my support. At the next meeting, I backed his suggestion for a reunion. The steering committee agreed to do the work, collect necessary data, send out invitations, etc. He was pleased, participated throughout the meeting, and agreed to distribute our minutes to the membership.

The steering committee as an innovative structure was responsive to the director's interests. His stress was decreased, and his involvement and commitment were increased. Acquiring and maintaining the commitment of key participants is always essential. Their support provides the context and sets the tone for other participants' cooperation.

The social worker seeks to keep the agreed-on change in people's minds and on the organizational agenda by assigning specific tasks to participants. If possible, a feedback system is built into the proposal such as regular progress reports to staff to provide monitoring and accountability (Zaltman, Duncan, and Holbeck 1973).

Some organizational structures are incompatible with particular innovations. Even organizational features that promote acceptance of innovation can nevertheless hinder its implementation. Organizations of low formality, for example, tend to encourage innovation, but also tend to hinder its institutionalization. In changing from a traditional to an open classroom approach, for example, a school maintained its rigid temporal schedules and grading system. These structures undermined the desired change (Gross, Giacquinta, and Bernstein 1971). While some structures are too rigid, others are too flexible to support and integrate the innovation. Therefore, even before an adopted change is implemented, the worker attempts to modify existing structures to increase the chance of success.

As a new format for team meetings was adopted, I realized that the time structure could cause frustration. At the first meeting under our new plan, I wondered aloud if there would be sufficient time to discuss patients scheduled for presentation at the end of the meeting. Staff agreed to extend rounds another fifteen minutes.

The staff found the additional time beneficial. It eliminated the potential for stress arising from many designated tasks competing for time. Now each would receive sufficient attention.

Staff assigned to carry out the innovation represent another potential obstacle to implementation. Expectations may be unclear, or the staff may unwittingly distort the objective. Participants may lack knowledge and skills for performing the required tasks. Others may lack sufficient motivation to commit themselves to the new way of doing things. Still others may be overwhelmed by the additional demands and competing time pressures. From the outset, social workers must concern themselves with organizational participants assigned responsibility for implementation. They are sensitive to and empathic with the anxiety aroused by changes in role expectations. They must provide a clear conception of role requirements, building into the implementation in-service training, consultation, and ongoing support necessary to ensure interest, motivation, and skilled task performance.

Throughout the implementation phase, the worker must pay careful attention to task performers and needs for approval and recognition. After a designated time, implementation is evaluated to determine whether the desired objective is being achieved and whether unexpected negative consequences have appeared. If modifications are needed, they are instituted before the innovation is standardized and formalized (Pressman and Wildavsky 1973).

Once an innovation is in place it is important to evaluate the extent to which the problem has been ameliorated. If the innovation has been successful, the "final task is to stabilize it to ensure its permanence in the system" (Holloway 1987:734). When the change in an organization's purpose, structure, and procedures or services arrangements is no longer perceived as change, but as an integral part of its ongoing activities, the innovation is institutionalized. Proof that an innovation is integrated into the organization's structure is its remaining essentially the same even though some initial participants are no longer involved. To assure continuity, the worker lodges the innovation with a person having staying power or who occupies a stable status.

> Every six months team composition changes with rotation of residents. In addition, the change of the chief resident means that a new personality and work style are introduced. The head nurse is key to maintaining stability, so the structural change was lodged with her. She orients new team members to the workings of the floor—the routines, procedures, etc.—and will see that the change is continued.

Other linking devices may be developed to ensure stability, such as inviting new staff to observe existing processes and procedures, or preparing a manual to formalize staff responsibilities. Whatever the method, the worker continues to monitor the institutionalization of the innovation.

TWELVE

INFLUENCING LEGISLATION, REGULATIONS, AND ELECTORAL POLITICS

Social work's commitment to social justice through political activity originated a century ago in the practice of settlement workers such as Jane Addams and charity organization workers such as Josephine Shaw Lowell (Germain and Hartman 1980).

Contemporary life-modeled practice actively embraces the commitment to a just society through the participation of practitioners in political activity.[1] The professional goal of political influencing by social workers is to attain more effective legislative and regulatory responses to human needs, especially those of the poor and other powerless populations. Political influencing, when based on knowledge of policy development, legislative and regulatory processes, and electoral politics is effective and valuable across local, state, provincial, and federal levels of government. In its simplest form, political influencing includes telephoning and writing letters to the decision-makers and persuading others to do the same. In its more complex forms political influencing includes lobbying, coalition-building, testifying, demonstrating, rallying public support, and working with the press and other media on behalf of desired legislation.

In a quite different mode, many social workers are engaged in paid or volunteer work in political campaigns of candidates who support social welfare issues. Some social workers run for elective office and increasing numbers are elected. Others serve as staff assistants or as consultants to a state legislator or a member of Congress, and still others fill appointed positions that carry political power, such as commissioners or directors of local, state, or federal agencies.

Political advocacy by social workers consists of:

1. influencing legislative policies by lobbying for or against new statutes and social policies or those being considered for modification. This requires knowledge of legislative process, existing law and policy, and methods and skills to influence policy development.
2. influencing official regulations that control how statutes and policies are carried out by lobbying the people who write the regulations. This requires knowledge of the regulatory process, existing regulations that bear on the particular concern, and methods and skills used to modify regulations that go beyond statutory authority or the spirit of the law.
3. influencing the electoral process through work in the political campaigns of candidates for elective office who support the advancement of social justice.

Influencing Legislation

The Legislative Process

The following description of the legislative process by which a bill becomes a law in one state (Mississippi) is similar to that in most other states. First, the original idea is drafted into a bill, which must be introduced by a legislator. The bill is then assigned to a committee and may be referred to a subcommittee for research. If rejected by the subcommittee, the bill dies. If approved, the bill then goes to the full committee for debate and amendment. If rejected by the committee, the bill dies. If approved, it proceeds to the full membership of the lower chamber for further debate and amendment. If rejected by the lower chamber, the bill dies. If approved, it proceeds to the higher chamber where it undergoes the same process. If the bill is passed in both chambers without change in language, it is sent to the governor, who has five days to sign or veto the bill. If it is signed or if no action is taken, the bill becomes law. If the governor vetoes the bill, it may still become law if the legislature overrides the veto by two-thirds vote in both chambers. If the bill had passed both chambers with a change of language, however, it goes to a joint committee for clarification and compromise of differences. The amended bill then goes back to both chambers for a vote and, if approved, it is sent to the governor for signature (Van Gheluwe and Barber 1986).

Social Work Lobbying

Successful social work lobbying requires information gathering, engaging legislators, actions to influence, networking, coalition building, and testifying.

Information gathering.   Researching bills is the base for effective lobby-ing, whether bills propose a new statute or seek to amend, revise, supple-ment, or delete an existing one. The social worker who seeks to influence the passage or defeat of a particular bill needs to undertake both substan-tive research on the contents of the bill and procedural research on its history.

Substantive research rests on a review of the existing laws that the bill seeks to change. This is followed by writing a position statement (especially important in testifying). The position statement includes:

1. an analysis of the modifications or additions to the present law as proposed by the bill, including strengths and weaknesses of the bill; new problems that the bill may create; and needed amendments to the bill (Kleinkauf 1981)
2. facts that support or negate key points in the bill
3. costs of implementing the bill; source of funding; and new positions required to carry out the legislation. This information is usually contained in the financial impact statement prepared by the legislative staff or the rele-vant governmental agency
4. Positions held on the bill by relevant governmental agencies and other groups. Their positions yield information on points made for and against the bill, and on potential allies or opponents.

In procedural research the social worker must determine the following:

1. which committee referrals the bill originally had and why; where it is now; and where it has yet to go
2. if a similar bill exists in the other chamber of the legislature and, if so, the committees to which it has been referred
3. if the bill has already been amended and if so, where, when, why, and how this was done. This information gives clues to what in the original bill was objectionable or unworkable and whether the bill has the support of key legislators
4. identify the sponsors of the bill and their motive in introducing it
5. review the legislature's rules of procedures for conducting legislative busi-ness. Copies are available from committee staff.

Analyzing the committee and its members is as important as analyzing the bill (Kleinkauf 1981, 1989). Data needed include:

1. details about each committee member such as background, constituencies, and interests. Other influences are personal philosophy, political conse-quences of the vote, party affiliation, and issues on which the member cam-paigned. From such information the social worker can construct a commit-tee profile useful in lobbying and preparing testimony.

2. voting records of committee members, although care should be exercised in generalizing from them to a likely vote on the bill.
3. information on committee practices, special procedures, and the protocol followed in the committee's hearings can be obtained from committee staff and by observing the committee in action.

In this and other research, the staff of legislative committees, the staff assistant of a friendly legislator, or a lobbyist from a NASW chapter or League of Women Voters can be of assistance, and it is well worth [taking] time to become acquainted with helpful people who are available. (Kleinkauf 1981:298–99)

Engaging legislators and influential officials.   The social worker seeking to influence legislation needs to develop personal relationships with legislators and initiate frequent contact with them (Mathews 1982:625). Regardless of the lobbyist social worker's party affiliation, legislators are likely to be influenced by the most active segments of their constituencies. Interest groups and individuals (including lobbyist social workers) who are the most influential maintain frequent contact with legislators and provide them with technical and political information. Reputation, professionalism, and the ability to influence constituents appear to be more important in legislators' assessment of lobbyists than party affiliation or ideology. It is important that the social worker stay involved and keep communicating to establish and maintain visibility, credibility, and identity (Mathews 1982:627).

Data needed to analyze the committee include:

1. details about each committee member such as background, constituencies, and interests. Other influences are personal philosophy, political consequences of the vote, party affiliation, and issues on which the member campaigned. From such information the social worker can construct a committee profile useful in lobbying and preparing testimony.
2. voting records of committee members, although care should be exercised in generalizing from them to a likely vote on the bill.
3. information on committee practices, special procedures, and the protocol followed in the committee's hearings can be obtained from committee staff and by observing the committee in action.

The social worker can set up an interview with a legislator through the legislator's secretary. Copies of the proposed bill and a typed position statement for the legislator should be left with the secretary in advance of the appointment. Such interviews are usually very brief. "Generally, the legislators' first (and maybe only) question is 'Who is against it?' They want to know who they'll offend if they support it. You have to give an honest answer, else you lose credibility" (Dempsey 1988). Occasionally, social workers have a chance to describe the merits of a bill they favor or the disadvantages of a bill they oppose. "But most often legislators plan to go along with the recommendation of the committee the bill came out of or to vote along party lines" (Dempsey 1988:25–26). In any event, an interview is likely to reveal the legislator's position on a bill.

The support of the governor is essential in light of the governor's veto privilege (Dear and Patti 1982). In order to influence his or her view of the proposed bill, it is wise to engage people close to the governor in arranging an interview (and perhaps a photo opportunity) to briefly present the proposed bill, other endorsements, and support of the relevant agency. If an interview is not possible, a brief letter can be left with the governor's executive assistant, together with copies of the proposed bill and the social worker's position on the bill. Administrators of relevant state agencies can be important sources of support because legislators listen seriously to agencies' representatives. Agency-requested legislation generally has a significantly better chance of passage than legislation without such a request.

Interventions used in legislative lobbying. Among a series of actions suggested for use by single-issue social workers who have limited power and resources (Dear and Patti 1982) are the following:

1. Ask more than one legislator to sponsor a bill. Multiple sponsors tend to make the bill more visible and they increase the power that will push the bill past legislative obstacles. They can press for a hearing, make necessary compromises and trade-offs to move the bill out of committee, push to get it scheduled by the rules committee, get it out of the rules committee and on to the floor of the legislature, and apply pressure to get it passed by both houses.

2. Obtain the sponsorship of the majority party. It is even more beneficial to obtain meaningful bipartisan sponsorship with a member of the majority as primary sponsor.

3. Enlist influential legislators willing to exercise their influence in promoting the bill. Committee chairs and committee members (looked to by other members because of their expertise in particular areas) are influential. When a bill touches on a concern of a legislator's constituency, active sponsorship is likely. Hence, the social worker's awareness of potential effects on a lawmaker's constituency is crucial in determining a legislator's position since the effects on the constituency are often the basis of the legislator's vote (Kleinkauf 1989). In controversial areas, legislators with secure electoral margins are more likely to be responsive to interest groups and to support unpopular causes (Dear and Patti 1982).

4. Use the amending process to promote a favorable outcome for a bill. Amendments are a means to achieve passage. Periodic reevaluation of legislators' positions on amended bills is useful, as their support and opposition to a bill shift as amendments are made. Keeping a running vote tally until

final passage is helpful so neutral committee members can be identified and given special attention.

Networking. A network of social workers who can push a bill is an important resource of the lobbyist social worker. Such networks might include practitioners who live in a legislator's district, those active in their party, social agencies with legislators on their board, and social worker politicians. For example, a social worker lobbyist asked a county commissioner to explain a social work licensing bill to her reluctant state senator. She did and convinced him of the need for the bill's passage (Dempsey 1980).

"Clearing the bill" is part of networking. It might include negotiating with state agencies and other groups that will be affected by a bill in order to gain their support. In lobbying for the social work licensing bill mentioned above, the social worker first cleared the bill with the state's department of social and health services, which employs social workers; with the department of licensing, which would administer the law; and with the department of personnel, which writes job specifications and professional exams. Clearing a bill also might include reaching compromises so that all parties are satisfied. When several state agencies are involved, however, satisfactory compromises are difficult to attain.

Networking also includes establishing working relations with legislative staff. For example, an Alaskan lobbyist social worker sought to influence legislation or budget appropriations for an AFDC grant increase. She found that legislative staff in the offices of the bill's sponsor and the committee chair were key to success. Advocate social workers have ready access to legislative staff, who are the links between their legislator and lobbyists (Kleinkauf 1988).

Of related interest is the experience of a social work professor and his students interested in political influencing. They met with the staff aides of a United States Senator and a member of Congress. Both meetings centered on AIDS. In discussion with the senator's staff aide on the issue of testing for HIV, a student described the agonizing dilemma of rape victims who do not know whether the rapist was infected. Given the civil liberties and privacy concerns involved, serious questions can arise for any social worker. The staff aide had not thought about the issue from this perspective. In the meeting with the Congress member's staff aide, another student described her frustration at not being able to find and provide services to infants who may be infected, and how this lack of services was a strong deterrent to finding and retaining foster parents. Again, the issue was entirely new to this staff aide. The social work professor comments,

> I tell students in class that social workers are uniquely situated to "witness" the effects of social policies on the lives of the people they serve and try to help.

In both instances, I was struck by the truth and importance [of being thus situated] that came from the mouths of students who were simply reporting difficulties which they and clients face as a result of policies designed and organized by others.　　　　　　　　　　　　　　　　　　　　　　　(Rosen 1988)

Networking among supporters is also carried out by groups of social workers in politically oriented task forces or committees. Group actions include sending out newsletters and legislative alerts, and establishing telephone "trees" for calling legislators when a vote on a bill is imminent. Political influencing sometimes requires the group to garner more widespread public support for a proposed bill from voters, prominent individuals, and organizations. Two highly successful advocacy groups drew on similar networking interventions (Van Gheluwe and Barber 1986; Bonilla-Santiago 1989):

- Gather information to justify the need for a bill's passage or defeat.
- Use the collected information in awareness and educational campaigns directed toward the public, professional groups, and legislators.
- Solicit written endorsements from professional groups or prominent individuals and signed petitions from voters.
- Send news releases to newspapers and organization newsletters.
- Offer presentations to groups and organizations on the issues.
- Prepare and broadcast radio spots.

Additional interventions identified by Gheluwe and Barber are included in a case illustration following the next section.

Coalition-building.　　Coalitions in the political arena are formed for a limited purpose and are usually temporary. When a coalition achieves its objective, the members may decide to dissolve it or to take advantage of the linkages that were developed and build a new coalition to address a new issue (Roberts-DeGennero 1986). Coalitions imply the joint use of resources, but resources are attached to each member and thus can be withdrawn at any time (Weisner 1983). Coalitions of organizations and social workers, other professionals, and interested community members can and do influence legislation, policy making, and they advocate for social change more effectively than separate and competing interest groups. Especially in a time of economic stringency, competition among agencies for limited resources heightens. It can be destructive of services, agency budgets, and interagency relationships, and is apt to be ineffective. During the 1980s, human services coalitions for legislative influencing grew in number and size in response to severe cuts in services and programs sorely needed by vulnerable families and individuals.

INFLUENCING LEGISLATION 403

If each interest group goes its own way . . . legislators will be bombarded with a disorganized collection of special interests fighting for their own human service programs and entitlements. This is not likely to be well received in state capitols or county seats, nor will it lead to an increase in the total amount of funds allocated for human service programs. It is also unlikely to serve the best interests of the poor and disadvantaged for whom such programs are intended.

(Weisner 1983:293)

Agencies and other groups that decide to band together in a coalition can benefit from pooling their resources and working cooperatively to "educate" and influence political decision-makers. Also, a broad-based, unified voice is more apt to be heard than is the cacophony of competing voices. For example, the Bay Area Advocates for Human Services, a coalition of agencies and advocacy groups, was founded in 1981 in response to state funding cuts in social programs. It grew to be a consolidating force in the San Francisco bay area. Perceived benefits included the passage of favorable legislation for the human services (a benefit for nonmembers as well) and increased referrals and publicity for member agencies. The most frequently mentioned benefit by participants was "their enhanced ability to gather and exchange information in an increasingly volatile and complex human services field" (Weisner 1983:304).

If an issue is specific and time-bound, then organizations with conflicting interests are more willing to overlook their differences and form a coalition for a more powerful impact. But if an issue is wide in scope, it is more likely to highlight differences that, in turn, could reinforce self-interest, discourage organizational cooperation, and promote narrow interest politics (Roberts-DeGennero 1986).

Hearings, preparing testimony, and testifying. Hearings draw media and public attention to a proposed bill, although they also run the risk of expanding public opposition. The social worker should press for open committee hearings. When such hearings are held, the social worker then attempts to arrange for testimony on behalf of the bill by expert witnesses, especially staff members of relevant governmental agencies. Depending on the nature of the bill, former or potential clients, practitioners, community leaders, representatives of special interest groups, and independent professionals can also be effective. Presentations based on research or intimate familiarity with the subject (case vignettes) are persuasive to legislators (Dear and Patti, 1982).

Preparing testimony. Substantive and procedural research, described in the first section of this chapter, are basic to effective testimony. Prior to the hearing, the social worker develops a position paper on the topic, setting forth a general philosophy of what is hoped to be achieved (approved by the social worker's organization). Next, written testimony is developed from the major points made in the position paper. Written testimony should not be read but spoken from an outline in order to maintain eye contact with committee members that sustains their interest.

Oral testimony should briefly describe the issue addressed by the bill and the position taken. Attention should be called to what the bill will and will not accomplish: objectivity enhances the credibility of testimony. Professional terminology and arguments based on values instead of facts should be avoided (Kleinkauf 1981:300). The social worker must be prepared to answer questions from the committee and to furnish additional information and comments on particular points of the bill. Copies of the position paper and the written testimony should be distributed to committee members beforehand, and copies should also be available at the hearing.

A community social worker on the staff of Seattle Legal Services lobbied the state legislature on behalf of senior citizens. In the following instance, she opposed an adult protective service bill sponsored by the Department of Social and Health Services:

> She first tried to persuade agency decision-makers to withdraw the bill, but was unsuccessful. Next, she wrote position papers, spoke to legislators, and testified against the bill, arguing that it was redundant and lacked the protection of due process. The bill died. The lobbyist social worker concluded "If you create enough controversy [when lobbying against a bill], there's a good chance [legislators] won't touch it with a ten-foot pole."   (Cohen 1980:27)

Table 12.1 summarizes social work lobbying at the state level:

An Illustration of Influencing Legislation

This example illustrates some of the various methods of legislative lobbying that were used to gain passage of the Limited Medically Needy Bill in Mississippi despite difficult economic conditions. The proposed bill provided (a) prenatal and delivery services for pregnant women who are married but are as poor as solo parent recipients of Medicaid, and (b) outpatient services for children from intact families who are as poor as families on welfare whose children receive those services. Need for the new law arose from a Mississippi Medicaid regulation that required recipients to be aged, blind, disabled, or living in families in which one parent had deserted, was disabled, or had died. Congress had passed an act in 1981 that addressed such budget constraints by allowing individual states to cover married poor people with partial rather than full Medicaid benefits. Partial benefits had to include prenatal and delivery services and outpatient health care for the children of eligible recipients.

Figure 12.1	State Legislative Process

- idea drafted into a bill
- introduced by legislator
- assigned to committee
- either referred to subcommittee for research or rejected
- goes to full committee, if approved, for debate and/or amendment
- proceeds, if approved, to the full membership of the chamber for further debate and/or amendment
- proceeds, if approved, to the other chamber where it undergoes the same process
- goes to joint committee for clarification if one chamber changes the language
- returns to both chambers for vote on amended bill
- sent to the governor, if approved by both chambers, who has five days to sign or veto
- becomes law, if bill is signed by governor
- becomes law, if legislature overrides veto by a two-thirds vote in both chambers

Health care advocates saw this enabling act as a cost-effective way to provide desperately needed services in the face of the state's high infant mortality rate, low per capita income, and growing unemployment. The Coalition for Mothers and Babies and other supporters of the idea of the Limited Medically Needed Program formed a task force for the bill's passage. It was composed of the following Mississippi state organizations: Health Care Commission, Conference on Social Welfare, Department of Health, NASW chapter, and Children's Defense Fund office. Strategy meetings were open to all. Strategies included information gathering, awareness and education, advocating and soliciting support, networking, and monitoring.

Information gathering. Data were compiled that would justify the need for the program. Reports on costs and numbers served were obtained from other states, and Mississippi statistics were analyzed. Information gathered was used in awareness and educational campaigns directed toward the public, professional groups, and legislators.

Awareness and education. In addition to networking activities mentioned in the earlier section, the task force developed a slide tape show and distributed it statewide. Public awareness packets were sent to the press and legislators. Information booths were set up at fairs and other activities around the state. These local functions received television coverage as did a legislative rally held in the state capitol. The latter included a press conference by parents in need of the proposed program.

Advocating and soliciting support. Over fifty organizations statewide gave written endorsements of the bill. Hundreds of petitions were signed. Key legislators were identified and lobbied by NASW and other groups to work actively for passage.

Networking. Supporters received continuously updated information through legislative alerts and a newsletter from the Coalition for Mothers and Babies. Through an extensive telephone tree, nine calls allowed over 400 people statewide to be given updated news about the bill's progress. At the point when a negative decision about the bill was about to be made, the tree was activated and within an hour over 100 calls were made to the capitol in support of the bill. The vote that followed was in favor of the bill.

Monitoring. Subcommittee, committee, and floor actions that dealt with the bill were constantly monitored by task force members. All discussion and voting on the bill was observed by one or more supporters to monitor legislators' voting patterns. This facilitated (a) passing on pertinent information to legislators who were supporting the bill, (b) soliciting statewide support at crucial times, (c) forwarding accurate information on the bill's progress to supporters around the state, and (d) securing an accurate count of who voted for and against the bill.

Outcome. The bill passed both houses and was signed by the governor on April 1, 1983, to be implemented by July 1984. During the 1984 legislative session, however, severe revenue problems led to reducing many state-funded programs. A bill was passed to delay implementation for two years. In light of the economic situation, program supporters agreed to a one-year delay and were successful in persuading the legislators to accept the change. In the 1985 session, funding was secured for the program.

Table 12.2 summarizes lobbying skills.

The Regulatory Process[2]

Regulatory Context

All publicly funded social welfare programs are carried out within a regulatory context. Such regulated programs include child welfare services, income maintenance (especially in appeals processes), aspects of services to the mentally ill, and health care. When social welfare legislation is enacted, the authority to implement the law is delegated to a governmental administrative agency that was created by the legislation or empowered by it to carry out the law. The agency develops regulations and rules about how service providers are to operate their programs that fall within the purview of the statute. The regulations must stay within the limits of the intent and policy goals of the legislation. At the federal and state levels judicial review "tests whether the agency has exceeded its constitutional or statutory authority, has properly interpreted the applicable law, has conducted a fair hearing, and has not acted capriciously and unreasonably" (Robinson and Gellhorn 1972:33, cited by Albert 1983).

Figure 12.2   Lobbying Skills of the Political Advocating Method

---

- *Gather substantive information:*   Review existing laws
                                        Study strengths and weaknesses of proposed bill
                                        Learn facts that support or negate key points
                                        Study implementation costs
                                        Research positions held on the bill by key actors
- *Gather procedural information:*   Review committee route for bill
                                        Explore current status
                                        Assess sponsors and their interests
                                        Learn legislature's rules and procedures
- *Engage legislators and*   Study legislator's background (voting
  influential officials: record, constituencies, interests)
                                        Develop personal relationships
                                        Maintain frequent contacts
                                        Develop and maintain contacts with persons close
                                           to the governor
                                        Gain support of administrators of relevant state
                                           agencies
- *Influence legislative processes:*   Seek multiple legislative sponsors
                                        Seek support of majority party
                                        Seek support of influential legislators
                                        Use amending process for promoting favorable outcome
- *Develop networks:*   Find others to support (social work politicians,
                                           social workers living in a legislator's district)
                                        Clear bill with other groups
                                        Find people to bear witness regarding need
                                        Send out newsletters and legislative alerts
- *Build coalitions:*   Join organizational and personnel resources
                                        Educate and influence political decision-makers

An administrative agency develops three kinds of regulations:

1. Procedural rules (methods of operation) are usually authorized by the statute and are binding on the administrative agency. For example, if a regulated unit such as a social agency can show that the administrative agency did not comply with its own rules, the administrative agency's decision can be reversed.
2. Interpretive rules are issued as a guide for the administrative agency's staff and regulated parties of how the agency will interpret its legislative mandate. Policy statements announced through a press release are subject to public scrutiny for the purpose of influencing the regulatory environment in which a social agency operates.
3. Substantive rules are actually administrative laws through which administrators exercise their constitutional administrative powers. Notice and hearing usually must precede issuance of a substantive rule.

Publishing regulations in the Federal Register (or, in the case of a state statute, in a State Register) prior to implementation fulfills requirements for notice to the public and allows sufficient time for public comment. Such comment may be written or, in some instances, offered at a public hearing. Following the comment period, comments are analyzed, and public influence, if any, has an effect. Final regulations are then adopted and published.

Influencing the Regulatory Process

As in the legislative context, a social worker advocate gains influence in the regulatory context through effective lobbying for or against particular regulations.

> Effective social work advocacy in the regulatory process will, as a practical matter, depend on [workers'] ability to analyze the regulations, properly organize written comments and testimony for hearings, and engage in pre- and post-notice activities to maximize their input.   (Albert 1983:477)

Analyzing the regulations.   Social workers must understand the statutory authority for the regulation before they can argue whether it is within the scope of the statute upon which it is based. In order to assess the validity of the statutory authority for the regulation, the following questions for social workers to ask themselves are suggested (Statsky 1975:140, cited by Albert 1983):

- Is there some statute in existence which gives the agency authority to pass regulations on the general subject matter of the regulations before you?
- Is there a statute which is the authority for the particular regulation before you?
- Is the agency's interpretation of its own regulation consistent with the statute upon which it is based?
- Is your interpretation of the regulation consistent with the statute upon which it is based?

Organizing for hearings.   The comment period is an opportunity for social workers to influence the scope and type of the final rules. Social work administrators and supervisors, for example, will understand a regulation's likely impact on social services. A carefully drafted written response to the agency or a well-structured presentation at a public hearing could be influential. And successful coalition-building might increase the number of people who write comments or provide testimony at the hearing. Hearings as formal settings require a more structured response than a written comment:

- Identify yourself and your agency's interest in the matter.
- Explain the regulation's impact on the people served and describe your agency's unique expertise.

- Provide the reasons for your agency's conclusions regarding the impact on those served.
- Recognize the legitimacy of other views, but refute them when necessary.
- Provide clear documentation (data, case examples) to support your agency's position and its long connection with the regulatory topic.

Pre- and postnotice activities. These activities can help to connect the analysis to the written comments or to hearing testimony. They emphasize mutual education, information sharing, and constituency-building to strengthen communication between the administrative agency and the social worker advocate. Both parties have an interest in the potential impact of the regulation; that fact can be used to facilitate negotiation on points of difference.

Prenotice activities include the following:

- Learn about the administrative agency's structure, decision-making hierarchy, jurisdiction, and policy statements.
- Become acquainted with the administrative agency's staff to identify sources of support or opposition.
- Share views so they will understand your professional interests and the extent to which they reflect the interests of other service providers.
- Identify staff within the administrative agency who have expert knowledge in the pertinent substantive areas.
- Research the administrative agency position to predict potential decisions and to identify interest groups that seem to dominate agency decision-making.

Postnotice activities following participation in the hearings include the following:
- Maintain communications with other affected service providers and sympathetic staff of the administrative agency in order to keep in touch with developments.

- Monitor the relevant regulations and their subsequent hearings for actual or potential implementation problems.
- Share relevant new information with your agency's staff and mobilize support among other service providers.
- Stand ready to organize service providers against a proposed or final regulation.

The philosophy underlying these pre- and postnotice activities in regard to administrative regulations and rules is congruent with the life-modeled practice emphasis on the exchanges between people and their environment and its efforts to improve the level of fit. Social worker advocate participation in the regulatory process is significant because many social services fall within some administrative agency's jurisdiction.

After those who are interested in or affected by the regulations have been given an opportunity to be heard, final regulations are issued.

A Case Study

An illustration of discriminatory actions against welfare recipients that went beyond any existing regulations in Quebec's welfare administration was reported by Torczyner (1991, 1987; Cotler and Torczyner 1988).

> [In 1986 a newly elected] Quebec Minister of Manpower and Income Security announced a new program whereby his department would spend $9 million to hire special investigators to weed out fraud among welfare recipients. He claimed that 20 percent of welfare recipients were frauds or cheats and that these actions would recoup some $80 million annually.   (Torczyner 1991:123)

No public hearings were held as the investigations were introduced as administrative changes that required no change either in law or in regulations. The investigators had no legal authority but they had extraordinary discretionary power:

> A 30-page instruction book detailed how to conduct the inspections to determine almost every aspect of a recipient's financial, personal, and private circumstances: searching for signs of men's clothing, checking bank transactions, looking for signs of concealed employment such as a sewing machine, estimating the value of furniture and books, and examining birth certificates to verify that the correct children were in residence. (124)
>
> Through a media campaign and a court challenge by community social workers and human rights advocates, the investigations were declared unconstitutional by the Quebec Human Rights Commission, a quasi-judicial body empowered to investigate and adjudicate allegations of discrimination that violate the Quebec Charter of Human Rights. (123)

Courtroom and media attention focused on the case of Mrs. Nguyan before the Quebec Human Rights Commission. Mrs. Nguyan was a welfare recipient, single, and a refugee from Southeast Asia living in Montreal. She spoke no English or French and had no relatives living in Canada. The case documented 100 violations of her rights during the time a welfare investigator sought to coerce her into implicating another welfare recipient in fraud. The Commission based its ruling on the Nguyan case. In June 1988 the Commission ruled that the investigations represented systematic violations of the rights of poor people. Its ruling restored the fundamental human rights of all welfare recipients in the province and eliminated the investigations program.

Electoral Politics

Work in Political Campaigns

Many social workers serve as volunteers or as paid organizers in the political campaigns of candidates whom they favor, or whom NASW supports by raising and contributing campaign funds through PACE (Political Action for Candidate Election).

For example, an Arizona social worker coordinated many campaigns for candidates seeking election as local and state legislators, and a United States senator. He canvassed Chicanos, African-Americans, American Indians, white upper-middle-class individuals, blue collar workers, and farmers. He rallied support through radio spots and telephone networks, prepared position papers on social issues for the candidates to use in speeches and interviews; and provided transportation on election day (DeGraw 1980).

> Each political campaign needs coordinators for telephoning, volunteer organizing, polling, canvassing, speech writing, direct mail work, fund raising, and election day activities. These coordinators, who are usually unpaid volunteers in legislative races, build the closest relationships with the candidate.
>
> (Abrams and Goldstein 1982:255–56)

Whether social workers occupy formal or informal leadership roles in a campaign, they can make a unique contribution to maintaining morale during the strains of campaigning. Using social work skills in human relations, the practitioner might help maintain a balance between expressive approaches oriented to feelings and instrumental, task-oriented, approaches to the activity of staff and volunteers, thereby preventing an overemphasis on either (Salcido 1984). For example, a social worker in one congressional campaign provided psychological support not only to staff but to the candidate's family members when they grew anxious about the campaign's outcome. The worker met with them as an existing group and helped them to control their fears and to identify and take on suggesting problem-solving tasks (Salcido 1984:191). Through group process, team building, and networking, social workers can help campaign staff and volunteers coordinate their work and extend support and encouragement to them. Such approaches help avoid common campaign problems of competitiveness and conflict.

Legislative Appointments

Still other social workers in politics are employed as congressional aides or as staff assistants and consultants to state and local legislators. Historically, Harry Hopkins served as Secretary of Commerce and adviser to Franklin D. Roosevelt throughout the years of the Great Depression and World

War II. Other social workers, presumably because of their political activity as well as their professional expertise, have been appointed to high federal posts. They included Wilbur Cohen, Secretary of Health Education and Welfare and Commissioner of Social Security through several administrations), Ada Deer (Assistant Secretary for Indian Affairs, Department of Interior), Thomas P. Glynn III (Deputy Secretary for Vocational and Adult Education, Department of Education), Wendy Sherman (Assistant Secretary, Office of Legislative Affairs, Department of State), Fernando Torres-Gil (Assistant Secretary of Aging, Administration on Aging, Department of Health and Human Services), and Wendell C. Townsend, Jr. (Assistant Secretary for Administration, Department of Agriculture).

A professional social worker served as a staff assistant to Congressman Ted Weiss (D. NY), whose district covered a large area of Manhattan. Her duties included providing help to constituents based on her extensive familiarity with local and governmental agencies. When constituents asked for help, she sought to involve them in solving their own problems (Wallach 1980). For example, she worked with large numbers of immigrants whenever the immigration system bogged down. If a constituent needed additional documents, Wallach determined what were needed, and then had the individual pull them together (recognizing that the ability to do so was limited in some instances). If the problem was resolved, an additional significance of the outcome to the constituent was that she or he had an effective role in collaboration with the congressman's office.

Social Workers in Electoral Politics

Many professional social workers hold high elective office at federal, state, and local levels. As of 1991 they included United States Senator Barbara Mikulski of Maryland; United States Congressmen Ronald Dellums of California and Edolphus Townes of New York; Sidney Barthelemy, mayor of New Orleans, Arthur Agnos, mayor of San Francisco; and Detroit City Council President Pro Tem, Maryann Mahaffey. NASW reported there were at least 120 social workers in office across the country (Goldstein 1991).

Social workers in electoral office bring social work knowledge and values to bear on their public responsibilities. For example, Ruth W. Messinger, a professional social worker, was elected to the New York City Council in 1977 and has been regularly re-elected every four years. Currently, she is Manhattan borough president. She functions in ways that are different from those of other members of the City Council. First, much of her legislative time and energy is devoted to the less popular human service issues. Second, she is sensitive to process, using her social work skills to "track what is happening in a debate and to intervene in ways that help clarify issues, determine possibilities, and build mutual understanding or agreement" (Messinger 1982:214). Third, and most important, the theme of her office is empowerment, "the transfer to others of the knowledge and skills they need to do more for themselves and on their own in future struggles" (Messinger 1985:28).

> The people most affected often know the most about what changes have to be made; that meaningful change will make many people more aware, self-reliant, and organized than they are now; that knowledge and skills social workers and other professionals have are not hard to share; and that we will all benefit if this sharing takes place.   (Messinger 1985:28)

When constituents request that something specific be done, Messinger or her staff undertake to do so. But they also "look for patterns in the work among constituents and for areas in which it is of mutual advantage to organize a lobbying and advocacy force rather than to just give help" (1985:29). In addressing meetings and in cooperating with coalitions and other advocacy groups she makes use of educational opportunities that such work provides. She might explain how to organize people to work on behalf of important issues through demonstrating, writing letters, organizing a petition campaign, and getting others to do so.

Sheldon R. Goldstein, the former Executive Director of NASW, reported (1991:2) that the full time government relations staff in the national office numbered six people, "improving our capacity to look out for the profession's interests on Capitol Hill and in federal regulatory agencies," and many chapters now have lobbyists on staff or under contract to influence the legislative process at the state level. Goldstein added that the most crucial step will be to increase the number of social workers who themselves hold office at all levels of government. In addition to their knowledge of policy development, the principles of persuasion and organizing, and the skills of mediation, social workers know only too well the effects of inadequate social policies on individuals and society. Our knowledge and skills are well suited to politics and policy making. Such activities "are simply logical extensions of our efforts to help people one to one." He invites social workers who are interested in running for office to consult the NASW political affairs office, which is ready to help them evaluate their situation and help to bring their candidacy about. "The sooner the profession begins to work for social worker candidates in every state, the sooner the profession and its values will have articulate voices in legislative committees and on floors of debate" (Abrams and Goldstein 1982:256).

A Study of Social Work Influence

The finding of a study of social workers' influence on lawmakers carried out by Mathews (1982) are disturbing. Twenty-four federal and state legislators representing southwestern Michigan were interviewed using a structured questionnaire. Seven were Democrats and seventeen were Republican. Five were federal lawmakers and nineteen were state legislators.

Those in the sample did not have an accurate picture of who social workers are and what they do. Two gave totally incorrect definitions. Sixteen gave partially adequate definitions, and six gave adequate definitions. Eighteen failed to mention either professional education in social work or human services employment as important in defining a social worker. A significant perception that social work is identical with governmental social services was held by some.

When asked what makes an organization influential, the legislators cited visibility and activity; getting involved in many issues; expertise (providing timely, pertinent, specialized information that the legislator can use); and reputation. Given the names of five professional organizations, NASW was the only organization that had never contacted the legislators in the sample, and it was totally unknown to some. This may be less true now, given NASW's greater emphasis on PACE.[3]

Seven legislators reported receiving twenty or more letters from individual social workers in the prior year. Five reported twenty or more telephone conversations, and five had twenty or more face-to-face contacts with social workers. Only one legislator reported not meeting with any social worker in the prior year. Reasons given for social workers' contacts included concern for programs and threats to their jobs. When legislators were asked how social work might be more effective in influencing the political process, the most frequent response was the development of personal relationships with legislators, followed by letter writing and then by knowledgeable input.

Mathews commented that,

> Social workers need to educate legislators as to who they are, how they are trained, and what it is that distinguishes them from other health and human service professionals. (624)
>
> Social workers should develop personal relationships with legislators and initiate frequent contact with them. (625)

Mathews believes that both as individuals and in their professional associations, social workers tend to align themselves exclusively with liberal, Democratic, urban politicians. Yet

> legislators of all persuasions may be most influenced by the most active section of their constituency, regardless of ideological "fit." This is borne out in comments made by more than one Republican respondent that social workers avoided them because of their conservative ideology. (625)

Increasingly, social workers are undertaking political activity and social agencies are employing social worker advocates. These practitioner advocates and agency advocates are committed to working politically to improve

the quality of life of the populations they serve. Yet given the many professional responsibilities already carried by social workers, why should we take
on such a difficult additional task as political influencing? The answer:

> Because there is a chance that by our "going out on a limb," we will begin a
> process of change that in the short run may benefit our clients and in the long
> run may really have an impact on the fabric of our country. . . . The profession
> will be seen both by clients and decision-makers as a professional resource for
> social planning and change. (Kinoy 1984:9).

Furthermore, in times of fiscal constraint and political conservatism, effective political advocacy by social workers could mean that social welfare programs will not be ignored in the competition for available funds.

> Of course, political advocacy is not always smooth sailing for constituents, leg-
> islators, or social workers. But the satisfaction of engagement itself and the vic-
> tories, however large or modest, continue to support practitioners' professional
> commitment to a just society and their knowledge-based efforts to secure social
> change through skilled political activity and client empowerment. What [social
> work] programs and services exist, who they are available to, and how they are
> funded are decided, at least in part, in the governmental arena, and anything
> decided in that sphere is affected by politics. . . . It would benefit us and our prac-
> tice if our behavior were political too. We . . . ought to be in there slugging, pro-
> fessionally and personally, to influence regulation, law, policy, and budget as
> they affect us and our clients. We . . . should run for office, seek appointment to
> appropriate government positions, appear as lobbyists, urge our professional
> and agency associations to lobby, be active in our communities, and vote—draw-
> ing . . . on our knowledge, our skill, and our professional and personal ethics.
> (Messinger 1982:223)

The social work profession has changed in the process of responding to traditional and new needs, knowledge and skills, and has incorporated new
aspirations and goals to meet new social and cultural conditions. Some
believe that social work is disengaging itself from its historic commitment
to the poor. Walz and Groze (1991) describe the flight from public welfare
work as more graduate students prepare for social work in industry, health
care, family therapy, and private practice which, in general, serve better
educated, more economically secure people. They report studies of current
students that found a shift among many from a desire to help others and to
work for social change, to motivation based on monetary reward. The
authors remind us that clinical resources

> must be given to the most oppressed and most needy people because they have
> no other resources. These clinical resources must be connected structurally to

the advocacy and political processes, both weak links in the current social work and welfare systems. . . . Clinicians should not be comforted by the fact that they may have helped a particular individual or family along the way; their measure of success should be in multiples of people helped through social change. (503)

We believe that many if not most social workers are indeed committed to the poor and oppressed. They serve the chronically mentally ill, the abused and misused, the homeless, those suffering from AIDS, newly arrived immigrants and refugees, poor people in hospital emergency rooms and rural clinics, frail and poor elderly living alone or in institutions, tenants in public housing, children in ghetto schools and their parents, the chronically physically ill, the physically challenged and their families, prisoners, parolees, and probationers.

Social work's professional purpose in society is more necessary and more complex than ever. Practice and education for practice must be consonant with new knowledge, new needs, now social conditions, cultural diversity, and the search for an end to oppression. The profession has always shown the courage and the will to move in new ways in response to social problems and societal failures. We believe that life-modeled practice, through its values and practice principles derived from the ecological perspective is well-suited to the social conditions of today's world and those likely to characterize the opening years of the twenty-first century. Life-modeled practice seeks to elevate the fit between people's needs and their environmental resources. In mediating the exchanges between people and their environments, social workers bear witness against social inequalities and injustice by mobilizing community resources to improve community life, influencing unresponsive organizations to develop responsive policies and services, and by politically influencing local, state, and federal legislation and regulations to support social justice.

Life-modeled practice is committed to responding constructively to changes within the profession and in pertinent new theory and research findings, and to increases in human and environmental diversity. It will continue its quest for ever-broadening understanding of, and respect for, the endless variety of human strengths, exemplified in the lives of all those whom social work serves.

This chapter concludes the journey that readers and the authors together have taken through the realms of life-modeled practice. We believe that the evolving nature of life-modeled practice with its openness to new theory makes it especially suitable for understanding and helping people as they confront new and old life stressors generated by new and emerging social conditions and increasingly difficult national and global issues.

EPILOGUE

This Epilogue presents a brief review of social, economic, cultural, demographic, and technological changes affecting social work practice. We also briefly examine concepts developed in feminism and social constructionism that are congruent with ecological thinking and life-modeled practice.

Societal Issues and Changes

Social Conditions

In the United States, the 1980s and early 1990s saw increasing rates of HIV infection and AIDS; the disappearance of affordable housing leading to homelessness; teenage pregnancy and childbearing, especially but not exclusively in impoverished communities; alcohol and drug abuse among all social and age groups; white-collar crime; drug-related killings, and children killing children; and family violence (Gitterman 1991).

Societal changes also include:

• the failure of public schools to educate or even to retain their pupils

• a growing gap between the rich and poor in which more and more people are at risk of becoming excluded and alienated from society. Especially at risk are minority adult and young adult males shut out from higher education and the job market

• the failure to provide both preventive and acute health care to poor children and their families, with extreme differences between whites and people of color in rates of longevity, morbidity, and infant mortality.

Social workers are engaged in all these issues as practitioners, policy and program analysts, researchers, and social change advocates.

Economic and Political Changes

The 1980s and 1990s saw severe cutbacks in services and programs developed during the eras of the New Deal and the Great Society. In addition to an intractable federal budget deficit and widespread opposition to tax increases, this will lead to even less funding of domestic needs including health care and AIDS research, social welfare, education, affordable housing, urban infrastructure repairs, the search for alternative energy sources, and environmental regulation and repair. Together with other industrialized nations, we must continue financial and technical aid to many developing countries in the effort to stave off the horrifying daily threats of famine, disease, and civil wars. To this must be added the anticipated need for aid to the newly liberated countries of Eastern Europe and the new republics emerging from the break-up of the former Soviet Union. Meanwhile, many American states and cities face profoundly difficult fiscal problems and are resorting to regressive forms of taxation that hurt those at lower economic levels the most.

At the same time, American manufacturing is moving to eastern and southern Asia and Mexico, where workers earn much less than American workers. Parallel to this is the marked shift from an economy based on production to one based on services. Professional services have increased in number and diversity while non-expert services no longer offer sufficient wages to maintain a family. Both trends have contributed to the loss of jobs for American and Canadian workers.

Cultural Changes

The feminist movement of the 1970s and 1980s sought to liberate women from the oppression of a patriarchal social order in family, work, and community life. Currently, the majority of women over age 18 are in the workforce, most because their earnings are needed for family support. Yet child care services lag far behind the need. Women still experience difficulty in entering and advancing in male-dominated professions and occupations, although some progress has been made. Sexual harassment at the workplace, colleges, and schools continues to increase despite the passage of laws that carry severe penalties.

The feminist movement also led to some change in gendered family roles, mostly among middle-class adults and particularly among those men who themselves are liberated from the masculine mystique with its emphasis on work achievement at the expense of family life and participation in child rearing. While committed relationships without marriage increased markedly in the 1970s and 1980s, marriage is still the preferred option, although studies show that men are more satisfied with married life than women are. The United States divorce rate has stabilized in the last several years: nevertheless, some 40% of American children are destined to live part of their childhood in solo parent families.

Gay men and lesbian women have achieved some reduction of negative public attitudes, social stigma, and punitive and discriminatory laws. Gay rights are recognized in some large cities, but the struggle continues elsewhere. The social work profession, however, is not much better than any other in its attention to gay rights. More of us need to become aware of our own and our agencies' homophobic attitudes, learn about gay and lesbian life styles and the strengths within gay communities, and become familiar with available resources for gays and lesbians so we are ready to undertake sensitive, ethical, empowering, and effective services, training, and teaching.

Independent living for those with physical or emotional challenges has also taken on the nature of a liberation movement with an emphasis on the right to physical and social access to all aspects of community life. Despite recent federal statutes, however, children and adults with emotional and developmental disabilities, AIDS, and chronic diseases have not fared very well, and their struggle continues.

Demographic Changes

Both the United States and Canada are pluralistic, multi-cultural societies: although settled primarily by northern Europeans, now the flow of immigrants into both countries is increasingly from South and Central America, Asia, and to a lesser degree from Africa. In the United States, newcomers from South and Central America, Mexico, and the Caribbean are increasing in numbers, either as legal immigrants and refugees requesting asylum or as undocumented aliens. The marvelous cultural diversity of immigrants from the Philippines, Korea, Laos, Vietnam, Afghanistan, India, China, Hong Kong, the central Asian republics of the former Soviet Union enriches North American society, while creating strains in education, health and mental health care, housing, and the social services which have not been adequately prepared for diverse values, norms, and needs. Indeed, the provision of culturally appropriate services and programs to American Indian, African-American, Puerto Rican and Mexican American populations is long overdue. Only since the mid-1970s have the United States and Canada embarked on self-direction and self-governance for some Indian, Eskimo, and Inuit populations in tribal affairs, including their own social services, education, and health care systems.

Another demographic change is the "graying of society." The population over 65 is the fastest growing segment in the United States, with the numbers of the very old, those older than 85, growing the fastest. Strains are felt as women—the traditional caregivers—are now in the work force. Strain is also felt in the health care system as the elderly have a higher utilization rate, and in institutional care, which frequently impoverishes those who need it. Controversy mounts over the cost and coverage of Social Security and Medicare. With growing numbers of the old and very old, social services become increasingly necessary.

Technological Changes

Technology has grown so fast and become so complex that it merits discussion. Medical technology has created means to reduce the impairment of some chronic and genetic diseases. In other instances, however, grave moral issues and ethical dilemmas accompany technological marvels. For example, persons in terminal and vegetative states whose lives a short time ago would have ended in natural death are now kept alive by machines. Similarly, extremely premature infants and gravely ill infants survive who, a short time ago, would have died in utero, at birth, or very soon postnatally. The moral and ethical issues raised by these advances are two-fold. One issue is the quality of life, a question made more complex by legal implications when the courts take over decision-making. The second issue, one that is avoided in public discussion, is the use of costly heroic lifesaving measures versus the lack of routine health maintenance, prevention, and treatment for poor infants, children, and adults.

Reproductive technology has enabled infertile couples to have children genetically related to one or both parents and fertile parents to control the number of offspring. Surgery and other treatments of a fetus in utero is now possible to prevent certain genetic or accidental conditions. These are the benefits of reproductive technology. But redefining motherhood, fatherhood, and the birth process may cause as yet unknown psychological consequences later.

Social workers in health care, child welfare, and family services increasingly confront complex ethical and moral dilemmas as they try to help individuals and couples reach difficult decisions created by reproductive and other medical technologies.

New Knowledge and Theory

Feminist Thought

Concepts from feminist theory have been entering the practice of many, if not most, social workers over the past two decades. Three feminist social workers call attention to some points of convergence in the feminist perspective and the ecological perspective and life-model practice in social work:

> Social work's integrated thinking with its ecological view of processes between the individual and the environment is consonant with feminist thought. Both ideologies envision the desirable as transactions between people and their environments that support individual well-being, dignity, and self-determination.

Both reflect a holistic consciousness not bound or limited by what feminists would argue are artificial androcentric polarities. (Collins 1886:216).

Feminist analysis mandates viewing reality in a holistic, integrated, and ecological fashion. The ecological perspective pertains to the interrelatedness inherent between persons and their environments.

(Van Den Bergh and Cooper 1986:4).

Life on earth is characterized by a web of connectedness and not by the hierarchy that a patriarchal culture projects onto it. "There is no hierarchy in nature among persons, between persons and the rest of the natural world, or among the many forms of nonhuman nature" (King 1983:124). Yet the assumed hierarchy projected on nature is used to justify exploitation of nature, all forms of domination, and coercive power. (We note some exceptions in nature not mentioned by King, such as hierarchies among some primates and other mammals.)

The rapidly accelerating rate of extinction of animal and plant species is as serious a problem as pollution. It "corresponds to reducing human diversity into faceless workers, or to the homogenization of taste and culture through mass consumer markets that cover the world" (King 1983).

Human survival requires a new/old understanding of our relationship to nature, our own biological nature, and nonhuman nature in which we are embedded.

We find an additional convergence between feminist thought and ecological thinking (including the values and principles of life-modeled practice) in their shared concern for the ultimate liberation of all people everywhere from oppression imposed by dehumanizing social, economic, and political institutions and structures. Feminists make us aware of gendered roles in family, work, political, and economic life, as well as historical and contemporary violence against women. These aspects of feminist theory are incorporated into the social work practice of many women and some men and into CSWE's curriculum policy and standards for accreditation.

The following values and principles run through feminist thought and the ecological perspective:

1. Concern for the dignity and worth of the human being.
2. Commitment to social justice.
3. A practice emphasis on social change to achieve growth and health promoting environments for all children and adults.
4. Helping those who suffer prejudicial discrimination to empower themselves.
5. Concern for achieving: (a) international peace; (b) an end to militarism; (c) alternatives to war in resolving international conflicts; and (d) protecting the well-being of the global environment, its peoples, and other forms of life now at risk from destructive, uncaring uses of certain technologies and scarce sources of energy.

The following feminist principles are specifically relevant to social work education and practice (Van Den Bergh and Cooper 1986:4–28):

a. Eliminating false dichotomies and artificial separations: Feminist practice shuns such dichotomies as specialist versus generalist practice and any view of direct practice as unconnected to indirect research, policy, and administration. Further, the vision decries the separation of work with individuals from work to improve social conditions.

b. Reconceptualizing power: Feminist social work practice seeks to facilitate client empowerment. It emphasizes assisting clients to develop skills needed to influence their environment, such as assertiveness training, improved communication skills, managing stress and time, conflict resolution, and negotiation and bargaining skills.

c. Valuing process as equally important as product:. "Discouraging dependency on the [practitioner] and encouraging challenging as well as risk-taking behaviors engender a therapeutic process by which independence is learned and validated" (19). The authors also emphasize the client's learning of skills that will be useful in future life situations and not only in the presenting one.

d. Validating renaming: "Claiming and renaming one's heritage is an empowering process and is integral within both ethnic-sensitive and feminist practice" (21). For example, Pinderhughes (1982) found that renaming her African-American heritage through genealogical research was both liberating and therapeutic. People can choose how they name their own experiences. Consciousness-raising groups for women and people of color, for example, lead to recognition of collective experiences and to reclaiming and renaming what it is to be what they are. Life stories, as we saw in earlier chapters, also reflect renaming processes.

e. Believing that the personal is political through the connections between personal troubles and political realities: "When a client encounters resistance in the way of a desired goal and is able to differentiate whether the restraint is internal or external, then that individual is indicating an evolving political consciousness" (23). External restraints refer to political, economic, and social systems and internal restraints refer to one's own resistance to changing one's maladaptive behaviors.

Social Constructionism

Since the late 1980s, a relatively new set of ideas about the personal, social, political, and cultural construction of reality has been examined with enthusiasm by many social workers (Laird 1993b). The earliest formulation was introduced by Berger and Luckmann (1967), followed by the work of the French philosopher, Foucault (1980) and the French psychoanalyst, Derrida (1986). The ideas were later taken up in the North American fields of literary criticism and textual analysis. Later still, the ideas entered social work via the work of psychologists (Anderson and Goolishian 1992; Bruner

1990, 1986; Sarbin 1986; Gergen 1985). Gergen's interpretations are reflected in the social work writings of Witkin (1990), Holland, Gallant, and Colosetti (1993), Laird (1993a), Hartman (1994:11–30), Middleman and Wood (1993), among others (see Laird 1993b).

Witkin (1990) describes Gergen's four assumptions as the basis of social constructionism:

1. Conventional understandings of the world are less dependent on observation and hypothesis testing and more dependent on language, culture, and history.
2. Language itself is the "product of social processes which are historically and culturally situated"(38).
3. Understandings of the world are not necessarily based on empirical standards, "but have more to do with socio-cultural rules and usefulness in achieving desired ends" (38).
4. Understandings "are not merely reflections of the way things are, but constitute modes of social action." (38).

Witkin suggests that certain qualities of constructionist thought fit well with social work's person-in-environment emphasis and the ecological perspective. It is consistent with social work values; and it offers an alternative, a "sense-making" worldview for both practice and research. He also draws attention to how language influences the ways in which we make sense of the world, and how the language of our theories affects how we perceive, think, and act. Despite science's claim of objectivity in research, social beliefs and values have always influenced scientific inquiry. Similarly, social work practice is permeated with value positions and moral concerns. These are usually translated into the language of psychology, so that values and morality define what "clients" and "problems" are (Witkins 1990:41–46).

Witkin concludes:

> Perhaps the most important implication of the moral and ethical focus of the constructionist perspective is that it encourages social workers to be actively involved with the truly important issues of our time. For example, homelessness, AIDS, the rights of people who are physically or mentally different, war and peace, and the death penalty are issues that, in a significant way, are socially defined and maintained. Each issue expresses certain values and is sustained by various societal (e.g., economic, political) forces. The thoughtful, informed, and critical analysis of social workers can be an important influence in the definition and response to these issues. Constructionism offers a useful perspective for this activity. (46)

This perspective is compatible with life-modeled practice, enhancing both approaches, as Witkin suggests.

Throughout this book we have referred to the ways that people attribute individual meanings to illness (Germain 1984), losses, and other negative life events and to positive life events such as the birth of a wanted child or positive relationships with others. We had viewed these processes as arising from personal and cultural positions. Holland, Gallant, and Colosetti (as cited by Witkin) elaborate this process further from a constructionist point of view:

> Our efforts to make sense of inner and outer experiences involve trying to formulate some coherence from streams of events. . . . Such contexts of meaning take on a narrative or story-like form, linking past, present, and anticipated future, involving movement toward or away from goals or the form may emphasize blockage or no change.   Witkin 1990:46

We conclude that, in general, some constructionist concepts are proving to be relevant to social work practice. As Middleman and Wood (1994:142) point out:

> Constructionism encourages awareness of multiple realities and hidden meanings . . . reduces the distance between . . . practitioner and client. It tames the practitioner's . . . desire and need to be the expert. It demolishes the claim of objectivity by practitioners and researchers. It suggests that categories are and should be suspect.

The Evolving Nature of Life-Modeled Practice

Social work's professional purpose in society is more necessary and more complex than ever. Practice and education for practice must be consonant with new knowledge, new needs, now social conditions, cultural diversity, and the search for an end to oppression. The profession has always shown the courage and the will to move in new ways in response to social problems and societal failures. We believe that life-modeled practice, through its values and practice principles derived from the ecological metaphor, and augmented by feminist and social constructionist thought, is well-suited to the social conditions of today's world and those likely to characterize the opening years of the twenty-first century. Life-modeled practice seeks to elevate the fit between people and their environments, especially between human needs and environmental resources. In mediating the exchanges between people and their environments, social workers bear witness against social inequalities and injustice by mobilizing community resources to improve community life, influencing unresponsive organizations to develop responsive policies and services, and by politically influencing local, state, and federal legislation and regulations to support social justice.

Life-modeled practice is committed to responding constructively to changes within the profession and in pertinent new theory and research findings, and to increased human and environmental diversity. It will continue its quest for ever-broadening understanding of, and respect for, the endless variety of human strengths, exemplified in the lives of all those whom social work serves. This commitment, rooted in the evolving, adaptive nature of the life model, helps ready its practitioners to meet new and old demands in the coming century.

And so the journey continues!

NASW CODE OF ETHICS (1993)

I. The Social Worker's Conduct and Comportment as a Social Worker

A. Propriety—The social worker should maintain high standards of personal conduct in the capacity or identity as social worker.

1. The private conduct of the social worker is a personal matter to the same degree as is any other person's, except when such conduct compromises the fulfillment of professional responsibilities.

2. The social worker should not participate in, condone, or be associated with dishonesty, fraud, deceit, or misrepresentation.

3. The social worker should distinguish clearly between statements and actions made as a private individual and as a representative of the social work profession or an organization or group.

B. Competence and Professional Development—The social worker should strive to become and remain proficient in professional practice and the performance of professional functions.

1. The social worker should accept responsibility or employment only on the basis of existing competence or the intention to acquire the necessary competence.

2. The social worker should not misrepresent professional qualifications, education, experience, or affiliations.

3. The social worker should not allow his or her own personal problems, psychosocial distress, substance abuse, or mental health difficulties to interfere with professional judgment and performance or jeopardize the best interests of those for whom the social worker has a professional responsibility.

4. The social worker whose personal problems, psychosocial distress, substance abuse, or mental health difficulties interfere with professional judgment and performance should immediately seek consultation and take appropriate remedial action by seeking professional help, making adjustments in workload, terminating practice, or taking any other steps necessary to protect clients and others.

C. Service—The social worker should regard as primary the service obligation of the social work profession.

1. The social worker should retain ultimate responsibility for the quality and extent of the service that individual assumes, assigns, or performs.

2. The social worker should act to prevent practices that are inhumane or discriminatory against any person or group of persons.

D. Integrity—The social worker should act in accordance with the highest standards of professional integrity and impartiality.

1. The social worker should be alert to and resist the influences and pressures that interfere with the exercise of professional discretion and impartial judgment required for the performance of professional functions.

2. The social worker should not exploit professional relationships for personal gain.

E. Scholarship and Research—The social worker engaged in study and research should be guided by the conventions of scholarly inquiry.

1. The social worker engaged in research should consider carefully its possible consequences for human beings.

2. The social worker engaged in research should ascertain that the consent of participants in the research is voluntary and informed, without any implied deprivation or penalty for refusal to participate, and with due regard for participants' privacy and dignity.

3. The social worker engaged in research should protect participants from unwarranted physical or mental discomfort, distress, harm, danger, or deprivation.

4. The social worker who engages in the evaluation of services or cases should discuss them only for the professional purposes and only with persons directly and professionally concerned with them.

5. Information obtained about participants in research should be treated as confidential.

6. The social worker should take credit only for work actually done in connection with scholarly and research endeavors and credit contributions made by others.

II. The Social Worker's Ethical Responsibility to Clients

F. Primacy of Clients' Interests—The social worker's primary responsibility is to clients.

1. The social worker should serve clients with devotion, loyalty, determination, and the maximum application of professional skill and competence.

2. The social worker should not exploit relationships with clients for personal advantage.

3. The social worker should not practice, condone, facilitate or collaborate with any form of discrimination on the basis of race, color, sex, sexual orientation, age, religion, national origin, marital status, political belief, mental or physical handicap, or any other preference or personal characteristic, condition or status.

4. The social worker should not condone or engage in any dual or multiple relationships with clients or former clients in which there is a risk of exploitation of or potential harm to the client. The social worker is responsible for setting clear, appropriate, and culturally sensitive boundaries.

5. The social worker should under no circumstances engage in sexual activities with clients.

6. The social worker should provide clients with accurate and complete information regarding the extent and nature of the services available to them.

7. The social worker should apprise clients of their risks, rights, opportunities, and obligations associated with social service to them.

8. The social worker should seek advice and counsel of colleagues and supervisors whenever such consultation is in the best interest of clients.

9. The social worker should terminate service to clients, and professional relationships with them, when such service and relationships are no longer required or no longer serve the clients' needs or interests.

10. The social worker should withdraw services precipitously only under unusual circumstances, giving careful consideration to all factors in the situation and taking care to minimize possible adverse effects.

11. The social worker who anticipates the termination or interruption of service to clients should notify clients promptly and seek the transfer, referral, or continuation of service in relation to the clients' needs and preferences.

G. Rights and Prerogatives of Clients—The social worker should make every effort to foster maximum self-determination on the part of the clients.

1. When the social worker must act on behalf of a client who has been adjudged legally incompetent, the social worker should safeguard the interest and rights of the client.

2. When another individual has been legally authorized to act in behalf of a client, the social worker should deal with that person always with the client's best interest in mind.

3. The social worker should not engage in any action that violates or diminishes the civil or legal rights of clients.

H. Confidentiality and Privacy—The social worker should respect the privacy of clients and hold in confidence all information obtained in the course of professional service.

1. The social worker should share with others confidences revealed by clients, without their consent, only for compelling professional reasons.

2. The social worker should inform clients fully about the limits of confidentiality in a given situation, the purposes for which information is obtained, and how it may be used.

3. The social worker should afford clients reasonable access to any official social work records concerning them.

4. When providing clients with access to records, the social worker should take due care to protect the confidences of others contained in those records.

5. The social worker should obtain informed consent of clients before taping, recording, or permitting third party observation of their activities.

I. Fees—When setting fees, the social worker should ensure that they are fair, reasonable, considerate, and commensurate with the service performed and with due regard for the clients' ability to pay.

1. The social worker should not accept anything of value for making a referral.

III. The Social Worker's Ethical Responsibility to Colleagues

J. Respect, Fairness, and Courtesy—The social worker should treat colleagues with respect courtesy, fairness, and good faith.

1. The social worker should cooperate with colleagues to promote professional interests and concerns.

2. The social worker should respect confidences shared by colleagues in the course of their professional relationships and transactions.

3. The social worker should create and maintain conditions of practice that facilitate ethical and competent professional performance by colleagues.

4. The social worker should treat with respect, and represent accurately and fairly, the qualifications, views, and findings of colleagues and use appropriate channels to express judgments on these matters.

5. The social worker who replaces or is replaced by a colleague in professional practice should act with consideration for the interest, character, and reputation of that colleague.

6. The social worker should not exploit a dispute between a colleague and employers to obtain a position or otherwise advance the social worker's interest.

7. The social worker should seek arbitration or mediation when conflicts with colleagues require resolution for compelling professional reasons.

8. The social worker should extend to colleagues of other professions the same respect and cooperation that is extended to social work colleagues.

9. The social worker who serves as an employer, supervisor, or mentor to colleagues should make orderly and explicit arrangements regarding the conditions of their continuing professional relationship.

10. The social worker who has the responsibility for employing and evaluating the performance of other staff members, should fulfill such responsibility in a fair, considerate, and equitable manner, on the basis of clearly enunciated criteria.

11. The social worker who has the responsibility for evaluating the performance of employees, supervisees, or students should share evaluations with them.

12. The social worker should not use a professional position vested with power, such as that of employer, supervisor, teacher, or consultant, to his or her advantage or to exploit others.

13. The social worker who has direct knowledge of a social work colleague's impairment due to personal problems, psychosocial distress, substance abuse, or mental health difficulties should consult with that colleague and assist the colleague in taking remedial action.

K. Dealing with Colleague's Clients—The social worker has the responsibility to relate to the clients of colleagues with full professional consideration.

1. The social worker should not assume professional responsibility for the clients of

another agency or a colleague without appropriate communication with that agency and colleague.

2. The social worker who serves the clients of colleagues, during a temporary absence or emergency, should serve those clients with the same consideration as that afforded any client.

IV. The Social Worker's Ethical Responsibility to Employers and Employing Organizations

L. Commitments to Employing Organization— The social worker should adhere to commitments made to the employing organization.

1. The social worker should work to improve the employing agency's policies and procedures, and the efficiency and effectiveness of its services.

2. The social worker should not accept employment or arrange student field placements in an organization which is currently under public sanction by NASW for violating personnel standards, or imposing limitations on or penalties for professional actions on behalf of clients.

3. The social worker should act to prevent and eliminate discrimination in the employing organization's work assignments and in its employment policies and practices.

4. The social worker should use with scrupulous regard, and only for the purpose for which they are intended, the resources of employing organization.

V. The Social Worker's Ethical Responsibility to the Social Work Profession

M. Maintaining the Integrity of the Profession—The social worker should uphold and advance the values, ethics, knowledge, and mission of the profession.

1. The social worker should protect and enhance the dignity and integrity of the profession and should be responsible and vigorous in discussion and criticism of the profession.

2. The social worker should take action through appropriate channels against unethical conduct by any other member of the profession.

3. The social worker should act to prevent the unauthorized and unqualified practice of social work.

4. The social worker should make no misrepresentation in advertising as to qualifications, competence, service, or results to be achieved.

N. Community Service—The social worker should assist the profession in making social services available to the general public.

1. The social worker should contribute time and professional expertise to activities that promote respect for the utility, the integrity, and the competence of the social work profession.

2. The social worker should support the formulation, development, enactment and implementation of social policies of concern to the profession.

O. Development of Knowledge—The social worker should take responsibility for identifying, developing, and fully utilizing knowledge for professional practice.

1. The social worker should base practice upon recognized knowledge relevant to social work.

2. The social worker should critically examine, and keep current with emerging knowledge relevant to social work.

3. The social worker should contribute to the knowledge base of social work and share research knowledge and practice wisdom with colleagues.

VI. The Social Worker's Ethical Responsibility to Society

P. Promoting the General Welfare—The social worker should promote the general welfare of society.

1. The social worker should act to prevent and eliminate discrimination against any person or group on the basis of race, color, sex, sexual orientation, age, religion, national origin, marital status, political belief, mental or physical handicap, or any other preference or personal characteristic, condition, or status.

2. The social worker should act to ensure that all persons have access to the resources, services, and opportunities which they require.

3. The social worker should act to expand choice and opportunity for all persons, with special regard for disadvantaged or oppressed groups and persons.

4. The social worker should promote conditions that encourage respect for the diversity of cultures which constitute American society.

5. The social worker should provide appropriate professional services in public emergencies.

6. The social worker should advocate changes in policy and legislation to improve social conditions and to promote social justice.

7. The social worker should encourage informed participation by the public in shaping social policies and institutions.

CASW SOCIAL WORK CODE
OF ETHICS (1994)

Definitions

In this Code,

Best Interest of Client

means

(a) that the wishes, desires, motivations, and plans of the client are taken by the social workers as the primary consideration in any intervention plan developed by the social worker subject to change only when the client's plans are documented to be unrealistic, unreasonable or potentially harmful to self or others or otherwise determined inappropriate when considered in relation to a mandated requirement.

(b) that all actions and interventions of the social worker are taken subject to the reasonable belief that the client will benefit from the action, and

(c) that the social worker will consider the client as an individual, a member of a family unit, a member of a community, a person with a distinct ancestry or culture and will consider those factors in any decision affecting the client.

Client[1]

means

(a) a person, family, group of persons, incorporated body, association or community on whose behalf a social worker provides or agrees to provide a service

(i) on request or with agreement[2] of the person, family, group of persons, incorporated body, association or community, or

(ii) as a result of a legislated responsibility, or

(b) a judge of a court of competent jurisdiction who orders the social worker to provide to the court an assessment.[3]

Conduct Unbecoming

means behavior or conduct that does not meet standard of care requirements and is therefore subject to discipline.[4]

Malpractice and Negligence

means behavior that is included as "conduct unbecoming" and relates to social work practice behavior within the parameters of the professional relationship that falls below the standard of practice and results in or aggravates an injury to a client. Without limiting the generality of the above,[5] it includes behavior which results in assault, deceit, fraudulent misrepresentations, defamation of character, breach of contract, violation of human rights, malicious prosecution, false imprisonment or criminal conviction.

Practice of Social Work

includes the assessment, redemption and prevention of social problems and the enhancement of social functioning of individuals, families, groups and communities by means of

(a) the provision of direct counselling services within an established relationship between a social worker and client:

(b) the development, promotion and delivery of human service programs, including that done in collaboration with other professionals;

(c) the development and promotion of social policies aimed at improving social conditions and equality;[6] and

(d) any other activities approved by CASW.[7]

Social Worker

means a person who is duly registered to practice social work in a province or territory or where mandatory registration does not exist, a person practicing social work who voluntarily agrees to be subject to this Code.

Standards of Practice

means the standard of care ordinarily expected of a competent social worker. It means that the public is assured that a social worker has the training, the skill and the diligence to provide them with professional social work services.

Preamble

Philosophy

The profession of social work is founded on humanitarian and egalitarian ideals. Social workers believe in the intrinsic worth and dignity of every human being and are committed to the values of acceptance, self-determination and respect of individuality. They believe in the obligation of all people, individually and collectively, to provide resources, services and opportunities for the overall benefit of humanity. The culture of individuals, families, groups, communities and nations has to be respected without prejudice.[8]

Social workers are dedicated to the welfare and self-realization of human beings; to the development and disciplined use of scientific knowledge regarding human and societal behaviors; to the development of resources to meet individual, group, national and international needs and aspirations; and to the achievement of social justice for all.

Professional Practice Conflicts

If a conflict arises in professional practice, the standards declared in this Code take precedence. Conflicts of interest may occur because of demands from the general public, workplace, organizations or clients. In all cases, if the ethical duties and obligations or ethical responsibilities of this Code would be compromised, the social worker must act in a manner consistent with this Code.

Nature of this Code

The first seven statements in this code establish ethical duties and obligations. These statements provide the basis of social worker's relationship with a client and are based on the values of social work. A breach of any of these statements forms the basis of a disciplinary action. The remaining three statements are characterized as ethical responsibilities and are to be seen as being different from the ethical duties and obligations. These ethical responsibilities are not likely to form the basis of any disciplinary action if breached. However these sections may form the basis of inquiry. These ethical responsibilities may be used in conjunction with breaches of other sections of this code and may form the basis of necessary background information in any action for discipline. Of equal importance, these ethical responsibilities are desirable goals to be achieved by the social work profession which by its nature is driven by an adherence to the values that form the basis of these desirable ethical behaviors.

Social Work Code of Ethics

Ethical Duties and Obligations

1. A social worker shall maintain the best interest of the client as the primary professional obligation.

2. A social worker shall carry out her or his professional duties and obligations with integrity and objectivity.

3. A social worker shall have and maintain competence in the provision of a social work service to a client.

4. A social worker shall not exploit the relationship with a client for personal benefit, gain or gratification.

5. A social worker shall protect the confidentiality of all information acquired from the client or others regarding the client and the client's family during the professional relationship unless

(a) the client authorizes in writing the release of specified information,

(b) the information is released under the authority of a statute or an order of a court of competent jurisdiction, or

(c) otherwise authorized by this Code.

6. A social worker who engages in another profession, occupation, affiliation or calling shall not allow these outside interests to affect the social work relationship with the client.

7. A social worker in private practice shall not conduct the business of provision of social work services for a fee in a manner that discredits the profession or diminishes the public's trust in the profession.

Ethical Responsibilities

8. A social worker shall advocate for workplace conditions and policies that are consistent with the Code.

9. A social worker shall promote excellence in the social work profession.

10. A social worker shall advocate change
    (a) in the best interest of the client, and
    (b) for the overall benefit of society, the environment and the global community.

Chapter 1

Primary Professional Obligation

1. A social worker shall maintain the best interest of the client as the primary professional obligation.

1.1 The social worker is to be guided primarily by this obligation. Any action which is substantially inconsistent with this obligation is an unethical action.

1.2 A social worker in the practice of social work shall not discriminate against any person on the basis of race, ethnic background, language, religion, marital status, sex, sexual orientation, age, abilities, socio-economic status, political affiliation or national ancestry.[9]

1.3 A social worker shall inform a client of the client's right to consult another professional at any time during the provision of social work services.

1.4 A social worker shall immediately inform the client of any factor, condition[10] or pressure that affects the social worker's ability to perform an acceptable level of service.

1.5 A social worker shall not become involved in a client's personal affairs that are not relevant to the service being provided.

1.6 A social worker shall not state an opinion, judgment or use a clinical diagnosis unless there is a documented assessment, observation or diagnosis to support the opinion, judgment or diagnosis.

1.7 Where possible, a social worker shall provide or secure social work services in the language chosen by the client.

Chapter 2

Integrity and Objectivity

2. A social worker shall carry out his or her professional duties and obligations with integrity and objectivity.[11]

2.1 A social worker shall identify and describe education, training, experience, professional affiliations, competence, nature of service in an honest an accurate manner.

2.2 The social worker shall explain to the client her or his education, experience, training, competence, nature of service and action at the request of the client.

2.3 A social worker shall cite an educational degree only after it has been received from the institution.

2.4 A social worker shall not claim formal social work education in an area of expertise or training solely by attending a lecture, demonstration, conference, panel discussion, workshop, seminar or other similar teaching presentation.[12]

2.5 The social worker shall not make false, misleading or exaggerated claim of efficacy regarding past or anticipated achievement with respect to clients.

2.6 The social worker shall distinguish between actions and statements made as a private citizen and actions and statements made as a social worker.[13]

Chapter 3

Competence in the Provision of Social Work Services

3. A social worker shall have and maintain competence in the provision of a social work service to a client.

3.1 The social worker shall not undertake a social work service unless the social worker has the competence to provide the service or the social worker can reasonably acquire the necessary competence without undue delay, risk or expense to the client.

3.2 Where a social worker cannot reasonably acquire the necessary competence in the provision of a service to a client, the social worker shall decline to provide the service to the client, advising the client of the reason and ensuring that the client is referred to another professional person if the client agrees to the referral.

3.3 The social worker, with the agreement of the client, may obtain advise from other professionals in the provision of service to a client.

3.4 A social worker shall maintain an acceptable level of health and well-being in order to provide a competent level of service to a client.[14]

3.5 Where social worker has a physical or mental health problem, disability or illness that affects the ability of the social worker to provide competent service or that would threaten the health or well-being of the client, the social worker shall discontinue the provision of social work service to a client

(a) advising the client of the reason[15] and,

(b) ensuring that the client is referred to another professional person if the client agrees to the referral.

3.6 The social worker shall have, maintain and endeavor periodically to update an acceptable level of knowledge and skills to meet the standards of practice of the profession.

Chapter 4

Limit on Professional Relationship

4. A social worker shall not exploit the relationship with a client for personal benefit, gain or gratification.

4.1 The social worker shall respect the client and act so that the dignity, individuality and rights of the person are protected.

4.2 The social worker shall assess and consider a client's motivation and physical and mental capacity in arranging for the provision of an appropriate service.

4.3 The social worker shall not have a sexual relationship with a client.

4.4 The social worker shall not have a business relationship with a client, borrow money from a client, or loan money to a client.[16]

4.5 The social worker shall not have a sexual relationship with a social work student assigned to the social worker.

4.6 The social worker shall not sexually harass any person.

Chapter 5

Confidential Information

5. A social worker shall protect the confidentiality[17] of all information acquired from the client or others regarding the client and the client's family during the professional relationship[18] unless

(a) the client authorizes in writing the release of specified information,[19]

(b) the information is released under the authority of a statute or an order of a court of relevant jurisdiction, or

(c) otherwise authorized under this Code.

5.1 The requirement of confidentiality also applies to social workers who work as

(a) supervisors,

(b) managers,

(c) educators, or

(d) administrators.

5.2 A social worker who works as a supervisor, manager or administrator shall establish policies and practices that protect the confidentiality of client information.

5.3 The social worker may disclose confidential information to other persons in the workplace who, by virtue of their responsibilities, have an identified need to know as determined by the social worker.

5.4 Clients shall be the initial or primary source of information about themselves and their problems unless the client is incapable or unwilling to give information or when corroborative reporting is required.

5.5 The social worker has the obligation to ensure that the client understands what is being asked, why and to what purpose the information will be used, and to understand the confidentiality policies and practices of the workplace setting.

5.6 Where information is required by law, the social worker shall explain to the client the consequences of refusing to provide the requested information.

5.7 Where information is required from the other sources, the social worker

(a) shall explain the requirement to the client, and

(b) shall attempt to involve the client in selecting the sources to be used.

5.8 The social worker shall take reasonable care to safeguard the client's personal papers or property if the social worker agrees to keep the property at the request of the client.

Recording Information

5.9 The social worker shall maintain only one master file on each client.[20]

5.10 The social worker shall record all relevant information, and keep all relevant documents in the file.

5.11 The social worker shall not record in a client's file any characterization that is not based on assessment or fact.

Accessibility of Records

5.12 The social worker who contracts for the delivery of social work services with a client is responsible to the client for maintaining the client record.

5.13 The social worker who is employed by a social agency that delivers social work services to clients is responsible

(a) to the client for the maintaining of a client record, and

(b) to the agency to maintain the records to facilitate the objectives of the agency.

5.14 A social worker is obligated to follow the provision of a statute that allows access to records by clients.

5.15 The social worker shall respect the client's right of access to a client record subject to the social worker's right to refuse access for just and reasonable cause.

5.16 Where a social worker refuses a client the right to access a file or part of a file, the social worker shall advise the client of the right to request a review of the decision in accordance with the relevant statue, workplace policy or other relevant procedure.

Disclosure

5.17 The social worker shall not disclose the identity of persons who have sought a social work service or disclose sources of information about clients unless compelled legally to do so.[21]

5.18 The obligation to maintain confidentiality continues indefinitely after the social worker has ceased contact with the client.

5.19 The social worker shall avoid unnecessary conversation regarding clients.

5.20 The social worker may divulge confidential information with consent of the client, preferably expressed in writing, where this is essential to a plan of care or treatment.

5.21 The social worker shall transfer information to another agency or individual, only with the informed consent of the client or guardian of the client and then only with the reasonable assurance that the receiving agency provides the same guarantee of confidentiality and respect for the right of privileged communication as provided by the sending agency.

5.22 The social worker shall explain to the client the disclosure of information requirements of the law or of the agency before the commencement of the provision of social work services.

5.23 The social worker in practice with groups and communities shall notify the participants of the likelihood that aspects of their private lives may be revealed in the course of their work together, and therefore require a commitment from each member to respect the privileged and confidential nature of the communication between and among members of the client group.

5.24 Subject to section 5.26, the social worker shall not disclose information acquired from one client to a member of the client's family without the informed consent of the client who provided the information.

5.25 A social worker shall disclose information acquired from one client to a member of the client's family where
(a) the information involves a threat of harm to self or others,[22]
(b) the information was acquired from a child of tender years and the social worker determines that its disclosure is in the best interests of the child.[23]

5.26 A social worker shall disclose information acquired from a client to a person or a police officer where the information involves a threat of harm to that person.

5.27 A social worker may release confidential information as part of a discipline hearing of a social worker as directed by the tribunal or disciplinary body.

5.28 When disclosure is required by order of a court, the social worker shall not divulge more information than is reasonably required and shall where possible notify the client of this requirement.

5.29 The social worker shall not use confidential information for the purpose of teaching, public education or research except with the informed consent of the client.

5.30 The social worker may use non-identifying information for the purpose of teaching, public education or research.

Retention and Disposition of Information

5.31 Where the social worker's documentation is stored in a place or computer maintained and operated by an employer, the social worker shall advocate for the responsible retention and disposition of information contained in the file.

Chapter 6

Outside Interest

6. A social worker who engages in another profession, occupation, affiliation or calling shall not allow these outside interests to affect the social work relationship with the client.

6.1 A social worker shall declare to the client any outside interests that would affect the social work relationship with the client.

6.2 A social worker shall not allow an outside interest:
(a) to affect the social worker's ability to practice social work;
(b) to present to the client or to the community that the social worker's ability to practice social work is affected; or
(c) to bring the profession of social work into disrepute.[24]

Chapter 7

Limit on Private Practice

7. A social worker in private practice shall not conduct the business of provision of social work services for a fee in a manner that discredits the profession or diminishes the public's trust in the profession.

7.1 A social worker shall not use the social work relationship within an agency to obtain clients for his or her private practice.

7.2 Subject to section 7.3, a social worker who enters in contract for service with a client

(a) shall disclose at the outset of the relationship, the fee schedule for the social work services,

(b) shall not charge a fee that is greater than that agreed to and disclosed to the client, and

(c) shall not charge for hours of service other than the reasonable hours of client services, research, consultation and administrative work directly connected to the case.

7.3 A social worker in private practice may charge differential fees for services except where an increased fee is charged based on race, ethnic background, language, religion, marital status, sex, sexual orientation, age, abilities, socio-economic status, political affiliation or national ancestry.

7.4 A social worker in private practice shall maintain adequate malpractice, defamation and liability insurance.

7.5 A social worker in private practice may charge a rate of interest on delinquent accounts as is allowed by law.[25]

7.6 Notwithstanding section 5.17 a social worker in private practice may pursue civil remedies to ensure payment for services to a client where the social worker has advised the client of this possibility at the outset of the social work service.

Chapter 8

Ethical Responsibilities to the Workplace

8. A social worker shall advocate for workplace conditions and policies that are consistent with the Code.

8.1 Where the responsibilities to an employer are in conflict with the social worker's obligations to the client, the social worker shall document the issue in writing and shall bring the situation to the attention of the employer.

8.2 Where a serious ethical conflict continues to exist after the issue has been brought to the attention of the employer, the social worker shall bring the issue to the attention of the Association or regulatory body.[26]

8.3 A social worker shall follow the principles in the Code when dealing with

(a) a social worker under the supervision of the social worker,

(b) an employee under the supervision of the social worker, and

(c) a social work student under the supervision of the social worker.

Chapter 9

Ethical Responsibilities to the Profession

9. A social worker shall promote excellence in the social work profession.

9.1 A social worker shall report to the appropriate association or regulatory body any breach of this Code by another social worker which adversely affects or harms a client or prevents the effective delivery of a social service.

9.2 A social worker shall report to the association or regulatory body any unqualified or unlicensed person who is practicing social work.

9.3 A social worker shall not intervene in the professional relationship of a social worker and client unless requested to do so by the client and unless convinced that the best interests and well-being of the client require such intervention.

9.4 Where a conflict arises between a social worker and other professionals, the social worker shall attempt to resolve the professional differences in ways that uphold the principles of this Code and the honor of the social work profession.

9.5 A social worker engaged in research shall ensure that the involvement of clients in the research is a result of informed consent.

Chapter 10

Ethical Responsibilities for Social Change

10. A social worker shall advocate change
(a) in the best interest of the client, and
(b) for the overall benefit of society, the environment and the global community.

10.1 A social worker shall identify a document and advocate for the elimination of discrimination.

10.2 A social worker shall advocate for the equal distribution of resources to all persons.

10.3 A social worker shall advocate for the equal access of all persons to resources, services and opportunities.

10.4 A social worker shall advocate for a clean and healthy environment and shall advocate the development of environmental strategies consistent with social work principles.

10.5 A social worker shall provide reasonable professional services in a state of emergency.

10.6 A social worker shall promote social justice.

Notes

1. A client ceases to be a client 2 years after the termination of a social work service. It is advisable for this termination to be clearly documented on the case file.

2. This sub-paragraph identifies two situations where a person may be considered a voluntary client. The person who requests a social work service is clearly a voluntary client. A person also may originally be as a result of the actions of a court or other legally mandated entity. This person may receive a service beyond that originally mandated and therefore be able to terminate voluntarily that aspect of the service. A situation where a person is referred by another professional or family ember clearly falls into this "voluntary service" relationship when the person agrees with the service to be provided. This type of social work relationship is clearly distinguishable from the relationship in sub-paragraph (ii) where the social worker does not seek or have agreement of the service to be provided.

3. In this situation, the social worker is providing an assessment, information or a professional opinion to a judge of competent jurisdiction to assist the judge in making a ruling or determination. In this situation, the relationship is with the judge an the person on whom the information, assessment or opinion is provided is not the client. The social worker still has some professional obligations towards that person, for example: competence and dignity.

4. In reaching a decision in *Re Mathews and Board of Directors of Physiotherapy* (1986) 54 O.R. (2d) 375, Saunders J. makes three important statements regarding standards of

practice and by implication Code of Ethics: (i) Standards of practice are inherent characteristics of any profession; (ii) Standards of practice may be written or unwritten; (iii) Some conduct is clearly regarded as misconduct and need not be written down whereas other conduct may be the subject of dispute within a profession.

5. The importance of the collective opinion of the profession in establishing and ultimately modifying the Code of Ethics was established in a 1884 case involving the medical profession. Lord Esher, M.R. stated:

If it is shown that a medical man, in the pursuit of his profession, has done something with regard to it which would be reasonably regarded as disgraceful or dishonorable by his professional brethren of good repute and competency

then it is open to General Medical Council to say that he has been guilty of "infamous conduct in a professional respect."

6. This definition except paragraph (d) has been taken from *An Act to Incorporate the New Brunswick Association of Social Workers*, chapter 78 of the Statutes of New Brunswick, 1988, section 2.

7. The procedure of adding activities under this paragraph will be established as a bylaw by the CASW Board of Directors.

8. Taken from *Teaching and Learning about Human Rights: A Manual for Schools of Social Work and the Social Work Profession*, U.N. Centre for Human Rights, Co-operation with International Federation of Social Workers and International Association of Schools of Social Workers, United Nations, New York, 1992.

9. This obligation goes beyond grounds of discrimination stated in most Human Rights Legislation and therefore there is a greater professional obligation than that stated in provincial legislation.

10. The term condition means a physical, mental or psychological condition. There is an implied obligation that the social worker shall actively seek diagnosis and treatment for any signs or warnings of a condition. A disclosure under this section may be of a general nature. See also 3.4.

11. The term objectivity is taken from the Québec Code of Professional Conduct. See Division 2: Integrity and Objectivity (6.0 Québec) November 5, 1979 Vol 2 No. 30. The term objectivity is stated in the following: 3.02.01. A social worker must discharge his professional duties with integrity and objectivity.

12. The provincial associations may regulate the areas of expertise to be stated or advertised by a social worker. This will vary in each province according to its enabling legislation. Where there is not sufficient legislative base for this regulation, the claim of an expertise without sufficient training may form the basis of a determination of unprofessional conduct.

13. Even with a distinction made under this section, a social worker's private actions or statements may be of such a nature that the social worker cannot avoid the responsibilities under this Code. See also 6.2(c).

14. This section should be considered in relation to section 1.4 and involves proper maintenance, prevention and treatment of any type of risk to the health or well-being of the social worker.

15. It is not necessary in all circumstances to explain specifically the nature of the problem.

16. Where a social worker does keep money or assets belonging to a client, the social worker should hold this money or asset in a trust account or hold the money or asset in conjunction with an additional professional person.

17. Confidentiality means that information received or observed about a client by a social worker will be held in confidence and disclosed only when the social worker is properly authorized or obligated legally or professionally to do so. This also means that professionally acquired information may be treated as privileged communication and ordinarily only the client has the right to waive privilege.

Privileged communication means statements made within a protected relationship (i.e. husband-wife, professional-client) which the law protects against disclosure. The extent of the privilege is governed by law and not by this Code.

Maintaining confidentiality of privileged communication means that information about clients does not have to be transmitted in any oral, written or recorded form. Such information, for example, does not have to be disclosed to a supervisor, written into a workplace record, stored in a computer or microfilm data base, held on an audio or videotape or discussed orally. The right of privileged communication is respected by the social worker in the practice of social work notwithstanding that this right is not ordinarily granted in law.

The disclosure of confidential information in social work practice involves the obligation to share information professionally with others in the workplace of the social worker as part of a reasonable service to the client. Social workers recognized the need to obtain permission from clients before releasing information about them to sources outside their workplace; and to inform clients at the outset of their relationship that some information acquired may be shared with the officers and personnel of the agency who maintain the case record and who have a reasonable need for the information in the performance of their duties.

18. The social worker's relationship with a client can be characterized as a fiduciary relationship.

In *Fiduciary Duties in Canada* by Ellis, fiduciary duty is described as follows:

> where one party has placed its "trust and confidence" in another and the latter has accepted—expressly or by operation of law—to act in a manner consistent with the reposing of such "trust and confidence," a fiduciary relationship has been established.

19. The "obligation of secrecy" was discussed by the Supreme Court of Canada in *Halls v. Mitchell*, (1928) S.C.R. 125, an action brought by a disabled CNR worker against a company doctor who had disclosed the employee's medical history, to the latter's detriment. Mr. Justice Duff reviewed the duty of confidentiality:

> We are not required, for the purposes of this appeal, to attempt to state with any sort of precision the limits of the obligation of secrecy which rests upon the medical practitioner in relation to the professional secrets acquired by him in the course of his practice. Nobody would dispute that a secret so acquired is the secret of the patient, and normally, is under his control, and not under that of the doctor. Prima facie, the patient has the right to require that the secret shall not be divulged; and that right is absolute, unless there is some paramount reason which overrides it.

Thus the right of secrecy/confidentiality rests squarely with the patient; the Court carefully provided that there is an "ownership" extant in the confidentiality of the personal information. Duff J. continued by allowing "paramount" criteria which vitiates from the right:

> Some reasons may arise, not doubt, from the existence of facts which bring into play overpowering considerations connected with public justice; and there may be cases in which reasons connected with the safety of individuals or of the public, physical or moral, would be sufficiently cogent to supersede or qualify the obligations prima facie imposed by the confidential relation.

Duff J. continued:

> The general duty of medical men to observe secrecy, in relation to information acquired by them confidentially from their patients is subject, no doubt, to some exceptions, which have no operation in the case of solicitors; but the grounds of the legal, social or moral imperatives affecting physicians and surgeons, touching the inviolability of professional confidences, are not any more than those affecting legal advisers, based exclusively upon the relations between the parties as individuals.

20. The master file refers to all relevant documents pertaining to the client consisting of such information as demographics, case recordings, court documents, assessments, correspondence, treatment plans, bills, etc. This information is often collected through various means including electronic and computer-driven sources. However the client master file exists as one unit, inclusive of all information pertaining to the client, despite the various sources of the recording process. The description and ownership of the master file is most often defined by workplace standards or policies. The client's master file should be prepared keeping in mind that it may have to be revealed to the client or disclosed in legal proceedings.

21. A social worker may be compelled to reveal information under the section when directly ordered by the court to do so. Before disclosing the information, the social worker shall advise the court of the professional obligations that exist under this section of the Code and where reasonably possible inform the client.

22. The case of *Tarasoff v. The Regents of the University of California et al.* (1976), 551 p.2d 334 (Cal. Supreme Court) focused on the obligation of a psychiatrist to maintain the confidentiality of his patients' statements in their discussions. In that case the patient told the psychiatrist that the patient had an intention to kill a certain woman. When the patient actually did kill this woman, her parents brought suit alleging that the psychiatrist owed a duty to tell the woman of the danger to her.

It was held that the psychiatrist did have a duty to tell the woman of the threat. The court recognized that the psychiatrist owed a duty to the patient to keep in confidence the statements the patient made in therapy sessions, but held there was also a duty to care to anyone whom the psychiatrist knew might be endangered by the patient. At a certain point the obligation of confidentiality would be overridden by the obligation to this third person. The psychiatrist's knowledge itself gave rise to a duty of care. What conduct would be sufficient to fulfill the duty to this third person would depend on the circumstances, but it might be necessary to give a warning that would reveal what the patient had said about the third party. The court in this case held that the psychiatrist had a duty to warn the woman about the patient's stated intention to kill her, and having failed to warn her the psychiatrist was liable in negligence. Moreover, the court stated that the principle of this duty of care belonged not just to a psychiatrist but also to a psychologist performing therapy. It would follow that the principle would also apply to social workers performing therapy.

23. For the purpose of this Code, a child of tender years shall usually be determined to be a child under the age of seven years subject to a determination by a social worker considering the child's social, physical, intellectual, emotional or psychological development.

24. This section brings the social worker's outside interest and personal actions in line with the professional duties and obligations as set out in this Code.

25. This rate shall be stated on all invoices or bills sent to the client.

26. In this situation the professional obligations outweigh any obligations to the workplace.

SOCIAL WORK PRACTICE
RESEARCH TRADITIONS

Scientific Traditions

Social work practice research and contributions to knowledge emerge from various distinct traditions. In the *case study method* the investigator tests out intervention hypotheses through detailed documentation of practice. This research method is grounded in the processes and details of a case and captures the subtle nuances of practice. However, problems of validity and the reliability of the investigator's observations represent a critical disadvantage of the case study method. The worker may not be a neutral observer, tending to over-claim one's "successes." Similarly, it is possible to over-generalize the findings with particular case in a particular setting and culture to the findings of other workers, or other clients, settings and cultures.

Increasing concerns about validity and reliability led clinical investigators to study comparison groups of patients. The *group comparison method* establishes two groups composed of people with similar background and problem characteristics. Interventions are provided to one group (the experimental group) while interventions are withheld from the other (the control group). By measuring the differences between the groups on some outcome measure, the investigator evaluates the effectiveness of the intervention on the clients in the experimental group. In a recent study, for example, the group comparison method was used to examine the treatment of depression by pharmacotherapy, interpersonal psychotherapy, and cognitive behavioral therapy. These three experimental groups were compared to a control group which was given a placebo and some general emotional support (Elkin, Parloff, Hadley, and Autry 1985). Validity and reliability are more effectively established in the group comparison approach than in the case study approach.

However, group comparison also has significant disadvantages. In aggregate data, the interventions' effect on an individual is averaged into a group score. Thus the individual response is lost in the aggregated data. Similarly, the impact of the environment is extremely difficult to control. A new job or a sudden loss of a relationship may have a more profound positive or negative effect than the professional intervention itself. Another disadvantage is that interventions are often defined ambiguously and not precisely specified (Wood 1978). Moreover, when interventions are specified, they are evaluated on their own terms as if they were separate from a worker's style and persona. The art of social work practice is removed from the science of social work practice. Individual practitioner skills and the reciprocal transactions between social worker and client are often ignored. Finally, withholding treatment from those in the control group, and technical sampling problems of composing two or more similar groups raise ethical issues.

An alternative to the group comparison method is the *single-case method*. It represents a more rigorous elaboration of the case study approach and a return of focus from the group to the individual. Currently, the single-case design is the predominant method of evaluating the effectiveness of a planned intervention, with much to offer the practitioner. It demands a specification of client outcomes and clarity about interventive methods. This demand alone often increases practice focus, discipline, and accountability. Moreover, when clients are actively involved in defining their life stressors, identifying hoped-for outcomes, and participating in the interventions, they become engaged in evaluating their own progress.

The sequence of the single-case method design consists of phase *A*—establishing a baseline measure of a person's behavior, perception, attitude or feeling; followed by phase *B*—introducing an intervention and remeasuring the behavior, perception, attitude or feeling (Blythe and Tripodi 1989). The first step in evaluating a practice outcome (the dependent variable) is the collection of baseline data at various points in time prior to the introduction of the treatment intervention (independent variable). If one collects baseline data at only one point in time, the standard may be idiosyncratic and not representative of the individual's behavioral patterns. To have confidence that the baseline is truly representative of the individual's behavioral pattern, data have to be collected at various points prior to the introduction of the helping interventions. Establishing baseline criteria is fundamental to single-case outcome evaluation of changes in behavior (perception, attitude, or feeling). At times, this complex process of remeasurement creates ethical dilemmas related to the postponement of needed services and the logistical problems of repeating baseline measurement (Barlow and Hersen 1973). For some clients, postponing services results in an unmanageable increase in stress, or impatience and dropout.

Nelson (1985) identifies four dimensions to be considered in defining the intervention: form, content, dosage, and context. Form refers to the type of communication used. Examining (breaking up large concerns into smaller, more manageable ones), for example, reflects a type of intervention. Content refers to the message provided by the intervention. Reaching for a client's anger, for example, may communicate that the emotion of anger is acceptable and legitimate to express. How extensively and intensively interventions are repeated reflects dosage. Context refers to such factors as the client's prior experiences with professional and social agencies, the worker's reactions to the client, the degree of trust and conditions of safety established in the helping relationship, and messages communicated in voice tone and nonverbal behaviors. These four dimensions are considered in the process of developing conceptual and operational definitions of the experimental intervention. However, a natural overlap between these dimensions makes the task of developing these definitions a most difficult and challenging step for the clinical investigator.

After establishing the baseline measure and conceptualizing the intervention, one introduces the intervention and then compares the client's starting point behavior to behavior at later points in time. For example, a worker requests that a woman suffering the symptoms of depression (e.g. difficulty sleeping and eating, internalizing anger, expressing self-doubts) complete a self-anchored depression scale and a problem inventory at three different times. After establishing a baseline measure of her depression through the self-anchored scale and identifying the major stressor as her boyfriend through the problem inventory (phase *A*), the worker helps her by teaching her assertiveness skills. After ten sessions, the woman completes the depression scale once again (phase *B*). A decrease in the depression score is suggestive of an effective and successful intervention.

However, factors other than the treatment intervention may confound or account for the outcome (Jayarante and Levy 1979; Nelson 1981). A major confounding factor which affects internal validity is a change in the person's environment. For example, the depressed woman's boyfriend may have been promoted on his job and, feeling better about himself, changed his behavior towards his girlfriend. This environmental change may be more responsible for her improvement than the helping intervention. Another factor is the individual's own internal development. The depressed person becomes "tired of being tired" and sets out to make changes in her life. Finally, the treatment environment may have its own build-in confounding factors. For example, the worker's unconditional support and nurturing of the depressed person may have had more to do with the improvement in her depressive state than the assertiveness intervention. Possibly, six months later, without the therapeutic relationship, the woman might have become as or even more depressed than the initial baseline measure of her depression. Finally, while single-subject investigators usually effectively conceptualize and operationalize an intervention, there is a tendency to not verify its actual use (Nelson 1985). The worker in this example may have modeled reasoning skills rather than assertiveness skills. Without the safeguard of external verification by independent observation, the specified intervention may be delivered in a manner other than intended.

To develop greater experimental controls, various adaptations of the *AB* design have been developed. One such adaptation is the *ABC* design, also referred to as the "successive interventions design" (Nelson 1988:371). In the case of the depressed woman, after establishing the baseline data (phase *A*), the assertiveness intervention is evaluated after ten weeks (phase *B*). If the person makes no or limited progress, a new intervention (e.g., an antidepressant) is applied and progress evaluated after ten additional weeks (phase *C*). This design can be further expanded. After establishing a new baseline, the worker introduces a new intervention (antidepressant and unconditional support) and after ten additional weeks evaluates this intervention (phase *D*). In this design external factors are not controlled. However, some impressionistic comparison of interventions can be made.

Another adaptation is the *ABAB* design which can be either a reversal design or a multiple baseline design. Like the *AB* and *ABC* designs, the reversal *ABAB* design begins with the establishment of baseline behavior (phase *A*) followed by the introduction of the experimental intervention and evaluation of the outcome (phase *B*). The outcome serves as the new baseline (second phase *A*), but this time the intervention is withdrawn and, after the same period of time, the outcome of the withdrawn intervention is evaluated (second phase *B*). If the person had improved after the original intervention was applied and regressed after it had been withdrawn, the effectiveness of the intervention is believed to be demonstrated. If the intervention can be reintroduced and the individual once again improves, there is greater confidence in the outcome. This final application actually expands the design to an *ABABAB*. To illustrate, after establishing the baseline behavior of a disruptive child in a group (phase *A*), the worker for a period of five sessions uses nonverbal methods to demonstrate acceptance of the child and evaluates the child's disruptions at the end of the time period (phase *B*). After establishing the new baseline (second phase *A*), the worker ignores the child's disruptive behavior for the next five sessions and evaluates the child's behavior at the end of this time period (second phase *B*). Finally, after establishing the new baseline (third phase *A*), the worker reintroduces the accepting nonverbal interventions for the next five weeks and then evaluates behavioral changes (third phase *B*). A decrease in the youngster's disruptive group behavior followed by a regression and increase in disruption, followed by subsequent decrease in d... uptions, establishes the positive impact of the worker's accepting, non-verbal interventions.

While this design has greater empirical controls, the withdrawal of a potentially effective intervention raises serious ethical and service issues for the social worker. To remove an effective intervention from the depressed woman in our example may do her irreparable harm. Even though the results might be more definitive, the human costs may be too great.

Pressure to demonstrate effectiveness may result in the selection of more motivated clients with less severe problems because they fit the design better than those less motivated for behavioral change and those economically disadvantaged. Thus the most significant problems may not be selected for outcome evaluation. In short, a finding might be statistically, but not clinically, significant.

In an attempt to gain acceptance and approval of university administrators and colleagues from other disciplines, social work scholars are primarily drawn to experimental quantitative designs to the exclusion of other methods that "fit" better with the complexities of real life and social work practice. We agree with Reagh's observation that:

> social work has gone too far in its quest to validate its existence when it forgets that clients can lose a great deal while they are "studied" in relation to the treatment outcome.   1994:81

Ecologically sensitive scientific traditions. There are other ways of studying and learning and contributing to the profession's knowledge base. The quest for a scientific base of social work is as old as the profession itself, and continues unabated today. Naturalistic qualitative methods widely used in anthropology and biology are compatible with social work's client-centered traditions. In naturalistic explorations, the investigator is the major instrument of study. The social worker skilled in inviting and exploring clients' stories is a natural investigator into people's transactions with their social and physical environment. By exploring, observing, and following cues, the practitioner is able to capture subtle nuances of meaning and behavior.

> The human instrument is the only instrument that can process a complex, holistic picture all at one time and be able to generate and test hypotheses immediately in the very situation in which they are created. The human instrument also has the unique capability of summarizing data on the spot and feeding them back to the respondent for clarification and explanation of any atypical or idiosyncratic responses that might have occurred.   (Reagh 1994:92)

By immersing themselves in clients' stories and environments, social workers are in a natural position to describe adaptive and dysfunctional patterns, as well as processes of change. Through detailed and rich descriptions, including direct quotes from clients and significant environmental figures, we capture the whole person within a life-course and ecological perspective. The biologist Albert Szent-Gyorgyi (1967:11) referred to the ecological field as the most complex and difficult to research. To study this field, "we must be in direct personal contact with it and we must use all our senses, including two outdated instruments: eyes and brains."

Suppose a social work administrator is asked to plan social work service in a new regional intensive-care neonatal nursery. She will need to learn how parents cope with the stress of having a seriously handicapped infant, so that the nursery staff will understand the nature of their needs and how best to provide the service. The administrator will need to learn from the parents and the staff how organizational policies and procedures affect them. She will need to learn which staff behaviors support or frustrate the parents. At the same time, by talking to parents and following their cues, social work staff learn about their coping skills and difficulties within the social and physical contexts in which their transactions with staff are embedded. The impact of the physical environment will need to be understood: its spatial design and accessibility, and its temporal features that either facilitate and or hinder parent-infant interaction and parent-staff interaction.

Life-modeled social work practice is based on our systematic examination of the detailed and rich descriptions of seasoned and student social workers' interventions over many years. By reviewing audio and videotapes, direct observation, records of service, critical incidents, process and summary recordings, we study the complexities of the transactions between person and environment, between client and worker. By examining this mass of information, we can deduce transactional patterns and practice principles. The primary advantage of inductive case patterning is that clinical generalizations develop from "inside" and represent an "insider's" view of the helping process.

To deal with a separation of process and outcomes and to further develop the process method of empirical inquiry, some social work practice scholars attempt to relate helping processes to differential client outcomes. Shulman initially investigated the association between twenty-two skills with the development of a positive relationship and client perception of worker helpfulness (Shulman 1978). He developed a category observation system for systematizing observations of interactions between workers and clients (Shulman 1981). In this early research, he examined the clients' perceptions of the helping process in an entire agency at one point in time. In his most recent study, a number of "hard" outcomes (such as maintaining children at home rather than in foster care, or court status) were added to client and worker subjective impressions about the helping process (Shulman 1991). He found that the professional skills of helping clients to manage their feelings showed a direct and strong path to caring. In turn, caring suggested a causal path to court status and number of days a child spends in foster care. Naturalistic inquiry is life-oriented and directed to context as well as people.

NOTES

Preface

1. We use the term *life model* interchangeably with *life-modeled practice* in order to add still more emphasis to the fact that the practice is patterned on natural life processes. We are less concerned with whether the approach is a model in the technical sense and more concerned with ensuring the embodiment of those real-life processes that release human potential and lead to continued growth, empowerment, satisfying bio-psycho-social functioning, and effective action to improve environments and contribute to social justice.

2. Nevertheless, the social policy, administration, and social work research specializations associated with community organization in many social work educational programs probably need to remain separate because of their highly specialized and technological nature—even though they rest on the same values and theoretical foundation as the rest of social work.

1. The Ecological Perspective

1. The first two sections of this chapter are adapted in part from Germain and Gitterman (1987, 1995) and Germain (1985a; 1990; 1991a).

2. We thank Professor Susan Kemp for her suggestion of a nonevent as a life stressor.

3. Among the best known life cycle models are those of Erikson (used in our 1980 book), Freud, Gould, Kohlberg, Levinson, and Vaillant.

4. We thank Dean Anita Lightburn for calling our attention to Broughton's work.

5. Even in biological development, in contrast to social and emotional development, individual and group difference may be due to genetic structures and their interplay with environment through accidents, serious illness, genetic mutations, social timetables, educational practices, and cultural meanings and responses.

2. The Life Model of Social Work Practice: A Brief Overview

1. Self-awareness regarding one's own values, beliefs, attitudes, and orientations is also essential to developing sensitivity to and acceptance of difference. Both field and classroom education in social work provide opportunities to enhance self-awareness and to acquire specialized knowledge pertaining to human diversity. When social work services are needed by newcomers not yet covered in educational programs, practitioners must obtain such specialized knowledge through consultation, reading, and attending seminars.

2. Buchanan (1978:372) defines paternalism as "interference with a person's freedom of action or freedom of information, or the deliberate dissemination of misinformation, where the alleged justification of interference or misinforming is that it is for the good of the person who is interfered with or misinformed"; cited by Reamer (1990:82).

3. Beginnings: Auspice, Modalities, Methods, and Skills

1. Crohn's disease is an inflammation of the digestive tract, most often resulting in the small intestine becoming thick, hard, and brittle. Deep ulcers, scarring and swelling may obstruct the intestinal tract and cause infections and severe pain.

2. As early as 1963, Robert Butler identified oral reminiscence as integrative activity characteristic of most older people. Practice experience in using elders' reminiscences for therapeutic purposes made it easy for many social workers to later work with the more complete life stories or narratives told to them by clients of all ages and circumstances.

5. Helping Individuals, Families, and Groups with Environmental Stressors

1. The lack of a viable network is also a source of stress. Mentally ill people, for example, often suffer from impoverished networks (Croty and Kulys 1985; Hamilton, Ponzoha, Cutler and Weigel 1989). Some residents of otherwise satisfactory housing experience stress because physical provision for the formation of social networks is lacking (Yacey 1971). Although slum areas might be physically deteriorated, many do have strong social networks that are lost in redevelopment.

2. Case management is a rapidly growing system of community-based care for defined populations who suffer profound, long-term, or permanent disabilities. The chronically mentally ill are the largest population served, followed by the physically and developmentally challenged. A growing population of older persons who are unable to provide adequately for their health, social, and economic needs without in-home services, are also maintained in the community through public and private case management agencies. Similarly, physically challenged persons in the community who require multiple social and health services in order to maintain independent living are served by case managers attached to rehabilitation agencies or provided by case management and community-based agencies, including those who also serve the elderly (Germain 1994b).

3. Social network intervention has probably characterized social work practice since its beginning. The settlement movement was conceived by its founders as good neighboring. College students and youthful professionals who became settlement house residents sought to be friendly neighbors to the poor among whom they lived. They wanted to help their neighbors organize themselves to improve the quality of neighborhood life through mutual help. They appreciated the ecological validity and value of intervening in networks within their community and cultural contexts. Now, more than a century

later, recognition of the importance of natural helpers in people's lives is growing and many such helpers coalesce into social networks.

6. Helping with Dysfunctional Family Processes

1. "Two-provider families" designates a working-class family in which both parents must work to stay solvent. "Two-career families" refers to middle-class families in which both parents work in professional positions for personal satisfaction as well as a higher standard of living.

2. We believe strongly that all social workers, and not only those in the mental health field, should know about commonly used psychotropic medications and their aims, contraindications to their use, and side effects. (See Bentley 1993; Bentley, Rosenson, and Zito 1990; Gerhart 1987; Libassi 1995.)

7. Helping with Dysfunctional Group Processes

1. This discussion is drawn from Gitterman 1989a.
2. The discussion and illustration is drawn from Gitterman, 1992.
3. The discussion and illustration is drawn from Gitterman, 1992.

8. Reducing Interpersonal Stress Between Worker and Client

1. This discussion draws from Gitterman 1983, 1989b.

9. Endings: Auspice, Modalities, Methods, and Skills

1. Kubler-Ross (1975) awakened the profession to understanding and teaching about the processes of death and dying. However, her fixed, sequential, universal stages of dying do not accurately describe these processes. We do not all die alike or mourn alike in predictable, uniform, separable stages, but uniquely as a consequence of many interacting factors which appear, recede, and come to the fore again and again. In place of Kubler-Ross's stages of dying, death and mourning follow unique pathways and trajectories (Dane 1991; Kavenaugh 1977; Nuland 1994; Pattison 1977; Rando 1985).

10. Influencing Community and Neighborhood Life

1. Some schools of social work continue to teach a "community organization" specialization which usually includes some of the following: management and administration, social planning, social policy analysis, fund-raising, grant writing, community research, and grass-roots organizing for social action—often on a large scale and in a context of serious opposition and controversy. At times, the social worker community organizer may also work collaboratively with affluent and influential community groups.

2. In addition to participation at this grassroots level, participation also includes a level of resident involvement that we merely note here. "As a means of recovering the lost sense of community and regenerating social institutions on the local level," Kramer and Specht (1983) advocate resident participation in planning bodies and neighborhood organizations, including involvement in decision-making processes. Additionally, the current interest in empowerment is reflected in an emphasis on participant decision-making in organizations.

3. Although started informally on a community level, many self-help groups have developed into large, formalized, powerful, national advocacy or research organizations. The question for groups that develop into formal organizations is how to simultaneously

meet the needs of new members for support and mutual aid and of long-term members for services such as fund-raising, research, and advocacy. Some organizations try to continue informal mutual aid at the local level.

4. Developmental disabilities, as defined by the Developmental Disabilities Assistance and Bill of Rights Act of 1990 (P.L. 101-496) are severe, chronic conditions that:

> are attributable to mental or physical impairments or a combination of both
> are manifested before age 22
> are likely to continue indefinitely
> result in substantial limitations in three or more major activity areas (self-care, receptive and expressive language, learning, mobility, self-direction, capacity for independent living, and economic self-sufficiency)
> require a combination and sequence of special, interdisciplinary, or generic care, treatment, or other services that are of extended or lifelong duration and are individually planned and coordinated. (Freedman 1995)

5. Gibbs's model for understanding African-American responses to consultation includes the following phases: (1) "sizing up" the consultant for personal authenticity; (2) investigation or "checking out" how the consultant relates to people of different educational, social, and cultural backgrounds; (3) involvement (if the consultant checked out favorably and was familiar with African-American culture, symbolic behaviors, attitudes, and values); (4) commitment to program (based on evaluation of consultant's empathic skills, demonstrated comprehension of the institution's problems and complexities, and support and non-judgmental attitudes when consultees expressed personal conflicts or professional frustrations); and (5) engagement (based on evaluation of the consultant's instrumental competence). Phases 4 and 5 overlap. "While black persons will make this commitment as a result of their evaluation of the consultant's interpersonal competence in the first four [phases], white persons will make this commitment in terms of the instrumental competence shown by the consultant up to this time" (p. 200).

11. Influencing the Practitioner's Organization

1. We continue to be grateful to Professor George Brager for referring us to the literature and sharing his ideas while we wrote the first edition of this work (1980).

2. This illustration and discussion draws on Gitterman and Miller 1989.

12. Influencing Legislation, Regulations, and Electoral Politics

1. Whatever the practice approach, the number of social workers engaging in political activism is growing. Despite NASW support for participation in political influencing by all social workers, the Council of Social Work Education (CSWE) has not yet mandated or even recommended curriculum content on political influencing in class and field.

2. This section draws in part on Albert (1983).

3. All political action committees (PACs) including PACE have become controversial but integral parts of the governmental process. A related NASW activity is its Educational Legislative Action Network (ELAN), which monitors legislative activity and alerts state chapter members when their letterwriting and telephone calls to members of Congress are needed in support of legislation favorable to social work and the populations we serve.

REFERENCES

Abrams, H.A. and S. Goldstein. 1982. "A State Chapter's Comprehensive Political Program." In M. Mahaffey and J. Hanks (Eds.). *Practical Politics: Social Work and Political Responsibility* pp. 241–60. Silver Spring, Md.: National Association of Social Workers.

Abramson, M. 1983. "A Model for Organizing Our Ethical Analysis of the Discharge Planning Process." *Social Work in Health Care* 9(1):45–52.

——. 1984. "Ethical Issues in Social Work Practice with Dying Persons." In L. Suszychi and M. Abramson, (Eds.) *Social Work Management and Terminal Care* pp. 126–35. New York: Praeger.

——. 1985. "The Autonomy-Paternalism Dilemma in Social Work Practice." *Social Casework* 66(7)387–93.

——. 1989. "Autonomy vs. Paternalistic Beneficence: Practice Strategies." *Social Casework* 70(2):101–5.

——. 1990. "Keeping Secrets: Social Workers and AIDS." *Social Work* 35(2):169–73.

Adams, R. G. and R. Blieszner. 1993. "Resources for Friendship Interventions." *Journal of Sociology and Social Welfare* 28(4):159–75.

Ahrons, C. R. and R. H. Rodgers. 1987. *Divorced Families and Multidisciplinary Developmental View*. New York: W. W. Norton.

Albert, J. 1994. "Rethinking Difference: A Cognitive Therapy Group for Chronic Mental Patients." *Social Work with Groups* 17(1/2):105–21.

Albert, R. 1983. "Social Work Advocacy in the Regulatory Process." *Social Casework* 64(October):473–81.

Alcabes, A. and J. Jones. 1985. "Structural Determinants of 'Clienthood.' " *Social Work.* 30(January-February):49–53.

Altman, I. 1975. *Environment and Social Behavior*. Monterey: Brooks/Cole.

Altman, I. and M. Gavain. 1981. "A Cross-Cultural and Dialectic Analysis of Homes." In L. Lieben, A. Paterson, and N. Newcombe (Eds.) *Spatial Representation and Behavior Across the Life Span* pp. 283–320. New York: Academic Press.

Ambrosino, S. 1984. "Family Advocacy" an interview with *Practice Digest* 7(3):5–6.

Anderson, C. and G. Hogarty. 1986. *Schizophrenia and the Family*. New York: Guilford Press.

Anderson, C., Reiss, D. J. and G. E. Hogarty. 1980. "Family Treatment of Adult Schizophrenic Patients: A Psycho-Educational Approach." *Schizophrenia Bulletin* 6:490–505.

Anderson, H. and H. A. Goolishian, 1992. "The Client is the Expert: A Not-Knowing Approach to Therapy." In S. McNamee and K. J. Gergen, (Eds.) *Therapy as Social Construction* pp. 25–39. Newbury Park, Cal.: Sage.

Antsey, M. 1982. "Scapegoating in Groups: Some Theoretical Perspectives and Case Record of Intervention." *Social Work with Groups* 5(3):51–63.

Aponte, H. J. 1976. "The Family-School Interview: An Eco-Structural Approach." *Family Process* 15(September):303–12.

Armstrong, B. 1991. "Adolescent Pregnancy." In A. Gitterman (ed.) *Handbook of Social Work Practice with Vulnerable Populations* pp. 319–44. New York: Columbia University Press.

Asser, E. 1978. "Social Class and Help-Seeking Behavior." *American Journal of Community Psychology.* 6(5):465–74.

"A State Chapter's Comprehensive Political Program." In Mahaffey, M. and J. W. Hanks, (Eds.). *Practical Politics: Social Work and Political Responsibility,* pp. 241–60. Silver Spring: National Association of Social Workers.

Auslander, G. and H. Levin. 1987. "The Parameters of Network Intervention: A Social Work Application." *Social Service Review* 61(June):305–18.

Bandler, B. 1963. "The Concept of Ego-Supportive Psychotherapy." In H. Parad and R. Miller (Eds.) *Ego-Oriented Casework: Problems and Perspectives* pp. 27–44. New York: Family Service Association of America.

Bank, S. P. and M. D. Kahn. 1982. *The Sibling Bond.* New York: Basic Books.

Banner, D. and E. Gagne. 1994. *Designing Effective Organizations.* Newbury Park, Cal.: Sage.

Barbarin, O. 1983. "Coping with Ecological Transitions by Black Families: A Psychosocial Model." *Journal of Community Psychology* 11(October):308–22.

Barlow, D. and M. Hersen. 1973. "Single Case Experimental Designs: Uses in Applied Clinical Research." *Archives of General Psychiatry* 29(3):319–25.

Barton, B. R. and A. S. Marshall. 1986. "Pivotal Partings: Forced Termination with a Sexually Abused Boy." *Clinical Social Work Journal* 14(2):149–59.

Baum, R. and P. Paulus. 1987. "Crowding." In D. Stokols and I. Altman (Eds.) *Handbook of Environmental Psychology* pp. 533–70. New York: Cambridge University Press.

Beck, D. F. and M. A. Jones. 1973. *Progress on Family Problems.* New York: Family Service Association of America.

Beck, R. 1987. "Redirecting Blaming in Marital Psychotherapy." *Clinical Social Work Journal* 15 (Summer):148–58.

Becker, G. 1993. "Continuity After a Stroke: Implications of Life Course Disruption in Old Age." *Gerontologist* 33(April):148–58.

Bentley, K. J. 1993. "The Right of Psychiatric Patients to Refuse Medication." *Social Work* 38(January):101–6.

Bentley, K. J., M. K. Rosenson and J. M. Zito. 1990. "Promoting Medication Compliance: Strategies for Working with Families of Mentally Ill People." *Social Work* 35(May):274–77.

Berg, I. and S. Miller. 1992. "Working with Asian Clients: One Person at a Time." *Families in Society* 73(June):356–63.

Berger, C. S. 1990. "Enhancing Social Work Influence in the Hospital: Identifying Sources of Power." *Social Work in Health Care* 15(2):77–93.

Berger, P. and T. Luckmann. 1966. *The Social Construction of Reality.* Garden City, New York: Doubleday.

Bergman, A. 1989. "Informal Support Systems for Pregnant Teenagers." *Social Casework* 70(9):525–33.

Berlin, S. 1983. "Cognitive-Behavioral Approaches." In A. Rosenblatt and D. Waldfogel (Eds.) *Handbook of Clinical Social Work* pp. 1095–1119. San Francisco: Jossey-Bass.

Berliner, A. 1989. "Misconduct in Social Work Practice." *Social Work* 34(1):69–72.

Berman-Rossi, T. 1991. "Elderly in Need of Long-Term Care." In A. Gitterman (Ed.) *Handbook of Social Work Practice with Vulnerable Populations* pp. 503–48. New York: Columbia University Press.

——.1992. "Empowering Groups through Understanding Stages of Group Development." *Social Work with Groups* 15(2/3):239–55.

——. 1994a. "The Fight Against Hopelessness and Despair: Institutionalized Aged." In A. Gitterman and L. Shulman (Eds.) *Mutual Aid Vulnerable Populations and the Life Cycle* pp. 385–409. New York: Columbia University Press.

—- (Ed.). 1994b. *Social Work: The Collected Writings of William Schwartz*. Itasca, Ill: F. E. Peacock.

Berman-Rossi, T. and M. Cohen. 1988. "Group Development and Shared Decision Making Working with Homeless Mentally Ill Women." *Social Work with Groups* 11(4):63–78.

Berman-Rossi, T. and P. Rossi. 1990. "Confidentiality and Informed Consent in School Social Work." *Social Work in Education* (April):195–207.

Berthold, S. M. 1989. "Spiritism as a Form of Psychotherapy: Implications for Social Work Practice." *Social Casework* 70(October):502–9.

Betcher, H. and F. Maple. 1985 "Elements and Issues in Group Composition." In Sundel, M., Glasser, P., Sarri, R., and R. Vinter (Eds.) *Individual Change Through Small Groups* pp. 180–202. New York: Free Press.

Biegel, D. E., E. M. Tracy, and K. N. Corvo. 1994. "Strengthening Social Networks: Intervention Strategies for Mental Health Case Managers." *Health and Social Work* 19(3):206–16.

Black, R. and J. Weiss. 1990. "Genetic Support Groups and Social Workers as Partners." *Health and Social Work* 15(2):91–99.

Black, R. B. and J. O. Weiss. 1991. "Chronic Physical Illness and Disability." In A. Gitterman (Ed.) *Handbook of Social Work Practice with Vulnerable Populations* pp. 137–64. New York: Columbia University Press.

Bloom, M. 1987. "Prevention." In *Encyclopedia of Social Work* 18th ed., pp. 303–15. Silver Spring: National Association of Social Workers.

Blumenfield, S. and J. Lowe. 1987. "A Template for Analyzing Ethical Dilemmas in Discharge Planning." *Health and Social Work* 12(1):47–56.

Blythe, B. and T. Tripoli. 1989. *Measurement in Direct Practice*. Newbury, Cal.: Sage.

Bogard, M. 1984. "Family Systems Approaches to Wife Battering: A Feminist Critique." *American Journal of Orthopsychiatry* 54(October):558–68.

Bonilla-Santiago, G. 1989. "Legislating Progress for Hispanic Women in New Jersey." *Social Work* 34(3):270–72.

Bower, S. and G. Bower. 1979. *Asserting Yourself*. Reading, Penn.: Addison-Wesley.

Bowlby, J. 1973. "Affectional Bonds: Their Nature and Origin." In R. S. Weiss (Ed.) *Loneliness: The Experience of Emotional and Social Isolation* pp. 38–52. Cambridge: MIT Press.

Bowlby, J. 1980. *Attachment and Loss, Vol.III, Loss*. New York: Basic Books.

Brabender, V. 1985. "Time Limited Inpatient Group Therapy: A Developmental Model." *International Journal of Group Psychotherapy* 35(3):373–90.

Brager, G. and S. Holloway. 1978. *Changing Human Service Organizations*. New York: Free Press.

——. 1992. "Assessing Prospects for Organizational Change." *Administration in Social Work* 16(3/4):15–28.

Brager G., Specht, H., and J. Torezyner. 1987. *Community Organizing*. New York: Columbia University Press.

Breton, M. 1984. "A Drop-In Program for Transient Women." *Social Work* 29(6):542–46.

Brice, J. 1982. "West Indian Families." In M. McGoldrick, J. Pearce, and J. Giordano (Eds.) *Ethnicity and Family Therapy* pp. 123–33. New York: Guilford.

Brickel, C. 1986. "Pet-Facilitated Therapies: A Review of the Literature and Clinical Implementation Considerations." *Clinical Gerontologist* 5(2):309–32.

Bridging Cultures: Southeast Asian Refugees in America. 1981. Los Angeles: Asian American Community Mental Health Training Center.

Broughton, J. 1986."The Psychology, History and Ideology of the Self." In K. Larsen (Ed.) *Dialectics and Ideology in Psychology.* Norwich, N.J.: Ablex.

Brown, A. and T. Mistry. 1994. "Group Work with 'Mixed Membership' Groups: Issues of Race and Gender." *Social Work with Groups* 17(3):5–21.

Brown, D. R. and L. E. Gary. 1987. "Stressful Life Events, Social Support Networks, and the Physical and Mental Health of Urban Black Adults." *Journal of Human Stress* 13:165–74.

Brown, J. 1994. "Agents of Change: A Group of Women in a Homeless Shelter." In A. Gitterman and L. Shulman (Eds.) *Mutual Aid Vulnerable Populations and the Life Cycle* pp. 273–96. New York: Columbia University Press.

Bruner, J. 1966. *Toward a Theory Of Instruction.* Cambridge: Harvard University Press.

———. 1986. *Actual Minds, Possible Worlds.* Cambridge: Harvard University Press.

———. 1990. *Acts of Meaning.* Cambridge: Harvard University Press.

Burghart, S. 1982. *Organizing for Community Action.* Beverly Hills: Sage.

Burruel, G. and N. Chavez. 1974. "Mental Health Outpatient Centers: Relevant or Irrelevant to Mexican Americans." In A. Tulipan, G. Attneave, and E. Kingstone (Eds.) *Beyond Clinic Walls* pp. 108–30. Tuscaloosa: The University of Alabama Press.

Butler, R. 1963. "The Life Review: An Interpretation of Reminiscence in the Aged." *Psychiatry* 26(1):65–76.

Cain, C. 1990. In J. A. Fickling (Ed.) *Social Problems with Health Consequences: Program Design, Implementation, and Evaluation* pp. 61–75. Columbia, SC: Proceedings of the BiRegional Conference for Public Health Social Workers in Regions IV and VI, The University of South Carolina College of Social Work.

Chiriboga, D. 1982. "Adaptation to Marital Separation In Later and Earlier Life." *Journal of Gerontology* 37(1):109–14.

Cingolani, J. 1984. "Social Conflict Perspective on Work with Involuntary Clients." *Social Work* 29(September-October):442–46.

Clarke, E. 1957. *My Mother Who Fathered Me.* London: Allen and Unwin.

Code of Ethics. 1993. Silver Spring: National Association of Social Workers.

Cohen, A. 1980. Quoted in "How to Clout the Issues." An interview with *Practice Digest* 3(3):25–27.

Cohen, S. 1989. "Life Transitions: Losing a Pet." Doctoral term paper. New York: Columbia University School of Social Work. June 9 (unpublished)

Cohen, S. and D. Horm-Wingerd. 1993. "Children and the Environment: Ecological Awareness among Preschool Children." *Environment and Behavior* 25(1):103–20.

Cohen, S. and S. Syme (Eds.). 1985. *Social Support and Health.* Orlando: Academic Press.

Cohen, S. and T. Willis. 1985. "Stress, Social Support and the Buffering Hypothesis." *Psychological Bulletin* 98(2):310–57.

Cohen-Mansfield, J., Werner, P., and M. Marx. 1990. "The Spatial Distribution of Agitation in Agitated Nursing Home Residents." *Environment and Behavior* 22(May):408–19.

Cohler, B. 1982. "Personal Narrative and Life Course." In P. B. Baltes and O. G. Brim, Jr. (Eds.) *Life-Span Development and Behavior* Vol. 4 pp. 205–41. New York: Academic Press.

Cole, J. B. 1986. *All American Women: Lines that Divide. Ties that Bind.* New York: Free Press.

Coleman, D. 1991. "Non-Verbal Cues Are Easy to Misinterpret." *The New York Times* (September 17)pp.C1, 9.

Collins, A. H. and D. Pancoast. 1976. *Natural Helping Networks*. Washington, D. C.: National Association of Social Workers.

Collins, A. H., Pancoast, D. L., and J. A. Dunn. 1977. *Consultation Case Book*. Portland, OR: Portland State University.

Collins, B. G. 1986. "Defining Feminist Social Work." *Social Work* 31(3):214–19.

Comer, J. and M. Hamilton-Lee. 1982. "Support Systems in the Black Community." In D. Biegel and A. Naparstek, Eds. *Community Support Systems and Mental Health: Practice, Policy, and Research* pp. 121–36. New York: Springer.

Congress, E. P. 1994. "The Use of Culturegrams to Assess and Empower Culturally Diverse Families." *Families in Society* 75(9):531–40.

Cooper, S. 1973. "A Look at the Effects of Racism on Clinical Work." *Social Casework* 54(2):76–84.

Coopersmith, S. 1967. *The Antecedents of Self-Esteem*. San Francisco: Freeman.

Coplon, J. and J. Strull. 1983. "Roles of the Professional in Mutual Aid Groups." *Social Casework* 64(5):259–66.

Cotler, I., and J. Torczyner. 1988. *Complainant's Reply* (Dossier No. 8606004542-0001-0). Montreal, Quebec: Commission des Droits de la Personne.

Cowger, C. D. 1994. "Assessing Client Strengths: Clinical Assessment for Clinical Empowerment." *Social Work* 39(3):262–68.

Coyne, J. and R. Lazarus. 1980. "Cognitive Style, Stress, Perception, and Coping." In I. Kutash and L. Schlesinger, (Eds.) *Handbook on Stress and Anxiety* pp. 103–27. San Francisco: Jossey-Bass.

Coyne, J., Wortman, C., and D. Lehman. 1988. "The Other Side of Support: Emotional Over Involvement and Miscarried Helping." In B. Gottlieb (Ed.) *Marshaling Social Support* pp. 305–30. Newbury Park, Cal.: Sage Publications.

Crotty, P. and R. Kulys. 1985. "Social Support Networks: The Views of Schizophrenic Clients and Their Significant Others." *Social Work* 30(4):301–11.

Croxton, T. 1985. "The Therapeutic Contract." In M. Sundel, P. Glasser, R. Sarri, and R. Vinter (Eds.) *Individual Change Through Small Groups* pp. 159–79. New York: Free Press.

Cwikel, J. and R. Cnaan. 1991. "Ethical Dilemmas in Applying Second-Wave Information Technology to Social Work Practice. *Social Work* 36(2):114–20.

Dahl, A. S., K. M. Cowgill, and R. Asmundsson. 1987. "Life in Remarriage Families." *Social Work* 32(Jan/Feb):40–44.

Daly, M. and R. Burton. 1983. "Self-Esteem and Irrational Beliefs: An Exploratory Investigation with Implications for Counselors." *Journal of Counseling Psychology* 30(3):361–66.

Dane, B. and B. Simon. 1991. "Resident Guests: Social Workers in Host Settings." *Social Work* 36(3):208–13.

Dane, B. O. 1991. "Death of a Child." In A. Gitterman (Ed.) *Handbook of Social Work Practice with Vulnerable Populations* pp. 446–70. New York: Columbia University Press.

Davenport, J. and J. Davenport. 1982. "Utilizing the Social Network in Rural Communities." *Social Casework* 63(1):106–13.

de Anda, D. and R. Becerra. 1984. "Support Networks for Adolescent Mothers." *Social Casework* 65(3):172–81.

Dean, R. G. and M. Rhodes. 1992. "Ethical-Clinical Tensions in Clinical Practice." *Social Work* 37(2):128–32.

Dear, R. B. and R. J. Patti. 1982. "Legislative Advocacy: Seven Effective Tactics." In Mahaffey, M. and Hanks, J. W. (Eds.) *Practical Politics: Social Work and Political Responsibility* pp. 99–117. Silver Spring: National Association of Social Workers.

DeGraw, R. 1980. Interview with *Practice Digest* 3(3):25–28.

DeJong, G. 1979. "Independent Living: From Social Movement to Analytical Paradigm." *Archives of Physical Medicine and Rehabilitation* 60:435–46.

Delgado, M. 1988. "Groups in Puerto Rican Spiritism: Implications for Clinicians." In Jacobs, C. and D. H. Bowles (Eds.) *Ethnicity and Race: Critical Concepts in Social Work* pp. 34–47. Silver Spring: National Association of Social Workers.

Delgado, M. and D. Humm-Delgado. 1982. "Natural Support Systems: Source of Strength in Hispanic Communities." *Social Work* 27(January):83–90.

DeLone, R. 1979. *Small Futures: Children, Inequality, and the Limits of Liberal Reform.* New York: Harcourt Brace Jovanovich.

Dempsey, D. 1980. Interview with *Practice Digest* 3(3):25–28.

DeNitto, D. M. and C. A. McNeece. 1990. *Social Work: Issues and Opportunities in a Challenging Profession.* Englewood Cliffs, NJ: Prentice Hall.

Derrida, J. 1986. In M.C. Taylor (Ed.) *Deconstruction in Context.* Chicago: University of Chicago Press.

Devlin, A. 1992. "Psychiatric Ward Renovation: Staff Perception and Patient Behavior." *Environment and Behavior* 24(January):66–84.

Devore, W. 1983. "Ethnic Reality: The Life Model and Work with Black Families." *Social Casework* 64(November):525–31.

Devore, W. and E. Schlesinger. 1995. *Ethnic-Sensitive Social Work Practice* 4th ed. Boston: Allyn Bacon.

Dolgoff, R. 1981. "Clinicians as Social Policymakers." *Social Casework* 62(May):284–92.

Dore, M. and A. Dumois. 1990. "Cultural Differences in the Meaning of Adolescent Pregnancy." *Families in Society* 71(February):93–101.

Drachman, D. and A. Shen-Ryan. 1991. "Immigrants and Refugees." In A. Gitterman (Ed.) *Handbook of Social Work Practice with Vulnerable Populations* pp. 618–46. New York: Columbia University Press.

Dubos, R. 1965. *Man Adapting.* New Haven: Yale University Press.

——. 1968. *So Human an Animal.* New York: Scribner's.

Duehn, W. and E. Proctor. 1977. "Initial Clinical Interventions and Premature Discontinuance in Treatment." *American Journal of Orthopsychiatry* 47(2):284–90.

Duffy, T. 1990. "Psychodrama in Beginning Recovery: An Illustration of Goals and Methods." *Alcoholism Treatment Quarterly* 7(2):97–109.

Duhl, B. 1983. *From the Inside Out and Other Metaphors.* New York: Brunner-Mazel.

Duhl, F. 1976. "Changing Sex Roles—Concepts, Values, and Tasks." *Social Casework* 57(February):87–92.

Duncan-Ricks, E. N. 1992. "Adolescent Sexuality and Peer Pressure." *Child and Adolescent Social Work Journal* 9(4):319–27.

Dunkel, J. and S. Hatfield. 1986. "Countertransference Issues in Working with Persons with AIDS." *Social Work* 31(2):114–18.

Dussy, J. 1977. *Egograms.* New York: Harper and Row.

Elbow, M. 1986. "From Caregiving to Parenting: Family Formation with Adopted Older Children." *Social Work* (September-October):323–29.

Elkin, I., M. Parloff, and J. Autry. 1985. "NIMH Treatment of Depression Collaborative Research Program." *Archives of General Psychiatry* 42(March):305-16.

Epstein, L. 1988. *Helping People: The Task-Centered Approach.* Columbus: Merrill.

Erikson, G. 1984. "A Framework and Themes for Social Network Interventions." *Family Process* 23(1):187–98.

Esterberg, K., P. Moen, and D. Dempster-McCain. 1994. "Transition to Divorce: A Life-Course Approach to Women's Marital Duration and Dissolution." *Sociological Quarterly* 35(May):289–307.

Evans, G. and S. Lepore. 1992. "Conceptual and Analytical Issues in Crowding Research." *Journal of Environmental Psychology* 12(1):163–73.

Falicov, C. J. (Ed.). 1983. *Cultural Perspectives in Family Therapy*. Rockville: Aspen Publishers.

Farquharson, A. 1978. "Self-Help Groups: A Health Resource." Victoria, BC: University of Victoria, School of Social Work. Mimeo.

Finkelhor, D. 1987. "Trauma of Child Sexual Abuse." *Journal of Interpersonal Violence* 2(4):348–66.

Finkelhor, D. and A. Browne. 1985. "The Traumatic Impact of Child Sexual Abuse: A Conceptualization." *American Journal of Orthopsychiatry* 55(4):530–41.

Fischer, F. and C. Siriani (eds.). 1994. *Critical Studies in Organization and Bureaucracy*. Philadelphia: Temple University Press.

Fisher, J., Goff, B., Nadler, A., and J. Chinsky. 1988. "Social Psychological Influences on Help Seeking and Support from Peers." In B. Gottlieb (Ed.) *Marshaling Social Support* pp. 267–304 Newbury Park, Cal.: Sage.

Fisher, R. 1994. *Beyond Machiavelli: Tools for Coping with Conflict*. Cambridge: Harvard University Press.

Fortune, A. 1987. "Grief Only? Client and Social Worker Reactions to Termination." *Clinical Social Work Journal* 15(2):159–71.

Fortune, A., Pearlingi, E., and C. D. Rochelle. 1991. "Criteria for Terminating Treatment." *Families in Society: The Journal of Contemporary Human Services* 72(6): 366–70.

——. 1992. "Reactions to Termination of Individual Treatment." *Social Work* 37(2): 171–78.

Foster M. and L. Perry. 1982. "Self-valuation Among Blacks." *Social Work* 27(January): 60–67.

Foucault, M. 1980. *Power/Knowledge: Selected Interviews and Other Writings*. New York: Pantheon.

Franklin, A. 1982. "Therapeutic Interventions With Urban Black Adolescents." In E. Jones and S. Korchin (Eds.) *Minority Mental Health* pp. 267–95. New York: Praeger.

Franklin, A. 1992. "Therapy with African Men." *Families in Society* 73(June):350–55.

Freedman, R. I. 1995. "Developmental Disabilities and Direct Practice." In *Encyclopedia of Social Work* 19th ed., pp. 721–29. Silver Spring: National Association of Social Workers.

Freeman, E. 1984. "Multiple Losses in the Elderly: An Ecological Approach." *Social Casework* 65(5):287–96.

Freeman, E. M. and M. Pennekamp. 1988. *Social Work Practice: Toward a Child, Family, School, Community Perspective*. Springfield: Thomas.

Freeman, M. 1984. "History, Narrative, and Life-Span Development Knowledge." *Human Development* 27(1):1–19.

Freire, P. 1979. *Pedagogy of the Oppressed*. New York: Continuum Press.

Frey, G. 1990. "A Framework for Promoting Organizational Change." *Families in Society* 71(3):142–47.

Friedrich, W. 1990. *Psychotherapy of Sexually Abused Children and their Families*. New York: Norton.

Galanter, M. 1993. "Network Therapy for Addiction: A Model for Office Practice." *American Journal of Psychiatry* 150(Jan):28–36.

Galinsky, M. and J. Schopler. 1985. "Patterns of Entry and Exists in Open-Ended Groups." *Social Work with Groups* 8(2):67–79.

——. 1989. "Developmental Patterns in Open-Ended Groups." *Social Work with Groups* 12(2):99–114.

Galo, F. 1982. "The Effects of Social Support Networks on the Health of the Elderly." *Social Work in Health Care* 8(2):65–74.

Gambrill, E. 1992. *Critical Thinking in Clinical Practice: Improving the Accuracy of Judgments and Decisions About Clients*. San Francisco: Jossey-Bass.

Garland, J., H. Jones, and R. Kolodny. 1968. "A Model of Stages of Group Development in Social Work Groups." In S. Bernstein (Ed.) *Explorations in Group Work* pp. 12–53. Boston: University School of Social Work.

Garvin, C. C. and B. Seabury. 1984. *Interpersonal Practice in Social Work: Processes and Procedures.* Engelwood Cliffs, NJ: Prentice Hall.

Gelinas, D. 1983. "The Persisting Negative Effects of Incest." *Psychiatry* 46(November): 312–32.

Gentry, M. E. 1987. "Coalition Formation and Processes." *Social Work with Groups* 10(3):39–54.

Gerard, D. 1985. "Clinical Social Workers as Primary Prevention Agents." In Germain, C. B. (Ed.) *Advances in Clinical Social Work Practice* pp. 84–89. Silver Spring: National Association of Social Workers.

Gergen, K. J. 1985. "The Social Constructionist Movement in Modern Psychology." *American Psychologist* 40:266–75.

Gerhart, U. C. 1987. "Psychotropic Medications." In *Encyclopedia of Social Work* 18th ed, pp. 405–9. Silver Spring: National Association of Social Workers.

Gerhart, U. C. and A. D. Brooks. 1983. "The Social Work Practitioner and Antipsychotic Medications." *Social Work* 28(November/December):454–60.

Germain, C. B. 1976. "Time: An Ecological Variable in Social Work Practice." *Social Casework* 57(July):419–26.

——. 1977. "An Ecological Perspective on Social Work Practice in Health Care." *Social Work in Health Care* 3(4):67–76.

——. 1978. "Space, an Ecological Variable in Social Work Practice." *Social Casework* 59(November):15–22.

——. 1982a. "Teaching Primary Prevention in Social Work: An Ecological Perspective." *Journal of Education for Social Work* 18(Winter):20–28.

——. 1982b. "Understanding Resistance: Seven Social Workers Debate." *Practice Digest* 63:5–23.

——. 1983. "Using Social and Physical Environments." In A. Rosenblatt and D. Waldfogel (Eds.) *Handbook of Clinical Social Work* pp. 110–34. San Francisco: Jossey-Bass.

——. 1984. *Social Work in Health Care.* New York: Free Press.

——. 1985a. "The Place of Community Work Within an Ecological Approach to Social Work Practice." In S. H. Taylor and R. W. Roberts (Eds.) *Theory and Practice of Community Social Work* pp. 30–55. New York: Columbia University Press.

——. 1985b. "Understanding and Changing Communities and Organizations in the Practice of Child Welfare." In J. Laird and A. Hartman (Eds.) *A Handbook of Child Welfare: Context, Knowledge, and Practice* pp. 122–48. New York: Free Press.

——. 1988. "School as a Living Environment within the Community." *Social Work in Education* 10(4):260–76.

——. 1990. "Life Forces and the Anatomy of Practice." *Smith College Studies in Social Work* 60(March):138–52.

——. 1991a. *Human Behavior in the Social Environment: An Ecological View.* New York: Columbia University Press.

——. 1991b. "Educational Reform, Power, and Practice in the 1990's." In R. Constable, J. P. Flynn, and S. McDonald (Eds.) *School Social Work: Practice and Research Perspectives* 2d ed., pp. 87–95. Chicago: Lyceum.

——. 1994a. "Emerging Conceptions of Family Development over the Life Course." *Families and Society: The Journal of Contemporary Human Services* 75(5):259–68.

——. 1994b. "Using An Ecological Perspective." In J. Rothman (Ed.). *Practice with Highly Vulnerable Clients: Case Management and Community Based Service* pp. 39–55. Engelwood Cliffs, NJ: Prentice Hall.

Germain, C. B. and A. Gitterman. 1979. "The Life Model of Social Work Practice." In F. Turner (ed.) *Social Work Treatment* pp. 361–84. New York: Free Press.

——. 1986. "The Life Model of Social Work Practice Revisited." In F. Turner (Ed.) *Social Work Treatment* pp. 618–44. New York: Free Press.

——. 1987. "Ecological Perspective." In *The Encyclopedia of Social Work* 18th ed., pp. 488–99. Silver Spring: National Association of Social Workers.

——. 1995. "Ecological Perspective." In *Encyclopedia of Social Work* 19th ed, pp. 816–24. Silver Spring: National Association of Social Workers.

Germain, C. B. and A. Hartman. 1980. "People and Ideas in the History of Social Work Practice." *Social Casework* 61(6):323–31.

Getzel, G. 1994. "No One is Alone: Groups During the Aids Pandemic." In A. Gitterman and L. Shulman (Eds.) *Mutual Aid Groups, Vulnerable Populations, and The Life Cycle*. New York: Columbia University Press.

Getzel, G. 1991. "AIDS." In A. Gitterman (Ed.) *Handbook of Social Work Practice with Vulnerable Populations* pp. 35–64. New York: Columbia University Press.

Ghali, S. B. 1977. "Cultural Sensitivity and the Puerto Rican Client." *Social Casework* 58(8):459–68.

Gibbs, J. T. 1980. "The Interpersonal Orientation in Mental Health Consultation: Toward a Model of Ethnic Variations in Consultation." *Journal of Community Psychology* 8:195–207.

Gingerich, W., M. Kleczewski, and S. Kirk. 1982. "Name Calling in Social Work." *Social Service Review* 56(3):366–74.

Gitterman, A. 1971. "Group Work in the Public Schools." In W. Schwartz and S. Zelba (Eds.) *The Practice of Group Work* pp. 45–72. New York: Columbia University Press.

——. 1977. "Social Work in the Public Schools." *Social Casework* 58(February):111–18.

——. 1982. "The Uses of Groups in Health Settings." In A. Lurie, G. Rosenberg, and S. Pinskey (Eds.) *Social Work with Groups in Health Settings* pp. 6–21. New York: Prodist.

——. 1983. "Uses of Resistance: A Transactional View." *Social Work* 28(March/April):127–31.

——. 1987. "Social Work Looks Forward." In St. Denis, G. (Ed.) *Implementing a Forward Plan: A Public Health Social Work Challenge* pp. 3–16. Pittsburgh: University of Pittsburgh.

——. 1988. "The Social Worker as Educator." *Health Care Practice Today: The Social Worker as Educator* pp. 13–22. New York: Columbia University School of Social Work.

——. 1989a. "Building Mutual Support in Groups." *Social Work in Groups* 12(2):5–22.

——. 1989b. "Testing Professional Authority and Boundaries." *Social Casework* 70(March):165–71.

——. 1991. "Introduction to Social Work Practice with Vulnerable Populations." In A. Gitterman (Ed.) *Handbook of Social Work Practice with Vulnerable Populations* pp. 1–34. New York: Columbia University Press.

——. 1992. "Creative Connections between Theory and Practice." In M. Weil, K. Chau, and D. Southerland (Eds.) *Theory, Practice, and Education* pp. 13–27. New York: Haworth Press.

——. 1994. "Developing a New Group Service." In Gitterman, A. and L. Shulman (Eds.) *Mutual Aid Groups, Vulnerable Populations and The Life Cycle* pp. 59–77. New York: Columbia University Press.

Gitterman, A. and C. B. Germain. 1976. "Social Work Practice: A Life Model." *Social Service Review* 50(December):601–10.

Gitterman, A. and I. Miller. 1989. "The Influence of the Organization on Clinical Practice." *Clinical Social Work Journal* 17(2):151–64.

Gitterman, A. and I. Miller. 1992. "Should Part of Social Workers' Salaries be Contingent on the Outcomes They Achieve with Their Clients? NO." In E. Gambrill and R. Pruger (Eds.) *Controversial Issues in Social Work* pp. 279–87. Boston: Allyn and Bacon.

Gitterman, A. and A. Schaeffer. 1972. "The White Worker and the Black Client." *Social Casework* 53(May):280–91.

Gitterman, A. and L. Shulman (Eds.). 1994. *Mutual Aid Groups, Vulnerable Populations and the Life Cycle*. New York: Columbia University Press.

Gitterman, N. 1991. "Learning Disabilities." In A. Gitterman, (Ed.). *Handbook of Social Work Practice with Vulnerable Populations* pp. 234–64. New York: Columbia University Press.

Givelber, D. J., Bowers, W. J. and C. L. Blitch. 1984. "Tarasoff, Myth and Reality: An Empirical Study of Private Law in Action." *Wisconsin Law Review* 2:443–97.

Glaser, J. S. 1972. "The Stairwell Society of Public Housing: From Small Groups to Social Organizations." *Small Group Behavior* (August):159–73.

Glassman, U. and L. Kates. 1986. "Techniques of Social Group Work: A Framework for Practice." *Social Work with Groups* 9(Spring):9–38.

Gliedman, J. and W. Roth. 1980. *The Unexpected Minority: Handicapped Children in America*. New York: Harcourt Brace Jovanovich.

Golan, N. 1986. "Crisis Theory." In F. Turner (Ed.) *Social Work Treatment* pp. 296–340. New York: Free Press.

Gold, N. 1990. "Motivation: The Crucial but Unexplored Component of Social Work Practice." *Social Work* 35(1):49–56.

Goldstein, H. 1983. "Starting Where the Client Is." *Social Casework* 64(May):267–75.

——. 1984. *Creative Change: A Cognitive-Humanistic Approach to Social Work Practice*. New York: Methuen.

Goldstein, S. R. 1993. "As I See It." *NASW NEWS* 38(1):2.

Goodman, C. 1984. "Natural Helping Among Older Adults." *Gerontologist* 24(April):138–43.

——. 1985. "Reciprocity Among Older Adult Peers." *Social Service Review* 59(June):269–82.

Googins, B. 1984. "Avoidance of the Alcoholic Client." *Social Work* 29(2):161–66.

Gordon, W. 1965. "Knowledge and Value: Their Distinction and Relationship in Clarifying Social Work Practice." *Social Work* 10(July):32–39.

Gottlieb, B. 1985. "Assessing and Strengthening the Impact of Social Support in Mental Health." *Social Work* 30(4):293–300.

——. 1988. "Marshalling Social Supports: The State of the Art In Research and Practice." In B. Gottlieb (Ed.) *Marshalling Social Support: Formats, Processes, and Effects*. Newbury Park, Cal.: Sage.

Gray, L. A. and A. K. Harding. 1988. "Confidentiality Limits with Clients Who Have the AIDS Virus." *Journal of Counseling and Development* 66:219–23.

Greene, M. J. and B. Orman. 1981. "Nurturing the Unnurtured." *Social Casework* 62(September):398–404.

Greene, R. 1986. "Countertransference Issues in Social Work with the Aged." *Journal of Gerontological Social Work* 9(3):79–88.

Gross, G., Giacquinta, J., and M. Bernstein. 1971. *Implementing Organizational Innovations*. New York: Basic Books.

Gross, J. 1987. "For a Teen-Age Mother, a Job and Guidance." *New York Times* (October 22):A-1, B-4.

Grosser, C. F. and J. Mondros. 1985. "Pluralism and Participation: The Political Action Approach." In S. H. Taylor and R. W. Roberts (Eds.) *Theory and Practice of Community Social Work* pp. 154–78. New York: Columbia University Press.

Guitierez, L. M. 1990. "Working with Women of Color: An Empowerment Perspective." *Social Work* 35(2):149–53.

Hage, J. and M. Aikens. 1970. *Social Change in Complex Organizations*. New York: Random House.

Haggstrom, W. 1987. "For a Democratic Revolution: The Grass-Roots Perspective." In Cox, F., Erlich, J., Rothman, J and J. Tropman (Eds.) *Tactics and Techniques of Community Practice* pp. 222–31. Itasca, IL: F. E. Peacock.

Hale, C. and J. Polt. 1985. "Using Pets as Therapists for Children with Developmental Disabilities." *Teaching Exceptional Children.* 17(3)

Hamilton, N., Ponzoha, C., Cutler, D., and R. Weigel. 1989. "Social Networks and Negative Versus Positive Symptoms of Schizophrenia." *Schizophrenia Bulletin* 15(4): 625–33.

Hanson, M. 1991. "Alcoholism and Other Drug Addictions." In A. Gitterman (Ed.) *Handbook of Social Work Practice with Vulnerable Populations* pp. 1–34. New York: Columbia University Press.

Hardman, D. 1977. "Not with My Daughter, You Don't." *Social Work* 20(July):278–85.

Hardy-Fanta, C. and E. MacMahon-Herrera. 1981. "Adapting Family Therapy to the Hispanic Family." *Social Casework* 62(March):138–48.

Hareven, T. K. 1982. "The Life Course and Aging in Historical Perspective." In T. K. Hareven and K. J. Adams (Eds.) *Aging and the Life Course Transitions: An Interdisciplinary Perspective* pp. 1–26. New York: Guilford Press.

Hartman, A. 1984. *Working with Adoptive Families: Beyond Placement*. New York: Child Welfare League of America.

——. 1994. *Reflections and Controversy, Essays on Social Work*. Washington, D.C.: NASW Press.

Hartman, A. and J. Laird. 1983. *Family-Centered Social Work Practice*. New York: Free Press.

Hartman, C. and D. Reynolds. 1987. "Resistant Clients: Confrontation, Interpretation, and Alliance." *Social Casework* (4):205–13.

Hasenfeld, Y. 1983. *Human Service Organizations*. Engelwood Cliffs, N.J.:Prentice Hall.

——. 1987. "Power in Social Work Practice." *Social Service Review* 61(September): 469–83.

——. 1992. *Human Services as Complex Organizations*. Newbury Park, Cal.: Sage.

Hasenfeld, Y. and H. Schmid. 1989. "The Life Cycle of Human Organizations: An Administrative Perspective." *Administration in Social Work* 13(3/4):243–69.

Hawkins, J. and M. Fraser. 1984. "Social Network Analysis and Drug Misuse." *Social Service Review* 58(March):81–97.

Heller, K., Swindel, R., and L. Dusenbury. 1986. "Component Social Support Processes: Comments and Integration." *Journal of Consulting and Clinical Psychology* 54(4):466–70.

Hepworth, D. and J. Larsen. 1986. *Direct Social Work Practice: Theory and Skills* pp. 146–51. Chicago: The Dorsey Press.

Herman, J. 1992. *Trauma and Recovery*. New York: Basic Books.

Hess, P. and T. Howard. 1981. "An Ecological Model for Assessing Psychosocial Difficulties in Children." *Child Welfare* 60(8):499–518.

Hirsch, B. J. 1981. "Social Networks and the Coping Process: Creating Personal Communities." In B. H. Gottleib (Ed.) *Social Networks and Social Support* pp. 149–70. Beverly Hills, CA: Sage.

Hoffman, L. 1980. "The Family Life Cycle and Discontinuous Change." In E. A. Carter and M. McGoldrick (Eds.) *The Family Life Cycle: A Framework for Family Therapy*. New York: Gardner Press.

Hoffman, R. G. 1991. "Companion Animals: A Therapeutic Measure for Elderly Patients." *Journal of Gerontological Social Work* 18(1/2):195–205.

Holland, T. P. 1995. "Organizational Context for Social Service Delivery." In *Encyclopedia of Social Work* 19th ed., pp. 1787–95. Silver Spring: National Association of Social Workers.

Holland, T. P., J. P. Gallant, and S. Colosetti. 1993. "Assessment of Teaching a Constructivist Approach to Social Work Practice." *Areté*:45–60.

Hollister, W. G. 1977. "Basic Strategies in Designing Primary Prevention Programs." In D. C. Klein and S. E. Goldston (Eds.) *Primary Prevention: An Idea Whose Time Has Come* pp. 41–48, Rockville: DHEW Publication N. (ADM)77–447.

Holloway, S. 1987. "Staff Initiated Organizational Change." *Encyclopedia of Social Work* 18th edition, pp. 729–36. Silver Spring: National Association of Social Workers.

——. 1991. "Homeless People." In A. Gitterman (Ed.) *Handbook of Social Work Practice with Vulnerable Populations* pp. 584–617. New York: Columbia University Press.

Holloway, S. and G. Brager. 1985. "Implicit Negotiations and Organizational Practice." *Administration on Social Work* 9(2):15–24.

Holroyd, K. and R. Lazarus. 1982. "Stress, Coping, and Somatic Adaptation." In L. Goldberger and S. Breznitz (Eds.) *Handbook of Stress: Theoretical and Clinical Aspects* pp. 21–35. New York: Free Press.

Hooker, C. 1976. "Learned Helplessness." *Social Work* 21(3):194–99.

Hooley, J., Orley, J. and J. Teasdale. 1986. "Levels of Expressed Emotion and Relapse in Depressed Patients." *British Journal of Psychiatry* 148(1):64–67.

House, J. 1981. *Work Stress and Social Support*. Reading, MA.: Addison-Wesley.

Hutcheon, L. 1989. *The Politics of Postmodernism*. New York: Routledge.

Hutchison, E. 1987. "Use of Authority in Direct Social Work Practice with Mandated Clients." *Social Service Review* 61(December):581–98.

Imber-Black, E. 1991. "Rituals of Stabilization and Change in Women's Lives." In M. McGoldrick, C. M. Anderson, and F. Walsh (Eds.) *Women in Families: A Framework for Family Therapy* pp. 451–69. New York: Norton.

Irizarry, C. and Y. Appel. 1994. "In Double Jeopardy: Preadolescents in the Inner City." In A. Gitterman and L. Shulman (Eds.) *Mutual Aid, Vulnerable Populations and the Life Cycle* pp. 119–49. New York: Columbia University Press.

Ivanoff, A., B. Blythe, and T. Tripodi. 1994. *Involuntary Clients in Social Work Practice: A Research Based Approach*. New York: Aldine Gruyter.

Jayarante, S. and R. Levy. 1979. *Empirical Clinical Practice*. New York: Columbia University Press.

Johnson, S. 1986. "Clinics Taking Birth-Control Help and Advice to the Teen-Agers." *New York Times* (March 12): C-1, C-12.

Jordon, J. V. 1991. "Empathy and Self Boundaries." In J. V. Jordon, A. G. Kaplan, J. B. Miller, I. Stiver and J. L. Surrey (Eds.) *Women's Growth In Connection: Writings from the Stone Center* pp. 67–80. New York: Guilford.

Joseph, Sr. M. V. and Sr. A. P. Conrad. 1980. "A Parish Neighborhood Model for Social Work Practice." *Social Casework* 6(September):423–32.

Joseph, V. 1985. "A Model for Ethical Decision Making in Clinical Practice." In C. Germain (Ed.) *Advances in Clinical Social Work* pp. 207–17. Silver Spring: National Association of Social Workers.

Kadushin, A. 1983. *The Social Work Interview*. New York: Columbia University Press.

Kahn, S. 1992. *Organizing: A Guide for Grassroots Leaders*. New York: McGraw Hill.

Karlins, M. and H. Abelson. 1970. *Persuasion: How Opinions and Attitudes Are Changed*. New York: Springer.

Karls, J. M. and K. E. Wandrei. 1995. "Person-in-Environment." In *Encyclopedia of Social Work* 19th ed., pp. 1818–27. Silver Spring: National Association of Social Workers.

Kasl, S. 1972. "Physical and Mental Health Effects of Involuntary Relocation and Institutionalization on the Elderly: A Review." *American Journal of Public Health* 62(3):377–84.

Katz, A. and E. Bender. (Eds.). 1990. *Helping One Another: Self-Help Groups in a Changing World.* Oakland, CA: Third Party Publishing.

Kavenaugh, R. E. 1977. "Humane Treatment of the Terminally Ill." In R. H. Moos (Ed.) *Coping with Physical Illness* pp. 413–20. New York: Plenum.

Kelley, M. L., McKay, S. and C. H. Nelson. 1985. "Indian Agency Development: An Ecological Practice Approach." *Social Casework* 66(10):594–602.

Kelley, P. and V. Kelley. 1985. "Supporting Natural Helpers: A Cross-Cultural Study." *Social Casework* 66(6):358–66.

Kerson, T. and L. A. Kerson. 1985. *Understanding Chronic Illness: The Medical and Psychosocial Dimensions of Nine Diseases.* New York: Free Press.

King, Y. 1983. "Toward an Ecological Feminism and a Feminist Ecology." In J. Rothschild (Ed.) *Machina Ex Dea* pp.118–29. New York: Pergamon.

Kinoy, S. K. 1984. "Advocacy: A Potent Antidote to Burnout." *NASW News* (November):9.

Kleinkauf, C. 1981. "A Guide to Giving Legislative Testimony." *Social Work* 26(4):297–303.

——. 1988. "Social Work Lobbies for Social Welfare: An Alaskan Example." *Social Work* 33(1): 56–57.

——. 1989. "Analyzing Social Welfare Legislation." *Social Work* 34(2):179–81.

Kopels, S. and J. D. Kagel. 1993. "Do Social Workers Have a Duty to Warn?" *Social Service Review* 67(1):101–26.

——. 1994. "Teaching Confidentiality Breaches as a Forum of Discrimination." *Areté* 19(1):1–9.

Koss, M. and J. Butcher. 1986. "Research on Brief Psychotherapy." In S. Gardfield and A. Bergin (Eds.) *Handbook of Psychotherapy and Behavior Change* pp. 627–70. New York: Wiley.

Koss, M. and M. Harvey. 1987. *The Rape Victim: Clinical and Community Approaches to Treatment.* MA: The Stephen Greene Press.

Kozol, J. 1991. *Savage Inequalities.* New York: Crown.

Kramer, R. M. and H. Specht. 1983. *Readings in Community Organization Practice* 3d ed. Englewood Cliffs, NJ: Prentice-Hall.

Kubler-Ross, E. 1975. *Death: The Final Stages of Life.* Englewood Cliffs, NJ: Prentice-Hall.

Kupers, T. A. 1988. *Ending Therapy: The Meaning of Termination.* New York: University Press.

Kurtz, L. and T. Powell. 1987. "Three Approaches to Understanding Self-Help Groups." *Social Work with Groups* 10(1):69–80.

Kurzman, P. A. 1985. "Program Development and Service Coordination as Components of Community Practice." In S. H. Taylor and R. W. Roberts (Eds.) *Theory and Practice of Community Social Work* pp. 95–124. New York: Columbia University Press.

Kutchins, H. 1991. "The Fiduciary Relationship: The Legal Basis of Social Workers' Relationships to Clients." *Social Work* 36(2):106–13.

Kutchins, H. and S. Kirk. 1987. "DSM-III and Social Work Malpractice." *Social Work* 32(May/June):205-12.

——. 1988. "The Business of Diagnosis: DSM-III and Clinical Social Work." *Social Work* 33(May/June):215-220.

Laird, J. 1984. "Sorcerers, Shamans, and Social Workers: The Use of Ritual in Social Work Practice." *Social Work* 29(March-April):123–29.

——. 1989. "Women and Stories: Restoring Women's Self-Constructions." In M. McGoldrick, F. Walsh, and C. Anderson (Eds.) *Women in Families* pp. 420–50. New York: Norton.

——. 1991. "Enactment of Power Through Ritual." In T. J. Goodrich (Ed.) *Women and Power: Perspectives for Family Therapy* pp. 123–47. New York: Norton.

——. 1993a. "Family-Centered Practice: Cultural and Constructionist Reflections." *Journal of Teaching in Social Work* 8 (1/2):77–110.

——. 1993b (Ed.). "Revisioning Social Work Education: A Social Constructionist Approach." *Journal of Teaching in Social Work* 8(1 and 2).

Laird, J. and A. Hartman (Eds.). 1985. *A Handbook of Child Welfare: Context, Knowledge, and Practice*. New York: Free Press.

Landy, D. 1960. "Problems of the Person Seeking Help in Our Culture." *Social Welfare Forum* pp. 127–45. New York: Columbia University Press.

Langelier, R. 1982. "French Canadian Families." In M. McGoldrick, J. K. Pearce and J. Giordano (Eds.) *Ethnicity and Family Therapy* pp. 229–46. New York: Guilford.

Lappin, B. 1985. "Community Development: Beginnings in Social Work Enabling." In S. H. Taylor, and R. W. Roberts (Eds.) *Theory and Practice of Community Social Work* pp. 59–94. New York: Columbia University Press.

Lazarus, R. 1980. "The Stress and Coping Paradigm." In L. Bond and J. Rosen (Eds.) *Competence and Coping During Adulthood* pp. 28–74. Hanover, NH: University Press of New England.

Lazurus, R. and S. Folkman. 1984. *Stress, Appraisal, and Coping*. New York: Springer.

Lee, J. A. B. 1992. Personal communication.

——. 1994a. *The Empowerment Approach to Social Work Practice*. New York: Columbia University Press.

——. 1994b. "No Place to Go: Homeless Women." In A. Gitterman and L. Shulman (eds.) *Mutual Aid Groups, Vulnerable Populations, and the Life Cycle* pp. 297–314. New York: Columbia University Press.

Lee, J. A. B. and C. Swenson. 1978. "A Community Social Service Agency: Theory in Action." *Social Casework* 59(June):359–69.

——. 1994. "The Concept of Mutual Aid." In A. Gitterman and L. Shulman (Eds.) *Mutual Aid Groups, Vulnerable Populations, and the Life Cycle* pp. 413–29. New York: Columbia University Press.

Lee, P. 1929. "Social Work: Cause and Function." *Proceedings, National Conference of Social Work* pp. 3–20. New York: Columbia University Press.

Lepore, S., Evans, G., and M. Schneider. 1992. "Role of Control and Social Support in Explaining the Stress of Hassles and Crowding." *Environment and Behavior* 24 (November):795–811.

Levine, K. and A. Lightburn. 1989. "Belief Systems and Social Work Practice." *Social Casework* 70(March):139–45.

Levy, C. S. 1976. *Social Work Ethics*. New York: Human Sciences Press.

Lewin, K. 1952. "Group Decisions and Social Change." In E. Maccoby, T. Newcomb, and E. Hartley (Eds.) *Readings in Social Psychology* pp. 207–11. New York: Holt, Rinehart, and Winston.

Lewis, E. and Z. E. Suarez. 1995. "Natural Helping Networks." In *Encyclopedia of Social Work* 19th ed., pp. 1765–72. Silver Spring: National Association of Social Workers.

Lewis, H. 1984. "Ethical Assessment." *Social Casework* 65(4):203–11.

Libassi, M. F. 1995. "Psychotropic Medications." In *Encyclopedia of Social Work* 19th ed., pp. 1961–66. Silver Spring: National Association of Social Workers.

Lide, P. 1966. "Dynamic Mental Representation: An Analysis of the Empathic Process." *Social Casework* 47(March):146–51.

Lightburn, A. and S. Kemp. 1994. "Family-Support Programs: Opportunities for Community-based Practice." *Families in Society* 75(1):16–26.

Lin, N., M. Woolfel and S. Light. 1985. "The Buffering Effect of Social Support Subsequent to an Important Life Event." *Journal of Health and Social Support* 26(3):247.

Lind, B. 1982. "Mental Patient Status, Work, and Income: An Examination of the Effects of a Psychiatric Label." *American Sociological Review* 47(April):202–15.

Lindholm, G. 1995. "Schoolyards: The Significance of Place Properties to Outdoor Activities in Schools." *Environment and Behavior* 27(3):259–93.

Loewenberg, F. and R. Dolgoff. 1992. *Ethical Decisions for Social Work Practice*. Itasca, IL: F. E. Peacock.

Logan, S., Freeman, E., and R. McRoy. 1990. *Social Work Practice with Black Families*. New York: Longman.

Luckey, I. 1994. "African American Elders: The Support Network of Generational Kin." *Families in Society* 75(Feb):82–89.

Mackenzie, T., Collins, N., and M. Popkin. 1980. "A Case of Fetal Abuse?" *American Journal of Orthopsychiatry* 52(4):699–703.

Mahaffey, M. 1987. "Political Action in Social Work." In *Encyclopedia of Social Work* 18th ed. pp. 283–94. Silver Spring: National Association of Social Workers.

Malekoff, A. 1994. "A Guideline for Group Work with Adolescents." *Social Work with Groups* 17(1/2):5–19.

Mallon, G. P. 1994. "Cow as Co-Therapist: Utilization of Farm Animals as Therapeutic Aides with Children in Residential Treatment." *Child and Adolescent Social Work Journal* 11(6):455–74.

Maluccio, A. 1979a. *Learning from Clients*. New York: The Free Press.

——. 1979b. "Perspective of Social Workers and Clients in Treatment Outcomes." *Social Casework* 60(7):394–401.

Maluccio, A. and W. Marlow. 1974. "The Case for the Contract." *Social Work* 19(January):28–36.

Manser, G. 1987. "Volunteers." In *Encyclopedia of Social Work*, 18th ed., pp. 842–51. Silver Spring: National Association of Social Workers.

Marsden, P. and V. Lin. (Eds.). 1982. *Social Structure and Network Analysis*. Beverly Hills: Sage.

Mathews, G. 1982. "Social Workers and Political Influence." *Social Service Review* 56(4):616–28.

Mayer, J. and A. Rosenblatt. 1964. "The Client's Social Context." *Social Casework* 45:(9)511–18.

Mayer, J. and N. Timms. 1969. "Clash in Perspectives Between Worker and Client." *Social Casework* 53(January):32–40.

——. 1970. *The Client Speaks*. New York: Atherton Press.

McFarlane, A. H., Norman, G. R., Streiner, D. L. and R. G. Roy. 1984. "Characteristics and Correlates of Effective and Ineffective Social Supports." *Journal of Psychosomatic Research* 28(6):501–9.

McGoldrick, M., J. Pearce and J. Giordano. (Eds.). 1982. *Ethnicity and Family Therapy*. New York: Guilford.

McGowan, B. 1978. "Strategies in Bureaucracies." in J. Mearing, (Ed.). *Working for Children: Ethical Issues Beyond Professional Guidelines* pp. 155–80. San Francisco: Jossey-Bass.

McGowan, B. 1987. "Advocacy." *Encyclopedia of Social Work* 18th ed., pp. 89–95. Silver Spring: National Association of Social Workers.

McMullin, P. and A. Gross. 1983. "Sex Differences, Sex Roles, and Health-Related Help-Seeking." In B. DePaulo, A. Nadler, and J. Fisher (Eds.) *New Directions In Helping* (Vol 2). New York: Academic Press.

McNeil, J. 1995. "Bereavement and Loss." In *Encyclopedia of Social Work* 19th ed., pp. 7–15. Silver Spring: National Association of Social Workers.

Messinger, R. W. 1982. "Empowerment: A Social Worker's Politics." In M. Mahaffey and J. W. Hanks (Eds.) *Practical Politics: Social Work and Political Responsibility* pp. 212–23. Silver Spring: National Association of Social Workers.

——. 1985. "The Ultimate Advocate: The Social Worker as Politician." *Practice Digest* 7(3):27–30.

Meyer, C. H. 1993. *Assessment in Social Work Practice.* New York: Columbia University Press.

Meyers, M. K. 1993. "Organizational Factors in the Integration of Services for Children." *Social Service Review* 67(4):547–75.

Mickelson, J. S. 1995. "Advocacy." In *Encyclopedia of Social Work* 19th ed., pp. 95–101. Silver Spring: National Association of Social Workers.

Middleman, R. 1980. "The Use of Program." *Social Work with Groups* 3(3):5–23.

Middleman, R. and G. G. Wood. 1993. "So Much for the Bell Curve: Power/Conflict, and the Structural Approach to Direct Practice in Social Work." *Journal of Education in Social Work* 8(1/2):129–46.

Milgrom, J. H., G. R. Schoener, J. C. Gonsiorek, E. T. Luepker, and R. M. Conroe. 1989. *Psychotherapists' Sexual Involvement with Clients.* Minneapolis: Walk-in Counseling Center (unpublished).

Miller, D. and W. Turnbull. 1986. "Expectancies and Interpersonal Processes." *Annual Review of Psychology* 37:233–56.

Miller, W. 1983. "Motivational Interviewing with Problem Drinkers." *Behavioral Psychotherapy* 11:142–47.

Miller, W. and S. Rollnick. 1991. *Motivational Interviewing: Preparing People to Change Addictive Behavior.* New York: Guilford Press.

Minami, H. and K. Tanaka. 1995. "Social and Environmental Psychology: Transaction Between Physical Space and Group-Dynamics Processes." *Environment and Behavior* 27(1):43–55.

Minuchin, S. H. and C. Fishman. 1981. *Family Therapy Techniques.* Cambridge: Harvard University Press.

Mitchell, M. 1986. "Utilizing Volunteers to Enhance Informal Social Networks." *Social Casework* 67(5):290–98.

Mizio, E. 1974. "Impact of External Systems on the Puerto Rican Family." *Social Casework* 55(2):76–83.

Mondros, J. and T. Berman-Rossi. 1994. "The Relevance of Stages of Group Development Theory to Community Organization Practice." *Social Work with Groups* 14(3/4):203–21.

Mondros, J. and S. Wilson. 1994. *Organizing for Power and Empowerment.* New York: Columbia University Press.

Monette, P. 1988. *Borrowed Time, an AIDS Memoir.* New York: Harcourt Brace.

Morgan, G. 1986. *Images of Organizations.* Beverly Hills, CA.: Sage.

Moriarty, A. and S. McDonald. 1991. "Theoretical Dimensions of School-Based Mediation." *Social Work in Education* 13(3):176–84.

Morrison, J. 1991. "The Black Church as a Support System for the Elderly." *Journal of Social Work with Groups* 17(1/2):105–20.

Moses, A. E. and R. O. Hawkins. 1982. *Counseling Lesbian Women and Gay Men: A Life-Issues Approach.* St. Louis: Mosby.

Nadelman, A. 1994. "Sharing the Hurt: Adolescents in a Residential Setting." In A. Gitterman and L. Shulman (Eds.) *Mutual Aid, Vulnerable Populations, and the Life Cycle* pp. 163–81. New York: Columbia University Press.

Nakhaima, J.M. 1994. "Network Family Counseling: The Overlooked Resource." *Areté* 19(1):46–56.

NASW News. 1992. Washington, D.C.: National Association of Social Workers.

NASW News. 1994. Washington, D.C.: National Association of Social Workers.

NASW Standards for Social Work Case Management. 1992. Washington, D.C.: National Association of Social Workers.

Neinstein, L. 1982. "Lowering Broken Appointment Rates at a Teenage Health Center." *Journal of Adolescent Health Care* 3(September):110–13.

Nelsen, J. 1975. "Dealing with Resistance in Social Work." *Social Casework* 56(10): 587–92.

——. 1980. "Support A Necessary Condition for Change." *Social Casework* 61 (September):388–92.

——. 1981. "Issues in Single-Subject Research for Nonbehaviorists." *Social Work Research and Abstracts* 17(Summer):31–37.

——. 1985. "Verifying the Independent Variable in Single-Subject Research." *Social Work Research and Abstracts* 21(Summer):3–8.

——. 1988. "Single-Subject Research." In R. Grinnell, Jr. (Ed.) *Social Work Research and Evaluation* pp. 362–99. Itasca, Ill: F. E. Peacock.

Netting, F. E., C. C. Wilson, and J.C. New. 1987. "The Human-Animal Bond." *Social Work* 32(1):60–64.

Neugarten, B. 1969. "Continuities and Discontinuities of Psychological Issues Into Adult Life." *Human Development* 12(2):121–30.

——. 1979. "Time, Age, and the Life Cycle." *American Journal of Psychiatry* 136(7): 887–94.

New York Times. 1988. "Teen-Agers With Plans, Not Babies." November 5: Editorial.

Newman, O. 1973. *Defensible Space.* New York: Collier.

Nieto, D. S. 1982. "Aiding the Single Father." *Social Work* 27(November):473–78.

Northen, H. 1982. *Clinical Social Work.* New York: Columbia University Press.

Nuland, S. W. 1994. *How We Die.* New York: Knopf.

Odum, E. 1964. "The New Ecology." *Bioscience* 14(7):14–16.

O'Looney, J. 1993. "Beyond Privitization and Service Integration: Organizational Models for Service Delivery." *Social Service Review* 67(4):501–34.

Orfield, G. 1991. "Cutback Policies, Declining Opportunities, and the Role of Social Service Providers." *Social Service Review* 65(4):516–30.

Osmand, H. 1970. "Function as the Basis of Psychiatric Ward Design." In H. Proshansky, W. Ittleson, and L. Rivlin (Eds.) *Environmental Psychology: Man and His Physical Setting* pp. 27–37. New York: Holt, Rinehart and Winston.

Palmer, S. 1983. "Authority: An Essential Part of Practice." *Social Work* 28(March-April):120–25.

Palumbo, J. 1982. "The Psychology of Self and the Termination of Treatment." *Clinical Social Work Journal* 10(Spring 1982):15–27.

Pancoast, D. L. 1980. "Finding and Enlisting Neighbors to Support Families." In Garbarino, J. and S. H. Stocking (Eds.) *Protecting Children from Abuse and Neglect: Developing and Maintaining Effective Support Systems for Families* pp. 109–32. San Francisco: Jossey-Bass.

Pancoast, D. L. and A. Collins. 1987. "Natural Helping Networks." In *Encyclopedia of Social Work* 18th ed., pp. 177–82. Silver Spring: National Association of Social Workers.

Parad, L. 1971. "Short-term Treatment: An Overview of Historical Trends, Issues, and Potentials." *Smith College Studies in Social Work* 41(February):119–46.

Patterson, S. L., C. B. Germain, E. M. Brennan, and J. Memmott. 1988. "Effectiveness of Rural Natural Helpers." *Social Casework* 69(5):272–79.

Patterson, S., J. Memmott, C. B. Germain, and E. Brennan. 1992. "Patterns of Natural Helping in Rural Areas: Social Work Research Implications." *Social Work Research and Abstracts* 28(3):22–28.

Patti, R. and H. Resnick. 1972. "Changing the Agency from Within." *Social Work* 17(7):48–57.

Pattison, E. M. (Ed.). 1977. *The Experience of Dying*. Englewood Cliffs, NJ: Prentice Hall.

Pernell, R. 1985. "Empowerment and Social Group Work." In M. Parenes (Ed.) *Innovations in Social Group Work: Feedback from Theory to Practice* pp. 107–19. New York: Haworth.

Perrow, C. and M. Guillen. 1990. *The AIDS Disaster: The Failure of Organizations in New York and the Nation*. New Haven: Yale University Press.

Peterson, M. R. 1992. *At Personal Risk: Boundary Violations in Professional-Client Relationships*. New York: Norton.

Pinderhughes, E. 1982a. "Family Functioning of Afro-Americans." *Social Work* 27(January):91–96.

——. 1982b. "Black Genealogy: Self Liberator and Therapeutic Tool." *Smith College Studies in Social Work* 59:93–106.

——. 1983. "Empowerment for Our Clients and for Ourselves." *Social Casework* 64(6):331–38.

——. 1989. *Understanding Race, Ethnicity, and Power*. New York: Free Press.

Powell, T. 1987. *Self-Help Organizations and Professional Practice*. Silver Spring: National Association of Social Workers.

——. 1990. *Working with Self-Help Groups*. Silver Spring: National Association of Social Workers.

Poynter-Berg, D. 1994. "Getting Connected: Institutionalized Schizophrenic Women." In A. Gitterman and L. Shulman (Eds.) *Mutual Aid Groups, Vulnerable Populations, and the Life Cycle* pp. 315–34. New York: Columbia University Press.

Practice Digest. 1980. "Helping 'Natural Helpers' Do What Comes Naturally." 5(1):5–9.

Presley, J. 1987. "The Clinical Dropout: A View from the Client's Perspective." *Social Casework* 68(10):603–8.

Pressman, J. and A. Wildavsky. 1973. *Implementation*. Berkeley: University of California Press.

Proshansky, H., W. Ittelson, and L. Revlin. 1976. *Environmental Psychology: People and their Settings*. New York: Holt, Rinehart and Winston.

Pruchno, R., N. Dempsey, N. Carder, and T. Koropeckyj-Cox. 1993. "Multigenerational Households of Caregiving Families: Negotiating Shared Space." *Environment and Behavior* 25(3):349–66.

Rando, T. A. 1985. "Bereaved Parents: Particular Difficulties, Unique Factors, and Treatment Issues." *Social Work* 30(January-February):19–23.

Rapoport, L. 1970. "Crisis Intervention as a Mode of Brief Treatment." In R. Roberts and R. Nee (Eds.) *Theories of Social Casework* pp. 265–311. Chicago: University of Chicago Press.

Rauch, J. 1978. "Gender as a Factor in Practice." *Social Work* 23(5):388–96.

Reagh, R. E. 1994. "What's Wrong with Prevention Research?" In J. A. Fickling (Ed.) *Social Problems with Health Consequences: Program Design, Implementation, and Evaluation* pp. 89–96. Columbia, SC: Proceedings of the BiRegional Conference for Public Health Social Workers in Regions IV and VI, The University of South Carolina College of Social Work.

Reamer, F. 1983. "Ethical Dilemmas in Social Work Practice." *Social Work* 28(1):31–35.

——. 1987. "Informed Consent in Social Work." *Social Work* 32(5):425–29.

——. 1990. *Ethical Dilemmas in Social Service*. New York: Columbia University Press.

——. 1994. *Social Work Practice and Liability: Strategies for Prevention*. New York: Columbia University Press.

——. 1995. *Social Work Values and Ethics*. New York: Columbia University Press.

Redfer, L. and J. Goodman. 1989. "Brief Report: Pet Facilitated Therapy with Autistic Children." *Journal of Autism and Developmental Disorder* 19(3):461–67.

Reid, W. 1992. *Task Strategies: An Empirical Approach to Clinical Social Work*. New York: Columbia University.

Reid, W. and A. Shyne. 1969. *Brief and Extended Casework*. New York: Columbia University Press.

Reisch, M. 1990. "Organizational Structure and Client Advocacy: Lessons from the 80's." *Social Work* 35(1):73–74.

Reiss, D. 1981. *The Family's Construction of Reality*. Cambridge: Harvard University Press.

Rene, K. 1987. "Networks of Social Support and the Outcome from Severe Head Injury." *Journal of Head Trauma Rehabilitation* 2(3):14–23.

Resnick, H. and B. Jaffee. 1982. "The Physical Environment and Social Welfare." *Social Casework* 63(6):354–62.

Reynolds, B. 1934. "Between Client and Community." *Smith College Studies in Social Work Journal* 5(1):entire issue.

Riley, M. W. 1985. "Women, Men, and the Lengthening of the Life Course." In A. S. Rossi (Ed.) *Aging and the Life Course* pp. 333–47. New York: Aldine.

Riley, P. 1971. "Family Advocacy: Case to Cause and Back to Case." *Child Welfare* 50(July):374–83.

Roberts-DeGennero, M. 1986. "Building Coalitions for Political Advocacy." *Social Work* 31(4):308–11.

Robinson, G. and O. Gelhorn. 1972. *The Administrative Process*. St.Paul: West.

Rogers, C. 1961. "The Characteristics of a Helping Relationship." In C. Rogers (Ed.) *On Becoming a Person* pp. 33–58. Boston: Houghton Mifflin.

Rodwell, M. and Blankebaker, A. 1992. "Strategies for Developing Cross-Cultural Sensitivity: Wounding as a Metaphor." *Journal of Social Work Education* 28(2):153–65.

Romeder, J. 1981. "Self-Help Groups and Mental Health: A Promising Avenue." *Canada's Mental Health* 21(1):10–12, 31.

Rooney, R. H. 1992. *Strategies for Work with Involuntary Clients*. New York: Columbia University Press.

Rosen, S. M. 1988. *Memorandum*. New York: Columbia University School of Social Work (unpublished)

Rosenberg, M. 1979. *Conceiving the Self*. New York: Basic Books.

Rothman, J. 1979. "Three Models of Community Organization Practice, Their Mixing and Phasing." In F. M. Cox, J. L. Erlich, J. Rothman and J. E. Tropman (Eds.) *Strategies of Community Organization* pp. 25–44. Itasca, IL: Peacock.

——. 1994. *Social Work with Highly Vulnerable Populations: Case Management and Community-Based Service*. Englewood Cliffs, NJ: Prentice-Hall.

Rothman, J., J. L. Erlich, and J. G. Teresa. 1979. *Promoting Innovation and Change in Organizations and Communities*. New York: Wiley.

Rotton, J. 1993. "Atmospheric and Temporal Correlates of Sex Crimes: Endogenous Factors Do Not Explain Seasonal Differences in Rape." *Environment and Behavior* 25(5):625–42.

Rowles, G. 1980. "Growing Old 'Inside': Aging and Attachment to Place in an Appalachian Community." In N. Datan and N. Lohman (Eds.) *Transitions of Aging*. New York: Academic Press.

——. 1983. "Geographical Dimensions of Social Support in Rural Appalachia." In G. Rowles and R. Ohta (Eds.) *Aging and Milieu: Environmental Perspectives on Growing Old* pp. 111–30. New York: Academic Press.

Rubin, A. 1987. "Case Management." In *Encyclopedia of Social Work* 18th ed., pp. 212–22. Silver Spring: National Association of Social Workers.

Rutter, M. 1986. "Myerian Psychobiology, Personality Development, and the Role of Life Experiences." *American Journal of Psychiatry* 143(9):1077–86.

Salcido, R. M. 1984. "Social Work Practice in Political Campaigns." *Social Work* 29(2): 189–91.

Salem, D. A., E. Seidman, and J. Rappaport. 1988. "Community Treatment of the Mentally Ill: The Promise of Mutual-Help Organizations." *Social Work* 33(5):403–8.

Salebry, D. 1994. "Culture, Theory, and Narrative: The Intersections of Meanings in Practice." *Social Work* 39(4):351–59.

Sales, B. D. and D. W. Shuman. 1994. "Mental Health Law and Mental Health Care: Introduction." *American Journal of Orthopsychiatry* 64(April):172–79.

Sarbin, T.R. 1986. *Narrative Psychology: The Storied Nature of Human Conduct.* New York: Prager.

Schaffer, S. and J. Pollak. 1987. "The Interruption and Resumption of Milieu Treatment with Children and Adolescents." *Child and Adolescent Social Work Journal* 4(1):41–49.

Schild, S. and R. Black. 1984. *Social Work and Genetics.* New York: Haworth.

Schilling, R. 1987. "Limitations of Social Support." *Social Service Review* 61(March): 19–31.

Schilling, R. and S. Schinke. 1983. "Social Support Networks in Developmental Disabilities." In J. Whittaker, J. Garbiano, and Associates (Eds.) *Social Support Networks: Informal Helping in the Human Services* pp. 383–404. New York: Aldine.

Schlesinger, E. G. and W. Devore. 1995. "Ethnic-Sensitive Practice." In *Encyclopedia of Social Work* 19th ed., pp. 902–8. Silver Spring: National Association of Social Workers.

Schmidt, H. 1992. "Relationships Between Decentralized Authority and Other Structural Properties in Human Service Organizations: Implications for Service Effectiveness." *Administration in Social Work* 16(1):25–39.

Schmidt, H. and Y. Hasenfeld. 1993. "Organizational Dilemmas in the Provision of Home-Care Services." *Social Services Review* 67(1):40–54.

Schopler, J.H. and M.J. Galinsky. 1995. "Group Practice Overview." In *Encyclopedia of Social Work* 19th ed., pp. 1129–44. Silver Spring: National Association of Social Workers.

Schwartz, M. 1978. "Helping the Worker with Countertransference." *Social Work* 23(May):204–9.

Schwartz, W. 1961. "The Social Worker in the Group." In *The Social Welfare Forum, Proceedings of the National Conference on Social Welfare.* New York: Columbia University Press.

——. 1969. "Private Troubles and Public Issues: One Job or Two?" *Social Welfare Forum, Proceedings of the National Conference on Social Work* pp. 22–43. New York: Columbia University Press.

——. 1971. "On the Use of Groups in Social Work Practice." In Schwartz, W. and S. Zelba (Eds.) *The Practice of Group Work* pp. 32–24. New York: Columbia University Press.

——. 1976. "Between Client and System: The Mediating Function." In R. Roberts and H. Northern (Eds.) *Theories of Social Work with Groups* pp. 171–97. New York: Columbia University Press.

Scott, R. and J. Meyer (eds.). 1994. *Institutional Environments and Organizations.* Newbury Park, Cal.: Sage.

Seabury, B. 1971. "Arrangements of Physical Space in Social Work Settings." *Social Work* 16(8):43–49.

——. 1976. "The Contract: Uses, Abuses, and Limitations." *Social Work* 21(January): 16–26.

——. 1979. "Negotiating Sound Contracts with Clients." *Public Welfare* 37(Spring): 33–38.

Searle, J. 1990. "The Storm Over the University." *The New York Review of Books*.

Searles, H. 1960. *The Non-Human Environment*. New York: International Universities Press.

Sebba, R. 1990. "The Landscapes of Childhood: The Reflections of Childhood's Environment in Adult Memories and in Children's Attitudes." *Environment and Behavior* 22(July):395–422.

Seligman, M. 1980. *Human Helplessness*. New York: Academic Press.

Shapiro, J. 1970. *Communities of the Alone*. New York: Association Press.

——. 1983. "Commitment to Disenfranchised Clients." In A. Rosenblatt and D. Waldfogel (Eds.) *Handbook of Clinical Social Work* pp. 888–903. San Francisco: Jossey Bass.

Sherman, S. 1976. "The Therapist and Changing Sex Roles." *Social Casework* 57(February):93–96.

Sherman, W. and S. Wenocur. 1993. "Empowering Public Welfare Workers Through Mutual Support." *Social Work* 28(5):375–79.

Shulman, L. 1967. "Scapegoats, Group Workers, and Pre-emptive Interventions." *Social Work* 12(April):37–43.

——. 1978. "A Study of Practice Skills." *Social Work* 23(4):274–81.

——. 1987. "Consultation." In *Social Work Encyclopedia* 18th ed., pp. 326–31. Silver Spring: National Association of Social Workers.

——. 1991. *Interactional Social Work Practice: Toward an Empirical Theory*. Itasca, Ill.: Peacock.

——. 1992. *The Skills of Helping: Individuals, Families, and Groups*. Itasca, IL.: F. E. Peacock.

Shulman, L. and W. Buchan. 1982. *The Impact of the Family Physician's Communication, Relationship, and Technical Skills on Patient Compliance, Satisfaction, Reassurance, Comprehension and Improvement*. Vancouver, B.C.: University of British Columbia.

Shulman, L., Robinson, E., and A. Luckyj. 1982. *A Study of Content, Context, and Skills of Supervision*. Vancouver: University of British Columbia.

Siebold, C. 1991. "Termination: When the Therapist Leaves." *Clinical Social Work Journal* 19(2):191–204.

Simon, B. L. 1994. *The Empowerment Tradition in American Social Work: A History*. New York: Columbia University Press.

Siporin, M. 1983. "Morality and Immorality in Working with Clients." *Social Thought* 9(Fall):10–28.

——. 1984. "Have You Heard the One About Social Work Humor?" *Social Casework* 65(October):459–64.

Smith, L. 1978. "A Review of Crisis Intervention Theory." *Social Casework* 59(July): 396–405.

Smith-Bell, M. and W. J. Winslade. 1994. "Privacy, Confidentiality, and Privilege in Psychotherapeutic Relationships." *American Journal of Orthopsychiatry* 64(April): 180–93.

Smothers, R. 1989. "Parley Aims at Nurturing Black Youths." *New York Times* May 4.

Social Casework. 1974. "Special Issue on Puerto Ricans: Contra Viento y Marea" [Against Stormy Seas] 55(3).

Social Casework. 1976. "Special Issue on Asian and Pacific Islander Americans: Heritage, Characteristics, Self-Image, Conflicts, Service Needs, Organization." 57(3).

Social Casework. 1980. "Special Issue on The Phoenix and the Flame: The American Indian Today." 61(8).

Social Work. 1982. "Issue on Social Work and People of Color." 27(January).

Social Work Code of Ethics. 1994. Ottawa, Ontario: Canadian Association of Social Workers.

Solomon, B. B. 1976. *Black Empowerment: Social Work in Minority Communities*. New York: Columbia University Press.

——. 1982. "Social Work Values and Skills to Empower Women." In A. Weick and S. T. Vandiver (Eds.) *Women, Power, and Change* pp. 206–14. Washington, D.C.: National Association of Social Workers.

Specht, H. 1985. "Managing Professional Interpersonal Interactions." *Social Work* 30(3):225–30.

——. 1986. "Social Support, Social Network, Social Exchange, and the Social Work Practice." *Social Service Review* 60(2):218–32.

Specht, H. and R. Specht. 1986. "Social Work Assessment: Route to Clienthood—Part I and Part II." *Social Casework* 67 (November; December):525–32; 587–93.

Spence, D. P. 1982. *Narrative Truth and Historical Truth: Meaning and Interpretation in Psychoanalysis*. New York: Norton.

Sprung, G. 1989. "Transferential Issues in Working with Older Adults." *Social Casework* 70(10):597–602.

Stack, C. B. 1974. *All Our Kin: Strategies for Survival in a Black Community*. New York: Harper Colophon.

Staples, L. 1987. "Community Development." In *Encyclopedia of Social Work* 18th ed., pp. 291–308. Silver Spring: National Association of Social Workers.

Statsky, W. P. 1975. *Legislative Analysis: How to Use Statutes and Regulations*. St. Paul: West.

Stern, D. 1977. *The First Relationship*. Cambridge: Harvard University Press.

——. 1985. *The Interpersonal World of Human Infants*. New York: Basic Books.

Suls, J. and B. Fletcher. 1985. "Self-Attention, Life Stress, and Illness: A Prospective Study." *Psychosomatic Medicine* 47:469–81.

Sundel, M. and C. F. Schanie. 1978. "Community Mental Health and Mass Media Preventive Education: The Alternatives Project." *Social Service Review* 52(June): 297–306.

Super, S. I. 1982. "Successful Transition: Therapeutic Intervention with the Transferred Client." *Clinical Social Work Journal* 10(Summer):113–22.

Susa, A. M. 1994. "The Effects of Playground Teasing on Pretend Play and Divergent Thinking." *Environment and Behavior* 26(4):560–79.

Swenson, C. 1979. "Social Networks, Mutual Aid, and the Life Model of Practice." In C. B. Germain (Ed.) *Social Work Practice: People and Environments* pp. 213–38. New York: Columbia University Press.

——. 1981a. Unpublished research data.

——. 1981b. "Using Natural Helping Networks to Promote Competence." In A. Maluccio (Ed.) *Promoting Competence in Clients* pp. 103–25. New York: Free Press.

Szent-Gyorgyi, A. 1967, *Collected Papers 1913–31, 1949–54*. Bethesda: NLM.

Terkelsen, K. G. 1980. "Toward a Theory of the Family Life Cycle." In E. A. Carter and M. McGoldrick (Eds.) *The Family Life Cycle: A Framework for Family Therapy* pp. 21–52. New York: Gardner.

Thoits, V. 1986. "Social Support as Coping Assistance." *Journal of Consulting and Clinical Psychology* 54(4):416–23.

Thomas, L. 1974. *Lives of a Cell*. New York: Viking.

Tice, K. 1990. "Gender and Social Work Education: Directions for the 1990's." *Journal of Social Work Education* 26(2):134–44.

Torczyner, J. 1991. "Discretion, Judgment, and Informed Consent: Ethical and Practice Issues in Social Action." *Social Work* 36(2):97–192.

Toseland, R. 1987. "Treatment Discontinuance." *Social Casework* 68(4):195–204.

Toseland, R. and R. Rivas. 1984. *An Introduction to Group Work Practice*. New York: Macmillan.

——. 1995. *Introduction to Group Work Practice* 2d ed. New York: Allyn and Bacon.

Truax, C. 1966. "Therapist Empathy, Warmth, Genuiness and Patient Personality Change in Group Psychotherapy: A Comparison Between Interaction Unit Measures,

Time Sample Measures, and Patient Perception Measures." *Journal of Clinical Psychology* 71(1):1–9.

Truax, C. and R. Carkhoff. 1967. *Toward Effective Counseling and Psychotherapy*. Chicago: Atherton.

Turnbull, J. 1991. "Depression." In A. Gitterman (Ed.) *Handbook of Social Work Practice with Vulnerable Populations* pp. 1–34. New York: Columbia University Press.

Turner, V. 1982. "Introduction." In V. Turner (Ed.) *Celebration, Studies in Festivity and Ritual* pp. 11–30. Washington, D.C.: Smithsonian Institution Press.

Valentine, C. A. and B. L. Valentine. 1970. "Making the Scene, Digging in Action, and Telling It Like It Is: Anthropologist at Work in a Dark Ghetto." In N. E. Whitten and J. F. Szwed (Eds.) *Afro-American Anthropology* pp. 403–18. New York: Free Press.

Valentine, D.P., M. Kiddoo, and B. Lafleur. 1993. "Psychosocial Implications of Service Dog Ownership for People Who Have Mobility or Hearing Impairments." *Social Work in Health Care* 19(1):109–25.

Van Den Bergh, N. and L. B. Cooper (Eds.). 1986. *Feminist Visions for Social Work*. Silver Spring: National Association of Social Workers.

Van Gheluwe, B. and J. K. Barber. 1986. "Legislative Advocacy in Action." *Social Work* 31(5):393–95.

Vandervelde, M. 1979. "The Semantics of Participation." *Administration in Social Work* 3 (1):65–78.

Videka-Sherman, L. 1991. "Child Abuse and Neglect." In A. Gitterman (Ed.) *Handbook of Social Work Practice with Vulnerable Populations* pp. 345–81. New York: Columbia University Press.

Vinter, R. 1985. "Program Activities: An Analysis of Their Effects on Participant Behavior." In M. Sundel, P. Glasser, R. Sarri and R. Vinter (Eds.) *Individual Change Through Small Groups* pp. 226–36. New York: Free Press.

Vosler, N. R. 1990. "Assessing Family Access to Basic Resources: An Essential Component of Social Work Practice." *Social Work* 35(5):434–41.

Waite, L.M. 1993. "Drama Therapy in Small Groups with the Developmentally Disabled." *Social Work with Groups* 16(4):95–108.

Wald, E. 1981. *The Remarried Family: Challenge and Promise*. New York: Family Service Association of America.

Walden, T., I. Wolock, and H. W. Demone Jr. 1990. "Ethical Decision Making in Human Services: A Comparative Study." *Families in Society* 71(1):67–75.

Wallach, E. 1980. "From Immigration to Leaky Roofs: Job of a Congressman's Aide." *Practice Digest* 3(5):23–25.

Walz, T. and V. Groze. 1991. "The Mission of Social Work Revisited: An Agenda for the 1990's." *Social Work* 36(6):500–4.

Wapner, S. and L. Craig-Bray. 1992. "Person in Environment Transitions." *Environment and Behavior* 24(March):161–88.

Warren, R. 1963. *The Community in America*. Chicago, IL: Rand McNally.

Weaver, D. R. 1982. "Empowering Treatment Skills for Helping Black Families." *Social Casework* 63(February):100–6.

Webb, N. B. 1985. "A Crisis Intervention Perspective on the Termination Process." *Clinical Social Work Journal* 13(Winter):329–40.

Webb, N. B. (Ed.). 1991. *Play Therapy With Children in Crisis: A Casebook for Practitioners*. New York: Guildford.

Weedon, C. 1987. *Feminist Practice and Poststructuralist Theory*. Oxford: Basil Blackwell.

Weick, A. 1982. "Issues of Power in Social Work Practice." In A. Weick and S. T. Vandiver (Eds.) *Women, Power, and Change* pp. 173–85. Washington, D.C.: National Association of Social Workers.

Weick, A. and S. T. Vandiver (Eds.) 1982. *Women, Power, and Change*. Washington, D. C.: National Association of Social Workers.

Weil, M. and L. Sanchez. 1983. "The Impact of the Tarasoff Decision on Clinical Social Worker Practice." *Social Service Review* 57(11):112–24.

Weiner, H. J., Akabas, S. and J. Sommer. 1973. *Mental Health Care in the World of Work.* New York: Association Press.

Weisner, S. 1983. "Fighting Back: A Critical Analysis of Coalition Building in the Human Services." *Social Service Review* 57(2):291–306.

Weiss, R. 1973. "The Nature of Loneliness." In R. Weiss, (Ed.) *Loneliness: The Experience of Emotional and Social Isolation* pp. 9–29. Cambridge: MIT Press.

——. 1982. "Attachment in Adult Life." In C. Parkes and J. Stevenson-Hinde (Eds.) *The Place of Attachment in Adult Life* pp. 171–83. New York: Basic Books.

Weissman, H., Epstein, I., and A. Savage. 1983. *Agency-Based Social Work.* Philadelphia: Temple University Press.

Wells, R. 1982. *Planned Short-Term Treatment.* New York: Free Press.

Werner, C., I. Altman, D. Oxley, and L. Haggard. 1987. "People, Place, and Time: A Transactional Analysis of Neighborhoods." In W. Jones and D. Perlman (Eds.) *Advances in Personal Relationships* pp. 243–75. New York: JAI Press.

Wethington, E. and R. Kessler. 1986. "Perceived Support, Received Support, and Adjustment to Stressful Life Events." *Journal of Health and Social Behavior* 27(1): 78–89.

Wheaton, B. 1983. "Stress, Personal Coping Resources, and Psychiatric Symptoms: An Investigation of Interactive Models." *Journal of Health and Social Behavior* 24(3): 208–29.

White, R. 1959. "Motivation Reconsidered: The Concept of Competence." *Psychological Review* 66(September):297–333.

Whiteman, M., D. Fanshel, and J. Grundy. 1987. "Cognitive-Behavioral Interventions Aimed at Anger of Parents at Risk of Child Abuse." *Social Work* 32(November-December):469–74.

Whittaker, J. and J. Garbarino. 1983. *Social Support Networks: Informal Helping in the Human Services.* New York: Aldine.

Wickler, M. 1986. "Pathways to Treatment: How Orthodox Jews Enter Treatment." *Social Casework* 67(2):113–18.

Williams, C. W. 1995. "Adolescent Pregnancy." In *Encyclopedia of Social Work* 19th ed., pp. 34–40. Silver Spring: National Association of Social Workers.

Williams, L. 1990. "The Challenge of Education to Social Work: The Case of Minority Children." *Social Work* 35(3):236–42.

Winters, W. G. and F. Easton. 1985. *The Practice of Social Work in the Schools: An Ecological Perspective.* New York: Free Press.

Witkin, S. L. 1990. "The Implications of Social Constructionism for Social Work Education." *Journal of Teaching in Social Work* 4 (2):37–48.

Wood, K. 1978. "Caseworkers Effectiveness: A New Look at Research Evidence." *Social Work* 23(4):437–58.

Woodrow, R. 1987. "Influences at Work: Orientations of Hospital Social Workers to Organizational Change Practice." New York: Columbia University School of Social Work, doctoral dissertation (unpublished)

Woods, M. and F. Hollis. 1990. *Casework: A Psychosocial Therapy.* New York: McGraw-Hill.

Yacey, W. 1971. "Architecture, Interaction, and Social Control: The Case of a Large-Scale Public Housing Project." *Environment and Behavior* 3(March):3–18.

Yalom, I. 1985. *The Theory and Practice of Group Psychotherapy.* New York: Basic Books.

Zaltman, G., R. Duncan, and J. Holbeck. 1973. *Innovations and Organizations.* New York: Wiley.

INDEX

Page references in italics indicate tables or figures